Windows® 2000 Secrets®

Windows® 2000 Secrets®

**Brian Livingston and Bruce Brown
with Bruce Kratofil**

IDG
BOOKS
WORLDWIDE

IDG Books Worldwide, Inc.
An International Data Group Company

Foster City, CA ♦ Chicago, IL ♦ Indianapolis, IN ♦ New York, NY

Windows® 2000 Secrets®

Published by
IDG Books Worldwide, Inc.
An International Data Group Company
919 E. Hillsdale Blvd., Suite 400
Foster City, CA 94404
www.idgbooks.com (IDG Books Worldwide Web site)

ISBN: 0-7645-3413-0

Printed in the United States of America

10 9 8 7 6 5 4 3 2

1B/SY/QR/QQ/FC

Distributed in the United States by IDG Books Worldwide, Inc.

Distributed by CDG Books Canada Inc. for Canada; by Transworld Publishers Limited in the United Kingdom; by IDG Norge Books for Norway; by IDG Sweden Books for Sweden; by IDG Books Australia Publishing Corporation Pty. Ltd. for Australia and New Zealand; by TransQuest Publishers Pte Ltd. for Singapore, Malaysia, Thailand, Indonesia, and Hong Kong; by Gotop Information Inc. for Taiwan; by ICG Muse, Inc. for Japan; by Intersoft for South Africa; by Eyrolles for France; by International Thomson Publishing for Germany, Austria and Switzerland; by Distribuidora Cuspide for Argentina; by LR International for Brazil; by Galileo Libros for Chile; by Ediciones ZETA S.C.R. Ltda. for Peru; by WS Computer Publishing Corporation, Inc., for the Philippines; by Contemporanea de Ediciones for Venezuela; by Express Computer Distributors for the Caribbean and West Indies; by Micronesia Media Distributor, Inc. for Micronesia; by Chips Computadoras S.A. de C.V. for Mexico; by Editorial Norma de Panama S.A. for Panama; by American Bookshops for Finland.

For general information on IDG Books Worldwide's books in the U.S., please call our Consumer Customer Service department at 800-762-2974. For reseller information, including discounts and premium sales, please call our Reseller Customer Service department at 800-434-3422.

For information on where to purchase IDG Books Worldwide's books outside the U.S., please contact our International Sales department at 317-596-5530 or fax 317-596-5692.

For consumer information on foreign language translations, please contact our Customer Service department at 800-434-3422, fax 317-596-5692, or e-mail rights@idgbooks.com.

For information on licensing foreign or domestic rights, please phone +1-650-655-3109.

For sales inquiries and special prices for bulk quantities, please contact our Sales department at 650-655-3200 or write to the address above.

For information on using IDG Books Worldwide's books in the classroom or for ordering examination copies, please contact our Educational Sales department at 800-434-2086 or fax 317-596-5499.

For press review copies, author interviews, or other publicity information, please contact our Public Relations department at 650-655-3000 or fax 650-655-3299.

For authorization to photocopy items for corporate, personal, or educational use, please contact Copyright Clearance Center, 222 Rosewood Drive, Danvers, MA 01923, or fax 978-750-4470.

Library of Congress Cataloging-in-Publication Data
Livingston, Brian.
    Windows 2000 Secrets /
    Brian Livingston and Bruce Brown, with
    Bruce Kratofil.
        p. cm.
    ISBN 0-7645-3413-0 (alk. paper)
    1. Microsoft Qindows (Computer file) 2. Operating systems (Computers) I. Brown, Bruce, 1950- II. Kratofil, Bruce. III. Title.
QA76.76.063 L595 1999
005.4'4769—dc21   99-048112

is a registered trademark or trademark under exclusive license to IDG Books Worldwide, Inc. from International Data Group, Inc. in the United States and/or other countries.

ABOUT IDG BOOKS WORLDWIDE

Welcome to the world of IDG Books Worldwide.

IDG Books Worldwide, Inc., is a subsidiary of International Data Group, the world's largest publisher of computer-related information and the leading global provider of information services on information technology. IDG was founded more than 30 years ago by Patrick J. McGovern and now employs more than 9,000 people worldwide. IDG publishes more than 290 computer publications in over 75 countries. More than 90 million people read one or more IDG publications each month.

Launched in 1990, IDG Books Worldwide is today the #1 publisher of best-selling computer books in the United States. We are proud to have received eight awards from the Computer Press Association in recognition of editorial excellence and three from Computer Currents' First Annual Readers' Choice Awards. Our best-selling ...For Dummies® series has more than 50 million copies in print with translations in 31 languages. IDG Books Worldwide, through a joint venture with IDG's Hi-Tech Beijing, became the first U.S. publisher to publish a computer book in the People's Republic of China. In record time, IDG Books Worldwide has become the first choice for millions of readers around the world who want to learn how to better manage their businesses.

Our mission is simple: Every one of our books is designed to bring extra value and skill-building instructions to the reader. Our books are written by experts who understand and care about our readers. The knowledge base of our editorial staff comes from years of experience in publishing, education, and journalism — experience we use to produce books to carry us into the new millennium. In short, we care about books, so we attract the best people. We devote special attention to details such as audience, interior design, use of icons, and illustrations. And because we use an efficient process of authoring, editing, and desktop publishing our books electronically, we can spend more time ensuring superior content and less time on the technicalities of making books.

You can count on our commitment to deliver high-quality books at competitive prices on topics you want to read about. At IDG Books Worldwide, we continue in the IDG tradition of delivering quality for more than 30 years. You'll find no better book on a subject than one from IDG Books Worldwide.

John Kilcullen
Chairman and CEO
IDG Books Worldwide, Inc.

Steven Berkowitz
President and Publisher
IDG Books Worldwide, Inc.

Eighth Annual Computer Press Awards ≥1992

Ninth Annual Computer Press Awards ≥1993

Tenth Annual Computer Press Awards ≥1994

Eleventh Annual Computer Press Awards ≥1995

Credits

Acquisitions Editor
Andy Cummings

Development Editor
Katharine Dvorak

Technical Editor
Don Murdoch, MCSE, MCT

Copy Editors
Sally Neuman
Ami Knox

CD-ROM
Media Development

Project Coordinator
Linda Marousek

Graphics and Production Specialists
Mario Amador
Stephanie Hollier
Jude Levinson
Ramses Ramirez
Dina Quan

Quality Control Specialist
Chris Weisbart

Book Designer
Liew Design

Illustrator
Mary Jo Richards
Shelley Norris

Proofreading and Indexing
York Production Services

E-Book Preparation
Dianna Stockdale

CD-ROM Setup Development
Bill Zitomer
Eric Robichaud
Allen Robichaud

About the Authors

Brian Livingston is the author of IDG Books Worldwide's best-selling *Windows Secrets* series, including *Windows 3.1 Secrets, 2nd Edition*; *Windows 95 Secrets*; *Windows 98 Secrets*; and *More Windows 98 Secrets*. His books are printed in more than 30 languages. In addition to writing books, Brian is a contributing editor of *InfoWorld* magazine, and has been a contributing editor of *PC Computing*, *PC World*, *Windows Sources*, and other magazines. He was a recipient of the 1991 Award for Technical Excellence from the National Microcomputer Managers Association.

Bruce Brown is the creator of BugNet and the author of numerous books, including the environmental classic, *Mountain in the Clouds*, and the comic cult favorite, *Dr. Whacko's Guide to Slow-pitch Softball*.

Bruce Kratofil is President of BJK Research in Cleveland, Ohio. He is the Senior Editor of BugNet, and was a contributing writer to "The Windows 95 Bug Collection." He previously taught economics and corporate finance, and serves as Webmaster for the National Association for Business Economics. When he's not sitting in front of a computer, he coaches his daughter's soccer and softball teams.

For Margie Livingston; Laurel and Shanna Brown; and Sharon and Rachel Kratofil

Contents at a Glance

Contents

Chapter 1

Read This First

In This Chapter

▶ A guide to the structure and contents of this book

▶ A summary of each of the chapters and what you can get out of them

▶ How to use Windows 2000 commands, as described in this book

▶ How the icons in the margins help you find the "naughty parts"

The Key to Windows 2000 Professional

Welcome to the ninth book in the Windows *Secrets* series from IDG Books Worldwide. This chapter holds the key to your unlocking the gems within. We hope you'll take a minute to scan this chapter before launching into the other parts you seek.

If this is your first Windows *Secrets* book, you hold in your hands the best secrets, little-known tricks, and life-saving workarounds we could find on Windows 2000 Professional. Hopefully, we've provided information that is unlike that in any other book on the subject.

If you've used previous books in the Windows *Secrets* series, you know you'll find within this book those hard-to-find facts and techniques that Microsoft never seems to get around to putting in their own books on the subject.

The "lineage" of this book—the nine books that bring us up to today—are:

■ *Windows 3 Secrets* (1990, the "1st Edition" of Windows *Secrets*)

■ *Windows 3.1 Secrets* (1991, the "2nd Edition")

■ *More Windows 3.1 Secrets* (1993, a completely new book)

■ *Windows Gizmos* (1993, a collection of Windows freeware and shareware)

■ *Windows 95 Secrets* (1995, the "3rd Edition")

■ *Windows 95 Secrets, 4th Edition* (a thoroughly updated Windows 95 book)

■ *Windows 98 Secrets* (1998, a totally new book)

- *More Windows 98 Secrets* (1999, another new book on Windows 98)

- *Windows 2000 Secrets* (1999, completely original research on Windows 2000)

Windows 2000 Secrets is the first book in the series based on Microsoft's NT product line (New Technology, or as Microsoft now calls it, "Network Technology"). As such, we have written *Windows 2000 Secrets* completely from scratch, with information that applies solely to the NT code base — not old information that applies only to Windows 9x.

In this book, you'll find only the best, most hard-to-find information on Windows 2000. We've collected this sought-after information from our friends within Microsoft, from hard-core experimenters who are survivors of the beta process, from labs that put the Windows 2000 betas through torture testing, and from our own experiences.

What You *Won't* Find in This Book

There are many gems in this book, but there are also many things of lesser value that you *won't* find within:

- **The Obvious.** If a topic is covered in the printed manual or Help system you get with Windows 2000, it's probably not in here. We've left out the obvious stuff so you get more "secret" stuff. Anyone can pull down a screen full of menus and describe what they do — and that's just what most computer books contain. But not this one — we've included only what's *not* in the manual.

- **The Old.** If it applies only to Windows 98, and not to Windows 2000, it's not in here. We already have eight other books on the old consumer Windows code base — why repeat that here? We've uncovered plenty of secrets that are specific to Windows 2000, and that's what we've put in between these covers.

- **The CIO Stuff.** If you're the Chief Information Officer of a multinational corporation — and you want to know how to run your global enterprise on NT 4.0 or Windows 2000 Server — you need a lot more help than this book can provide. But if you're a normal, intelligent power user who's running Windows 2000 because you *want* to (or because you *have* to, due to the requirements of your job), then this book is for you. We cover everything that's common to users of both Windows 2000 Professional (the desktop operating system) and Windows 2000 Server (the high-end operating system).

We've written this book to help those just beginning to use Windows 2000, as well as for the more experienced users of Windows 2000. You'll need a different book than this if you desire the most high-end, technical details of Windows 2000 Server. But this book should be just what the doctor ordered for users of Windows 2000 Professional and Windows 2000 Server who just want it to work the way *they want it to work*.

The Five Parts of This Book

Windows 2000 Secrets is organized into five parts. Each is further organized into a number of chapters to give you a convenient way to get just what you need out of this book.

Part I: Setup and Configuration

Part I should be read by everyone — especially people who've already installed Windows 2000 Professional (or bought a PC with Win 2000 already installed). We cover many tricks that can improve the configuration, even after it's been installed.

Part II: The User Interface

Part II consists of a rich set of tricks to make your Windows 2000 system conform more to your liking. In this part, we discuss the basic Windows conventions and features, how to take control of your system, how to customize your environment, and how to have fun with Windows 2000 applets.

Part III: Communications

The third part of this book reveals the secrets of Windows 2000 Professional communications — everything from connecting to the outside world with modems, DSL, and cable, to dial-up networking and working with Internet Explorer 5 and Outlook Express.

Part IV: Hardware

Making Windows 2000 work with all the different kinds of hardware out there can be a challenge. In this section, we try to give you the help you need to succeed, including information on managing your computer with the Control Panel, managing your system with the Microsoft Management Console, understanding the registry, managing drives, and working with printers and fonts.

Part V: Networking with Windows 2000 Professional

There's a lot of networking you can do with Windows 2000 Professional computers — even if you also have Windows 2000 Server on your LAN. This part delves deeply into the secrets of networking, installing network hardware, and networking with Windows 2000 Professional.

Getting the Most out of Windows Commands

While Windows relies on the mouse for most things, there are times when a good old typed-in command is just the thing you need to get the result you want.

In this book, the following styles show you what to type, and when.

```
notepad {/p} filename
```

When you need to type a command, it's shown in a special font, like the line above.

Parameters that are optional are shown in curly braces {like this}.

Items that are to be typed exactly as shown are in roman type, such as the /p in {/p}. (For example, /p indicates that Notepad is to print the filename that follows.)

Terms that should be replaced with real words or numbers are shown in *italics,* such as *filename.* In this case, you don't type the letters f-i-l-e-n-a-m-e. You substitute the name of the file you want to operate on, such as readme.txt.

To open the readme.txt file in the C:\Winnt folder, for example, you would click the Start button, click Run, and then type the following and click OK:

```
notepad c:\winnt\readme.txt
```

To print the same file, you would type the following instead:

```
notepad /p c:\winnt\readme.txt
```

There are usually several different ways to represent the name of file, and each way can describe the same file. For example, if you are at a command prompt and are currently in the c:\winnt folder, all of the following commands work the same way to open the setuplog.txt file:

```
notepad c:\winnt\setuplog.txt
notepad c:\winnt\setuplog
Notepad Setuplog
NOTEPAD SETUPLOG.TXT
```

Special keys on your keyboard are shown in the book with an initial capital letter. This includes Enter, Backspace, Tab, Alt (alternate), Ctrl (control), Esc (escape), and so on.

If we want you to hold down one special key while you press another, a plus sign (+) appears between the two keys. For example, *Ctrl+A* means *hold down the Ctrl key, press and release the A key, and then release the Ctrl key.*

If we want you to press and release each of a series of keys in turn, commas appear between the keys. For example, *press Alt, F, O* means *press and release the Alt key, then press and release the F key, and then press and release the O key.* (This runs the File ⇨ Open command in most Windows applications.)

Sometimes the mouse is all you need to run a command, but you can also run it with a keyboard combination. We don't necessarily spell out the keyboard equivalent, but if there is one, you can use it if you like. For example, when we say *click File ⇨ Open* you could pull down the File menu, and then click Open with your mouse. Alternatively, you could press Alt, F, O to do the same thing. The choice is yours.

Keys to the Naughty Bits

The following icons can lead you to "juicy" parts of *Windows 2000 Secrets:*

Secret

The **Secret** icon marks items that are not documented in the manual you get with Windows 2000 Professional, or are little-known facts that are not obvious for most Windows 2000 users. This information may be written down *somewhere* by Microsoft, but not in a way that's easy for users to find.

Tip

The **Tip** icon indicates a technique that may involve items on the menu or in the manual, but the trick is not obvious or well-explained by Microsoft.

Note

The **Note** icon points out items of interest or importance that we want to draw your attention to.

The **New in 2000** icon shows you features that are new to Windows 2000, compared with Windows NT 4.0 or Windows 98.

Caution

The **Caution** icon warns you about side effects you should watch out for or precautions you should take before doing something that may have a negative impact on your system.

Cross-
Reference

The **Cross-Reference** icon points you to different parts of the book where more information on a particular topic can be found.

Take Windows 2000 to New Heights

With this book, we hope you will find ways to make Windows 2000 do things you never before thought possible.

This book would not be possible without many unsung individuals who've shared their knowledge in newsgroups and with us personally. We've tried to credit these individuals in the pages of the book, at the point where their contribution most helped us explain how Windows 2000 actually works.

Have a good compute!

Part I

Setup and Configuration

Chapter 2

Installing Windows 2000 Professional

Preparations You Should Take

The upgrade path from Windows NT 4.0 to Windows 2000 Professional is the easiest upgrade. Both of these versions of Windows share the same registry database and structure, and they each have the same file system and folder architecture. They also share the same security architecture, operating system kernel architecture, and device driver model. Although this means the upgrade process is supposed to be straightforward and smooth, any time you upgrade an operating system, it pays to both plan ahead and to take precautions.

Checking minimum hardware requirements

First, you need to see if your computer is up to the task. Table 2-1 shows the minimum hardware requirements recommended by Microsoft, as well as a consensus opinion of what you really need to run Windows 2000 with adequate performance.

Table 2-1   Hardware Requirements for Windows 2000

Component	Microsoft Requirements	Realistic Minimums
Processor	133 MHz Pentium or higher	300 MHz Pentium II or higher
RAM	32MB minimum; 64MB recommended	At least 96MB
Hard Drive	2GB, with 650MB free	4GB
Video	VGA or better	SVGA

The realistic minimums have come from discussions in newsgroups, as well as from reviews of beta versions of the operating system. In practical terms, if your hardware is anywhere near the realistic minimum, you probably shouldn't upgrade unless you are forced to for compatibility reasons. Windows 2000 is a heavyweight operating system, and it needs the hardware to carry the load.

Back up

If you are upgrading an existing computer, the first thing you want to do is back up all your data. If you are upgrading—rather than doing a clean install—all your programs and files should be waiting for you there at the end, but don't count on it. Any number of bad things can happen during an upgrade, and there is always a chance that you can lose files. So back up all your data files, such as your word processing documents, spreadsheets, and the like, first.

There are many other valuable pieces of information scattered elsewhere on your hard drive, so you should make sure you back those up, as well. This includes your e-mail address book, Web site passwords stored in cookie files, preferences stored in .INI files, Registry .DAT files, and so forth. Depending on the size of your hard drive and the type of backup media you use, it might be best to do a complete backup.

Collect drivers

Windows 2000 ships with an extensive list of drivers for most common hardware devices. To see if your hardware is supported, check the Hardware Compatibility List (HCL) located in the \Support folder of the Windows 2000 Professional CD-ROM. If your device is not on the list, you either need to locate the disks or CD-ROMs that came with it, or contact the hardware manufacturer to see if they have a Windows 2000 driver available. If the devices are Plug and Play, then you (probably) won't need to get drivers.

If you are not sure what drivers you may need, don't worry. In one of the first installation steps, the Setup Wizard will scan your hardware for problem devices and report them to you. If your system hardware is okay, Windows 2000 will go ahead and install. If not, the areas of conflict will be identified for you.

Tip

Any last minute changes, cautions, or warnings from Microsoft will be included in a number of files that usually can be found in the root directory of the Windows 2000 CD-ROM. These include the Read First Notes, the Setup text file, the Advanced Setup text file, and the Release Notes. There may be valuable information about incompatibilities, or about things you should not do while installing, and the information is typically more current than that which is contained in the printed material accompanying the CD-ROM.

Caution

While there are safeguards built in to the Windows 2000 Setup Wizard that should prevent you from incapacitating your computer, you should still make sure you have an Emergency Boot Disk from your current operating system. Depending on how — or when — the Windows 2000 setup was interrupted, this might allow you to restore your computer to something resembling its previous state should a problem occur.

Upgrade or Clean Install?

When you actually begin the installation process, one of the first questions you will be asked is whether you want to upgrade your existing operating system or perform a new (or clean) installation. What you decide here will have important ramifications on your workload immediately after the operating system installation is complete. When you upgrade, you replace your existing operating system files with the Windows 2000 files. However, your applications, settings, and data files should remain intact, and will be ready for use when Setup is over. During a new installation, Windows 2000 is installed into a new folder, leaving your old operating system files in place. You must then reinstall all of your applications and reset all of your preferences so that the new operating system knows about them.

In general, you should perform an upgrade if you answer yes to *all* of the following three questions:

■ Does your current operating system support an upgrade to Windows 2000? (All releases of Windows 95 and 98 do. So does Windows NT 3.51 and 4.0, with all their service packs.)

■ Do you want to replace your previous Windows operating system files with Windows 2000? (This saves hard drive space.)

■ Do you want to keep your existing data and preferences? (An upgrade should allow all your applications to remain in place.)

There are four questions to answer if you are considering a new installation. If you answer yes to *any* of these, then you should perform a new installation:

- Do you have an empty hard drive? (No operating system is installed.)

- Does your current operating system not support an upgrade to Windows 2000? (DOS, Windows 3.1, or OS/2, for instance.)

- Do you want to get rid of your existing data and preferences and make a fresh start?

- Do you want to have a dual-boot configuration with Windows 2000 and your existing operating system version? (You need two disk partitions to do this.)

Note that the Windows 2000 files can take as much as 650MB of space for a full installation on your hard drive. Space limitations may play a factor in your decision on whether to do an upgrade or a clean installation, if you don't think you have room for two operating systems.

Secret

While it may seem a bit drastic, some experienced computer users swear by a housecleaning procedure whereby once every six months or so, they back up their data files, reformat their hard drives, and then reinstall their operating system and all their applications from scratch. They say this "spring cleaning" helps clear out a lot of unneeded settings, files, and assorted clutter, and helps their computer run more quickly and efficiently. If this sounds like a good idea, then a new install might be for you.

What File System Should You Use?

Another decision you may need to make is determining what file system you will use on your hard drive. The file system is the way your files are organized on your hard drive. Windows 2000 can work with the NT file system (NTFS), as well as the two legacy systems, File Allocation Table (FAT), and File Allocation Table (32-bit) (FAT32). If your hard drive is already using NTFS, you have no decision to make, because once you have gone to NTFS, you can't go back without reformatting your hard drive.

NTFS is the native file system for Windows 2000, and it is the system that Microsoft recommends you use for Windows 2000. It has both advantages and disadvantages over FAT systems. By using NTFS, you will have more secure files, better disk compression, and better scalability to larger drives. It also uses large hard drives more efficiently than FAT. The major disadvantage is that it is only recognized by Windows NT and Windows 2000. Other operating systems, such as Windows 95 and 98, cannot read from or write to NTFS partitions.

To add to the confusion, the version of NTFS that ships with Windows NT 4 is NTFS 4. When Windows 2000 is installed, it upgrades this version to NTFS 5. The only version of Windows NT that can read NTFS 5 partitions is NT 4.0, Service Pack 4. If there is any chance you will have to go back to Windows NT, you must have installed Service Pack 4 first, or you will not be able to read from your drive. The only way you can recover from this is to reformat your drive.

Tip

On a large hard drive, NTFS partitions are more efficient. If you use FAT on a 2GB hard drive, each cluster on the drive will be 32K in size. Since two files cannot share a cluster, even a 1K file will occupy 32K of space on a drive. If a drive is formatted as NTFS, each cluster is 2K. The smaller clusters are more efficient — converting a 2GB drive from FAT to NTFS could easily free up 300MB of space on a drive.

Tip

If you plan to use a dual-boot system with Windows 2000 and an earlier operating system (Windows 3.1, Windows 95, Windows 98, OS/2, or Windows NT Service Pack 3 or earlier) occupying different partitions, you should use FAT, or you should use FAT32 if the second operating system is Windows 95 OSR2 or Windows 98. The older operating systems will not be able to access NTFS 5 partitions. See Chapter 3 for more information about dual-boot systems.

A Guided Tour of the Upgrade Process

Once you have backed up your data, collected any drivers you need, and decided on the type of installation and file system, it's time to actually perform the upgrade. Don't worry, though; you haven't reached the point of no return yet. You will have a number of opportunities to change your mind during the early stages of the upgrade process.

Installing from the CD-ROM

The installation process is simple if you are upgrading from the CD-ROM. Boot your computer using your existing operating system. Then, insert the Windows 2000 CD-ROM disc into the drive. It should start automatically and give you the message, "This CD-ROM contains a newer version of Windows than the one your are presently using. Would you like to upgrade to Windows 2000?" If you respond Yes, you will see the Welcome screen for the Windows 2000 Setup Wizard, as shown in Figure 2-1.

If the Windows 2000 CD-ROM disc does not automatically start, click Start ➪ Run and type the following command in the Open text box (where d: is the letter that actually represents your CD-ROM drive):

```
d:\i386\winnt32.exe
```

Make sure that the correct radio button is selected for the decision you made earlier in the section, "Should you upgrade or do a clean install?" and then click Next. You will see the Microsoft License Agreement as shown in Figure 2-2. To move on to the next step, you must select "I accept this agreement." (Fortunately, you only need to accept the agreement. You don't have to show that you understand it.)

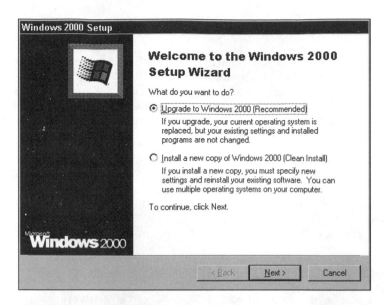

Figure 2-1: The Windows 2000 Setup Wizard. If you are upgrading from a supported operating system, the upgrade is usually the recommended option.

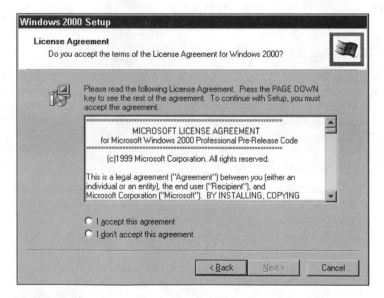

Figure 2-2: The Microsoft License Agreement for Windows 2000. You must agree to continue the installation.

If your current drive is partitioned as a FAT or FAT32 partition, you will be asked next if you want to upgrade to NTFS. (If you already have an NTFS partition, you won't see this step.) Instead, you will automatically be upgraded to NTFS 5 later in the installation process.

The next step is a critical step. It is the System Compatibility Check, where the Setup Wizard scans your system looking for devices that are incompatible with Windows 2000. A typical screen is shown in Figure 2-3.

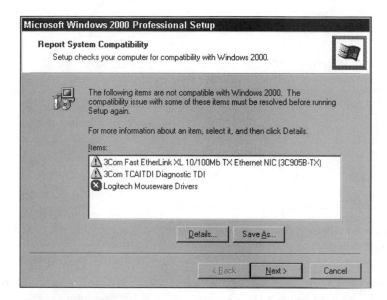

Figure 2-3: The System Compatibility Check. A red circle here is a temporary dead end.

A yellow triangle is a caution symbol. It means that Windows 2000 does not have a driver for the indicated device. Select this line and then click Details to read the warning. Typically, you will have three choices here. You can tell the Wizard that you have a disk with the correct driver. If you don't have a disk, you can still proceed with the installation, but the device won't work properly after the installation. Finally, you can cancel the installation until you can obtain the correct driver.

A red circle in the compatibility check resembles a stop sign, and that is exactly what it means here. The Setup Wizard has detected a problem that will prevent the installation from proceeding. Clicking the Details button will often provide a potential remedy, like the one for the Logitech Mouseware Drivers shown in Figure 2-4.

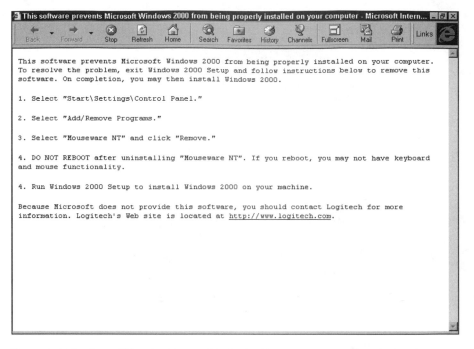

Figure 2-4: The Setup Wizard might provide detailed instructions on how to deal with an offending device.

If you click Continue after a red warning sign, the Setup Wizard will terminate. Once you have followed the Wizard's advice (or found another way around the problem), you can begin the installation process again. On the other hand, if there are no more red warnings, the installation process will really begin. At this point, you just need to sit back and wait. Messages will flash by as files are copied from the CD, the system is rebooted a number of times, and the setup procedure runs in earnest. For an upgrade, the Setup Wizard will use your existing values for user information, language, date and time settings, and so forth.

Tip

At certain times, you might be prompted to supply a floppy disk or CD-ROM disc containing a specific device driver. The Setup Wizard might find the files automatically, or it might prompt you to browse the disk so it can find a particular file.

Reaching your goal — the Windows 2000 Welcome

Eventually, after following all the instructions, Windows 2000 will start. After a successful upgrade, you should see most of your previous Desktop shortcuts, Start Menu items, and preferences still in place. You can use your existing user name and password to log on. The Windows 2000 Welcome screen should be displayed (see Figure 2-5).

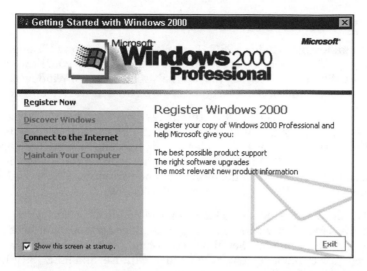

Figure 2-5: The Windows 2000 Welcome Screen. It signifies a successful setup.

Upgrading over a network

Instead of installing from a CD-ROM disc, you can upgrade your computer over your network (where applicable). Your network administrator will tell you which shared network folder contains the Windows 2000 setup files. After you start your computer, connect to that folder. If you are running Windows 95, Windows 98, or Windows NT, go to the command prompt and type the path to winnt32.exe. If you are using some other operating system, you should type the path to winnt.exe. In either case, you will be asked if you want to upgrade to Windows 2000 Professional. Click Yes, and then follow the installation instructions.

Connecting to a network during installation

If you want to connect to a network during the Windows 2000 installation, you also might need to provide some network information. During an upgrade, if you already belong to a domain, your existing computer account will be used. If you didn't have an account, you will need to provide that information to the Wizard. You should determine your domain and account information before you begin the setup process. If you don't have this information, join a workgroup instead of a domain. You can join an existing workgroup, provide a new workgroup, or just use the default workgroup name that the Wizard suggests.

Tip

You can change all your network settings later, or you can set up new network connections. If you are not sure what answer to provide, it should be safe for you to accept the default suggestions and move on.

Upgrading from Windows 95 and 98

The upgrade from Windows 95/98 is similar to the Windows NT upgrade. The Setup Wizard is still going to do a lot of the work for you. However, there are more differences between the internal architecture of Windows 95/98 and Windows 2000, so it will not be quite as automated as the NT upgrade process.

There is a greater chance that there will be driver problems, especially coming from Windows 95. If any of your hardware drivers use the older virtual driver model (VxD), you will need to replace them, because they are not supported under Windows 2000. Drivers written specifically for Windows 98 should work, because they are based on the newer common Windows Driver Model (WDM) architecture that Windows 98 shares with Windows 2000.

Note

The Windows Driver Model is based on the Windows NT driver model. In theory, any WDM driver should support devices for both Windows 98 and Windows 2000. Universal Serial Bus (USB) and other Plug and Play (PNP) devices, power management, audio, video capture, and IEEE 1394 devices will all be based on WDM.

Once you have confirmed that you have a compatible set of drivers, you need to make sure that your Windows 95/98 applications will work in Windows 2000. If you have access to a Windows 2000 computer, you might want to do some testing yourself.

Because of differences between the Windows 95/98 and the Windows 2000 Registries, you will not achieve as complete a transfer of information as you would in with an upgrade from Windows NT. Therefore, you may need to supply more information to the Setup Wizard during the setup process. As with the upgrade from Windows NT, you may be prompted to supply a floppy disk or CD-ROM disc with specific device driver. The Setup Wizard may find the files automatically, or it might prompt you to browse the disk so that it can find a particular file.

Doing a Clean Install

There are two different starting points when performing a clean installation. For example, you might have a hard drive with no operating system installed at all, providing you with no normal way to start the computer. The second example might be that an existing operating system is already installed. If you perform a clean install on a PC that already has Windows 95 or 98 installed, you will need to reinstall all your applications, as well as reconfigure the system to your liking.

Performing a clean install with no operating system installed

With the blank hard disk example, you need some way to boot your computer so that you can start the Windows 2000 installation. With some newer computers, you can configure the computer to boot from the CD-ROM drive. If your computer works this way, you can start the computer with the Windows 2000 CD-ROM in place, which should automatically start the Setup Wizard once the computer starts.

If you are unable to boot from the CD-ROM drive, you will need to use the Windows 2000 Setup floppy disks. Insert the first disk into your floppy drive and turn on your computer. The Setup Wizard should begin. If you don't have the Setup floppy disks, you can create a set using the following steps. (If you use 1.44MB, 3.5-inch diskettes, you will need four disks and a working computer.)

STEPS:

Creating the Windows 2000 Setup disks

Step 1. Insert a blank diskette into the floppy drive.

Step 2. Insert the Windows 2000 CD-ROM into your CD-ROM drive.

Step 3. In Windows 95, 98, and NT, click Start ➪ Run, and then type the following (where d: is your CD-ROM drive letter):

```
d:\bootdisk\makeboot.bat a:
```

Step 4. Follow the on-screen instructions, labeling the disks "Setup 1," "Setup 2," and so on, as the program instructs you to do.

Clean install from an existing operating system

If your target computer has an existing operating system installed, you do not need to create the Setup floppy disks. Instead, take the following steps:

STEPS:

Clean install

Step 1. Insert the Windows 2000 CD-ROM disc into the CD-ROM drive.

Step 2. Start your computer as usual.

Step 3. If the Windows 2000 Setup Wizard automatically starts, you can skip the rest of these steps, and move the next section.

Step 4. If the Setup Wizard doesn't start automatically, and you are running Windows 95, 98, or NT 4.0, click Start ➪ Run. If you are running Windows NT 3.51 or Windows 3.1, click File ➪ Run from the Program Manager.

Continued

STEPS:

Clean install *(continued)*

Step 5.   In Windows 95, 98, NT 3.51 or NT 4.0, type the following command in the Open text box (where d: is your CD-ROM drive letter):

        `d:\i386\winnt32.exe`

Step 6.   In Windows 3.1, type the following command at the DOS prompt (where d: is your CD-ROM drive letter):

        `d:\i386\winnt.exe`

Step 7.   Press Enter to start the Setup Wizard.

Clean install information

A clean install does not use any of your existing information, so you will have more questions to answer during the Setup Wizard. As with an upgrade, you have to agree to the License Agreement, and you then need to decide which file system to use. Following those steps, you will be asked to select your preferences for the following options:

- From the Special Options page, you can choose your language and accessibility options.

- From the Regional Settings page, you can choose additional settings to match your country or language preferences.

- From the Personalize Software page, you will be asked to type your name and, if applicable, your organization name in the spaces provided.

- From the Computer Name and Administrator Password page, you will be asked to provide a unique name for your computer. (If you won't be connecting to a network, the answers you provide here are not critical.) During Setup, an Administrator account will be created. (See Chapter 15 for more information on Administrators and accounts.) You will be asked to select a password for this account, which you should immediately write down for safekeeping.

- Date, Time, and Time Zone Settings. You also can let Windows 2000 keep track of Daylight Savings Time so that your clock will automatically switch when the time zone changes.

- In Networking Settings, you can either select Typical or Custom. If you are going to be on a network, your network administrator can supply you with information.

- Next, you need to join either a workgroup, which is a small group of workstations, or a domain, which is a set of centrally managed computers, users, and groups. If you aren't going to be on a network, then choose workgroup. If you are going to be on a network, you need to determine your domain information, or add this later.

- If you are upgrading from Windows 95 or 98, there may be software upgrades or service packs that will also upgrade your software for Windows 2000. You should get these from your software vendor, if they are available and needed.

Running Setup from the Command Line

You also can install Windows 2000 from the command line. You might want to choose this route this so that you can customize your installation, or so that you can perform an unattended installation. If you are upgrading from the Windows NT, Windows 98, or Windows 95 command prompt, the syntax of the command-line prompt is as follows (where d: is your CD-ROM drive letter):

```
d:\i386\winnt32.exe {options}
```

Table 2-2 outlines the command-line switches for the winnt32 setup.

Table 2-2 Command-Line Switches for WINNT32 Setup	
/s:*sourcepath*	Points to the location of the Windows 2000 installation and CAB files. You can have multiple source parameters, such as when you need to copy files from multiple drives or servers.
/syspart:*drive*	Lets you copy the Setup startup files to an active partition on your hard drive. You can install that drive in another computer so that when that computer starts, Setup resumes with the next step. You must also use the /tempdrive switch if you use the /syspart switch. Example: /syspart:d:
/tempdrive:*drive*	Tells the Setup program to put its temporary files on the specified drive, and then to install on the specified drive.
/copydir:*foldername*	Creates an additional folder within the Windows 2000 folder. Files within the source folder of the same name will then be copied to the location specified. You can use the new folder to hold custom files. (This switch is used in place of the /r switch.) Example: /copydir:oemfile
/copysource:*foldername*	Creates an additional folder, like /copydir above, but temporary folder is deleted after Setup is complete.
/cmd:*command*	Executes the specified command prior to the final Setup step, after the computer restarts the second time. Example: /cmd:special.bat

Continued

Table 2-2 *(continued)*	
debug[n][:*filename*]	Creates a debug log of the level specified by n. The default level is 2, or Warning. Example: /debug[2][:debug.log]
/i:*Dosnet.inf*	The filename, without a path, of the setup information file. The default filename is Dosnet.inf.
/x	Prevents Setup from creating Setup boot floppies.
/unattend	Upgrades your previous version of Windows. All user settings will be maintained from your previous installation, which means that no user input will be needed during Setup.
/unattend[num]:*answerfile*	Performs a new installation of Windows 2000. Answers to setup questions will be taken from the specified answer file. The value of [num] will be the number of seconds after Setup finishes copying files and the time Setup restarts.
/r:*directory*	Adds an additional directory in the directory tree where Windows 2000 is installed. This can be used multiple times. It creates an empty directory, unlike /copydir:*foldername*.
/e:*command*	Executes the specified command after Setup has completed and Windows 2000 has been installed.
/udf:*id* [,*UDF_file*]	An identifier (ID) for Setup to use to specify how a Uniqueness Database File (UDF) can change an answer file.

Be Prepared

By now, you should have a computer running a functional Windows 2000 operating system. You will soon be making changes as you install hardware and software, as well change the configuration to fit your working style. While it is touted as the most stable version of Windows yet, there is still a chance that some changes you make could temporarily render your computer helpless.

Chapter 5 will cover troubleshooting in greater depth, but there is still one precaution you should take right away. You should create an Emergency Repair Disk in Windows 2000. The Emergency Repair Disk is designed to help you fix problems with your system files, your Registry, and your hard disk structure. The Emergency Repair Disk is part of the Windows Backup Program, shown in Figure 2-6.

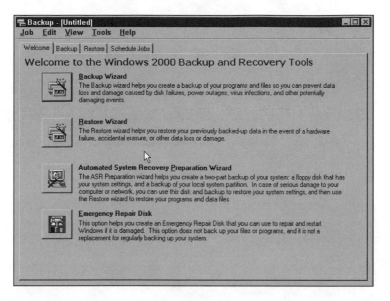

Figure 2-6: The Emergency Repair Disk is part of the Windows Backup program.

To create an Emergency Repair Disk, follow these steps:

STEPS:

Creating an Emergency Repair Disk

Step 1. Before you begin, you will need to prepare a blank, formatted 1.44MB floppy disk.

Step 2. Click Start ⇨ Programs ⇨ Accessories ⇨ System Tools, and then click Backup.

Step 3. From the menu, click Tools ⇨ Create an Emergency Repair Disk.

Step 4. The program will prompt you to insert a floppy disk into the drive. Click OK.

Step 5. Once the process is complete, you will see the dialog box shown in Figure 2-7.

Continued

STEPS:

Creating an Emergency Repair Disk *(continued)*

Figure 2-7: You will see this dialog box when you successfully create an Emergency Repair Disk.

Label the disk and put it away in a safe location where you will easily be able to find it. The last thing you want to do during an emergency is rummage through a large pile of floppy disks looking for this disk.

Tip

If you change your computer's configuration, you will want to create a new Emergency Repair Disk. The old disk will only be able to take you back to your old configuration, which will no longer be valid.

Secret Installation Roadmap

If you are curious to see how Windows 2000 knows where everything goes when it is installed, you can see from the roadmap that it leaves behind. Within the Windows 2000 system folder, which is probably called c:\winnt, is a subfolder called \INF. (There are two different tools, My Computer and Windows Explorer, that can be used to look at these folders. See Chapter 7 for more information on how to use them.) This subfolder is packed with INF and PNF files that contain setup information for Windows 2000 and other applications.

To see the roadmap, follow these steps:

1. Use Windows Explorer or My Computer to locate your Windows 2000 folder.

2. Scroll down this list of files until you find one called syssetup.inf.

3. Right click on this file, and select Open with. This displays the list of programs you can use to open this file. Scroll down until you find Notepad.

4. Select Notepad and click OK.

The syssetup.inf file is a list of instructions that shows what gets installed, and in what folders, for both upgrades and clean installs. The following portion of the file, for instance, shows the instructions for setting up the groups in the Start Menu's Program section.

```
;    The following section lists
all the groups under 'Start
Menu\Programs' that should
;    be created on a clean install
and upgrade. The format of the
items in this section
;    is:
;
;
;    [StartMenuGroups]
;    <group_name_id> =
<description>,<common_group>
;
;    where:
;
;        <description> is the name
of the group to be created;
;        <common_group> is a
number: 0 indicates private group
;
1 indicates common group
;
;
```

```
[StartMenuGroups]
Accessories = %accessories%,0
Accessibility = %accessibility%,0
Startup = %startup%,0
StartupCommon = %startup%,1
AdminTools = %admintools%,1
Entertainment =
%accessories_entertainment%,0
StartMenuCommon =
%startmenucommon%,0
SystemTools = %systemtools%,1
```

Syssetup.inf is not the only file that reveals these instructions. You may also find these files in the \INF folder:

- cdrom.inf sets up files for your CD-ROM drive.

- disk.inf sets up files for hard drives.

- msoe50.inf holds the information for setting up Outlook Express 5.0

along with many other similar files. One note of caution—unless you know what you are doing, this is a place where you should look but don't touch. Changing one of the instructions could cause problems if you have to install things again.

Troubleshooting Steps for Setup

Microsoft has included a series of troubleshooting steps to help you with installation issues. They are installed under Start ⇨ Help, but without a successful installation of Windows 2000, they won't be much use to you. If you have access to another computer that has a successful Windows 2000 installation, you can run the Windows Troubleshooter by clicking Start ⇨ Help, and then clicking the Troubleshooting icon in the right window, as shown in Figure 2-8.

Included with a number of Windows 2000 hardware and software trouble shooting guides is the System Setup Troubleshooter, which suggests some remedies for problems with your Windows 2000 setup. Figure 2-9 shows the potential problem points that you might find solutions for. (Note: this assumes that your computer has passed the System Compatibility Check at the beginning of the setup process.) Try the steps that follow, and then try again to install after each step.

Figure 2-8: Windows 2000 Help and the Troubleshooting Guide.

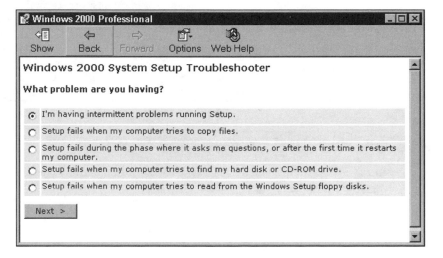

Figure 2-9: Windows 2000 System Setup Troubleshooter

Caution

Many of the suggestions involve tinkering with your computer's BIOS or CMOS settings. Making a mistake in these areas can cause serious problems with your computer. Carefully consult your hardware reference manual, or contact your computer manufacturer if you are not sure what to do.

STEPS:

Troubleshooting intermittent problems

Step 1. If you are having intermittent problems installing Windows 2000, the first suggestion is to temporarily disable your system cache memory. Instructions on how to do this are specific to various computer models, so you should consult your hardware guide or manufacturer for this information.

Step 2. Make sure your RAM modules have the correct specification and that they are correctly installed. (Problems here would have appeared using your previous operating system, too.)

Step 3. Check to see if your computer is infected with a boot sector virus.

Step 4. If your system is clean, you might need to add a wait state to your RAM settings. This is typically done through BIOS or CMOS settings and again, differs by computer.

STEPS:

Troubleshooting Setup failures when copying files

Step 1. Make sure your hard drive and CD-ROM have the correct drivers, and that they are properly configured. This should be done at the CMOS or BIOS levels, not with your previous operating system's Control Panel application.

Step 2 Make sure that all drive jumper settings are correct. If your drives are connected to the primary IDE channel, and your secondary IDE channel is enabled in your CMOS, that you move your CD-ROM drive cable to the secondary channel, and then configure it as a master.

Step 3. If that doesn't work, ensure that there are no hardware conflicts on your system, and check that you are using the correct IDE controller settings in the system BIOS.

Step 4. The next step, if the files still won't copy, is to see if your system's motherboard, controller, or hard disk have problems with a high-speed data transfer, also called PIO mode. You might need to lower this setting in your CMOS configuration.

Step 5. If you are still having problems, you might need to disable your system cache memory, which may be causing a conflict during Setup.

Step 6. Ensure that your RAM modules are the correct specifications and that they are correctly installed.

Continued

STEPS:

Troubleshooting Setup failures when copying files *(continued)*

Step 7.   Try adding a wait state to your RAM, again through your CMOS settings.

Step 8.   Make sure that all your drive cables are connected and working properly.

STEPS:

Troubleshooting setup failures during questions, or after first reboot

Step 1   Make sure your hard drive and CD-ROM have the correct drivers, and that they are properly configured. This should be done at the CMOS or BIOS levels, not with your previous operating system's Control Panel application.

Step 2.   Make sure that all drive jumper settings are correct. If your drives are connected to the primary IDE channel, and your secondary IDE channel is enabled in your CMOS, that you move your CD-ROM drive cable to the secondary channel, and then configure it as a master.

Step 3.   If that doesn't work, ensure that there are no hardware conflicts on your system, and check that you are using the correct IDE controller settings in the system BIOS.

Step 4.   If Setup is still failing, see if your system's motherboard, controller, or hard disk have problems with a high data transfer speed, or PIO mode. You may have to lower this in your CMOS configuration.

Step 5.   If you are still having problems, you might need to disable your system cache memory, which may be causing a conflict during Setup.

Step 6.   Ensure that your RAM modules are the correct specifications and that they are correctly installed.

Step 7.   Check to see if your computer is infected with a boot sector virus.

Step 8.   If your system is clean, you might need to add a wait state to your RAM settings. This is typically done through BIOS or CMOS settings and again, differs by computer.

STEPS:

Troubleshooting setup failure when looking for CD-ROM

Step 1. Make sure that your hardware configuration lets you boot from the CD-ROM drive.

Step 2. If it does, you need to check the Windows 2000 Hardware Compatibility List to make sure your drive and drive controller are supported. If they are not on the list, you need to contact the manufacturer for drivers.

Step 3. If they are supported, make sure your hard drive and CD-ROM have the correct drivers, and that they are properly configured. This should be done at the CMOS or BIOS levels, not with your previous operating system's Control Panel application.

Step 4. Make sure that all drive jumper settings are correct. If your drives are connected to the primary IDE channel, and your secondary IDE channel is enabled in your CMOS, that you move your CD-ROM drive cable to the secondary channel, and then configure it as a master.

Step 5. Check to make sure your CMOS boot order is set correctly. At startup, the CD-ROM should be accessed before the hard drive if you want to boot from it. As a quick test, the CD-ROM's busy light should flicker before your hard drive starts.

Step 6. Ensure that there are no hardware conflicts on your system, and check that you are using the correct IDE controller settings in the system BIOS.

Step 7. If there are no conflicts, see if your system's motherboard, controller, or hard disk have problems with a high data transfer speed, or PIO mode. You may have to lower this in your CMOS configuration.

Step 8. Check to see if your computer is infected with a boot sector virus.

Step 9. Make sure all your cables are connected properly.

STEPS:

Troubleshooting failures reading Windows Setup floppy disks

Step 1. If you are trying to install from floppy diskettes, make sure they are undamaged. See if you can read their directories using the Windows Explorer or using a DOS DIR command.

Continued

STEPS:

Troubleshooting failures reading Windows Setup floppy disks
(continued)

Step 2. If the diskettes appear to be bad, try to create new ones from the Windows 2000 CD-ROM. In Windows 95, 98 or Windows NT, click Start ⇨ Run, and then type d:\bootdisk\makeboot.bat a: in the Open text box (where d: is your CD-ROM drive letter and a: is your floppy drive letter).

Step 3. If the diskettes are good, check your CMOS to make sure that your system's boot order checks the floppy drive first.

Step 4. Next, make sure that the floppy drive works. If you can boot to your previous operating system, try accessing the drive by reading from or writing to it.

Summary

In this chapter, we looked at the most common situations in a Windows 2000 installation.

▶ We look at the preparation steps: hardware requirements, backup, collecting drivers, and so forth.

▶ We look at the considerations for an upgrade vs. a clean install.

▶ We look at the file system options available in Windows 2000.

▶ We take a guided tour of the upgrade process.

▶ We see how to perform a clean installation.

▶ We see how to run installation from the command line.

▶ We create an Emergency Repair Disk.

▶ We look at some troubleshooting steps.

Chapter 3

Advanced Windows 2000 Professional Installation

In This Chapter

We look at some advanced installation issues, including:

▶ Installing Windows 2000 on a dual-boot system.

▶ Installing the Resource Kit, including Setup Manager.

▶ Installing Windows 2000 Professional unattended.

Installing Windows 2000 on a Dual-Boot System

If you have to ask why anyone would ever want to set up Windows 2000 in a dual-boot configuration, read no further. Most individual users and most organizations will never need to boot the computer between alternate operating systems.

Various power users, however, will most definitely want to be able to dual-boot their systems. Some are high-end developers and IS administrators who need to work on a variety of platforms; others are kids who want to be able to run some of the cool classic games from the DOS, Windows 3.x, and Windows 95 eras.

Still others have decided they don't want to burn all their bridges to the past, so they opt to preserve the option to run their PC using their previous Windows operating system and Windows 2000.

Be forewarned, however: setting up a dual-boot system is not a simple process, and it will take you into a dark part of the Windows forest where the Wizards are scarce and help is expensive.

Windows 2000 can dual-boot with these operating systems:

■ Windows NT 3.51

■ Windows NT 4.0

- Windows 95
- Windows 98
- Windows 3.1 and Windows for Workgroups 3.11
- MS-DOS
- OS/2

Windows 2000 also can be dual-booted with other operating systems, but only through the use of other companies' products. Windows 2000 does not provide a way to dual-boot between them. Operating systems in this category include:

- UNIX
- Netware
- Linux

Tip

If you are worried that some of your legacy applications will not be compatible with Windows 2000, and you have a large hard drive to hold multiple operating systems, then dual-booting might be for you.

Disk Partitions

In a dual-boot environment, Windows 2000 can have either its own hard drive or have its own disk partition. Therefore, the first step in the dual-boot installation process is to decide where on your hard drive (or its primary partitions) you want your operating systems to be installed.

Note

The Windows 2000 disk partition should be at least 1GB in size. While the *minimum* installation size of the Windows 2000 files is roughly 500MB, you also need room on this partition for any updates, Service Packs, and so forth. Also, some programs — even if installed on another drive or partition — might insist on installing some files into the Windows 2000 directory.

File System

After you determine where you want to install Windows 2000 and your other OS(s), the next step is to decide what file system to use.

In general, to obtain the full benefits of Windows 2000 security and file compression, you need to use the NTFS file system. However, there are other factors to consider when you are setting up a dual-boot system.

The biggest factor you need to consider involves backward compatibility. If you use the NTFS file system — which the Windows 2000 Setup program will upgrade to NTFS 5 — only Windows 2000 will be able to access files created on that partition. Windows NT 4.0 Service Pack 4 or later will be able to read files on NTFS 5, but earlier operating systems will not.

Here are some general guidelines:

■ If you are going to dual-boot between Windows 2000 and MS-DOS, Windows 3.1, Windows 3.11, OS/2, Windows 95 and 98, Windows NT 3.51, or Windows NT 4.0 with Service Pack 2 or earlier, then you must use FAT. Your partition must be 2GB or less in size.

■ If you are going to dual-boot between Windows 2000 and Windows 95 OSR2 or Windows 98, you should use FAT32. You need a hard drive of at least 512MB.

Caution

If you do convert to NTFS 5, you cannot go back to any of the earlier file systems without first backing up all your files, reformatting the partition, and then restoring all your files from your backup afterward.

Secret

If you have an NTFS file system, earlier versions of Windows (such as Windows 95 OSR1) on a dual-boot system will not be able to access the NTFS partitions of their own local hard drive. But, if you have set up a peer-to-peer computer network between a Windows 2000 PC and a PC running an earlier version of Windows (such as Windows 95 OSR1), the older version of Windows *will* be able to access the files on the NTFS portion of the Windows 2000 PC's hard drive over the network.

Advantages of NTFS

If you use either FAT or FAT32 instead of NTFS 5, you will not be able to use the following Windows 2000 features:

■ Increased security settings: under NTFS, you can assign permissions to individual files and folders.

■ Recovery log of disk activities: users should rarely need to run any disk repair program on an NTFS volume, according to Microsoft.

■ Flexible formatting options, volume extensions, striped volumes, encryption, volume extensions without restart, disk quotas, distributed link tracking, mount points, and full text and property indexing.

Advantages of FAT

Of course, the major advantage to FAT and FAT32 is that it is the only file structure the older operating systems understand. Also, on a smaller hard drive, FAT can provide faster performance, both because the FAT file structure is simpler, and because the FAT folder size is smaller for an equal number of files.

A quick and dirty dual-boot scorecard

There are many variables to consider when contemplating a *paseo doble*. Table 3-1 lists some of the dual-boot issues that might affect you, depending on your situation and needs:

Table 3-1	Dual-Boot Considerations
Factor	*Considerations*
Partitions	Each operating system should ideally have its own drive or disk partition, and the operating system boot files normally must be located on the first physical hard drive in order to be bootable.
Applications	Since dual-booting requires a clean installation of your applications under Windows 2000, you will need to reinstall all your applications afterward.
Installation order	If your system is going to be configured with MS-DOS or Windows 95 and Windows 2000, you should install Windows 2000 last to avoid overwriting important files. Generally, you want to install dual-boot operating systems in the chronological order of their creation, except in the case of OS/2, which must be installed last.
File system	Your choice of file systems (FAT, FAT32, or NTFS) will be determined by your mix of operating systems.
Existing dual-boot systems	If you plan to add Windows 2000 to a system that is already set up to dual-boot between MS-DOS and OS/2, the Windows 2000 Setup program will configure your system so that you can dual-boot between Windows 2000 and the operating system you most recently used before you ran Windows 2000 setup.
Compressed drives	Windows 2000 can only be installed on a compressed drive if it uses the NTFS file compression utility. If you are going to dual-boot with Windows 95 or 98, you don't have to decompress DriveSpace or DoubleSpace volumes, but the compressed volumes won't be available while you are running Windows 2000.
Hardware settings	Microsoft warns that the first time you use Windows 95 or 98, they might reconfigure your hardware settings, which might cause problems with Windows 2000.
Application sharing	For applications to be able to run under both operating systems, they must be installed in each operating system. If you want to preserve settings in an application across operating systems, it is recommended that you reinstall each application under each operating system into the same folder.

Dual-boot scenarios

Each possible Windows 2000 dual-boot scenario has its own tricks and wrinkles, as you'll see below. Before we begin, though, we strongly urge you to prepare for the unexpected.

Caution

You should make sure you have good backups of all your data. It's also a very good idea to have a Windows 2000 startup floppy disk on hand so that you can boot the PC if your hard drive gets toasted. For more information on creating an emergency boot disk, see Chapter 2.

Tip

If your hard disk has partitions containing Windows 2000, Windows NT, Windows 98 or 95, Windows 3.x, DOS, or OS/2, you can choose which operating system your PC boots up to by changing the active partition.

Booting from the root

To boot into Windows 2000, Windows 2000's system partition (which contains all the files necessary to load Windows 2000 — Boot.ini, Bootsect.dos, and Ntdetect.com) must be located on the active partition of the computer's first hard drive.

You can use the DiskProbe tool in the Windows 2000 Resource Kit (see "Installing the Windows 2000 Resource Kit," later in this chapter) to determine which partition is the active partition on your hard drive. The value of the Boot Indicator field in DiskProbe will be *80* for the active partition, while the Boot Indicator field value of the non-active, non-boot partitions will be *00*.

To install and load one or more additional operating systems on your x86-based PC, you must change the active partition so that each OS's partition is the active partition at the time of installation.

Use Windows 2000's Disk Management snap-in (see Figure 3-1), which you can access through the Control Panel, to designate a new active partition.

STEPS:

Using The Disk Management Snap-In to Set the Active Partition

Step 1. Click Start ⇨ Settings ⇨ Control Panel, and click the Administrative tools icon.

Step 2. Click Computer Management, and then expand Storage in the left pane so that you can see Disk Management.

Step 3. In Disk Management Snap-in, click a logical drive or primary partition.

Continued

Step 4. Open the Partition menu.

Step 5. Set a non-active partition as active by clicking Mark Active.

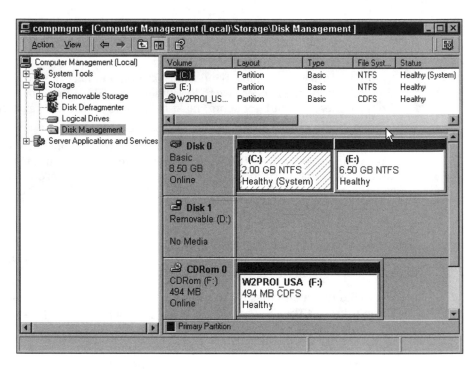

Figure 3-1: The Disk Management snap-in.

The only problem with this method is that you need to be running Windows
2000 to use it. If you can't run Windows 2000, you can use the MS-DOS
Fdisk.exe program to accomplish the same thing.

STEPS:

Using DOS Fdisk to Set the Active Partition

Step 1. Boot your system to the MS-DOS prompt using a startup disk
containing Fdisk.exe.

Step 2. Type a:fdisk at the DOS prompt and press Enter.

Step 3. Type the numeral 2 in the Enter Choice box.

Step 4. Make sure one of the columns has an A in the Status column, indicating that it is the active partition.

Step 5. To change the active — or system — partition, type the number of the partition you want to set as the active partition, and then repeat Step 4.

Tip

If you want to dual boot between DOS and Windows 95 or Windows 98, you'll need to edit the multiboot line of your Msdos.sys file, which should be located in the root directory of your hard drive. First locate the file in Windows Explorer, choose properties and change the file attributes so that Read Only and Hidden are unchecked. Then open the file in a text editor and make sure multiboot=1. Microsoft says that by changing the value from 0 to 1, you can "start MS-DOS by pressing F4 (or by pressing F8 to use the Windows Startup menu)."

Installing DOS and Windows 2000 dual-boot

Do yourself a favor and install MS-DOS before you install Windows 2000. Use the steps described above to change one of the primary partitions on your hard drive to the active partition, and then install MS-DOS to that partition as directed by your MS-DOS manual. Then, install Windows 2000 to another partition on your hard drive, which the Windows 2000 Setup program will change to be the active or boot partition as described above. Any partitions you want MS-DOS to be able to see must be formatted as FAT or FAT32.

Installing Windows 3.x and Windows 2000 dual-boot

Again, it's best to install the older OS, Windows 3.x, first into a separate partition. Any partitions you want Windows 3.x to be able to see must be formatted as FAT.

Installing Windows 95 or 98 and Windows 2000 dual-boot

You cannot install both Windows 95 and Windows 98 to then dual-boot with Windows 2000. You must choose one or the other. Finally, you should make sure the partition where you install Windows 95 or 98 is formatted to FAT for Windows 95 OSR1, and either FAT or FAT32 for Windows 95 OSR2 and Windows 98.

Installing Windows NT and Windows 2000 dual-boot

This is the easiest Windows 2000 upgrade path. However, if you experience trouble, you might find it helpful to install Windows 2000 and Windows NT interactively, without the winnt/u or winnt32/u commands.

Installing OS/2 and Windows 2000 dual-boot

Here's another place where the general rules don't apply. Even though OS/2 is one of the oldest OSs here, you should install it last in a dual-boot installation sequence. Thus, if you wanted to be able to boot to Windows 95, Windows 2000, and OS/2, you'd install Windows 95 first, Windows 2000 next, and OS/2 last. Also note that Windows 2000 only supports OS/2 version 1.

Tip

On a dual-boot PC that uses FAT, FAT32 and NTFS volumes, you can use the Windows 2000's Disk Management snap-in to assign drive letters to the FAT and NTFS volumes. If you begin with the first drive letter after the one assigned to the last FAT volume, you can ensure that the FAT drive letters appear the same for each file system. This also helps to ensure that your migrated paths are accurate and valid.

Installing UNIX, Netware or Linux and Windows 2000 dual-boot

The same general rule applies here: install UNIX or another non-Microsoft operating system in a separate partition from the one that contains Windows 2000. You can then use either the other operating system's boot manager, or a third-party partitioning and boot management tool (such PowerQuest Partition Magic, IBM Boot Manager or V Communications System Commander) to choose the partition you want to boot to. Be careful, though. If your dual-boot environment includes any NTFS 5 partitions, make sure that the third-party tool can handle NTFS 5.

Secret

We know of one individual at Microsoft with a multiboot system running Windows 98, Windows NT 4, Linux, and Solaris UNIX. Since Windows 2000 doesn't provide a way to do this, he uses System Commander from V Communications to manage the boot process.

What to expect when the Windows 2000 Setup program is run in a dual-boot environment

You've installed one or more operating system on one or more partitions of your hard drive which you have made active as needed. Now, you want to install Windows 2000. Piece of cake.

You can designate the partition where you want to install Windows 2000 as the active partition, as discussed above. Setup and installation is one of the places where a great deal of effort has been invested to make things simpler, and it shows.

When the Windows 2000 Setup program runs, it checks your existing hard drive configuration. Depending on what it finds, you might have these options during setup:

- If setup finds an unpartitioned hard drive, you will be given the opportunity to create and size a partition for Windows 2000.

- If the hard drive has a partition with insufficient room for Windows 2000, but there is enough unpartitioned disk space available, you will be able to use the unpartitioned space for the installation.

- If the hard drive has a partition that is big enough for Windows 2000, you can use that.

- You can delete an existing partition to create more unpartitioned disk space for a Windows 2000 installation. Deleting a partition will erase any data on that partition.

Tip

During Windows 2000 setup, create only the partition you need for Windows 2000. After it has been installed, you can use the Windows 2000 Disk Management snap-in to make changes or to create new partitions.

How does dual-booting work in Windows 2000?

The dual-boot function in Windows 2000 is managed by Bootsect.dos. This hidden, read-only system file is recreated each time the Windows 2000 Setup program is run.

When you install Windows 2000 on an x86-based computer, Windows 2000 copies the boot sector for the active partition of the computer to the file Bootsect.dos. Windows 2000 Setup then replaces the boot sector on the active partition with its own boot sector.

When you start your computer and Windows 2000 is on the active partition in a multiboot system, Windows 2000 automatically starts the Boot Loader (NTLDR). The Boot Loader allows you to choose between installed operating systems.

The Final Step: Installing — and reinstalling — all your apps

Once you've succeeded in installing two or more operating systems, you then get to reinstall all your applications — not just once, but once for each operating system you have installed. Microsoft recommends that these digital genuflections be performed in the privacy of a common folder — in other words, that you install and reinstall each application to the same program folder on your system. Even so, you'll probably find that not all settings will be transferred, and you will then need to manually reconfigure each application to some degree.

Secret

Here's one the folks in Redmond find very restful. If you install a Windows program to a common folder on a dual-boot Windows 2000 computer, you can run the exact same program under different versions of Windows on the same computer.

Installing the Windows 2000 Resource Kit

The Windows 2000 Resource Kit contains a collection of management tools, support utilities, and documents that can help you manage and configure your Windows 2000 computer. It is not installed during the default Windows 2000 installation, so you need to install it separately after you have Windows 2000 up and running.

Among other things, the Resource Kit contains DiskProbe and Setup Manager (which eases the task of unattended Windows 2000 installations), which is the next topic we'll address in this chapter. The general tool groups in the Resource Kit are: Deployment, Diagnostics, Computer Management, Network Management, and Storage Management.

To install the Resource Kit, follow these steps:

STEPS:

Installing the Resource Kit

Step 1.   Start your Windows 2000 computer.

Step 2.   Insert the Windows 2000 CD-ROM into the CD-ROM drive and wait for the AutoRun screen. If the AutoRun screen doesn't appear, see Step 6.

Step 3.   When the AutoRun screen appears, click Browse this CD.

Step 4.   Using the Browse window, navigate to the \Support\Reskit folder.

Step 5.   Click Setup.exe, and then follow the installation instructions.

Step 6.   If the AutoRun screen doesn't appear after you insert the CD-ROM, click Start ⇨ Run.

Step 7.   Type the following command into the Open text box on the Run dialog box (where D: is your CD-ROM drive letter):

```
D:\SUPPORT\RESKIT\SETUP.EXE
```

The setup program will install the Resource Kit tools onto your hard drive (see Figure 3-2). The default installation directory is \Program Files\Resource

Kit, and the tools will occupy about 8MB of disk space. It will also add shortcuts to your Start ⇨ Programs menu.

Secret

During the Windows 2000 beta testing program, many users of the third beta release had problems installing the Resource Kit from the CD-ROM; the installation would fail with an error message. The workaround? Copy the entire \Support\Reskit\ folder to a temporary folder on your hard drive, and then run setup from your hard drive.

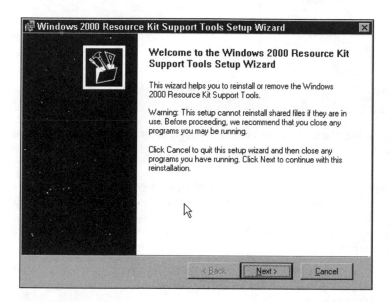

Figure 3-2: Starting the Resource Kit installation

The tools that come with the Resource Kit are accessed through the Microsoft Management Console (MMC), which is a shell program you can use to manage various utility and configuration programs that either come with Windows 2000, or that can be added later. When you run the Resource Kit, you will see a window similar to Figure 3-3. In the left pane, you can search for the particular tool you want to use, which can then be run by simply clicking or double-clicking it in the right pane. For more information on the MMC, see Chapter 15.

Unattended Installation

One of the greatest weaknesses of Windows NT 4, the immediate predecessor of Windows 2000, was the headaches it gave system administrators trying to installing it across oftentimes quite extensive networks.

With Windows NT 4, you had to individually run setup on every machine on a network, which consumed 45 to 60 minutes of IS time for each machine to which you installed or which you upgraded. And it gets better!

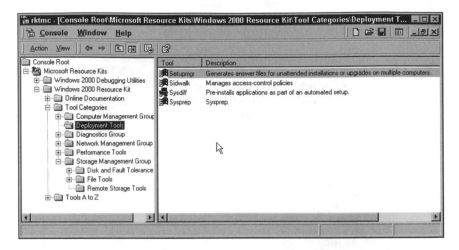

Figure 3-3: The Resource Kit includes the Setup Manager, which helps you manage unattended installations.

Among the endearing qualities of Windows NT 4 was the fact that every time you added new hardware you had to rerun every service pack you'd ever applied to a machine each time you changed the hardware configuration! Say what? Well, actually, the system administrators we know said a lot more than *what*.

Some of these graphic expressions were apparently communicated back to Microsoft, because Windows 2000 boasts a much richer array of automated installation tools:

- Fully automated installation scripts with Setup Manager
- Disk imaging with System Preparation Tool
- Remote Installation Server
- Electronic software distribution with Systems Management Server 2.0

Automatic installation by scripting

The biggest addition — and the addition Microsoft is obviously proudest of — is the fully scriptable installation now available through the Setup Manager Wizard shown in Figure 3-4 (see "Installing the Windows 2000 Resource Kit," earlier in this chapter, if you don't already have Setup Manager installed on your system).

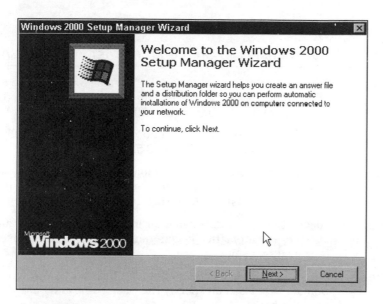

Figure 3-4: Windows 2000's new Setup Manager Wizard automates the creation of answer files.

Answer files are used to answer questions during Setup. Windows 2000 takes the answer file concept in Windows NT 4 further, allowing you to automatically install even the gnarliest peripherals. For instance, Windows 2000 lets you can script the installation of sound cards with an answer file. Better still, the Windows 2000 Setup program won't abort if a peripheral such as a modem doesn't install properly.

The Windows 2000 Setup Manager Wizard will walk you through the process of creating an answer file without requiring you to actually write any script yourself. Answer files can be used to both upgrade and create new systems.

By creating automated installation scripts with answer files, system admininstrators can now avoid having to physically send a technician to every desktop and spend up to an hour there.

STEPS:

Using Setup Manager to Create an Answer File

Step 1. Start the Setup Manager from the Windows 2000 Resource Kit (see "Installing the Windows 2000 Resource Kit," earlier in this chapter).

Continued

STEPS:

Using Setup Manager to Create an Answer File *(continued)*

Step 2.   Choose "Create a new answer file." You also can choose to edit an existing answer file, or you can create an answer file that is a duplicate of the PC that is currently running the Setup Manager.

Step 3.   Select the level of user interaction desired, including fully automated, as shown in Figure 3-5.

Step 4.   Enter default information for Name and Organization. If you leave this information blank, no name or organization will be passed to the PC by the answer file during installation.

Step 5.   Specify the computer's name, or instruct the Windows 2000 Setup Manager to automatically generate computer names based on organization name.

Step 6.   Automatically enroll destination computers in a Workgroup or Domain. You also can specify the User Name and Password for the machine here.

Step 7.   Choose the folder into which you want Windows 2000 installed.

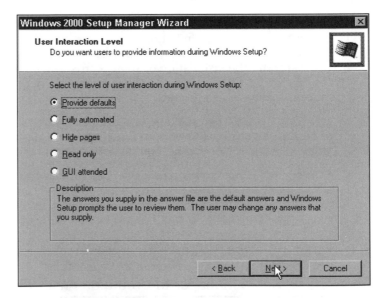

Figure 3-5: Windows 2000's new Setup Manager lets you set the level of automation you want for scripted Windows 2000 installation.

A sample answer file

To perform an unattended installation of Windows 2000, you would type the following command:

```
winnt[32] /unattend:<answer file> /s:<install source>
[/syspart:<target drive>]
```

where the parameters are as listed in Table 3-2:

Table 3-2   Unattended Install Parameters

Parameter	Explanation
<answer file>	The file containing the answers to the installation questions.
<install source>	The location of the Windows NT installation files.
/syspart	This will copy all of the boot and temporary files to a target drive and then mark the target as active. You use this switch if the target drive is going to be duplicated and then put into another computer as the primary drive.

Obviously, your answer file must be carefully constructed so that it supplies the correct answers to installation questions. A sample answer file called UNATTEND.TXT can be found in the \I386 folder on the Windows 2000 CD-ROM.

A sample file uses the following format:

```
; Sample Unattended Setup Answer File
;
; This file contains information about how to automate the
installation
; or upgrade of Windows NT Workstation and Windows NT Server so the
; Setup program runs without requiring user input.
;
; For information on how to use this file, read the appropriate
sections
; of the Windows NT 5.0 Resource Kit.

[Unattended]
Unattendmode = FullUnattended
OemPreinstall = NO
TargetPath = WINNT
Filesystem = LeaveAlone

[UserData]
FullName = "Your User Name"
OrgName = "Your Organization Name"
ComputerName = "COMPUTER_NAME"
```

```
[GuiUnattended]
TimeZone = "004"
; Sets the Admin Password to NULL
AdminPassword = *
; Turn AutoLogon on
AutoLogon = Yes

;For Server installs
[LicenseFilePrintData]
AutoMode = "PerServer"
AutoUsers = "0"

[GuiRunOnce]
; List the programs that you want to launch when the machine is logged
into for the first time
; "Notepad %WINDIR%\Setuperr.log"

[Display]
BitsPerPel = 4
XResolution = 800
YResolution = 600
VRefresh = 70

[Networking]
; When set to YES, setup will install default networking components.
The components to be set are
; TCP/IP, File and Print Sharing, and the Client for Microsoft
Networks.
InstallDefaultComponents = YES

[Identification]
JoinWorkgroup = Workgroup
```

Automatic installation by disk imaging

The System Preparation Tool (also in the Windows 2000 Resource Kit) provides for the use of the same disk image across multiple Windows 2000 machines — even where the hardware is not uniform. The reason that disk image deployment can work across a relatively heterogeneous network is that the Windows 2000 Setup program automatically runs the process of detecting and installing hardware after the operating system files have been copied to the target machine.

Caution

The only way to make sure that disk image deployment of Windows 2000 will work is to rigorously test beforehand. There can be many unexpected pitfalls. For instance, the mass storage controller on both the master and the target images must be the same. For instance, you'll come to grief if one PC has a Symbios Logic controller and the other has an Adaptec controller.

Automatic installation by remote installation server

Microsoft has leveraged Windows 2000's new Active Directory feature to make possible a new method of automatic installation in Windows 2000 — remote OS installation. Remote OS installation can use Microsoft's new Pre-boot eXecution Environment (PXE) remote boot technology and server-based services to install copies of Windows 2000 Professional on workstations throughout an enterprise.

Tip   Remote Installation Server deployment of Windows 2000 is only suited to organizations that already have an Active Directory infrastructure, where the target machines are all new and support PXE.

Automatic installation by electronic software distribution

And for the really Big Boys — those who have bought into Microsoft's Systems Management Server (SMS), Windows 2000 offers even more bells and whistles. In addition to rolling out Windows 2000 Professional, SMS 2.0 provides detailed software and hardware inventory and monitoring, as well as remote troubleshooting tools.

Summary

In this chapter, we examined several advanced Windows 2000 Professional installation issues, including:

▶ Installing Windows 2000 on a dual-boot system

▶ Installing the Windows 2000 Resource Kit, including Setup Manager

▶ Various tactics for unattended Windows 2000 Professional installation

Chapter 4

Hardware and Software Compatibility

In This Chapter

We show you how to manage and configure your computer using the Control Panel. You will learn:

▶ What you need to think about regarding compatibility and Windows 2000.

▶ Which software and hardware products will and won't function under Windows 2000.

▶ What "Windows 2000-compatible" really means.

▶ Windows 2000 changes to MS-DOS commands.

Compatibility Not Spoken Here

When addressing the subject of Windows 2000 compatibility with existing PC software and hardware, one is almost moved to speak in hushed tones: so many have fallen here, so much blood has been shed.

Compatibility — or the lack thereof — has been, by design, one of the main weaknesses of Windows since the beginning. In designing Windows 2000, the Windows and Windows NT architects decided to build a pure system, one that would make precious few compromises with the messy, retrograde realities of PC hardware and software.

Since they would not take the mountain to Mohammed, the rest of the PC vendor community was simply going to have to come to Mount NT, re-designing their programs and products to meet Windows 2000 specifications.

Not surprisingly, Windows and Windows NT both have a history of compatibility problems with applications, networks, modems, printers, and so forth. For example, using NT 4.0 Service Pack 1, installing Corel WordPerfect 8 would result in a thoroughly trashed system. With NT Service Pack 2, you'd see the infamous blue screen of death and the dreaded STOP 0x0000000A error if you unwisely tried to access your floppy or CD-ROM drive while antivirus software was running.

Windows 2000's immediate predecessor, Windows NT 4.0, also coyly manifested incompatibility problems in areas completely unrelated to the actual problem. For instance, printing in Windows NT 4.0 had a strange way of affecting functions that might, at first, appear to be totally separate. If your network printers were set as the default printers and you lost your network connection, any 16-bit Windows-based applications, such as Write, might either load very slowly or appear to hang completely.

No hardware or software has been immune from Windows compatibility problems. Even some of Microsoft's own applications have had difficulties, and Microsoft acknowledges that certified device drivers might also crash (see the sidebar, "Microsoft Windows NT Crash Study Casts Harsh Light On Device Drivers," later in this chapter). Nothing seemed to bring out the worst in the Dr. Jekyll and Mr. Hyde print persona more, though, than third-party network print managers.

Happily, all these problems have been fixed in Windows 2000. In fact, Microsoft has taken significant steps toward merging NT into the PC mainstream, such as Windows 2000's adoption of the Windows 98 Windows Driver Model (WDM).

Mohammed has not moved very much, though. The mountain of Windows software and hardware that will need to move if it is to run on Windows 2000 systems. What does this mean? For the first time since the late 1980s, compatibility is an issue you need to stay on top of.

Not Good Enough, Right Out of the Box

Right off the bat, Microsoft wrote off a fairly large number of products in terms of Windows 2000 compatibility. Here some of the error messages you'll encounter if you try to install one of the nearly 150 products that won't work with Windows 2000 — right out of the box, as they say.

You'll recognize some familiar names here: — Adaptec RAID controllers, Phoenix PC Card controller software, Calcomp tablets, Wacom tablets, Traveling Software's LapLink, McAfee VirusScan, Logitech mice, and others

- Your Adaptec AAA or ARO series RAID controller will not function under Microsoft Windows 2000 with the driver that is currently installed.

- Adaptec CD-R Filter Driver (required by Adaptec CD Creator) versions 2.4 and earlier are not compatible with Windows 2000. Therefore, this software will be disabled during the upgrade.

- This audio adapter is based on the Avance Logic ALS120 chipset and will not function under Microsoft Windows 2000 with the driver that is currently installed.

- The Calcomp tablet will not function under Microsoft Windows 2000 with the driver that is currently installed.

- InocuLAN by Cheyenne (a division of Computer Associates) is not compatible with Windows 2000 and must be uninstalled before the upgrade can continue. To uninstall this software, quit Windows 2000 Setup and follow the instructions below.

- Version 2.0 of the Handwriter software by CIC is not compatible with Windows 2000. The tablet will no longer function, and the following message will appear each time the system is started.

- Compaq CPQ32FS2 — The Windows NT 4.0 driver installed for this hardware is not compatible with Windows 2000 and will be disabled during the upgrade process.

- The Crystalware audio device is not compatible with Windows 2000 and will be disabled during the upgrade.

- The manufacturer of your computer (Digital Equipment Corporation, a subsidiary of Compaq) has requested that Microsoft stop providing support in Microsoft Windows 2000 for the model of computer you have. For this reason, the files your computer needs to run Windows 2000 are not available from Microsoft. Contact your computer manufacturer for information.

- Dell's "OpenManage Client" Software installed on the computer will not function under Windows 2000 with the driver that is currently installed.

- The currently installed driver for the Dell Auto-Shutdown Service is not compatible with Windows 2000 and will be disabled during the upgrade.

- The currently installed driver for the Dell Thermal Shutdown Service is not compatible with Windows 2000 and will be disabled during the upgrade.

- One of the drivers required by the HP Colorado Backup II 6.0 software installed on this machine is not compatible with Windows 2000 and will be disabled during the upgrade.

- This display adapter may not be compatible with Microsoft Windows 2000 it's driver, glint.sys will be disabled before upgrading to Microsoft Windows 2000.

- The HP LaserJet printer will not function properly using the driver that is currently installed.

- Hewlett Packard Desktop Management Interface (DMI) Components are not compatible with Windows 2000.

- The version of Hewlett-Packard HP Lock that is currently installed on your computer does not support Windows 2000.

- The version of the Hewlett-Packard C4734 Extended Keyboard driver that is currently installed on your computer is not compatible with Windows 2000.

- The HP 1150c scanner software is not compatible with Microsoft Windows 2000. You may want to uninstall the 1150c software before upgrading to Windows 2000.

- The version of Hewlett-Packard TopTools Device Manager that is currently installed on your computer does not support Windows 2000.

- The driver that is currently installed for the IBM ServeRAID II SCSI Host Adapter is incompatible with Windows 2000 and must be uninstalled before the upgrade can continue.

- The Low Speed IRDA Driver by IBM Corporation is not compatible with Windows 2000 and will be disabled during the upgrade.

- The [MCI] MPEG-2 Decoder driver by IBM Corporation is not compatible with Windows 2000 and must be uninstalled before the upgrade can continue.

- The TrackPoint driver by IBM Corporation is not compatible with Windows 2000 and will be disabled during the upgrade.

- The 9397 Video Capture driver by IBM Corporation is not compatible with Windows 2000 and will be disabled during the upgrade.

- The driver that is currently installed for the Imation Parallel Port SuperDisk Drive is incompatible with Windows 2000 and must be uninstalled before the upgrade can continue.

- The SCSI adapter in this computer is based on the Initio INI-910 chip and will not function under Windows 2000 with the driver that is currently installed. The driver must be uninstalled before the upgrade can continue.

- Portions of the Intel LANDesk Client Manager installed on your system are incompatible with Windows 2000 and will be disabled during the upgrade.

- Setup has detected an Iomega Zip drive connected to the parallel port on your computer. The drivers for this device will be disabled upon upgrade, as Windows 2000 has embedded support for the Iomega Zip drive.

- This version of the Interphase Fibre Channel driver is not compatible with Windows 2000 and will be disabled during the upgrade process.

- Windows 2000 will not function with the version of Microsoft Intellipoint Software for the Microsoft Mouse installed on this system. During the upgrade process this software will be disabled.

- The PC Card controller software by Phoenix is not compatible with Windows 2000 and must be uninstalled before the upgrade can continue. The uninstaller is usually found in the Program Files\Card Executive directory and is called Uninstall.exe. Removing this software will disable the Cards.sys and Enabler.sys files that are known to be incompatible with Windows 2000.

- The OnStream Echo Backup Software is not compatible with Windows 2000.

- The Phoenix Power Management service on your system will not function under Microsoft Windows 2000 with the driver that is currently installed (Phnixad.sys) and will be disabled during the upgrade process.

- DeskOn which is part of DeskView by Siemens is not compatible with Windows 2000. Therefore DeskOn must be uninstalled before the upgrade can continue.

- DeskWOL which is part of DeskView by Siemens is not compatible with Windows 2000. Therefore DeskWOL must be uninstalled before the upgrade can continue.

- The LapLink program by Traveling Software is not compatible with Windows 2000 and must be uninstalled before the upgrade can continue.

- The Lexmark printer will not function properly using the driver that is currently installed.

- Logitech MouseWare drivers are not compatible with Windows 2000. Therefore, this software will be disabled during the upgrade.

- The Lucent Technologies Modem Driver for NT 4 is not compatible with Windows 2000. Therefore, this driver will be disabled during the upgrade.

- Portions of the McAfee ViruScan driver installed on your system are incompatible with Windows 2000 and will be disabled during the upgrade.

- The Powerdesk Utilities installed on this computer will no longer continue to work properly.

- Message Queuing 1.0 Information Store was found on this computer. If you continue to upgrade to Windows 2000, the Message Queuing service and data will not be available.

- The Panda Anti-Virus software installed on your computer is not compatible with Windows 2000. The software will be disabled for the upgrade to continue.

- The pcAnywhere software by Symantec is not compatible with Windows 2000 and must be uninstalled before the upgrade can continue.

- The Real Time Monitor of PC-Cillin NT, by Trend Micro, is not compatible with Windows 2000 and PC-Cillin NT and will be disabled for the upgrade to continue.

- The Rockwell Riptide audio driver on your system is not compatible with Windows 2000.

- The SIIG application titled "CYBER PCI" installed on this computer will not function under Windows 2000 with the driver that is currently installed, and will be disabled.

- The STB video adapter in this computer will not function under Windows 2000 with the driver that is currently installed. Multiple monitor functionality will be disabled. If you continue, Setup will remove this video driver and install a Plug and Play video driver on this computer.

- The "DeskOff Driver" which is part of DeskView by Siemens is not compatible with Windows 2000. Therefore DeskOff must be uninstalled before the upgrade.

- "DeskView System Monitoring" which is part of DeskView by Siemens is not compatible with Windows 2000 and will be disabled during the upgrade.

- Toshiba Power Management System on your system is not compatible with Windows 2000 and the most part of power management feature will be provided by Windows 2000 itself. Therefore this feature will be disabled for the upgrade to continue.

- Toshiba Video Capture software installed on your system is not compatible with Windows 2000. Therefore, this software will be disabled during the upgrade.

- Toshiba System Configuration Interface drivers are not compatible with Windows 2000. Therefore, this software must be uninstalled prior to upgrading to Windows 2000.

- The UMAX VistaScan version 2.40 scanner software is not compatible with Windows 2000 and will be disabled during the upgrade. Setup will install a new UMAX DS driver so that your scanner will function under Windows 2000.

- The Wacom Digital Writing device installed on this computer will not function under Microsoft Windows 2000 with the driver that is currently installed. The device will be disabled during the upgrade process.

- Windows 2000 Setup cannot determine the version of Windows CE Services installed on this computer.

- Windows CE Services requires version 2.2 to properly communicate with Windows 2000

Musical Chairs: Round Two

The second group of Windows 2000 dropouts — incompatibilities that Microsoft decided to live with rather than fix — is revealed in additions made by Microsoft to the Microsoft Knowledge Base (MSKB) during the late beta phase of Windows 2000 and listed in Table 4-1.

Although some of these compatibility issues will be fixed by the time final product ships, experience with previous versions of Windows suggests that most — if not all — of the compatibility issues are present in the version that ships.

You'll find issues with Netscape Communicator 4.04, Electronic Arts Need For Speed III, Symantec Norton Anti-Virus Deluxe 4.0, America Online 4.0, as well as Microsoft products like Word 2000 and the IntelliPoint mouse software.

For more information, see the online version of the MSKB at http://support. microsoft.com/support/c.asp (you'll have to register first to access this page).

Table 4-1   Late Breaking Windows 2000 Compatibility Issues

MSKB Article Number	Synopsis of Compatibility Problem
Q202581	IntelliPoint Software Reports Errors in Windows 2000 When you start the Microsoft IntelliPoint software, the Mouse Properties dialog box may open with some options disabled.
Q226042	Error Messages with Communicator 4.04 After Windows 2000 Upgrade After you upgrade a computer running Microsoft Windows NT 3.51 with Netscape Communicator version 4.04 installed to Windows 2000, you may get the error: NETSCAPE caused an access violation in OLETHK32.DLL.
Q226140	Wrong MS-DOS Version Is Displayed in Compaq Diagnostics After you upgrade a Compaq computer from Windows NT 4.0 to Windows 2000, you may note that the MS-DOS version displayed in the Compaq Diagnostics program is incorrect.
Q227697	Cannot Uninstall Norton "Your Eyes Only" in Windows 2000 You can install and run the Norton Your Eyes Only software in Windows 2000, but you cannot uninstall it using Windows 2000's Add/Remove Programs tool.
Q206675	Need for Speed III Not Compatible with Microsoft Windows 2000 If you upgrade Microsoft Windows 95 or Microsoft Windows 98 to Microsoft Windows 2000 Professional, the Electronic Arts Need For Speed III game will not run properly.
Q226031	NEC Card Wizard Does Not Work After Windows 2000 Upgrade If you upgrade from Microsoft Windows NT 4.0 to Windows 2000, the NEC Card Wizard program may no longer function.
Q226302	Manta Handwriter 2.0 Handwriting Practice Does Not Work in Windows 2000 If you upgrade from Microsoft Windows 95 to Windows 2000, the Manta Handwriter 2.0 graphics tablet may not work any more.
Q220683	Invalid Page Fault with Office 2000 Assistant Character That Has Fewer Than 256 Colors In Windows 2000 if you choose an Office 2000 Assistant in the Office Assistant Gallery, the operation may freeze and shut down.

Continued

Table 4-1   *(continued)*

MSKB Article Number	Synopsis of Compatibility Problem
Q226380	Epson Print Utilities Removed During Windows 2000 Upgrade
	If you upgrade to Windows 2000 on a computer that has Windows 95 installed and an Epson Stylus Color 800 printer, the Epson print utility programs will no longer available.
Q227309	Cannot Quit Norton Anti-Virus Deluxe 4.0 Rescue Disk Tool
	If you want to upgrade a Microsoft Windows 98-based computer to Windows 2000, you must first uninstall Norton Anti-virus Deluxe 4.0.
Q227467	Access Violations Opening Multiple Documents in Quattro Pro
	If you open multiple documents in Corel Quattro Pro 7.0, your computer may stop freeze.
Q227652	Cannot Install "You Don't Know Jack Sports" in Windows 2000
	If you try to install the You Don't Know Jack Sports software in Windows 2000, you will find you can not.
Q228086	America Online 4.0 Cannot Establish Modem Connection in Windows 2000
	If you upgrade from Microsoft Windows 95 or Microsoft Windows 98 to Windows 2000, America Online (AOL) 4.0 may not be able to establish a modem connection.
Q227967	Cannot Use Internal Touchpad When You Connect an IntelliMouse
	With Windows 2000, if you connect a Microsoft IntelliMouse to a laptop that uses an internal touchpad, the touchpad may be disabled.
Q211241	Problems with SoundBlaster Live and Windows 2000
	If you restart your computer after loading and selecting the "8MB midi bank" in the AudioHQ SoundFont program included with the Creative Labs SoundBlaster Live sound card, you may get a critical stop error, better known as the blue screen of death.
Q229453	Unable to Install Office 2000 Server Extensions on Cyrix CPU
	You can not install Microsoft Office Server Extensions on PCs with Cyrix 233-333 megahertz (MHz) MII CPUs.
Q234803	No ClipArt Displayed in Microsoft Clip Gallery After Installation
	If you point to Picture on the Insert menu and click ClipArt in any of the Microsoft Office 2000 programs, you see no images in the Clip Gallery.

MSKB Article Number	Synopsis of Compatibility Problem
Q235306	Error Message "The Microsoft Map data file EUROPE.IND was not found."
	If you attempt to insert a Microsoft Map graphic into a Microsoft Excel worksheet, you may receive an error.
Q226778	Animated GIFs Lose Animation When Dragged from Word 2000
	When you insert an animated GIF file into Microsoft Word 2000, and then drag this animated GIF from Word into Microsoft PowerPoint 2000, it may lose its animated qualities.
Q227425	CD-ROM Changer Mapped as Single Drive Letter in Windows 2000
	Upon installing or upgrading to Windows 2000, you may find there is only a single drive letter for your ATAPI CD-ROM changer.
Q227452	PS/2 Mouse May Not Work on Laptop Docking Station
	If you install Windows 2000 on a laptop computer that is set up to use a docking station with a PS/2-style mouse, the mouse may not function properly.

Microsoft Windows NT Crash Study Casts Harsh Light On Device Drivers

The Windows 2000 reliability issue is like the smell of the dog — it just won't go away.

Supposedly built from the ground up for greater security and stability than prior versions of Windows, NT is the OS that put the term "blue screen of death" on the map.

Now a couple of new Windows NT crash studies reveal something about the curious scope and shape of the problem.

In one Giga Information Group study involving 1,300 corporate NT sites, the good and the bad news are nestled down right next to each other.

Microsoft has been talking up the Giga study's finding that 60 percent of the participants only had to reboot their NT servers once every six months, which is good.

What smells like dog is the fact that the same survey shows that 15 percent have to reboot between daily and monthly. So the majority get reliable performance from NT, but a significant minority get poor, even unacceptable reliability.

What's the deal? Another study, this one conducted by Microsoft itself on 700 NT crashes, sheds some interesting light on what causes NT trouble. According to Vince Orgovan, Microsoft Program Manager for Windows NT Reliability, half of all NT crashes were associated with device drivers.

Anti-virus products were also a hot spot, with 8 percent of NT crashes associated with this product category. Orgovan said "one third of all drivers submitted [to Microsoft] for NT certification have some sort of crash experience."

Continued

(continued)

This is hardly news to old NT hands, of course, who know all too well how peevish and poorly behaved NT can be in the presence of even mainstream peripherals.

What is a little surprising is Orgovan's revelation that in Microsoft's root crash analysis of 700 NT flameouts; Microsoft certified NT drivers caused more trouble than uncertified drivers. According to Orgovan, 7 percent of the crashes were associated with uncertified device drivers, while 18 percent were associated with drivers that Microsoft had certified for use with NT.

Hmmm.

What Is Compatible with Windows 2000?

Because of the Registry tweaking noted in the Secret above, most relatively new mainstream business applications run pretty well under Windows 2000.

Of course, "pretty well" might not be good enough if one of the few broken features is one feature you absolutely need. What about complete, reliable, mission-critical compatibility?

Microsoft's Web site boasts that more than 4,000 products are already compatible with Windows 2000, but closer examination reveals this to be a bit of an exaggeration. At the same time Microsoft claims 4,272 Windows 2000-compatible products, there are actually none that are *certified* ready for Windows 2000. In fact, there are fewer than 500 actually dubbed "ready" for Windows 2000; the rest are planned to be ready.

Figure 4-1 displays some of the programs that are reportedly compatible with Windows 2000, as shown in the Registry Editor, but are not on the Windows 2000 Compatibility list.

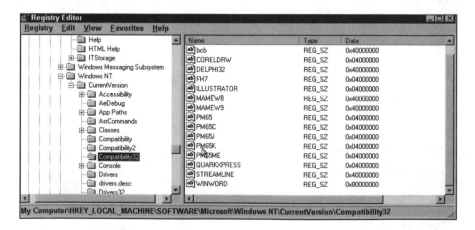

Figure 4-1: The Undead: The Registry Editor displays some of the programs that are reportedly compatible with Windows 2000, but which are not on the Windows 2000 Compatibility List.

Closer examination of those 500 applications that are ready for Windows 2000 reveals something else: there are very few big names here, and very few mainline core applications. You will, however, find the Italian version of Aurora and the Brazilian version of BusinessObjects among the compatible. Based on software that is ready for Windows 2000 right now, you'd expect Windows 2000 to be popular in very small overseas niche markets.

Note

An area of particular weakness for Windows 2000—just as it has been for previous versions of Windows—is games. Microsoft acknowledged late in the beta process that 75 percent of existing games won't run on Windows 2000.

Not even Microsoft itself has much to offer that is compatible with Windows 2000 beyond its Office 2000 Suite, but they do offer an Arabic version of Office 2000 that is Windows 2000 compatible.

From a compatibility standpoint, the highlight of the late beta phase of Windows 2000 was Microsoft's struggle for Windows 2000 to support the latest NetWare protocol from Novell. Although this issue has undoubtedly been resolved by now, it reinforces the importance of staying on top of Windows 2000 compatibility issues. Table 4-2 lists the products that are ready for Windows 2000, according to Microsoft.

Table 4-2   Applications That Are Ready for Windows 2000

Vendor	Products
690593 Ontario Ltd.	POSTERM, English, Ver. 5.0
80-20 Software, Inc.	Document Mgmt Extensions for Microsoft
A.P.System s.r.l.	AziWin, Italian, Ver. 01.03
A2i, Inc.	Catalog Builder, English, Ver. 1.00
Aardvark Software Inc.	Polisher for Visual Basic, English, Ver. 6.0
Absolute Infotech Ltd	E-Cash, English, Ver. 2.0, EAT, English, Ver. 3.0
Accounting Programming Company	WallPaper Plus 99, English, Ver. 1.0
AccountMate Software Corporation	Visual AccountMate, English, Ver. 4.0
AccuSoft Enterprises	AccuTerm 97, English, Ver. 3.1e
Achilles Software	Matrix 3D, English, Ver. 1.0
acotec GmbH	Acotec RAM — Remote Access Manager, English, Ver. 2.0
Active+ Software	Service-It Control, English, Ver. 1.1.11
AdenaCorp, Inc.	ConversionCalc, English, Ver. 4
adenin technologies	Enterprise NetPortal, English, Ver. 1.0, Enterprise NetPortal, German, Ver. 1.0

Continued

Table 4-2   *(continued)*

Vendor	Products
Adiscon GmbH	EvntSLog, English, Ver. 3.0
Adkins Resource, Inc.	Hyena, English, Ver. v2.0
Advanced Systems Concepts, Inc.	BQMS, the Batch Queue Management System, English, Ver. 2, XLNT, English, Ver. 2
Agendum Software	AgDigital, English, Ver. 1.7, AgFastformVB5, English, Ver. 3, AgFastformVB6, English, Ver. 3, AgMapthat, English, Ver. 3.6.4, AgOnlineUpdate, English, Ver. 3.4, AgProgressive D/L, English, Ver. 2.0
Ahrens Online	WebShop, German, Ver. 1.2
Alexandre Fernandes	Contas a Pagar e a Receber para Windows, Portuguese, Ver. 1.0
AlphaPad	AlphaPad, English, Ver. 2.0
AP Automation + Productivity AG	P2, German, Ver. 2.7
Application Techniques	CaptureEze 97, English, Ver. 6.0
arcplan Information Services GmbH	dynaSight, English, Ver. 2.4, dynaSight, German, Ver. 2.4, inSight, English, Ver. 2.4, inSight, German, Ver. 2.4
Arioch SofTech	WeatherWatcher, English, Ver. 1.0
ArtLogic	codex, Greek, Ver. 1.00
ARvee Systems	millennium::OMS, English, Ver. 99h
Asset Management Systems, Inc.	Asset Tracking for Schools, English, Ver. 7.0
ATIO Corporation	Cybercall, English, Ver. 3.0
Aurora Systems, Inc.	Aurora, English, Ver. 3.0, Aurora, French, Ver. 3.0, Aurora, German, Ver. 3.0, Aurora, Italian, Ver. 3.0, Aurora, Spanish, Ver. 3.0
Avensoft	Perfect Tracker, English, Ver. 3.5
Azure Dragon Software	Thirty5, English, Ver. 1
BAV Software, Inc.	InitiaLink, English, Ver. 1.6
Beagle Software	ClockWatch, English, Ver. 1.3.0, ClockWatch, English, Ver. 1.3.4
BindView Development Corporation	BindView EMS/NOSadmin for Windows NT, English, Ver. 6.1, BindView Enterprise Management System, English, Ver. 6.1
Black Cat Software	Dealership sales management, English, Ver. 1.0

Vendor	Products
Blighty Design	Sam Spade, English, Ver. 1.07
Block Financial	Stallion, English, Ver. 2
Blue Forest Software	Seasonal Trader's Lab 2000, English, Ver. 1.4, Seasonal Trader's Lab 2000, German, Ver. 1.4
Blue Gulf Software	GlobalWorks, English, Ver. 1.21.20, GlobalWorks, Spanish, Ver. 1.21.20
Bluecurve, Inc.	Dynameasure Enterprise, English, Ver. 2.0
Broadband Associates, Inc.	M.SHOW, English, Ver. 2.0
Broadcast Software International	WaveStation, English, Ver. 3.0
Bug - Desenvolvimento de Software Lda	Gestao Hoteleira, English, Ver. 2.2, Gestao Hoteleira, Brazilian, Ver. 2.2, Gestao Hoteleira, Portuguese, Ver. 2.2
Business Objects	BusinessObjects, English, Ver. 5.0, BusinessObjects, Brazilian, Ver. 5.0
C & F Associates - Spofford	PlayTrac, English, Ver. 2.0
Caldwell Consulting	ZoomSpy, English, Ver. 0.98
Camellia Software Corporation	Batch Job Server, English, Ver. 2.1, EventLogger, English, Ver. 1.2
CASE Partners, Inc.	DevCenter, English, Ver. 3
Centurion Enterprises	ECDB, English, Ver. 6.0
ChatSpace, Inc.	ChatSpace Server Edition, English, Ver. 1.5
Clarinet Systems Inc.	EthIR, English, Ver. 1.0
Cloanto Corporation	Cloanto Currency Server, English, Ver. 2.1, Cloanto Euro Calculator, English, Ver. 2.0, Cloanto Euro Calculator, German, Ver. 2.0, Cloanto Euro Calculator, Italian, Ver. 2.0
Cloanto Italia srl	Amiga Forever, English, Ver. 3.0, Amiga Forever Online Edition, English, Ver. 3.0
Coastal Technologies Group	Telecom OSS Modules, English, Ver. 3.0
Cognitus Consultoria S/C Ltda.	Castro Alves, Brazilian, Ver. 1, Castro Alves, Brazilian, Ver. 1, Castro Alves, Brazilian, Ver. 1, Koogan Houaiss Enciclopedia, Brazilian, Ver. 1, Koogan-Houaiss 99, Brazilian, Ver. 2.0, Koogan-Houaiss 99, Brazilian, Ver. 2.0, Koogan-Houaiss 99, Brazilian, Ver. 2.0, Koogan-Houaiss 99, Brazilian, Ver. 2.0

Continued

Table 4-2   *(continued)*

Vendor	Products
Compaq	Compaq Work Expeditor, English, Ver. V1.2, Compaq Work Expeditor, French, Ver. V1.2, Compaq Work Expeditor, German, Ver. V1.2, Compaq Work Expeditor, Italian, Ver. V1.2, Compaq Work Expeditor, Russian, Ver. V1.2, Compaq Work Expeditor, Japanese, Ver. V1.2, Compaq Work Expeditor, Simplified Chinese, Ver. V1.2, Compaq Work Expeditor, Traditional Chinese, Ver. V1.2, Compaq Work Expeditor, Korean, Ver. V1.2, Compaq Work Expeditor, Hebrew, Ver. V1.2, Compaq Work Expeditor, Thai, Ver. V1.2, Compaq Work Expeditor, Swedish, Ver. V1.2, Compaq Work Expeditor, Dutch, Ver. V1.2, Compaq Work Expeditor, Brazilian, Ver. V1.2, Compaq Work Expeditor, Norwegian, Ver. V1.2, Compaq Work Expeditor, Danish, Ver. V1.2, Compaq Work Expeditor, Finnish, Ver. V1.2, Compaq Work Expeditor, Czech, Ver. V1.2, Compaq Work Expeditor, Polish, Ver. V1.2, Compaq Work Expeditor, Hungarian, Ver. V1.2, Compaq Work Expeditor, Portuguese, Ver. V1.2, Compaq Work Expeditor, Spanish, Ver. V1.2
Comprehensive Pharmacy Services	COMSTAT, English, Ver. 1.0
Compté	Compté Accounting, English, Ver. 1.0
Compu/Quest	BizActionY2K, English, Ver. 1.0
Compuware Corporation	EcoTOOLS, English, Ver. 6
Connectrix Technology LLC	Alphabet Soup(tm), English, Ver. 2.0
Conqueror Design and Engineering Limited	EaziForm, English, Ver. 1.0, Majic, English, Ver. 2.0, X-NC Machinist, English, Ver. 3.0
CONSYS GmbH	consys-dent für Windows, German, Ver. 3.1
Corex Technologies Corp.	CardScan, English, Ver. 4.0
CppSolutions	FunPad, English, Ver. v1.0
Creative Services Software, Inc.	PacTerm 98, English, Ver. 1.3.1, PK-Term '99, English, Ver. 1.3.1
Critical Mass	GameSpy, English, Ver. 2.0, MP3Spy, English, Ver. 1.0
Crowe Chizek - Software Products Group	FAMAS 2000, English, Ver. v. 1
CTN Agency	Agenda Legislativa, English, Ver. 6

Vendor	*Products*
Custom Insurance Solutions LLC	Agency Information Manager, English, Ver. 3.01a
CYMA Systems	CYMA IV Accounting for Windows, English, Ver. 1.5.2
D.I.E. CAD und Statik Software	XFEMily, German, Ver. 5.0
D.T.Portable Digital	Year End Countdown, English, Ver. 1.0
DataFocus Incorporated	NuTCRACKER Professional, English, Ver. 4.2
DataNet Quality Systems (DQS)	WinSPC C/S Enterprise, English, Ver. 1.2.0
DataSolutions	CargoStore, Dutch, Ver. 2000, CargoStore, Dutch, Ver. 805, Horeca Accounting Plus, Dutch, Ver. 805, Horeca Analyse Overzicht, Dutch, Ver. 805
Datastream Systems	MaintainIt Pro, English, Ver. 3.0, MaintainIt Pro, Danish, Ver. 3.0, mp2, English, Ver. 6.0, MP2 Enterprise, English, Ver. 5.0
Decisionism	Aclue Decision Supportware, English, Ver. 2.3
Dentisoft Inc.	Dentisoft, English, Ver. 6.1
Design Resources	SyncUp, English, Ver. 1.0
Deterministic Networks Inc.	Application Management Probe (AMP), English, Ver. 1.1
dhs Dietermann & Heuser GmbH	dhs Image Database, English, Ver. 5.0, dhs Image Solution Database, German, Ver. 5.0
Digital Design	DataSpider, English, Ver. 2.0, DataSpider, Russian, Ver. 2.0
DNA Digital	Voice Surf, English, Ver. 0.5
DOCS, Inc.	SOAPware, English, Ver. 3.0
Dolphin Computer Access	Hal Screen Reader, English, Ver. 3.03, Hal Screen Reader, German, Ver. 3.03, Supernova Reader Magnifier, English, Ver. 3.03, Supernova Reader Magnifier, German, Ver. 3.03
Dr. Computer	DataMorf, English, Ver. 1.0
DWSoft Corporation	DWGuide: Navigator, English, Ver. 1
Eagle Express Car Wash Systems	Alert Watch, English, Ver. 1.02
Eastek Ltd.	Jiva Sales Automation, English, Ver. 3.0

Continued

Table 4-2   *(continued)*

Vendor	Products
Eicon Technology	Connections for Windows NT, English, Ver. V4R2a, DIVA, English, Ver. 2.01, DIVA, French, Ver. 2.01, DIVA, German, Ver. 2.01, DIVA, Dutch, Ver. 2.01, DIVA, Spanish, Ver. 2.01, DIVA Mobile V.90 PC Card, English, Ver. 2, DIVA Mobile V.90 PC Card, French, Ver. 2, DIVA Mobile V.90 PC Card, German, Ver. 2, DIVA Pro, English, Ver. 2.0, DIVA Pro, French, Ver. 2.0, DIVA Pro, German, Ver. 2.0, DIVA Pro, Dutch, Ver. 2.0, DIVA Server BRI, English, Ver. 1, Eicon Card C31, English, Ver. V4R2A, Eicon Card C31, French, Ver. V4R2A, Eicon Card C31, German, Ver. V4R2A, Eicon Card C31, Dutch, Ver. V4R2A, Eicon Card C31, Spanish, Ver. V4R2A, EiconCard C20, English, Ver. V4R2A, EiconCard C20, French, Ver. V4R2A, EiconCard C20, German, Ver. V4R2A, EiconCard C20, Italian, Ver. V4R2A, EiconCard C20, Dutch, Ver. V4R2A, EiconCard C20, Spanish, Ver. V4R2A, EiconCard C21, English, Ver. V4R2A, EiconCard C21, French, Ver. V4R2A, EiconCard C21, German, Ver. V4R2A, EiconCard C21, Italian, Ver. V4R2A, EiconCard C21, Dutch, Ver. V4R2A, EiconCard C21, Spanish, Ver. V4R2A, EiconCard C30, English, Ver. V4R2A, EiconCard C30, French, Ver. V4R2A, EiconCard C30, German, Ver. V4R2A, EiconCard C30, Italian, Ver. V4R2A, EiconCard C30, Dutch, Ver. V4R2A, EiconCard C30, Spanish, Ver. V4R2A, EiconCard P92 for Windows NT, English, Ver. V4R2A, EiconCard P92 for Windows NT, French, Ver. V4R2A, EiconCard P92 for Windows NT, German, Ver. V4R2A, EiconCard P92 for Windows NT, Italian, Ver. V4R2A, EiconCard P92 for Windows NT, Dutch, Ver. V4R2A, EiconCard P92 for Windows NT, Spanish, Ver. V4R2A, EiconCard s50, English, Ver. V4R2A, EiconCard s50, French, Ver. V4R2A, EiconCard s50, German, Ver. V4R2A, EiconCard s50, Italian, Ver. V4R2A, EiconCard s50, Dutch, Ver. V4R2A, EiconCard s50, Spanish, Ver. V4R2A, Eiconcard S51, English, Ver. V4R2A, Eiconcard S51, French, Ver. V4R2A, Eiconcard S51, German, Ver. V4R2A, Eiconcard S51, Italian, Ver. V4R2A, Eiconcard S51, Dutch, Ver. V4R2A, Eiconcard S51, Spanish, Ver. V4R2A, EiconCard S52, English, Ver. V4R2A, EiconCard S52, French, Ver. V4R2A, EiconCard S52, German, Ver. V4R2A, EiconCard S52, Italian, Ver. V4R2A, EiconCard S52, Dutch, Ver. V4R2A, EiconCard S52, Spanish, Ver. V4R2A, EiconCard S90, English, Ver. V4R2A, EiconCard S90, French, Ver. V4R2A, EiconCard S90, German, Ver. V4R2A, EiconCard S90, Italian, Ver. V4R2A, EiconCard S90, Dutch, Ver. V4R2A, EiconCard S90, Spanish, Ver. V4R2A, Eiconcard S91, English, Ver. V4R2A, Eiconcard S91, French, Ver. V4R2A, Eiconcard S91, German, Ver. V4R2A, Eiconcard S91, Italian, Ver. V4R2A, Eiconcard S91, Dutch, Ver. V4R2A,

Vendor	*Products*
Eicon Technology (Continued)	Eiconcard S91, Spanish, Ver. V4R2A, EiconCard s94, English, Ver. V4R2A, EiconCard s94, French, Ver. V4R2A, EiconCard s94, German, Ver. V4R2A, EiconCard s94, Italian, Ver. V4R2A, EiconCard s94, Dutch, Ver. V4R2A, EiconCard s94, Spanish, Vor. V4R2A
Elcom Ltd.	Advanced Office 97 Password Recovery, English, Ver. 1.0, Advanced Office 97 Password Recovery, Russian, Ver. 1.0, Advanced ZIP Password Recovery, English, Ver. 2.2
Electronic Imaging Systems	Hotels, Lodging Facilities, Czech, Ver. 2.0
Elephant Software AG	EleAdress, German, Ver. 2.0, EleOffice, German, Ver. 3.0
elitedevelopments	preHTML, English, Ver. 1.1 Beta-3
Equilibrium	DeBabelizer Pro, English, Ver. 4.5, DeBabelizer Pro, French, Ver. 4.5
Equilibrium	DeBabelizer Pro, Japanese, Ver. 4.5
EXE Technologies	EXceed WMS, English, Ver. 4000
Executive Software International	Diskeeper for Windows NT, English, Ver. 4.0, Diskeeper for Windows NT, English, Ver. 4.0, Diskeeper for Windows NT, French, Ver. 4.0, Diskeeper for Windows NT, French, Ver. 4.0, Diskeeper for Windows NT, German, Ver. 4.0, Diskeeper for Windows NT, German, Ver. 4.0, Diskeeper for Windows NT, Japanese, Ver. 4.0, Diskeeper for Windows NT, Japanese, Ver. 4.0, Undelete for Windows NT, English, Ver. 1.0, Undelete for Windows NT, English, Ver. 1.0
Express Technologies Corporation	World Watch, English, Ver. 5.0.1310
Eytcheson Software	Multi-Remote Registry Change, English, Ver. 3.1
Fabasoft	Fabasoft Components, English, Ver. 3.0, Fabasoft Components, German, Ver. 3.0
FacetCorp	FacetWin, English, Ver. 2, FacetWin, French, Ver. 2, FacetWin, German, Ver. 2, FacetWin, Italian, Ver. 2, FacetWin, Russian, Ver. 2, FacetWin, Swedish, Ver. 2, FacetWin, Dutch, Ver. 2, FacetWin, Brazilian, Ver. 2, FacetWin, Norwegian, Ver. 2, FacetWin, Danish, Ver. 2, FacetWin, Finnish, Ver. 2, FacetWin, Czech, Ver. 2, FacetWin, Polish, Ver. 2, FacetWin, Hungarian, Ver. 2, FacetWin, Portuguese, Ver. 2, FacetWin, Greek, Ver. 2, FacetWin, Turkish, Ver. 2, FacetWin, Spanish, Ver. 2
Facility Innovations	Time and Place, English, Ver. 2.0, Time and Place Extended, English, Ver. 2.0
Fermion Consultancy	Mocha!, English, Ver. 2.0

Continued

Table 4-2 *(continued)*

Vendor	Products
Final Draft, Inc.	Final Draft, English, Ver. 5
Financia, Inc.	Financia, English, Ver. 6.5
Fine Point Technologies, Inc.	Total Internet, English, Ver. 3.5
FMS, Inc	Total Visual Agent, English, Ver. 9
FPS CONSULTORIA E INFORMATICA	Banzay2000, Brazilian, Ver. 6
Freshwater Software, Inc.	SiteScope for NT, English, Ver. 4.0
Frontix Development BV	Frontix Site Manager, English, Ver. 1.5, Frontix Site Manager, Dutch, Ver. 1.5
Fujitsu Software Corporation	Fujitsu COBOL, English, Ver. 4.2
Full Armor Corporation	Full Armor Zero Administration 2000, English, Ver. 7.0
Garlon Business Systems	ICIS, English, Ver. 1.0
Gaylord Information Systems	Polaris, English, Ver. 1.3
Gemplus Corporation	GCR410P Serial Smart Card Reader, English, Ver. 1.0, GemSAFE Smart Card, English, Ver. 2.0, GPR400 PC-CARD Smart Card Reader, English, Ver. 1.0
GEO-SLOPE International	SEEP/W, English, Ver. 4.2, SIGMA/W, English, Ver. 4.2, SLOPE/W, English, Ver. 4.2, TEMP/W, English, Ver. 4.2
Geometique	Geometique, English, Ver. 1.0
GIANT Systems	GIANT Office Software, English, Ver. 5.0
GIM Archive	Genealogical Information Manager (GIM), English, Ver. 3.18
Glosser Software	Wilderness Trakker, English, Ver. 3.1.0, Wilderness Trakker, English, Ver. 3.1.0
Glück&Kanja GmbH	CryptoEx Security Suite, English, Ver. 2.1, CryptoEx Security Suite, German, Ver. 2.1
Go-get Networks	ESM Development Wizard, English, Ver. 2.0, ESM Development Wizard, English, Ver. 2.0
goldcom inc.	CableTools, English, Ver. 2.5
GRATCO	tarot2000, English, Ver. 1.00
Heroix Corporation	RoboMon NT, English, Ver. 7.5
Hiawatha Island Software LLC	Hi-verify for FrontPage(r) 98 and 2000, English, Ver. 1.0.5, Hi-Visibility for FrontPage 98 and 2000, English, Ver. 1.0.5b, TagGen for FrontPage 98 and 2000, English, Ver. 1.0.5

Vendor	Products
Hill Computing Services	ActiveX Document Loader w/control, English, Ver. 1.0
Hill Technologies	Ultimate Pattern Tracker, English, Ver. 2.01
HiTecSoft Corp.	WebConsole for NT, English, Ver. 3.0
HMR Inc	e-image server, English, Ver. 1.0
HMS Software	TimeControl, English, Ver. 3.1
Houston Solutions, Inc.	AutoMagic Accounting, English, Ver. 4.0
Hyperionics	HyperCam, English, Ver. 1.4, HyperSnap-DX, English, Ver. 3.40, Scribbler, English, Ver. 1.8
I.S.C.	SecretAgent, English, Ver. 3.14
iDREAM Software	Jio, English, Ver. v1.1, Realism 3D, English, Ver. v2.0
IM Systems Ltd.	IMS Suite, English, Ver. 1.1
IMAGE-X International	A FREE FAX, English, Ver. 1.4, CO-MINER, English, Ver. 2.3, E-Filing, English, Ver. 2.1, IMAGE-X DOCUMENT IMAGING SYSTEM, English, Ver. 4.0, IMAGEflow, English, Ver. 3.2
imagine LAN, Inc.	ConfigSafe, English, Ver. 2.00.09, ConfigSafe, French, Ver. 2.00.09, ConfigSafe, German, Ver. 2.00.09, ConfigSafe, Italian, Ver. 2.00.09, ConfigSafe, Japanese, Ver. 2.00.09, ConfigSafe, Simplified Chinese, Ver. 2.00.09, ConfigSafe, Traditional Chinese, Ver. 2.00.09, ConfigSafe, Portuguese, Ver. 2.00.09, ConfigSafe, Spanish, Ver. 2.00.09
ImaginOn	WebZinger, English, Ver. 6, WebZinger for Kids, English, Ver. 6
IMG Inc.	The Magnifier, English, Ver. 1.20, The Right Touch!, English, Ver. 1.10
Incentive Systems, Inc.	Incentive, English, Ver. 1.0, INCENTIVE, English, Ver. 1.0
INDESOFT LTDA	Contabilidad efikaz, Spanish, Ver. 3.5
InfoAccess Inc.	HTML Transit, English, Ver. 4.0
Ingenieurbuero fuer Software-Technologie	TimeNet, English, Ver. 6.06
INOSOFT GmbH	InfoManager, English, Ver. 1.0, InfoManager, German, Ver. 1.0, InfoManager, German, Ver. 1.0, InfoManager, German, Ver. 1.0, VendorBase 2000, English, Ver. 2.0, VendorBase 2000, English, Ver. 2.0, VendorBase 2000, English, Ver. 2.0, VendorBase 2000, French, Ver. 2.0, VendorBase 2000, French, Ver. 2.0, VendorBase 2000, German, Ver. 2.0
InstallShield Corporation	InstallFromTheWeb, English, Ver. 2.3, InstallShield Express 2, English, Ver. 2.1, InstallShield for Windows Installer, English, Ver. 1.0

Continued

Table 4-2 *(continued)*

Vendor	Products
Insyst! Information Systems, Inc.	ShopWerks, English, Ver. 1.x
Integrated Visions	KaratePointofSaleManager, English, Ver. 2.0, KarateTournamentManager, English, Ver. 2.0
Integrity Software	The eOS, English, Ver. 1.0
Intelisys Electronic Commerce LLC	IEC Enterprise, English, Ver. 3.0
Intelitech	SecurFiles, English, Ver. 3.3, SecurInst, English, Ver. 3.3
Interactive System Designs Inc.	Load Center, English, Ver. 1.2
InterCan Tech	AdsOff!, English, Ver. 1.0
International Business Solutions, LLC	DemandLink, English, Ver. 1.6
International Technical Institute	Adabas Budget, English, Ver. 2.1, Adabas Budget, Spanish, Ver. 2.1
Intersect Inc	ActiveStart, English, Ver. 99
Intersect Software Services	ActiveStart 99, English, Ver. 2, ActiveStart 99, French, Ver. 2
Intranet 2001, Inc.	HierOlap/iHierOlap, English, Ver. 1.0
Intriguing Concepts Inc.	NetMeeting Super Enhancer, English, Ver. 1.1
Intuitive Manufacturing Systems Inc.	MRP9000, English, Ver. 3.7
IP Metrics Software, Inc.	NIC Express, English, Ver. 1.1c
iPlay, Inc.	iPlay Bompers, English, Ver. 1.0
IQ Technologies	IQ Business, English, Ver. 2.0, IQ Business, French, Ver. 2.0, IQ Business, German, Ver. 2.0, IQ Business, Italian, Ver. 2.0, IQ Business, Brazilian, Ver. 2.0, IQ Business, Czech, Ver. 2.0, IQ Business, Portuguese, Ver. 2.0, IQ Business, Spanish, Ver. 2.0
iSOFT plc	iSOFT2000, English, Ver. 1.1, Ivo MACHULDA - INFOS informaèní poèítaèové
systémy	WinPUB98, English, Ver. 2.06, WinPUB98, German, Ver. 2.06, WinPUB98, Czech, Ver. 2.06
iWorker, Inc.	ModelSheet, English, Ver. 1.0
J.D. Edwards World Source Company	OneWorld, German, Ver. B7331
JAC Enterprises	InetCOM, English, Ver. 1.0

Vendor	Products
JavaBear Systems	RingWorld Server, English, Ver. 1.0
jBASE Software, Inc.	jBASE, English, Ver. 3.1/3.2/4.
JH Marketing	EZ E-Commerce, English, Ver. 1.2
K.W. Sellick & Associates	Btrieve Connection, English, Ver. 2.1
Kaspersky Lab.	Antiviral Toolkit pro by Eugene Kaspersky, English, Ver. 3.0, Antiviral Toolkit pro by Eugene Kaspersky, Russian, Ver. 3.0
KD SOFTWARE	Verne, English, Ver. 2.0, Verne, German, Ver. 2.0, Verne, Czech, Ver. 2.0, Verne, Czech, Ver. 2.0, Verne, Czech, Ver. 2.0, Verne, Czech, Ver. 2.0, Verne, Czech, Ver. 2.0, Verne, Polish, Ver. 2.0
Keyboard Technologies Ltd	Keyboard Pro Millennium Edition, English, Ver. 2.1
Kids Page	Help Me!, English, Ver. 2, Help Me!, Spanish, Ver. 2
Kinook Software	Visual Build, English, Ver. 1.0
Knosys Inc.	ProClarity, English, Ver. 2.0
KPI Technologies INc	KPI Enterprise, English, Ver. 4.0, KPI Manager, English, Ver. 3.7
Landmark Systems Corporation	PerformanceWorks, English, Ver. 3.0.x
LaRonde Technologies Corporation	Telcom FaxCast, English, Ver. 4
Latin Technologies	Healthcare Applications Provider, English, Ver. 1.0
Lavenir Technology, Inc.	ViewMaster, English, Ver. 6.0.3, ViewMate, English, Ver. 6.0.3
LC Technology International, Inc	RecoverNT, English, Ver. 3.1, RecoverNT, English, Ver. 3.1, RecoverNT, English, Ver. 3.1
Les Logiciels Avantage	Integrated Accounting, English, Ver. 7.2, Integrated Accounting, French, Ver. 7.2
Lieberman and Associates	LAN Server to NT Migration Wizard, English, Ver. 1.6N, Server-to-Server Password Synchronizer, English, Ver. 3.11, User Manager Pro, English, Ver. 1.12
Lilac Software	HomeBuyer's Assist, English, Ver. 1.0, Medical Laboratory Test Directory, English, Ver. 1.0
Literate Systems, Inc.	Literate Time Manager, English, Ver. 2.00
Lockstep Systems	IGetMail, English, Ver. 1.0.1
Logisoft, Inc.	Logisoft X/Page OCX, English, Ver. 1.0
Luc Bouchard & Associates Ltd.	LBA G2, English, Ver. 2.80, LBA G2, French, Ver. 2.80

Continued

Table 4-2   *(continued)*

Vendor	Products
Luxor Software Inc.	Task-Xplorer, English, Ver. 1.0
Ly & Associates	Power NT, English, Ver. 1.0
M-Tech	P-Synch, English, Ver. 3.5
M.I.C.S.	BIS for Windows, English, Ver. 99
MagicByte Software	MagicINSTALL 5, German, Ver. 5.0.011
Main Street Software	Boulevard, English, Ver. 6.0
MAIN Training GmbH	ZAM - Zentrales AdreßManagement, German, Ver. 1.2
MAJIQ	MAJIQTrim, English, Ver. 1.3, QuikView 2, English, Ver. 2.1.3
Major Micro Systems,	ASPdb, English, Ver. 1.09 Inc.
Manawatu Software	Aladdins - Envelopes and Labels, English, Ver. 5 Solutions
MCDS GmbH	HANDICRAFT, German, Ver. 3/99
McFall Associates Inc	Cricket, English, Ver. 3
McRae Software	GridWiz, English, Ver. 3.7 International, Inc.
MEDIA Consulting	Media Consulting 351, Italian, Ver. 7.0, Media Consulting 400, Italian, Ver. 7.0, Media Consulting MRP, Italian, Ver. 7.0, MEDIA Consulting Rubik, English, Ver. 7.0
MediaTonic	MailVerify, English, Ver. 1.5
Medlin Accounting Shareware	Medlin Accounting Shareware, English, Ver. 3.0
Melach Ges.m.b.H.	TEAMWORK-2000, English, Ver. 2b, TEAMWORK-2000, German, Ver. 2b
MerTech Data systems Inc	SQLFlex(tm), English, Ver. 2.0 S
Microsoft	Microsoft Access, English, Ver. 2000, Microsoft Excel, English, Ver. 2000, Microsoft FrontPage, English, Ver. 2000, Microsoft Office 2000 Premium, English, Ver. 2000, Microsoft Office 2000 Professional, English, Ver. 2000, Microsoft Office 2000 Professional, Arabic, Ver. 2000, Microsoft Office 2000 Small Business, English, Ver. 2000, Microsoft Office 2000 Standard, English, Ver. 2000, Microsoft Outlook, English, Ver. 2000, Microsoft PowerPoint, English, Ver. 2000, Microsoft Publisher, English, Ver. 2000, Microsoft Word, English, Ver. 2000
MindQuake Interactive	Jotter 2000, English, Ver. 1.0 Inc.
MinServ (Mineral Services)	The WinRock Wizard, English, Ver. V1.x, WinRock, English, Ver. V3.x, XPlotter, English, Ver. V1.x, XRDCALC, English, Ver. V4.x
Monotype Typography	Enhanced Screen Quality Fonts, English, Ver. 1.0 Inc

Vendor	Products
Mountain Systems, Inc.	BusyBuster, English, Ver. 1.0, CallAudit Client, English, Ver. 4.0
Mutek Solutions ltd	Bugtrapper, English, Ver. 2.0
National Instruments	ComponentWorks, English, Ver. 2.0
Navision Software A/S	Navision Financials, English, Ver. 2.01, Navision Financials, French, Ver. 2.01, Navision Financials, German, Ver. 2.01, Navision Financials, Italian, Ver. 2.01, Navision Financials, Russian, Ver. 2.01, Navision Financials, Swedish, Ver. 2.01, Navision Financials, Dutch, Ver. 2.01, Navision Financials, Norwegian, Ver. 2.01, Navision Financials, Danish, Ver. 2.01, Navision Financials, Czech, Ver. 2.01, Navision Financials, Polish, Ver. 2.01, Navision Financials, Spanish, Ver. 2.01
Neatware	Ladybug98 Player, English, Ver. 1998
Neil Freeman Consultants	netconferencing, English, Ver. 1.0, Power Management System, English, Ver. 1.1
Netier Technologies, Inc.	Rapport, English, Ver. 1.4
NetIQ	NetIQ AppManager Suite, English, Ver. 3.0, NetIQ AppManager Suite, Japanese, Ver. 3.0
ObjectAutomation	OAenterprise99, German, Ver. 1.0
Obvious Choices	TradeIt! for Windows, English, Ver. 3.82
OCS Software Division	PrimeInfo 2000, English, Ver. 1.00
Odyssey Computing, Inc.	BizCalc, English, Ver. 4
Omm Software	Mantracalc, English, Ver. 1.0
On!Contact Software	Client Management Software (CMS), English, Ver. 4.0, Client Management Software (CMS), French, Ver. 4.0
ONYX Software Corporation	Onyx Customer Center, English, Ver. 4.5, Onyx Customer Center, French, Ver. 4.5, Onyx Customer Center, German, Ver. 4.5, Onyx Customer Center, Spanish, Ver. 4.5
OOPadelic software	Resolver, English, Ver. 2.0
Option Wizard	Option Wizard, English, Ver. Online
ORANGE Digital Systems Inc.	EMPulse Series - Time & Attendance, English, Ver. 3.0
ORCASoftware	ORCA! 2000, English, Ver. 7.0
Pacific Edge Software	Project Office, English, Ver. 2.0, Project Office Express, English, Ver. 2.0
Pacific Software Associates, Inc.	WoodResource C/S, English, Ver. v1.R5
PacificRim Consulting	MedDent Mgr, English, Ver. 1.0

Continued

Table 4-2 *(continued)*

Vendor	Products
Palm Technology	QikKids, English, Ver. 1.76, QikKids, English, Ver. 2
Parakeet Publications	E-Studio, English, Ver. 1.0, E-Studio Web, English, Ver. 2.0
parmac inc	Broker, English, Ver. 2.1, Broker, Brazilian, Ver. 2.1, Broker, Portuguese, Ver. 2.1, Broker, Spanish, Ver. 2.1, THESYS, English, Ver. 2.3, THESYS, Brazilian, Ver. 2.3, THESYS, Portuguese, Ver. 2.3, THESYS, Spanish, Ver. 2.3
Parwan Electronics Corporation	CallAhead, English, Ver. 2.1, CallAhead, French, Ver. 2.1, CallAhead, Spanish, Ver. 2.1, Insight IVR, English, Ver. 2.5, Insight IVR, French, Ver. 2.5, Insight IVR, Spanish, Ver. 2.5, Reminder, English, Ver. 1.0, Reminder, Spanish, Ver. 1.0, VoiceSaver, English, Ver. 2.1, VoiceSaver, French, Ver. 2.1, VoiceSaver, Spanish, Ver. 2.1
PassLogix, Inc.	v-GO Visual Password, English, Ver. 1.0
Passware	Administrator Password Recovery Kit, English, Ver. 2.0
PC-studio gmbh	PCS-call!, German, Ver. 4.11
Pearl Software	Cyber Snoop, English, Ver. 3.0, Cyber Snoop Pro, English, Ver. 3.0
Pegasus Disk Technologies	InveStore Storage Management Software, English, Ver. 3.x, InveStore Storage Management Software for NT, English, Ver. 3.x
Personal MicroCosms	Vault, English, Ver. 1.36
PhatWare Corp.	HPC Notes, English, Ver. 2.03
Phillips Computer Telephony	Automated Obituary Line, English, Ver. 2.0, Q-Page Dispatch System, English, Ver. 2.0
PIM+ Ltd.	xReminder Pro, English, Ver. 2.6
Pinard Software	CMStatus, English, Ver. 1.0
Pivotal Software, Inc.	eRelationship, English, Ver. 1.0, eRelationship, French, Ver. 1.0, eRelationship, German, Ver. 1.0, eRelationship, Italian, Ver. 1.0, eRelationship, Japanese, Ver. 1.0, eRelationship, Swedish, Ver. 1.0, eRelationship, Norwegian, Ver. 1.0, eRelationship, Danish, Ver. 1.0, eRelationship, Finnish, Ver. 1.0, Relationship, English, Ver. 99/SQL7, Relationship, English, Ver. 99/SQL7, Relationship, French, Ver. 99/SQL7, Relationship, German, Ver. 99/SQL7, Relationship, Italian, Ver. 99/SQL7, Relationship, Japanese, Ver. 99/SQL7, Relationship, Hebrew, Ver. 99/SQL7, Relationship, Swedish, Ver. 99/SQL7, Relationship, Dutch, Ver. 99/SQL7, Relationship, Norwegian, Ver. 99/SQL7, Relationship, Danish, Ver. 99/SQL7, Relationship, Finnish, Ver. 99/SQL7, Relationship, Turkish, Ver. 99/SQL7, Relationship, Spanish, Ver. 99/SQL7

Vendor	Products
PixelSoft Software Development Corporation	Clarity, English, Ver. 3.1, Patches, English, Ver. 4.1
Positive Support Review, Inc.	Zinnote, English, Ver. 5.6a
PPL	T-Card, English, Ver. 1.0
PQ Systems	SQCpack 2000, English, Ver. 4.0
Practice Masters, LLC	Practice Master - Dental, English, Ver. 6.2
Premier Automation Inc.	P I D-Premier Instrumentation Directory, English, Ver. 8.1, P I Dc - Premier Instrumentation Directory, English, Ver. 1998, PRISM 9000, English, Ver. 3.08, PRISMc9000, English, Ver. 3.08
Premier Software	Scriptum Web Professional, English, Ver. 5.1
Pro-ShopKeeper Computer Software Co. Inc.	Pro-ShopKeeper, English, Ver. 4.0i
Profitus Lda	WinMax '98 - Gestão Comercial, Portuguese, Ver. 1.0
Profitus Lda	WinMax 2000 - Gestão Comercial, Portuguese, Ver. 1.0, WinMax 2000 - Shop, Portuguese, Ver. 1.0
ProLaw Software	ProLaw, English, Ver. 7
Purklesoft	D-Member, English, Ver. 1.0, GSA Financial Tools, English, Ver. 1.1
Purple Solutions,Inc.	Pansophy, English, Ver. 1.0
QUAD Solutions	Minerva Knowledge Base, English, Ver. 1, Minerva Knowledge Base, Dutch, Ver. 1
Quantum Research & Technologies	BookMark2000, English, Ver. 4.3
R+R	Ultranet, English, Ver. 2000
Radex Co.	Konwerter, Polish, Ver. 1.2
RealityWave Inc.	RealityWave Server, English, Ver. 1.2
ReGet Software	ReGet Pro, English, Ver. 1.4, ReGet Pro, German, Ver. 1.4, ReGet Pro, Russian, Ver. 1.4, ReGet Pro, Japanese, Ver. 1.4
Relian Software	QuickLink, English, Ver. 1.0
Replica Technology	Interior Design Collection for Office 97 and 2000, English, Ver. 1.0, The Millenium 3D Font Collection for MSOffice 2000, English, Ver. 1.0

Continued

Table 4-2 *(continued)*

Vendor	Products
RGE, Inc.	IP Sentry, English, Ver. 4.0
Rhino Software	InterQuick, English, Ver. 1.0
RimStar	RimStar Programmer's Editor, English, Ver. 4.0
RIS	DICOM 3 Image File Reformatter, English, Ver. 1.0, Medical Image Grab Client/Server, English, Ver. 1.10, Radiology Scan and View System (RSVS), English, Ver. 4.10
Rockliffe Systems, Inc.	MailSite, English, Ver. 3.4.1
Ron Sarver Consulting	Profit Prophet (Standalone), English, Ver. 2.0
RVS Datentechnik	RVS-COM, French, Ver. 1.62, RVS-COM, Japanese, Ver. 1.62, RVS-COM, Korean, Ver. 1.62, RVS-COM, Swedish, Ver. 1.62, RVS-COM, Czech, Ver. 1.62, RVS-COM, Polish, Ver. 1.62, RVS-COM, Portuguese, Ver. 1.62
RWT Corporation	OnTrack, English, Ver. 2.0
Safetynet Inc.	Yes2K NT, Swedish, Ver. 3.0
SAI	CB Data, English, Ver. 5.1
SAPIEN Technologies, Inc.	PrimalSCRIPT, English, Ver. 1.0
SAS Institute	The SAS System, English, Ver. 8
Seagate Software	Backup Exec, English, Ver. 8.0
SekChek Information Protection Services	SekChek, English, Ver. 4.3.3
Sensation	SensatioNet, English, Ver. 1.1
Silicon Energy Corp	Enerscape, English, Ver. 1.3
Silverwand Software Corporation	BasicCryption, English, Ver. 1.0
Smart Shop Software, Inc.	Smart Manager, English, Ver. 6.2
SmartLine Inc.	DeviceLock, English, Ver. 3.2.1, DeviceLock, German, Ver. 3.2.1, DeviceLock, Russian, Ver. 3.2.1, DeviceLock (DEC Alpha), English, Ver. 3.2.1, DeviceLock (DEC Alpha), German, Ver. 3.2.1, DeviceLock (DEC Alpha), Russian, Ver. 3.2.1, Remote Task Manager, English, Ver. 1.5.1, Remote Task Manager (DEC Alpha), English, Ver. 1.5.1
SMD Informática SA	Officeworks, English, Ver. 1.1.0, Officeworks, Brazilian, Ver. 1.1.0, Officeworks, Portuguese, Ver. 1.1.0, Officeworks, Spanish, Ver. 1.1.0
SnapSoft	SnapSoft Web Server Control, English, Ver. 2.2

Vendor	Products
Soft Class	Soft Class para Abogados, Spanish, Ver. 98
SoftAid Medical Management Systems	The Medical Office, English, Ver. 3.0, The Medical Office, English, Ver. Pro, The Medical Office, English, Ver. SQL, The Medical Office, Spanish, Ver. 3.0, The Medical Office, Spanish, Ver. Pro, The Medical Office, Spanish, Ver. SQL
SOFTNET	SOFTFA, English, Ver. 1.0, SOFTFA, English, Ver. 1.0
Software Pursuits, Inc.	SureSync, English, Ver. 2.0
SolveTech Corporation	Appointment Reminder System, English, Ver. 3.1
Sound Linked Data Inc. (MLI Inc.)	Max Hearing System, English, Ver. 4.0
SPK Consulting, Inc.	SPK 3D Game Engine, English, Ver. .8
Squicciarini Software	Central Information System, English, Ver. 1.0
STAS	Power Monitor, French, Ver. 1.1
StoragePoint, Inc.	WebDrive, English, Ver. 2
Svetlana Software	AudioSphere, English, Ver. 1.07
Sylvain Nantel	Truck Fleet Managment / Gest de flotte, English, Ver. 1.0.0
Symbolic Source Group	Of Gold and Maiden, English, Ver. 1.0
Synaptec Software, Inc.	FileBase, English, Ver. 2000, LawBase, English, Ver. 2000, LawBase, English, Ver. 2000
T. H. E. Solution	C++ Framework and ToolKit for Control Applications, English, Ver. 0.04
Tailor Made Software	Flat Out!, English, Ver. 4.0, Hp2Design Pro, English, Ver. 5.3
Talley Software	Hippee, English, Ver. 1.0
TCAC	Pearl, English, Ver. 1.0
Tech Hackers Inc	@nalyst, English, Ver. 2000
Technolutions, Inc.	Technolutions 2084, English, Ver. 3.0, Technolutions 2084, French, Ver. 3.0, Technolutions 2084, Spanish, Ver. 3.0, Technolutions webTools, English, Ver. 3.0
Technos Corporation	INTELLIDENT Office, English, Ver. 2.0
TechVision, Inc.	AccuForm SDK, English, Ver. 2.0, FormIDEA for Microsoft Excel 97/2000, English, Ver. 2.0
Teconomics (dbgroups)	Dispatch, French, Ver. 2.0
Textware Solutions	Instant Text, English, Ver. 3
The Bradford Group Ltd.	Call Center Display, English, Ver. 3.01, Call Center Messaging, English, Ver. 1.20
The Business Solution	Contact Manager, English, Ver. 1.1

Continued

Table 4-2   *(continued)*

Vendor	Products
The ComWorks Group	WebAdemics Live Virtual Campus, English, Ver. 1.0
The Welsh Paterson Group	MikMod DLL, English, Ver. 5.11
ThermoAnalytics, Inc.	WinTherm, English, Ver. 4.0
Time/system International	TaskTimer, English, Ver. 5, TaskTimer, French, Ver. 5, TaskTimer, German, Ver. 5, TaskTimer, Swedish, Ver. 5, TaskTimer, Dutch, Ver. 5, TaskTimer, Danish, Ver. 5
TLi	CallTracx, English, Ver. 3.5, CallTracx, English, Ver. 3.5
Trafficware	SimTraffic, English, Ver. 4.0, SimTraffic, English, Ver. 1.1, SimTraffic CI, English, Ver. 1.0, Synchro, English, Ver. 3.2
Transoft International, Inc.	OptiCa$h, English, Ver. 4.1, Virtual ATM Simulator - Test, English, Ver. 1.1
Treasoft	TreasuryAnalyst, English, Ver. 0.99 beta
Tritium Technologies	eCode, English, Ver. 1.0, Encrypto 2000, English, Ver. 1.0
Twin Rivers Interactive, Inc.	WebAurora 98, English, Ver. 1.0
Ultimate Software	UltiPro HRMS/Payroll, English, Ver. 3.0
Unigraphics Solutions, Inc.	Solid Edge, English, Ver. V7
Unisyn	AutoMate Enterprise Server, English, Ver. 4, AutoMate Professional, English, Ver. 4.3
Universal Imaging Corporation	MetaMorph, English, Ver. 4.0
USDATA Corporation	FactoryLink ECS, English, Ver. 6.6, WebClient, English, Ver. 6.6, Xfactory, English, Ver. 1.3
Vadem	PenOffice, English, Ver. 1.1
VALIS International	VSecure-store, English, Ver. beta
Variable Solutions	BoltWare, English, Ver. 1.00
Velox Software Development	VelHotel for Windows (32), Danish, Ver. 1.24
Virasoft Corporation	ProScriptio, English, Ver. 1.0
Vishwak Associates	EasyStruct, English, Ver. 3.0
Visio Corp.	Visio 2000 Standard Edition, English, Ver. 2000, Visio Enterprise, English, Ver. 5.0, Visio Standard, English, Ver. 5.0, Visio Technical, English, Ver. 5.0 Plus
Vision-Quest	IntelliTrax, English, Ver. 1.2

Vendor	*Products*
VisualCommerce	VisualCommerce Constructor, English, Ver. 1.5
VSCL Inc.	Conceal, English, Ver. 2.01
Vtopia, Inc.	Woodstock <Hypertext>, English, Ver. 4.1
VyPRESS Research	Vypress Auvis, English, Ver. 1.5.1, Vypress Messenger, English, Ver. 2.5.5
W. Quinn Associates	QuotaAdvisor, English, Ver. 4.0
WA Technologies	AMPS 2000, English, Ver. Bv1.1
Webplanet Corporation	Webplanet - Tools, English, Ver. 4.0, Webplanet - Tools, German, Ver. 4.0
WebTrends	WebTrends Enterprise Suite, English, Ver. 3.5, WebTrends for Firewalls and VPNs, English, Ver. 1.2, WebTrends Log Analyzer, English, Ver. 4.5, WebTrends Professional Suite, English, Ver. 3.0, WebTrends Security Analyzer, English, Ver. 2.1
Whizel Technologies Ltd	TestWizard, English, Ver. 1.0
WinJewel	WinJewel, English, Ver. 5.0
Wise Owl Consulting, Inc.	Zandia, English, Ver. 2.0
Wise Solutions	Wise for Windows Installer, English, Ver. 1.0
Witzend Software	Witzend Search Library, English, Ver. 2.1
WizSoft Inc.	WizRule, English, Ver. 3.02, WizWhy, English, Ver. 2.5.1
WM Software, Inc.	ShutdownPlus, English, Ver. 3.7
YearLook Enterprises	CompuCampus, English, Ver. 1.0
Zero G Software	InstallAnywhere Enterprise Edition, English, Ver. 3

Windows 2000 Compatible—What Does It Mean?

Do glossy little corporate icons thrill you? Then you'll love the Microsoft compatibility program for Windows 2000. It offers a zippy little star for applications that are "certified" Windows 2000-compatible—a business-like check mark for applications that are Windows 2000 "ready,"—and a hollow, but hopeful, circle for applications that the vendors "plan" to be Windows 2000-compatible.

Certified is the highest level, and the most rigorous, requiring two levels of compliance testing. It also gets the coolest icon, the coveted Windows 2000-compatible logo. In general terms, Microsoft specifies that certified applications must:

Continued

(continued)

■ "Provide a robust, self-repairing installation that helps minimize conflicts among shared components to enable better co-existence of applications.

■ "Facilitate easier software deployment and management for organizations.

■ "Correctly maintain user preferences and computer settings to ensure a good 'roaming user' experience, support for multiple users per machine, and regeneration of application settings in machine.

■ "Run in a tightly controlled network environment, to enable network administrators to secure and control corporate desktops.

■ "Provide a consistent user experience and supports accessibility standards to reduce support and training costs.

■ "Provide a smooth transition of the application for users that upgrade from Windows 95 or later operating systems.

■ "Support OnNow power management for a better mobile computing experience."

Sounds good, but here's the kicker. As of this moment, there are no Windows 2000 certified applications—not even from Microsoft.

So what have we got? As of now, there are several hundred Windows 2000 ready applications. Ready means that the software vendor "has tested the application for Windows 2000 compatibility" and has agreed to provide support for the product running under Windows 2000. Notice, however, that it doesn't guarantee the degree of compatibility, nor does it guarantee the specific feature that you need will work.

The lowest level of Windows 2000 compatibility is the planned level, which means the software vendor has pledged to deliver a ready or certified Windows 2000-compatible application in the future. The vast majority of the Windows 2000-compatible applications listed on Microsoft's own Web site are in the planned category.

Windows 2000 Hardware Compatibility

Hardware compatibility is a relative bright spot for Windows 2000. After years of struggling with limited offerings for Windows 95, 98, and NT in every major hardware category, Microsoft has finally gotten the big hardware vendors on board for Windows 2000.

There still might not be as many offerings available as there are for Windows 9x, but Windows 2000 closes much of the gap, especially if you're looking at new equipment. There are already hundreds of Windows 2000-compatible modems, video boards, network cards, and so on.

However, when you look closely, you see that there are a gazillion Windows 2000-compatible monitors and printers, but only a paucity in some other categories. Tables 4-3, 4-4, and 4-5 list some of the products that Microsoft says are compatible with Windows 2000.

Table 4-3   Windows 2000 Compatible Imaging Hardware

Vendor	Product
Hewlett-Packard	ScanJet 3p, ScanJet 4100C, ScanJet 4p, ScanJet 5100C, ScanJet 5200C, ScanJet 5p, ScanJet 6100c or 4c/3c, ScanJet 6200C, ScanJet IIc, ScanJet IIcx, ScanJet IIp
Intel	USB Video Camera for Proshare technology YC76 Camera
Kodak	DVC 300 Digital Video Camera, DVC323 Digital Video Camera
Logitech	USB QuickCam Home (the rectangular version ONLY)
Microsoft	SanDisk USB ImagingMate
Philips	CE Philips CIF Digital Camera
Sony	1394 CCM-DS250 Desktop Camera
Logitech	PageScan USB TI 1394 MC680-DCC Desktop Camera

Table 4-4   Windows 2000 Compatible Network/ISDN Hardware

Vendor	Product
AVM Berlin GmbH	AVM ISDN-Controller B1 ISA, AVM ISDN-Controller B1 PCI, AVM ISDN-Controller B1 PCMCIA, AVM ISDN-Controller B1 USB, AVM ISDN-Controller FRITZ!Card Classic, AVM ISDN-Controller FRITZ!Card PCI, AVM ISDN-Controller FRITZ!Card PCMCIA, AVM ISDN-Controller FRITZ!Card PnP, AVM ISDN-Controller FRITZ!Card USB
Digi International	Datafire /4 ST, Datafire PRIme (PCI), Datafire PRIme 2-Port ISA, S/T ISA, U ISA
Eicon Technology	DIVA (PCMCIA), DIVA 2.0 (ISA-PnP), DIVA 2.0 (PCI), DIVA 2.0 /U (ISA-PnP), DIVA 2.0 /U (PCI), DIVA 2.01 (ISA-PnP), DIVA Piccola (ISA-PnP), DIVA Pro (ISA-PnP), DIVA Pro (PCMCIA), DIVA Pro 2.0 (ISA-PnP), DIVA Pro 2.0 (PCI), DIVA Pro 2.0 /U (ISA-PnP), DIVA Pro 2.0 /U (PCI), DIVA Server BRI (ISA-PnP), DIVA Server PRI (PCI), EiconCard C21 (ISDN), EiconCard S51/S50 (ISDN)
Tiger Jet Network Inc.	PCI ISDN-S/T, PCI ISDN-U
USR	Sportster 128K

Table 4-5   Windows 2000 Compatible USB Hub Hardware

Vendor	Product
ADS	(TI) Hub
Behavior Tech Computer Corp.	8112
CTX	USB Hub
EIZO	USB Hub
Entrega	Hub4U, Hub7U
Fujitsu	USB Bus Powered Hub
Granite Microsystems	USB Hub
I/O	NetworksHubport/7
Iiyama	USB Hub
Intel 8x930Hx	USB Hub
KC Technology	USB Hub
LiteOn Lite On	USB Hub
Microsoft	Keyboard Hub
MultiVideo Labs	USB Hub
National Semiconductor	USB Hub
NEC	F14T41B, F14T41W, F15R41B, Intellibase USB Hub, USB 4-port Hub
Nokia	USB Hub Type P
Peracom	Hub
Peracom	Quad Hub
Philips Semiconductors	CICT USB Hub
Philips	USB Hub
Sand	USB Hub
Solid Year	ACK-298H
Sony	USB HUB
Taxan (Europe) Ltd.	Ergovision 755 TC099
Teac	FD-05 PUB
TI	General purpose USB Hub
Winbond	USB Hub

What's New or Different in MS-DOS

Windows 2000 retains and enhances almost all of the functionality of MS-DOS. Tables 4-6, 4-7, and 4-8 identify new Windows 2000 commands not found in MS-DOS, changes to MS-DOS commands, and unavailable MS-DOS commands.

Table 4-6 Windows 2000 system commands not found in MS-DOS	
Command	*Function*
at	Schedules commands and programs to run on a computer at a specified time and on a specified date.
cacls	Displays or modifies access control lists (ACLs) of files.
convert	Converts file systems from FAT to NTFS.
dosonly	Prevents starting applications other than MS-DOS-based applications from the Command prompt.
echoconfig	Displays messages when reading the MS-DOS subsystem Config.nt file.
endlocal	Ends localization of environment variables.
findstr	Searches for text in files using regular expressions.
ntcmdprompt	Runs the Windows 2000 command interpreter, Cmd.exe, rather than Command.com after running a TSR or after starting the command prompt from within an MS-DOS application.
popd	Changes to the directory last set with the **pushd** command.
pushd	Saves the current directory for use by the **popd** command, and then changes to the specified directory.
setlocal	Begins localization of environmental variables.
start	Runs a specified program or command in a secondary window and in its own memory space.
Title	Sets the title of the command prompt window.
&&	Command following this symbol runs only if the command preceding the symbol succeeds.
||	Command following this symbol runs only if the command preceding the symbol fails.
&	Separates multiple commands on the command line.
( )	Groups commands.
^	Escape character. Allows typing command symbols as text.
; or ,	Separates parameters.

Table 4-7   Windows 2000 changes and improvements to MS-DOS commands

Command	Changed features
chcp	Changes code pages for full-screen mode only.
cmd	Cmd.exe replaces Command.com.
del	New switches provide many more functions.
dir	New switches provide many more functions.
diskcomp	Switches /1 and /8 are not supported.
diskcopy	Switch /1 is not supported.
doskey	Available for all character-based programs that accept buffered input. **Doskey** has been improved by a series of enhancements.
format	20.8 MB optical drive supported. Switches /b, /s, and /u are not supported.
label	The symbols ^ and & can be used in a volume label.
mode	Extensive changes.
more	New switches provide many more functions.
path	The %PATH%environment variable appends the current path to a new setting at the command prompt.
print	Switches /b, /c, /m, /p, /q, /s, /t, and /u are not supported.
prompt	New character combinations allow you to add ampersands ($a), parentheses ($c and $f), and spaces ($s) to your prompt.
recover	Recovers files.
rmdir	New /s switch deletes directories containing files and subdirectories.
sort	Does not require TEMP environment variable. File size is unlimited.
xcopy	New switches provide many more functions.

Table 4-8   MS-DOS commands not available at the command prompt when running Windows 2000

Command	New procedure or reason for obsolescence
assign	Not supported in Windows 2000.
backup	Not currently supported.
choice	Not currently supported.
ctty	Not currently supported.
dblspace	Not supported.
defrag	Windows 2000 automatically optimizes disk use.

Command	New procedure or reason for obsolescence
deltree	The **rmdir /s** command deletes directories containing files and subdirectories.
diskperf	Not currently supported.
dosshell	Unnecessary with Windows 2000.
drvspace	The Drvspace program is not currently supported.
emm386	Unnecessary with Windows 2000.
fasthelp	This MS-DOS 6.0 command is the same as the Windows 2000 command **help**. Windows 2000 also provides an online command reference.
fdisk	Disk Administrator prepares hard disks for use with Windows 2000.
include	Multiple configurations of the MS-DOS subsystem are not supported.
interlnk	The Interlnk program is not supported.
intersrv	The Intersrv program is not supported.
join	Increased partition size and an improved file system eliminate the need to join drives.
memmaker	Windows 2000 automatically optimizes the MS-DOS subsystem's memory use.
menucolor	Multiple configurations of the MS-DOS subsystem are not supported.
menudefault	Multiple configurations of the MS-DOS subsystem are not supported.
menuitem	Multiple configurations of the MS-DOS subsystem are not supported.
mirror	Not supported in Windows 2000.
msav	The Msav program is not supported.
msbackup	Windows 2000 provides the Backup utility (in the Administrative Tools in Control Panel) for computers with tape drives, or the **xcopy** command for computers without tape drives.
mscdex	It is unnecessary to configure the MS-DOS subsystem to use a CD-ROM drives. Windows 2000 provides access to CD-ROM drives for the MS-DOS subsystem.
msd	Use the System Information snap-in. To start System Information, click **Start**, click **Run**, and then type msinfo32.
numlock	Not currently supported.
power	The Power utility is not supported.
restore	Not currently supported.
scandisk	The Scandisk utility is not supported.
smartdrv	Windows 2000 automatically provides caching for the MS-DOS subsystem.

Table 4-8   *(Continued)*

Command	New procedure or reason for obsolescence
submenu	Multiple configurations of the MS-DOS subsystem are not supported.
sys	Windows 2000 will not fit on a standard 1.2 MB or 1.44 MB floppy disk.
undelete	Not supported in Windows 2000.
Unformat	Not supported in Windows 2000.
Vsafe	The Vsafe program is not supported.

Summary

We learned how to manage and configure your computer with the Control Panel, including:

▶ Why you need to think about compatibility with Windows 2000.

▶ Which software and hardware products Microsoft wrote off for Windows 2000, "right out of the box."

▶ Which products should work with Windows 2000.

▶ What Windows 2000 compatible means.

▶ Windows 2000 changes to MS-DOS commands.

Chapter 5

Troubleshooting

In This Chapter

We help prepare you for problems and emergencies. While one of Microsoft's goals for Windows 2000 is to make it their most stable operating system, there are still going to be the inevitable crashes, freezes, and lockups. We will look at:

▶ Preventative medicine: How to be ready with an Emergency Repair Disk and the System State backup.

▶ Startup problems: How to boot into Safe Mode, and what can you do to start your computer.

▶ How to work at the Recovery Console and the Command Prompt.

▶ How to deal with hardware problems and conflicts.

▶ How to use diagnostic tools and troubleshooters that come with Windows 2000.

Preventative Medicine

The word is *when*, not *if*.

Don't think of it as "If I ever have computer problems...;" you should be thinking of it as "When I have computer problems...." Use Windows 2000 long enough, and something inevitably will go wrong. It might be a hardware failure, or it might be a software failure. It might be a bug in the software, or it might be that you did something stupid. But at some point, plan on problems to occur.

The first thing to do is follow the old Boy Scout motto: "Be Prepared." We will show you three things to do now, while things are running well, so that you can help yourself later, when things go bad. Store these things in a safe place so that you know where your troubleshooting tools can be found.

Emergency Repair Disk

We learned in Chapter 2 how to prepare an Emergency Repair Disk. Your Emergency Repair Disk is used in conjunction with either the Windows 2000 CD-ROM, or with the four installation floppy disks that you can create. (Creating installation diskettes is also covered in Chapter 2.) When you create your installation diskettes, Windows 2000 writes three files to the first floppy disk: Autoexec.nt, Config.nt, and System.log. These three files contain the minimum pieces of information you will need to restore your system. (The exact contents will vary, depending on your system setup.) You create the Emergency Repair Disk from the Windows Backup menu, as shown in Figure 5-1.

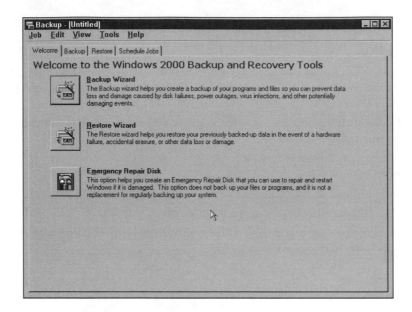

Figure 5-1: Create an Emergency Repair Disk.

Once you have created the Emergency Repair Disk, you will find a file named autoexec.nt and a file named config.nt, which will be similar to the file contents displayed in Listing 5-1 and 5-2, respectively.

Listing 5-1: Contents of the autoexec.nt

```
@echo off

REM AUTOEXEC.BAT is not used to initialize the MS-DOS environment.
REM AUTOEXEC.NT is used to initialize the MS-DOS environment unless a
REM different startup file is specified in an application's PIF.
REM Install CD ROM extensions
lh %SystemRoot%\system32\mscdexnt.exe

REM Install network redirector (load before dosx.exe)
lh %SystemRoot%\system32\redir
REM Install DPMI support
lh %SystemRoot%\system32\dosx
REM Install network redirector

lh %SystemRoot%\system32\nw16

lh %SystemRoot%\system32\vwipxspx
```

Config.NT is much larger, but only due to the presence of a lot of REMarked instructions. The actual content is only a few lines.

Listing 5-2: Contents of Config.NT

```
REM Windows NT MS-DOS Startup File
REM
dos=high, umb
device=%SystemRoot%\system32\himem.sys
files=20
```

The third file, setup.log, is a listing of files to be installed, and to what directory the files are to be installed in. These files, together with the Windows 2000 CD-ROM or floppy disks, are intended to replace missing files that might have disrupted your startup procedure.

Tip

Changing your computer's configuration will change the information stored in the setup.log file. After you modify your configuration, you should make a new Emergency Repair Disk. Make sure to write the date on the disk so you can easily determine your most recent copy. The three files, at least on our Windows 2000 system, only consume 137K.

System State backup

The System State backup, also found in the Windows Backup program, backs up key files that allow your system to be restored. For Windows 2000 Professional, the System State includes the Registry, the system boot files, and all the key system files. (These are the digitally signed files that Microsoft deems crucial to Windows 2000. These files are protected and can't be overwritten by another program.)

STEPS:

Do a System State backup

Step 1. Click Start ➪ Programs ➪ Accessories ➪ System Tools ➪ Backup.

Step 2. Select the Backup tab.

Step 3. In the left pane, check the System State option.

Step 4. In the Backup media or filename, select the drive to which you want to backup. (Given the size of the System State data, as shown in the Note above, the minimum size of your backup media should probably be 100MB, such as a Zip or SuperDisk disk. You would not want to select a floppy drive unless you have a lot of time to feed diskettes to the drive.)

Step 5. Click Start Backup.

If you need to restore the System State backup, the procedure is similar to these steps. However, you will need to select the Restore tab in Step 2, and then select the backup file you want to restore.

Data backup

The System state backup tools might help restore your computer to working order. Settings will be restored, profiles will be replaced, and your desktop should be restored to the same state it was previously in. However, it does not replace the most crucial files on your system — your data. You should also develop a plan to regularly back up your data to some other medium (tape, removable drives, CD-R discs, or even to floppies). Windows 2000 comes with a backup program, and the Backup Wizard will guide you through the backup and restore processes. If you have a large media drive such as a Zip or Jaz drive, backup software is typically provided by the vendor. The same is true for tape drives. The most important prevention step you can take is to regularly back up your data files.

Secret

Originally, Windows 2000 was going to include another recovery feature called Automated System Recovery. This was dropped from the final Beta 3 edition, although a number of prerelease documents and help files continue to refer to it.

Microsoft's Preventative Medicine

One of Microsoft's goals for Windows 2000 was greater reliability. Quite probably, they were tired of jokes like "I was driving down a road and came up behind a car whose license plate said NT GURU. I immediately turned off the road because I figured that car was going to turn blue and crash violently." In their programming efforts, they added some preventative medicine to help further that goal. Two areas of focus were driver reliability and system file protection.

Driver signatures

You can obtain device drivers that have been digitally signed by Microsoft. The digital signature implies that the driver has passed a certain amount of compatibility testing, and also that the driver has not been altered by another program installation. To check whether a driver has been digitally signed, check its driver details in Device Manager using the following steps.

Secret

While many third-party device drivers will be provided and digitally signed by Microsoft, they are often written by the driver's manufacturer — or jointly by the manufacturer and Microsoft — and included with Windows 2000.

STEPS:

Checking driver signatures

Step 1. Click Start ⇨ Settings ⇨ Control Panel.

Step 2. Select Administrative Tools, and then select Computer Management.

Step 3. Expand System Tools in the console tree in the left pane, and then select Device Manager.

Step 4. You must select a device category in the right pane, such as Sound, Video, and Game Controllers, and then expand it by clicking the plus sign to its left.

Step 5. Right-click one of the devices shown, such as your sound card, and then select Properties.

Step 6. Select the Drivers tab. You should see the name of the provider of the driver, it's the driver's version number and date, and the source of the driver's digital signature, as shown in Figure 5-2.

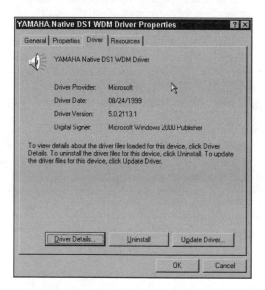

Figure 5-2: The Driver tab in a device's Properties dialog box will display the driver provider name and the driver's digital signature details. In the figure, the Yamaha sound card driver was provided by Microsoft.

System file protection

A major cause of incompatibility and crashes is something affectionately referred to as *DLL Hell*. Symptoms of this anomaly are that an application might overwrite files with a similar name belonging to other applications. Often, these are dynamic link library (DLL) files that get placed in the C:\Winnt\System32 folder during an application's installation.

As a way to protect the files that are installed by Windows 2000 and other applications, Microsoft developed a process called system file protection, which is a background process that monitors whether any of the system files are replaced or moved. System file protection prevents these files from being overwritten except under the following circumstances:

- Installation of a Windows 2000 Service Pack.

- Installation of a Windows 2000 Hot fix.

- Installation of a Windows 2000 upgrade using Winnt32.exe.

- Updates using the built-in Windows Update feature.

Protected System files are backed up each time you perform a System State backup. A command prompt utility called System File Checker (Sfc.exe) is also available that will scan and verify all of your protected system files. If it finds that one of your protected system files has been overwritten, it will retrieve a copy from the C:*%systemroot%*\system32\dllcache folder. To use the System File Checker, click Start ⇨ Programs ⇨ Command Prompt, and type the following command into the Open text box:

```
c:\sfc {options}
```

The System File Checker options are listed in Table 5-1.

Table 5-1 System File Checker Options	
Option	*Description*
/scannow	Runs System File Checker immediately.
/scanonce	Runs System File Checker only once — the next time the system is booted.
/scanboot	Runs System File Checker each time the system is booted.
/cancel	Cancels all scheduled future scans.
/quiet	Runs the scan in quiet mode, without any prompts.
/purgecache	Purges the file cache and performs an immediate scan.
/enable	Turns on Windows File Protection during normal operation.
/cachesize=*num*	Sets the file cache size equal to the value in *num*.

File Signature Verification

File Signature Verification is a tool that lets you scan selected portions of your system to look for files that have not been digitally signed.

STEPS:

Running File Signature Verification

Step 1. Click Start ➪ Run, type sigverif into the Open text box, and then press Enter or click OK.

Step 2. At the opening screen, click the Advanced button to set options, as shown in Figure 5-3.

Figure 5-3: In addition to scanning System Files, you can use File Signature Verification to search for unsigned files.

Step 3. By default, File Signature Verification only searches System Files. You can extend your scan by selecting other folders and their subfolders. The most crucial place to search is your Windows 2000 folder and subfolders.

Step 4. Select the Logging tab. You can have output sent to a log file, which you can then examine or print later. If you use the default log file, sigverif.txt, you can either append to or overwrite any existing log.

Step 5. Click OK to close the Advanced Options dialog. Then, click Start.

Continued

Step 6. After the scan is complete, you will see a window showing the results of the files that were found without digitally signatures, as shown in Figure 5-4.

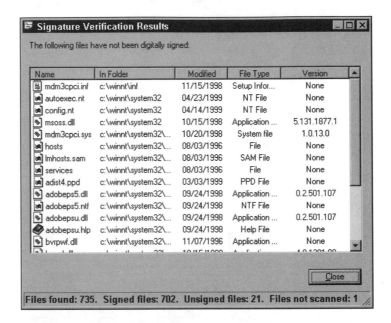

Figure 5-4: The results of the File Signature Verification scan are shown here. If you also kept the optional log file, you can view or print the report.

If you extended your scan beyond system files, you will probably see a number of unsigned files listed in your report. Is this bad? Probably not. Configuration and data files will not be signed, nor will many files added by third party or legacy applications. However, if you see some core Windows 2000 applications, such as Explorer.exe or Regedit.exe, displayed in the list of unsigned files, you should suspect that some of your files have been overwritten or damaged.

Secret

Most of the important Windows 2000 DLLs reside in the C:\%systemroot%\ system32 folder. The vast majority of the files here are signed. On one of our Windows 2000 computers, there were 1,913 files in this folder and its subfolders, with 1,588 having digital signatures. Many of the unsigned files were configuration files that frequently get changed, or files from legacy applications written prior to the advent of digital signatures.

The Windows 2000 Boot Procedure

Before we talk about specific troubleshooting steps, it will help you to see what happens when Windows 2000 first starts.

The Windows 2000 boot sequence is very similar to the way in which Windows NT boots, but it is quite different from the way in which both Windows 95 and Windows 98 boot. The latter two use Io.sys, Msdos.sys, Config.sys, and Autoexec.bat, which are not used in the Windows 2000 boot process.

The BIOS (basic input/output system) is in charge when you first apply power to your computer. Typically, it first conducts a power-on self-test, and it then loads some of the most basic drivers for essential equipment, such as your video card and disk drives. The BIOS then gives the command to run the program on the boot sector of your start-up drive.

Note

Most computers are set up so that the BIOS first looks to the floppy drive — drive A: — for system files with which to boot, and it then looks to your system drive — usually your C: drive. This is a safety measure. If your hard drive has malfunctioned, you can still boot the computer by inserting a boot diskette into the floppy drive. It is also the reason why you will see an error message "Non-system or disk error" if you have a non-bootable floppy in the drive when you turn on your computer.

The first file in the boot sequence is Ntldr (NT Loader), a hidden system file located in the root directory of your hard drive. Ntlrstarts the initial boot loading phase, and carries out a couple of jobs: it switches the microprocessor into 32-bit flat memory mode, and it then starts the minifile system drivers built-in to Ntldr, which are used to find the Windows 2000 files from their location on the hard drive.

Next, Ntldr looks for the Boot.ini file, which is what provides the text menu that asks which operating system you wish to load. Boot.ini is actually a small text file in the root directory of your hard drive.

Listing 5-3: A typical Boot.ini file used on a single-boot system

```
[boot loader]
timeout=30
default=multi(0)disk(0)rdisk(0)partition(1)\WINNT
[operating systems]
multi(0)disk(0)rdisk(0)partition(1)\WINNT="Microsoft Windows 2000
Professional" /fastdetect
```

If you had a dual-boot system prior to installing Windows 2000, additional entries would be listed here from which you could choose the operating system you wanted to load. On dual-boot systems, one operating system is always designated as the default. If you don't make a choice before the timeout period expires, the default operating system is loaded.

After Ntldr completes its required processes, Ntdetect begins looking for installed hardware. It creates a list of all the currently installed hardware and sends this information to Ntldr so that Ntldr can open the Registry. Some of the hardware detected by Ntdetect includes: the installed bus and adapter types; the number and type of installed communications and parallel ports; the floating-point processor type; the number of installed floppy disk drives; the number of installed hard disk drives; the type of keyboard installed; the number and type of attached pointing devices; the type of video adapter installed; and, the number and type of SCSI (small computer system interface) adapters that are installed.

If you have different hardware profiles established on your computer (see Chapter 14 for information on creating hardware profiles), you will then see a menu from which you can choose which profile you wish to load. Otherwise, the default profile will be loaded. After all the hardware detection and setup is complete, Ntoskrnl then takes over.

It is only when you reach the log on screen — where you enter your user name and password — that your user profile is loaded. That means that any customized settings, such as a left-handed mouse configuration , are available only after you log on.

Troubleshooting Startup Problems

The Windows 2000 Online Help files contain a number of interactive troubleshooters that step you through solutions to particular problems. These can be an excellent source of help for many problems with your computer. To reach the troubleshooters, follow these steps:

STEPS:

Using the Interactive Troubleshooters

Step 1.   Click Start ⇨ Help.

Step 2.   Select the Contents tab in the left pane of the Help window.

Step 3.   Click Troubleshooting and Maintenance to expand it.

Step 4.   Select Windows 2000 Troubleshooters in the left pane.

Step 5.   In the right pane, click the troubleshooter for your particular problem.

There is one problem that these interactive troubleshooters can't help you with: if you can't get your computer started in the first place, you certainly won't be able to reach the troubleshooters, let alone use them.

After you power up your computer, Windows 2000 may fail to start. In some cases, you might see an error message telling you what the problem is. Other times, the computer will appear to hang. At this point, there are a number of things you can try to restart your system. These options include:

- Booting into Windows 2000 Safe Mode
- Using the Emergency Repair Disk
- Using the Windows 2000 Recovery Console

Windows 2000 Safe Mode

To boot your computer in safe mode, you circumvent the normal operating system start up process. There are actually a number of different options available to you in safe mode. You choose the option you want from a menu, which you can reach using the following steps

STEPS:

Booting into Safe Mode

Step 1. Apply power to your computer.

Step 2. Wait for the message, "Please select the operating system to start."

Step 3. As soon as you see this message, press the F8 key. You may not have a lot of time to do this before the automatic boot sequence begins.

Step 4. If you successfully reach the boot menu, you will see a number of choices from which you can select (these choices are explained following these steps).

Step 5. Use the keyboard arrow keys to highlight the selection you want, and then press the Enter key.

Step 6. A text screen will be displayed from which you select the operating system you wish to boot to. If you have a dual-boot system, choose Windows 2000.

Tip

The window of opportunity for pressing F8 is rather short. It normally lasts only as long as the message "Please select the operating system to start" displays during a normal boot process. Have your finger poised over the F8 key early so you won't miss your window of opportunity.

The choices available to you normally include the following.

- Safe Mode

- Safe Mode with Networking

- Safe Mode with command prompt

- Enable Boot Logging

- Enable VGA Mode

- Last Known Good Configuration

- Debugging Mode

- Normal Boot

There may be additional options listed on your menu, particularly if you have used the Remote Install Services. The option you choose depends, to some extent, on what problems you are having.

Secret

By setting things up ahead of time, you can use another method to boot into safe mode. Microsoft Knowledge Base Article Number Q239780 details switches you can add to your Boot.ini file that enable you to choose one of the safe mode boot options from the operating system menu you see when you first start Windows 2000. If you often find yourself booting into safe mode or one of its variations, it may be easier to simply choose your option from the menu.

The switches used for the various safe-modes follow:

- Safe Mode switch: /SAFEBOOT:MINIMAL /SOS /BOOTLOG /NOGUIBOOT

- Safe Mode with Networking switch: /SAFEBOOT:NETWORK /SOS / BOOTLOG /NOGUIBOOT

- Safe Mode with Command Prompt switch: /SAFEBOOT:MINIMAL (ALTERNATESHELL) /SOS /BOOTLOG /NOGUIBOOT

- Enable Boot Logging switch: /BOOTLOG

- Enable VGA Mode switch: /BASEVIDEO

- Directory Services Restore Mode (Domain Controllers Only) switch: /SAFEBOOT:DSREPAIR /SOS

- Debugging Mode switch: /DEBUG

Your boot.ini file would look something like what is shown in Listing 5-4:

Listing 5-4: Boot.ini with safe mode options

```
[boot loader]
timeout=30
default=multi(0)disk(0)rdisk(0)partition(1)\WINNT
[operating systems]
multi(0)disk(0)rdisk(0)partition(1)\WINNT="Microsoft Windows 2000
Professional" /fastdetect
multi(0)disk(0)rdisk(0)partition(1)\WINNT="Microsoft Windows 2000
Professional" /fastdetect /SAFEBOOT:MINIMAL /SOS /BOOTLOG /NOGUIBOOT
```

Note that you are not required to add any of these switches to boot into safe mode; you can still do so by pressing F8 at startupand then selecting a boot mode option from the Safe Mode menu. However, if you often find yourself using one of these options, it might be more convenient to have them appear on the startup menu. Each menu option — with available switches is described below.

Safe Mode

This starts Windows 2000, but only with the most basic drivers and files. Since there is a problem somewhere, safe mode will load only the minimum system files required, simplifying its own environment. You will see a list of the drivers and services that do load scroll on your screen. Once you reach the Windows 2000 Desktop, you will find yourself in 640x480 video mode with a very basic color scheme. You should also see "Safe Mode" displayed on your Desktop.

Once you have booted your computer in safe mode, you might have to perform additional troubleshooting, such as examining the event logs (event logs are covered in Chapter 15), or viewing the hardware troubleshooters, to determine what the problem is. If safe mode doesn't help you solve your system problems, and your system still won't boot, you might need to use one of the other available boot options.

Secret

USB ports are not supported in safe mode; its drivers are among those omitted in this boot mode. This means that anything you might attach to your computer through a USB port, such as a mouse, a keyboard, or a Zip drive, will not be accessible in safe mode.

Secret

It is probably not a complete list, but if you want to see some of the things that are not available in Safe mode, check the Event Log. There should be a whole string of error messages, detailing services or devices that could not start because something else is missing.

Safe Mode with networking

This is the same as the standard safe mode option, plus it adds support for network connections. This enables you connect to your network if you need to copy files or call on other network resources.

Safe Mode with command prompt

This dispenses with the Windows 2000 GUI (graphical user interface), mouse support, and other modern conveniences. Choosing this menu option will take you straight to the command prompt, where you can use command-line utilities (all those MS-DOS commands that are long forgotten). Later in this chapter, the Recovery Console section covers many of the command-line utilities you can use.

Secret

If you boot into Safe mode with Command Prompt, you will not be able to use many of the computer management tools that are accessed via the Control Panel or the Microsoft Management Console. One important tool that would be unavailable is the Event Viewer, which lets you view the three Event Logs, which record events such as errors and warnings that occur on your computer. There is a Command Prompt utility available in the Windows 2000 Resource Kit that will let you dump the contents of an Event Log to a tab delimited text file. This text file can then be viewed with the Type command from the Command Prompt.

At the Command Prompt, give this command:

```
dumpel -f filename {options}
```

The parameters for Dump Event Log are listed in Table 5-2.

Table 5-2   Dump Event Log commands

Parameter	Meaning
-f *filename*	This is the filename for the output file. There is no default output file, so you must give a filename.
-s *server*	If you have a network connection, you can save the event log to a server.
-l *logname*	This tells which of the three log files (system, security, application) you want to dump. If you don't give a log file, or give an invalid log file name, the application log will be dumped by default.
-m *source*	This will dump records only from a specified source, such as RemoteAccess or DHCP. You can only specify one source. If you don't give this parameter, the entire log is dumped.
-e *n1, n2,...n10*	This lets you specify up to ten events to scan for and dump. If you don't use this switch, everything is dumped. This must be used together with the -m switch.
-r	This reverses the selection for -e; all events except those specified will be dumped to the text file.
-t	This will use a tab as the delimiter in the text file. If you don't use this, then spaces will be used as the delimiter.
-d *n*	This will dump events for the past *n* days.

Secret

If you aren't sure what codes are used for sources and events, there is a Microsoft Access 97 database file in the Windows 2000 Resource Kit that contains all the Event Log messages. The database has 2768 different Event Log messages in the database. The name of the file is ntevntlg.mdb, and you can find it in the Windows 2000 Resource Kit, under the Diagnostic Tools category. If you don't have Access 97 or another program that can open the file, take a look at one of the Event Logs before you get in trouble. You will be able to see the sources and events that get recorded.

Another useful Microsoft Management Console tool that would be unavailable if you are at the Safe Mode Command prompt is the System Information tool. The Windows 2000 Resource Kit has a command line version of this tool, called WinMsdp. It also collects information about your system, only it sends the information to a text file named Msdrpt.txt, which can then be viewed onscreen using the Type command. To use it from the Safe Mode Command Prompt, and assuming the Resource Kit has been installed in its default folder, give these commands:

```
cd progra~1
cd resour~1
cd ntrk
winmsdp {options}
```

The options for WinMsdp tell what information to put into the report. The selections are listed in Table 5-3.

Table 5-3   Optional Reports for WinMsdp

Parameter	Report
/a	All settings
/d	Drive information
/e	Environment information
/il	Interrupt resources
/n	Network information
/p	Port information
/r	Driver information
/s	Services information
/w	Hardware information
/y	Memory information

The full report, which you get by giving the /a command, can be quite large. A sample report generated for one of our Windows 2000 computers totaled 142 K.

Enable boot logging

This does a normal Windows 2000 startup, keeping a log of all of the drivers and services that were loaded during the boot process (including details about those having problems). The bootlog file will be saved in a file called ntbtlog.txt in your Windows 2000 directory.

Chances are that if Windows 2000 wouldn't start before, it still won't start. However, the ntbtlog.txt file might very well tell you why it didn't start properly. You will then need to start Windows 2000 in safe mode (or by choosing the option Safe Mode with Command Prompt). You can then view or print the file, which might lead you toward resolving the cause of your problem. The Type and More commands, for example (which are available at the Command Prompt or the Recovery Console), are tools you can use to view the ntbtlog.txt file. Listing 5-5 is an example ntbtlog.txt file. It shows, in part, which services and devices were loaded for the last startup. If there was an error in loading a driver or program, that information also will be shown, and it might be a valuable clue to assist you in your troubleshooting.

Listing 5-5: Excerpt: Sample Ntbtlog.txt file

```
Microsoft (R) Windows 2000 (R) Version 5.0 (Build 2031)
 8 13 1999 17:12:56.500
Loaded driver \WINNT\System32\ntoskrnl.exe
Loaded driver \WINNT\System32\hal.dll
Loaded driver \WINNT\System32\BOOTVID.DLL
Loaded driver ACPI.sys
Loaded driver \WINNT\System32\DRIVERS\WMILIB.SYS
Loaded driver pci.sys
Loaded driver isapnp.sys
Loaded driver ftdisk.sys
Loaded driver intelide.sys
Loaded driver \WINNT\System32\DRIVERS\PCIIDEX.SYS
```

The full log file would be much larger, of course. With a safe mode startup, many of the drivers and services you normally use would not be loaded; they would be reported like this:

```
Did not load driver Audio Codecs
Did not load driver Legacy Audio Drivers
Did not load driver Media Control Devices
Did not load driver Legacy Video Capture Devices
Did not load driver Video Codecs
```

Enable VGA mode

If you just upgraded your video driver and Windows 2000 will no longer start, the problem may be that new driver. This command starts a full Windows 2000 startup using a basic VGA driver—the same basic driver that is used when you boot in safe mode. If Windows 2000 starts, you should reinstall your previous driver.

Last known good configuration

If the error messages you see when Windows 2000 starts up indicate some problem with the Registry, you might be in luck. Windows 2000 keeps a backup copy of the last known good Registry configuration with which you successfully started Windows. Try this option to see if it solves your startup problem. (For more information on this feature, see Chapter 16.)

Debugging mode

If your computer is linked to another computer through a serial cable, you can use this option to send debugging information over the cable to the other computer.

Using the Recovery Console

The Recovery Console is a new feature of Windows. Using the Recovery Console is similar to booting using the Safe Mode Command Prompt mode in that you will have a command prompt from which you can use various utilities to try to fix your system. There are a couple of differences, however. Some of these additional utilities can only be run from the Recovery Console. Also, you reach the Recovery Console from the operating system selection menu, completely bypassing Windows 2000.

Setting up ahead of time

You can get to the Recovery Console after a problem has occurred. To do so, you will need to start your computer using the four Windows 2000 boot disks. (See Chapter 2 for instructions on how to create these diskettes.) If you haven't created these boot disks ahead of time, and your computer won't start, you can use another computer even a non-Windows 2000 computer — to create a set of diskettes from the Windows 2000 CD-ROM.

The best choice, of course, is to be prepared ahead of time. You install the Recovery Console from the Windows 2000 CD-ROM using the following steps:

STEPS:

Installing the Recovery Console

Step 1.   Insert the Windows 2000 CD-ROM disc into your CD-ROM drive.

Step 2.   If the CD automatically starts and you see the Windows 2000 installation screen, exit from it.

Step 3.   Click Start ⇨ Run, and then type the following command (where d: is the drive letter for your CD-ROM drive):

```
d:\i386\winnt32 /cmdcons:
```

Continued

STEPS

Installing the Recovery Console *(continued)*

Step 4. You will see the Recovery Console introductory screen shown in Figure 5-5. Click the Yes button to continue.

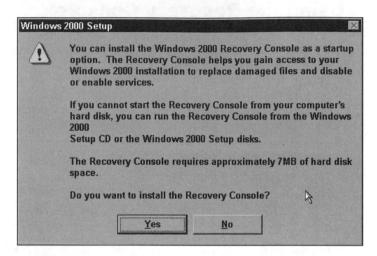

Figure 5-5: Click the Yes button to install the Windows 2000 Recovery Console. It adds files to your system, and gives you another choice on your operating system selection menu that you can see when you start your system.

Once the Recovery Console has been installed, you will have a new choice on the Operating System selection menu that you will be able to choose when you first boot your computer. If you view the Boot.ini file, you will see the extra selection added to the bottom (If you have a dual-boot system, there will be additional entries in the Boot.ini file, as well.)

Listing 5-6: Boot.ini with Recovery Console added

```
[boot loader]
timeout=30
default=multi(0)disk(0)rdisk(0)partition(1)\WINNT
[operating systems]
multi(0)disk(0)rdisk(0)partition(1)\WINNT="Microsoft Windows 2000
Professional" /fastdetect
C:\CMDCONS\BOOTSECT.DAT="Microsoft Windows 2000 Command Console"
/cmdcons
```

Using the Console

If you select the Recovery Console option when you boot your computer, you will first see a screen asking which Windows 2000 installation you wish to log into. If you have multiple installations, make your choice. You will then be prompted for the Administrator's password.

Tip

The Recovery Console looks in the Registry's Security Accounts Manager hive for the password information. If this hive is damaged or deleted, you will not be able to use the Recovery Console. You might have to boot into safe mode instead by pressing the F8 key at the operating system menu, and then choosing the option to restore the last known good Registry files.

Caution

At the Recovery Console, you will find two important limitations. First, you cannot get beyond the Windows 2000 installation that you are currently booted into. If you have multiple operating systems installed, you will not be able to see the other operating systems. Second, you will not be able to copy a file from the hard disk to a floppy disk. This means that if you have been lax in backing up your data, you won't be able to use the Recovery Console to get in and rescue a copy of crucial data files.

Once you are at the Recovery Console, you can use the following utilities to make whatever repairs are needed to your system. You exit the Recovery Console by typing **EXIT** at the command prompt, which then closes the Recovery Console and restarts your system.

Deleting the Recovery Console

If you wish to delete the Recovery Console, there are two things you need to delete: the \Cmdcons folder beneath your root directory, and the file cmldr, also in the root directory. (Note that both the folder and the file are hidden, so you will have to configure Windows Explorer to show hidden files and folders first. See Chapter 7 for help.)

Recovery Console utilities

Once you've reached the Recovery Console, there are a number of command-line utilities you can use.(Most of these utilities have counterparts that can be used at the command prompt when Windows 2000 is running normally, or if you boot into Safe Mode with Command Prompt mode. If you've used computers in pre-Windows (MS-DOS) days, or if you have used the command prompt in prior Windows versions, these utilities will seem quite familiar to you. Note that many of these commands, such as COPY and DEL, actually have less options at the Recovery Console than they would when at the Command Prompt.

If you are going to be able to successfully fix a problem using the Recovery Console in Safe Mode with Command Prompt mode, you might need to use one or more of the following utilities. (Optional parameters or command-line switches are shown in italic text.)

CHDIR (or CD) — Change Directory

Changes the current folder to the one given in the command. The syntax is:

```
c:\cd {/d} [drive:][path]
```

The *{/d}* parameter changes to a different drive, which will be specified in the *[drive:]* parameter. If you omit the /d parameter, the command will change to the specified folder on the current drive. There are three special symbols that you can substitute for the *[path]* parameter:

```
cd..
```

will return you to the parent folder of your current folder (up one folder level), and

```
cd\
```

will take you to the root folder of the current drive. This will be your only means of navigating between folders if you are using the Recovery Console or command prompt.

```
cd..\
```

takes you to the another subfolder of the same level as the current folder, but still beneath the parent folder. For example, you can type cd ..\system at the c:\winnt\applog folder prompt to change to the c:\winnt\system folder.

CHKDSK — Check Disk

CHKDSK is a troubleshooting tool that checks a disk for errors, optionally fixing errors if specified. The syntax and options for CHKDSK at the Recovery Console, shown in Table 5-4, are different than the parameters for the regular CHKDSK command used at the Command Prompt, which are covered in Chapter 17.

```
chkdsk drive: {options}
```

Table 5-4   Recovery Console CHKDSK options

Option	Meaning
none	If there are no options given, then the status of the current drive will be displayed.
/p	This will perform an exhaustive check of the drive, but does not make changes to it.
/r	This will find bad sectors on the drive and recover information from them. Giving the /r command implies giving the /p command.

CLS — Clear Screen

Clears the screen. As you type commands at the Recovery Console or the command prompt, the commands you type, along with their results, stay on the screen until they scroll off the top. This can make the display appear somewhat cluttered. Think of this as a squeegie that wipes the screen clean.

COPY

If you find a damaged or missing file — or if you just want to copy a file from one location to another — use the Copy command. The syntax is:

```
copy source  destination
```

Both *source* and *destination* can be any combination of drive letter, path, and/or filename. If the drive letter or path is omitted, the default is the current drive and folder. If the destination filename is omitted, the existing filename will be used at the destination. The source directory can be any directory within the system directories of the Windows installation, the root directory of any drive, local installation sources, the Cmdcons directory or removable media. The destination drive can be the same locations as the source directory, except for removable media.

Note

The Move command is not available when you are working in the Recovery Console or at the command prompt. You will need to copy the file to a new folder, and then delete the original file using the DEL command discussed later in this chapter.

ERASE (or DEL) — Erase (or Delete)

This command will delete a specified file. The syntax is:

```
c:\del [drive:] [path] [filename]
```

If the drive and path are omitted, the current directory will be used. There is another DEL command that can be used at the Command prompt, that has additional options. Those options do not apply at the Recovery Console. You will only be able to use the DEL command in the system directories of the current Windows installation, the root directory of any hard disk partition, the local installation sources, and removable media.

DIR — Directory

This command will show you the files and subfolders in a given directory. The syntax is:

```
c:\dir [drive:] [path] [filename]
```

The output of DIR will look something like what is shown in Figure 5-6.

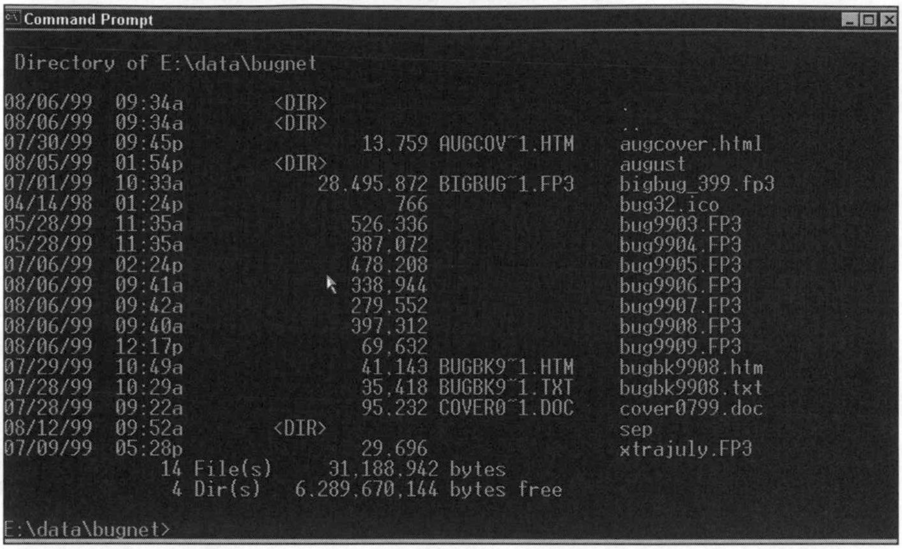

```
Command Prompt                                                        _ □ ×

Directory of E:\data\bugnet

08/06/99   09:34a      <DIR>                              .
08/06/99   09:34a      <DIR>                              ..
07/30/99   09:45p               13,759  AUGCOV~1.HTM      augcover.html
08/05/99   01:54p      <DIR>                              august
07/01/99   10:33a           28,495,872  BIGBUG~1.FP3      bigbug_399.fp3
04/14/98   01:24p                  766                    bug32.ico
05/28/99   11:35a              526,336                    bug9903.FP3
05/28/99   11:35a              387,072                    bug9904.FP3
07/06/99   02:24p              478,208                    bug9905.FP3
08/06/99   09:41a           ▸  338,944                    bug9906.FP3
08/06/99   09:42a              279,552                    bug9907.FP3
08/06/99   09:40a              997,312                    bug9908.FP3
08/06/99   12:17p               69,632                    bug9909.FP3
07/29/99   10:49a               41,143  BUGBK9~1.HTM      bugbk9908.htm
07/28/99   10:29a               35,418  BUGBK9~1.TXT      bugbk9908.txt
07/28/99   09:22a               95,232  COVER0~1.DOC      cover0799.doc
08/12/99   09:52a      <DIR>                              sep
07/09/99   05:28p               29,696                    xtrajuly.FP3
               14 File(s)      31,188,942 bytes
                4 Dir(s)    6,289,670,144 bytes free

E:\data\bugnet>
```

Figure 5-6: The output of the DIR command will show the date and time stamp of a file or folder, its size, its short (MS-DOS) filename, and its long (Windows) filename.

Each line in a DIR command represents a single file. You will see the date and time stamp, the size of the file, its short (MS-DOS) filename if necessary, and its long (Windows) filename. At the top of the display, you will see the path name of the folder; at the bottom of the display, you will see the size of the folder and the amount of free space on the drive. You will also see the file attributes, if any, for a file. These attributes are shown in Table 5-5.

Table 5-5	File Attributes
Abbreviation	**Attribute**
a	A file ready for archiving.
c	A compressed file.
d	A directory.
e	An encrypted file.
h	A hidden file.
p	A reparse point.
r	A read-only file.
s	A system file.

The DIR parameters and switches are listed in Table 5-6.

Table 5-6	DIR parameters and switches
Parameter	**Description**
drive: path	The folder for which you want to see a directory listing. If you omit the drive letter, the current drive will be displayed. If you omit the path name, the current folder will be displayed.
filename	Returns information only for the file specified, rather than showing all the files in the folder. You can use wildcards for filenames.

You also can use wildcard characters in place of the *filename* specification. If you type the following command:

```
c:\dir f*.*
```

it will return all of the files in the current directory beginning with the letter f.

The DIR command can be especially useful if you are having problems starting your computer. Often, startup problems happen because a crucial file gets erased or overwritten, although System File Protection is supposed to prevent this. You can either look for the file, or you can check its attributes to see if it has somehow been changed. For instance, many of your system files should have a time stamp matching the date that the operating system was installed. If they all suddenly have today's date, you know something has happened.

DISABLE

This command can only be used at the Windows 2000 Recovery Console; it can't be used from the command prompt. If your computer isn't starting correctly because of a service or driver, you can disable the culprit using the following command:

```
disable [service] | [device driver]
```

where *[service]* is the specified service, and *[driver]* is the specified driver that you want to disable, or turn off.

Cross-Reference

If you are already in Windows 2000, you can disable services from the Computer Management Console, which is covered in Chapter 15.

When you disable a command, a message will be displayed stating the start-up type for the service. You will need to remember this information if you are going to later use the ENABLE command to again enable the service.

ENABLE

The ENABLE command is the companion to the DISABLE command. It only works from the Windows 2000 Recovery Console, not from command prompt. To start a specific service or driver, type the following command:

```
enable [service] | [device driver] {startup type}
```

There are five driver startup types. The first three are similar to the startup options you find in the Services Console in the Computer Management Console. (See Chapter 15 for information on how to manage services when Windows 2000 is running.) These five types are:

- SERVICE_AUTO_START: same as Automatic.

- SERVICE_DISABLED: same as Disabled.

- SERVICE_DEMAND_START: same as Manual.

- SERVICE_BOOT_START: starts when the computer boots up.

- SERVICE_SYSTEM_START: starts when Windows 2000 boots up.

Tip

If you don't specify the start type, the current start type for the service will be displayed. If you change the start type, make a note of the original type so that you can restore it later if necessary.

EXIT

This command closes the Windows 2000 Recovery Console and restarts your computer. It is not available from the command prompt. (To close the command prompt, close its window.)

EXPAND

Sometimes a file gets corrupted or deleted. The EXPAND command is used to retrieve a driver from a cabinet (.CAB) file, or from a compressed file on the Windows 2000 CD. The syntax of the command is

```
expand {options}source | source.cab /F:filename {destination}
```

The parameters and options for the EXPAND command are shown in Table 5-7.

Table 5-7   EXPAND parameters and Switches

Parameter	Meaning
source	You specify this if your source file is a single file you need to extract from
source.cab /F:filename	Use this if you need to extract from a cabinet file, using the filename to specify which file to extract. You can use wildcards for the filename.
destination	Shows where you want the extracted file to go.

Parameter	Meaning
{Options}	
/d	This will only list files that are stored in a cabinet, without extracting any.
/y	This option will surpress the warning when you are overwriting a file.

Caution

You can use the wildcard specification *.* to extract all the files from a cabinet. However, some of the driver cabinet files on the Windows 2000 CD have a thousand files in them. It is far better to extract only the one you want than to extract all of them, and sort through for the relevant one.

FIXBOOT

Normally, when your computer starts, it looks for a particular segment of one hard drive—often called the system drive—for its boot files. These files are generally stored in the boot sector. The FIXBOOT command will either change this to a different drive or, if there is no parameter, it will write a new partition boot sector to the current drive. Type the following command:

```
fixboot [drive:]
```

where *[drive:]* is a specific drive letter. This command only works from the Windows Recovery Console, and it only works on Intel-based computers. It will not work on Compaq-Alpha computers.

FIXMBR—Fix Master Boot Record

This is another command that is available only from the Windows Recovery Console. It will write a new master boot record to the specified hard drive. Type the following command:

```
fixmbr [device]
```

where *[device]* is the name of the device—and not the drive letter—of the drive to which you want to write the new master boot record. You can use the MAP command to determine the device name of your drive, which may look something like \Device\HardDisk0. This command is only available on Intel-based computers.

FORMAT

The FORMAT command prepares your disk to accept data. The FORMAT command available from the Windows Recovery Console only has a subset of the parameters available from FORMAT run from the command prompt. From the Recovery Console, the command syntax is

```
format drive: {/q} {/fs:filesystem}
```

The drive parameter indicates what drive to format. From the Recovery Console, you will not be able to format a floppy disk. The optional /q only does a quick format, and does not scan the drive for bad sectors, so you should only use this switch if you know this drive is good. With the /fs: switch, you indicate which file system to use when formatting, eith FAT, FAT32, or NTFS. If you omit this, then the existing file format will be used.

Full details on using the regular FORMAT command from the Command prompt are available in Chapter 17.

LISTSVC

This command, which has no optional parameters, will show what services and drivers are available on this computer. It can only be used from the Recovery Console.

LOGON

From the Windows Recovery Console, this command will search the network for any instances of Windows 2000 or Windows NT. It will list all that it finds, and it will then ask you for the Administrator password.

MAP

This will MAP — or show the relationship — between drive letters and physical device names on your computer. You might need to run this utility to determine the device names before using the FIXBOOT, FIXMBR, or FDISK commands. The command syntax is as follows:

```
MAP {arc}
```

If you use the optional *{arc}* switch, MAP will show the Advanced RISC Computing device names. By default, it will show the Windows 2000 device names. This command is only available from the Windows Recovery Console.

MKDIR (or MD) — Make Directory

This command will create a new folder (directory). The syntax for this command is as follows:

```
mkdir {drive:} path
md {drive:} path
```

If you don't specify a drive on which to create a new folder, the new folder will be created on the current drive. *Path* will be the location and name of the new folder. If you type just the new folder name as the sole argument, as in the following example:

```
md newdir
```

a subfolder named *newdir* will be created in the current folder.

MORE

When you are at the Windows 2000 Recovery, you might want to view the contents of a text or log file. You can type the following command:

```
type filename.txt
```

If this file is large, it will quickly scroll off the top of the screen, before you can read it. The MORE command will allow you to see a screen load (approximately 24 lines) at a time. The syntax is as follows:

```
type | more filename
```

If you are using the MORE command on an NTFS drive, then any file name, which has spaces must be enclosed in quotation marks. There is another MORE command, which can be used at the Command Prompt, which has a different set of options.

RMDIR (or RD) — Remove Directory

This command removes a folder (directory). The syntax is as follows:

```
rmdir {drive:path} directory
rd {drive:path} directory
```

If no drive or path is specified , the folder specified will be deleted. This command can only be used on an empty directory. It also will only work in the system directories of the Windows installation, on removable media, the root directory of any hard disk partition, or local installation sources. There is an alternative RMDIR that can be used at the Command Prompt.

RENAME (or REN)

This renames a file, which can be handy when troubleshooting. You might want to replace a driver or a configuration file, while still keeping the original file available as a fallback. You can rename the original file using the following syntax:

```
Rename {drive:path} oldfilename newfilename
Ren {drive:path} oldfilename newfilename
```

If you do not specify a drive and path, the current folder will be searched by default. The newly named file must be placed in the same directory, you cannot specify a new location for it during the rename process.

SET

You can use the SET command to modify certain environment settings. It can be very useful to circumvent certain built-in limitations of some of the Recovery Console commands. From the Recovery Console, the syntax of the command is

```
set variable=string
```

The variables that can be set from the Recovery Console are shown in Table 5-8.

Table 5-8   Environment Variables at the Recovery Console

Environment Variable	Meaning
AllowWildCards	This will let you use wildcards with commands such as DEL.
AllowAllPaths	This will let you access all files and directories on the system.
AllowRemovableMedia	This will let you copy files to removable media.
NoCopyPrompt	This will turn off the warning given before you overwrite a file.

Secret

The SET command will not work at the Recovery Console by default, because Microsoft has disabled it. According to the Help files that accompany Windows 2000 Release Candidate 2, there should be a setting in the Security Template, at Local Computer Policy/Computer Configuration/Windows Settings/Security Settings/Local Policies/Security Options, called Enables the Set command for the Recovery Console. However, this setting is not actually in the Release Candidate 2 Security snap-in. There is a setting there called Recovery Console:Allow floppy copy and access for all drives and folders, which is the equivalent of the AllowAllPaths in Table 5-8. For more information on the Security snap-in, see Chapter 15.

SYSTEMROOT

This command is only available from the Windows Recovery Console. It makes the current folder the systemroot folder, which is the folder in which the Windows 2000 system files are located. While this would normally be drive C: drive, you can switch it to another drive. You might want to change the systemroot folder if, for some reason, your Windows 2000 files get hopelessly mangled, and you then want to install a fresh copy on another drive or in another partition.

TYPE

Displays the specified file on your screen. The syntax is as follows:

```
type {drive:path} filename
```

If no drive or path name is specified, the current folder is used. The TYPE command is often combined with the MORE command, discussed earlier, to examine a long file on a screen-by-screen basis.

If you are having problems starting Windows 2000, one troubleshooting step you can try is to boot into safe mode, and then enable boot logging to track all the devices and services that are loaded — or that fail to load. Enabling logging will write the information to the ntbtlog.txt file in your Windows directory. If you can't boot into safe mode — landing in Safe Mode Command Prompt mode instead, you can type the following commands at the command prompt:

```
c:\cd winnt
c:\type ntbtlog.txt |more
```

This will display a screen-by-screen view of the log file, which you then can examine for any errors in services or drivers to provide clues as to why Windows 2000 is not starting.

Secret

Why would anyone want to use the TYPE command to send output to the screen? Well, this command has its roots deep in computer history. Most output went to teletype machines rather than video screens; hence, the command TYPE.

Using the Emergency Repair Disk

If none of these procedures work in getting your computer started again, it is time to use the Emergency Repair Disk. We saw how to create this disk in the Preventative Medicine section. To use the disk, follow these steps:

STEPS:

Using the Emergency Repair Disk

Step 1. Start your computer using the four Windows 2000 Setup disks.

Step 2. A number of files will be copied to your computer. When the copying is complete, your computer will restart.

Step 3. When you see the "Welcome to Setup" screen, press the letter R on your keyboard.

Step 4. You will be given a choice of either Manual Repair or Fast Repair. It's best to choose Manual Repair at this stage. The Fast Repair option will erase a lot of configuration information because sit restores the first complete set of Registry files that were created after a successful Windows 2000 installation.

Step 5. Follow the prompts to insert your Emergency Repair Disk in drive A:, and then press the letter L on your keyboard to locate Windows 2000.

Step 6. Follow any additional prompts. The Manual Repair installation can verify your files from the original Windows 2000 CD-ROM while it performs the repair process.

Any configuration changes made after you last created an Emergency Repair Disk will be lost—replaced by the original Windows 2000 files.

Troubleshooting Hardware Problems

One of the major goals in the Windows 2000 development process was to decrease the number of hardware problems, especially compared to Windows NT 4.0. A new Windows Driver Model—where both Windows 98 and Windows 2000 can use the same hardware drivers—should mean less problems with compatibility than were present in Windows NT 4.0.

Hardware compatibility list

The first step in dealing with hardware problems, especially newly installed hardware, is to check the Windows 2000 Hardware Compatibility List. A version of this list is included on your Windows 2000 CD-ROM disk in the \Support folder; the filename is HCL.TXT. This list should conform to the version of Windows 2000 that is on your CD-ROM disc. However, the HCL is a dynamic list, undergoing almost daily changes as more devices become certified and when devices are dropped as incompatibilities are noted.

Tip

The most up-to-date HCL can be found on the Microsoft web site. You can find the list at ftp://ftp.microsoft.com/services/whql/win2000hcl.txt. If Microsoft moves this file, you can find a link to it on the Windows 2000 page at http://www.microsoft.com/windows/professional/default.asp.

Hardware troubleshooting tools

If you are experiencing hardware problems, there are a number of built-in troubleshooting and diagnostic tools that you can use. Many of these are snap-in tools that are accessed from the Microsoft Management Console. (See Chapter 15 for more information about the Microsoft Management Console.)

Device Manager

To see what hardware devices are installed on your computer, use the Device Manager, as shown in Figure 5-7. Click Start ⇨ Settings ⇨ Control Panel ⇨ System, , and select the Hardware tab. The first thing you should notice here is an alternative path to running the Add Hardware Wizard (which you can start by clicking the top button).

To go to the Device Manager, click the Device Manager button. This opens a hierarchical view of your computer, with devices sorted into categories (Drives, Ports, and so on).

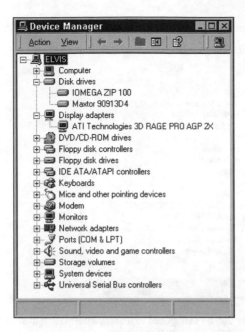

Figure 5-7: The Device Manager shows all the Hardware currently installed on your system.

The Windows 2000 Device Manager is different from the Device Manager in previous versions of Windows. It is now a snap-in component in the Microsoft Management Console, which is a shell program designed to provide a common user interface to most of the available configuration and management tools. You also can access the Device Manager by selecting Start ⇨ Control Panel ⇨ Administrative Tools ⇨ Computer Management. There is more on the MMC in Chapter 15.

The Device Manager can be configured to show a variety of different views (see Figure 5-8). By default, the Device Manager will show the devices as Devices by Type, which displays an alphabetical list of installed devices. Click View on the Device Manager menu, and then select the Resources by Type option to see how Direct Memory Access (DMA), Input/Output (IO), Interrupt Requests (IRQ), and Memory are being allocated. Click the plus sign next to Interrupt Request to expand the device tree and see which devices are sharing interrupts. You also can view Devices by Connection, as well as Resources by Connection.

Tip

In addition to displaying this information on screen, you can click View ⇨ Print to display either a System Summary report or an All devices and system summary report. On a fully loaded computer, the All devices report was 34 pages long, while the summary was only 3 pages long.

Figure 5-8: The Device Manager can be configured to display information in several different ways. Here, all the devices are listed by their IRQ assignment.

Click the plus sign next to one of the categories — such as Disk Drives — to view the actual devices installed. To view details about a particular device, right-click the device and select Properties from the shortcut menu. All Windows 2000 hardware devices will have a similar Properties dialog box, although some may present additional tabs, depending on the device type. For example, Figure 5-9 shows the Properties dialog box for a fairly common piece of hardware: an Iomega Zip Drive. The General tab will display a Device Status box to report if the device is working correctly. If the device is not working properly, you can click the Troubleshooter button, which will open the Windows 2000 Help file to an appropriate troubleshooter (if available).

Note

The Troubleshooter may lack specifics, depending on what it is you want to troubleshoot. Clicking Troubleshoot on the Iomega Properties tab offered a troubleshooter for CD-ROM drives and hard drives, but nothing specifically designed for a Zip drive.

When you select the Driver tab of a device's Properties dialog box, you will see information about the driver provider, the driver date, the driver version, and the digital signer (if there is one). If you click the Driver Details button, you will see a list of the path and filenames for all the driver and resource files for this device.

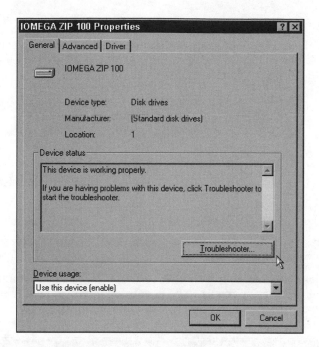

Figure 5-9: The Properties dialog box for all devices share a common look.

You also can use the Add/Remove Hardware Wizard to troubleshoot device conflicts. For troubleshooting, follow these steps:

STEPS:

Troubleshooting Hardware

Step 1. Click Start ⇨ Settings ⇨ Control Panel, and then click Add/Remove Hardware.

Step 2. Click Next to move beyond the splash screen, and then Select Add/Troubleshoot a Device and click Next.

Step 3. The wizard will begin looking for new hardware. If it does not find any, it will present you with a list of the devices it has found. Select the one you want to troubleshoot and click Next.

One possible reason for trouble is that Windows 2000 has lost track of the device and its settings, and the device needs to be reinstalled. Click Add a New Device, and then follow any instructions on the screen.

Conflicts

Sometimes problems arise with hardware because two or more pieces of hardware are trying to use the same resource, such as a hardware interrupt. To check for these kinds of conflicts, follow these steps:

STEPS:

Checking for hardware conflicts

Step 1. Click Start ⇨ Settings ⇨ Control Panel, and select Administrative Tools.

Step 2. Select Computer Management.

Step 3. Expand System Tools in the console tree, expand System Information, and then expand Hardware Resources.

Step 4. Click Conflicts/Sharing in the left pane. Wait a few seconds for the conflict/sharing report to be generated. It will appear in the details pane on the right side, as shown in Figure 5-10.

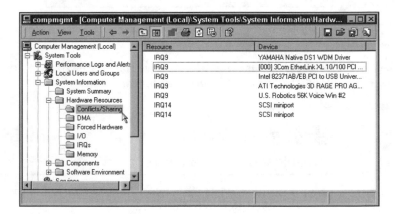

Figure 5-10: The Hardware Resources Conflict Checker shows if hardware devices are sharing the same resources. Here, the sound card, network interface card, USB controller, modem, and video card are all sharing the same IRQ — IRQ 9.

Just because different hardware devices are sharing the same interrupt doesn't mean you must change things. In Figure 5-10 shown earlier, a number of devices are sharing IRQ 9; yet, all the devices are working correctly. The

Windows 2000 Plug and Play Manager automatically allocates hardware resources as needed. However, if one of the devices is not a Plug and Play device, or if it is not working properly, you might have to manually adjust its resources. (See Chapter 14 for more information on managing hardware.)

Note

This portion of the Computer Management Console only collects information. You cannot make any configuration changes here. Use the Device Manager if you need to make changes.

Tip

If a hardware device is having problems, always check to see if there is a new driver available. First, check the hardware manufacturer's web site. Most vendors will have a Support page where you can search for the latest hardware drivers. You also can search the Microsoft Knowledge Base at http://support.microsoft.com/support.

Troubleshooting Video Problems

If you are having problems with your display—especially with video, animation, and special effects—or you are having problems with sound, the problem might actually be with the DirectX drivers. Windows 2000 includes DirectX version 7.0 drivers (DirectX Microsoft's technology that provides support for multimedia).

The Windows 2000 Resource Kit includes a DirectX troubleshooting utility. If you haven't yet installed the Resource Kit, you can learn how in Chapter 3. To run the troubleshooter, follow these steps:

STEPS:

Using the DirectX troubleshooter

Step 1.   Click Start ➪ Programs ➪ Resource Kit ➪ Tools Management Console. (This is the default location of the shortcut to the Resource Kit.)

Step 2.   Select Windows 2000 Resource Kit ➪ Tool Categories ➪ Diagnostic Tools in the console tree.

Step 3.   Select DirectX Diagnostic Tool in the details pane.

The DirectX Diagnostic Tool has eight tabs. The purpose of some of these tabs is to gather information. Select the DirectX Files tab, as shown in Figure 5-11. In this particular example, the Diagnostic Tool is displaying a yellow caution sign on many of the files, each of which is explained in the Notes

pane at the bottom of the dialog box. One of the DirectX files — dplayx.dll —
is marked as Version 5.00.2017.001, while all the others have slightly older
version numbers — 5.00.2008.001 or 5.00.2008.001. Potentially, a mismatch of
files can cause incompatibility problems, although these version numbers are
very close. There would be more cause for concern if some were Version
5.00.2, while others were Version 5.00.3. The attributes for these files are
displayed as Final Retail; if they were displayed as Beta or Debug, you should
look for newer versions of the drivers.

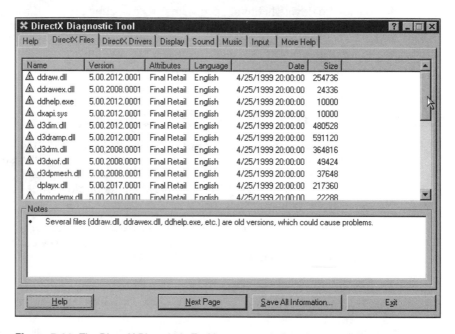

Figure 5-11: The DirectX Diagnostic Tool has two main functions — gathering information
and running diagnostic tests. Here, you see what versions of the DirectX driver file are
installed on your system.

The Display, Sound, and Music tabs allow you to run diagnostic tests on that
particular aspect of the DirectX subsystem. When you click the Test button,
either a graphic image will be displayed or a sound will be played, and you
will then be asked if you saw a particular feature (such as a spinning cube). If
a particular feature — such as DirectDraw Acceleration — has problems, you
can click the Disable button to turn that feature off. Once it is disabled, the
button changes to read Enable, allowing you to turn the feature back on. Note
that the Display and Sound tabs also report information on the driver, as well
as whether the driver is certified. If a file is certified, it means that it has been
tested by the Microsoft Windows Hardware Quality Labs for compatibility
with Windows 2000. In Figure 5-12, you can see that this particular driver is
uncertified, although it is working properly. (Since the driver was obtained
during the beta testing period, not all the tests had been run.) In general,
certified drivers should be less likely to give you trouble.

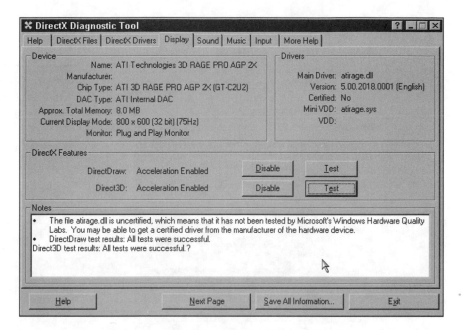

Figure 5-12: The Display tab, as well as the Sound and Music tabs, let you test DirectX functionality. The Notes section will show information about the test, and will also note other information. Here, you see that the main video driver has not yet passed the Microsoft compatibility tests, hence its lack of certification.

The More Help tab leads you to still more tools. If you have upgraded the drivers on this computer, you might see a button that you can click to restore your old drivers. Clicking the Save All Information button will save all the diagnostic information from this session into a file that you can view later. This file can be e-mailed to a tech support person if your own troubleshooting is unsuccessful.

One additional step you can take, if you are having video problems, is to override the DirectDraw Refresh rate. Take the following steps:

STEPS:

Override DirectDraw Refresh Rate

Step 1.   Within the DirectX Diagnostics Tool, select the More Help tab.

Step 2.   Click the Override button.

Step 3.   In the Override DirectDraw Refresh Behavior dialog box, shown in Figure 5-13, select Override Value instead of Default, and then supply a new value. This must be a value that is valid for your monitor type. Check your monitor documentation for details.

Continued

STEPS:

Override DirectDraw Refresh Rate *(continued)*

Step 4.   If you want to switch back to the default at any time, repeat Step 1
and Step 2, and then select Default in the Refresh Rate portion of
the dialog box.

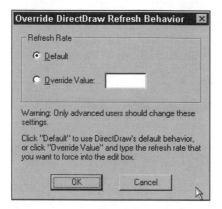

Figure 5-13: You can override the DirectDraw refresh rate and select a rate that
is better for your monitor. The new value must be supplied from your monitor's
documentation or help files.

TweakUI Repair Tools

TweakUI is a customization tool that allows you to achieve greater
customization over your user interface. It also provides a repair tool that you
can use to fix some specific problems that might crop up. (To see how to
install TweakUI, see Chapter 14.)

When TweakUI is first installed, it installs an applet in the Control Panel
from which you can access its many features. To open TweakUI, click Start ⇨
Settings ⇨ Control Panel, and then click the TweakUI icon. Then select the
Repair tab, which provides a handful of tools you can use to fix specific some
of the following user interface options Windows 2000 (see Figure 5-14):

■ Rebuild Icons: Use this to repair the display of your desktop icons, or if
you're seeing the wrong icons for your desktop shortcuts.

■ Repair Font Folder: Use this if your font folder has lost its functionality.

- Repair Regedit: If RegEdit is no longer showing all of its columns, you can use this tool to restore the defaults.

- Repair Temporary Internet Files: If your disk cache doesn't seem to be working correctly in Internet Explorer, its folder may need to be repaired. When you view your cache folder in the Windows Explorer using the Details view, should display custom columns labeled Internet Address and Expired. If not, repair this folder.

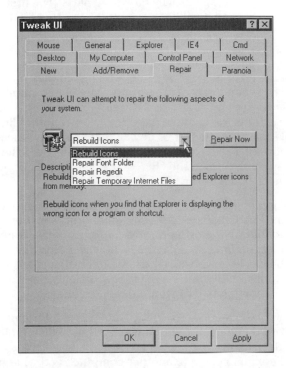

Figure 5-14: TweakUI has tools that will fix some damaged portions of Windows 2000.

Diagnosing Errors

One of Microsoft's design goals for Windows 2000 was to make error messages less cryptic and more informative. If you do see error messages, you also should see a Help button that will provide you with more information about what the error really means, and what steps you might take to fix the error. The Windows 2000 Resource Kit contains a comprehensive list of error messages, and diagnostic tools like Dr. Watson are still available.

Stop messages

A stop message occurs when the Windows 2000 kernel runs into a problem from which it can't recover. Since it cannot recover, it stops (which is where it gets its name), and it then generates a character-mode message with white letters on a blue background. A message like this is referred to — with no affection whatsoever — as the "Blue Screen of Death," or BSOD.

A Windows 2000 stop message usually has three parts. The first part is the bug check information, and it will look something like this:

```
*** STOP: 0x0000001E (0xC0000005, 0xFDE38AF9, 0x00000001, 0x7E8B0EB4)
KMODE_EXCEPTION_NOT_HANDLED ***
```

The first part of the error is the Stop Code, which identifies the type of error that occurred. The second part of the error is a set of four numbers in parentheses that represent the optional developer-defined parameters. The third part of the error is the name of the error. Often, another line of information will identify the driver or device that generated the error. Much of this information will seem like so much technobabble, but the Stop Code can be used as a search term in the Microsoft Knowledge Base and other technical references (such as the Microsoft TechNet).

The second portion of the blue screen is meant to be read for its descriptive nature. It contains Recommended User Action information. Sometimes, the recommended actions are just generic advice (for example, "Check with your vendor for any BIOS updates."). Sometimes, however, tips that are specific to the current problem will be shown. Often, the only advice is to restart the computer. Sometimes, these blue screens are seemingly random, triggered by a momentary incompatibility that would rarely occur again.

The third portion of the blue screen is the Debug port information. It tells you whether a memory dump occurred that was written to disk, which you can use as a tool to determine what happened. It also advises if the debug information was communicated to another computer, and what port was used to send that communication.

Tip

If you get a stop error message, make a note of the parameters that are displayed. You will need them to compare to later if the error occurs again, if you need to look up information about the error, or if you eventually have to talk with technical support representatives about the problem.

What to do

If the error message does not contain specific information about a fix, here are some general things you can do:

■ Do nothing: Actually, just restart the computer and see if the error recurs. If it doesn't, write it off as a random event and don't worry about it.

■ If you just added some new hardware and it triggers errors, remove the hardware and see if the problem disappears. Then, check whether the hardware is on the Windows 2000 Hardware Compatibility List, or check with the vendor about new or updated Windows 2000 device drivers.

- If you just added new software and you suddenly begin seeing error messages, uninstall the software. (See Chapter 14 for information on how to uninstall software the correct way.)

- Use an up-to-date virus scanner to see if your computer has been infected with a virus. A virus can corrupt important system files which, in turn, can trigger stop errors.

- Search the Microsoft Knowledge Base to see if there are any articles about your particular problem.

Tip

When searching the Microsoft Knowledge Base (which has over 200,000 articles), try using a keyword search with the keyword winnt (Windows 2000 articles still seem to be using winnt as a keyword) and the stop number, such as 0x00000079.

Secret

The forthcoming Windows 2000 Server Resource Kit refers to the Microsoft Knowledge Base article Q103059 as "Description of Bug Codes for Windows 2000," although the title of that article in the Knowledge Base, as this book is being written, was still "Description of Bug Codes in Windows NT."

- Check to see if there have been any service packs issued for Windows 2000. Service packs are collections of bug fixes, and your problem may be fixed in a specific service pack.

- Check for Windows 2000 hot fixes. A hot fix is a fix to a problem that is issued between service packs. While there are no hot fixes available as of the writing of this book, a likely place to find them will be ftp://ftp.microsoft.com/bussys/winnt/winnt-public/fixes/. Hot fixes, while made available by Microsoft, are still undergoing testing and generally should not be applied unless the hot fix cures a specific problem you are having.

Other error messages

While stop code — or Blue Screen of Death — messages are usually fatal, you might also experience non-fatal errors. These will usually occur within their own window, and they will often provide a Help button you can click to receive additional information. Depending on the error, there will be additional buttons with which you ca close the application having the error, or with which you can try to resume the application.

Secret

The Windows 2000 Resource Kit ships with a database containing details about Windows 2000 error messages. This database comes in two forms. One version is a compiled hypertext file that can be viewed using the Help engine that ships with Windows 2000. The other version is a Microsoft Access 97 database, which you can use only if you have Access 97 installed on your computer.

To view the Windows 2000 error message hypertext file, follow these steps.

STEPS:

View the Windows 2000 Error Messages

Step 1.   Click Start ⇨ Programs ⇨ Resource Kit ⇨ Tools Management Console. (This is the default location for the Resource Kit shortcut.)

Step 2.   Expand the Windows 2000 Resource Kit in the console tree, expand Tool Categories, and then expand Computer Management Tools.

Step 3.   Select Windows 2000 Error Messages in the details pane.

Step 4.   This opens a help page for the error message database. Select the Open Messages Now link.

The error message database is organized by functional errors — that is, where the errors may have occurred (see Figure 5-15). In the left pane, you can expand each book, which may contain other books. For example , the Accessories book contains books for the Calculator, the CD player, and so on. One way to search for details about an error is to locate the application that triggered the error, and then to browse down the list until you find the specific error message. The details pane on the right will then display an explanation of the problem, as well as a possible solution. In some cases, the only advice will be to call technical support.

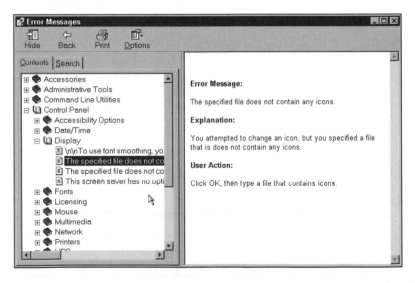

Figure 5-15: The Windows 2000 error message database is organized by the location in which an error might have occurred. The error shown here would normally occur when you have the Control Panel's Display dialog box open.

A better way to use the database is to use the search function, which is built-in to the Help file itself. For example, you might see the following error message: "No serial device was successfully initialized." Select the Search tab above the left pane. Then, in the Keywords text box, type **serial device**. The search will display about ten error messages that include your search term, and you can then find your error in the list, as shown in Figure 5-16. For this particular error message, you are referred to the Event Log, where you can find a more exact error message.

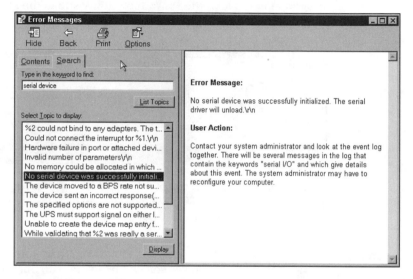

Figure 5-16: The results of searching for the term "serial device" in the Windows 2000 error message database.

Gather clues with Dr. Watson

Dr. Watson is the name of a program error debugging utility that is automatically installed with Windows 2000. If an error occurs in a program, and it is not handled by the program itself, Dr. Watson is automatically activated and will write information about the error to a log file. If you don't think Dr. Watson has been enabled, you can check the settings in the Registry. (See Chapter 16 for information on how to use the Registry Editor.)

STEPS:

Verifying Dr. Watson settings

Step 1. Click Start ⇨ Run, and then type regedit into the Open text box.

Step 2. Click the Enter button to open the Registry Editor.

Continued

STEPS:

Verifying Dr. Watson settings *(continued)*

Step 3.   In the left pane, navigate to the following registry key: HKEY_LOCAL_MACHINE\SOFTWARE\Microsoft\Windows NT\ CurrentVersion\AeDebug

Step 4.   The data value for Auto in the right pane should be set to 1, and the command to load the Dr. Watson utility should be shown as the value for Debugger, as shown in Figure 5-17.

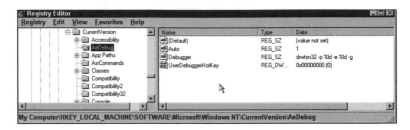

Figure 5-17: If Dr. Watson is configured as your debugger, the Registry settings in HKEY_LOCAL_MACHINE\SOFTWARE\Microsoft\Windows NT\CurrentVersion\AeDebug should look similar to the ones here.

Step 5.   If the settings are not as shown in Figure 5-17, and you want to change them so that Dr. Watson will be loaded, do not edit the Registry here.

Step 6.   Closet he Registry Editor. Click Start ⇨ Programs ⇨ Command Prompt, and then type the following command:

```
c:\drwatsn32 -I
```

Step 7.   Close the command prompt dialog box. Dr. Watson will now be configured as your debugger.

There are a number of options you can set for Dr. Watson. To set the configuration options, follow these steps:

STEPS:

Configuring Dr. Watson

Step 1.   Click Start ⇨ Run, and type drwtsn32 into the Open text box.

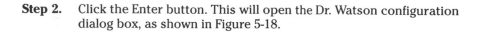

Step 2. Click the Enter button. This will open the Dr. Watson configuration dialog box, as shown in Figure 5-18.

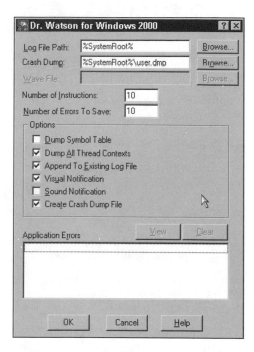

Figure 5-18: The Dr. Watson configuration dialog box. When you set up Windows 2000, Dr. Watson is automatically enabled.

Step 3. There are two different log files that Dr. Watson can generate for errors. The first file is a standard error file, which is a text file named drwtsn32.log. You can choose in which folder you want to save this log file, although the default folder is the Windows 2000 folder.

Step 4. The second file is named user.dmp. It is a binary file that captures the system status, and it can become quite large. If you don't want to save this file, clear the Create Crash Dump File check box.

Step 5. You can choose to append any Dr. Watson output to the existing log file. You also can set the number of times to append the output by changing the value in the Number of Errors to Save text box.

The Dr. Watson log file can be opened in any text editor or word processor. It also can be e-mailed as an attachment to a technical support person so they can see what was happening on your computer when the error occurred. The initial portion of a Dr. Watson log file is shown in Listing 5-7.

Listing 5-7: Sample Dr. Watson Log File

```
Application exception occurred:
        App: msimn.exe (pid=1000)
        When: 08/06/1999 @ 13:54:51.715
        Exception number: c0000005 (access violation)

*----> System Information <----*
        Computer Name: ELVIS
        User Name: Administrator
        Number of Processors: 1
        Processor Type: x86 Family 6 Model 5 Stepping 2
        Windows 2000 Version: 5.0
        Current Build: 2031
        Service Pack: None
        Current Type: Uniprocessor Free
        Registered Organization: Stupendomungus Corp
        Registered Owner: Bruce Kratofil

*----> Task List <----*
    0 Idle.exe
    8 System.exe
```

Summary

In this chapter, you learned what to do when you have problems. You saw how to:

▶ Take precautions ahead of time to prepare for emergencies.

▶ Follow the Windows 2000 boot process.

▶ Use Safe Mode to solve startup problems.

▶ Work at the Windows Recovery Console and the Command Prompt.

▶ Troubleshoot hardware problems.

▶ Decipher error messages.

Part II

User Interface

Chapter 6

What You See on the Screen

In This Chapter

We look at the things you see in the Windows 2000 environment, and we cover the basic Windows conventions, including:

▶ The Desktop and its contents.

▶ Using the Mouse.

▶ The Start Menu.

▶ The Taskbar.

▶ Common Windows 2000 tasks.

▶ Keyboard shortcuts.

▶ Closing Windows 2000.

Quick Tour: The Desktop and Its Contents

If you have migrated from Windows 95, Windows 98, or Windows NT, you will feel right at home in Windows 2000. The familiar Desktop metaphor is still here, as are the Start menu, the Taskbar, and the Desktop icons. For those of you who might be coming from some other operating systems, a tour is in order.

The *Desktop* is the blank area that takes up most of your display. Like a regular Desktop, you place objects on it. The Windows 2000 Desktop can hold documents, shortcuts, programs, and more. You also can decorate it with pictures and patterns. It is an *active Desktop*, meaning that you can configure it to display as a Web page, as well. When you begin, though, about the only items on the Desktop are icons. The icons shown in Figure 6-1 are those that are configured to display by default on the Windows 2000 Desktop.

Figure 6-1: The Windows 2000 Desktop.

An *icon* can represent many different things. It can represent an actual program, like the Internet Explorer icon. It might also be a folder like My Documents, which is used to hold other objects or items. It also can represent a data file, such as a word processing document or a spreadsheet file. Most commonly, however, it is a shortcut to an item or an object. You can tell the icon is a shortcut if there is a black arrow in the icon's lower-left corner.

A *shortcut* is a link or pointer to some other item. It might be a shortcut to a program; clicking or double-clicking the shortcut opens the program. It could be a shortcut to a document; clicking or double-clicking first opens the associated program, and then loads the document. It could be a link to a folder or to another computer on your network. It also could be a link to some location on the Internet. Most of the items on your Start Menu are actually shortcuts to programs or documents.

The default Windows 2000 Desktop only has a handful of icons, but they are important. We will look at My Computer in Chapter 7; the icon looks like a computer, and it represents your computer and its contents. My Network Places is a replacement for Network Neighborhood in Windows 95 and 98; it represents the network you are connected to, if applicable. My Documents is the default folder where your data files are stored. (With these names, Microsoft apparently wants you to bond with your computer. If you find them too cloying, you can easily rename them.) The Recycle Bin is a purgatory for files you delete from your computer. Internet Explorer and Outlook Express are the Web browser and e-mail clients, respectively, that are an integral part of Windows 2000 (they are covered in Chapters 12 and 13).

Microsoft's usability studies reveal that most Windows users mistakenly try to delete unwanted programs by dragging the program shortcut icons to the Recycle Bin. In prior versions of Windows, this wouldn't work. Instead, you were forced to delete programs through the Control Panel's Add/Remove Programs application. In Windows 2000, however, if you drag a program's shortcut to the Recycle Bin, you'll be prompted whether you want to remove the program, and you'll then be if so asked to use the Add/Remove Programs application in Control Panel if you do.

A somewhat unpopular new feature in Windows 98 was the Channel Bar. It was present by default when you first booted your computer. The Channel Bar had buttons from which you selected channels; each button was a shortcut or link to a Web site having rapidly changing content. In Windows 2000, the Channel Bar is still around, but it is disabled by default.

Caution

If you are upgrading from Windows 3.x, there is one crucial difference in icons from Windows 2000: deleting an icon for a program did not delete the program itself; you still had to delete the program file or files. In Windows 2000, however, if the icon is not a shortcut, deleting the icon also deletes the underlying program or document.

At the bottom of your display, you will find the Taskbar with a Start button in the lower-left corner. If you don't see the Taskbar or the Start button, Windows 2000 might be configured to automatically hide the Taskbar. To bring it back, follow these steps:

STEPS:

Showing the Taskbar

Step 1. Move your mouse pointer to the bottom of the screen. The Taskbar should appear.

Step 2. Right-click an empty portion of the Taskbar. (If you're not sure how to use the mouse, see "Using the Mouse," in the next section.)

Step 3. Choose Properties from the context menu.

Step 4. Clear the Auto hide check box, and then click OK.

Not wild about the way all this looks? Don't worry. Just about everything on the Desktop can be customized more to your liking, as we'll explore in Chapter 8.

Using the Mouse

There are two basic input devices: a mouse and a keyboard. The mouse is usually the quickest way to navigate on the Desktop. A Windows-compatible mouse will have a minimum of two buttons. Some mouse devices have more than two buttons, while others might have wheels, trackballs, or other controls. Instead of a mouse, you might have a pressure-sensitive stylus (which looks like a pen with buttons), or you might have a trackball (which is essentially a mouse with the roller ball on the top of the mouse). If you are using a laptop, you might have a pointing stick, a touchpad, or both. Regardless of the type of mouse device you have, they all work on a similar principle: you move the mouse pointer around the screen and make your selections with the mouse buttons.

The primary mouse button is the one below your index finger. For right-handed mouse users, it is the left button; for left-handed mouse users, it is the right button. The primary button is the one you press to start most activities. Some actions, such as clicking the Start button, require a single click. Other actions require a double-click — two clicks in rapid succession. If you click the secondary mouse button (often called *right-clicking*), a context menu of shortcuts will be pop up. The context menu is specific to the area in which you right-click; in other words, it will contain different actions depending on where you click. You also can move items on your Desktop by hovering over them with your mouse pointer, clicking and holding the primary button, and then dragging the selected item with your mouse to another destination. This is commonly referred to as a *click and drag* or *drag and drop*.

Tip

You can set your mouse up as a right-hand mouse, or as a left-hand mouse, depending on your preferences.

STEPS:

Configuring Your Mouse

Step 1.   Click Start ➪ Settings ➪ Control Panel.

Step 2.   Double-click the mouse icon. The Mouse Properties dialog box appears, as shown in Figure 6-2.

Step 3.   Click the Buttons tab, and select either Right-handed or Left-handed for your button configuration.

Step 4.   While you are in the Mouse Properties dialog box, you might want to adjust your double-click settings to respond to slower or faster clicks. Double-click within the test area to test and adjust your mouse's clicking speed. Click and drag the slider to the left to respond to slower clicks, or to the right to respond to faster clicks.

Step 5.   Click OK to accept your changes.

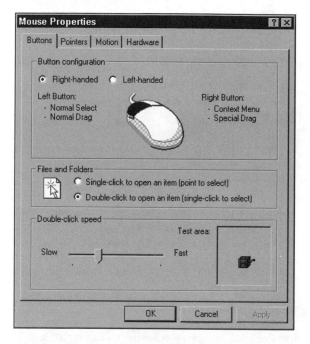

Figure 6-2: The Mouse Properties dialog box.

The mouse is represented on your screen by a pointer or cursor that can take many different shapes, depending on the action you are taking. The default shape on the Windows 2000 Desktop is a white arrow. When you click something, it is important that the tip of this arrow be over the item you want to click.

The Start Menu

The Start Menu has remained essentially the same since Windows 95. Click Start to see the menu shown in Figure 6-3.

Figure 6-3: The Start Menu.

Notice that the Start Menu is vertically divided by a thin line. Items below this thin line are standard and will be seen on any computer (although Windows 2000 lets you add some additional options here). Items above the thin line can be customized, and some application programs frequently add their own shortcuts here.

Cross-Reference

See Chapter 8, "Customizing Your Work Environment," to learn how to make changes.

If a menu item has an arrow pointing to the right, it indicates that the menu leads to another menu. You can access these additional menus simply by moving your mouse pointer up to that item—you don't have to click. The new menu will spill out to the right.

Programs

The Programs Menu leads the way to your application and utility program shortcuts (see Figure 6-4). Many of these shortcuts are added by Windows 2000. Still others come from applications or utilities that might have been installed by your computer manufacturer. Still more will be added as you install additional applications and tools on your computer. To reduce the clutter once you have installed many programs on your computer, you can organize your program menu shortcuts into additional submenus.

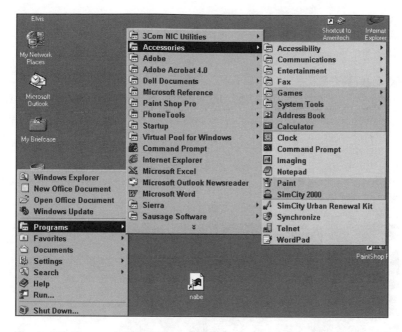

Figure 6-4: The expanded Programs Menu.

One way to reduce menu clutter is new in Windows 2000: Personalized Menus. Windows 2000 keeps track of how often you use a particular menu shortcut. Those that you use infrequently are hidden from view, while those that you use frequently will gravitate toward the top of the menu. Hidden items can be displayed by clicking the chevron emblem on the bottom of any menu. Personalized Menus won't instantaneously appear; Windows 2000 needs to first learn your habits.

Tip

If you decide that Personalized Menus are an insufferable infringement of your liberty, you can disable them.

STEPS:

Turning Off Personalized Menus

Step 1.   Click Start ➪ Settings ➪ Taskbar & Start Menu.

Step 2.   Click the General tab.

Step 3.   Clear the Use Personalized Menus check box at the bottom of the dialog.

Step 4.   If you later decide that Personalized Menus are a good idea after all, you can turn them back on by reversing the above steps.

Tip

To show your Web Favorites folder on your Start Menu, go to the Advanced tab and click Favorites in the Start Menu ⇨ Settings list.

Documents

Below Programs on the Start Menu is your Documents Menu (if you followed the preceding tip, it will also be below the Favorites menu), shown in Figure 6-5. The Documents Menu shows the last fifteen documents saved on your computer. Clicking a file on the Documents Menu is often the fastest way to resume work on a file. You can easily clear the documents from the list by clicking Start ⇨ Settings ⇨ Taskbar & Start Menu, selecting the Advanced tab, and then clicking Clear.

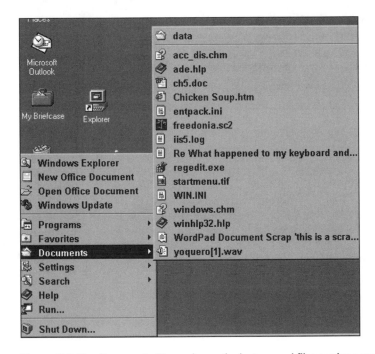

Figure 6-5: The Documents Menu shows the last several files you've accessed.

Settings

The Settings menu, shown in Figure 6-6, takes you to dialog boxes that let you change things on your computer. In later chapters, we will see how to use the Control Panel to configure your computer, add hardware and software, and do much to personalize your computer.

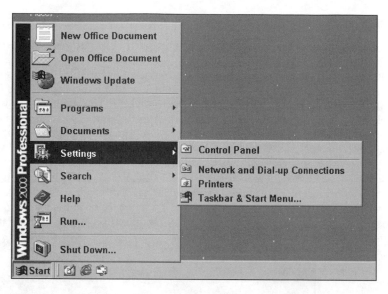

Figure 6-6: The Settings Menu lets you take control of your computer.

The Search menu, shown in Figure 6-7, replaces the Find menu in Windows 95/98. You can use it to find files on your computer, and you also can use it as a shortcut to the Search function in Internet Explorer 5.

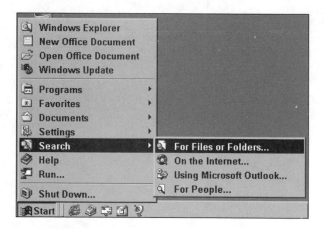

Figure 6-7: The Search Menu.

Help

Unlike previous versions of Windows that used a standard help file format, Windows 2000 Online Help is essentially a glorified Web page; the help files are compiled HTML documents providing a two-pane view, as shown in Figure 6-8. (A compiled HTML file has a file extension of .CHM.) The left pane has four tabs. Click Contents to see a list of closed book icons that represent topics within the help file. Click a book to expand it and see its contents, which may include more books (which, in turn, can be expanded). It might also be page symbol with a question mark; these represent pages of information; click a page and you will see the contents in the right pane. This is hypertext, which means it contains clickable links to other sections in the Help file. Because the help file is in HTML format, the links also can take you—through the Internet—to a Web site that contains updated information. Since the list of topics remains visible on the left, there is less chance of getting lost than there might be using traditional hypertext help files.

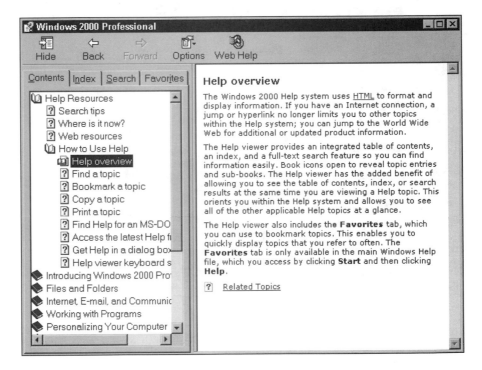

Figure 6-8: Windows 2000 Online Help.

There are three other tabs, in addition to Contents. Index functions just like the index of a book, with an alphabetical list of entries that you can click (see Figure 6-9). The Search tab lets you type in keywords. Click List Topics and you will see a list of pages that contain your keyword. Favorites lets you bookmark a page in the help file (see Figure 6-10). If you find a page that you want to refer to in the future, you can click Favorites, and then choose Add, and the displayed page will be added to your list of favorite help pages.

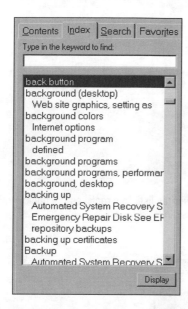

Figure 6-9: The Search Help dialog box.

Run

While almost all your programs can be accessed from a shortcut on the Start menu, this is not always true. Some applications are installed without shortcuts (MS-DOS programs, for instance). Often times, Microsoft tries to make it difficult to find a program because they might not encourage its use (such as RegEdit). For times like these, you can use the Run Menu (see Figure 6-11).

Figure 6-10: Adding a Help Page to your Favorites list. This replaces the bookmarking feature of the old Windows Help system.

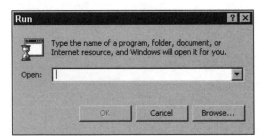

Figure 6-11: The Run Menu.

If you know the exact path and filename for the program you wish to run, type the path and filename in the Open text box and click OK. If you aren't sure of the exact path or name, click Browse. This opens up the Browse dialog box, shown in Figure 6-12, which is used in many different places throughout Windows 2000. This lets you explore your computer (or other computers on your network) to find the file that you want to open.

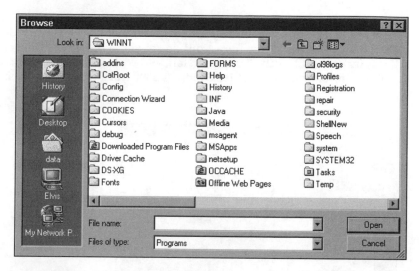

Figure 6-12: Use the Browse dialog box to browse your computer.

The Taskbar

The Taskbar has special areas on both the left and right, and an empty area in the middle. This empty area will fill up once you start some programs, with buttons that represent running programs. The Taskbar gets its name because it shows what programs — or tasks — are running on your computer. The area just to the right of the Start button is called the Quick Launch Bar, and it is a place where you can store shortcuts to programs, files, and other objects. If you disabled the Taskbar Auto hide feature, these shortcuts will always be visible and a single click away. By default, Windows 2000 loads the following shortcuts on the Quick Launch Bar:

- Internet Explorer, which launches the Web browser.

- Outlook Express, for e-mail and newsgroups.

- Desktop, which looks like a desk blotter. It minimizes (drops to the Task bar) all open windows, giving you a clear view of the Desktop.

- View Channels, which looks like a satellite dish. It lets you view Active Channels.

Cross-Reference

If you decide later that you want more shortcuts here (or you wish to remove some of these), see Chapter 8.

On the right side of the Taskbar is a slightly indented area called the System Tray — or SysTray. It also holds icons, but usually only for programs that are running. Typically, it is used by utilities or background programs, and it lets you quickly configure running programs by pointing and then clicking or right-clicking the icon. When Windows 2000 is first installed, you might only see two items here: a clock and — if you have a sound card installed — a loudspeaker icon representing your sound card's volume control. Double-click the clock and you will see your computer's Date/Time Properties, as shown in Figure 6-13. From here, you can set your computer's time and date if it is incorrect. Click the Time Zone tab, and you can designate the time zone you live in, and you also can let Windows 2000 track of Daylight Savings Time for you.

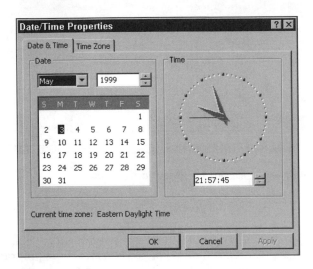

Figure 6-13: The Date/Time Properties dialog box.

While, by default, the Taskbar sits at the bottom of the Desktop, it doesn't have to stay there. To move the Taskbar to another edge of the Desktop, follow these steps:

STEPS:

Moving the Taskbar

Step 1. Move your mouse pointer over an empty area of the Taskbar (not over the Quick Launch Bar, Tray, or any other button). Click and hold down the primary mouse button.

Step 2. With the mouse button still held down, drag the Taskbar to one of the sides or to the top of your Desktop.

Step 4. When you arrive at the top, left, or right edge, an outline of the Taskbar will appear. Release the mouse button.

Step 5. To move the Taskbar back to it's original position, repeat Steps 1-4.

Common Windows Tasks

In this section, we will see how to do some of the most common Windows tasks. Most of these work the same way as they did in Windows 95, Windows 98, and Windows NT.

Start a program

As an example, we will start the Calculator program that comes with Windows 2000, and then show you how to manage its window.

STEPS:

Starting a Program

Step 1.   Click Start, and then slide the mouse up to Programs, over to Accessories, and then down to Calculator.

Step 2.   Click Calculator.

Step 3.   The Calculator program will appear, as shown in Figure 6-14, running in its own window. Note that a button now appears on the Taskbar with the Calculator icon and name.

Figure 6-14: The Calculator program in its own window.

Continued

STEPS:

Starting a Program *(continued)*

Step 4.   Click and hold down the mouse on the blue bar (called the Title Bar) at the top of the Calculator program window. Drag the mouse to move the window.

Step 5.   There are three gray buttons on the right side of the Title Bar. Click the inner-most button, which looks like an underscore character.

Step 6.   This minimizes the Calculator. It is still running, because there is still a Calculator button on the Taskbar. Click this button to restore the Calculator.

Step 7.   To close the program, click the gray button with the X in the upper-right corner. This closes the program window.

Windows 2000 is a multitasking operating system, which means that you can run more than one application program at a time. To see how to manage multiple windows, repeat steps 1 and 2 above to restart the Calculator and leave it running. Then, start another program—Notepad—by doing the following:

STEPS:

Switching Between Programs

Step 1.   Click Start ➪ Programs ➪ Accessories.

Step 2.   Click Notepad. Note that you will now have two buttons on the Taskbar—one for each program that is running.

Step 3.   Although more than one program can be running, only one can be the active program at any one time. The active program will have a blue title bar, while inactive program windows will have a gray title bar. Notepad should be the active window on your screen. (The active program's Taskbar button will also appear depressed.)

Step 4.   To make Calculator the active window, click anywhere within its window. Note the change in colors of the title bar reflects which one window is active.

Step 5.   Make Notepad the active window again by clicking its Taskbar button. This is another way to switch between programs, which can be useful if a program window takes up the entire screen and you can't see the other program window.

Tip Many experienced Windows users prefer to switch between programs using the tried-and-true Windows 3.x Alt-Tab keyboard shortcut. (See the keyboard shortcut list at the end of this chapter for more information on useful Windows 2000 keyboard shortcuts.)

No matter how much real estate your monitor provides, there will always be times when there isn't enough space to let you see everything at once. That's when you'll start to resize and arrange windows so you can see what you need to see.

STEPS:

Resizing a Program Window

Step 1.   The Notepad program window can be resized. Hover the mouse pointer right over the edge of the window. When the pointer changes to a double-headed arrow, click and drag in the direction of one of the arrows. This will change the size of the window. Clicking and dragging one of the corners of the program's window will let you resize the window in two directions at once.

Step 2.   Click the middle of the three buttons on right end of the Notepad title bar. This will maximize the window, so that the program window takes up the full screen.

Step 3.   Click the middle button again. It restores the window to its previous size.

Step 4.   In Notepad, click File ⇨ Exit. This also closes the program.

Step 5.   Right-click the Calculator button on the Taskbar. Select Close from the context menu. This is yet another way to close a program. Figure 6-15 shows the Calculator and Notebook windows together.

Secret   Do you find it hard to actually click your mouse on the darned little icons in the upper-right corner of a program window? You can toggle between full screen and partial screen view for a particular program by double-clicking the program's title bar. It is much easier to access this way because it extends all the way across the top of the program's window.

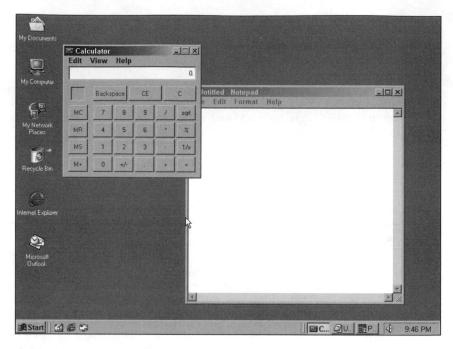

Figure 6-15: Calculator and Notepad together. (Your window position and sizes will vary.)

Activating your Desktop

You can actually set up your Desktop in two different ways. The first is referred to as the Windows Classic style, and is how the Desktop has worked since Windows 95. You select an item using a single click, outlining the item in blue. To activate an icon, you double-click it. Starting with Windows 98, a new organizational metaphor was introduced: the Web view. With Web view, your computer behaves more like a Web browser. Setting up your Desktop to use Web view has functional, as well as aesthetic, ramifications.

Single-clicking vs. double-clicking

If you are viewing a Web page in your browser and you want to follow a link, you single-click that link. Your Desktop can work that way, too.

STEPS:

Single-click the Desktop

Step 1.   Click Start ➪ Settings ➪ Control Panel.

Step 2.   Double-click the Folder Options Icon.

Step 3.   Select the General Tab. In the Click items as follows section, select the Single-click to open an item (point to select) option.

Step 4.   If you want your icon titles to be underlined — such as in a Web hyperlink — select Underline items consistent with my browser. If you decide that change makes your screen look too cluttered, select Underline items only when I point to them.

These changes will make your Desktop behave like a Web page, but you also can make it look like one by letting it display Active Content. For example, you might frequently visit a specific Web page with stock market news, breaking news stories, or sports scores. You can open a window on your Active Desktop to keep these pages on display all the time.

STEPS:

Adding Active Content to the Desktop

Step 1.   Turn on the Active Desktop first. Right-click an empty portion of the Desktop, point to Active Desktop in the menu, and then click Show Web Content.

Step 2.   Right-click an empty portion of the Desktop again, point to Active Desktop, and then click Customize my Desktop.

Step 3.   Make sure the Web tab is selected in the Display Properties dialog box. Click to enable Show Web content on my Active Desktop.

Step 4.   In the box beneath that, select what you want to see. If it isn't listed, click New.

Step 5.   To view the IDG Books Worldwide home page, type its URL in the box: http://www.idgbooks.com. Click OK twice.

Step 6.   A window should now be open on the Desktop showing a portion of the IDG Books Worldwide home page.

For Active Content to really be active, of course, you need to be connected to the Internet. See Chapters 11 and 12 for more information.

Folders and files

The file folder metaphor should be familiar to anyone who has had to organize a sheaf of papers. It is one of the conceptual legacies of Windows 95, as a user-friendly replacement for the term directory, and remains vital to the workings of Windows 2000 (although in many cases, its workings are hidden from the user). This is a brief introduction to working with folders and files. (See Chapter 7 for more information.)

Folders

You will probably be using your computer to store information. To see where all this information goes, click or double-click the My Computer icon. The My Computer window displays icons representing the drives available on your computer. (Note that the exact icons you will see differ from those shown in Figure 6-16, depending on the hardware installed on your system.)

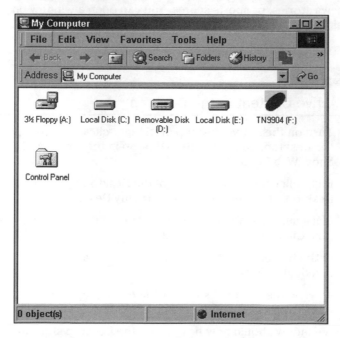

Figure 6-16: The My Computer Window: the drives on this computer are floppy drive labeled 31/2 Floppy (A:), hard drive partitions labeled Local Disk (C:) and Local Disk (E:), a removable drive labeled Removable Disk (D:), and a CD-ROM drive labeled TN9904 (F:).

There is actually less in the Windows 2000 My Computer window than there is in Windows 95 and Windows 98, since the Printers and Dial-Up Networking folders have been moved to the Control Panel (which still has an icon here). Otherwise, each drive on your system is represented by an icon. To see the contents of your primary hard drive — which is probably labeled Local Drive (C:) — click or double-click its icon. Again, while the exact contents of your primary hard drive will be different, it will look similar to the one shown in Figure 6-17.

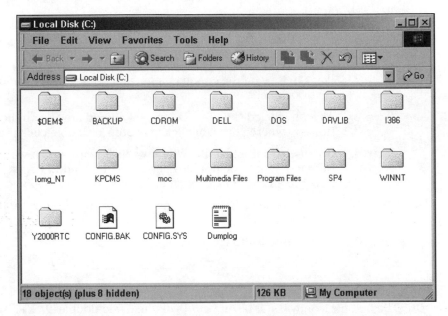

Figure 6-17: Local Disk (C:). Folders and files on this drive are represented by icons.

Hard drives can hold massive amounts of data, so some organization or structure is crucial. The manila folder icons in the primary hard drive window represent folders. A folder on your hard drive can contain either more folders or it can contain files (or both); otherwise, it really is the same thing as a directory. Files are represented by icons. If Windows 2000 recognizes type of file, it will use a special icon for that file. Text files appear with notepad symbols, settings files appear with gear symbols, and so on. Clicking one of the folder icons will open a new window to display the contents of that particular folder. (My Computer will be covered in much greater depth in Chapter 7.)

Files

For a first experience in working with files, we will create a simple file and then save it to the Desktop. Then, after editing the file, we will see how to get remove it.

STEPS:

Working with a file

Step 1.   Right-click an empty portion of the Desktop to access the context menu.

Step 2.   Point to New on the context menu, and then slide over and click Text Document.

Step 3.   An icon labeled New Text Document should now be on the Desktop where you right-clicked in Step 1. Double-click this icon.

Step 4.   Because this is a text file, Windows 2000 associates it with Notepad. When you double-click the icon, Windows opens Notepad and your new text file, and you are then ready to write.

Step 5.   Type "The quick brown dog jumped over the lazy fox," and then click File ⇨ Save.

Step 6.   Click File ⇨ Exit to close Notepad.

The text file icon will still be on your Desktop. If you double-click it, Notepad will open again, and it will then open your file; you will see your sentence. Close the window again. If you want, you can click and drag on this icon to move it to a different location on your Desktop. To delete this file entirely, follow these steps:

STEPS:

Deleting a file

Step 1.   Select the text icon for the file you want to delete and press the Delete key. Alternatively, if want to mouse around, you can select the file icon and, while holding down the mouse button, drag it over to the Recycle Bin on the Desktop.

Step 2.   When your mouse pointer and the icon are over the Recycle Bin, let go of the mouse button. If you have not deleted anything on your system, the Recycle Bin icon will appear as an empty waste basket icon. As soon as you drop the file, it will change to a full waste basket icon.

What if deleting that file was a mistake? Good news! Your file isn't actually gone. It has just been moved to a special folder on your hard drive called the Recycle Bin. You can still rescue your file.

STEPS:

Retrieving a File from the Recycle Bin

Step 1.   Click or double-click the Recycle Bin icon to open it. Its window looks much like the My Computer window, but its contents should only be New Text Document.txt (see Figure 6-18). (Note that if you have deleted other files, they will be listed, as well.)

Step 2.   Click and drag the file icon out of the Recycle Bin window, and then drop it back on the Desktop.

Step 3.   To completely delete the file, repeat Steps 1 and 2. Click or double-click the Recycle Bin to open it.

Step 4.   Now, click File ⇨ Empty Recycle Bin. The Confirm File Deletion window will appear (if you haven't disabled this feature), to check whether you really want to remove this file.

Step 5.   Click Yes. Your Recycle Bin window should now be clear. Close the Recycle Bin.

Tip   Any file you delete from your hard drive will remain in the Recycle Bin until you empty it. If you don't occasionally empty the trash, all your deleted files will remain on your hard drive, and you won't recover any hard disk space.

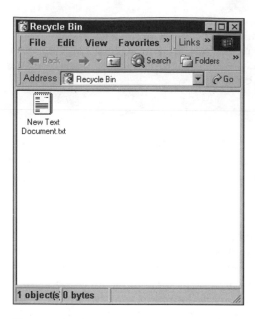

Figure 6-18: The Recycle Bin. It holds the files you have deleted since you last emptied the trash.

Create a shortcut on the Desktop

Let's say you use the Windows Notepad a lot (in real life, you'll probably use a full-featured word processing application for your writing chores), and you want to be able to access to it quickly, rather than having to use the Start menu. You can create a shortcut to Notepad right on your Desktop using the following steps:

STEPS:

Creating a shortcut

Step 1.   Right-click an empty spot on your Desktop.

Step 2.   Point to New on the context menu, and then click Shortcut. This starts the Create Shortcut Wizard shown in Figure 6-19.

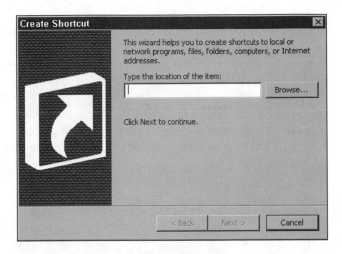

Figure 6-19: The Create Shortcut Wizard.

Step 3.   If you know the path and filename of the program or file for which you want to create a shortcut, type it's path and filename in the box. Otherwise, click Browse to locate it.

Step 4.   In the Browse for Folder window shown in Figure 6-20, click the plus (+) sign next to the C: drive to expand its contents. Then, click to select the folder where Windows 2000 is installed, most commonly in the C:\WINNT\ directory.

Figure 6-20: The Browse for Folder window. Clicking the plus sign next to a drive or folder will let you see its contents.

Continued

Step 5.   There should be many folders and files in your Windows folder.
Scroll down through the list until you find Notepad.exe. Select it
and click OK.

Step 6.   This brings you back to the Create Shortcut Wizard, and the path
and filename for Notepad is already filled in for you. Click Next.

Step 7.   Windows suggest notepad.exe as the name for your shortcut. You
can accept it by clicking Finish, or you can give it a different name
before clicking.

Your new shortcut should now be in place on your Desktop. You can
create shortcuts to programs, folders, documents, and any other item you
want to appear on your Desktop. If you decide you don't no longer need the
shortcuts, delete them by dragging them to the Recycle Bin and dropping
them in. Since they are shortcuts, deleting them does not delete the
underlying file. (Shortcuts will be covered in greater detail in Chapter 8.)

Keyboard Shortcuts

There is nothing more personal than the way in which individuals interact
with their personal computers. Some people love the mouse interface where
you choose options from menus, while others vow Death to Mice! and then
perform many of the same tasks using keyboard shortcuts.

The tradeoff is ease of navigation versus speed of execution. Whatever else
you want to say about the mouse, it is not always the fastest way to give a
command to your computer — especially if you are a touch-typist who is
more productive when your fingers are closest to the keyboard. In many
cases, reaching for the mouse slows you down rather than speeds you up.

In these instances — when the command you are trying to execute is buried
three or four dialog boxes deep in the Windows interface — a simple
keyboard shortcut that gets the job done immediately can be a real blessing.
On the other hand, the main drawback of keyboard shortcuts is that you
have to memorize them, and few are intuitive.

A large number of keyboard shortcuts are built-in to the Windows 2000
environment, and most will be familiar to users of earlier versions of
Windows. See Table 6-1 for a complete list.

Secret

You can move and resize windows using the keyboard, with the help of some
little known keyboard shortcuts.

STEPS:

Moving a window with the keyboard

Step 1. Start with a restored window — one that is not maximized on the screen.

Step 2. Press Alt+Spacebar. This opens the System Menu in the upper-left corner of the window.

Step 3. Use the arrow keys to select Move, and then press Enter. You also can type M, the underlined letter in Move.

Step 4. The mouse pointer will change to a four-headed arrow. Use the arrow keys to move the window to a new location.

Step 5. When you are satisfied with the new location, press Enter.

You can use a similar technique to resize a window. In step 3 above, select Size instead of Move. Again, you will see the four-headed arrow. Press the arrow key for the side that you want to move (the left-arrow for the left side, the up-arrow for the top, and so on). This moves the pointer to the window edge, and the arrow keys will enable you to shrink or size the window.

Table 6-1 Windows 2000 Keyboard Shortcuts

Key Combination	Action
F1	Brings up the Help window. From the Windows 2000 Desktop, it will bring you the Windows 2000 help file. From an application, it will bring you the application's help file.
F2	Renames the selected item.
F3	Brings up the "Search for Files or Folders" dialog box.
F4	In My Computer or Windows Explorer, it will bring up the address bar.
F5	Refreshes the active window.
F6	Cycles through screen elements in the active window or Desktop.
F10	Brings up the menu in the active window. Alt+F does this, too.
Alt+Tab	Switches between open items. This may be the quickest way to jump between running programs. Hold down the Alt key with your thumb and tap the Tab key with your index or middle finger until the icon for the program you want is highlighted. Then release both keys at the same time and you'll be switched to the program you chose.

Continued

Table 6-1 *(continued)*

Key Combination	Action
Alt+Esc	Switches between items in the order they were opened.
Alt+Enter	Views the properties for a selected item.
Alt+F4	Either closes the active item, or quits the active program.
Alt+Backspace	Undo. The same as Ctrl+Z.
Alt+Spacebar	Displays the system menu of the active window.
Alt+underlined letter in a menu item	Opens that menu.
Ctrl+C	Copies selection.
Ctrl+X	Cuts selection.
Ctrl+V	Pastes the previously copied or cut selection.
Ctrl+Z	Undo last action.
Ctrl+A	Selects all.
Ctrl+O	Open.
Ctrl+Esc	Displays the Start Menu.
Ctrl+F4	Closes the active document in applications that allow multiple opened documents.

Some keyboards, such as the Microsoft Natural Keyboard and other compatible keyboards, contain two extra keys which are usually located on the bottom row near the spacebar. The Windows key has the Microsoft Windows logo on it. The Application key looks like a drop-down menu. Table 6-2 lists the Natural Keyboard shortcuts.

Table 6-2   Microsoft Natural Keyboard Shortcuts

Optional Keys	On Microsoft Natural Keyboards, and other compatible keyboards
Windows Key	Shows or hides the Start menu.
Windows+D	Minimizes or restores all windows.
Windows+E	Opens My Computer.
Windows+F	Opens Search for File or Folders.
Windows+R	Opens the Run dialog box.
Windows+U	Opens the Utility Manager.

Optional Keys	*On Microsoft Natural Keyboards, and other compatible keyboards*
Windows+F1	Opens Windows 2000 Help.
Windows+Break	Opens Systems Properties.
Ctrl+Windows+F	Searches for computers (on a network).
Application Key	Key that looks like a drop-down menu. Displays the shortcut menu for selected item.

If a dialog box is active, the keyboard shortcuts listed in Table 6-3 are available.

Table 6-3   Dialog Box Keyboard Shortcuts

Tab	Move forward through dialog box options.
Shift-Tab	Move backward through dialog box options.
Ctrl+Tab	Moves forward through dialog box tabs.
Ctrl+Shift+Tab	Moves backward through dialog box tabs.
Enter	Carry out the active option or button.
Alt+underlined letter	Carry out the command that corresponds to the letter, or select the corresponding option.
Spacebar	If active option is a checkbox, toggles it on or off.
Arrow keys	If active option is a group of option buttons, selects a button.
F1	Displays help file for this dialog box.
F4	Shows the active list.
Backspace	In an Open or Save As dialog box, moves you up one level if a folder is selected.

Note that many other applications will also have keyboard shortcuts that let you perform particular functions.

If Sticky Keys (one of the Windows Accessibility Features) are enabled, some of these combination keyboard shortcuts might not work.

Closing Windows 2000

Ready to quit? To successfully shut down Windows 2000, you have to follow a shut-down procedure similar to Windows 95, Windows 98, and Windows NT. You can't just hit the power button like you could in DOS or Windows 3.x. (Well, you can, but at the risk of corrupting your computer's settings, or causing some errors on your hard drive.) To quit, follow these steps:

STEPS:

Shutting down your computer

Step 1. Click Start ⇨ Shut Down.

Step 2. Click the drop-down menu in the Shut Down Dialog box, shown in Figure 6-21, and select the type of shut down you want:

- **Logging off <username>** closes all running programs and disconnects you from the network, but leaves the computer running, ready for someone else to log on.

- **Shut down** saves any Windows settings that have been changed, and writes any information in memory to the hard drive. It then prepares the computer to be shut off.

- **Restart** is like a shutdown, but instead of powering down, it reboots the computer.

- **Standby**, if available, puts your computer into a low power consumption mode, but makes it available almost instantly. It doesn't save settings or memory, so that if the computer loses power during Standby, these are lost.

- **Hibernate**, if available, saves all information and shuts down the computer. However, when the computer comes back on, the Desktop is restored to where it was before shutdown.

Step 3. If your computer supports the Windows 2000 Advanced Power Management features, it will turn itself off. Otherwise, wait for a message saying it is okay to turn off your computer, and then power down.

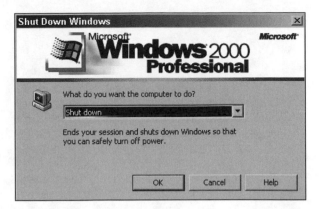

Figure 6-21: The Windows 2000 Shut Down dialog box.

The Standby and Hibernate features rely on the ability of your computer to support the power management scheme of Windows 2000, which is called Advanced Configuration and Power Interface (ACPI). To learn more about power management, see Part IV.

Summary

In this chapter, we learned the basic parts of the Windows 2000 environment, and we learned how to do basic tasks:

▶ The parts of the Desktop, Start Menu, and Taskbar.

▶ How to use and adjust the mouse.

▶ Where things are on the Start menu.

▶ How to start a program and manipulate its window, and how to manage multiple windows.

▶ How to create a shortcut.

▶ Time-saving keyboard shortcuts.

▶ The correct way to close Windows 2000.

Chapter 7

Take Control of Your System

In This Chapter

We show you how to take control of your computer using My Computer and the Windows Explorer. You will see:

▶ How your computer is organized with files and folders.

▶ How to find your way around with My Computer and the Windows Explorer.

▶ How to customize My Computer and the Windows Explorer.

▶ How to create, delete, and move folders.

▶ How to copy, delete, and move files.

Before You Begin: Click Once or Click Twice?

In Windows 95 and Windows NT, to select an item you clicked it once, and to open it you clicked it twice. This is part of what is termed the Windows Classic interface. (Has Windows been around long enough to pass itself off as Classic?) Windows 98 introduced an optional Web-style interface, where just placing the mouse pointer over an item (hovering) selects it, and a single click opens it. This style is also available in Windows 2000.

To set the style of clicking you want to use, click Start ⇨ Settings ⇨ Control Panel ⇨ Folder Options. On the lower portion of the View tab, you can choose a click style: Single-click to open an item (point to select), or Double-click to open an item (single-click to select). Switching to the single-click style might take some getting used to, especially if you have been double-clicking for a number of years. But you'll find, after awhile, that all those saved clicks add up to less wear and tear on both your fingers and your mouse.

In this book, we will use the term click interchangeably for both methods. When we refer to a click in this book, substitute a double-click if you have chosen the Windows Classic interface. When we say to select an icon by hovering or pointing with a mouse, you will need to single-click if you are using the Windows Classic interface.

How Your Computer Is Organized

Today's computers can hold thousands of files. These files might be either program files, or they might be data files. This many files would be very hard to manage if they were all in one huge pile, just like the contents of a filing cabinet would be difficult to access if all the files were jumbled into one huge pile on the floor (just ask *Windows 2000 Secrets* coauthor Bruce Brown). To help manage this massive quantity of files, modern operating systems sort files into directories. Directories can hold both subdirectories and files. In order to sound more user-friendly, the Microsoft Windows family of operating systems has replaced the words *directory* and *subdirectory* with the words *folder* and *subfolder*. But it is more than just a name change: folders provide some additional capabilities that DOS directories can't provide.

Beginning with Windows 95, two folder and file management tools have been provided: My Computer and the Windows Explorer (which should not be mistaken for Internet Explorer, the Web browser). My Computer has seemingly been pushed as the more important tool. It gets placed in the most prominent spot, the upper-left corner of the Desktop, while the Windows Explorer is buried somewhere on the Start ⇨ Programs menu. Yet, most users will probably agree that the Windows Explorer—with its two-pane window—is a far more powerful and useful utility for managing files.

While the default view for My Computer in Windows 2000 looks much the same as it did in Windows 95 and 98, you can transform it into a tool that is virtually indistinguishable from the Windows Explorer and Internet Explorer by tweaking some views and adding some toolbars. The three programs are essentially the same tool. By customizing the views, the Explorer Bar, or the toolbars, you can make them look and act the same.

Change your computer's name to Elvis

As computers move out of their technical/hobbyist niche and into the mainstream, Microsoft has tried to hide much of the more technical aspects of and terms in the operating system, replacing them instead with a friendlier vocabulary. Windows 95 introduced us to My Computer—a way to get us to bond with the machine. "It's not just a computer, it's *My Computer*!" Instead of being attached to a network, we belonged to a Network Neighborhood. (Can you picture Bill Gates in a zippered cardigan, singing "Won't you be my neighbor?") Windows 2000 takes it one step further. Network Neighborhood is now My Network Places; if you click it, you will see a new place called Computers Near Me.

If this is too much for you, don't worry. You can change the name of My Computer to something else if you like. If you are on a network, your computer has a name. You can rename My Computer so that it uses that name. If you are not on a network, you can use nearly any name you want by taking the following steps:

STEPS:

Rename My Computer

Step 1.   Right-click the My Computer icon.

Step 2.   Select Rename from the context menu.

Step 3.   The label "My Computer" beneath the icon is now highlighted in blue. Type in a replacement name; call it Elvis or Bertha or any other name you like.

Step 4.   Press Enter.

Tip

When you rename something, the old name is highlighted in blue. The highlighted material will be replaced by what you type. If you only want to make a small change in a name and you don't want to retype the whole name, you can edit the name instead. Pressing the Home or End key, or clicking somewhere within the existing name, will switch you into Edit mode so you can make changes to the existing name.

Changing My Computer

Start My Computer by clicking its icon. This will open a window where you see icons for all of your hard drives, your removable drives, and your CD-ROM drives. You also will see the Control Panel folder. This is an alternate route to the Control Panel, which you also can reach by clicking Start ⇨ Settings, where you will do most of the customization on your computer. Two folders that were in My Computer in Windows 95/98/NT are gone: the Printers and Dial-Up Networking folders. These folders have been moved to the Control Panel with the other configuration tools, where they rightfully belong.

Secret

While they are called folders and they use the folders icon, the Control Panel, Printers, Network and Dialup Connections, and Scheduled Tasks folders are not really folders in the literal sense. The contents of the Control Panel folders are really files in the Windows\System folder that have the extension .cpl. The other folders aren't really folders, either. They are simply containers for information that is stored in the Registry—a special data file that holds most of your user and system settings.

In Windows 2000, it is easy to configure My Computer to show you much more. First, click the View menu in My Computer. You have a choice of showing Large Icons, Small Icons, List, or Details. Select Details. Click Choose Columns, and then select Type, Total Size, and Free Space, to display more information about your drives. Click OK. If all the information doesn't fit in your window, but some of the columns have a lot of empty space, you can adjust the column size. Move your mouse up to the gray column headers and hover over one of the dividers between the columns. When the mouse pointer changes to a two-headed arrow, click and drag to resize the columns. You also can double-click the divider and the column will automatically adjust to fit the widest entry.

My Computer is now telling us a lot more than before, but we can do better. Click View again, and then move down to the Explorer Bar and select Folders. My Computer has transformed into what looks like the Windows Explorer, as shown in see Figure 7-1.

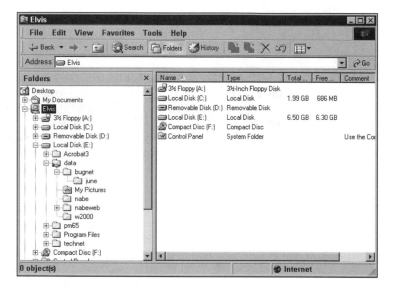

Figure 7-1: The My Computer window with folders enabled. It now resembles the Windows Explorer.

Tip

To automatically open My Computer in a two-pane view, right-click its icon and select Explore from the context menu.

Both My Computer and the Windows Explorer allow you to see the contents of the drives and folders in your computer, yet they both let you do more than just look. If you click an application in My Computer or the Windows Explorer, you will start that application. Click a data file and you will open both the data file and its associated program in a single step. (We will look at the way Windows keeps track of what files go with what applications below.)

My Computer window properties

If you right-click an empty portion of the My Computer window, you will see a context menu that allows you to change the view of the window by selecting large icons, small icons, list, or details. The context menu also provides a Properties selection.

Tip

Selecting Properties will take you the Windows 2000 System Properties Dialog box. You also can reach this dialog box by right-clicking My Computer and choosing Properties, or you can reach it through the Control Panel by double-clicking the System icon. From this dialog box, you can manage most of the hardware settings for your computer, which will be covered in Part IV of this book.

Note

If you ever need to find your Windows 2000 serial number, it is located here in the My Computer properties dialog box.

Order the icons

You can specify the order in which your icons are displayed in a window. Click View ➪ Arrange Icons, and then choose the desired option from the submenu. If you are looking at the top-level My Computer window (the one you see when you first click My Computer), your choices are By Drive Letter, By Type, By Size, and By Free Space. If you are looking at other folders, your choices are usually By Name, By Type, By Size, and By Date, although this might vary a little, depending on which folder you are viewing.

A first look at the Windows Explorer

The Windows Explorer looks just like My Computer, but by default, it opens with a two-pane view — again, with the folders on the left and the contents of the selected folder on the right (see Figure 7-2). The two panes are connected in this way, but they are also independent. You can view the contents of one folder in the right pane and, without disturbing that view, expand the tree in the left pane to find another folder. You also can scroll up or down to see other portions of the folder tree.

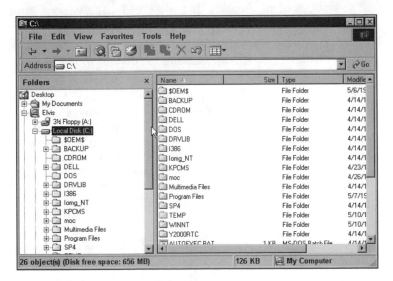

Figure 7-2: The Windows Explorer displaying the contents of the C: drive in the right pane.

Tip

To scroll either of the panes, you can click the arrows above or below the vertical scrollbars to move one line at a time. To scroll more quickly, click and drag the button on the scrollbar.

In the left pane, you must click a folder to display its contents. Hovering will not work. However, you can hover to select in the right pane.

Because the Windows Explorer allows you to do so much, one of the first things you need to do is make finding it easier. By default, it is buried in the Start ➪ Programs ➪ Accessories menu, when it deserves a place on the desktop just like My Computer. Create a shortcut to the Windows Explorer on your Desktop, and then change some of its settings, following these steps:

STEPS:
Customize the Windows Explorer

Step 1.   Create a shortcut on the Desktop for the Windows Explorer (see Chapter 6). The location of the executable file Explorer.exe is your Windows 2000 folder.

Step 2.   Click your shortcut to start the Windows Explorer. It will open with a two-pane view showing folders in the left pane and the contents of the current folder in the right pane. If the folder contains subfolders, they will be listed first, before any files.

Step 3.   By default, the right pane will display large icons. Click View ➪ Details to show more information about each file or folder. Click View ➪ Columns; in addition to displaying the name, also select size, type, modified, and attributes. Note that there are additional pieces of information that you could display (see Figure 7-3).

Step 4.   You can adjust the size of the columns the same way you did in My Computer, by clicking and dragging the column heading divider, or by double-clicking the divider to size the column to fit the widest entry.

Step 5.   By default, the items in the right pane are listed in alphabetical order by name. Sometimes — especially when working with data files — you might want your files arranged differently. Click ➪ View ➪ Arrange Icons ➪ By Date if you want your newest files and folders to be listed at the top. This makes it easier to find your most recently used files. (You can always change back to alphabetical order if you like, or you can sort them by type or size instead.)

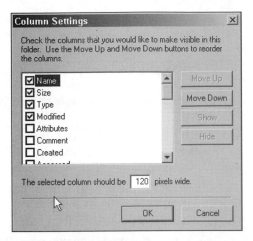

Figure 7-3: The Column Settings dialog box. You can let the Windows Explorer display many different pieces of information about a file or a folder.

You also can change the sort order by clicking the gray column heading of the column in which you want to sort. A new feature in Windows 2000 is a faint gray triangle that will appear beside the column heading text of the sorted column. It will be pointed upward if the sort order is ascending. If you want to switch from ascending to descending order or back again, click the column header and the arrow will switch to reflect the new sort order.

Secret

You also can configure a folder in the Windows Explorer — but not in My Computer — to display a background image using the Customize this folder option. While some of the images included with Windows 2000 do a pretty good job of obscuring the contents of the folders, you might want to add background images for certain folders to make it easy to tell at a glance what folder you are viewing.

STEPS:

Customize an Explorer Folder

Step 1. Open the folder you want to customize.

Step 2. Click View ⇨ Customize this Folder to begin the Customization Wizard.

Continued

STEPS:

Customize an Explorer Folder *(continued)*

Step 3.   To begin, click Next.

Step 4.   Select Modify Background picture and filename appearance, and then click Next.

Step 5.   Windows 2000 ships with a variety of bitmap images you can use for backgrounds. You also can choose your own by clicking Browse and locating the bitmap image you want to use.

Step 6.   Depending on the background color of your bitmap image, you might want to change the text color for your folder, as well, so that it displays against the background. Click Next.

Step 7.   The customization will appear the next time you open the folder.

If all this makes your folder a visual mess, you can always reverse your changes. Run the Customization Wizard again by repeating Steps 1-3, and then choose Remove Customization.

Secret

When you customize a folder, the settings are kept in a hidden file within the folder called Desktop.ini. (See the View tab section below for information on how to display hidden files.) Each folder that has been customized will have one of these files. If you open it in Notepad, you can see the customization instructions, which are rather cryptic, as can be seen in Listing 7-1.

Listing 7-1: Typical Desktop.ini file

```
[ExtShellFolderViews]
Default={5984FFE0-28D4-11CF-AE66-08002B2E1262}
{5984FFE0-28D4-11CF-AE66-08002B2E1262}={5984FFE0-28D4-
11CF-AE66-08002B2E1262}

[{5984FFE0-28D4-11CF-AE66-08002B2E1262}]
WebViewTemplate.NT5=file://Folder.htt

[.ShellClassInfo]
ConfirmFileOp=0
```

Through these changes, you can configure My Computer and the Windows Explorer to look and act the same. Throughout the rest of this chapter, almost all of the folder and file management techniques we discuss will work equally in both, provided they are set up for two-pane view.

Tip

Following some of these customization steps, you can make My Computer look and act like the more powerful Windows Explorer. It only takes a couple of keystrokes or mouse clicks to do this. In most cases, you will save time by just going straight to the Windows Explorer.

Freshening up the folder window

A folder window might not always accurately display the actual contents of the folder. Sometimes file moves or copies are not immediately updated in the display. If you think you have a stale window, you can freshen it by pressing the F5 key. You also can click View ➪ Refresh, or you can right-click the client area of the My Computer window, and then click Refresh.

Folder options

You can carefully configure a view in My Computer or the Windows Explorer to show just those details you want to see — icons, details, and so forth. But when you click another folder, those settings are gone — replaced by the default settings. Luckily, you don't have to go through the customization process for every folder. The Folder Options tool allows you to set these choices as the default for all folders.

Folder Options got a promotion in Windows 2000. In Windows 95, there were very limited Options settings to configure. In Windows 98, it became the more powerful Folder Options, but it was located under the View menu in both the Windows Explorer and My Computer. In Windows 2000, it has been moved to the Tools menu, and it also has its own icon in the Control Panel.

The General tab

The General tab in the Folder Options dialog box (shown in Figure 7-4) lets you set some very important options both on your desktop and in folders. The first choice allows you to display Web content on your desktop, or it retains the Windows classic look, which is discussed in Chapter 12. The second option sets your folders up to display Web content. Select Enable Web content in folders, and then close the Folder Options dialog box. In the Windows Explorer, this will split the right pane, adding a graphic section that displays file information. Note that this is the same information you will see if you select View ➪ Details, and select the columns you want to display. If My Computer is set to a single-pane view, the Web content section will be on the left side. If you enable the Explorer Bar, the Web content will share the right pane.

Note

It's a matter of personal preference whether the information shown by Web content in the folders is worth the amount of screen real estate it consumes. You can experiment with it both enabled and disable and then decide for yourself which view you prefer.

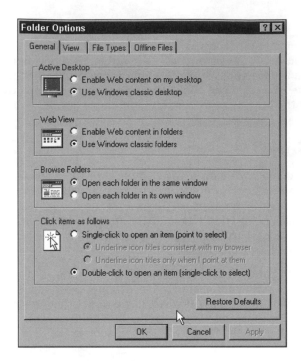

Figure 7-4: The Folder Options General tab.

The next option on the General tab determines how you browse through folders in My Computer. If it is set to Open each folder in the same window, the new view replaces the previous view in My Computer when you click a drive or folder to display its contents. If you select Open each folder in its own window, you will see the contents of your selected drive in a new window, but your old folder will still be in view. This has advantages and disadvantages. The major advantage is that with two or more open windows, you can quickly perform certain file maintenance tasks, as we will see below. The major disadvantage is that you can quickly clutter your screen with a number of windows if you need to move down a few levels in your folder tree.

Secret

If you drill down through a folder and its subfolders, with each opening in a different window, the result will be a screen full of windows. It can be tedious to close them all, one by one. Instead, hold down the Shift key as you click the Close button to close not only the window that has the current focus, but also all the parent windows.

The last option on the General tab allows either single- or double-clicking. (See the beginning of this chapter for more information.)

The View tab

Possibly the most powerful choice in the Folder Options dialog box is on the View tab (see Figure 7-5). Configuration choices made from the View Menu or within the Folder Options dialog box affect only the currently open folder. However, if you configure the folder so that it is just the way you like it, and then select the View tab and click the Like Current Folder button, your configuration will then be applied to all your folders. You are not locked into this view, however. By clicking the other button—Reset All Folders—everything changes back to the default Windows 2000 settings. You also can fine-tune your folder views. You can make universal changes through the Like Current folder button, and then change a view in a specific folder that will remain only for that folder.

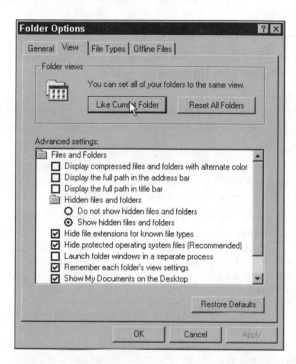

Figure 7-5: You can apply the view for your current folder to all your folder views by clicking the Like current folder button.

The View tab also has a number of advanced options from which you can select. Some of these settings are cosmetic, and some are designed to keep you away from things on your own computer where you might do harm.

- You can elect to display compressed files and folders using a different color. If you do use compression, the color will help provide you with a visual clue as to the file type.

- The next two options will show the full path of your selected item in the Address Bar and the Title Bar. Enable both of these options; they will help you to see how the computer is organized.

- By default, files that have a hidden attribute will not display in the Windows Explorer. After all, they are hidden. If you decide that you don't want your computer keeping secrets from you, you can select the Show hidden files and folders options.

- Windows 2000 uses file extensions to keep track of what files go with what programs. When a program is installed, it registers its file types with the Windows Registry. By default, Windows 2000 will not display know file extensions. You can change this so that the file extensions will display in the Windows Explorer.

- The next thing that you can unhide is protected operating system files.

Secret

This is the only option where Windows 2000 adds a Recommended label. It doesn't want you tinkering with these files.

Caution

Some of these operating system files can be edited or changed by advanced users, if they know what they are doing and it is done in the correct fashion. But be aware that serious consequences can result if you accidentally change or delete these files.

- You can open each Explorer folder in a separate part of memory by selecting the next option. If you do, you can increase the stability of Windows 2000, but at a slight decrease in performance.

- If you have gone to all this trouble to set your folder options just so, enable the box to Remember each folder's view settings. Likewise, make sure the option to show My Documents on the Desktop is enabled so that you can retain this useful shortcut, and enable the pop-up descriptions (these are the little balloon captions that pop up when you hover your mouse pointer over an object).

File Types

The third tab in the Folder Options dialog box is File Types, shown in Figure 7-6. Windows 2000 keeps track of which applications open which data file by means of the file extensions — the three (and now four) characters that follow the period in the filename.

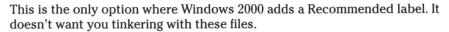

Note

It's old hat if you have upgraded from Windows 95, 98 or NT, but if you are coming from Windows 3.x, the strict limits on filenames are no more. You now have a total of 255 characters, including spaces — but excluding the following characters: \ / : * ? " < > |. Be aware, however, that some programs might not be capable of correctly handling extremely long filenames.

Scrolling through the list of registered file types in the Folder Options dialog box shows the various file extensions that Windows 2000 knows. Some file associations between programs and extensions are created when Windows 2000 is installed; for example, .TXT indicates a text file that can be opened with Notepad or WordPad. Other file associations are created when you install other applications. If you install Adobe Acrobat, for example, it will claim the .PDF file extension.

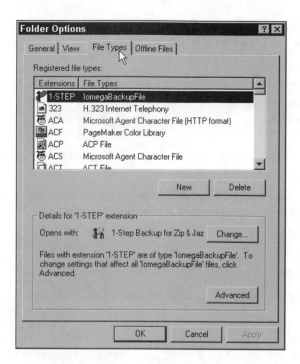

Figure 7-6: The File Type tab in the Folder Options dialog box shows which file extensions are associated with which applications.

In previous versions of Windows, a particular file type could only be associated with only one program, which led to constant warfare between some programs for the rights to a particular extension. The best example of this is probably Netscape Navigator and Internet Explorer's endless jostling for the .HTM file extension. Windows 2000 attempts to make peace between programs by allowing more than one program to be associated with a particular file extension. If you've ever opened a file with a particular program, that program will be available in the Open With context menu. Just highlight the file you want to open in the Windows Explorer, right-click and choose Open With, and then select the program you want to open the file with from the context menu.

Caution

If you change a file extension when you rename a file, you run the risk of Windows 2000 losing track of the file's associated application. You will then see the warning message shown in Figure 7-7 when you change a file extension. This normally does not make a file unusable, though. Many programs will still be able to open their data files, even when they do not have their normally associated file extension; they just won't be able to do so automatically.

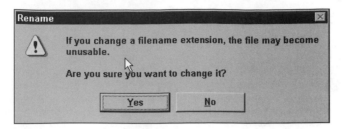

Figure 7-7: You will see this warning message when you change a file's extension.

We will look at some of the customizations you can perform with file-type icons in Chapter 8. The final tab of the File Options dialog box, Offline Files, will be discussed in Part V.

Folder trees

In the two-pane view of either My Computer or the Windows Explorer, you get a better idea of the hierarchical arrangement of your computer; at least you would if Windows didn't take some liberties with how it display files, folders, and so forth. When you look in the Folders pane on the left side, you see that the top-most item is the Desktop. If you click it, you will see all the objects that inhabit your Desktop in the right pane, including My Computer, the Recycle Bin, and any shortcuts that you might have created on your Desktop. In the Folders window, descending downward from the Desktop in the right pane, you will see a dotted line that connects to My Documents, My Computer, My Network Places, and a few other special folders. When you click the plus sign next to My Computer, you will see icons for your floppy and hard drives, your CD-ROM drive, and the Control Panel. The icons make it appear as though these other folders and icons branch directly off the desktop. If, in the previous section, you enabled the option to show full folder addresses, you would see the path of the Desktop as C:*windows*\\Profiles*username*\\Desktop — it is actually a subfolder under your Windows directory (if you installed Windows 2000 as an upgrade).

Secret

In actuality, both the Desktop and the My Documents folder in the Explorer Bar are simply shortcuts — or pointers — to special folders within your computer that help you work more efficiently. The actual top level of your computer is My Computer. (The role of My Documents is discussed later in this chapter.)

In the Folders pane, a plus sign to the left of a drive or folder icon means that there are subfolders beneath the drive or folder. Clicking the plus sign will expand the drive or folder so that all its sub-folders are visible on the left. Once expanded, the plus sign changes to a minus sign. Click the minus sign to collapse the folder.

Tip

Selecting a drive or folder and then pressing the asterisk key on the numeric keyboard (with NumLock on) will also expand all the subfolders for your selection. (See Table 7-3 for more keyboard shortcuts.)

Caution

Computers are faster than ever before, but at the same time, hard drives are larger. Pressing the asterisk key shortcut can take some time to complete.

Expanding the folders in this way shows how folders and subfolders use a hierarchical organization. In fact, this organizational structure is often referred to as a tree, with folders having subfolders branching from the trunk (or root) of the tree.

My Computer menu and toolbar buttons

The toolbar in My Computer closely resembles both the Windows Explorer the Internet Explorer toolbars(see Figure 7-8). Each toolbar helps you navigate through your computer, just like Internet Explorer helps you navigate through the World Wide Web. To see the name of a button, hover the mouse pointer over it, and a tooltip will pop up with the button's name.

Figure 7-8: The My Computer toolbar.

STEPS:

Using the My Computer Icons to Navigate

Step 1. Click My Computer. It should be open in a single-pane view.

Step 2. Click the C: drive folder to display its contents.

Step 3. The left-pointing arrow on the toolbar is now active. It represents the Back button, and clicking it will take you back to your previous view. Click it to go back to My Computer.

Step 4. You can now click the right-pointing arrow, which stands for Forward, to trace your steps back to the C: drive.

Step 5. The upward-pointing arrow on the toolbar is the Up button, which takes you up one level in the computer's folder hierarchy. In this case, it takes you back to My Computer. If you have moved down through a folder and a number of subfolders, you might have to click the Up button a number of times to get back to My Computer.

The remaining buttons open the Search, History, and Folder views, the same as if you clicked View ⇨ Explorer Bar and chosen of those options.

Search Assistant

In addition to having a Folder view in the Explorer Bar, you also have other choices. Clicking View ⇨ Explorer Bar ⇨ Search will open the Search Assistant, which is identical to the Search window you see when you click Start ⇨ Help.

The Search Assistant replaces the Find Files or Folders utility found in previous versions of Windows, and more closely resembles the Search function in Internet Explorer. You can call the Search Assistant in My Computer, Internet Explorer, and the Windows Explorer, as well as in any specialized folder view such as the Recycle Bin or the Control Panel.

If you need to find a file and you are not sure what folder it is in, the Search window will help you avoid a long and aimless search through a series of folders. You can search for exact filenames, and you also can use wildcard characters if you are not certain of the exact filename (see Figure 7-9).

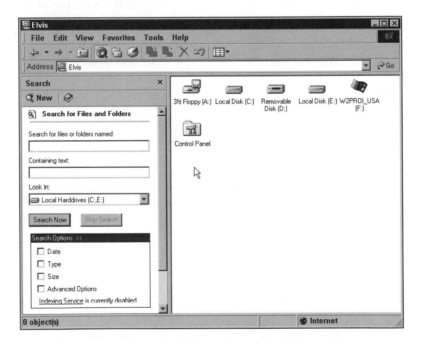

Figure 7-9: The Search window helps you search for files on your computer.

If you know the exact filename, you type the name into the Search for files or folders named text box. You can limit your search to specific drives, or you can search your entire computer. After clicking the Search Now button, the results of the search will appear in the right pane. Clicking the filename will then open that file in its associated application.

If you are not sure of the exact filename, but you have a pretty good idea, you can use wildcards. The asterisk (*) symbol can be substituted for unknown characters: *.doc will look for all documents with the file extension .doc; b*.doc will search for all doc files that begin with the letter b. (An asterisk (*) character will return results of any length.) A search for b*.doc will find ba.doc, bad.doc, and backflip.doc. A question mark (?) can be substituted for a single character. A search for b?.doc will turn up ba.doc or bb.doc and ignore bad.doc. Table 7-1 shows how you can use wildcard characters in searches.

Table 7-1	Searching with Wildcards
Searching for this	*Will find this*
.	All files and folders (this is pronounced "start dot star").
*.	Files, but will not find folders unless the folder has a period within its name.
.exe	Nothing, because no filenames or folder names begin with a period.
exe	Files with the characters exe in the name, including files such as explorer.exe and bexely.doc.
*.exe	Will find all files with the extension .exe.
br*.*	All files that begin with br, including bruce.doc and brian.doc.
br?.*	Any files with a three-letter name that begins with br, such as br1.doc, but not bruce.doc.
?.*	Any file that has a one-character name.

Indexing Service

What do you do if you can't remember what the filename is, but you remember what's in the file? You can search for files containing a specific text string. This can be a lengthy search on a computer having many documents.

Secret

The Windows 2000 Indexing Service will compile indexes of both the contents and the properties of files both on your hard drives and any shared network drives for the following document types: HTML, Text, Office 95 (or later) files, and, Internet mail and news files. If the Indexing Service is running, text searches will be much faster.

The Indexing Service is disabled by default. To enable this service, click the Search Options link directly below the Search Now button to open the advanced features page. Click the link to the Indexing Service to open the Indexing Service Settings dialog box shown in Figure 7-10. Once it is enabled, Windows 2000 will create an index to both the contents and the properties of the data files mentioned above. Indexing works in the background; when it is enabled, it will speed up any full-text searches on your computer, and it also will provide a status report on whether it has completed an index, as well as if it is working on one.

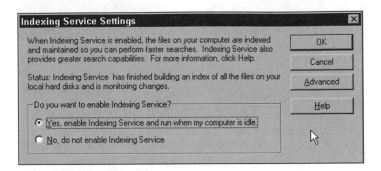

Figure 7-10: The Indexing Service dialog box. You can enable the Indexing Service here. For full configuration of the Service, you need to use the Indexing Service Tool in the Microsoft Management Console.

The Indexing Service is run through the Microsoft Management Console (MMC), which is a framework for using administrative tools on Windows 2000. To see the complete configuration settings for the Indexing Service, follow these steps:

STEPS:

Indexing Service in the MMC

Step 1.   Click Start ⇨ Settings ⇨ Control Panel.

Step 2.   Click the Administrative Tools icon, and then select Computer Management.

Step 3.   In the Computer Management Console, expand Services and Applications, and then click Indexing Service ⇨ System ⇨ Directories.

Step 4.   In the right pane, you can exclude a drive from being indexed, or you can add a drive or directory by clicking Action ⇨ New.

Tip

While the Indexing Service is running, it maintains its index information in a catalog file. The size of this catalog will cover approximately 15 percent of the documents you will be indexing, if you use the NTFS file systems, and closer to 30 percent if you use a FAT or FAT32 system.

Note

The speed of indexing comes with a tradeoff: the need for additional hard drive space. If you rarely use full-text searching, and your hard drive is running low on free space, the Indexing Service might be a luxury you could do without. On the other hand, Indexing does significantly speed up your searches.

To disable the Indexing Service, go back to the Search Assistant, click the Indexing Service link, and then select No to disable the service. (For more information on using the MMC to manage your computer, see Chapter 15.)

Advanced searches

You can specify where on your system you want your search to be performed using the drop-down menu. The search can be limited to a specific drive or folder, or you can search your entire hard drive (see Figure 7-11). By default, subfolders are included in the search path.

Tip

Don't know the name or the drive, but you know you saved the file yesterday? You can search for files by modification date. Selecting Date in the Search Options dialog box will open a date selection dialog box where you can specify the date range within which you want to search. You can search by Creation date, Modified date, or Last Accessed date.

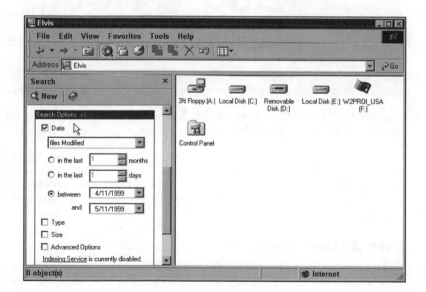

Figure 7-11: You can search for files created or saved over a specific modification date range.

Turn My Computer into a Web browser

If you click View ⇨ Explorer Bar, you can add your Favorites list to the left pane. Click one of the favorites; if the page is available offline (because it is stored in your browser cache), it will appear in the right pane. This transforms My Computer into Internet Explorer, as shown in Figure 7-12.

Tip

If the page is not available offline, the shortcut will be unavailable (grayed out) on the menu. If you click the shortcut, you will see the message "This page is not available offline. Do you wish to connect?" Click Yes, and your Internet connection will begin.

This is a literal transformation. The toolbar changes to the Internet Explorer toolbar, and the menu bar becomes the Internet Explorer menu bar. If you click Help ⇨ About, you will see that you are now using Internet Explorer 5.

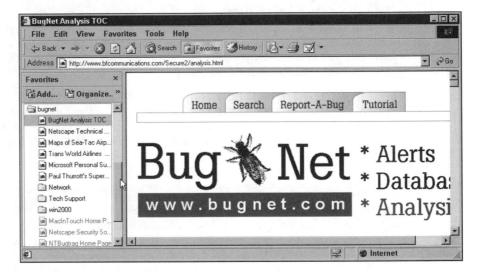

Figure 7-12: My Computer transformed into Internet Explorer, after adding your Favorites to the Explorer Bar, and then selecting a web site shortcut.

In addition to jumping to a location on the Web by adding your Favorites to the left pane, you also can click View ⇨ Explorer Bar ⇨ History to add a list of Web sites you have visited. (See Chapter 12 for more information on how to use the Internet Explorer history panel.)

File Action icons

In the next section of the toolbar are buttons that let you perform actions on selected files or folders. Select an item within the My Computer window, and then click the Move button. This opens the Browse folders dialog box, where you can choose a folder to which you can move your selection. The Copy button works in a similar fashion. The button displaying an X will delete your selection, and the button displaying a bent arrow will undo your last action. (You also can undo your last action by selecting Edit ⇨ Undo.)

Secret

Windows 2000 lets you undo more than just your last action. It keeps a stack — or list — of changes. You can undo your changes in the reverse order in which they were executed by repeatedly clicking Undo. If you right-click the right pane, you will see Undo, along with your last action, as a choice on the context menu. For example, if you have just renamed a file, then you will see Undo Rename on the menu.

Tip

The keyboard shortcut to undo your most recent action is Ctrl+Z.

The View button, which is the last icon on the right side of the toolbar, allows you to select a specific folder view. You can change your view to display using the following settings: Large Icons, Small Icons, List, Details, and Thumbnail View.

Customizing the toolbar

If you aren't satisfied with the way the toolbar appears in either My Computer or the Windows Explorer, or if you don't like the shortcuts that the toolbar provides, you can change that. Right-click an empty spot on the toolbar, and then click Customize. The Customize Toolbar dialog box, shown in Figure 7-13, appears.

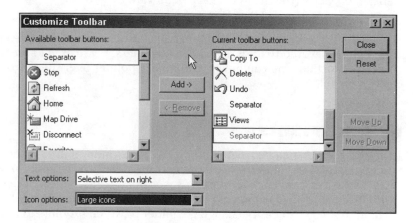

Figure 7-13: You can change both the appearance and the icons in the Windows Explorer and My Computer in the Customize Toolbar dialog box.

Most of the space in the Customize Toolbar dialog box is comprised of button selection options. The selection box on the left shows the toolbar buttons that you can are add to your toolbar, and the selection box on the right displays the buttons you currently have enabled on your toolbar. Some of the buttons make more sense in Internet Explorer than they would in the Windows Explorer. For example, the Home button will open your home page in Internet

Explorer. (The home page is the first page you see when you start your browser. We will cover Internet Explorer in greater detail in Chapter 12.) To add a button, select the button in the left pane, and then click the Add button to add the button to the right pane. If you find that you never use a particular button on your toolbar, select it and click the Remove button.

Tip

There are two ways to control the placement of new buttons on the toolbar. Before you add a button, select the button in the right pane where you want the new button to be placed. Then click the Add button. If a button is not located where you want it to be, select the button in the right pane, and then click either Move Up or Move Down to change its position on your toolbar.

Secret

Use the Separator button to add the thin vertical line between groups of icons on the icon bar.

If your customization efforts result in confusion, click the Reset button to restore the default toolbar buttons.

In addition to controlling which buttons to display on the toolbar, you also can control their appearance. In the Text Options dialog box, you can choose to display text labels beneath each toolbar button, you can choose to display only a few to the right of the buttons, or you can choose to display no text labels at all. The latter makes the toolbar thinner and provides more screen real estate to your folder views. You also can choose between Large and Small Icon views (the default is Large Icon view).

Tip

Once you know which buttons are which, you can turn off the text labels beneath the toolbar icons so that you have more screen real estate space that can be devoted to folders and their contents. If you aren't sure about a button's function, you can hover your mouse pointer over the button to see its tooltip text.

My Documents

One major difference between Windows 95 and Windows 2000 is the prominent placement of the My Documents folder on your Desktop. Windows 2000 looks here first each it opens or saves documents. The My Document folder is located in C:*windows r*\Profiles*user name*\My Documents by default, but you can easily change the folder to which it points to any folder you want to use.

NEW IN 2000

One of the requirements of the Windows 2000 logo program is that an application defaults to My Documents for saving and opening files.

If you have installed Windows 2000 as an upgrade, by default the My Document folder is C:*windows folder*\Profiles*user name*\My Documents, but you can actually configure it to point to any other directory. If Windows 2000 has been set up as a fresh install, you will find the My Documents folder in c:\Documents and Settings*Username*.

Windows 2000's built-in multiuser capabilities are enabled by default. Two users can configure the same computer to work differently through the different preferences they each set. As illustrated in the default \Profiles*username* path shown above. When a user logs on at the Windows 2000 startup screen, the profile for that user name is automatically loaded.

STEPS:

Change the Target for My Documents

Step 1. From the Windows Explorer, right-click the My Documents folder in the left pane. (You also can right-click the My Documents folder on the Desktop.)

Step 2. Click Properties on the context menu.

Step 3. Click the Target tab.

Step 4. In Target Folder Location, click Move.

Step 5. In the Browse for Folder window, choose a new default location for your document. This new location must already exist.

Most experienced Windows users logically divide their hard drives into multiple partitions (see Chapter 17 for more on drive management). If your hard drive is partitioned into two or more logical drives, you can move your My Documents folder to another drive. For example, if you need to reinstall your operating system software on the C: drive, and your date files are stored on your D: drive, your data files normally will not be affected (though you should still back them up anyway before undertaking actions such as formatting partitions and reinstalling software).

The placement of the My Documents folder at the top of the folder hierarchy might be viewed by some as an oddity. The My Documents folder seems to appear twice: once at the top of the folder hierarchy, and again in what would be its normal place within the folder tree. For example, the hard drive reflected in Figure 7-13 has been configured so that the My Documents folder points to the data folder on drive E:. When you click and expand the E:\data folder in the left pane, you will see that it has an identical subdirectory structure to that shown in the My Documents section which, in effect, is simply a mirror image of your real data folder. While they appear twice, you don't have two copies of the folder on your hard drive.

Many applications — including the Microsoft Office applications — use the My Documents folder for saving and retrieving files by default. While you might want to change the name of the folder or change the drive upon which the folder is stored, it's a good idea to store your data files in a central location. Doing so will make backing up your data files more convenient, and it also will make searching for lost files faster and easier.

Note that the My Documents folder shown in Figure 7-14 has a number of subfolders contained within it. How you create new subfolders — and the reason you should create more subfolders — is explained in the next section.

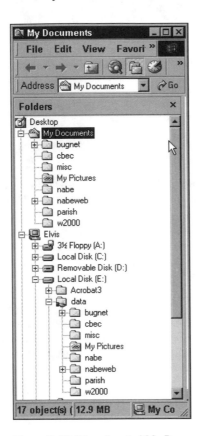

Figure 7-14: The relocated My Documents folder.

Create a New Folder

Since Windows 2000 will make you super productive, you will most likely be creating a lot of data files on your computer. But if all your data files are stored in a single folder, you would soon find it difficult to locate your files. Luckily, you can easily create any number of subfolders beneath a folder.

STEPS:

Creating a New Folder

Step 1. In the Folders pane, click the folder beneath which you want to create a new subfolder.

Step 2. Click File ➪ New ➪ Folder.

Step 3. In the right pane, a new folder icon will appear with the name New Folder already highlighted. Type the name you want for the new folder.

Step 4. Press Enter.

Tip

Take some time to design an organizational scheme for your My Documents folder. You might want a folder for each project, or even a folder for each client. Your scheme could even mirror whatever system you use for filing paper in your office.

Common Windows Explorer Tasks

In this section, we look at some of the common folder and file operations you can perform in the Windows Explorer. Unless otherwise noted, they also can be performed in My Computer (when it is configured to use a two-pane view).

Moving a file to another folder

There are a number of different ways to move a file from one folder to another. It is generally easiest to accomplish, however if you have both the source and destination folders showing in the Windows Explorer.

STEPS:

Moving a File with Drag and Drop

Step 1. In the left pane, click the folder that contains the file you want to move. If necessary, expand your folders so you can locate the file in its subfolder.

Step 2. The file you want to move should now be displayed in the right pane. Select it.

Continued

STEPS:

Moving a File with Drag and Drop *(continued)*

Step 3.   Without clicking any other folder, scroll the left pane so that the destination folder is also showing. You can click the plus sign to the left of a folder to expand its contents, but if you click the folder itself, you will lose your view in the right pane, because it will switch to display the contents of the folder you just selected.

Step 4.   Back in the right pane, again select the file you want to move but don't release the mouse button. While holding down the mouse button, drag the file over into the left pane until your mouse pointer is directly on top of your target folder. You will see a ghosted image of the file moving right along with your mouse pointer.

Step 5.   Release the mouse button to complete the move.

Note

When the source and destination folders are on located the same drive, dragging and dropping results in moving the selected file; it will no longer be located in the source folder. When the source and destination folders are located on different drives, dragging and dropping the file results Windows creating a copy of the file in the destination folder; the file in the source folder remains in place.

Secret

When you drag and drop an executable (application) file to another folder, Windows 2000 creates a shortcut to the application when you release the mouse button. The application file stays in place; in the destination folder, you've created a shortcut pointing back to the original application file.

If you want to copy a file between two folders located on the same drive, follow the steps above, but click and drag with the right mouse button instead. When you release the mouse button, the context menu will appear with the following four choices: Copy Here, Move Here, Create Shortcut Here, and Cancel. Select Copy Here to create a copy of the file in the destination folder.

Caution

If you move or copy a file and the destination folder already has a file of the same name, you will see the warning message shown in Figure 7-15. Carefully check the file dates to see if you are mistakenly overwriting a newer file with an older file.

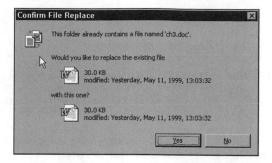

Figure 7-15: The Confirm File Replace warning message. In this case, the two files are identical, so it doesn't matter if one replaces the other.

STEPS:

Moving a File by Right-Clicking

Step 1. In the left pane, click the folder that contains the file you want to move. If necessary, expand your folders until you find it.

Step 2. The file you want to move should now be displayed in the right pane. Right-click it.

Step 3. Click Cut on the context menu.

Step 4. Right-click the destination folder in the left pane, and then click Paste on the context menu.

In the above steps, you also can use the keyboard shortcuts for cut (Ctrl+X) and paste (Ctrl+V) instead of right-clicking. If you want to copy a file, use the keyboard shortcut for copy (Ctrl+C) instead.

STEPS:

Copying a File Using the Ctrl Key

Step 1. In the left pane, click the folder that contains the file you want to move. If necessary, expand your folders until you find it.

Step 2. The file you want to move should now be displayed in the right pane. Select it.

Continued

STEPS:

Copying a File Using the Ctrl Key *(continued)*

Step 3. Without clicking any other folder, scroll the left pane so that the destination folder is showing. You can click the plus sign to expand a folder, but if you click any other folder, you will lose your view in the right pane.

Step 4. While holding down the Ctrl key, click the file you want to move. The, still holding down the mouse button, drag the file over to the left pane until you are directly on top of the target folder.

Step 5. Release the mouse button and the Ctrl key. This will copy the file to its new location and leave the original file in place in the source folder.

Deleting a file

To delete a file from within the Windows Explorer or My Computer, right-click the filename and click Delete from the context menu. Windows will present a dialog box asking: "Are you sure you want to send *filename* to the Recycle Bin?" Click yes, and the file will be sent to the Recycle Bin. (You also can select the file and then press the Delete key.) As we discussed in the last chapter, the Recycle Bin is a safety net, of sorts. Even after a file has been sent there, it can still be restored.

You also can delete a file by dragging it to the Recycle Bin and dropping it. This delete method will bypass the Delete Confirm dialog box.

Moving and deleting folders

Any of the copy, move, and delete functions you perform with files also can be performed with folders. Just select a folder instead of a file. The folder and all of its contents will be copied, moved, or deleted.

Tip

You can delete a file or folder and completely bypass the Recycle Bin. After you right-click the file or folder you want to delete, hold down the Shift key before you click Delete on the context menu. This method bypasses the Recycle Bin and deletes the file or folder in one step.

Other right-click actions

In the above example, when you right-clicked on a file or folder, you probably noticed a number of other options. Table 7-2 lists the right-click options available in Explorer.

Table 7-2   Right-Click Options in the Windows Explorer

Selection	Action
Open	Opens the file with its associated application. If you choose an application, the application will start.
Print	Sends the item to the printer.
Open with	Open a file in a program other than its default, associated program. For example, you might have Internet Explorer as your default Web browser, but you also have Netscape Navigator installed on your system. Right-clicking an .HTM file and choosing Open With will let you choose one or the other.
Send to	Copies the file or folder to a preselected list of destinations. (This list is kept in the SendTo folder.)
Cut	Moves the file or folder out of its current location and to the Clipboard.
Copy	Copies the file or folder to the Clipboard, leaving the original in place.
Create Shortcut	Creates a shortcut to the file or folder.
Delete	Sends the file or folder to the Recycle Bin.
Rename	Gives the file or folder a new name.
Properties	Displays the properties of this file or folder. While the exact properties will differ depending on which file is clicked, it will show when the file was created and modified, as well as its security and custom settings.

Selecting multiple files for action

When you select a file or folder in the right pane of the Widows Explorer, it is normally highlighted in blue. When you select another object, the highlighting moves from the original object and to the new object. Sometimes, however, you want to select multiple objects so that you can copy, delete, or move them.

STEPS:

Moving Adjacent Items

Step 1.   Select the first item.

Step 2.   Hold down the Shift key, and then select the last item.

Continued

STEPS:

Moving Adjacent Items *(continued)*

Step 3.   All the items between the first and the last should now be highlighted. Release the Shift key.

Step 4.   Click and hold the mouse button on the selected items, and then drag the selection to your destination folder. You will see a ghost image of the entire selection moving right along with the mouse pointer.

Step 5.   When you get to your destination folder, release the mouse button.

Caution

If you have enabled single-clicking, remember that pointing at a file selects it. If the mouse pointer strays over a folder and lingers, you might unintentionally add the folder to your multiple selection.

While this shows how to move a group of physically adjacent items, you would use the same technique to cut, copy or delete physically adjacent items.

STEPS:

Moving Non-adjacent Items

Step 1.   Select the first file you want to move.

Step 2.   Hold down the Ctrl key. Then, click each remaining item, one at a time, that you want to move.

Step 3.   When all the items you want to move have been selected, release the Ctrl key.

Step 4.   Click and hold any of the selected items. Then drag the selection to the destination folder. The selected items will move to the destination at one time.

Step 5.   When you reach the destination folder, release the mouse button.

Note

When you make multiple selections with either the Shift or the Ctrl key, it is crucial—once you reach Step 4—to click and hold and not just click. A click and release will cause you to lose all your earlier selections.

If your window is in List view, your icons are lined up in adjacent columns. You can select multiple icons by drawing a rectangle (a lasso) around or through the icons that you want to select.

Secret

You can select a group of icons by dragging a rectangle around the icons. Move the mouse pointer to an area near—but not directly over—the icons. Click and hold down the left mouse button. Drag the mouse pointer over the additional icons you want to select. As you surround them, they will be added to the selection. Release the mouse button when you have highlighted all the items you want to select.

Select everything

You can quickly select everything in a window. Click Edit ⇨ Select All. The Ctrl+A keyboard shortcut also does this.

Select everything but

You can quickly select all but just a few items. First, select the few that you don't want to include using any of the selection methods we've already discussed. Then, click Edit ⇨ Invert Selection. Everything that wasn't in the original selection is now selected, and those original selections are now deselected.

Deselect with Ctrl+Hover

You might have a large group of adjacent items you want to select, but there are a few in between that you don't want to select. Here is how to clear those selections. First, select all the items pressing the Shift key and hovering, or by drawing a rectangle around them. Now, press the Ctrl key and hover over each of the icons you want to deselect. (This does not work if use Double-clicking instead of Single-clicking.)

Grabbing the icon group

If you have selected a group of icons and want to move or copy them with drag and drop you need to drag them all together. To left- or right-click and drag the group, point to one of the selected items and start dragging—you'll bring the whole group with you. If you start dragging when the mouse pointer is between the selected icons, you will deselect the icons.

Copying and moving between windows

Another way to move or copy files is to use the multiple window option in My Computer. To do so, first make sure that this option is turned on. Open My Computer, click Folder Options, and select Open Each Folder in its own window.

STEPS:

Copying and Moving between Windows

Step 1.   Starting in My Computer, click to open the drive or folder that contains your source file. You might have to open multiple folders to do this.

Step 2.   Open the Destination folder in My Computer. You might have to open multiple folders to do this.

Step 3.   Arrange the windows so that you can see both the Source and Destination folders on your desktop. If necessary, close any other unneeded folders.

Step 4.   Click the file or folder you want to move and hold the mouse button down. Drag the file or folder to the destination folder.

Step 5.   Release the mouse button.

If the two windows are on the same drive, these steps move the file; it will no longer be in the source directory. If the two folders are on different drives, these steps copy the file, and the original remains in the source directory. If the folders are on the same drive, and you want to make a copy, hold down the Ctrl key before you drag the file.

How to escape danger

If there is a problem while you are in the middle of dragging a file or group of files around, you can't just release the mouse button; you might drop your selection somewhere you didn't intend to drop it. Instead, press the Esc key to abort any drag operation, leaving your selection intact.

The Windows Explorer keyboard shortcuts

You can use the mouse to send commands to the Windows Explorer. There are also a number of keyboard shortcuts you can use, as listed in Table 7-3.

Table 7-3 The Windows Explorer Keyboard Shortcuts	
Key press	*Does This*
End	Go to the last item in the active window.
Home	Go to the first item in the active window.
Num Lock+ numeric keypad asterisk	Expand all subfolders under the currently selected folder.

Key press	*Does This*
Num Lock + numeric keypad plus	Expand the selected folder.
Num Lock + numeric keypad minus	Collapse the selected folder.
Left arrow	Collapse the current selection, if it is expanded. If not, move to the parent folder.
Right arrow	Expand the current selection, if is collapsed. If not, move to the first subfolder.

Summary

My Computer and the Windows Explorer are tools that let you manage your files and folders.

▶ We looked at the difference between the Windows Classic and Web views.

▶ We customized My Computer, and we used it to look at the folders and files on your hard drive.

▶ We saw how the Windows Explorer two-pane view allows you to perform many file management tasks.

▶ We learned how to customize folders.

▶ We learned how to search for files.

▶ We learned how to move and copy single files and groups of files.

Chapter 8

Customizing Your Working Environment

In This Chapter

We show you how to personalize your computer to make you more efficient. You will learn the following:

▶ How to set up your Desktop.

▶ What the Taskbar Options are.

▶ The ins and outs of creating shortcuts to your files.

▶ Rearranging the Start Menu to make you more productive.

▶ Edit your file types so that you can take control of your file associations.

Taking Control

When you first launch Windows 2000, it is configured using defaults based on Microsoft's usability studies. These defaults represent an optimal setup for the average user.

However, you are not the average user. You already have your own working habits, developed either from working with other operating systems, or developed from your own real world experience in life. This chapter is about making Windows 2000 work in a way that's comfortable for you. Some changes we'll show you are cosmetic, while others can greatly speed you through your work.

When you first change a setting, such as moving the Taskbar to the top or to the side of your Desktop, the new environment may seem strange. However, after working in it for a while, not only will you become accustomed to it, but you will also see that it makes working in Windows 2000 easier.

User Profiles

There are many different ways in which to customize your computer. Windows 2000 keeps track of your customizations in a User Profile. By default, you are required to log on to Windows 2000 with a user name and password. When a new user is created on a Windows 2000 computer, the default user settings are copied into a new User Profile. These settings control the Desktop, the Taskbar, your Start Menu's appearance, your Favorites list, your local settings, your Internet settings; and so forth. As you begin to customize these settings, your changes are stored in your individual User Profile. Other users who log on to this computer and use their own profile will not be affected by the changes that other users make.

If you are on a network, you can store your preferences on a central server. This way, no matter where on the network you log on, your preferences will be available for you. Also, network administrators can — if they choose — set up preferences from a centralized, secure location if they don't want individual users making changes. Both of these features will be covered in Part V.

Tip

If you are the only person who is going to be using your Windows 2000 computer, and you are not connected to a network, you can disable the logon procedures. Click Start ⇨ Settings ⇨ Control Panel, and then click the Users and Passwords icon. Clear the selection Users enter a user name and password to use this computer.

Setting Up Your Desktop

You are going to be looking at your computer screen a lot, so it will probably be worthwhile for you to make your Desktop look attractive. You can do this in much the way you would decorate a physical Desktop, by adding pictures and other objects. In addition to decorative elements, you also can fine-tune your screen settings to suit your tastes, or just to make things easier to see.

Display Properties

The Display Properties dialog box is a mix of both decorative and hardware settings that determine how your Desktop looks. You can find Display Properties by clicking Start ⇨ Settings ⇨ Control Panel, and then clicking the Display icon. A faster way is to right-click an empty spot of your Desktop, and then click Properties on the shortcut menu.

Background tab

The Display Properties dialog box has six tabs that group together the many different settings that you can change. The first tab is for Background settings, as shown in Figure 8-1. The most important choice here is the ability to choose a picture to use as *wallpaper* on your Desktop. This picture can be centered, so that it displays in its actual size in the middle of your screen; tiled, so that it repeats over and over again; or stretched, so that the one image takes up the whole screen.

The selections you see in the list are all default bitmapped graphic files that come with Windows 2000. They are in your \Windows directory. You are not limited to just these choices. Any bitmapped graphic file having a .BMP extension can be used. You can even have one of your favorite pictures scanned — or find a graphic on the Web — to use as your wallpaper.

Tip

If you have a picture in .JPG or .GIF format, you can convert it to a .BMP file using the Microsoft Paint program located on the Start ⇨ Programs ⇨ Accessories Menu. If you have a graphic file in another format, you will have to use some other graphics editing program, such as Corel Draw or Paint Shop Pro, to convert the file.

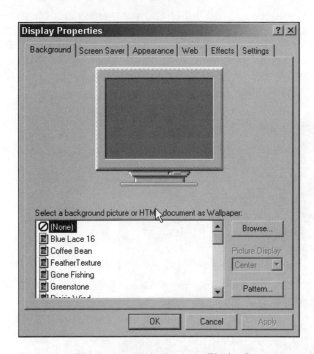

Figure 8-1: The Background tab on the Display Properties dialog box lets you add pictures to your Desktop.

Secret

If you browse the Web and see a graphic image you like, right-click the graphic and select Set As Wallpaper from the context menu. The graphic will be automatically downloaded and saved to your hard disk, and the Desktop will be configured to use it as wallpaper.

Caution

Graphic images on a Web site are generally covered by copyright laws. While most Web sites don't mind if you save one of their graphic files to display only on your computer, they certainly will object if you try to repackage and sell their image. Always ask. In addition to a picture, you also can select a pattern that will fill all the empty portions of your Desktop. By clicking the Patterns button, you can choose one of a number of eyestrain-inducing patterns that have been known to cause splitting headaches. Of course, it's all a matter of taste. With both wallpaper and patterns, you can always go back and choose None for both options to gain a less cluttered appearance.

Screen Saver tab

In the early days of PCs, monitors were susceptible to something called *burn-in*. If the same screen was constantly displayed on a monitor, the monitor would gradually develop a faint, but permanent, ghost image of that screen. To save your screen from this type of condition, screen savers were invented. After a certain period of screen inactivity, these programs would kick in and randomly fill your screen with images that prevented burn-in.

Modern monitors — together with built-in power management features — aren't nearly as prone to this kind of damage, but ever-more inventive screen savers have remained popular for their sheer entertainment value. To see the selection of screen savers that come with Windows 2000, select the Screen Saver tab, as shown in Figure 8-2, and then click the down arrow to the right of the list box to display your choices.

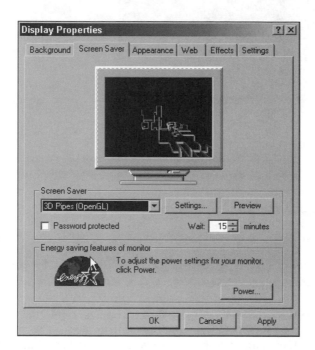

Figure 8-2: The Screen Savers that come with Windows 2000.

Some of the screen savers are quite venerable, such as Mystify, Scrolling Marquee, and Starfield Simulation, which makes it feel like you are back playing Atari Star Raiders. With more powerful graphics cards and processors, a number of quite mesmerizing 3D OpenGL screen savers were introduced with the Active Desktop.

The most important setting for screen savers is Wait Time, which is how long your system will wait before the screen saver kicks in. Once a screen saver has started, either a key press or a mouse movement will turn it off and restore your screen. For extra security when you are away from your computer, you can have your screen saver password protected, so that you have to type in your password to turn it off.

Tip
If a screen saver has activated while a word processor or similar program is running, turning off the screen saver with a key press might introduce an unwanted character into your work. Moving the mouse to turn off the screen saver is safer.

Individual screen savers also have settings that allow you to customize them. The 3D Text and the Scrolling Marquee screen savers allow you to type in your own message and select a font. Other screen savers allow you to tweak their settings in various ways. If you have subscriptions to any of the Active Channels over the Internet, you can choose them as your screen saver, as well.

Appearance tab

The Appearance tab shown in Figure 8-3 has controls that let you adjust individual settings of your screen's appearance. There are actually two ways you can make changes here: you can either choose one of Microsoft's predefined color schemes, or you can make changes to individual items and create your own color scheme.

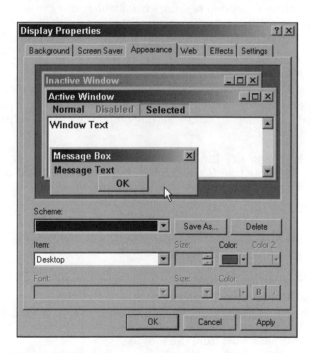

Figure 8-3: On the Appearance tab, you can make changes to individual screen elements.

A number of predefined color schemes come with Windows 2000 and can be selected from the Schemes drop-down list box. In addition to the Windows Standard, there are high contrast schemes, large font schemes, and some mood-setting schemes like Desert, Eggplant, Lilac, and Rainy Day. If you don't like any of the schemes, you can create your own. There are 18 individual screen elements that can be customized. Choose one of the individual screen elements from the drop-down list, such as Desktop (Figure 8-3), and then apply your own color scheme using the steps in the following exercise:

STEPS:
Changing the Desktop Color

Step 1.   Right-click an empty spot of your Desktop.

Step 2.   Click Properties from the shortcut menu.

Step 3.   Click the Appearance tab on the Display Properties dialog box.

Step 4.   Select Desktop from the items drop-down list.

Step 5.   Click the Color list. If none of the colors on the drop-down list interest you, click Other.

Step 6.   An enhanced selection of colors from which you can select a color are available from this dialog box. Select one and click OK, and then click OK again to close the Display Properties dialog box.

Note

The number of color options you have available will depend on the color depth setting you have selected on the Settings tab of the Display Properties dialog box.

The default font for menus in Windows 2000 is Tahoma. If you would like to change it back to the more traditional MS Sans Serif—or even to a more decorative font—follow these steps:

STEPS
Changing the Font Menu

Step 1.   Repeat Steps 1–3 in "Changing the Desktop Color."

Step 2.   Select Menu from the Item drop-down list.

Step 3.   Select MS Sans Serif from the font list.

Step 4.   You can make the menu choices larger by increasing the font size. Note that the font size, which is on the lower row of the dialog box, shouldn't exceed the menu size, which is the choice immediately above it.

Step 5. Click OK, if you are finished making changes, or click Apply to save your changes and leave the dialog box open for further changes.

Tip

If you work through the list and create your own scheme, click the Save As button, name it, and then add your creation to the rest of the schemes. This way, you can switch to the Windows Standard scheme, but still come back to your own scheme later.

Web tab

The Web tab is where you add Active Content to your Desktop (see Figure 8-4). We introduced Active Content in Chapter 6.

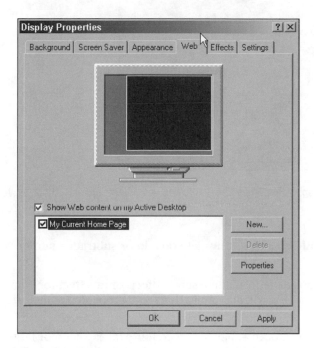

Figure 8-4: The Web tab lets you add Active Content to your Desktop.

Effects

The Effects tab, shown in Figure 8-5, lets you make some advanced adjustments to your Desktop preferences. The upper box lets you change the icon for the basic Desktop objects such as My Computer, My Network Places, and the Recycle Bin. Select the icon you would like to change and click the Change Icon button.

Secret

You will be presented with a choice of icons that Microsoft has included in the windows\system32\shell32.dll file. If you have your own custom icons, you can use those either by typing in their path and filename in the box, or by searching for them with the Browse button.

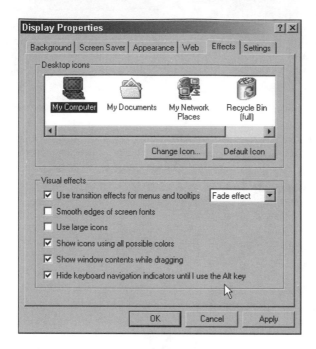

Figure 8-5: The Display Properties Effects tab lets you adjust various settings on your Desktop.

The rest of the Effects tab settings let you add or subtract a number of other visual effects:

- You can choose a fade effect, a scroll effect, or no effect for your menus and ToolTips. This will add animations to the opening and closing of these items.

- The option to smooth edges of screen fonts takes effect for large fonts, and it aims to avoid the jagged edges they sometimes have. This option won't work unless your video card and monitor support 256-color mode, and they work best in high color, or 16-bit, mode.

- You can choose to use large icons on your Desktop, rather than the standard icons. A drawback to this is that large icons use more memory than small icons, and they could slow down your system's performance.

- Using all possible colors when displaying the icons is primarily a cosmetic setting, and will appear more often in the icons as a color fade effect, rather than as solid colors.

■ The next item, Show window contents while dragging, could have a performance effect. When it is enabled and you drag a window, you will see the entire window moving across the screen in real time. If it is disabled, the window stays in place, and all you see is the outline of the window as it moves.

Tip If you have a 400 MHz processor and 8MB of video RAM, it doesn't make a difference if Show Window content is enabled or disabled; the window will drag smoothly across the screen. If you are running Windows 2000 on an underpowered system and this option is enabled, there may be a slight delay while the screen redraws.

■ The last item, Hide keyboard navigation characters until I use the Alt key, will suppress the underlined characters in menus and controls, as well as the dotted rectangles around objects, until you start using the keyboard to navigate in Windows.

Settings tab

Some of the most powerful changes you can make to your display can be found on the Settings tab, shown in Figure 8-6. From this tab, you can change both your screen resolution and your color depth, both of which have a tremendous effect on the appearance of your screen.

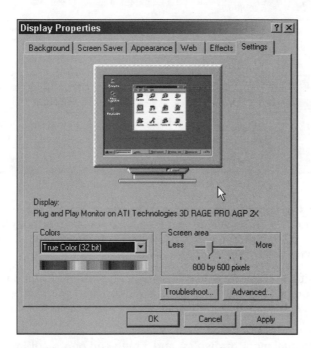

Figure 8-6: You can change your screen resolution and your color depth from the Settings tab.

Your Settings tab may appear slightly different than the one shown, because your options depend on your display adapter and monitor, which will be listed under the mock display of your Desktop at the top of the dialog box. Your color depth shows the maximum number of colors that can be displayed on your screen at one time. You have the choice of: 256 colors; High Color — which can display a maximum of 65536 colors — and True Color — which can show over 16 million colors at once.

Tip

If you want a photo-realistic color display, you need to increase your color depth to True Color. The higher the color resolution, the more processor power is needed to handle it. Fast computers with an abundance of video RAM can handle the load with no problems. If your machine doesn't have that power, you may want to move down to High Color or lower.

The Screen area control lets you determine how much information you can display on your screen, and how big or small that information will appear. Table 8-1 shows the alternative screen resolutions available, although not all will be supported on your hardware. The measurements are in shown pixels, which is shorthand for picture elements.

Table 8-1   Alternative Video Resolutions

Width	Height	Comment
640	480	With a 13- or 14-inch monitor, this may be your optimal screen resolution.
800	600	Works well with a 15-inch monitor.
1024	768	Things will be very small unless you have a 19-inch or larger monitor.
1152	864	Not all monitors and display adapters support the higher resolutions.
1280	1024	Super high resolution.

The lower the resolution, the larger items will appear on your screen; however, the overall Desktop will appear small. As you switch to higher resolutions, your overall screen area will appear to increase, but all the individual items on the screen will be smaller.

Note

There is an inevitable trade-off: you can display more information on your screen, but as you increase the resolution, you increase the risk of eyestrain. Experimentation is the key to finding your most comfortable working environment.

Secret

If you are using a dual monitor display, and a high-end photo editing application like Adobe Photoshop, you can set the primary monitor, which displays your photo, in super-high resolution. You can then locate the toolbars to the second monitor, which can be set at a lower resolution.

Need glasses?

While many people are interested in seeing how they can get more information onto the screen, there are others who, due to poor eyesight, want to make things easier to read. Here are some things to try:

STEPS:

To make the screen easier to read

Step 1.   Right-click an empty area of the Desktop, and then click Properties from the shortcut menu.

Step 2.   Click the Settings tab.

Step 3.   Slide the Screen Area selector all the way to the left, until it selects 640 x 480. Click Apply.

Step 4.   Click the Appearance tab.

Step 5.   Click the button to the right of the Schemes drop-down list, and select either Windows Standard Large, or Windows Standard Extra Large. Click OK.

Step 6.   Click Start ➪ Settings ➪ Control Panel. Click the Mouse Properties icon.

Step 7.   Click the Pointers tab. In the Schemes list, try either the Windows Standard Large or Windows Standard Extra Large settings. Click OK.

Tip

If you have problems with colors, experiment with one of the high contrast color schemes.

Bringing order to icons

When Windows 2000 is first installed, the icons are lined up in a column on the left side of your screen. As you add more icons, you can place them randomly on your Desktop, or you can use some of the organizing tools that come with Windows 2000 to bring some order to your Desktop.

While you can't see it, there is a grid on your Desktop that can hold and center your icons. The default size of each of the cells in this grid is 75 pixels. To see how this grid works, you need to mess up your Desktop first.

STEPS:

Using icon controls

Step 1. By clicking and dragging, move your Desktop icons (My Computer, the Recycle Bin, and others) to random spots on your Desktop.

Step 2. Right-click the Desktop and click Line Up icons. This will cause the icons to center themselves in the grid. While the icons may still be scattered around the Desktop, they will be centered within their grid cells, appearing to be lined up evenly with one another.

Step 3. Right-click the Desktop again, click Arrange Icons, and then select Auto Arrange. This will arrange all your icons in a column or columns, starting with the upper-left corner of the Desktop. The icons will again be centered within the grid cells.

Step 4. Auto Arrange works as a toggle switch. Once you select Auto Arrange, it stays selected, displaying a check mark next to it on the menu, until you disable it. Try to click and drag one of your icons to some other spot on the Desktop. It will spring back into the columns, moving to the end of the line, with the other icons moving up to fill in the empty spot.

If you want to arrange icons in your own fashion, you will need to disable Auto Arrange. This will give you full control of your icon placement.

Tip

Some users organize icons by function. Icons for Internet-related programs, such as Internet Explorer or Outlook Express, might go in the upper-right corner, while shortcuts to documents they are working on go in the lower-right corner. Others like to keep their icons lined up on the left so they know where they are.

You can change the size of the icon grid to give either more or less space between your icons. To do this, follow these steps:

STEPS:

Changing icon spacing

Step 1. Right-click the Desktop and choose Properties.

Step 2. Select the Appearance tab.

Step 3. Open the Item field by clicking its drop-down arrow.

Step 4. Select Icon Spacing ⇨ Horizontal. Decrease the spacing from the default 43 to 40. Click Apply.

Step 5. Repeat Steps 3 and 4 for Icon Spacing ⇨ Vertical. Click OK.

Taking these steps decreases the size of the grid from 75 pixels (the 43 for the spacing plus the 32-pixel width of the icon) to 72 pixels. When you right-click the Desktop and choose either Line up Icons or Auto Arrange, the icons will be closer together. You can try for even closer spacing between the icons by decreasing the spacing even more, or you can spread things out farther by increasing the spacing.

If you decrease the spacing too much, the icons might begin to overlap. This will make it difficult to select the correct icon when you click with the mouse.

Customizing the Taskbar

You do not have to accept the appearance of the Taskbar as a given. There are a number of adjustments you can make so that it will be more useful to you.

Taskbar toolbars

Right-clicking an empty area of the Taskbar brings up a shortcut menu that lets you enhance your Taskbar. Select the Toolbars option at the top to see the toolbars you can add to your Taskbar (see Figure 8-7).

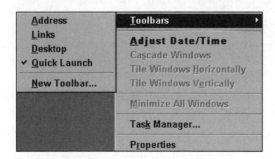

Figure 8-7: You can add these additional toolbars to the Taskbar.

■ The **Address Bar** allows you to type in an address to display, either for a file or folder on your computer, or you can type in a Web page address to start your browser and connect to the Internet.

■ The **Links** toolbar displays the special toolbar that you can configure in Internet Explorer 5. (See Chapter 12 for more information.)

- The **Desktop** toolbar can place copies of all your Desktop icons onto your toolbar.

- The **Quick Launch** toolbar is enabled by default in Windows 2000, but you can also disable it here.

A line appears on the upper edge of every toolbar. Hover the mouse pointer over the line and the cursor changes to a double-headed arrow. You can click and drag to expand or contract a toolbar. If the entire toolbar can't be shown, you will see a chevron symbol on the right side, similar to the chevron on the personalized menus. Clicking this chevron will display the rest of the toolbar.

Toolbars are not limited to being placed on the Taskbar, either. Point with the mouse cursor to the line, and then click and drag it until it is over the Desktop. Then, release the mouse button. The toolbar then becomes a window on the Desktop that can be moved or resized like any other window. Right-click the toolbar, and then select Always on Top from the context menu to have the toolbar display on top of any application window. If it gets in your way, click the Close button in the upper-right corner to remove the toolbar. If you want it back, right-click the Taskbar, click Toolbars, and then select it again. This will bring it back to the Taskbar.

You also can create a new toolbar to place on the Taskbar using the following steps:

STEPS:

Adding a new toolbar to the Taskbar

Step 1. Right-click an empty portion of the Taskbar.

Step 2. From the context menu, click Toolbars ⇨ New Toolbars.

Step 3. This will open the New Toolbar selection dialog box. You can choose a folder on your computer, or you can type in an Internet address.

Step 4. Click the Control Panel. This will display the Control Panel icons as a toolbar on your Taskbar.

Step 5. To remove the new toolbar, repeat Steps 1 and 2, and deselect the new toolbar.

Tip

How can all these toolbars fit on the Taskbar? You can make the Taskbar larger. Hover the mouse pointer on the upper edge of the Taskbar, and the pointer changes into a double-headed arrow. Clicking and dragging upward will let you expand the Taskbar until it takes up as much as half of your screen.

Quick Launch toolbar

The Quick Launch toolbar was introduced in Windows 98. It is a container for shortcuts. The Quick Launch toolbar is expandable by clicking and dragging its right border. To add a shortcut from the Desktop to the Quick Launch toolbar, simply click and drag the shortcut and drop it onto the Quick Launch toolbar. To delete a shortcut already on the toolbar, right-click the shortcut it and click Delete.

Tip

The icon that looks like a desk blotter isn't actually a shortcut, but a Windows Explorer command. It minimizes all your open windows; in other words, it functions as a shortcut to your Desktop. However, that is not the only way to minimize all open windows. If you right-click the Taskbar, you can choose Minimize all Windows from the shortcut menu. If you have a Windows Logo key on your keyboard, pressing the Windows key+D keyboard combination also works as a toggle switch to minimize and maximize all windows.

Moving the Taskbar

You can move the Taskbar to a different spot on the Desktop. Since most applications have a menu at the top of their window that requires mouse clicks, moving the Taskbar to the top of the Desktop saves you from moving the pointer from the top to the bottom of the Desktop.

STEPS:

Moving the Taskbar

Step 1. Move your mouse pointer over an empty area of the Taskbar (not over the Quick Launch Bar, system tray, or a program button).

Step 2. Click and hold the mouse button.

Step 3. With the mouse button still held down, move the taskbar to one of the sides, or to the top, of your Desktop.

Step 4. When you arrive at one of the edges, an outline of the Taskbar will appear. Release the mouse button.

Step 5. To move the taskbar back, repeat the preceding steps, but moving the taskbar back to its original position on the lower edge of your screen.

Taskbar properties

There are a number of other adjustments you can make to the Taskbar. Right-click an empty portion of the Taskbar and click Properties, or click Start ⇨ Settings ⇨ Taskbar & Start Menu.

Always on Top

If Always on Top is enabled, no other window will be able to obstruct the Taskbar; it should always be visible. When it is disabled, other windows will be free to expand over the Taskbar. Sometimes, they will do such a good job of it that it will be difficult to find the Taskbar without closing or shrinking some windows.

Tip

If you have a keyboard with the Windows logo key, you can use this key to quickly bring the Taskbar into view.

Auto Hide

When Auto Hide is checked, the Taskbar disappears when you click something else. It will stay hidden until you move your mouse back to the edge of the screen where the Taskbar is docked. If you don't click the Taskbar and you move your mouse more than ten pixels away, it will hide again. Clicking the Taskbar after it appears gives it the focus, and it will remain in view until you click something else. It will stay in view even if you move the mouse pointer elsewhere.

Tip

To make sure you can see the Taskbar, make sure Always on Top is checked if you Auto Hide. Otherwise, when the Taskbar comes back, it could be hidden behind other windows. You will either have to move the other windows, or use the Windows logo key to restore the Taskbar.

The major advantage of hiding the Taskbar is to gain screen real estate. However, you may find yourself accidentally restoring the Taskbar if the mouse pointer strays into its territory. You may find yourself with awkward pauses as you wait for your screen to redraw.

If Auto Hide is disabled, most windows will stay out of the Taskbar's way so that it is always visible. Other windows also might have an Always on Top property, too, which means that if they have the focus, they will still be on top of the Taskbar.

Small icons

Selecting the Show Small Icons in Start menu option will shrink the total size of the Start Menu, which will allow you to add more shortcuts to it without it becoming too large for your screen. (See "Customizing the Start Menu," later in this chapter.) Figure 8-8 shows an example of both small and large icons in the Start Menu.

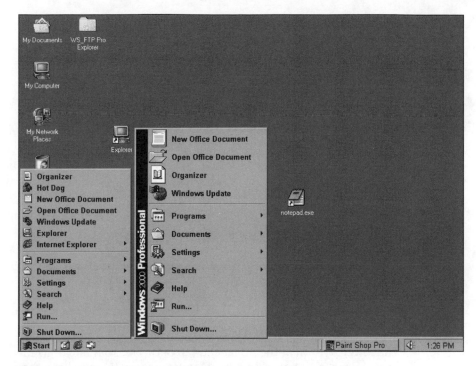

Figure 8-8: Using small icons for the Start Menu, compared to large icons.

The Start Menu

The Start Menu is also configurable. You have a number of choices to make in displaying items, in addition to adding, subtracting, and rearranging the shortcuts on the Start ➪ Programs Menu. Click Start ➪ Settings ➪ Taskbar & Start menu and go to the Advanced tab. The upper portion of the Advanced tab of the Taskbar and Start Menu Properties dialog box (shown in Figure 8-9) lets you do this. We will see how to manipulate shortcuts in the next section.

The middle portion of this dialog box lets you clear your Documents Menu. The Documents Menu lists your most recently opened files, and it also provides a shortcut for you to quickly open these documents. Some applications, however, cannot add their files to the Documents Menu.

Figure 8-9: The Start Menu Options section of the Taskbar and Start Menu Properties dialog box.

Start Menu options

The lower portion of the Advanced tab of the Taskbar and Start Menus Properties dialog box is new. It lets you add selections to both the Programs Menu (which you could do in Windows 98 using the Customize Start Menu dialog box) and to the Start Menu. The following items can be added to the Start Menu:

■ **Favorites**: a copy of your Favorites Menu from the Internet Explorer 5 (or the Favorites panel in the Explorer Bar). This feature was added in Windows 98.

■ **Logoff**: an option to log off as the current user can be added next to the Shut Down option. You also can access the Logoff option from the drop-down list after selecting Shut Down.

Other options in this dialog box either let you add entries to the Program Menu or let you expand other entries. Display Administrative Tools adds a shortcut to the Administrative Tools folder on your Programs Menu. The other way to access it is in the Control Panel.

 Expand My Documents: At the top of the Documents Menu is an entry for the My Documents folder. Clicking this will open the My Documents folder in a single pane folder view. If Expand My Documents is selected, clicking Start ⇨ Documents ⇨ My Documents becomes an extension of the Start Menu instead, with each subfolder under My Documents having its own expanding menu.

You can also change the Control Panel, Network and Dial up Connections, and Printers folders into extensions of the Start Menu. This way, if you click Start ⇨ Settings ⇨ Control Panel, you will get another menu with all of the Control Panel icons, rather than just seeing the Control Panel folder itself.

Personalized menus

Windows 2000 introduces a major new usability feature: Personalized Menus. Windows 2000 tracks how often you use the various shortcuts on your Start ⇨ Programs Menu. After awhile, it will begin to hide shortcuts that you almost never use, promote shortcuts (show them higher on the menu) that you use the most, and demote shortcuts that are less frequently used.

Even if this feature is enabled, personalized menus will not be immediately visible. It will take some time for Windows 2000 to track your usage patterns and decide which icons are frequently or infrequently used. You will realize this is working when you click Start ⇨ Programs, and suddenly say "Hey. Where did all my shortcuts go!" You will note a chevron symbol at the bottom of the Program Menu. Clicking this symbol or hovering your mouse pointer over a personalized menu for a few seconds will restore the entire menu. Submenus that branch out from the Program Menu also have the chevron symbol, and they also can be expanded to reveal the hidden shortcuts, as shown in Figure 8-10.

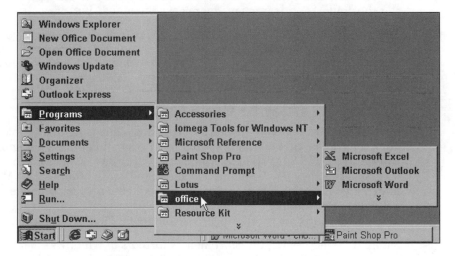

Figure 8-10: To expand the personalized menus, either click the chevron symbol, or leave the menu open and wait a few seconds.

If you decide you do not want to use Personalized Menus, click Start ⇨ Settings ⇨ Taskbar & Start Menu. Click the Advanced tab. Then, in Start Menu Settings, clear the Use Personalized Menus check box.

It will take longer for items to move to the hidden portion of the menu than it will for items to be promoted or demoted.

Arranging Start Menu items

When new shortcuts are added to the Start Menu, they often end up in inconvenient spots. Some suites, like Microsoft Office, put all their entries directly on the Programs Menu, which can lead to long, cumbersome menus. Others insist on adding a folder to the Start Menu, even if there is only going to be a single item in the folder. There are a number of ways in which you can rearrange and reorganize menu items to make your Programs Menu more productive.

Changing the order of shortcuts

One of the simplest steps you can take is to change the order of shortcuts on the menu. You can move an entry so that it appears higher, lower, or somewhere in between. This can be done directly on the Start ⇨ Programs Menu.

To change the order of an item, expand the Start Menu until you see the item you want to move. Click the shortcut and hold the mouse button down. Then drag the shortcut to its new location. A heavy black line will indicate where the shortcut will appear when you release the mouse button.

You are not restricted to having an item stay on the same menu. If you move up to where another menu branches off, the menu will expand, and you can then drop the shortcut there. You also can move it to the left, and then drop it on top of the Start Menu.

Adding a folder to the Start Menu

Each expanding menu on the Start ⇨ Programs menu is actually a folder in your user profile that contains shortcuts. The location differs depending on whether you have upgraded to Windows 2000, or have done a clean install. If an upgrade, they will be in the *Windows*\Profiles*username*\Start Menu folder. If you have done a clean install, they will be in your \Documents and Settings folder, found under the appropriate user name. You can add new menus and shortcuts by viewing these folders in Windows Explorer.

Similar to Windows NT, the Start Menu shortcuts in Windows 2000 actually come from two different folders. Each individual user has a Start Menu, plus there is a common All Users Menu that is shared by everyone. When you create a shortcut, it can be placed either in your individual menu, or the shared menu (see Figure 8-11).

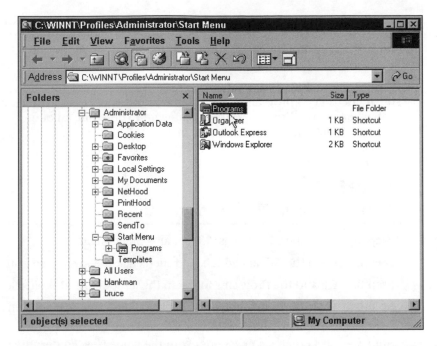

Figure 8-11: The Administrator's Start menu. On this computer, there are also settings for the other users (bruce, blankman) and for All Users.

STEPS:

Configuring Start Menu Shortcuts

Step 1.   Click Start ⇨ Settings ⇨ Taskbar & Start Menu.

Step 2.   Click the Advanced tab, and then click the Advanced button.

Step 3.   This will open the Windows Explorer at your Start Menu shortcuts, which is in your *Windows*\Profiles folder. If you are logged on as the Administrator, you will see all the other user profiles. If you are logged on as a User, you will see only your own profile.

Step 4.   Expand the Programs folder by clicking the plus sign to the left of the Programs folder. Select the Programs folder in the left pane to see its contents in the right pane.

At this point, you can use all of the folder and file manipulation tricks from Chapter 7 to add folders, delete folders, make one folder a subfolder of another, or any other step that makes your Start Menu more useful to you. A few examples follow.

When you install Microsoft Office on your computer, it installs individual shortcuts to all its programs on the Start ⇨ Programs Menu — the first menu that expands from Programs. You might want to combine all of these into a submenu to limit the size of this first menu.

STEPS:

Combining the MS Office shortcuts

Step 1.   Click Start ⇨ Settings ⇨ Taskbar & Start Menu.

Step 2.   Go to the Advanced tab, and then click the Advanced button.

Step 3.   Expand the Programs folder in the left pane, and then select it.

Step 4.   Create a new subfolder by clicking File ⇨ New ⇨ Folder on the menu.

Step 5.   This creates a new folder with the name New Folder; the name will be highlighted in the right pane. Type a new name for the folder, such as Office or MSOffice, and then press Enter.

Step 6.   Click and drag the individual Microsoft Office application shortcuts (Microsoft Word, Microsoft Excel, and so on) to your new folder, which will then reduce the number of shortcuts in the Programs folder.

Instead of moving shortcuts to a subfolder so that an additional menu has to expand in order to can reach them, you can give a program a promotion.

Tip

Clicking and dragging either a folder or a shortcut and dropping it onto the Start folder in the left pane will move the folder or shortcut to the top of the Start Menu. This is a handy spot to put shortcuts for your most-used programs.

Secret

Here is a great little secret that showed up on the Windows 2000 beta pages. Drag and drop your My Computer icon on to your Start button. Not only do you get a shortcut to My Computer, like you would if you did this in Windows 95 or 98, but this is expandable. Select it, and it will expand, with each drive icon getting its own menu entry. Select one of the drives, and it will expand to show the folders or files it contains. Select one of the folders, and it will expand. With this shortcut, everything in your computer will be accessible from the Start menu.

Tip

You are not limited to creating shortcuts to programs. You also can create shortcuts to folders, and even to data files. If the target of your shortcut is a data file, the file will be opened in its associated program (see the next section, as well as "Customizing File Types," later in this chapter.)

The Startup folder

There is a special folder on the Start ➪ Programs Menu called Startup. Any shortcuts to programs in the Startup folder will be run automatically when you start Windows 2000. Some installation programs, like Microsoft Office, automatically add some shortcuts here. Utility programs may also place shortcuts here. If you decide you do not want to have these programs run when you start up, you can either delete the shortcuts or, better yet, move them to a new folder you create called NotStart. This way, if you decide you really need these shortcuts, it will be easy to move them back to the Startup folder.

Shortcuts

The most versatile tool for making your computer more productive is the shortcut. Shortcuts are used on the Desktop, and they make up most of the entries on the Start Menu. They also appear in toolbars, in documents, and in the Explorer. You can create a shortcut to just about anything — a program, a data file, a folder, or an Internet site.

If we didn't have shortcuts, there would be two ways in which you could run a program on your computer. You could use My Computer or the Windows Explorer to open the folder that holds the program, and then click on its icon; you could type in the program's name in either the Start ➪ Run dialog box or at the Command Prompt (like the good old DOS days). In either case, it would be a cumbersome process. By using shortcuts creatively, you can organize your workspace just about any way you like, and that speeds access to your work in the long run.

Shortcuts on the Desktop

Icons on your Desktop are shortcuts if there is a black and white arrow in the lower-left corner of the icon. The arrow is the ideal symbol for a shortcut; think of it as a pointer to a file.

STEPS:

Creating a Shortcut

Step 1. Right-click an empty portion of your Desktop.

Continued

STEPS:

Creating a Shortcut *(continued)*

Step 2. Point to New on the menu and then click Shortcut. This opens the Create Shortcut Wizard.

Step 3. If you know the path and filename of the program or file for which you want to create a shortcut, type it in the text box. Otherwise, click Browse to look for it.

Step 4. In the Browse for folder window, you may need to click the plus sign next to a drive or folder to expand its contents.

Step 5. In Windows 95/98, when you browsed for your target file, you were only shown program files by default, although you could configure the browse window to show all files. In Windows 2000, you are shown all files by default.

Step 6. Once you have found your target, select it and click Next. Then you need to name your shortcut. By default, the name of the file will be used, but you can name it anything you want. At the very least, you can dispense with the .exe on the end.

If the target of your shortcut is a data file, Windows 2000 will open the associated application and then load the file.

When you create a shortcut on the Desktop, the only thing being stored in the Desktop folder is the shortcut, not the actual item that the shortcut points to. Deleting the shortcut does not delete the target.

Microsoft's usability studies have shown that many people do not know that the underlying program is not deleted when you delete a shortcut. Therefore, when you delete a shortcut for most (but not all) programs, you will see the warning message shown in Figure 8-12.

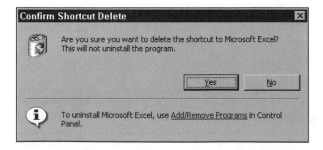

Figure 8-12: Deleting the shortcut will not delete the underlying program.

Tip

You can create shortcuts to the data files that you are currently working on. If you are writing a book, you can create a shortcut to your current chapter so that you can open it quickly. When you are done with that chapter and move on to the next, you can create a shortcut to your new chapter and delete the old shortcut. You also could create a shortcut to the folder that holds all your chapters. Clicking the shortcut opens the folder, and you can choose which file you want to open.

Shortcuts on the Start Menu

The entries you see on the Start ⇨ Programs Menu are actually shortcuts. Some of them are created when Windows 2000 is installed, some are automatically placed there when you install programs, and others can be created manually.

STEPS:

Creating a Start Menu shortcut

Step 1. Click Start ⇨ Settings ⇨ Taskbar & Start Menu.

Step 2. Go to the Advanced tab.

Step 3. In the Customize Start Menu section, click Add. The Create Shortcut Wizard appears, as shown in Figure 8-13.

Figure 8-13: Type or find the name of the shortcut's target.

Step 4. Choose the program or document you want as your target. If you don't know the path and filename, click the Browse button to find it. Click Next.

Continued

STEPS

Creating a Start Menu shortcut *(continued)*

Step 5. Now choose where on the Programs Menu you want the shortcut to appear (see Figure 8-14). To place the shortcut on a submenu, click the plus sign to the left of the parent menu.

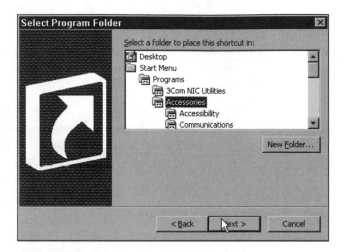

Figure 8-14: Choose where you want the shortcut to be placed on the Start or the Programs Menu.

Step 6. Finally, give the shortcut a name. The name of the program is used by default.

Tip

If you select the Start Menu folder as the destination for the shortcut, it will be placed on the Start Menu directly above the Programs Menu. This lets you quickly find a shortcut.

Shortcuts are interchangeable

If you have created a shortcut on your Desktop that you would like on the Start Menu, click and drag the shortcut over to the Start button, and release the mouse button. The shortcut will remain on the Desktop, but a copy will also appear at the top of the Start Menu.

You also can move or copy a shortcut from the Start Menu and place it on the Desktop.

STEPS:

Moving a shortcut from the Start Menu to the Desktop

Step 1. Expand the Start ⇨ Programs Menu until you see the shortcut you want to move.

Step 2. Right-click the shortcut and click Copy.

Step 3. To close the Start Menu without starting a program, click somewhere off the Start Menu.

Step 4. Right-click the Desktop and click Paste Shortcut.

Removing Shortcuts from the Start Menu

There are two ways to delete a shortcut from the Start Menu. If you are on Advanced tab of the Taskbar Properties dialog box (see Figure 8-9 earlier in this chapter), you can click the Remove button. It will open the Remove Shortcuts dialog box, which will let you choose which shortcuts you want to delete. You also can simply open the Start ⇨ Programs Menu, right-click the shortcut you want to delete, and then select Delete.

Shortcuts to drives and folders

You can create shortcuts to folders and drives, as well as to files. Open My Computer, and then click and drag one of the drive icons out of the My Computer window and onto the Desktop. When you release the mouse button, you will see the error message shown in Figure 8-15.

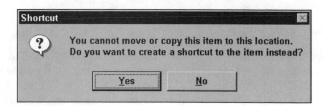

Figure 8-15: Dragging a drive icon to create a shortcut on the Desktop gives you this message.

Click Yes to create the shortcut. If you are connected to a network, you also can create shortcuts to shared folders or drives on the network.

Shortcut Properties

After a shortcut is created, you can make adjustments to how the shortcut behaves to make it more useful. Right-click a shortcut, either on the Desktop or on the Start Menu, to see the Explorer Properties dialog box shown in Figure 8-16. In Windows 2000, the dialog box has three tabs. The General tab is mostly informational, telling when the shortcut was created, last modified, and last accessed. You can rename the shortcut by changing the name in the text box near the top of the dialog box. You also can change the attributes of the shortcut to make it hidden or read-only.

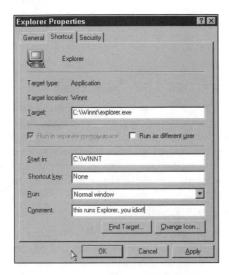

Figure 8-16: The Explorer Properties dialog box.

Change your target

The second tab in the Explorer Properties dialog box — the Shortcut tab — is where you can change a lot of the behaviors of the shortcut. If you want to change the target file for the shortcut, you can do so in the Target text box. If the filename can be used with optional arguments, you can add those arguments here. For instance, in the shortcut properties dialog box, the Windows Explorer executable file is the target. If you wanted the Windows Explorer to open showing the contents of the C:\ drive, you would modify the target to read:

```
C:\windows\explorer.exe c:
```

If your target is a data file, it would normally be opened by the program with which it is associated. For example, if the file is a text file, it would be opened with Notepad. If you want to open the text file with WordPad instead, you would change the target to read:

```
C:\Program Files\MSOffice\Office\WINWORD.EXE" e:\data\myfile.txt
```

Secret

If your target path has a space within the path's name, like C:\Program Files, you need to place the filename between quotation marks.

Run as other user

In the Target text box, you will find an option check box that lets you run this program as another user. When you click the shortcut, you will see the Run As Other User dialog box shown in Figure 8-17.

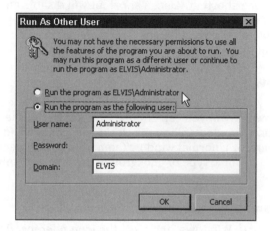

Figure 8-17: You can run a shortcut as another user, or you can keep your own identity.

You can either choose to run the target program with the current user name under which you are logged in, or you can switch to another user name, as long as you know the password. The other user must have the necessary permissions to run the program.

Start in

Some applications are particular about the folders in which they start. They may need to find some other files, or they may need to be able to look in the correct folder for data files. This is often referred to as the working directory. If your program has these requirements, you can fill in the correct directory in the Start in field. Most times, you will not need to enter anything here. An application can usually run without any problems from the directory in which it's located.

Tip

By default, Notepad will save the text documents it creates in your Windows folder — not a very good place for them. The Windows folder is jam-packed with important files. You can navigate elsewhere, but that can be tedious. If you have a shortcut to Notepad, display its properties and set its Start in location to your My Documents folder. That way, by default, your files go with your other data files.

Shortcut keys for shortcuts

You can specify a key combination that works as a keyboard shortcut, which is sometimes called a hot key. Pressing the key combination is the same as clicking the shortcut with the mouse. All shortcuts begin with Ctrl+Alt, which is added automatically in the dialog box. For example, if you type a Q in the box, the shortcut will be Ctrl+Alt+Q.

Note

You are not allowed to use the Esc, Enter, Tab, Spacebar, Print Screen, or the Backspace keys as part of a shortcut. Also, a shortcut will disable any access key in any program. For example, if you use Ctrl+Alt+F as the hot key for a shortcut, you will disable Alt+F (which opens the File Menu in any of the Microsoft Office applications).

Run in a window

The Run selection tells you what size window the application will be run in. By clicking the drop-down arrow, you can choose whether to run the application in a maximized window (filling the Desktop), a minimized window (a button on the Taskbar), or a normal window (something in between.) If this shortcut is pointing to some type of background process, you might opt to leave it minimized.

Change the icon

When you create a shortcut, Windows 2000 uses the icon referenced by the executable file. Some programs, such as the Windows Explorer, have multiple icons associated with them. If you created a shortcut to the Windows Explorer, right-click it, click Properties, and then click Change Icon. You will see the icon choices that are self-contained within the Windows Explorer, as shown in Figure 8-18.

Figure 8-18: These icons come with the Windows Explorer.

You wouldn't want to use many of these icons. They would be confusing, and you don't want to confuse the Windows Explorer with the Recycle Bin. However, there are some other files in Windows 2000 that hold a number of multi-purpose icons, and you can choose from among any of those. Click the Browse button in the Change icon dialog box, and then navigate to *Windows*\system32\SHELL32.dll, which has a large number of icons from which you can choose. There may also be a moricons.dll file in this folder, which holds other icons, many from some rather venerable applications.

Secret

You aren't limited to these icons. There are many icon library files available for downloading from the Internet, as well as icon editors and icon managers. You can even create your own icons in the Microsoft Paint applet. (See Chapter 9.)

Send to shortcuts

The SendTo Menu is available when you right-click an object on the Desktop, or from within My Computer or the Windows Explorer. The contents of this menu are also shortcuts that are contained in a special folder.

Open Windows Explorer and navigate to the Sendto folder. If you have upgraded to Windows 2000, it will be *Windows*\Profiles*username*\Sendto folder. If you have done a clean install, it will be in \Documents and Settings\. This folder contains shortcuts as well as some special links installed by either Windows 2000 or other installed applications, as shown in Figure 8-19. You can create your own shortcuts in the SendTo folder that will show up when you right-click an item.

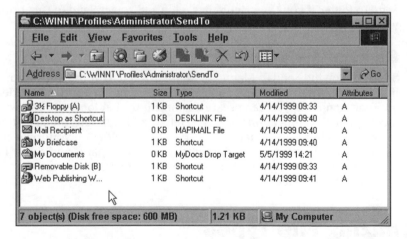

Figure 8-19: The SendTo folder contains shortcuts to drives, folders, devices, and programs.

Secret

You may run across small files with unassociated file extensions. These are often text files that contain settings or configuration information. To open these in Notepad, you can create a shortcut to Notepad in the SendTo folder.

STEPS:

Notepad shortcut in SendTo

Step 1.   In the Windows Explorer, locate the *Windows*\Profiles*username*\SendTo folder.

Step 2.   Click File ⇨ New ⇨ Shortcut.

Step 3.   Create a shortcut to Notepad.exe, either by typing in the path and filename, or by using the Browse dialog box.

Step 4.   Name the shortcut Notepad. Click Finish.

Now, if you right-click an object, you will have the choice of sending it to Notepad. (If it is not a text file, you will only see a mass of unintelligible symbols when you open the file.)

There should already be shortcuts to My Documents and to the A: drive in the SendTo folder, but you also can create shortcuts to other drives or folders, and even to printers, on your system. You can right-click, and then drag and drop one of the printer icons in your Printers folder over to your SendTo folder. If you then right-click a file and select SendTo this printer, you will be able to quickly print a file.

Shortcuts across a network

Shortcuts on the SendTo Menu are not restricted to your own computer. If you are on a network and you have access rights to a drive or folder on another computer, you can create a shortcut to that location. You will need to locate your target location using My Network Places, and then right-click the target and select Copy. Then, open The SendTo folder on your own computer using the Windows Explorer, right-click in the right pane, and select Paste Shortcut. You also might want to rename this shortcut to make the destination more clear.

Customizing File Types

Starting with Windows 95, Microsoft started to shift focus toward a document-first operating system (it's often been referred to as a docucentric concept). No longer would you need to start your word processing program and then load the document you wanted to work on. Now, you could just point to the document you wanted to work on, and let the operating system worry about opening the correct program.

This is most evident on the Documents Menu. You can click Start ⇨ Documents, and then click Chapter8.doc, and Windows 2000 would know that it needs to open Microsoft Word and then load Chapter8.doc. It knows this because it has associated the program Microsoft Word with the file extension .doc. When a program is installed in Windows 2000, it tells the operating system what file extensions it wants to claim. This information is stored in the Registry, and is used in opening files.

There is one problem with this: some file types are going to be claimed by more than one program. The most notorious example is probably the fight over the .htm and .html extensions by Netscape and Internet Explorer. You might also have two different graphics editing programs on your computer. You want your .bmp files opened with one, but they are associated with the other program.

Windows 2000 has enhanced flexibility with regard to file associations. To manage these associations, click Start ⇨ Settings ⇨ Control Panel, and then click the Folder Options icon. Click the File Types tab to display the dialog box shown in Figure 8-20.

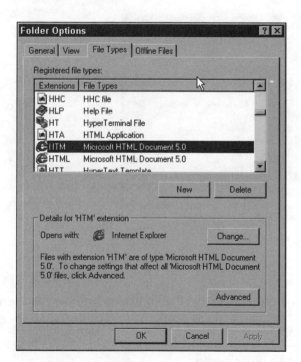

Figure 8-20: The File Types tab of the Folder Options dialog box shows what program is set to open a given file extension. Here, any .htm files will be opened by Microsoft Internet Explorer.

The scrolling window in the top of this dialog shows all the registered file types for this particular computer. To change the file association for text files, follow these steps:

STEPS:

Changing a file association

Step 1. Click Start ➪ Settings ➪ Control Panel.

Step 2. Click the Folder Options icon, and then click the File Types tab.

Step 3. Scroll down the list of registered file types until you find the entry for .txt files. Select it.

Step 4. In the Details section, you see that .TXT documents are associated with Notepad. To change this, click Change.

Step 5. In the Open With dialog box, shown in Figure 8-21, scroll down through the list of programs, until you find Word Pad. Select it, and then click OK.

Figure 8-21: Choose which program to open this file type.

Step 6. More customization can be done by clicking the Advanced button.

Step 7. This displays the Edit File Type. Click Change Icon to use a different icon with this file type. This is the icon that you see in My Computer or the Windows Explorer. You can either use one of the icons that comes with Windows 2000, or you can click Browse to choose a custom icon.

If you make changes, using these steps, a Restore button will appear, which you can use to go back to the default situation.

The Advanced button also can be used to add, delete, or change the file associations. Figure 8-21 shows the Open With dialog box for files having the .htm extension. Windows 2000 comes with both Internet Explorer and FrontPage Express, an HTML editor. When you click an HTM file in the Windows Explorer or My Computer, the default command — which is in boldface in the list — is invoked. Selecting open in the list and then clicking Edit will show that this file will be opened with the Internet Explorer.

Note

Results on your own computer may differ, depending on what programs you have installed, and what other file associations have been made.

Because this particular computer has the Hot Dog Web editor installed, there are two choices for editing this file. If you right-click an HTM file in the Windows Explorer, the shortcut menu will have a selection for Edit, which will open this file in FrontPage Express. There also will be a shortcut to Edit With Hot Dog, if you would rather use that program. In this particular case, the Hot Dog installation program added this file association. Figure 8-22 shows these associations between programs and file extensions.

Tip

If you want to add another option for editing, you can. Click New. Call the action Edit_with_Notepad. In Application Used to perform action, choose Notepad.exe (which should be in your Windows directory.) Now, when you right-click a file with this extension, you also have the choice to edit the file in Notepad.

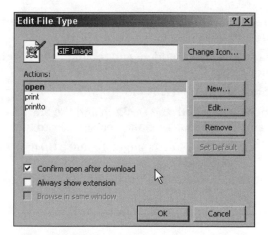

Figure 8-22: The associations between file types and programs for opening and editing are made in this dialog box.

Right Click Open With

When you make one of these changes in the file associations, it will work uniformly across your computer. Instead, if you face a one-time situation where you want to open a file with a different program, you can. Simply right-click the file and select Open With. You will then see a number of possible choices for opening a file, as well as Choose Program. Clicking this will open the Open With dialog box (shown previously in Figure 8-21). Note that there is a check box next to Always use this program to open this file. Do not select this box if you don't want to make this a system-wide, permanent change.

Accessibility Options

Microsoft has built a number of accessibility options into Windows 2000 for those with special computing needs. Some of the tools for eyesight accessibility were discussed in the Display Properties section; however, there are also tools for hearing and motor skills needs.

A basic set of tools can be found by clicking Start ⇨ Settings ⇨ Control Panel, and then clicking the Accessibility Options icon.

Summary

We show you the various ways in which you can customize your computer so that it works best for you:

- ▶ Most elements of the Desktop can be changed. Colors, sizes, and settings can all be manipulated, and decorative elements can be added.
- ▶ The Taskbar can be repositioned and hidden, and toolbars can be added to give easier access to shortcuts.
- ▶ We can customize the Start Menu to give us more options.
- ▶ We show how to add shortcuts to both the Desktop and the Start Menu. We also show how to rearrange the menus to make items easier to find.
- ▶ Individual properties of shortcuts can be changed to make them behave differently.
- ▶ We can edit file associations to open or edit files with different programs.

Chapter 9

Secrets of the Windows 2000 Applets

In This Chapter

We delve into little-known features of the small applications — or *applets* — that accompany Windows 2000. (These Windows applets should not be confused with *Java applets,* which are programs used in World Wide Web sites.) In this chapter, we discuss:

▶ The Registry Editor — or RegEdit — and its big brother, RegEdt32, and the roles they play in controlling your system configuration.

▶ Character Map, a utility that helps you insert any character or combination of characters from any fonts you have installed.

▶ Private Character Editor, a hidden applet that you can use in conjunction with Character Map to edit or insert your own custom characters within your documents.

▶ Calculator, an old but surprisingly useful scientific and statistical tool.

▶ The Windows 2000 games — Solitaire, Minesweeper, and FreeCell — including secret ways in which to manipulate them and even beat the house!

▶ Task Manager, a powerful weapon in the battle to keep your system running smoothly and efficiently.

▶ Notepad, which has gained additional new power under Windows 2000.

Secrets of the Registry Editor

By far the most powerful tools in the Windows 2000 arsenal are the Registry Editors. These utilities, also known as RegEdit (after its filename, regedit.exe) and RegEdit32, can do serious damage to your system if you mistakenly use them to delete items from your Windows 2000 Registry. They also can be your best friend when you need to change an obscure configuration setting in Windows.

The use of RegEdit and its sibling, RegEdt32.exe can help you find a configuration setting, troubleshoot problems, and make technical changes in Windows 2000, as well as in applications that use the Registry to store preferences. RegEdit's big brother, RegEdt32, has features that RegEdit does not, but both tools have their uses.

Neither RegEdit nor RegEdt32 appear on the default menus in Windows 2000. To use them, you must type their names into the Open text box in the Run dialog box, or create shortcuts for them on your desktop from which to launch either tool. Of course, since these utilities are advanced power tools, you might not *want* them to be easily available. If you use them frequently, however, you'll want them a click away.

STEPS:

Running RegEdit and RegEdt32

Step 1.　Click Start ⇨ Run.

Step 2.　In the Run dialog box's Open text box, type regedit or regedt32.

Step 3.　Click OK.

Figure 9-1 shows RegEdit just after its window has opened and you have clicked the plus sign to the left of the HKEY_CURRENT_USER key to expand its contents.

At this point, you can expand and explore:

- *keys,* which are shown in the left pane of RegEdit and RegEdt32; and,
- *value entries,* which are shown in the right pane.

Value entries have three parts:

- *names* shown in the right pane define the values contained by a key;
- *data types* determine the kind of data that is allowed in a value. Data types may be one of three styles:
  1. *string value,* which may consist of any characters of text;
  2. *binary value,* which is actually displayed as a hexadecimal value; or,
  3. *DWORD value,* which consists of four 8-bit bytes.
- *values,* which are the data associated with a name.

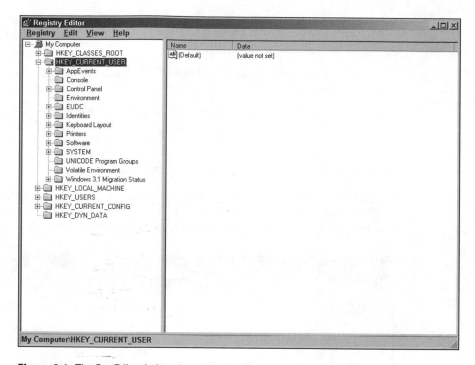

Figure 9-1: The RegEdit window, immediately after RegEdit opens regedit and expanding the HKEY_CURRENT_USER registry key.

Cross-Reference

More information about the Registry and what you might want or need to change in it is located in Chapter 16. In this chapter, what we are more interested in is how to use RegEdit and RegEdt32 as applets to quickly gain access to the registry keys we choose to inspect or alter.

Secret

Many people don't know that they can quickly expand all the subkeys within an entire major key (or all the subkeys within the entire Registry) using RegEdit. It's easy to do using the undocumented Alt+Keypad Asterisk keyboard combination.

STEPS:

Quickly expanding the Registry or a Registry key

Step 1. Run RegEdit.

Step 2. In RegEdit's left pane, click the folder icon near the key you want to expand, such as HKEY_CURRENT_USER.

Step 3. Hold down the Alt key, and then press the Asterisk (*) key on the numeric keypad. (Alt+Asterisk or Alt+Shift+8 on the main keyboard doesn't work.)

Secret

In RegEdt32, the key combination to expand all subkeys is Ctrl+Asterisk. In this case, you can use the asterisk key either on the numeric keypad or on the main keyboard (Ctrl+Shift+8).

To collapse a key you've expanded in RegEdt32, double-click the key or press the minus key on the numeric keypad or the main keyboard.

In RegEdit, pressing Alt+Keypad Asterisk immediately begins expanding the key you selected — including each subkey beneath the selected key. This is very handy if you don't remember exactly where the key you're looking for is located. It's much faster to press Alt+Keypad Asterisk than to manually click every plus sign to expand keys until you find the spot you want.

Figure 9-2 shows the effect of expanding all subkeys of the HKEY_CURRENT _USER registry key. The subkeys of this key, of course, continue far beyond the limits of the window we are able to show you in the figure.

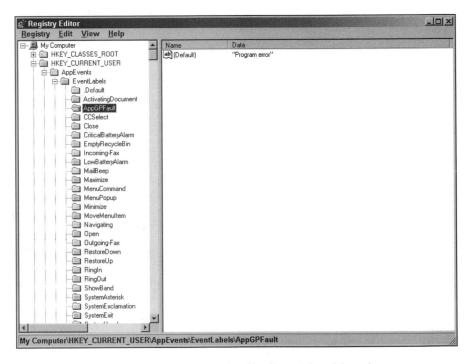

Figure 9-2: The RegEdit window, after pressing Alt+Keypad Asterisk on the HKEY_CURRENT_USER key, and then selecting the AppGPFault key in the left pane.

If you first select the My Computer icon before pressing Alt+Keypad Asterisk, this key combination will expand every key and subkey in the entire Registry. This can take a few minutes to complete, so plan to go get a cup of coffee if you choose to expand the entire Registry.

If it's taking too long to expand the keys you selected (or if you already see the subkey you want), you can stop the expansion process by pressing the Esc key.

There is one very mild side-effect of expanding every subkey within a key. When you collapse the key and then expand it again, it shows every subkey expanded exactly the way it was when the selected key was collapsed.

You might prefer to collapse a key and then expand it only to the first level of subkeys below it. (This is the original, default behavior when you expand a key.) It's easy to restore the original behavior, no matter how far you've expanded a key, by pressing the F5 key.

STEPS:

Restoring the default expansion behavior to a Registry key

Step 1. In RegEdit, collapse a key in the left pane by clicking the minus sign to the left of the folder you wish to collapse.

Step 2. Press the F5 key. When you expand this key by clicking its plus sign, the folder will expand only to the first level of subkeys.

RegEdit is documented by two compiled Windows Help files: RegEdit.hlp and RegEdit.chm. Of the two, RegEdit.chm is, by far, the more informative.

This file contains tips on how to search for a particular key, name, or value; how to add, modify, and delete keys and values; how to connect and edit a Registry across a network; and many other topics.

In Figure 9-2, for example, we see the AppGPFault subkey within the expanded HKEY_CURRENT_USER key. The AppGPFault subkey contains a default text string that is displayed when something crashes (in other words, when a General Protection Fault occurs). Using the techniques documented in RegEdit.chm to change a value, you could right-click the name Default, click Modify, and then change the string "Program error" to "Microsoft error." We're not suggesting that anyone actually do this, of course.

If you like, it's easy to read RegEdit.chm without even opening RegEdit. Simply type regedit.chm into the Run dialog box's Open text box, or right-click the file to open it with the Internet Explorer (see Figure 9-3).

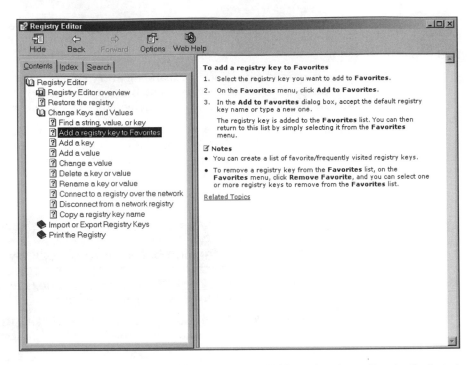

Figure 9-3: The RegEdit.chm help file, with the topic "Add a registry key to Favorites" selected.

RegEdit's big brother, RegEdt32, is more useful when you want to compare the contents of two different keys side-by-side.

RegEdt32 provides a *multiple document interface (MDI)* for the five major keys within the Registry. This means that you can see more than one window at a time. Figure 9-4 shows a copy of RegEdt32 with the Console key selected beneath the HKEY_CURRENT_USER key in the left pane of the foreground window.

As you can see, Figure 9-4 shows the five major keys in five windows that are *cascaded.* To see a part of all five windows at once, pull down the Window menu, and then click Tile. The Tile command resizes all five windows. You can then drag the windows with your mouse until the two windows you want to compare are in positions you want.

RegEdt32 uses a different set of conventions than RegEdit. For example, instead of single-clicking the plus sign to the left of a folder you wish to expand, as in RegEdit, you must double-click a folder you wish to expand in RegEdt32, or you must press the plus key on the numeric keypad or the main keyboard.

You also must double-click value entries you want to modify in the right pane of RegEdt32, instead of right-clicking the entries and then clicking Modify, as you do in RegEdit.

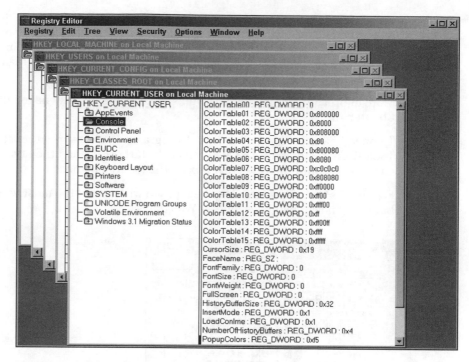

Figure 9-4: The RegEdt32 window with the Console key selected.

RegEdt32 supports several features that RegEdit does not. The most important incremental features are on the Security menu: Permissions, Auditing, and Ownership. The uses of these options are adequately described when you pull down RegEdt32's Help menu, click Contents, and then select Maintain Registry Security.

Separate from RegEdit's help file, RegEdt32 is documented by its own file — regedt32.chm.

Character Map

Character Map is an important applet for Windows users who wish to insert special characters into their documents. It's even more significant now that Windows 2000 includes full *multilingual support,* as well as *Unicode.*

Multilingual support enables you to install fonts that provide all the characters used by virtually all the written languages of the world. Unicode is an international standard with more than 65,000 possible characters (or *glyphs,* as they are known in typographical land). Over 38,000 Unicode glyphs have been defined as of this writing, with about 21,000 being used for Chinese characters alone.

Unicode uses 16 bits of data to encode each character, while the older ANSI standard in Windows 9x used 8 bits. This doesn't necessarily mean a document that uses Unicode will be twice as large, however. Word processing documents with substantial overhead, for example, may be less than twice the size in Unicode, compared with ANSI.

Cross-Reference

More information on multilingual support and Unicode may be found in Chapter 18.

To open Character Map, click Start ⇨ Programs ⇨ Accessories ⇨ System Tools ⇨ Character Map. You also can click Start ⇨ Run, and then type charmap.exe into the Open text box on the Run dialog box.

Figure 9-5 shows Character Map being used with one of the most versatile, but little-known, Windows fonts — Wingdings.

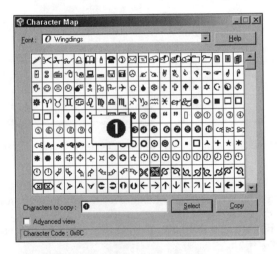

Figure 9-5: The CharMap applet in its standard view, with the Wingdings symbol font displayed. The "bulleted 1" symbol (Alt+0140) has been selected and copied to the Clipboard.

Tip

The Wingdings font, which contains over 200 useful and scalable Open Type symbols, has been installed by default on all Windows systems since Windows 3.1. For this reason, you can include Wingdings characters in any document that will be opened by users of Windows 3.1, Windows 9x, Windows NT, or Windows 2000. Users of any of these versions of Windows will be able to view and print the symbols you've included in your document.

Character Map enables you to select a special character from any installed font and insert that character into a document — without knowing the numerical position of that character within the font file.

To insert a "bulleted 1" symbol into a document manually, for example, follow these steps:

STEPS:

Manually inserting a Wingdings character into a document

Step 1. In an application that supports different fonts, select Wingdings.

Step 2. Make sure the NumLock light is on.

Step 3. Hold down the Alt key, type 0140 on the numeric keypad to insert a "bulleted 1" character, and then release the Alt key.

Step 4. Change the current font back to the original font you were using.

Using Character Map, you also could insert this character into a document without knowing its numerical value:

STEPS:

Inserting a Wingdings character using Character Map

Step 1. Click Start ⇨ Run, type charmap.exe, and then select the Wingdings font.

Step 2. Double-click the "bulleted 1" character (or click it, and then click the Select button). After you've selected all the characters you want, click the Copy button.

Step 3. In your application, click Edit ⇨ Paste. Your selected characters appear at the current cursor position in your document.

Character Map might be even more useful to you in inserting characters from languages other than the main keyboard language used in your system. Figure 9-6 shows the Windows 2000 Arabic Transparent font, which includes most Western characters, as well as an extensive collection of the glyphs used in the Arabic language.

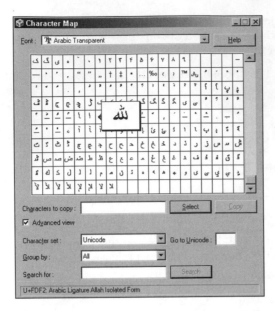

Figure 9-6: The CharMap applet, with the Arabic Transparent font selected and Unicode character FDF2 selected.

The Arabic Transparent TrueType font available for installation with Windows 2000 (as well as other fonts, such as Traditional Arabic) includes initial, isolated, final, and ligature forms of each glyph, where appropriate. Characters in Arabic can require a different form depending on whether they appear at the beginning, middle, or end of a word. The lack of different forms for such characters was a severe flaw in earlier attempts at supporting the Arabic language in computers.

More information about these and other Windows 2000 fonts — including character charts showing the symbols you can insert into documents — can be found in Chapter 18.

Private Character Editor

One of the benefits of fonts that support the Unicode standard is their support for *private characters*. These are characters that occupy "empty" positions in the font — in other words, no other character already resides in that numeric sequence. Unicode fonts include many such positions into which anyone can insert extra characters of their choice — perhaps a special symbol or a glyph that is used in for a single company.

Secret

One of the intriguing new features related to Character Map is the hidden Private Character Editor. This applet (eudcedit.exe) enables you to change the appearance of standard characters and to store the new character within one or all of the fonts on your system. The new character can then be used in any of your documents.

Figure 9-7 shows the Private Character Editor being used to change the registered trademark symbol (Alt+0174) into a circle-P character. This character is often used in the recording industry as part of the legal notices for a music album.

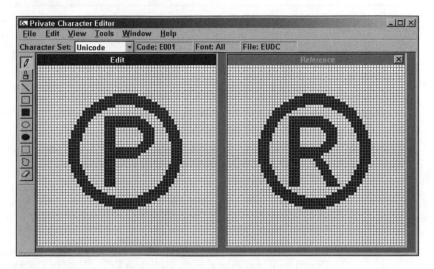

Figure 9-7: The Private Character Editor, with a registered trademark symbol (right) being edited into a new circle-P symbol like the one used in the recording industry (left).

Here's how to start and use the Private Character Editor (it doesn't show up on any of the Windows 2000 menus):

STEPS:

Using Private Character Editor to create special characters

Step 1. To start Private Character Editor, click Start ➪ Run, and then type eudcedit.exe into the Open text box. Click OK.

Step 2. When the Select Code dialog box appears, select a position in which to insert your new character, or accept the default choice of Unicode position E000. Click OK.

Step 3. If you do not want your new character to exist in all installed fonts, pull down the File menu and choose Font Links. In the Font Links dialog box, click Link with Selected Fonts, and then select a font to link your new character to. Click OK, select a filename for your new character, and then click OK.

Step 4. Pull down the Edit menu, and then click Choose Character.

Continued

STEPS:

Using Private Character Editor to create special characters

(continued)

Step 5. In the Copy Character dialog box, click the Font button. Select the font you want to use for the sample character (such as Arial). Click OK.

Step 6. Select the character you want to edit, such as the registered trademark symbol. Click OK.

Step 7. Back in the main Private Character Editor dialog box, pull down the Window menu and click Reference.

Step 8. In the Reference dialog box, click the Font button. Select the font you want to use for the reference character (probably the same font you selected in Step 3, such as Arial). Click OK.

Step 9. Select the character you want to use as a reference (probably the same character you selected in Step 4, such as the registered trademark symbol).

Step 10. Back in the main Private Character Editor dialog box, select the Pencil tool and edit the glyph in the Edit window. Clicking the left mouse button over a pixel turns that pixel black (writes). Clicking the right mouse button turns a pixel white (erases). Select other tools to paint areas or draw shapes.

Step 11. Select the Rectangular Selection button or the Freeform Selection button to select an area within the Edit window and move it. (For example, after removing the "tail" from the R to change it into a P, move the P two pixels to the right to center it.)

Step 12. When you've completed editing, pull down the Edit menu and click Save Character As. In the Save Character As dialog box, accept the default choice or select a new position.

For tips on how to insert your new character into a document, pull down the Help menu in Private Character Editor, click Help Topics, select "Use your private characters in a program," and then follow the instructions. (See Figure 9-8.)

Having said all this, Private Character Editor isn't a very good editor for TrueType and OpenType fonts. If you're interested in a serious redesign of one or more characters, you should use a commercial font editing program. Some Web sites with comparative reviews of such programs are listed here:

Web Site	URL
TrueType Typography Page	http://www.truetype.demon.co.uk/tttools.htm
Microsoft's comments on the best font tools	http://www.microsoft.com/typography/links/news.asp?NID=695
Nicholas Fabian's reviews of current font-editing utilities	http://webcom.net/~nfhome/digital.htm
Guide to font editors and font resources	http://graphicdesign.miningco.com/msubfont.htm

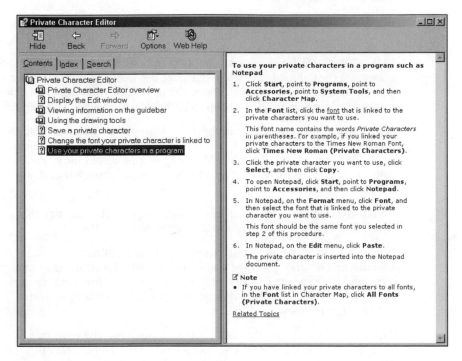

Figure 9-8: Private Character Editor Help describes ways you can use your new characters in documents.

Calculator

The Windows 2000 calculator (calc.exe) is based on a design that has been around since Windows 3.0 (1990). When you need to add or subtract some numbers — or when you want to compute sophisticated formulae or statistics — Calculator is handy to keep next to your major applications as a friendly tool.

Calculator comes in two *views*: Standard and Scientific. The standard view is shown in Figure 9-9.

Figure 9-9: In Calculator's standard view, only a few basic functions are available.

In Windows 2000, Calculator can support numbers up to at least 32 digits. As shown on the Calculator window in Figure 9-9, using 32-digit numbers means you can use figures up to 100 million million million million million (minus 1). In other words, you can calculate up to 99,999,999,999,999,999,999,999,999,999.

In some cases, even larger numbers are supported. When Calculator exceeds its display limits, it switches to scientific notation, such as 9.9e+35. The "e+35" means "times 10 to the 35th power." You would move the decimal point of 9.9 to the right 35 places to get an approximation of the intended result.

Tip

If your displayed number has one or more digits after the decimal place, these digits count as part of the 32-digit theoretical limit.

Because switching views zeroes out whatever number you had in the Calculator's display window, you can't use Calculator in the standard view and then switch to the scientific view to get a function the standard view doesn't have. For this reason, many Windows users operate Calculator in the scientific view at all times.

Tip

There is a workaround that allows you to preserve the contents of Calculator's display window across a change of views. First click Calculator's **MS** button, which stores the displayed number in the memory register. Then, change views and click the **MR** button to retrieve the number from memory.

Caution

If you use the above method to switch from scientific to standard view, and the number you stored using the **MS** button was in hexadecimal, octal, or binary format, retrieving it using **MR** will convert the number to decimal format (the only format supported in standard view).

Ever since Windows 3.0, Calculator has had a weird quirk that Microsoft has never fixed. The problem is that the standard view supports a square root key (SQRT in the upper-right corner), but the square root key disappears when you switch to the scientific view — where you're more likely to really need it!

Secret

If you like to keep Calculator in its scientific view (and why not — it only takes up a fraction of your screen), there's a way to get the square root functionality back when you need it. Simply press the **y** key on your keyboard before and after typing **.5** on your keyboard or with your mouse on Calculator's keys. This raises the number in the display to the power of 0.5, which always results in the square root.

Here are the steps to do this:

STEPS:

Getting the Square Root function back in scientific view

Step 1. In Calculator's scientific view, enter a number such as 10. (See Figure 9-10.)

Step 2. On your main keyboard, type **y.5y**.

Step 3. The square root appears in the display window as soon as you press **y** the second time. In this case, the square root of 10 is 3.162277660168. . . . (see Figure 9-11).

Figure 9-10: In Calculator's scientific view, the square root (SQRT) key has mysteriously disappeared from sight.

This trick works because Calculator supports a wide variety of keyboard shortcuts. These shortcuts can make Calculator much easier and faster to use than trying to click every key with your mouse. If you've avoided using Calculator because it seemed like too much trouble, try using your keyboard instead of your mouse.

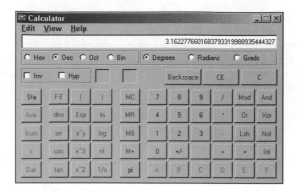

Figure 9-11: After you type **y.5y**, the display window shows the square root of 10, which is 3.162277660168. . . .

Table 9-1 shows keyboard shortcuts for Calculator.

Table 9-1   Keyboard Shortcuts for Calculator

Button	Key
A-F	A-F
And	&
Ave	CTRL+A
Backspace	BACKSPACE
Bin	F8
Byte	F4
C	ESC
CE	DEL
Cos	o
Dat	INS
Dec	F6
Degrees	F2
Dms	m
Dword	F2
Exp	x
F-E	v
Grads	F4
Hex	F5
Hyp	h

Button	Key
Int	;
Inv	i
Ln	n
Log	l
Lsh	<
M+	CTRL+P
MC	CTRL+L
Mod	%
MR	CTRL+R
MS	CTRL+M
n!	!
Not	~
Oct	F7
Or	|(pipe)
Pi	p
Qword	F12
Radians	F3
S	CTRL+D
Sin	s
Sqrt	@
Sta	CTRL+S
Sum	CTRL+T
Tan	t
Word	F3
Xor	^
x^2	@
x^3	#
x^y	y
%	%
(	(
)	)
*	*

Continued

Table 9-1   *(continued)*

Button	Key
+	+
+/-	F9
-	-
.	. *or* ,
/	/
0-9	0-9
1/x	r
=	ENTER

In Table 9-1, you can see that pressing the **y** key on your keyboard is the same as clicking the **x^y** key in Calculator with your mouse. Pressing **y** before and after **.5** computes the square root of the displayed number.

Tip

You can paste text from other applications into Calculator's display window, and Calculator will compute the result for you. This makes it convenient for you to store complex formulae and paste them into Calculator whenever you need them (perhaps adding a new number at the end of the calculation as appropriate for each new calculation).

Calculator supports another set of key sequences to activate functions when you are pasting in a formula. These key sequences allow you to clear the display, use scientific notation, retrieve the contents of the memory register, and more.

Table 9-2 shows the key sequences that activate functions.

Table 9-2   Keyboard Sequences for Calculator Functions

Sequence	Function
:c	Clears memory.
:e	Enables you to type scientific notation numbers in decimal form.
:m	Stores the displayed number in memory.
:p	Adds the displayed number to the number in memory.
:q	Clears the current calculation.
:r	Displays the number stored in memory.
\	Functions the same as Dat. Click Sta (statistics) before using this key.

The following steps provide an example of how you would use these functions to paste data into Calculator. Let's say customers usually purchase two movie tickets for $8 each, and you must then reduce the total by a different discount, depending on whom the customer is.

STEPS:

Pasting a mathematical function into Calculator

Step 1.   In an application such as a word processor, select the following text that you have previously stored, and then press Ctrl+C to copy the text to the Clipboard:

:c8:p:q8:p:r

In this formula, :c clears memory, :p adds 8 to the memory register, :q clears the display, and :r displays the memory register.

Step 2.   Switch to Calculator and press Ctrl+V to paste the text into the display. The display should show 16 (8 + 8).

Step 3.   Press the asterisk (*) key, and then type the discount rate for a particular customer. For example, if the customer qualifies for a 10% discount, type **.9** and then press Enter. The display should show 14.4, which is 90% of 16.

For more information on Calculator's functions, you can run the Calculator help file separate from Calculator itself by typing Start ⇨ Run, and then typing **calc.chm** into the Run dialog box's Open text box.

The Task Manager

In Windows 3.*x*, the Task Manager was displayed when you pressed the Ctrl+Esc keyboard combination. When Microsoft introduced Windows 95, the Start Button took over the Ctrl+Esc key combination, and you had to run **taskman.exe** to display the Task Manager.

In Windows 2000, simply right-click a vacant space on the Task Bar, and then click the Task Manager to display this applet, as shown in Figure 9-12. As an alternative, press Ctrl+Alt+Del and click the Task Manager button from the Log Off window. The latest Task Manager is far more powerful than those that inhabited Windows 3.*x* or 9*x*.

Figure 9-12: The Applications tab of the Task Manager shows the names and status of programs that are loaded.

Tip The Applications tab of the Task Manager, as shown in Figure 9-12, is the best way to shut down applications that are unresponsive or that have crashed. Simply select the program and click the End Task button. You also can run a program by clicking New Task.

Tip The Task Manager's Processes tab is an even more finely-grained view of the use of your system's resources. The Processes window shown in Figure 9-13 displays the percentage of CPU time and memory each process is consuming. This includes many routines that are started automatically by Windows 2000 — such as Explorer.exe — as well as visible applications like WordPad.

In Figure 9-14, a long directory (DIR) command is running in a background console session. The command processor, cmd.exe, is consuming 7 percent of CPU time, while a service, csrss.exe, is consuming 58 percent. This leaves 36 percent of the CPU time idle. (This doesn't add up to 100 percent due to rounding in the Task Manager.)

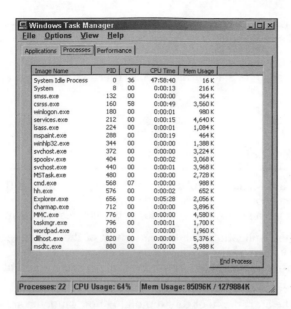

Figure 9-13: If your system feels sluggish, it may be because a program unknown to you is consuming CPU time or memory. The Processes tab makes this easy to check.

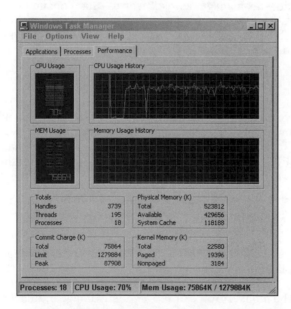

Figure 9-14: The Performance tab displays real-time graphs of CPU demand, memory usage, and other statistics on your system.

Figure 9-14 shows one of the Task Manager's most powerful uses — a dynamic picture of the CPU and memory usage of all your programs and services.

A great way to use this feature is to monitor how much CPU time and memory your applications use in the background. To do this, follow these steps:

STEPS:
Finding resource-hogging applications

Step 1. In the Task Manager, pull down the Options menu, and then select the Always on Top option. This keeps the Task Manager visible as you launch a series of applications that you want to test.

Step 2. Click the Applications tab to see a chart of the CPU time and memory used by the application you are about to open. Alternatively, click the Performance tab to see a graph of CPU and memory usage as you launch each application.

Step 3. Using the Start menu or the Run dialog box, launch a series of applications that you think may be using more CPU time or memory than you would like. As each application opens, watch the indicators in the Task Manager. We once found a commercial program — fax-management software — that consumed more than 50% of CPU time on a Pentium while it waited for a fax to arrive. The problem was cured with a later version of the program, which reduced the CPU demand to less than 5%.

In Figure 9-14, we've enabled the View menu's Show Kernel Times option. This is a menu choice that is only visible when the Performance tab is the foreground in the Task Manager. This option shows total CPU demand as a green line in the CPU Usage History window. The CPU demand on the kernel (the core Windows executables) is shown as a red line beneath the green line.

The CPU Usage History window shown in Figure 9-14 displays an initial spike to 100% as the Task Manager is loaded. After dropping to nearly zero, the CPU usage rises to about 70% utilization.

Secret

How did we manage to consume 70% of the CPU's time to create Figure 9-14 — with no applications doing anything? We consumed 70% of CPU time simply by dragging the Connect to the Internet icon rapidly in circles around the Desktop with the mouse. (You can see a ghostly image of this icon and the mouse pointer on the right side of the screen.) Just mousing around in little loops took up the majority of the computing power of a 450 MHz Pentium III! The moral is: don't idly drag icons in circles if you need your PC's full capacity for other, more important processes.

Notepad

No discussion of Windows 2000 applets would be complete without a section on Notepad. This little tool has been around for years, and it has changed form and added new powers as it's aged. Now it's better than ever.

As always, Notepad is still with us to open and edit plain text files. But Windows 2000 introduces a new power to the old faithful text editor.

The Notepad in Windows 2000 is no longer limited to loading and editing files of 50K or smaller. The new Notepad can edit almost any size text file you're likely to run into.

Under Windows 3.x and 9x, Notepad was a program compiled by Microsoft using the *small memory model*. This means that the text file and Notepad's code needed to fit within a 64K memory space, making Notepad fast, but also restricted to fairly small text files. In Windows 95, Microsoft added Notepad's big brother, WordPad (yes, they capitalized the "P" differently). When opening a file larger than about 50K, Notepad asked if you wanted to open it in WordPad instead, which worked with much larger files.

That step is no longer necessary for large text files in Windows 2000. Notepad works fine, eliminating the need to work on large text files in WordPad (raising the possibility that you might accidentally save them in one of WordPad's formats that would be incompatible with plain text).

Notepad has some other powers that aren't usually associated with text files:

Tip

You can insert the current time and date by pressing F5, or by pulling down the Edit menu and clicking Time/Date. This inserts the time format (without the seconds) using the short date format. These are the formats you've selected in the Control Panel's Regional Settings dialog box.

Tip

You can change the information that's printed in the header and footer of each page. This data isn't added to the text file when you save it, but Notepad uses your configuration choices to format the printed output.

To change the header or footer, pull down the File menu and click Page Setup. Table 9-3 lists the commands you can use to insert various pieces of information into text files:

Table 9-3	Notepad Page Setup Commands for Headers and Footers
Command	*Function*
&f	Inserts filename.
&d	Inserts current date when printed.
&t	Inserts current time when printed.
&p	Inserts page number.
&&	Prints an ampersand (&).

You can force any information to be printed in the left or right margin, or in the center of the header or footer, by combining the information with the commands listed in Table 9-4:

Command	Function
&l	Left alignment.
&r	Right alignment.
&c	Centered alignment.

Table 9-4   Notepad Commands for Left, Right, and Centered Alignment

Cheating at Solitaire

Solitaire has been a productivity feature of PCs since Windows 3.0. As one of the first games to be included with a version of Windows, Solitaire has probably been played by more people than any other Windows diversion.

Solitaire still has many of the old tricks that have delighted players since the early days. This is fortunate for people who don't take their games so seriously that they can't cheat a little now and then!

Secret

If you're playing the three-card draw version of Solitaire, you can find a secret keyboard combination the programmer added just for you. Say that you can see the card you need, but it's not the top card in the pile. You can click Game ⇨ Undo to return the last three cards to the deck. Then simultaneously hold down the Ctrl+Shift+Alt keys as you click the deck. Voilá! Only one card at a time turns from the deck. When you release the Ctrl, Shift, and Alt keys, the cards again turn normally—three cards at a time (see Figure 9-15).

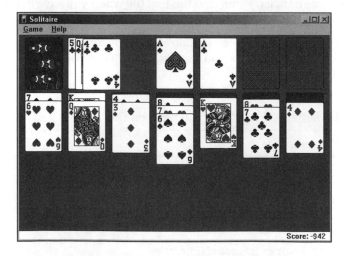

Figure 9-15: While playing three-card draw, you may find you need the black Queen and the black 5, as shown here.

How to cheat at three-card draw

Step 1.   To start Solitaire, click Start ⇨ Programs ⇨ Accessories ⇨ Games ⇨ Solitaire.

Step 2.   Pull down Solitaire's Game menu, and then click Options. Make sure the option Draw Three is selected. Configure the other options any way you want.

Step 3.   After clicking the deck with your mouse, turning over three cards at a time, you can click Game ⇨ Undo. Then, press and hold the Ctrl+Shift+Alt keys to turn over only one card at a time until the card you need is at the top of the stack. (See Figure 9-16.)

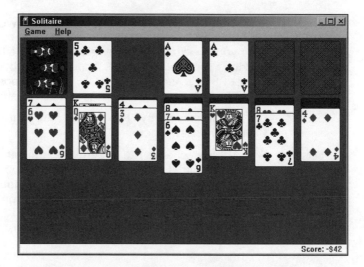

Figure 9-16: By clicking Game ⇨ Undo, and then turning over one card at a time, you can reveal the black 5 (as shown here), the black Queen, and so on.

Cheating at Minesweeper

Minesweeper is a small board game that's been played by kids and adults for eons. The object of the game is to click all the squares that *don't* have mines beneath them. If you click a square that hides a mine, you're dead and you lose the game.

That's okay, because you can just click Game ⇨ New to start a new game.

When you click a square that doesn't conceal a mine, but there are mines in any of the eight squares surrounding that square, a number from 1 to 8 appears on the square you clicked. The number, of course, indicates the number of mines hidden in those 8 squares. This is supposed to let you determine which other squares conceal mines so you can avoid them.

Secret

For beginners (and inveterate cheaters), there is another way to learn how to find mines before they find you. The programmer of Minesweeper added a secret keyboard combination into the game to help him (and you) see in advance which squares conceal mines.

STEPS:

Activating the secret key sequence in Minesweeper

Step 1.   Turn your desktop black by right-clicking the Desktop, and then clicking Properties. Click the Appearance tab, change the Desktop color to Black, and then click OK. (If you choose a color other than black, it may not be as easy to see the effect of this trick.)

Step 2.   Open Minesweeper by clicking Start, Programs ⇨ Accessories ⇨ Games ⇨ Minesweeper.

Step 3.   With Minesweeper as the foreground application, type **xyzzy**, and then press Shift+Enter. Nothing will appear on the screen when you press these keystrokes. But when your mouse is hovered over a "safe" square, a one-pixel white spot will appear in the upper-left corner of your screen, as shown in Figure 9-17. If your mouse is over a "bomb," the white spot will disappear.

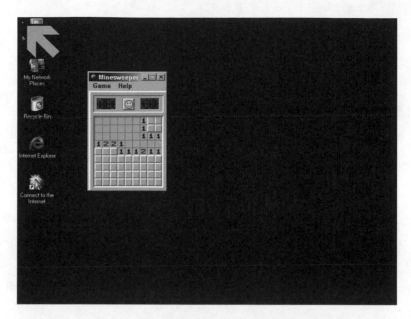

Figure 9-17: Minesweeper displays a white pixel in the upper-left corner of a black Windows 2000 desktop (indicated by the arrow) when you've activated the secret key sequence and your mouse is hovered over a "safe" square

Minesweeper has several other tricks that can help you learn the game and dazzle your friends:

Mark squares

To visualize where you think mines lie, based on the number shown on the playing field, you can "mark" squares with a flag or a question mark. If you think a square conceals a bomb, right-click the square once to place a flag icon there. If you're not sure, right-click the flag to change the flag into a question mark.

When you think you've marked all the mines around a square with a number in it, click that square with both mouse buttons at once to uncover all the remaining squares. (The easiest way to do this is to press and hold the left mouse button down, and then press and release the right mouse button.) If some squares you haven't marked *do* conceal mines, the squares will flash. That is, they will appear recessed and then flip back to their former state.

Turn off the timer

If you want more time to think (and, by the way, totally defeat the object of the clock), you can turn off the timer. Press and hold both mouse buttons down on the numbers in the time display. The smiley face changes into a face with an "O" for a mouth. With both buttons still held down, press the Esc key and the timer stops.

As a humorous note, when you turn off the timer, the Minesweeper title bar changes to "**budget.xls**." To complete the illusion, the title bar now sports an Excel icon. You can minimize the Minesweeper window and no one who walks into your office will know you're in the middle of playing a game — even if they look right at your Task Bar!

To restart the clock, restore the Minesweeper window after minimizing it.

Tip

Once you've mastered the default 9-by-9 Minesweeper board, you can make things more interesting by increasing the size of the board. Pull down Minesweeper's Game menu, and then click Custom. Change the board size (and the number of hidden mines) to whatever you like.

Cheating at FreeCell

FreeCell is another card game, somewhat in the spirit of its more famous brother, Solitaire. The object of the game is to move all your cards to the home cells in the upper-right corner. Free cells in the upper-left corner are used as cardholders (see Figure 9-18).

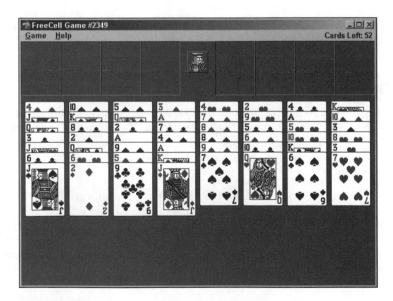

Figure 9-18: Clicking Game ⇨ New Game in FreeCell displays eight columns of cards.

Secret

While playing the game, you can press the Ctrl+Shift+F10 keyboard shortcut to win or retry the game. Clicking the Abort button lets you win (after you complete any move), while clicking Retry lets you retry the same game.

Summary

In this chapter, we described several tricks and secrets of Windows 2000 applets.

▶ The powers of RegEdit, which displays the Windows 2000 Registry in a hierarchical view, and its big brother, RegEdt32, which uses a multiple document interface to display different Registry branches side by side.

▶ The use of Character Map to insert characters from any font into documents, and the hidden Private Character Editor associated with Character Map.

▶ Little-known uses for the ancient, but surprisingly powerful, Calculator applet.

▶ Fun features of Solitaire, Minesweeper, and FreeCell, including secret key combinations embedded into them to help you learn about or cheat these games.

▶ Employing the Task Manager to help you find resource-hogging applications and processes.

▶ How Notepad has grown out of its old 50K text file limitation.

Part III

Communications

Chapter 10

Modems

In This Chapter

We learn secrets on how to manage your modem, and how to use it to make calls. In this chapter, you will learn:

▶ How to install a modem.

▶ How to configure modems and COM ports.

▶ How to set up dialing rules.

▶ How to use calling cards to place long-distance calls.

Modems

Modems are actually a gigantic workaround. They were invented to do something—send digital signals—over a medium that was not designed to transport digital signals: our ordinary copper phone lines. Computers function based on the digits one and zero. Telephone lines, on the other hand, are designed to carry analog signals. A modem, or *modulator/demodulator*, is designed to convert digital signals to analog signals, and back again.

Modems can be either internal modems—an add-in cards inserted into an expansion slot in your computer—or they can be external modems, connected by a cable to one of your computer's external serial (or COM) ports.

Modem manufacturers have been engaged in a speed race for years, bringing faster and faster communications to the computing public. Whenever a modem vendor developed another big jump in speed, such as the jump from 28.8K to 56K, other manufacturers would come up with different technologies for doing the same thing. At 56K, you saw this battle between the 3Com/US Robotics x2 standard and the Rockwell/Lucent K56 flex standard. Eventually the International Telecommunications Union (ITU) adopted a compromise standard between the two, known as V.90.

Since the original 1200 baud modems hit the computer store shelves, it has been forecast that we would eventually reach a technological limit for modem speed. Most advances beyond 56K, such as DSL, ISDN, and cable modems, will be digital technology. While we may still call them modems, they will no longer need to convert digital signals to analog as we do today.

Installing a Modem

Installing a modem in Windows 2000 can be easy, because Microsoft has designed Windows 2000 to be a true Plug and Play operating system. This means that if both your computer and your modem are Plug and Play compatible, your modem should be automatically recognized and installed by Windows 2000. (See Chapter 14 for more information on hardware and Plug and Play compatibility.) You are not limited to Plug and Play modems, however. If you have a valid Windows NT 4.0 driver for your modem, you can, in most cases, still install it in Windows 2000. Of course, installing a modem can still be difficult if there are any unforeseen incompatibilities.

Tip

If you want to see which modems are on the Windows 2000 Hardware Compatibility List, you can view the Hardware Compatibility List located on your Windows 2000 CD-ROM by opening HCL.TXT located in the \Support folder. You also can retrieve a copy of the current the Hardware Compatibility list online from Microsoft's FTP server at ftp://ftp.microsoft.com/services/whql/win2000hcl.txt, which you can then view offline.

Note

If your modem is not listed on the Windows 2000 Hardware Compatibility List, check with your modem manufacturer to see if an upgraded driver has been released for your modem to run under Windows 2000.

STEPS:

Install a Plug and Play Modem

Step 1.   Make sure the modem is installed and connected according to the manufacturer's instructions. When you have completed the physical installation, restart your computer and wait for the Windows 2000 desktop to appear.

Step 2.   Click Start ⇨ Settings ⇨ Control Panel, and then click Phone and Modem Options.

Step 3.   Select the Modems tab. If you see your modem already listed under installed modems, you are all set. Otherwise, click Add to start the Install New Modem Wizard shown in Figure 10-1.

Step 4.   Click Next to start the first step of the Modem Wizard. In the first dialog box, you will have two choices: allow the Wizard to search for your modem, or select your modem from a list. If you want to choose your modem from a list, check the box on the lower portion of the screen, and then click Next. If you want the Wizard to search for your modem, click Next. Since the modem we are installing in this example is a Plug and Play modem, we're leaving the box unchecked.

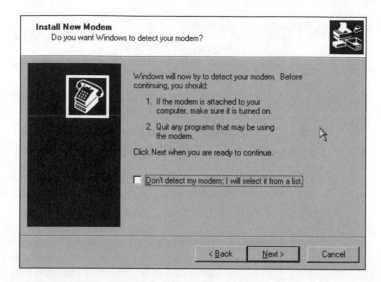

Figure 10-1: You can have the Install Modem Wizard look for your wizard, or you can select the check box at the bottom of the screen.

Step 5. Windows 2000 will then search for your modem. When it finds it, it should automatically begin installing the necessary drivers. You may be prompted to insert the diskettes or a CD-ROM that accompanied your modem so that Windows can copy the necessary files to install your modem.

Step 6. You should go through a few more automated steps, until you finally see the Success dialog box. Your modem should now be configured and ready to go.

If your modem is not a Plug and Play modem, it can still be installed as long as you have a valid driver for the modem.

STEPS:

Installing an unsupported modem

Step 1. Make sure your modem is correctly installed or connected according to the manufacturer's instructions.

Step 2. Click Start ➪ Settings ➪ Control Panel, and then click Phone and Modem Options.

Continued

STEPS:

Installing an unsupported modem (*continued*)

Step 3. Select the Modems tab. If you see your modem already listed under installed modems, you are all set. Otherwise, click Add to start the Install New Modem Wizard, and then click Next to begin.

Step 4. Since you are installing an unsupported modem, Windows 2000 might not recognize it. Select the check box "Don't detect my modem. I will select it from the list." (See figure 10-1 above.) You can always ask Windows 2000 to try to select your modem anyway. If that fails, you will automatically be taken to the next step. Click Next.

Step 5. Select your modem manufacturer from the left pane, as shown in Figure 10-2. Then, find your specific modem model in the list in the right pane. If your exact model is not listed, choose the modem that is the closest to the one you can have. (For example, select a modem having the same speed as the modem you are installing.)

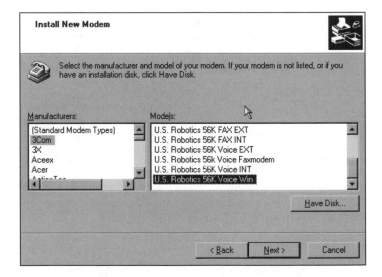

Figure 10-2: Choose your modem from the list by selecting the manufacturer in the left pane, and then selecting the modem model in the right pane.

Step 6. If there is no match from which to choose, click the Have Disk button, and then click Next.

Step 7. Follow the rest of the instructions on screen. At some point, you might be prompted to insert the modem driver disk or CD-ROM.

Secret

Do you have a really off-brand or generic modem, and the manufacturer doesn't appear anywhere on the list? Check the documentation that accompanied your modem. It may list a compatible modem from which you can then configure your modem. If not, select Standard Modem Types at the top of the manufacturer list in the left pane, and then select the appropriate speed for your modem from the list in the right pane.

Once you have worked through the Modem Installation Wizard, your modem should be correctly installed and assigned to an available COM port. To see your configuration details, do the following:

STEPS:

Check your modem configuration

Step 1.   Click Start ➪ Settings ➪ Control Panel, and then click Phone and Modem.

Step 2.   Select the Modem tab. Your modem should be listed as being installed. It will also show which COM port your modem is assigned to.

Step 3.   Make sure your modem is selected, and then click Properties. All your modem configuration settings are listed here.

Secret

Your modem's installation is guided by an .INF file in the \winnt\INF folder. Modem files typically start with the letters "mdm." If you open your modem file in Notepad, you will see that it contains setup information, and it also lists all the commands that the modem recognizes.

Caution

Do not modify the contents of this file. Making the wrong change can cripple your modem.

Installation troubleshooting

If you open the Phone and Modem Properties applet and find that your modem is not listed, there are a number of things you can check. The first is a rather easy step, especially if you believe your modem is a Plug and Play-compatible modem. Shut down your computer, and then start it up again. Sometimes, a setting gets configured incorrectly , and the modem is not recognized by Windows 2000. But, when you boot your computer again and Windows 2000 checks your hardware, it might find the modem and then automatically repair the problem. Often, though, it takes more than that. Here are some other things you will want to check if you are still having difficulty configuring your modem.

COM ports

Sometimes, the problem isn't the modem; rather, it is the COM port to which the modem is assigned. To see what COM port the modem is using, repeat Steps 1 and 2 in the previous exercise, "Check modem configurations." Then, check to ensure that your COM port is correctly configured using the following steps:

STEPS:

Check COM port settings

Step 1. Click Start ⇨ Settings ⇨ Control Panel, and click System.

Step 2. Select the Hardware tab, and then click Device Manager.

Step 3. Click the plus sign to the left of Ports (COM & LPT).

Step 4. Verify that none of the installed ports have an error symbol next to them. Error symbols include a yellow exclamation point symbol, a question mark symbol, or a red X symbol. If any of the installed ports have an error symbol, double-click that port and review the Device Status information, which will appear similar to the information shown in Figure 10-3, to see if there is an explanation for the error symbol.

Figure 10-3: In the Device Status information screen, your COM port should be reported as working properly, and the port should be enabled.

Step 5. If the port is disabled, enable it by selecting the option Use this device (enable) from the Device usage drop-down list box on the lower portion of the dialog box.

Step 6. Select the Resources tab.

Step 7. Review the resources used by the COM port. They should appear similar to those shown in Table 10-1, unless your computer is configured to use different settings.

Step 8. Microsoft recommends that the Use Automatic settings check box be selected. If you need to change the settings to agree with your modem documentation, clear the check box.

Step 9. Click Change Settings and type the new values. Click OK to close the COM port properties dialog box, and then click OK again to close the Device Manager.

Table 10-1   Standard COM port Settings

Port	Input/Output Range	Interrupt Request
COM 1	03F8-03FF	04
COM 2	02F8-02FF	03
COM 3	03E8-03EF	04
COM 4	02E8-02EF	03

Modem diagnostics

If your COM port is working correctly, it is time to check your modem. There is a Modem Diagnostics tool that you can use to see whether your modem can respond to some common modem commands. Use the following steps to check your modem responses:

STEPS:

Running modem diagnostics

Step 1. Click Start ➪ Settings ➪ Control Panel, and then click Phone and Modem Properties.

Step 2. Select the Modem tab, and then click Properties.

Step 3. Select the Diagnostics tab, as shown in Figure 10-4.

Continued

STEPS:

Running modem diagnostics *(continued)*

Step 4. Click Query Modem. This will send a series of commands to your modem. The modem will respond, and both the commands and the responses will be shown in the lower panel.

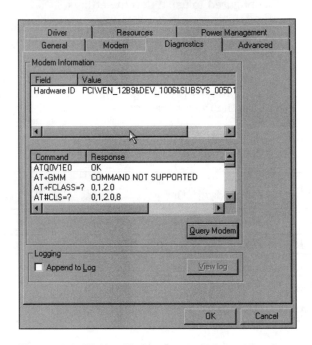

Figure 10-4: Clicking Modem Query sends a series of commands to the modem. A correctly configured modem will be able to respond to these commands.

The AT+GMM command, the second one sent by the diagnostics test, is the Model Identification command. It is not supported by all modems. However, your modem should respond to the other commands if it is correctly configured.

In Windows 2000 Professional, modem commands are automatically sent to a log file. The file will be located in your Windows folder with the name ModemLog_*modemname*.txt. This log file is overwritten each time you start Windows 2000, unless you click the Append to log option. If you do choose to append commands to a single log file, you will eventually have a very large file growing in your Windows folder. You can view this log file with a text editor such as Notepad, or in a word processing program.

Secret

If you purchased an internal Plug and Play modem for an NT computer, you may have had to manually configure it by setting jumpers or DIP switches on the modem card. If you then move this modem to a Windows 2000 computer, the changed configuration may prevent Windows 2000 from automatically recognizing it. You will have to change its settings back to the default so that the Windows 2000 Plug and Play manager will recognize it.

Configuring your Modem

When modems were used mainly to connect to BBSes or online services like CompuServe or America Online, you often had to configure your modem to match the different destinations to which you connected. Now that most modems are used only to connect to the Internet, we often only need to call one place — our Internet Service Provider. Once your modem is properly configured to dial your ISP, you no longer need to worry about configuring multiple destinations.

However, if you do need to change some modem settings, this is where they are located. All the locations in Table 10-2 assume that you have already opened the Control Panel, clicked Phone and Modem Options, and then selected the Modem tab.

Table 10-2   Location of Modem Configuration Settings

Setting	Where it is	What it does
Speaker Volume	Properties, General	Lets you hear the melodious squeal of your modem as you connect. Slide the slider to Off to mute sounds.
Maximum Port Speed	Properties, General	This is the speed at which programs can send data to the modem. It can be set as high as four times the speed of the modem, if the modem supports data compression. If you are getting errors, check your modem specifications for the highest speed your modem can handle and adjust this setting to match.

Continued

Table 10-2 *(continued)*

Setting	Where it is	What it does
Wait for dial tone	Properties, General	The modem won't dial until it hears a recognizable dial tone. Some dial tones, such as those with voice mail systems, might have a stutter that will confuse the modem. If so, disable this option.
Extra initialization commands	Properties, Advanced	Some modems require extra commands, which can be added here. They will override regular initialization commands, since they are sent afterward.
Manual disconnection	Properties, Advanced, Change Default Preferences, General	Your modem can automatically disconnect if it has been idle more than the time specified. You also can have the modem cancel the call if it hasn't connected within a set time limit. (See Figure 10-5.)
Port speed	Properties, Advanced, Change Default Preferences, General	This sets your computer-to-modem speed. If you lower the maximum port speed setting, it will affect this setting. If your modem is not working correctly, and this speed is greater than 115200, try reducing it.
Data Protocol	Properties, Advanced, Change Default Preferences, General	This sets the error correction settings for your connection. If it is set to Standard EC, the actual error correction will be negotiated between your modem and the modem to which you are connecting. If it is set to Forced EC, your modem will insist on a V.42 connection; if the modem to which you are connecting doesn't agree with this setting, it will hang up. Sometimes, your modem will not be able to negotiate a protocol that is fast enough, causing the other modem to time out (fail) the connection. In this scenario, you will have to disabled this setting, but at the risk of receiving garbled data.

Setting	Where it is	What it does
Compression	Properties, Advanced, Change Default Preferences, General	Enables or disables data compression by the modem, which helps speed up data transfer in most cases. If you are transferring data that has already been compressed (.ZIP, .ARC, or .SIT files, for example), hardware compression can actually slow things down.
Flow Control	Properties, Advanced, Change Default Preferences, General	Sets the modem to either hardware or software flow control (XON/XOFF). Some programs are incompatible with hardware flow control.
Data bits	Properties, Advanced, Change Default Preferences, Advanced	For most ISP and PC-to-PC connections, this should be set to 8 data bits. If you are dialing directly into a mainframe computer, you may need to set this to 7.
Parity	Properties, Advanced, Change Default Preferences, Advanced	This is a fairly primitive form of error checking. Your most likely setting should be None, leaving error checking to one of the advanced protocols. This setting must agree with the modem to which you are connecting.
Stop bits	Properties, Advanced, Change Default Preferences, Advanced	A stop bit marks the end of a packet of information. Almost all computers and modems set this value to 1.
Modulation	Properties, Advanced, Change Default Preferences, Advanced	The method used by modems to convert digital to analog signals. Both modems need to use the same method, which is normally the Standard method. However, there are a couple of other methods; non-standard for Bell and HST, and V.23 used by Minitel, the French system.

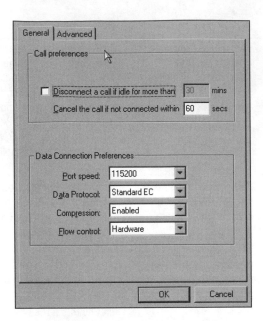

Figure 10-5: While you normally won't need to change these settings for regular Internet connections, you may need to make some changes when you are trying to connect to a BBS or a specialized computer, such as a mainframe.

Dialing Rules

Dialing rules aren't terribly important for a desktop computer; you don't often move it to another location before dialing out through the modem. But for portable computers, dialing rules can be a big productivity enhancer. If you are dialing out through a PBX system with your laptop, you might need to dial the phone in a specific way, such as having to dial a number to access an outside line first. From home, however, you normally won't need to dial to an outside line prior to calling your ISP. When you're traveling, you might need to dial an arcane set of codes from your hotel room to the home office using your telephone calling card codes. And of course, when you are vacating at the beach house, you'll surely want to retrieve your e-mail. (Of course, it would probably be nice to get a vacation from your e-mail, too.)

Any application that makes use of the Windows 2000 Telephony API can use this location information. That includes the Phone Dialer and Microsoft FAX that accompany Windows 2000, as well as many third-party applications.

A location can be defined by more than just its physical location. If you ever have to make adjustments due to area code changes, access to outside lines, calling cards, or different long-distance carriers, you can do this using dialing rules.

Create a new rule

You are planning a trip, say, to Washington, DC, and you want to be able to check your e-mail from your hotel room. Follow these steps to create a new dialing rule:

STEPS:

Create a dialing rule for another location

Step 1. Click Start ⇨ Settings ⇨ Control Panel, and then click Phone and Modem Options.

Step 2. Select the Dialing Rules tab, and then click New.

Step 3. Starting at the General tab, give a name to your new Location Rule. There are no real limits on the name you use, so make it something that makes sense to you (DC Hotel, for example, as shown in Figure 10-6).

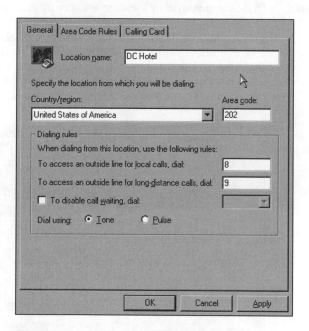

Figure 10-6: Creating a dialing rule that will work with a typical hotel telephone system for the 202 (Washington, DC) area code.

Step 4. Make sure that the country and area code are correct for your location.

Continued

STEPS:

Create a dialing rule for another location *(continued)*

Step 5. If you are going to be dialing through some sort of PBX system, such as from a hotel room or your office, you might need to dial an extra number first to get an outside line. Type those numbers for local and long-distance calls in these fields. Otherwise, leave them blank.

Step 6. Make sure you have selected the correct dialing style for the Dial using option: pulse or tone.

Step 7. Optional: By default, if the number you are going to dial is in the same area code as the area code you typed in Step 4, only the seven-digit phone number will be dialed. If the area codes are different, the default behavior is to dial 1, the area code, and then the seven-digit phone number. Now that any medium-large metropolitan area has three or four area codes, you may have to create some special area code rules, which we cover in "Area Code rules," later in this chapter.

Step 8. Optional: If your new location is away from home, and you will be making long-distance calls, you will most likely use a calling card for your computer calls. Select the Calling Card tab, as shown in Figure 10-7. A number of the most popular calling card types are already set up for you to use. If your card type is in the list, select it, and then fill in your account and PIN numbers. If you need to create a brand new calling card account, see "Calling Cards," later in this chapter.

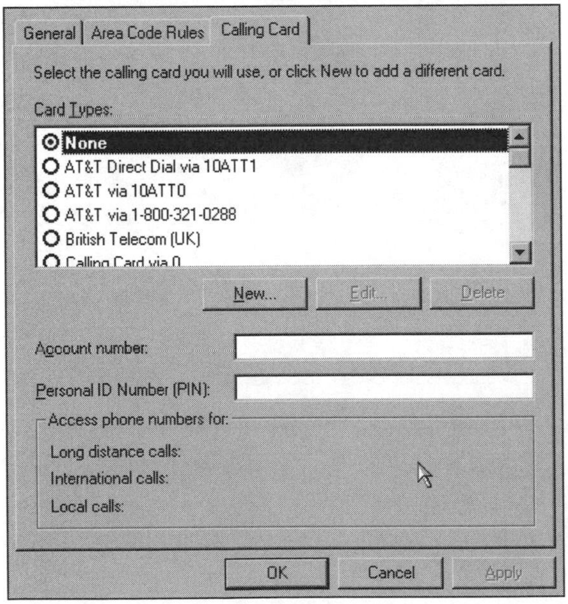

Figure 10-7: If you want to use your calling card rule to place a call, choose from among the predefined card types in the list, or create your own.

Step 9.   Click OK to save your new dialing rule.

Tip

You can use multiple calling cards by making two different dialing rules, with one rule for card A and another rule for card B. Include the name of the calling card in the Dialing rules name.

When you take your computer to your new location, tell the computer what your new location is by selecting the dialing rule you want to use before you make your first call.

STEPS:

Choose your dialing rule

Step 1.   Click Start ⇨ Settings ⇨ Control Panel, and then click Phone and Modem options.

Step 2.   Select your new location from the list, as shown in Figure 10-8.

Step 3.   Later, when you have returned home or you have moved to another location, repeat Steps 1 through 3.

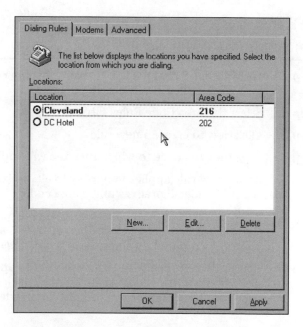

Figure 10-8: Select your dialing location from the list.

Note

When you connect to an ISP using Dial-Up Networking, you normally are not prompted for a dialing rule to use. Dial-Up Networking will use the dialing rule that has been selected. You need to select your location first, and then start the call.

Area Code rules

Dialing the telephone used to be a lot easier. With area codes few and far between, it was easier to tell which call was a local call, which call was a long-distance call, when you needed to dial 1 first, and so on. Now, the area code explosion has made knowing what to dial much more difficult.

Area code rules are a way to make it easier for your computer to dial the telephone. Area code rules are created to accompany a particular dialing rule, since they are dependent on the physical location of your computer.

The default dialing rule is: when the area code of the number to be dialed is different than your current location, then 1, the area code, and the telephone number is dialed. If the area codes are the same, only the telephone number is dialed. If you need something different from this rule, you must create an area code rule. (This is the optional Step 7 from the previous exercise, "Create a dialing rule from another location.")

STEPS:

Create an area code rule

Step 1.   Follow Steps 1 through 6 in "Create a dialing rule from another location," earlier in this chapter.

Step 2.   Select the Area Code Rules tab.

Step 3.   Click New to create a new rule.

Step 4.   Type the area code to which this rule will apply (see Figure 10-9).

Step 5.   If your new rule applies uniformly to all prefixes in this area code, select Include all prefixes in the area code.

Step 6.   If this new rule applies only to certain prefixes, select Include only the prefixes in the list below. Then click Add and list all the prefixes, separated by commas, in the dialog box. Click OK.

Step 7.   Now you must specify the rule you want to apply. If you need to dial 1 or any other numbers, select the check box and specify the numbers. Then choose whether the area code should be dialed.

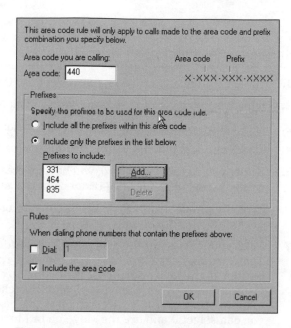

Figure 10-9: This area code rule applies to three prefixes in the 440 area code.

Step 8. Click OK. If you need to create more rules for this dialing location, repeat these steps. (A dialing location can have multiple area code rules.)

Calling cards

You can set up your computer to place calls through a long-distance calling card, as we saw in Step 8 in the exercise, "Create a dialing rule from another location." A number of popular long-distance calling cards are already preformatted and available for your use. You select the calling card you want to use, and then you add your card and PIN numbers.

If you have a calling card that is not on the list, you can still use it. You simply create a new calling card.

STEPS:
Create a new calling card

Step 1.   While creating a new dialing rule, select the Calling Card tab.

Step 2.   If the card you want to use is not listed, click New.

Step 3.   Select the General tab, and give the card a name.

Step 4.   Type your account and your PIN numbers for the calling card.

Step 5.   Before you can save this card, you have to create rules for when it can be used. Select the Long-Distance tab, as shown in Figure 10-10.

Step 6.   Type the phone number you need to dial to use this card in the Access number text box.

Step 7.   Next, you must enter the dialing procedure for using this card. There are six possible actions you can take, represented by the six buttons in the lower portion of the dialog box. Follow the instructions for your calling card, and then click these buttons following the order of your card. If you click a step out of order, you can select it and use the Move up or Move down button to change the order of the steps.

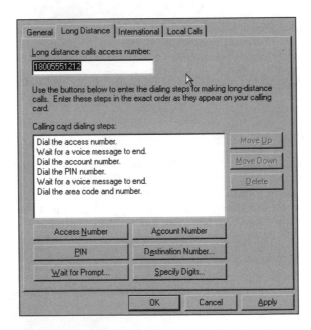

Figure 10-10: Enter the steps you must follow by clicking the appropriate button to use your calling card.

Step 8. If you need to wait for a prompt before taking another step, select Wait for Prompt. There are three different ways in which you can have the dialing rule wait: wait for a dial tone, wait for a voice message to end, or wait a specified time interval.

Step 9. If you also want to use this card for international calls, select the International tab. Follow Steps 6 through 8.

Step 10. There is also a tab for local calls. If you want to dial local calls normally, without the use of the calling card, leave all the entries on this page blank. If you do want to use the calling card for local calls, repeat Steps 6 through 8.

Step 11. Click OK to return to the Dialing Location dialog box.

Summary

In this chapter, we have looked at the first steps you must take to install and configure a modem in Windows 2000.

▶ We learned how to install a modem driver.

▶ We learned how to configure a modem to place different types of calls.

▶ We learned how to create dialing rules so that we can place calls using the computer in different locations.

▶ We learned how to set up area code rules to cope with the problem of numerous area codes.

▶ We learned how to set up and use calling cards in dialing rules in order to place calls.

Chapter 11

Connecting to an ISP with Dial-up Networking

In This Chapter

With a modem and Dial-up Networking, it's easier than ever to connect to an Internet Service Provider. We will explore:

▶ The different types of Internet Service Providers.

▶ How to use the Internet Connection Wizard to establish a connection.

▶ Troubleshooting steps you can take when you can't make a connection.

Getting onto the Internet

Personal computers are no longer isolated pieces of hardware. If the 1980s saw PCs grow from geeky obscurity into significant technological forces, the 1990s saw PCs link virtually the entire planet into a new communication network using the Internet.

Windows NT was designed from the ground up as a networking platform, of course, but even the largest Local Area Networks (LAN) and Wide Area Networks (WAN) pale by comparison to the vast, constantly shifting Internet. Fortunately, the Internet capabilities in Windows NT have been significantly extended and refined. Windows 2000 comes fully Internet-aware, complete with all the software you need to go online.

If your computer is part of a large network—either at work or on a campus— your Internet connection is probably made through the network. (These types of connections will be discussed in Part V of the book.) But if you are on a peer-to-peer network in a small office, or you are on a standalone computer, you probably connect to an Internet Service Provider (ISP) using Dial-up Networking, which is the topic of this chapter.

Internet Service Providers

If you want to connect to the Internet, you need to open an account with an Internet Service Provider. There are a huge number of options from which you can choose, and competition has forced prices into a very narrow range. In fact, your decision should be based not on dollar values, but on service considerations.

Online Services

The major online services — America Online, CompuServe, Prodigy, and the Microsoft Network — were, at one point, closed networks offering a mix of proprietary offerings to their subscribers. However, they are all either partially or completely moving away from that model (in the case of Prodigy) and are changing to the role of ISP, even offering subscribers a way to connect to the broader World Wide Web. They each have local dial-up numbers coast to coast, and their software is often pre-installed on new computers.

If you wanted to use America Online as your ISP with Windows 2000, you might have to wait a bit longer. A connection to AOL requires the use of proprietary dialing software that was never compatible with Windows NT. AOL 4.0 does not work with Windows 2000. Rumors say that AOL will eventually have a version for both Windows NT and Windows 2000. In the meantime, if you already have an Internet connection with Windows 2000, you will be able to connect to the AOL Web site.

National ISPs

National ISPs are similar to the online services, but without the proprietary connections. Well-known companies such as AT&T and Sprint, as well as Internet-only companies like Mindspring, Earthlink, and Concentric Network, are also duking it out to gain customers. They also have coast-to-coast local access numbers, and they often have toll-free access numbers for other areas. Many provide automated installation routines to set up your connection. However, this chapter will teach you everything you need to know about setting up your connection, because using their provided software can often make it harder to configure things your own way later on.

Local ISPs

Though there is a clear industry trend toward company mergers, there are still many local ISPs who cover only one city or one region. In addition to independent ISPs, many of the local telephone companies also compete in this area. For many of these smaller ISPs, customer service is usually their strongest point, because they are closer to their customers.

Here are some of the important factors you need to consider when you choose an ISP:

- **The ratio of modems to callers:** You don't want to have to constantly dial and redial because you keep getting a busy signal.

- **Speed of their modems:** The standard modem speed on new computers is 56K. That speed won't help you if your ISP uses 33.6K modems

- **No proprietary software:** If you prefer Netscape Navigator over Internet Explorer (or vice versa), you should be able to make that choice. If you want to choose your own e-mail program, go right ahead. Avoid any ISP that locks you into one type of software, or that requires the use of their installation software.

- **Type of account:** This is not as much an issue these days, since most ISPs deal exclusively with PPP (Point-to-Point protocol) accounts, rather than SLIP (Serial Line/Internet protocol) or shell accounts. You want a PPP account, if at all possible.

■ **Web site:** Most ISPs provide web site hosting services, also providing your web site with an address that looks something like *www.ispname.com/members/yourname.*

Windows 95 and Windows 98 both ship with several proprietary online services pre-installed. Windows 98 provides an Online Services folder, where certain providers placed their installation and configuration software. The online services got this nice piece of virtual real estate on millions of computers being sold with Windows in return for promising to use the Microsoft Internet Explorer as their preferred web browser.

You won't see an Online Services folder in Windows 2000, however. This cozy *quid pro quo* is one of the alleged monopolistic practices that prompted the U.S. Government's antitrust suit against Microsoft. The final chapter of that saga has yet to be written. But now that Microsoft has successfully cut off Netscape's air supply (as Microsoft Group Vice President Paul Maritz put it), effectively destroying Netscape's browser business and forcing the company's sale to AOL, Microsoft seems to be cooling it on the Online Services folder front.

Making a Connection

In previous versions of Windows, you could create an Internet connection through the Dial-up Networking folder in My Computer. Just to keep you on your toes, Microsoft has changed the location of this folder under Windows 2000.

Long -time Windows hands take note: the Dial-up Networking folder has been moved to the Control Panel, where it has been combined with networking configuration in the Network and Dial-up Connections folder.

Actually, there are many paths to making a connection. You can click Start ⇨ Settings ⇨ Network and Dial-up Connections. You also might have a shortcut at Start ⇨ Programs ⇨ Accessories ⇨ Communications for both the Internet Connection Wizard and the Network and Dial-up Connections folder. Before you make a connection, however, there are some preliminary steps you need to take.

Tip

To make a connection, a modem must be installed and configured on your computer, which was the topic of the last chapter. To see if your computer has an installed modem, access the Control Panel and click the Phone & Modem Options icon. Then, click the Modem tab. If your modem is listed, then it should be correctly configured.

Preparation

The Internet Connection Wizard assumes you already have an account with an ISP, and it is going to ask you questions about that account. Before you start, here is the information you need to have ready:

■ The phone number you dial for your connection.

- Your user name (sometimes called your logon name) and password.

- A specific IP address (optional with some ISPs. In most cases, this will be assigned dynamically at login by your ISP, so you don't have to worry about it).

- IP Header compression (optional with some ISPs).

- Primary and Secondary DNS servers. (These may also be assigned automatically, so you won't need them.)

- Any other optional settings your ISP may provide for you.

- If you are going to be setting up e-mail and news accounts, you will need the ISPs mail and news server addresses, as well. These can be configured later using Outlook Express.

Tip

If you already have an account with an ISP on another computer, and you are transferring your settings to your new Windows 2000 computer, you can collect all this information by going to the Dial-up Networking folder, right-clicking the account connectoid, and then selecting Properties from the context menu. You also can call your ISPs Customer Service Department to obtain the information.

The Internet Connection Wizard

Once you have all your information ready, it is time to create a connection. The quickest way to start the Internet Connection Wizard is to click Start ⇨ Settings ⇨ Network and Dial-up Connections, and then choose Make a New Connection. You also can start the Wizard from the Network and Dial-up Connections folder in the Control Panel, or you can start it from a shortcut on the Start ⇨ Programs ⇨ Accessories ⇨ Communications menu. In any case, here is what to do:

STEPS:

Using the Internet Connection Wizard

Step 1. After starting the Wizard, you will see a welcome screen. Click Next.

Step 2. Here, you will need to select your network connection type (see Figure 11-1). All choices might not be available to you; it depends on your networking configuration or hardware setup. To connect to your ISP, you would choose the option Dial-up to the Internet. The option to dial-up to a private network, as well as to connect to a private network over the Internet (virtual private networking), will be covered in Chapter 21.

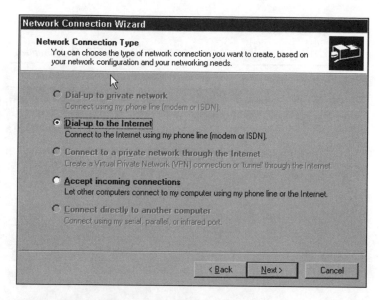

Figure 11-1: Choosing your connection type. To connect by modem to an ISP, select Dial-up to the Internet.

Step 3.   After clicking Next, you need to choose whether your Internet connection is made through your network (where your connection is made using your network interface card) or through your modem and telephone lines. Select Phone line, and then click Next.

Step 4.   In the next window, you need to choose whether you want to create a new connection or to edit an existing connection. If you have an existing connection, it will be displayed in the list box. After making your choice, click Next.

Step 5.   Now you need to type the phone number you will dial to make your connection. Your area code should already be listed; Windows 2000 gets this from the dialing rules you set up when you installed your modem. If you do not need to dial the area code when you call your ISP, clear the check box. (See Chapter 10 for more information on handling area codes.)

Step 6.   Click the Advanced button, and go to the Connection tab, shown in Figure 11-2. In most cases, you won't need to change these values. The most common connection type, as discussed above, is Point-to-Point Protocol, or PPP. Your ISP will tell you if you need to change this to a SLIP connection type, or if you need to disable LCP. If you need to use a logon script, the name of your script is specified here.

Continued

STEPS:
Using the Internet Connection Wizard *(continued)*

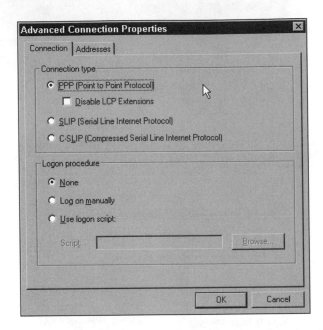

Figure 11-2: The Advanced Connection Properties dialog box. For most ISPs, you can accept the default settings.

Step 7.   The Addresses tab of the Advanced Connection Properties dialog box is where you specify your IP Address, as shown in Figure 11-3. Many ISPs dynamically assign an IP address to your connection each time you log on, while others require a static—or fixed—IP address that you will use each time. The IP address you use will be a series of four numbers separated by periods, looking something like 127.75.75.1. Most ISPs will also dynamically assign a DNS address. Think of a Domain Name System as an address book. It is what translates the domain names you type—such as www.yahoo.com—into their equivalent numeric IP address.

Step 8.   Click OK to close the dialog box and return to Step 1. Then, click Next.

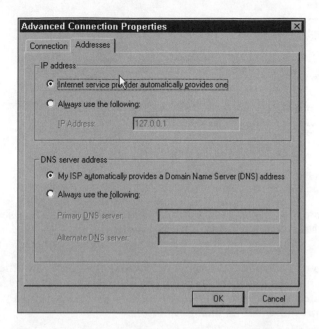

Figure 11-3: Some ISPs dynamically assign IP addresses and DNS addresses, which are the defaults in this dialog box.

Step 9. In Step 2, you need to supply your user name and password for your ISP. Note that these are probably not the same as your Windows 2000 user name and password. Your password will not appear in the box as you type; what you type will be masked by asterisk characters. Click Next.

Step 10. All of this connection information is being collected into a Dial-up Networking connection file. You need to give your connection a name, such as the name of the ISP to which you connect. Click Next.

Step 11. You've reached the finish line. Click Finish to save your settings.

Now, if you open the Network and Dial-up Connections folder again, as shown in Figure 11-4, you should see your new connection.

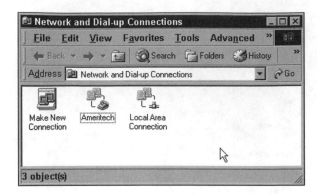

Figure 11-4: Your new connection will appear as an icon — often called a connectoid — in the Networking and Dial-up Connections folder.

You can connect to your ISP by opening this folder and then clicking the connectoid. However, to make the connection more convenient, you can place a shortcut to your connectoid on your Desktop, in your Startup group, or in your Quick Launch toolbar.

Tip

With the Networking and Dial-up Connections folder open, click and drag the connection icon, and then drop it onto the Start menu. This will add a shortcut to your connectoid on the Start menu. You can drag and drop it on the Desktop, as well. When you do, you will see the following message:

"You cannot move or copy this item to this location. Do you want to create a shortcut to the item instead?"

Click yes, and you a shortcut will appear on your Desktop. You also can drag and drop it onto the Quick Launch toolbar.

Connecting to the Internet

Now that you have completed the necessary configurations, it's time to dial your ISP. If you start your Web browser or e-mail program prior to dialing your ISP, they each can be configured to automatically dial your ISP for you. You also can click one of the shortcuts you created above to directly open the Connect window, as shown in Figure 11-5.

The user name and phone number should be the same as you supplied in the Connection Wizard. The password also should be the same, but it displays asterisks as placeholders for each character. If you want Windows 2000 to remember the password for you, click the Save Password check box.

Tip

User names and passwords are normally case-sensitive. Note the capitalization as you type your user name and password, and verify the status of your Caps Lock key, as well.

Figure 11-5: The Connect dialog box shows the information you supplied during the Internet Connection Wizard setup process.

Tip

If you want your password to be forgotten, uncheck the Save Password box, and delete the password from the text box.

Caution

Computers — unlike humans — usually never forget things. However, they are more likely than people to display symptoms of total lobotomy patients (in other words, have a catastrophic crash that forces you to reinstall your operating system), wiping out any saved password information. Be sure to keep a written record of all your passwords.

Save some time: Disable the connection window

The Windows 2000 Connection dialog box is nice, but it takes up valuable screen space and requires a couple of mouse clicks to banish. There might be times when you just want it to go away. Here's how.

STEPS:

Turning Off the Connection Dialog Box

Step 1. Click your connectoid or shortcut to display the Connection dialog box.

Step 2. Click Properties, and then select the Options tab.

Continued

Step 3.   Clear the check boxes for Display progress while connecting, Prompt for name, password, certificate, and Prompt for phone number.

Step 4.   Click OK.

Any time you want to display the Connection dialog box again, just reverse these steps.

Connection properties

To connect to your ISP, you click the Dial button. Before you do, however, first click Properties. The Properties dialog box for your dial-up connectoid contains the information you provided when you set up your dial-up connection

Tip

On the General tab, check the box that says Show icon in task bar when connected. This puts a miniature version of the Connection icon in your Systray or Taskbar tray, the "indented" space on the right side of your Taskbar. Hovering over this icon with your mouse when you are connected will display your connection speed along with the number of bytes sent and received. Enable the Display Progress while connecting check box on the Options tab so you can display your connection progress.

If your connection is successful, you won't have to do anything else in the Properties dialog box. Click OK to close the dialog box, and then click the Dial button to start your connection.

A successful connection can take anywhere from 5 to 20 seconds (and sometimes more) to complete. You will see a progress on the screen as the connection progresses. When the connection is successful, the connection window will minimize to your system tray on the right side of your Taskbar. If you hover your mouse pointer over the system tray icon for your connection, you also should see a pop-up ToolTip telling you about your current connection speed and other details. Once you're connected, you can open any Internet application you want, such as browser or your e-mail program.

Even if you never make a direct Internet connection (preferring to do so through your browser, e-mail program, or FTP client instead), it's helpful for you to know how to pull the plug when you need to.

STEPS:

Disconnecting from the Internet

Step 1. Click the connection icon in the system tray.

Step 2. Choose Disconnect from the Connections Status box, as shown in Figure 11-6, to disconnect your modem from your ISP.

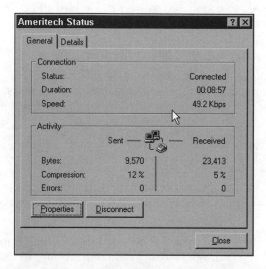

Figure 11-6: Once you have an open connection, the status box displays your connection details.

Secret

One of the ways in which integration of the operating system with Internet functions has hurt users is a simple matter of keyboard access to active Internet connection icons. In Windows 95, 98, and Windows NT 3.51, you could toggle between open processes using the handy Alt-Tab keyboard shortcut method. Once the Internet functions became a part of the operating system, however, users were then forced to click a tiny little icon in the system tray to disconnect or to check the connection's Status dialog box. Fortunately, there is a nifty way around this: display your connection's Status dialog box, and then press the Alt-Tab keys to switch to another open process. The next time you press the Alt-Tab keys, you'll see your open Internet connection icons, and can select one to either disconnect or to display your connection status.

Tip

Click the Details tab to see the server and client IP addresses for your connection, as well as the connection type. Properties on the General tab will take you back to the connection's Properties dialog box that you normally see before dialing your ISP.

Secret

The settings for your dial-up connections are saved in the Windows\System32\ras\rasphone.pbk file. There is a section for each connection. The settings can be viewed in a text editor like Notepad, but it's probably better to try to make changes in the connection's Properties dialog box.

If you successfully connected to your ISP, you're all set. You can move on to your browser or your e-mail program.

Manual and scripted connections

Some ISP's do not provide a completely automated logon process. Instead, after the connection is made, a terminal window appears, into which you need to type information when you are prompted. This information may include:

- Type of account; this could be PPP or SLIP.

- User name and password.

- If you have a SLIP account with dynamically assigned IP addresses, you will see yours. Write this down, because you may have to type this in later.

Tip

Microsoft includes a scripting tool called the Dial-up Scripting. You can assign a script to run with any of your connections. To assign a script, do the following.

Alternatively, your ISP may provide a script file for you to use, which details the necessary logon information the ISP's system will request.

Although used less frequently than in the days of Windows 95 and Windows NT 3.5, scripting remains a very useful function. Here's how to assign a script you have received from your ISP to a dial-up connectoid.

STEPS:

Assigning a Script to a Dial-up Connection

Step 1.   Click Start ➪ Settings ➪ Network and Dial-up Connections.

Step 2.   Right-click the connection to which you want to assign the script. Then, click the Properties button.

Step 3.   A number of basic scripts that work with common Internet connections are included in the *windows*\system32\ras folder. Click the list box to find one that matches your account, as shown in Figure 11-7.

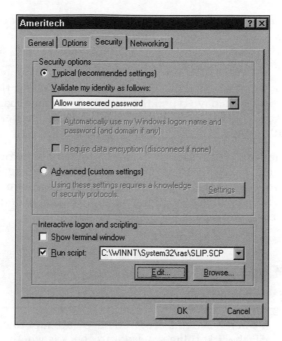

Figure 11-7: Check the Run script box and then choose a sample script.

Step 4. The scripts that have been provided by Microsoft are generic scripts. You will need to edit them so that they include the specific prompts required by your ISP. Click OK to save your connection's new properties.

Secret

If your ISP calls for something out of the ordinary, you might need to develop a custom script. Documentation for the Dial-up Scripting language can be found in the Windows 2000 Help file, under the topic "Automating the dial-up logon process by using Windows scripting."

Secret

The extension used for script files is .SCP. Almost every other program in the world uses the .SCR extension for script files. Microsoft has already assigned the .SCR extension to screen saver files.

Troubleshooting Connections

If you have an Internet connection, chances are good that you will have to troubleshoot it at some point. Often, the problem will be some transient problem with the Internet. In cases like these, all you can do is wait and try again later. Other times, what you should do often depends on the error message you receive, or the point in the connection process where things break down. The following troubleshooting steps assume you have never been able to make a connection. They represent some of the more common errors, and what you can do to correct them.

Tip

Before you adjust any of these advanced settings, check the simple things first. Make sure you have typed the correct user name, password, and phone number. Also, check that to be sure your modem is properly configured. (See Chapter 10.)

Tip

In the Windows 2000 online help, search on the term Error messages. You will be able to find a page that lists many of the error messages you may get with both Network and Dialup Connections. The messages are numbered, and there are 752 of them, although not all apply to Dialup connections. If you get a specific error message, try looking it up here.

STEPS

Error 5: Access Is Denied

Step 1.   If you receive this error when you attempt to connect to your ISP, the first thing you want to check is whether your encryption settings are correct. Right-click your connection, select Properties, and click the Security tab. Make sure that Typical is selected. In the Validate my identity as follows option, choose Allow unsecured password. You also should check with your ISP to ensure that you have set the correct encryption settings.

Step 2.   Some ISPs, such as the Earthlink Network, require a prefix before your username, such as ELN/*username*. Be sure to add any required prefix before your username. (The MSN part of the username is an example of a realm.)

STEPS

Error 629: The Port Was Disconnected by the Remote Machine

Step 1.   Request a terminal window, and manually enter your user name and password (see Figure 11-8). To open a terminal window, right-click the connection icon and choose Properties, and then click the Security tab. Check Show Terminal Window.

Step 2.   Check your modem control properties. In the connection's Properties dialog box, select the General tab, and then click Configure. Make sure that Enable hardware flow control, Enable modem error control, and Enable modem compression are all checked.

Step 3. Click the connection's icon and choose Properties, and then select the Networking tab. Click Settings, and ensure that Enable software compression is checked.

Step 4. The remote server may not support LCP extensions. Right-click the connection's icon and choose Properties, select the Networking tab, and then click Settings. Clear the Enable LCP extensions check box.

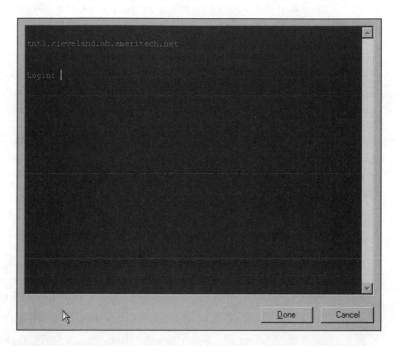

Figure 11-8: The Terminal Services window lets you perform an interactive logon.

Error 640: A NetBios error has occurred

You may be able to make a connection if you slow down your modem speed. Microsoft suggests dropping the speed to 9600 bps. To do this, follow these steps:

STEPS
Slowing Down Your Modem

Step 1. Click Start ➪ Settings ➪ Network and Dial-up Connections.

Step 2. Right-click your connection's icon, and then click Properties.

Continued

STEPS:

Slowing Down Your Modem *(continued)*

Step 3. Select the General tab, and then click Configure.

Step 4. Set your modem's maximum speed to 9600 bps.

If this works, you can go back later and try increasing the speed in single-step increments until you reach a speed where you can't connect. (You don't want to operate at 9600 bps if you can help it.)

Error: Remote PPP Peer is not responding

When you receive this error, you might need to manually connect to your ISP — this also helps you monitor what is happening. You will need to use a terminal window.

STEPS:

Opening a Terminal Window

Step 1. Click Start ⇨ Settings ⇨ Network and Dial-up Connections.

Step 2. Right-click your connection's icon, and then click Properties.

Step 3. Select the Security tab. Then, check Show Terminal Window.

TCP/IP Utilities do not work

If you make a connection to a server, but you can't get TCP/IP utilities like ping or tracert to work, you may have to turn off IP header compression. To do this, follow these steps:

STEPS:

Disabling IP Header Compression

Step 1. Click Start ⇨ Settings ⇨ Network and Dial-up Connections.

Step 2. Right-click your connection's icon, and then click Properties.

Step 3. Select the Networking tab.

Step 4. Select Internet Protocol (TCP/IP) from the installed components list, and then click Properties.

Step 5. Click the Advanced button, and then clear the Use IP header compression check box (see Figure 11-9).

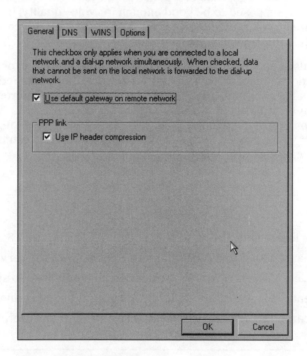

Figure 11-9: If TCP/IP programs won't work, you might have to clear the Use IP header compression check box.

Error: No dial tone

This might mean a physical error with the connection. Make sure that your phone line is connected to your modem, and that your modem is correctly configured and connected to the COM port on the back of your computer. (See Chapter 10.)

Once you are connected

Even after you have a working connection, things can occasionally go bad, and you can't make a connection. The first thing to do is wait and try a few minutes later. Your ISP may have had a temporary outage, your initial data transmission may have gotten mangled, or there could have even been sun spot activity.

Secret

Instead of blaming your software or your hardware, maybe its time to blame the phone company. Noise and static on phone lines may either prevent connections from occurring, or slow down high-speed connections. You probably won't get much response from the phone company, either. Their lines are supposed to be good enough for voice quality, but they aren't required to guarantee the lines for data quality. It's not called POTS (Plain Old Telephone Service) for nothing.

Secret

You also can blame the squirrels. This happened to one of the authors, who had increasing problems making connections with his modem due to static on his line. The static finally became bad enough to interfere with voice calls, which brought the phone company repair person out. Squirrels had been chewing on the phone line, and they made a hole big enough to let in the rain water, which seeped to the low point in the wire between the house and the pole, causing the short-circuits.

Summary

We have learned how to create a connection to an Internet Service Provider.

▶ We learned what to look for in an ISP, and some of the services they provide.

▶ We learned how to use the Internet Connection Wizard to set up a connection.

▶ We learned how to start, monitor, and stop a dial-up connection.

▶ We learned some basic troubleshooting steps for an Internet connection.

Chapter 12

Internet Explorer 5

In This Chapter

We learn some of the secrets of Internet Explorer 5:

▶ How to configure its startup options.

▶ How to set security just the way you want it, to give some discipline to applets, cookies, and ActiveX controls.

▶ How to get the most out of the Favorites menu.

▶ How to make your browsing more secure.

Integration of the Browser and the OS

Windows 2000 comes with Internet Explorer 5, Microsoft's newest browser. Microsoft argues that the browser is an integral part of the operating system, and indeed, a number of the newer features make navigating between the Web and local files almost seamless.

Whether these features could also be achieved without the integrated browser can be left for others to decide. In fact, as this book goes to press, a Federal judge is deciding the outcome of the Federal government and nineteen state government's antitrust suit against Microsoft. A key issue in this suit is whether a browser should be bundled with the operating system or not. There is always a chance that, as a consequence of this suit, Microsoft will be ordered to remove Internet Explorer 5 from Windows 2000, in which case some of this chapter will be wrong. However, we have written this chapter with the idea that there will be no changes to Internet Explorer's place within the operating system.

My Computer, the Windows Explorer, and the Internet Explorer all have the same basic look and feel, especially if you have chosen the Single Click style in Folder Options (see Chapter 7). Internet Explorer also has the Explorer bar, so it can be set up with a two-pane view. The left pane can be set for folder view, or for Search, Favorites, or History views.

Starting Internet Explorer

To show how tightly their browser is tied to the operating system, Microsoft gives you many different ways to start Internet Explorer. In fact, just about anywhere you turn, you trip over a way to start Internet Explorer:

- There is a shortcut for the Internet Explorer on the desktop.

- There is a shortcut for the Internet Explorer on the Quick Launch toolbar.

- There is a shortcut for the Internet Explorer on the Start ➪ Programs menu.

- Type a URL into the Address Bar in My Computer or the Windows Explorer, and they morph to become Internet Explorer.

- Select an HTML document from your hard drive using My Computer or the Windows Explorer, and the document will open in the Internet Explorer.

- If you are displaying your Favorites on the Start menu, click one of them.

- Click Start ➪ Run, and then type the URL.

Tip

You don't have to type the http:// portion of the URL to connect. Just type the rest of the address, such as www.idgbooks.com. If you're accessing a non-Web address such as an FTP server, you will have to supply the beginning portion of the address, as in ftp://ftp.microsoft.com.

Secret

If you are typing an address in Internet Explorer's Address Bar, pressing Ctrl+Enter will automatically add the "www." string to the beginning of the address you type, plus the "com" string to the end of the address.

Making your connection

If you already have an established connection to the Internet, either through a network or because you have already started a dial-up connection, you will be taken to the address that you typed or clicked. If you aren't connected, you may see the message shown in Figure 12-1.

Figure 12-1: This page isn't available locally. You will have to connect to the Internet to view it.

You may be able to see a Web page that you visited recently, if it is still stored in your cache. (See "Managing your disk cache," later in this chapter.) If you click Connect, you will then see the Dial-up Connection dialog box, similar to the dialog box you see when you click a Dial-up Networking connectoid. If you have multiple Dial-up networking connections, you can choose the connection you want to use from the list box, as shown in Figure 12-2, and then click the Connect button to reach the Web.

Tip

If you just want to connect directly to the Web, check the box that says Connect automatically. You will still see the Dial-up Connection dialog box, but you won't need to click the button. You don't want to do this if you often need to make changes to your connections.

Figure 12-2: The Internet Explorer Dial-up Connection dialog box. You can make additional modifications to your settings from Internet Explorer Options.

For additional control on how the Internet Explorer automatically connects to the Internet, start the Internet Explorer and click Tools ⇨ Internet Options. (You can also reach this dialog box without starting your browser by clicking Start ⇨ Settings ⇨ Control Panel, and then clicking the Internet Options icon.) Finally, click the Connections tab in the Internet Options dialog box for additional connection settings.

If you have established multiple dial-up connections, you can choose the connection you want to use as your default. From this dialog box, you also can modify the dialing behavior for your connections.

STEPS:

Modifying Dialing Behavior

Step 1. Within the Internet Explorer, click Tools ⇨ Internet Options, and select the Connections tab.

Step 2. Highlight the connection you want to change, and click the Settings button.

Step 3. In the Dial-up Settings section, click the Advanced button.

Step 4. In Advanced Dial-Up dialog box shown in Figure 12-3, you can choose how many times the connection will be attempted (invaluable if you often get busy signals from your ISP) and how long to wait between each attempt.

Step 5. You can specify how long your connection should remain open if there is no activity on your computer. If you have to pay either connection or long distance charges, you may want to adjust this time downward.

Step 6. You also can tell Internet Explorer to terminate the connection when you no longer need the connection open. How does the Internet Explorer know when it is not needed? The Internet Explorer waits until you have closed all your Internet applications (browser, e-mail, chat programs, and so on).

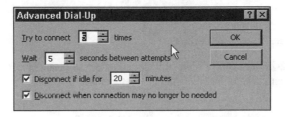

Figure 12-3: Advanced Dial-up settings can help you initiate or terminate a connection.

Your home page

If you started the Internet Explorer by clicking one of its shortcuts, rather than typing a specific Web address, the first place you will go once you are online is your home page. Well, it's not really your home page; it's probably the home page of someone who wants to sell lots of advertising.

The latest hot trend that is going to make everybody on the Web rich (as this book is being written) is the Internet Portal. A *portal* is your doorway to the Web — a site where the Internet Explorer first takes you when you start your browser. By all accounts, it was Netscape's Netcenter portal that made the company worth $10 billion to America Online (AOL). After all, Netscape's other main product, Communicator, is given away free.

By default, the Internet Explorer 5 takes you to the home page of the Microsoft Network, just as Netscape Navigator, by default, takes you to the Netscape Netcenter. Many computer OEMs (Original Equipment Manufacturers) change this. For example, a Dell computer may be configured to take you to a Dell-customized page provided by Excite, or your ISP may set its own page as your Home Page when you use their installation disk to set up your Internet connection. Why? To drive eyeballs to their sites. The more visitors they have, and the more click-throughs they have on their advertisements, the more they can charge their advertisers.

You may actually like the site that someone else has chosen for your home page. Some home pages can even be customized to show local news, weather, sports scores, and the like. But you might have a site in mind that you would prefer to see first. To change your browser home page, follow these steps:

STEPS:

Changing Your Browser Home Page

Step 1.   Start the Internet Explorer.

Step 2.   Click Tools ⇨ Internet Options. Make sure the General tab is forward.

Step 3.   In the Home Page text box, type the address of your new home page, as shown in Figure 12-4.

Step 4.   Not sure what address to use? Close the dialog box, and then navigate to the page you want to use. Then, repeat Step 2.

Step 5.   Click Use Current to configure the page you are viewing as your home page.

Step 6.   If you decide you want to go back to the original page someone else selected for you, click Use Default.

Step 7.   You don't need a home page at all. You can click the Use Blank button to display a blank page when you start the Internet Explorer.

Continued

STEPS:

Changing Your Browser Home Page *(continued)*

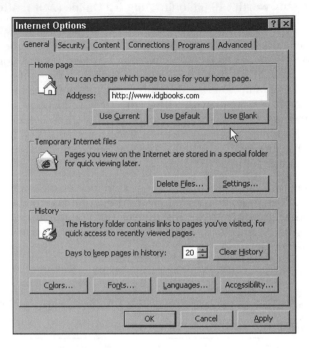

Figure 12-4: You can choose what home page you want to display each time you start Internet Explorer.

Secret

Tired of all this Web portal idiocy? You can create your own personal, non-commercial portal to the World Wide Web, even if you don't have access to a Web server. Simply create a document in a program like Microsoft Word that contains links to the Web pages you most often want to visit, and then save the document in .HTM format to your hard drive. Finally, open the .HTM file you just saved on your hard drive in the Internet Explorer, and designate it as your home page using the method described in the previous exercise.

The familiar ways of navigating in the Internet Explorer — clicking a link or using the Favorites list — are still available. However, Microsoft has tweaked a number of other features to help ease navigation.

Explorer Bar

Using the Explorer Bar, you can set up the Internet Explorer in a two-pane view, with either Folders (the contents of your computer), Favorites, History, or Search in the left pane. To display one of these, click View ➪ Explorer Bar within the Internet Explorer, and then choose the contents of the left pane. Selecting Folders will transform the Internet Explorer into the Windows Explorer, allowing you to browse your computer. Selecting Favorites will duplicate the drop-down Favorites list from the menu into the left pane. If your Favorites are organized in folders (see "Organize your Favorites," later in this chapter), clicking a folder will then expand it.

Note

If you are offline, any of your Favorites that are not cached — and thus not available offline — will be grayed out. Click one of them and you will be presented with a dialog box asking if you want to go online.

Using the Search Assistant

The Search Assistant has become more powerful in Internet Explorer 5. It now allows you to designate a search engine of your choice (Lycos, Excite, Yahoo!, and so forth). You also can run your search across several search engines in a meta-search style.

To change your Search Assistant settings, display the Search Assistant Customize Search Settings dialog box and follow these steps:

STEPS:
Customize Your Searching

Step 1. In the Internet Explorer, click View ➪ Explorer Bar, and then select Search.

Step 2. Click Customize in the left pane.

Step 3. Each category that you can search — Web pages, addresses, businesses, maps, and previous searches — each has its own customization section. You can choose which search engines tools the Search Assistant should use for each type of search.

Step 4. In each category, you should select one of the search engines as your primary search provider. Select it in the list box, and then click the up arrow button beneath the list box to move it to the top of the list.

Step 5. You can choose to use only one search engine (your primary search provider) by selecting Use one search service for all searches, as shown in Figure 12-5.

Continued

STEPS:

Customize Your Searching (continued)

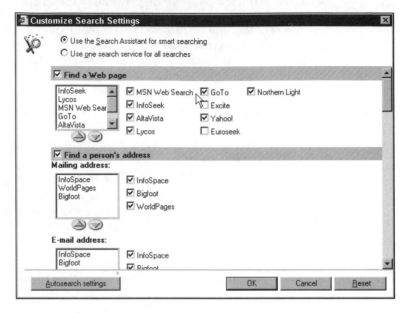

Figure 12-5: Customize Search dialog boxes. You can select which search engines you want to use for your searches. The search engine listed at the top of the list is your primary search engine.

Using the Search Assistant for smart searching

If you customize the settings in Search Assistant to enable smart searching of more than one search engine (see previous section), you can create a personal search tool that behaves much like Dogpile (www.dogpile.com) and WebCrawler (www.webcrawler.com) meta-search engines. The only difference is the way in which the results are displayed. With the Internet Explorer 5's Search Assistant, you cannot scroll through the collective results of all the various search engines used in your meta-search. Instead, you need to click the Next icon located in the navigation bar above the left search result pane to switch from the results of one search engine to the results of the next.

That's just the beginning of what Search Assistant's smart searching can do. If you select Customize, you can also configure the Search Assistant to find: a person's mailing and e-mail address; businesses; find maps; place names; an encyclopedia, atlas, dictionary, or thesaurus; pictures; and newsgroups. As a bonus, you can even customize a search based on your previous ten searches.

Another way to search is with the Related links tool. Use the Internet Explorer to access a page that interests you. Then, click Tools ⇨ Show Related Links to open the Explorer Bar with a list of sites that are similar to the one you are viewing. These similar links are prepared by a Web navigation service called *Alexa*. Alexa is one of a number of web accessories offered either by Microsoft or by third party vendors that add more functionality to Internet Explorer.

After you have displayed the related links in the Explorer Bar, you can download the full Alexa service by clicking the provided Alexa full service link. Once the full service has been loaded, Alexa can be displayed Alexa either in the Explorer Bar, or in a window along the lower edge of the browser window. Once you display a particular site, Alexa will display related links, and it will show additional information about a site if you request it to do so.

History bar

If you recently visited a cool page, but you forgot to add the address to your Favorites list, you might still be able to find it in your Internet Explorer History list. To see your History list, click View ⇨ Explorer Bar ⇨ History. The Explorer Bar now displays a series of folders resembling the pages of a calendar; each page holds a link to the pages you've visited by week, as well as the current and previous day.

The Internet Explorer History list will show only as many days as you have set on the General tab in the Internet Options dialog box. Select the number of days of Web activity you want your History folder to save. Increasing the number of days to maintain will increase the size of your History folder on your hard drive. To temporarily free up disk space, or to erase record of where you have been on the Web, click the Clear History button.

You can change the way the History folder is viewed. You can sort by date, by site, by most frequently visited, and by the order visited today.

If you know you visited the site yesterday, click View ⇨ By Date, and then click the page that represents yesterday (see Figure 12-6). The folder will expand to show all the sites you visited that day, arranged in alphabetical order. (Domain names do not include the www. in a Web address.) Click the link to see a list of all the pages in the site that you visited. Then, simply Click the link to the page to return to the site.

The Search, Favorites, and History Bars also can be displayed using the keyboard shortcuts Ctrl+E, Ctrl+I, and Ctrl+H. By default, the Internet Explorer toolbar also has icons that will display the folders: the globe, the folder, and the sundial.

Figure 12-6: The History folder is set to remember the last 20 days. Thus, the maximum number of days you can view history for is just under three weeks.

Web Accessories

Web accessories are add-ins from Microsoft and third parties—often major Web sites—that add extra features or functionality to Internet Explorer 5. (Some of the accessories are available for other browsers, as well.) Web accessories can be additional Explorer Bars, toolbar buttons, and even extra menu selections. Accessories that are supplied by Microsoft can be downloaded by clicking Tools ⇨ Windows Update. Some Microsoft web accessories include:

- **Quick Search:** Type "av bugs" in the Address Bar to do a quick search for bugs via Alta Vista.

- **Zoom in/Zoom out:** Right-click an image, and you can choose either to zoom in or zoom out.

- **Image Toggler:** Displaying images takes time. Put this switch on the Links toolbar to quickly disable them.

- **Web Search:** Select keywords on a Web page, and then right-click the keyword and

click Web search to send your selected words to a default search engine.

Other interesting third-party accessories, such as the New York Times Explorer Bar, are also available. Microsoft provides several web accessories—and links to other accessories—at http://www.microsoft.com/windows/ie/webaccess/, such as:

- Alexa Explorer Bar

- Alta Vista Explorer Bar

- Bloomberg Explorer Bar

- Microsoft Power Tweaks Web Accessories

- New York Times Explorer Bar

To enable Alexa, follow these steps:

1. Click View on the Explorer Bar.

2. Select Explorer Bar.

3. Choose either Alexa Vertical or Alexa Horizontal.

There is an easier way to enable the Alexa toolbar. Once you find a Web page on which you want Alexa to run, simply place your mouse pointer in the white area of the Search Bar, right-click, and then select Show Alexa from the context menu.

In addition to offering related links, Alexa can tell you a lot more about the page being viewed than you might expect. Typically you can expect information such as: traffic and web reviews; contact information, site statistics, related links, news, reference, and help.

Later, if you decide you want to remove any of these Web accessories, you use the Control Panel's Add/Remove Programs icon to remove them, as shown in the following steps:

1. Click Start ⇨ Settings ⇨ Control Panel.

2. Click the Add/Remove Programs icon.

3. In the list of installed programs, find the Web accessory you want to remove and highlight it.

4. Click the Change/Remove button. Sometimes the program will be automatically removed, while other times, you may need to work with the program's uninstall utility.

The Alexa toolbar can provide background information about your site, some site ratings, and show you a list of similar sites.

The Address Bar

The Search Bar and the History Bar are two navigational tools you can use if you don't know the address (the URL) that you want to visit. On the other hand, if you do know the address, the fastest way to get there is using the Address Bar.

Note

If the Address Bar is not displayed in your Internet Explorer window, click View ⇨ Toolbars ⇨ Address Bar to enable it. If it is sharing space with another toolbar, you can expand or contract it by clicking and dragging the selection handle to the right of the respective toolbar. You also can drag it upward to share space with another toolbar.

Typing a URL within the Address Bar is enhanced by the AutoComplete feature of Windows 2000, which applies not only to URLs within the Internet Explorer, but also in many other places where you type in a selection, including dialog boxes, Run, Forms, Mapping Network Drives, and the Windows Explorer. If you begin to type a Web address, the Internet Explorer will examine its History folder for similar addresses, as shown in Figure 12-7. AutoComplete can only look into the past, not to the future. If you haven't visited a page before, it will not appear as a choice in the AutoComplete list.

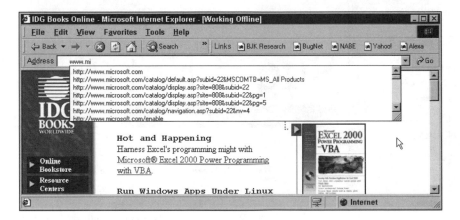

Figure 12-7: AutoComplete: By typing in www.mi, Internet Explorer displays a list of pages in the History folder that begin with these characters.

Once a number of possible AutoComplete selections are displayed, click an entry to select it. Alternatively, you can use the keyboard up arrow or down arrow keys to cycle through the list, and then select the link you want by pressing the Enter key.

Clicking the down arrow to the right of the Address Bar will expand it to show recent addresses that you typed into the Address Bar. However, it will not show URLs that you have accessed through other means, such as following a link or using your Favorites list.

Tip

AutoComplete can be used to fill in forms and passwords, as well as Web addresses. It also will fill in user names and passwords on Web forms. To select which information you want AutoComplete to handle, select Tools ⇨ Internet Options, and then click the Content tab. Click the AutoComplete button in the Personal Information section. (See Figure 12-8.)

Figure 12-8: You can adjust and clear your AutoComplete settings in the AutoComplete dialog box. If you don't want it to remember information typed into forms (like credit card numbers), disable here.

Caution

For AutoComplete to work, it must store this information on your hard drive. If you have stored sensitive information, and someone else may be using your computer, access the AutoComplete settings dialog box and click both the Clear Forms and Clear Passwords buttons to clear the details. While the information is encrypted, another user might still be able to use the encrypted data to enter a secured Web site.

Secret

You can clear your History folder by clicking a button; you also can empty your cache by clicking a button. However, if you want to clear the typed addresses that you can view in the Address Bar, you have to edit the Registry. Before editing the registry, you might want to review Chapter 16 for important safety information.

STEPS:

Erasing the Stored Addresses in the Address Bar

Step 1.   Close Internet Explorer.

Step 2.   Click Start ⇨ Run, and type Regedit.exe in the Open text box.

Continued

STEPS:

Erasing the Stored Addresses in the Address Bar *(continued)*

Step 3.   Within the Registry, navigate to the following key:

HKEY_CURRENT_USER\Software\Microsoft\Internet
Explorer\TypedURLs

Step 4   URLs that have been typed into the Address Bar will be listed as
Url1, Url2, and so on, in this registry key. You will need to delete
all but the Default keys. Right-click the key you want to delete, and
then select Delete from the context menu.

Step 5.   If you delete some of the keys, but leave others, and you then see
a gap in the numbering, the entries after the gap will not display
properly. Rename the remaining keys so that they are in numerical
order, if you want to be able to see the remaining entries.

Favorites

The fastest way to navigate is to compile and use a Favorites list. This is
Microsoft's version of Netscape's Bookmarks, only Microsoft's Favorites
have more flexibility. Favorites are nothing more than shortcuts, with each
Favorite becoming a separate file within your Favorites folder. If you have
upgraded to Windows 2000 from Windows 95, 98, or NT, the location of your
Favorites is probably *windows*\Profiles*username*\Favorites. If you did a
clean install of Windows 2000, your Favorites will be in the \Documents and
Settings folder. The location of your Favorites folder can be found in the
Registry at HKEY_CURRENT_USER\Software\Microsoft\Windows\
CurrentVersion\Explorer\Shell Folders.

You can display your Favorites as a cascading menu right from your
Start menu by configuring your Start Menu properties, as shown in the
following steps:

STEPS:

Adding Favorites to the Start Menu

Step 1.   Click Start ➪ Settings ➪ Taskbar & Start Menu.

Step 2.   Click the Advanced tab.

Step 3.   In the Start Menu Settings list, select Display Favorites.

Step 4.   Click OK.

Organize the Favorites menu

If you spend much time on the Web at all, you will soon collect a large number of Favorites. Just as you wouldn't want to save all your documents in one folder, you also should avoid storing all your Favorites in one folder by organizing your favorites into a number of subfolders, as well. Initially, the Favorites folder will have only a few subfolders, as shown in Figure 12-9. To open the folder in the Internet Explorer, click Favorites ➪ Organize Favorites.

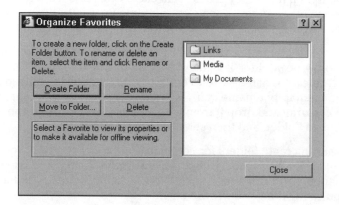

Figure 12-9: In your Favorites folder, you can create subfolders to hold categories of favorites: Tech Support, News, Sports, or any other category you like.

Oddly enough, while Favorites are nothing more than shortcut files within folders, and Microsoft has the Windows Explorer, the Internet Explorer, and My Computer converging toward a common look and feel, the Organize Folders tool does not use the same window in which to organize your folders as the Explorers do. Instead, the Organize Folders tool for your Favorites has a look and feel all its own. Unless your copy of the Internet Explorer 5 has been customized by your computer manufacturer or your ISP, you will probably see only a couple of folders there. One, called Media, has links to a number of Microsoft partners who offer audio or video over the Web. Another, called Channels, links to active content — or push — providers. Still another, called Links, is normally filled with shortcuts to a number of Microsoft sites that will guide you around the Web.

The reason the Links folder is important is because you can display it either on your Internet Explorer toolbar or on your Taskbar, so that you can quickly get to these links. However, you don't have to be content with the default Links that someone else might have placed there. If you want, you can delete all of them using the Organize Favorites dialog box, and then fill the Links Bar with your own quick favorites. To delete one of the Favorites, simply expand its folder within the Organize Favorites dialog box, select the link, and then click the Delete button.

Tip

If you think you might want to visit a quick favorite link someday, move it to some less prominent folder instead of deleting it. It's sort of like stashing some of your old clothes up in the attic, in the hope that they will one day come back into style. (Hey, fashions from the 70's have come back, which just goes to prove that anything is possible.) You can even create a Favorites folder called Attic just for this use.

Secret

To display the Links Bar on your Internet Explorer toolbar, click View ⇨ Toolbars, and then make sure Links is checked. Once it is displayed, you can drag it to some other spot; it can go on the same level with the menu, it can share space with the Address Bar, or you can drag it down to a line of its own.

To create a new folder in the Organize Favorites window, click the Create Folder button. A new folder, imaginatively called New Folder, will appear in the list box. Since the name — New Folder — is highlighted, typing in a new name will immediately rename it. If you want to move a Favorite into this new folder, you can drag and drop it from the Favorites list. You also can highlight it, click Move to Folder, and then select its new home.

You may want to create folders for common groups of Favorites. You can have one folder for News, one for Sports, one for Shopping, and one for a particular hobby. You can create subfolders within a Favorites folder, too, just like you can within your My Documents folder.

Secret

You can bypass the Organize Favorites folder and use the full power of the Windows Explorer instead. Just navigate to the Favorites folder within the Windows Explorer and use all of the copying, deleting, moving, and renaming secrets you learned in Chapter 7. You also can create new Favorites folders within the Windows Explorer.

Changing Favorites order

You can rearrange the order of shortcuts on your Favorites menu without going to the Organize Favorites window. Just click the Favorites menu in the Internet Explorer to display it. Then click and drag a Favorite or a folder to move it either up or down the list. If you want to move it to one of your subfolders, hover your mouse pointer over the subfolder until its menu expands, and then drop the shortcut onto a folder in the list.

Adding Favorites

You can add Web pages to your Favorites list, one at a time, by navigating to a page you want to add, and then clicking Favorites ⇨ Add to Favorites. However, there are faster ways to add favorites — especially if you have quite a few to add — and you can find links to them all on the same page.

Tip

In the Internet Explorer, click View ⇨ Explorer Bar ⇨ Favorites (or press Ctrl+I). This opens a pane with all your Favorites folders on the left. If you see a hyperlink that you would like to add to a folder, click and drag the hyperlink, and then drop it into the folder you want to add it to.

Another way to add a Favorite is through a right-click. If you see a hyperlink you want to add to your Favorites, right-click it and select Add to Favorites from the context menu. This will open the Add Favorites dialog box, where you can select the folder you want the Favorite to go to.

The Personalized Menus feature that hides rarely used entries on your Start Menu also enhances (afflicts?) your Favorites menu. It can be enabled or disabled, so you can experiment with whether you like this new feature.

STEPS:

Changing the Personalized Favorites Setting

Step 1. In Internet Explorer, click Tools ⇨ Internet Options.

Step 2. Click the Advanced tab.

Step 3. In the Settings, Browsing list, locate Enable Personalized Favorites menu.

Step 4. To hide your rarely used favorites, select this box. To always see the full list, clear it. Then click OK.

Step 5. If you have it enabled, click the chevron symbol on the Favorites menu to see the full menu.

Importing and exporting Favorites

The Internet Explorer recognizes that other applications — even (gasp!) Netscape Navigator — may want to use its shortcuts. An Import and Export Wizard has been added to the Internet Explorer file menu specifically to deal with these situations.

Netscape Navigator — the browser within the Netscape Communicator package — organizes Favorites, which it calls Bookmarks, differently than Internet Explorer. Bookmarks are kept in an HTML file, with each Bookmark a hypertext link in the file. Internet Explorer 5 has an Import and Export Wizard that will let you exchange favorites/bookmarks with Netscape Navigator.

STEPS:

Importing Favorites

Step 1. In Internet Explorer click File ⇨ Import and Export to open the Import/Export Wizard welcome page. Then, click Next.

Step 2. Select what you want to do. Let's Import Netscape Favorites, so select Import Favorites and click Next.

Continued

Step 3. Your Netscape bookmarks are probably kept in a file called bookmark.htm, which is located in your Netscape user profile folder. Click Browse to find it. (Check in C:\Program Files\Netscape\Users*username.*) Click Next.

Step 4. Now, select a Favorites folder to import the bookmarks into, and then click Next.

Step 5. When you come to the last screen of the wizard, click Finish. You will then find your imported bookmarks in the Favorites folder you selected in Step 4. If the bookmark file had separate sections, each section will appear in a subfolder.

The process is similar for exporting Favorites. You can select your entire Favorites folder, or a single subfolder, to export. You will need to provide a filename for your converted bookmarks.

Caution

The default filename for an export is bookmark.htm. This is the same name as the Netscape bookmark file. If you save it in your Netscape user profile folder, you will overwrite your existing Netscape bookmarks. Save it with a different name, and the two files can coexist. (You can load alternative bookmark files in Navigator.)

Secret

If you export your favorites to an HTML page, you can use this page as your default home page, using the steps shown earlier in this chapter.

Working with Web Information

In addition to designating a Web page as a Favorite so that you can easily visit it again, there are many other ways in which you can use the data you find on the Web.

Saving pages

A new feature in Internet Explorer 5 is its ability to save not only a Web page, but also all the graphics files displayed on the page. In previous versions of Internet Explorer, if you saved a page with the File ➪ Save As command, only the text would be saved. When you later opened the saved file in your browser, the page would display, but in place of the various graphics files would be the symbol for a missing file.

With the Internet Explorer 5, when you use the File ⇨ Save as command, you now have the ability to save the complete Web page by default. The text itself will be saved in the folder you specify in the Save Web Page dialog box (see Figure 12-10). All of the graphics files from the page will be saved in a subfolder beneath the Save location. The subfolder will have the same name as the file you save, and the file and folder will remain linked. If you delete the saved Web page, the subfolder will also be deleted. If you delete the folder, the file goes, too.

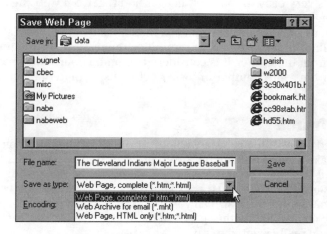

Figure 12-10: You can save a complete Web page, including all of its graphics files, or you can just save the HTML portion of the page.

If you are only interested in the text, and you don't want a bunch of folders full of data files, choose Save as type and select the HTML only option. For either type of save, the default filename chosen by the Internet Explorer 5 is the title of the page (found in the HTML header information). The title might need to be shortened if it's too long.

 You can save a Web page without viewing it as long as you have a hyperlink to it. Right-click the hyperlink, and then click Save Target As to save that particular page to your hard drive.

Tip

Save a graphic

To save a graphic file that you see on a Web page, right-click the graphic. The shortcut menu provides you with a number of save options: Save Picture as will let you save the picture as an ordinary graphic file, as either a JPEG (.JPG) file or as a bitmap (.BMP) file. The Set as Wallpaper option will let you use the graphic as wallpaper on your Desktop.

Note

When you choose the Set as Wallpaper option, the graphic is saved as a bitmapped file in your Windows directory with the filename Internet Explorer Wallpaper.bmp. To remove the saved wallpaper, you must change your Desktop properties. (See Chapter 8 for more information.)

Tip

If your Explorer Bar opens in Folder view, you can click and drag a graphic image from a Web page and then drop it into a folder to then save a copy of the graphic in the folder.

Caution

Although it is very easy to "borrow" images and text from Web sites, most of the content is protected by copyright law. Although there are probably few restrictions on your private, non-commercial use of the material, you normally cannot repackage, sell, or reproduce the material without written permission from the author. It is considered common courtesy to request permission from a site's author or owner before using material found on their web site.

Save a frame

While framed pages often allow a Webmaster to do certain things on a page, they also make it more difficult for a Web browser to do certain things. If you find a framed page, and want to save the contents of the main content frame, you will be out of luck if you just click File ⇨ Save. Commonly, you will save only the frame set for this page; all you will save is a very simple page that contains the names of the other pages that are displayed in the frames — the pages that you really wanted to save.

On a framed page, right-click the frame you want to save, and then select Save from the context menu to save the content of the frame as a standalone page.

Printing pages

There are a number of ways in which to print a page through the Internet Explorer. If the page you want to print is displayed, simply click the Print button on the Internet Explorer toolbar (or click File ⇨ Print). If you right-click a link to the article you want to print, you can then select Print Target. You also can use the keyboard shortcut Ctrl+P to print the page or active frame.

Tip

If you only want to print one frame of a Web page, right-click in the frame you want, and then select Print.

Tip

You can print a table of all of the links associated with a Web page. Click File ⇨ Print to open the Print dialog box. Then, click the Options tab and select Print Table of Links. You also can select the option to Print All Linked Document from this page to print every page for which the current page has a link.

If you are viewing a framed page and want to print just one of the frames, right-click the frame, and choose Print from the shortcut menu. This will open the Print dialog box shown in Figure 12-11. Click the Options tab. You can choose to print only the selected frame, all the frames individually, or to print the page as it is laid out on the screen. You can access this dialog box by clicking File ➪ Print, but at the risk of not being sure which is your selected frame.

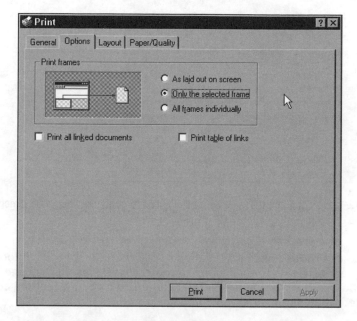

Figure 12-11: You have more flexibility in printing frames: you can print only the selected frame, or you can print all of the frames.

If you print a Web page that has frames, the Internet Explorer may leave some temporary files behind in your Temporary Internet Files folder. If you see any files in that folder beginning with the characters TRB, you can delete them.

Printing layout options

To make adjustments to Internet Explorer printouts, click File ➪ Page Setup. In the Page Setup dialog box shown in Figure 12-12, you can choose between portrait and landscape modes, and you also can adjust the margin size and change the paper source.

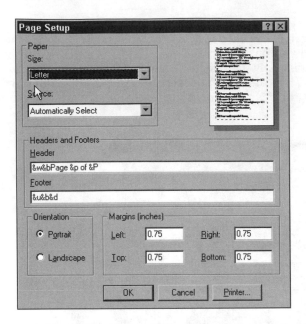

Figure 12-12: You can use the Page Setup dialog box to configure your page dimensions and to include document information in the page headers and footers.

You also can choose what information to print into the header or footer of a page by adding fields to the header or footer text boxes on the Page Setup dialog box, as listed in Table 12-1. All header and footer formatting codes are preceded by an ampersand (&) character.

Table 12-1   Header and Footer Options

Field control code	Prints this information
&w	Prints the window title.
&u	Prints the page's URL (address).
&d	Prints the date using the short format selected in Control Panel, Regional Settings.
&D	Prints the date using the long format selected in Control Panel, Regional Settings.
&t	Prints the current time using Control Panel, Regional Settings.
&T	Prints the time value using 24-hour format.
&p	Prints the current page number.
&P	Prints the total number of pages.
&b	Prints the text following the code as centered.

Field control code	Prints this information
&b&b	Prints the text following the code as right-aligned.
&&	Prints an ampersand character.

Secret

Many Web pages use colored backgrounds, or background images, for decorations. If you wanted to print one of these pages, they could use up a lot of ink or toner, and they might not be as readable on paper as they are on screen. Go to Tools ⇨ Internet Options, and click the Advanced Tab. In the Printing section, you can disable the Print background colors and images option to avoid this problem.

Managing your disk cache

Why, you might ask, should I *want* to manage my disk cache. I mean, why not do something really exciting like rearranging your sock drawer?

The reason is that, eventually, even the largest hard drives become cramped, and you'll find yourself needing to get rid of old, unneeded files to make more space. That's when you want to manage your Internet Explorer disk cache. Trimming the cache size is one of the easiest ways to recover disk space.

Here's how the cache works. To help speed your browsing, Internet Explorer saves the files it views in a cache that is called Temporary Internet Files. The location of these files can be found in the Registry at HKEY_CURRENT_USER\ Software\Microsoft\Windows\CurrentVersion\Explorer\Shell Folders. It is also listed in the Temporary Internet Files Settings dialog box. This cache file can greatly speed up your browsing. Depending on the settings you select, the Internet Explorer actually requests the page from your hard drive, rather than retrieving it from the Internet, if the page is in your cache. After all, hard drives work much faster than modems. The size and location, of the cache — along with other settings — can be set in the Internet Options dialog box. To make changes, follow these steps:

STEPS:

Managing your Temporary Internet Files

Step 1.   From Internet Explorer, click Tools ⇨ Internet Options.

Step 2.   If Internet Explorer is not open, click Start ⇨ Settings ⇨ Control Panel, and then click the Internet Options icon.

Step 3.   Make sure the General tab is selected. In the Temporary Internet files section, click the Settings button to see the Settings dialog box shown in Figure 12-13.

Continued

STEPS:

Managing your Temporary Internet Files *(continued)*

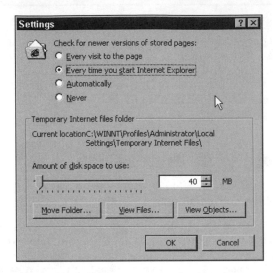

Figure 12-13: You manage your cache settings from the Temporary Internet Files ⇨ Settings dialog box. The less often Internet Explorer needs to check for newer pages, the faster your browsing will be.

The selection at the top of the Settings dialog box is crucial for your cache management. Table 12-2 explains how this choice affects your browsing speed.

Table 12-2 Temporary Internet Files Options

Check for newer versions of stored pages	What it really means
Every visit to the page	If you want to see a page that you have previously visited, the Internet Explorer will first check to see if the page has changed. If it has, it will download a newer version.
Every time you start Internet Explorer	In every browser session (from opening the Internet Explorer until you close it), the Internet Explorer will check for a new page the first time. On each subsequent visit, it will use the version stored in the cache. This increases the speed of your Web browsing.

Check for newer versions of stored pages	What it really means
Automatically	This option lets the Internet Explorer decide. It will only check for new content if you go back to a page that you last viewed either in an earlier session or on an earlier day. If the Internet Explorer determines that the page is not changing frequently, it will check for new information less often.
Never	Any time you go back to a page you have visited previously, the Internet Explorer will get the information from the cache rather than from the Web. This setting provides for the fastest browsing, but at the cost of missing new information.

Note If you are using one of the last three settings in Table 12-2, you can always force the Internet Explorer to retrieve the page from the Web. With the page in view, click the Refresh button on the Toolbar, or right-click the page (not on a link) and select Refresh (or press the F5 key). This overrides the selection you have made above, and gets a fresh copy of the page from the Web.

Tip If the pages you frequently view are not constantly updated, and they have a lot of graphical elements (navigation bars and the like), selecting the option Every time you start Internet Explorer is a good compromise between speed and missing updates.

From the Settings dialog box, you also can specify how much space to allocate to your cache. Unlike earlier versions of Internet Explorer, the size is now specified in terms of megabytes, rather than as a percentage of your hard drive space. To devote more space to the cache—and thus speed Web browsing—increase the space setting either by sliding the selector to the right, or by increasing the size using the spinner bar. Conversely, if you are running short on disk space, you can reduce the size of the cache and reclaim some disk space.

Tip If you need to quickly reclaim a lot of hard disk space, you can empty your cache. To do so, close the Settings dialog box so that you are back on the General tab of the Internet Options dialog box. Click the Delete Files button. Once you start browsing, your cache will start to fill up again.

Tip By default, your Temporary Internet Files are located on your system drive, where all your Windows 2000 files are located. If this drive is getting crowded, and you have another hard drive installed, move your Temporary Internet files folder to the other hard drive.

STEPS:

Moving Your Temporary Internet Files

Step 1.   Open Internet Explorer.

Step 2.   Click Tools ⇨ Internet Options. Then in the Temporary Internet Files section, click the Settings button.

Step 3.   Click the Move Files button, and then select a new location in the Browse folders window.

Step 4.   Click OK to go back to the Internet Options window, and then click OK again.

Step 5.   Windows 2000 will tell you that it needs to restart Windows. If your cache is full, you may hear quite a bit of disk activity as all the files are moved.

Managing downloads

If you want to download a file rather than view it, you can right-click its link and select File ⇨ Save Target As. If you click on a link to a file that Internet Explorer doesn't know how to display, you will see a dialog box that asks whether you want to save or run this file.

Secret

Internet Explorer saves downloaded files by default to the location stored in HKEY_CURRENT_USER\Software\Microsoft\Internet Explorer. You can easily change this. Find this key in the Registry, right-click Download Directory in the right pane, select Modify, and then type in a new download directory and press Enter.

Synchronize Files

The cache works automatically, and its intent is to help speed your Web browsing, especially when you repeatedly visit a page. It also allows you to go back and read pages when you are offline. A new feature of the Internet Explorer extends that capability to read Web pages offline, even pages you haven't visited in your last session. This feature is called *synchronization*.

Internet Security

While browsing the Internet, you do more than just download words and pictures from Web pages. To enable interaction between a Web user and Web site, a number of technologies have been developed. These new technologies mean that actual programs containing code that runs on your computer, can be downloaded, along with other bits of information. These (usually small) programs have a number of different forms:

- Active X controls
- Java applets
- Cookies
- Scripting: VBScript, Jscript.

While this enables all kinds of useful features, it also opens a potential security risk on your computer. You might download something that doesn't work quite right, or you might download some malicious code that has been written to do some intentional harm to your computer or data.

Security zones

Caesar divided Gaul into three parts. Microsoft's approach to security is to divide the computing world into four zones, as shown by the icons in Figure 12-14. You can assign sites to which you connect into one of these four security zones. Each zone provides a different security level. You can accept the suggested security settings for each zone, or you can customize these settings to suit your needs. Table 12-3 lists these four security zones and their default settings.

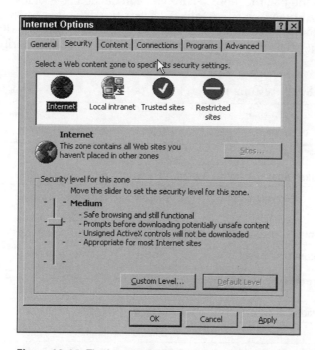

Figure 12-14: The Internet Security Zones. The icon for each site's zone will be displayed on the Internet Explorer status bar.

Table 12-3   Internet Security Zones

Zone	Description	Default Security Settings
Internet	This is the default zone. Every site is placed in this zone until you assign it to another zone.	Medium
Local Intranet	These are sites on your organization's Intranet.	Medium
Trusted Sites	You trust these sites not to damage your computer or data.	Low
Restricted Sites	These are the sites that worry you. You are unsure about malicious content they might contain.	High

The Internet Explorer also assumes — perhaps wrongly — that anything that is already on your computer is safe and can be trusted.

The security settings for each zone are a list of items that are either enabled (allowed to run without warning), prompted (requests your permission before downloading or running), or disabled. For each zone, you can move the security slider bar to change the settings for the zone. The higher the slider is set on the bar, the more secure you will be, at a cost of lost functionality on some Web sites. Table 12-4 lists the default security settings. As Table 12-4 shows, almost nothing is allowed (enabled) with the High Security setting, while just about anything goes with the Low Security setting.

Table 12-4   Security Zone Default Settings

Type of Control or Content	High	Medium	Medium low	Low
Download signed ActiveX controls	Disable	Prompt	Prompt	Enable
Download unsigned ActiveX controls	Disable	Disable	Disable	Prompt
Initialize ActiveX controls not marked safe	Disable	Disable	Disable	Prompt
Run ActiveX control or plug-in	Disable	Enable	Enable	Enable
Script ActiveX controls marked safe for scripting	Enable	Enable	Enable	Enable
Store Cookies	Disable	Enable	Enable	Enable
Accept per session Cookie	Disable	Enable	Enable	Enable
File Downloads	Disable	Enable	Enable	Enable
Font Downloads	Prompt	Enable	Enable	Enable

Type of Control or Content	High	Medium	Medium low	Low
Java Permission Safety	High	High	Medium	Low
Access data sources across domains	Disable	Disable	Prompt	Enable
Drag & Drop or Copy and Paste files	Prompt	Enable	Enable	Enable
Install desktop items	Disable	Prompt	Prompt	Enable
Launch programs and files in IFRAME	Disable	Prompt	Prompt	Enable
Navigate sub-frames across different domains	Disable	Enable	Enable	Enable
Software channel permissions	High	Medium	Medium	Low
Submit non-encrypted form data	Prompt	Prompt	Enable	Enable
User data persistence	Disable	Enable	Enable	Enable
Active Scripting	Enable	Enable	Enable	Enable
Allow paste via script	Enable	Enable	Enable	Enable
Java applet scripting	Disable	Enable	Enable	Enable

You can make big changes to each zone's security settings by moving the security setting up or down with the slider bar. But you can make smaller adjustments, too, if you decide you don't want one particular item to be enabled, but you don't want to make all the changes that come about by changing the security level for a zone. For example, let's suppose you want a better idea about what cookies are being stored on your computer, so you want to change the cookie setting for the Internet Zone. Here's how:

STEPS:

Customizing the Security Settings

Step 1. In Internet Explorer, click Tools ⇨ Internet Options.

Step 2. Click the Security Tab, and then select the Internet zone by clicking its icon.

Step 3. Click Custom Level, and then scroll down the list until you see the option Allow cookies that are stored on your computer.

Step 4. Change the setting to Prompt. You can still receive a cookie from a Web site, but you will be asked first if you want to receive it.

Step 5. Click OK. You will be asked whether you want to change settings for this level. Click Yes. Click OK once more to close the dialog box.

If you later decide that it is too much bother to always be prompted for cookies, you can change back. Repeat the steps above; in Step 4, choose Enable. You also can click the Reset button to restore the default security settings (from Table 12-4) for this zone.

Caution

None of these settings explicitly protects against viruses, although running with your security settings set to high will make it less likely that you would get a virus through your Web browsing. Virus protection is another matter entirely; in general, you need anti-virus software to protect yourself.

Adding a Web site to a security zone

By default, the entire World Wide Web is placed in the Internet Zone, which has a medium security level. If you decide that a site you visit has enough safeguards that you can trust its content, you can move it from the Internet Zone to the Trusted Zone. To do this, follow these steps:

STEPS:

Adding a Site to the Trusted Zone

Step 1. In Internet Explorer, click Tools ⇨ Internet Options, and select the Security tab.

Step 2. Click the icon for Trusted Sites. This will show you the security settings for Trusted Zones. It will also activate the Sites button. Click it.

Step 3. Type the address of the site you want to trust (see Figure 12-15). For instance, if you want to add the Microsoft Web site to your trusted sites list, type **http://www.microsoft.com**.

Step 4. If you know this site uses server verification (it would have https: in its address rather than just http:), make sure the option box is checked. Otherwise, clear it.

Step 5. Click Add, and then click OK twice.

If you begin to have second thoughts about whether you should trust the site, repeat Steps 1 and 2. Highlight the site that you no longer trust, and then click the Remove button.

Cookies

For something with such an innocuous sounding name, cookies have managed to stir up a heap of controversy on the World Wide Web.

Cookies are small text files that Web sites on your computer. Each user name will have a Cookies folder within the user Profiles folders, where these files are kept. The location of your cookies files is stored in the Registry at HKEY_CURRENT_USER\Software\Microsoft\ Windows\CurrentVersion\Explorer\Shell Folders. A Web site can only view its own cookies; it cannot view cookies left by other sites. And being text files, they should not be able to do any harm to your computer

A Web site may use cookies for many things. Some Web sites that require registration (a user name and password) store this information in a cookie on your computer. When you request to view one of secure or restricted pages, the Web site looks for its own cookie and reads the user information. Other sites use cookies to record actions that you have already taken at the Web site, such as selecting preferences, so you don't have to repeat those steps on subsequent visits. If you've ever wondered how you can go to a

Web page and see "Welcome Back" and your name, they have probably used cookies.

If they do such useful things, why are so many people concerned with cookies? One possible reason is that many people don't like the idea of some site depositing files on their computer without their knowledge. (This can be changed by following the previous exercise, "Customizing the security settings.") Others are afraid that Web sites will be able to read some of this information, or to use cookies to track your path across the World Wide Web. (By the way, if you think cookies are another nefarious plot by Microsoft to spy on your computing habits, they're not. Cookies were actually invented by Netscape.)

A number of sites devoted to the security aspects of cookies can be found at http://dir. yahoo.com/Computers_and_Internet/Internet/ World_Wide_Web/HTTP/Information_and_ Documentation/Persistent_Cookies/Security_Iss ues/. Karen Kenworthy of *Windows* Magazine has written a handy utility called Coolie Viewer, that will display the contents of all your cookies for you. You can read about and download this utility at http://www.winmag.com/library/1998/ 0901/how0063.htm.

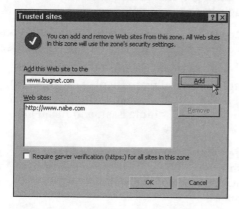

Figure 12-15: To add a site to your Trusted Zone list, type its URL in the text box and click Add.

Keeping up to date on security threats

The whole issue of security on the Internet is in flux. Holes in security are found, exploited, and patched with great rapidity. To stay current on threats and fixes, here are some sites to add to your Favorites list:

- Microsoft Security Site: http://www.microsoft.com/security/default.asp
- Netscape Security Site: http://home.netscape.com/products/security/index.html
- General Internet Security Site: http://www.w3.org/Security/

Customizing Internet Explorer

There are a number of things you can do to customize Internet Explorer. Some of these changes the look of IE, and some of these affect more substantive changes regarding what other programs work with IE. Since you will be using your browser as the interface for more and more tasks in the future, you may want to experiment to get a configuration with which you are comfortable.

Cosmetic changes

Just like the Windows Explorer and My Computer, you can customize the Internet Explorer toolbar. Right-click an empty portion of the toolbar and select Customize to go to the Customize Toolbar dialog box, as shown in Figure 12-16. Here, you can add additional toolbar buttons to add functionality to the Internet Explorer. Some of the additional buttons you may want to add include:

- **Full Screen:** clicking the Full Screen button will eliminate the Title Bar and Address Bar, leaving you with only the Toolbar buttons at the top of the browser window — leaving more screen space for the Web page. Click Full Screen again to toggle back to normal view.

- **Size Button:** click this to see a drop-down menu that allows you to increase or decrease the size of the text displayed in the browser.

- **Encoding:** If you often visit non-English Web sites that use a different alphabet, you can change the encoding to display the different characters. The default is Western European (Windows), but there is a full selection of eastern European, Middle East, and Asian alphabets from which you can choose.

Like in the Windows Explorer, you also can change the appearance of the Toolbar buttons. You can show text labels for the Toolbar buttons, show Selective labels on the right, or show no labels at all. You also can switch between large and small icons.

You can change to the no labels look to save some screen real estate. If you aren't displaying labels and you forget what a button does, hover over it with the mouse pointer to see its ToolTip.

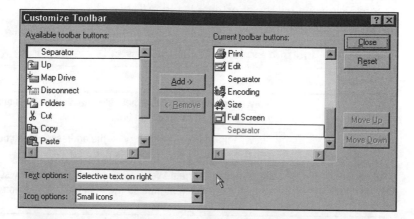

Figure 12-16: You can add buttons to or subtract buttons from the Internet Explorer Toolbar. You also can add labels to or remove labels from the buttons, as well as make them smaller.

You can change the size and placement of any of the toolbars. By clicking and dragging the Selector to the left of the Toolbar, Address Bar, or Links Bar, you can contract or expand their size. You also can drag one of these bars up or down to another level. The Links Bar and the Address Bar can share a row, or you can drag one of them up next to the Menu, if you like.

Changing Internet Explorer behavior

Microsoft actually makes it somewhat easy to choose other programs for Internet services. The various Internet tools that come with Windows 2000 along with Internet Explorer are configured as the default choices. But you can change them. Click Tools ⇨ Internet Options, and go to the Programs tab. There you can pick alternative programs for your HTML editor, your e-mail program, your news reader, your Internet conferencing, your calendar, and your contact list. In fact, if it is installed, it will let you use Netscape Messenger as your e-mail program.

When you click Tools ⇨ Internet Options, and click the Advanced tab, you will see a number of other customization features. If some of the features are unclear, click the question mark icon in the upper right corner of the Internet Options dialog box, and click the option in question.

 The Internet Explorer 5 will display friendly HTTP error messages. What's friendly about error messages? Error messages generally provide textual explanation of what happened, and often provides suggestions on how you can work around the error.

Internet Explorer Keyboard Shortcuts

There are many keyboard shortcuts built-in to the Internet Explorer. If you prefer to browse with your hands on the keyboard rather than holding on to a mouse, you can try the shortcuts listed in Table 12-5.

Table 12-5	Internet Explorer Keyboard Shortcuts
Key combination	*Results*
F1	Shows the Internet Explorer help file. If a dialog box is open, it will show help for that dialog box.
F4	Shows the Address Bar history — the addresses that you have typed in manually in the Address Bar.
F5	Refreshes the current Web page, but only if the locally stored version has a different time stamp than the Web version. (Also Ctrl+R.)
F6	Moves forward between frames. (Also Ctrl+Tab)
F11	Toggles the browser into full screen mode and regular viewing mode. Full screen mode reduces all the menus and icons in the upper portion of the the window to a single row.
Tab	Moves you forward from link to link on a page and then to the Address Bar.
Shift-Tab	Moves you backward from link to link on a page and then to the Address Bar.
Enter	Takes you to the selected link.
Up arrow	Scrolls toward]s the beginning of a page
Down Arrow	Scroll towards the end of a page.
PageUp	Scrolls toward the beginning of a page, almost a full screen at a time.
PageDown	Scrolls toward the end of a page, almost a full screen at a time.
Home	Moves to the top of a document.
End	Moves to the bottom of a document.
Esc	Stops the retrieval of a requested Web page.
Backspace	Takes you to the previous page.
Alt+Right-arrow	Takes you to the next page. (This only works if you have moved back at some point using the Alt+Left-arrow or backspace keys.)
Alt+Left-arrow	Goes to the previous page, if available. (Also Backspace key.)
Alt+Home	Takes you to your home page.
Alt+D	Selects the Address Bar text.

Key combination	Results
Ctrl+B	Takes you to the Organize Favorites dialog box.
Ctrl+D	Adds the current page to your Favorites list.
Ctrl+E	Opens the Search window in the Explorer Bar.
Ctrl I F	Finds a text string on the current page.
Ctrl+H	Opens the History window in the Explorer Bar.
Ctrl+I	Opens the Favorites window in the Explorer bar.
Ctrl+L	Takes you to a new location. This opens up a browse window where you can type an address to go to, and it is an alternative way to type an address in the Address Bar. (Same as Ctrl+O.)
Ctrl+N	Opens up a new browser window.
Ctrl+P	Prints either the current page or the active frame.
Ctrl+R	Refreshes the current page, but only if the locally stored version has a different time stamp than the Web version. (Also F5.)
Ctrl+S	Saves the current page to disk.
Ctrl+W	Closes the current window.
Ctrl+Left-arrow	Moves the cursor to the left of the first break if the cursor is in the Address Bar (either. or /).
Ctrl+Right-arrow	Moves the cursor to the right of the first break if your cursor is in the Address Bar (either . or /).
Shift+F10	Displays a shortcut menu for a link.

Summary

In this chapter we learned how to take Internet Explorer 5, and make it work more the way you want. We saw how to:

▶ Set your own home page.

▶ Search the Internet.

▶ Use Web accessories.

▶ Manage your Favorites.

▶ Manage your disk cache.

▶ Keep safe on the Internet.

▶ Customize Internet Explorer.

Chapter 13

Outlook Express

In This Chapter

We will see how to use Outlook Express, the Windows 2000 e-mail and newsreader programs. We will see:

▶ How to set up Internet connections through Outlook Express.

▶ How to set up multiple identities.

▶ How to configure the Outlook Express screen to maximize usability.

▶ How to manage your incoming e-mail.

▶ How to save your incoming e-mail.

▶ How to use newsgroups.

Getting Started

Outlook Express is the e-mail and newsreader program that comes bundled with Windows 2000. (It is also bundled with Windows 98.) It should not be confused with Microsoft Outlook, which is a full-featured e-mail program and personal information manager bundled with Microsoft Office. Rather, Outlook Express is the companion e-mail and newsreader program for Internet Explorer 5. Figure 13-1 shows the Outlook Express main screen.

Outlook Express shares its Internet connection with Internet Explorer. The first time you start Outlook Express, it looks for an Internet connectoid. If it can't find one, the Internet Connection Wizard automatically opens and begins the process of configuring a dial-up connection for you. (See Chapter 11 for details on this process.) As part of the Internet Connection Wizard, you will be asked if you want to set up e-mail and news accounts. If you say no, you will have the opportunity to do so as soon as Outlook Express opens.

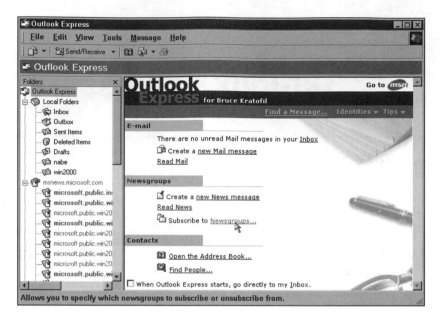

Figure 13-1: The Outlook Express main screen.

Once Outlook Express opens, you are taken through another wizard that collects the information you need to be able to send and receive e-mail. You will be asked for:

- Your name: This is the name you want to appear on your e-mail messages. It should be the name by which others refer to you, and not your Windows 2000 logon name or your user name for your ISP account.

- Your e-mail address.

- Your e-mail server name: Many ISPs use different servers for incoming and outgoing e-mail. The incoming server will be something like pop3.ispname.com, and the outgoing server will be something like smtp.ispname.com. Check with your ISP if you don't know what the server names are.

- Your user name: This will usually be the same user name you use to log on to your ISP. (It is the portion of your e-mail address that comes before the @ sign.)

- Your password: This will be the same password you use to log on to your ISP.

After you fill in this information, you finally reach the Outlook Express main screen. There will already be an e-mail message waiting for you — a welcoming message from Microsoft that provides a brief description of some of Outlook Express's features.

Outlook Express 5 will not work for e-mail accounts that require Microsoft Mail, Lotus cc:Mail, CompuServe, America Online, or any Microsoft Exchange Server prior to Microsoft Exchange version 5.

Establishing an Identity

Windows 2000 supports multiple users on a single computer. When you log on with your user name and password, your own personal (user) preferences are loaded. This means that one computer can maintain the identities and preferences for several users.

Outlook Express amplifies this chameleon quality by supporting multiple identities as well. To configure Outlook Express for multiple identities, open Outlook Express to see its main screen, as shown in Figure 13-1. Click Identities in the right pane to add, change, or delete identities.

One reason OE may account for separate identities is to enable individuals to share one computer for all their e-mail accounts. Multiple identities can also be managed using individual Windows 2000 identities, but this way, if password protection is disabled, they all have access to the others' files, which you might need if one individual is out of the office.

There are a number of reasons why you would want to have multiple identities for yourself. You might want to keep your work and your personal e-mail separate, in which case you set up an identity for each type of e-mail. You might also have different e-mail accounts, and it would be easier to set up a separate identity for each in order to manage the separate accounts.

STEPS:
Adding a New Identity

Step 1. Click File ⇨ Identities ⇨ Add New Identity. (If you are at the Outlook Express welcome screen, you can click Identities ⇨ Add Identities in the upper-right corner.)

Step 2. If this is the first time you have added an identity, your default identity is named Main Identity. You will be able to personalize this identity in the New Identity dialog box shown in Figure 13-2.

Step 3. If you want to add password protection to this identity, select the Require a password checkbox. In either case, click OK.

Step 4. Next, you will be asked whether you want to switch to this identity. Click Yes. After a brief pause, Outlook Express will reopen with the Internet Connection Wizard so that you can tell Outlook Express how this identity will connect to the Internet.

Continued

STEPS:

Adding a New Identity *(continued)*

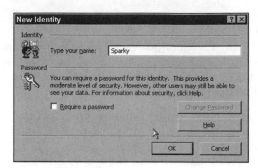

Figure 13-2: To add an identity, type an identity in the New Identity dialog box which is different from any existing identity setting.

Step 5. You can choose to use an existing Internet account if you want. If so, the Connection Wizard will then go through its steps using the information you originally provided for your existing account. If you decide to set up a new account, you will go through the Wizard much like you did earlier.

Step 6. If you have Internet e-mail messages and addresses from another program on your computer, you can choose to import your messages and Address Book in the next step of the Wizard. If you want to start fresh, click No.

Once all the setup wizards have completed, Outlook Express restarts using your new identity.

Once you have established multiple identities, you can switch between them by clicking File ⇨ Switch Identities. This will bring up the Switch Identities dialog box, shown in Figure 13-3, where you can choose the identity you want to use.

Note

Each time you create a new identity, it will start with the Outlook Express default preferences. You can view these settings by clicking Tools ⇨ Options. Because you start with the default view, any additional news or directory accounts that were set up in one identity will not appear in other identities; they must be manually added or imported.

Tip

If you click Manage Identities from the Switch Identities dialog box, or if you click File ⇨ Identities ⇨ Manage Identities from the menu, you can choose your default identity by selecting the Default to this identity checkbox, and then choosing which identity you want to use as your default identity.

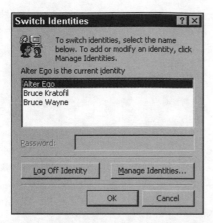

Figure 13-3: To switch identities, click the identity you wish to use.

Tip

To see which identity is currently in use, make sure that your Folder Bar is displayed. Click View ⇨ Layout. In the Layout dialog box, make sure that Folder Bar is selected. The Folder Bar is just below the Toolbar, and it displays your current folder name on the left and your current identity on the right.

Secret

Windows 2000 actually keeps track of identities using a long alphanumeric string called a Class ID (CLSID). You can see these numbers in the Registry at HKEY_CURRENT_USER\Identities. An identity key will look something like this: 0771C1B2-F98C-11D2-AB18-005004707D0A.

Customizing Views, Panes, and Toolbars

If you are an active e-mail and Internet newsgroup user, you will no doubt be collecting a lot of messages with Outlook Express. There are a number of customization features built-in to Outlook Express that let you manage this information, and that also make Outlook Express easier to use. The first thing you need to do, however, is make some changes to Outlook Express's defaults.

In Outlook Express, click View ⇨ Layout to make decisions about what you want to see on the Outlook main screen. If you clear all the check boxes in the Window Layout Properties dialog box shown in Figure 13-4, you will be left with the menu and two panes that split the screen horizontally. The top pane will show the contents of your current folder, and the bottom pane will show the currently selected message. However, you might want to see more than what this minimalist view displays. Other portions of the screen that can be enabled are discussed in the next section:

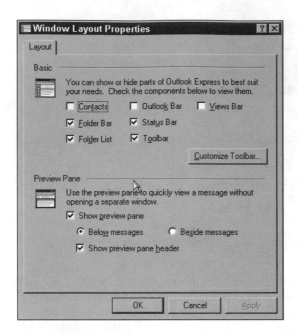

Figure 13-4: From the Window Layout Properties dialog box, you can decide what portions of the Outlook Express screen to display.

Contacts

Selecting Contacts in the Window Layout Properties dialog box will add an Address Book icon below the Folder List icon. Clicking a name in this list will open a new e-mail message, already pre-addressed to the individual whose name you clicked. The Contacts List has limited usefulness. It shows only the name, and it will only display your Contacts in First Name order.

Right-clicking a name in the Contacts List will let you see its Properties, which is just a fancy way of saying it will open your Address Book to that person's entry. You can then add or edit contact information about that person. (See "Managing the Windows Address Book," later in this chapter.)

Folder Bar

The Folder Bar is a narrow horizontal strip that appears just below the toolbar. Its only function is to display the name of the current folder and the name of your current identity. If your Folder List is displayed, you will see the current folder selected. If you won't be switching identities often, you can probably do without the Folder Bar.

Folder List

The Folder List option in the Window Layout Properties dialog box will add a vertical pane along the left side of the screen, showing all the local folders you have created, as well as folders for all the newsgroups to which you subscribe. If you navigate with your mouse, clicking a folder will open it, which is just a quick way to navigate between folders.

 Tip If you don't display the Folder List, you can navigate between folders by clicking View ⇨ Go to Folder, and then choosing your destination from the list of folders. You also can press Ctrl+Y to see the Folder List.

Outlook Bar

The Outlook Bar will add a vertical pane on the left side of the screen. It is named after the bar that first appeared in Microsoft Outlook, which appears in the Save dialog boxes of many Windows 2000 applications such as Notepad. The Outlook Bar contains icons to display Outlook Express's default local folders. If you create other folders, they also can be added to the Outlook Bar by right-clicking the folder and selecting Add to Outlook Bar from the context menu.

The Outlook Bar is redundant if the Folder List is also displayed. However, if you want an easier target for your mouse clicks, you can disable the Folder List and use the Outlook Bar instead. If you right-click the Outlook Bar, you can select small icons from the context menu to show more icons on the bar.

Status Bar

The Status Bar is displayed at the lower edge of each Outlook Express window. When the Status Bar is enabled, you will be able to see how many messages are in your current folder, as well as how many remain unread. It also tells you if a specific view has been applied to the selected folder — but not what view has been selected. The Status Bar also provides you with one important piece of information: whether you are working online or offline. (See "Working Offline," later in this chapter.)

Toolbar

Like the toolbar in other program windows, the Toolbar contains buttons for many of your most commonly used commands. You can customize the Toolbar by adding additional buttons to it by or removing buttons from it that you don't need. Right-click the Toolbar and select Customize, or click Customize Toolbar in the Window Layout Properties dialog box.

You also might decide to use small icons, as well as enable the Selective text on right feature for your toolbar buttons so that you can shrink your Toolbar a little. Taking these steps will give you more room in which to add extra icons to your toolbar, which we will practice in the next exercise.

STEPS:

Adding a Button

Step 1. Click View ➪ Layout.

Step 2. Click the Customize Toolbar button.

Step 3. In Available toolbar buttons list, find Mark All, and then select it.

Step 4. Click the Add button to move the Mark All button to the Current toolbar buttons list.

Step 5. If you don't like the position of the button in the list, select it in the Current toolbar buttons list, and then click the Move Up or the Move Down buttons to move it to another position.

Step 6. When you are satisfied with the toolbar buttons you have selected, click the Close button, and then click the OK button to return to the Outlook main screen.

The Mark All button allows you to select all the messages in the current folder, and perform some action on your selection, such as marking all the messages as having been read.

You can repeat the process to add more buttons to the Toolbar.

Tip

You don't need the Toolbar. Every button has a corresponding command somewhere on a menu. The Toolbar simply speeds up the action process if you're a mouse user.

Views Bar

The Views Bar lets you quickly select a view to apply to a folder. Among other things, Views allow you to specify what messages will be displayed, and they can help you sort through messages more quickly—especially in newsgroup folders. Table 13-1 lists some of the possible views available in Outlook Express.

Table 13-1	Outlook Express Views
View	**Results of View**
Show all messages	Every message will be displayed.
Hide Read Messages	Hides any messages you have already read after a few seconds have elapsed.
Show downloaded messages	Available only on IMAP and news servers. This will display only those messages that arrived when you last retrieved your e-mail messages.
Show replies to my messages	Available only in newsgroups. This option will display only those messages that are replies to messages you have sent.
Hide Read or ignored messages	Messages that have been flagged as Ignore Conversation or that have been read by you.

Once you set a View for a folder, it will be in effect for that folder until you change it. Views also can be set on a folder-by-folder basis. If you don't want to show the Views bar, you can change views by clicking View ⇨ Current View, and then selecting a view type from the menu.

Tip

The Views Bar is very narrow. If your screen resolution is set to at least 800by600, you should have room for it to the right of your menu. Select it in the Layout dialog box. Then, click and drag its selector and drop it just to the right of the Help command on your menu.

Views are especially useful in newsgroups. By selecting Hide Read messages, you can quickly find the new messages in a newsgroup, skipping the messages you have already seen.

Info Pane

If you received your copy of Outlook Express 5 from a third party, such as your ISP or your computer vendor, your version of Outlook Express might display an additional panel called the Info Pane. The Info Pane is basically a billboard that runs across the lower portion of the Outlook main screen sporting a company logo. You can delete it from the layout without losing any information, if you like.

Sending E-mail

There are at least three ways to create a new message in Outlook Express:

- Click the New Message icon on the Toolbar.
- Click Message ⇨ New Message.
- Press Ctrl+N.

You can also add Outlook Express to your New menu. When you right-click your Desktop and select New, you can have an Outlook Express mail item as one of your choices. For this to work, you need to install TweakUI. (See Chapter 14 for details on how to install TweakUI.) Then, follow these steps:

STEPS:

Adding Outlook Express mail messages to your New menu

Step 1. Right-click an empty portion of your Desktop.

Step 2. Select New ⇨ Text Document.

Step 3. It will be created with the name New Text Document. Rename it New.eml.

Step 4. You will see a warning that changing the extension may make this file unusable. Click Yes.

Step 5. Click Start ⇨ Settings ⇨ Control Panel, and select TweakUI.

Step 6. Go to the New tab of TweakUI. Drag and drop the New.eml icon on to the New tab. This should create a new item in the list of new documents in TweakUI called Outlook Express Mail Message.

Step 7. Close TweakUI.

Addressing messages

In the New Message window, clicking the Address Book icon to the left of the To: or Cc: buttons will open the Select Recipients dialog box. In the Contacts pane, highlight the person to whom you want to send the message, and then click the To:, Cc:, or Bcc: button, as shown in Figure 13-5. You can select as many recipients as you want in the To: or Cc: fields.

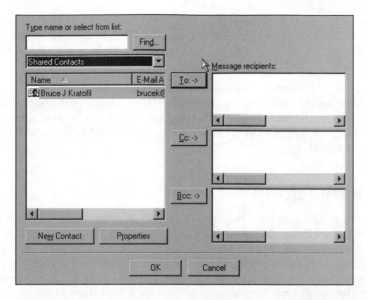

Figure 13-5: Select a contact from your Address Book, and then add them to the To:, Cc:, or Bcc: field.

Bcc: means blind carbon copy. The recipient of a Bcc message receives a copy of the message, but they do not see the other addressees of the message. This avoids a long block of addresses in your e-mail message, which consequently makes it look less like bulk e-mail. Equally important in some circumstances, the recipients of Bcc: messages are not visible to other recipients of your message. You can add a Bcc: field in the New Message window. Click View ⇨ All Headers to enable the Bcc: field.

You can avoid a trip to your Address Book if you know at least a portion of your intended recipient's e-mail name and you also have AutoComplete enabled. From the Outlook Express window, click Tools ⇨ Options, and select the Send tab. Make sure that the option Automatically Complete e-mail messages when composing is selected. If not, you can always manually complete an e-mail address. In the New Message window, begin typing a name or an e-mail address, and then click Tools ⇨ Check Name (or use the Ctrl+K keyboard shortcut). This will display a selection dialog box that lists all the possible matches for the name or address you have typed.

Drafts

If you begin composing a message, but you know you are not quite ready to send the message on its way, click File ⇨ Save to save the message in your Drafts folder. When you want to work on the message again, select the Drafts folder, and then double-click the header to open the message.

If you save a plain text message in the Drafts folder, Outlook Express will wrap all the lines at the default line length (which is set at 76 characters by default) and insert hard returns. To keep this from happening, save your drafts in HTML format instead.

Outlook Express breaks plain text lines at 76 characters in case they are displayed on old-fashioned character-based display terminals. If you want to reset this length, click Tools ⇨ Options, and select the Send tab. Click the Plain Text Settings button in the Mail Sending Format section, and then set a new line length.

Spell Checking

If Microsoft Office is installed on your computer, you can use the Office spell checker. Click Tools ⇨ Options ⇨ Spelling to check your spelling before you send your message. You also can let the spell checker suggest replacement spellings, as well as to ignore uppercase words, Internet addresses, and words with numbers. If Microsoft Office isn't installed on your computer, visit CompuBridge at http://www.spellchecker.com, for information about their shareware Speller for Microsoft Internet Products, which work with a variety of e-mail programs.

Sent mail

To track your outgoing e-mail, Outlook Express can be configured so that it saves a copy of all your outgoing e-mail messages in your Sent Items folder. Click Tools ⇨ Options, and then select the Send tab. Choose the first option, Save copy of sent messages in the `Sent Items' folder.

Even if you only use e-mail on a moderate basis, your Sent Items folder can become quite large over time. To see where this information is kept, right-click the Sent Items folder in your folder list and choose Properties from the context menu. It should show that the name of the file in which all your sent e-mail is stored is named Sent Items.dbx. Its folder location will depend on whether you moved your message store, as discussed later in the chapter. Periodically, you may wish to delete the older messages in your Sent Items folder, to keep its size under control.

When you delete your messages, they actually go to the Deleted Messages folder. To make sure that this folder is emptied each time you close Outlook Express, click Tools ⇨ Options, and select the Maintenance tab. Select the option Empty messages from the 'Deleted Items' folder on exit.

Annoy your friends: Use stationery

Outlook Express lets you choose between several formatting styles to increase the heft of your messages. One of your first choices is whether you want to send your e-mail messages using plain text or HTML-formatted messages.

In Outlook Express, click Tools ⇨ Options, and then select the Send tab. In the Mail Sending Format section, you choose between sending e-mail formatted as plain text or formatted as HTML. If you choose HTML format, a number of formatting tools will be available to you when you create a new e-mail message, as shown in Figure 13-6.

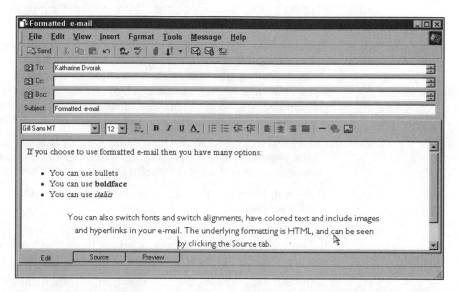

Figure 13-6: If you set your e-mail formatting preference to HTML format, you will have these formatting buttons and options available in the New Message window.

With HTML formatted e-mail, you can select fonts and font sizes, and you can select bold, italic, and underlined text. You can add a number of other graphic embellishments as well. If you really want to dress up your messages, you can use *stationery*. Click the down arrow to the right of the New Message icon, or click Message, New Message Using, and then select the stationery design you want to use. Stationery designs include a background image, as well as fonts, colors, and other enhancements. When you select a design to use, you will have a number of selections to choose from on the drop-down list, and you also can click Select Stationery to choose from an even more extensive list of designs.

Create your own stationery

You do not have to limit yourself to the stationery designs provided by Outlook Express. You also can create your own, letting the Outlook Express stationery wizard guide you.

STEPS:

Using the Stationery Wizard

Step 1. In Outlook Express, click Message ⇨ New Message Using ⇨ Select Stationery.

Step 2. In the Select Stationery dialog box, click Create New.

Step 3. This starts the Stationery Setup Wizard. Click Next to move past the Introduction dialog box.

Step 4. You will first need to choose a background picture or graphic to use. Outlook Express comes with a number of graphic images that are appropriate for letters (baby announcements, birthday invitations, and so on), or you can browse your hard disk to choose your own graphic image. (Since these stationery designs are really HTML pages, you can only include .GIF or .JPG images.)

Step 5. Once you have selected the image you want to use, set its position on the page, and also select whether you want the picture tiled (repeated over and over for a solid background). Then click Next.

Step 6. Choose the font you want for this stationery, as well as its size and color. Click Next.

Step 7. Adjust the margins for your e-mail messages. If you are using a background graphic, you probably want to set the margins so that your text does not display over the graphic.

Step 8. In the last step, name your new creation, and then click Finish. Your new stationery design will now be available for you to use.

Caution

What your stationery-based e-mail messages will look like on arrival also depends on your recipient's e-mail program. If they are not using Outlook or Outlook Express, some or all of the formatting may be lost. In some cases, the formatting — or at least the graphic — is added as an attachment. Some programs will display the underlying HTML code, which will make your message unintelligible and extremely annoying to your recipient. Other times, the attached graphic will show up as a solid block of numbers — very ugly.

Your stationery will be stored in the C:\Program Files\Common Files\Microsoft Shared\Stationery\ folder. If you want to edit your the stationery design — or any of the Microsoft-provided stationery designs — simply edit the HTML files. Many HTML editors, such as Microsoft FrontPage and FrontPage Express, are going to add a lot of hidden code that will make the file unusable as stationery. Instead, you should use the built-in editor within Outlook Express to make your changes.

STEPS:

Edit Your Stationery

Step 1.   In Outlook Express, open a new message window using the stationery you want to edit.

Step 2.   In the New Message window, click View ⇨ Source Edit.

Step 3.   In the lower portion of the window, click Source. This will display the HTML code for your selected stationery.

Step 4.   After you make your changes, click File ⇨ Save as Stationery.

Set default stationery

You can choose a single stationery design as your default for e-mail messages, and another design for your news messages. To set these defaults, follow these steps:

STEPS:

Setting Default Stationery

Step 1.   In Outlook Express, click Tools ⇨ Options, and select the Compose tab, as shown in Figure 13-7. In the Stationery section, select Mail to activate the default Stationery selection. Click the Select button to choose a stationery design you already have installed on your computer.

Step 2.   If you don't like your current selection, you can click Create New, which will start the Stationery Setup Wizard discussed above.

Step 3.   Click the Download More button to visit the Home Publishing Web site at http://home-publishing.com/outlookexpress/stationery.htm, which is a Microsoft Web site done in conjunction with Hallmark. From here, you can download even more stationery examples.

Step 4.   From the Compose Tab, you also can set your stationery options for newsgroup messages. Beware, however—many people who read newsgroups will not be happy downloading graphics-filled messages.

Continued

STEPS

Setting Default Stationery *(continued)*

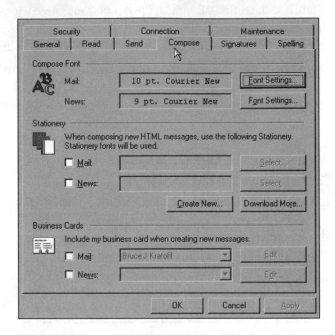

Figure 13-7: You can make your default stationery selections on the Compose tab of the Tools ⇨ Options dialog box.

Step 5.   When you are done setting your defaults, click OK.

Secret

On the Send tab of the Tools ⇨ Options menu, you can select Plain Text or HTML for your e-mail and news message format. If you select Plain Text here, and then select the Compose tab and choose a default stationery, it will override your Plain Text selection. To go back to plain text, you have to clear any mail or news stationery setting, and then select plain text on the Send tab.

In the previous exercise, we noted that many newsgroup readers will not take kindly to messages composed with stationery, since a 1K or 2K message may carry ten times the bandwidth overhead with the included graphics. This may also be true with your e-mail recipients. People with a slow connection, or who pay for connect times, might not like to receive stationery-based e-mail either.

More Stationery Choices

If you are not sure you are creative enough to design your own stationery, there are other sites on the Web where you can look. Some of these sites are:

- Kenja's Stationery at http://www.kenja. com/stationery/ has over 300 different choices for Outlook Express and Outlook.

- Outlook Express Stationery by Wen at http://members.tripod.com/~WenAnn/ index.html.

- Stationery by Teresa at http://www.geocities. com/EnchantedForest/Tower/6026/stationery .html.

- There is a newsgroup devoted to Outlook Express Stationery at microsoft.public. windows.inetexplorer.ie5.outlookexpress.st ationery.

Please note: there are compatibility issues between some stationery created for Outlook Express 4 (which shipped with Internet Explorer 4) and Outlook Express 5.

Identify yourself

There are a number of ways in which you can identify yourself on your outgoing e-mail messages. You can add a plain-text signature, you can attach an electronic business card to your e-mail, and you can obtain a digital signature that can be used to verify your identity.

Plain text signatures

Outlook Express can automatically attach a plain-text signature to the bottom of every e-mail message you send. You also can create a variety of different e-mail signatures from which you can choose to include on your messages.

STEPS:
Adding a Signature to a Message

Step 1. In Outlook Express, click Tools ⇨ Options, and select the Signatures tab.

Step 2. Click New. A new signature with a default name will be listed in the Signatures pane. In the Edit Signature text box, type the text you want to appear. For a multiline signature, press Enter at the end of each line.

Step 3. Make sure that the new signature is selected in the Signature pane, and then click the Rename button. Save it with an easy-to-remember name.

Continued

Step 4.   You can create more signatures by repeating Steps 3 and 4.

Step 5.   If you want Outlook Express to automatically add signatures, you need to choose one as your default. Select it in the Signatures pane, and then click Set as Default.

Step 6.   If you want signatures automatically added, select the option Add Signatures to all outgoing messages. You can choose to not add a signature to replies and forwards, if you want. Click OK.

Step 7.   If you selected to have signatures added automatically, each time you create a new message, your default signature will be added to the end of the message text. If you want to use a different signature, delete the default signature and click Insert ➪ Signature. All of your available signatures will be on available the Signatures menu, as shown in Figure 13-8.

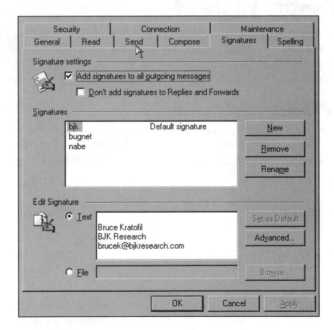

Figure 13-8: You can create multiple signatures that can be added to e-mail messages.

Add your e-mail address or your Web site URL to your signature file, in addition to your name. You also can add any other contact information you might want to include, such as a telephone or fax number.

Adding vCards

You can include even more information about yourself in an e-mail message by attaching a *vCard*. A vCard is an electronic version of a business card. They follow the standards established by the Internet Mail Consortium (http://www.imc.org) as a way of passing data between a variety of electronic devices, including computer e-mail programs, personal digital assistants, Web browsers, and digital telephones.

You create a vCard from information in the Outlook Express Address Book. The first thing you must do is create an entry for yourself in the Address Book, adding as much information as you want to pass along with your vCard. After you create the entry, select it and click File ⇨ Export, and then select Business Card (vCard). You will see the File ⇨ Save dialog box, which is already set to save a .VCF file. (VCF is the file extension for a vCard file, or virtual card file.) Choose a directory in which to save your new .VCF file.

If you moved all your Outlook Express message stores to a folder within your My Documents folder, save your vCard file there. This keeps all your related e-mail information in one place.

After you have created a vCard, you can automatically add it to all outgoing messages. Click the Tools ⇨ Options, and then select the Compose tab. In the Business Card section, check the Mail box to add your business card to e-mail messages (and your news messages, too, if you want), and then locate your vCard file in the list box.

If you don't want to add your vCard to every outgoing message, you can still include it with selected messages. When composing a new message, click Insert ⇨ My Business Card. Whether you insert a vCard automatically or manually, the vCard will be included as a file attachment.

Attachments

If you need to send a file—such as a word processing document or a spreadsheet file—along with your e-mail, you add them as a file attachment. From a message window, click Insert ⇨ File Attachment, which opens a browse window so that you can select the file you want to include. As a shortcut, you also can click the paperclip button on the toolbar to choose a file to attach.

You also can attach sound files to the e-mail message itself, which will play when the e-mail is opened by your recipient. To do this, you must first click Tools ⇨ Options ⇨ Send, and make sure that your e-mail is set as HTML rather than as plain text. Then, as you compose a new message, click Format ⇨

Background ⇨ Sound. Use the Browse button to search for the sound file you want to attach (.wav, .snd, .au, .aif, .aifc, or .aiff formats) and select how many times you want the sound repeated in the background — or if you want it played continuously. Note that the recipient needs a sound card and software support installed for whatever file format you send to be able to hear it.

You can use the Format ⇨ Background ⇨ Picture command to add a picture to the background of your e-mail. This is a quicker way to add a graphic than setting up stationery.

Tip

There are two ways to format attachments to your e-mail, MIME and UUENCODE. If you know your recipients are using an up-to-date e-mail program, you want to choose MIME encoding, which is the default in Outlook Express. If you are e-mailing to someone who uses UNIX, or if you are e-mailing to news servers, you want to switch to UUENCODE.

STEPS:
Switching to UUENCODING

Step 1. Click Tools ⇨ Options, and select the Send tab.

Step 2. In your Mail Sending Format, click the mail format you are using: HTML Settings or Plain Text Settings.

Step 3. In Message Format, select UUENCODE.

Step 4. Click OK, and then click OK again to close the dialog box.

Receiving E-mail

With the increasing importance of e-mail for both business and personal use, it is important to set up Outlook Express so that you can quickly check, sort, save, and back up your messages. Here are a number of techniques you can use.

Check your e-mail

Most people will want to check their inbox right away to see if there are any new messages. There are two ways to go directly to your Inbox:

- At the bottom of the Outlook Express opening screen is a check box that says When Outlook Express Starts, go directly to my Inbox. Selecting this will bypass the opening screen.

- You also can move directly to the Inbox, or disable this feature, from the Options dialog box, as explained in the following exercise:

STEPS:

Go Directly to the Inbox

Step 1.   Click Tools ⇨ Options, and select the General tab.

Step 2.   Select the option When Starting, go directly to my Inbox.

Step 3.   If you are going straight there, you may as well have your e-mail ready for you. In the Send/Receive section, select the option Send and Receive Messages at Start-up.

Step 4.   While you are online, you might want Outlook Express to periodically check for new e-mail messages. You can set this interval here, in minutes, as shown in Figure 13-9.

Step 5.   While you can have Outlook Express check for messages, you also can override this setting when you are offline. In the list box If my computer is not connected at this time, you can choose Do Not Connect, Connect only when not working offline, or Connect even if working offline. The last two choices will open the Connection dialog box. You can cancel the connection attempt by closing the dialog box.

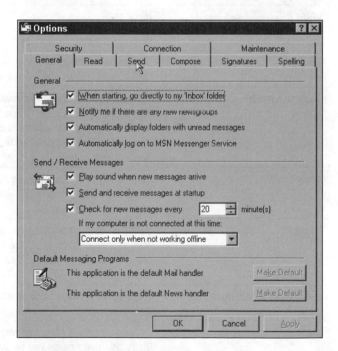

Figure 13-9: You can determine when Outlook Express checks for new messages.

You don't have to wait for a scheduled e-mail check. You can force one at any time by clicking the Send/Receive button on the Toolbar, or by clicking Tools ➪ Send and Receive ➪ Send and Receive All.

Tip

You also can choose just to send or just to receive e-mail. These options are on the Tools ➪ Send and Receive menu, or you can click the down arrow to the right of the Send and Receive button on the Toolbar.

Read your e-mail

To read e-mail, click a message header to view it in the preview pane. If you double-click a message header, it will open in its own window. In both cases, the Internet header — the technical information at the beginning of an e-mail message will be hidden. If you want to view it, right-click a message header, choose Properties, and then select Details.

There are quite a few other shortcuts available when you right-click a message header. They are listed in Table 13-2.

Table 13-2 Right-click Message Actions

Right Click and Select . . .	Does This . . .
Open	Displays the message in its own window.
Print	Opens the Print dialog box, which will enable you to configure and print the message.
Reply to sender	Opens a new message window with a reply addressed to the sender. The original message will be added to the reply, if you have clicked Tools ➪ Options ➪ Send and enabled the Include Message in Reply option.
Reply to All	Same as above, except that your reply will go to any additional addressees or individuals who were cc'ed on the original message.
Forward	Sends a copy of the message to another recipient. A new message window will be opened, and the original message will be added. You need to address the message.
Forward as Attachment	The original message will be attached as a file to a new message.
Mark as read/Mark as unread	Depending on the status of your message, one of these two commands will be available. The other will be grayed out.

Right Click and Select . . .	Does This . . .
Move to folder	Opens the Folder selection dialog box so that you can choose the folder to which you want to move the selected message. The original will be deleted from the Inbox.
Copy to folder	Opens the Folder selection dialog box so that you can choose the folder to which you Want to copy the selected message. The original will remain in the Inbox.
Delete	Sends the selected message to the Deleted Items folder.
Add sender to Address Book	Creates a new entry in the Address Book. The name of the entry will be taken from the message header information. You can open the Address Book and change this later.

Manage incoming e-mail

By default, Outlook Express has local folders labeled Inbox, Outbox, Sent Items, Deleted Items, and Drafts. While they are called folders, they are not the same folders you see in the Windows Explorer. They are actually a special type of file — called a message store, with a .dbx extension — that, by default, is buried deep within your user profiles. This is a change in architecture from earlier versions of Outlook Express, which used .mbx, .idx, and .nch files.

To see where these folders store their messages, right-click your Inbox, and select Properties. The Properties dialog box will show the location for the Inbox message store, which will be something like C:\WINNT\Profiles\ *username*\Local Settings\Application Data\Identities*identity*\Microsoft\ Outlook Express\Inbox.dbx. (This path is so long, it will probably extend past the Properties dialog box. Click it, and then use either the right-arrow key or the End key to see the rest of the path.)

Creating additional e-mail folders

Just like you would create additional subfolders within your My Documents folder to manage your data files, you will want to create additional e-mail folders to store important e-mail that you may receive and want to save. If your Folder List is being displayed, right-click the Local Folders icon, and then select New Folder. The Create Folder dialog box, shown in Figure 13-10, will be displayed, and you can type the name of your new folder.

If your Folder List is not being displayed, you can create a folder by clicking File ➪ New ➪ Folder, or by using the Ctrl+Shift+E keyboard shortcut.

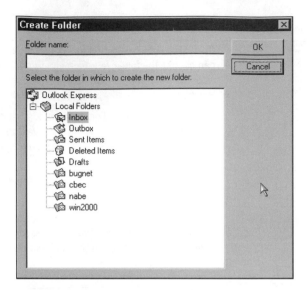

Figure 13-10: Name your new folder in the Create Folder dialog box. You can use these folders to store e-mail and news messages.

You can create a subfolder beneath another folder that you have already created. Simply right-click the parent folder under which you want the new folder to appear — rather than right-clicking the Local folders icon — and then select New Folder.

Once you create a new folder, a new .mbx file with the name of the folder is created within your message store. To move an e-mail message from your Inbox to one of these new folders, follow these steps:

STEPS:

Moving an E-Mail Message to a Local Folder

Step 1.   Go to your Inbox by clicking it in the Folder List or the Outlook Bar.

Step 2.   Click and drag the message from the Folder Content pane over to the destination folder in the Folder List. Release the mouse button.

Step 3.   If you don't have the Folder List or Outlook Bar displayed, you can move the message by right-clicking the message in the Folder Contents pane, and then selecting Move to Folder.

Step 4.   Select the destination folder from the dialog box.

Tip

If you don't want to use the mouse, you can use the Ctrl+Shift+V keyboard shortcut to open the list of folders. Then, use the keyboard arrow keys to select the destination folder.

Tip

You can create any number of new folders to store e-mail messages. You can have a folder for each client, for each project, or for any organizational scheme that works for you. Keeping all your important messages piled up in the in basket will probably cause you frustration in the long run as you search for important messages.

Moving your messages

In Windows 2000, there are advantages to having a centralized place the My Documents folder to store all your documents. As discussed in Chapter 7, this makes it easier to search for documents, and it makes it easier to back up, as well. In fact, having My Documents as the default save location is one of the requirements of the Windows 2000 compatibility logo.

Unfortunately, Microsoft doesn't always follow its own advice. Your incoming and outgoing e-mail messages, — especially the messages you save — are important documents. But instead of going into the My Documents folder with your other important files, they are buried deep within your Profiles folder. However, at least Microsoft has provided a way for you to move your e-mail folders.

STEPS:

Moving Outlook Express Messages to My Documents

Step 1. When you move your messages, they must go into an existing folder, which we will create. Start the Windows Explorer and highlight the My Documents folder. (Note that you may have renamed your My Documents folder.)

Step 2. Select New ⇨ Folder. Give the folder an appropriate name, such as Mail.

Step 3. Start Outlook Express. Click Tools ⇨ Options, and click the Maintenance tab, as shown in Figure 13-11.

Continued

STEPS

Moving Outlook Express Messages to My Documents *(continued)*

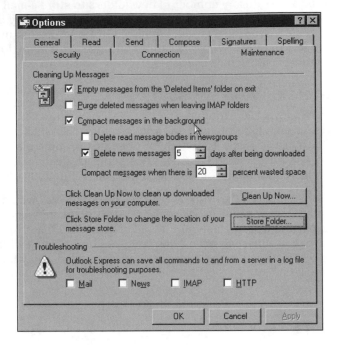

Figure 13-11: Click Store Folder to move your messages. If you store your messages with your other important data, it will be easier to back them up.

Step 4. Click Store Folder.

Step 5. This will bring up a small dialog box, as shown in Figure 13-12, showing the current location of your message store. Click Change.

Figure 13-12: The location of the Outlook Express Message Store.

Step 6. In the Browse window, navigate to the new folder you created in Step 2. Click OK.

Step 7. This brings you back to the window shown if Figure 13-12. The path should now show the new location. If it does, click OK. If not, click Change and find the new folder again.

Step 8. The change will not take place until you exit and restart Outlook Express. Close all the open dialog boxes, and then exit Outlook Express.

Step 9. Restart Outlook Express. There should be a slight pause while a message briefly reports that files are being copied.

Now, if you back up the My Documents folder, all your saved e-mail messages will also be backed up.

Move your Address Book

You also can move you Outlook Express Address Book to your My Documents folder to keep it with the rest of your valuable documents. Unfortunately, there is no easy migration tool like there is for your e-mail messages. Instead, you will have to edit your Registry.

Note

Each Windows 2000 user will have a separate Windows Address Book. If a user then sets up multiple identities within Outlook Express, each of those identities can have a separate address book.

STEPS:

Moving Your Address Book

Step 1. Close Outlook Express.

Step 2. Start the Registry Editor by clicking Start ➪ Run, and then typing regedit.exe in the Open text box.

Step 3. Find the following registry key: HKEY_CURRENT_USER\Software\ Microsoft\WAB\WAB4\Wab File Name. This is the current location of the Windows Address Book (see Figure 13-13). Make a note of it, as you will have to go to this folder later in Windows Explorer.

Continued

STEPS

Moving Your Address Book *(continued)*

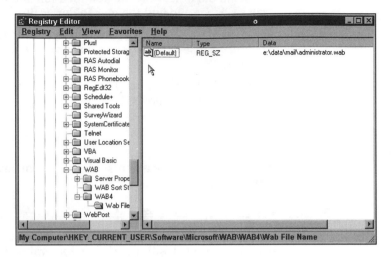

Figure 13-13: The location of the Windows Address Book is stored in this key:
HKEY_CURRENT_USER\Software\Microsoft\WAB\WAB4\Wab File Name

Step 4.   Double-click the icon in the right panel to display the Edit String
dialog box, shown in Figure 13-14, which enables you to change
the value of this Registry key.

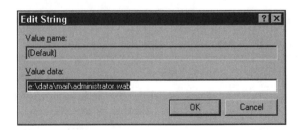

Figure 13-14: Type in the new path and name of your Windows Address Book.

Step 5.   In the Edit String dialog box, type the new path and name for your
Windows Address Book. A good place to put it is in the new folder
you created earlier for your message store.

Step 6.   Click OK, and then close the Registry Editor.

Step 7.   Open the Windows Explorer, and then move the *username*.wab file
from its original spot (the location noted in Step 3) to the new
folder you specified in Step 5.

Now your Address Book and messages files will be stored with the rest of your data files.

Note

Doing these two things — moving your message store and moving your address book — allow you to concentrate more of your valuable "eggs" into one basket. Now make sure you take care of that basket, with frequent backups and whatever security measures are appropriate.

Secret

For fast access to your Address Book, you can create a shortcut to it. The shortcut can be in any of the usual places — your desktop, the Quick Launch Toolbar, the Start Menu, and so on. When you create the shortcut, point to the *username*.wab file you moved above. If the shortcut is on the Desktop, clicking will open the Address book. Then, right-clicking a contact will open a New Message window so that you can compose an e-mail message. When you click Send, it will be stored in the Outlook Express outbox until the next time you send and receive messages.

Manage e-mail with rules

You can set up automated rules in Outlook Express to help manage your flow of e-mail. While these rules can't promise to eliminate spam (unwanted mass e-mail) they may take some of the drudgery out of the process.

Blocking senders

If there is someone from whom you don't want to receive messages, either by e-mail or in a newsgroup, you can add them to your blocked message list, something that is often referred to as a "kill file." Highlight one of their messages, and then click Message ➪ Block Sender. You will see the message shown in Figure 13-15.

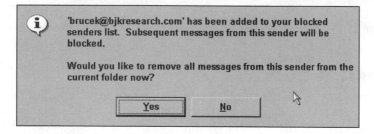

Figure 13-15: You have successfully blocked messages from this e-mail address.

Outlook Express keeps a list of blocked senders. To further manage the list, click Tools ➪ Message Rules ➪ Blocked Senders list. This dialog box will show all the people who have been added to the Blocked Senders list. If they were originally added to the list from an e-mail message, there will be a check mark in the e-mail box. If they were added from a newsgroup, you will only see a check for news. You can block both, or you can remove them from the list entirely by selecting the name and clicking Remove (see Figure 13-16). When you remove them from the list, you will again be able to receive messages.

Tip

Select an entry and click Modify. You can make changes to an e-mail address, or you can block an entire domain. For instance, if you don't want to receive any more e-mail from Microsoft, you would change the address to just the domain which, in this case, would be microsoft.com. More than likely, if you are constantly receiving e-mail invitations for Get Rich Quick schemes or from pornographic or other objectionable sites, and they all appear to be coming from the same domain, you can block that entire domain.

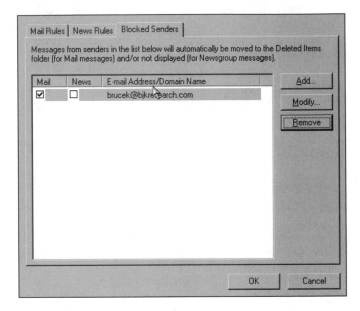

Figure 13-16: You can modify or delete senders from your Blocked Message list.

Message rules

You can do more than just block messages. You can set up rules that look at the properties of incoming e-mail for some specific details, and then choose an action to perform when one of these messages are encountered.

Possibly the easiest way to do this is a rule-by-example feature built into Outlook Express. To use it, find a message that is an example of the type of rule you want. For example, say you want to make a rule that highlights any e-mail that comes from Bruce Brown. To do this, follow these steps:

STEPS:
Setting Up a Message Rule

Step 1. Find an e-mail message from Bruce Brown and select it.

Step 2. Click Message ⇨ Create Rule From Message.

Step 3. This will display the New Mail Rule dialog box shown in Figure 13-17.

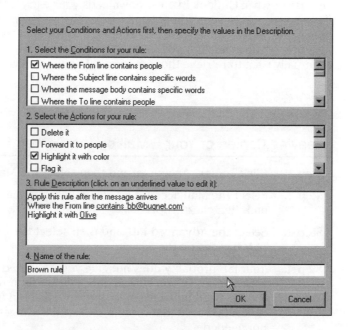

Figure 13-17: Set up your mail rule.

Step 4. In the first window of the dialog box, select the condition that Outlook Express is going to look for. In this case, the rule to apply is Where the From line contains people. The From line of the current message will be extracted and used for this rule.

Step 5. In the second window, pick your action. In this example, we want to choose the option Highlight it with color. You can see that there are many other possible actions you can choose from.

Step 6. In the third window, you can click one of the links so that you can modify the arguments. Select Highlight it with color and then click the color link in the third window and choose a color from the list. It would be appropriate to highlight messages from someone named Brown with brown, but since brown isn't one of the colors, we will highlight his messages in the closest color, which is olive.

Step 7. Give the rule a name. We will call it the Brown Rule. Click OK.

Once you have created a rule, you can modify it by clicking Tools ➪ Message Rules. You can modify existing rules, create new rules, or delete old rules.

Secret

A small item in the Outlook Express Release Notes reports that junkmail filtering is not available in Outlook Express 5. What is undocumented is that this is partially due to legal proceedings between Microsoft and Blue Mountain Arts, an electronic greeting card company whose products were being screened out by Outlook Express.

Tip

Ordinarily, when Outlook Express downloads your e-mail messages from your ISP's mail server to your computer, it deletes the messages from the mail server. Sometimes, you might want to leave copies of the messages on the server; for instance, you are checking your e-mail from someone else's computer, and you eventually want to retrieve those messages to your own computer.

STEPS:

Leaving Copies of Your E-Mail on the Server

Step 1. Click Tools ➪ Accounts, and then select the Mail tab.

Step 2. Select the Mail account where you wish to leave your messages, and then click Properties.

Step 3. Select the Advanced tab, and then select the option Leave A Copy of Messages on the Server.

Step 4. Your ISP probably does not give you unlimited storage space on their server, so you should check either Remove from server after X days, or Remove from Server when deleted from 'Deleted Items'. At least be sure that disable this option altogether when it is not needed.

Managing the Windows Address Book

Outlook Express uses the Windows Address Book to store its Contact information. Earlier, we saw how to move your Address Book to the My Documents folder.

The Windows Address Book is more than just a list of names and e-mail addresses. It has the capacity to hold almost as much information as a full-fledged Contact Manager — with separate tabs for work, home, personal, and digital ID and NetMeeting information. It rivals the contact information kept by both Microsoft Outlook 98 and 2000, which is Microsoft's Personal Information Manager.

Adding contacts

There are a number of ways in which you can add contacts to your
Address Book:

- There is the hard way: just sit down and start typing information.

- When you receive a message, you can right-click the message header and
  select Add Sender to Address Book.

- Under Tools ➪ Options ➪ Send, you can select Automatically put people I
  reply to in my Address Book.

- If a vCard is attached to e-mail, the information can be imported into
  your Address Book.

- You can import Address Book information from other e-mail programs.
  Outlook can import information from the following programs: Eudora Pro
  or Light through version 3.0; LDIF and LDAP Data Interchange Format;
  Microsoft Exchange Personal Address Book; Microsoft Internet Mail for
  Windows 3.1; Netscape Address Book version 2 or 3; Netscape
  Communicator 4; and comma separated value (CSV) Text files.

As an example, here is how to import address information from Eudora Pro:

STEPS:

Importing Information from Other Programs

Step 1.   Open the Address Book.

Step 2.   Click File ➪ Import ➪ Other Address Book.

Step 3.   Choose the address book format from which you will be importing
from the list. Then, click Import.

Step 4.   Outlook Express will attempt to find the address book. If it can't,
you will see the message shown in Figure 13-18. Click Yes.

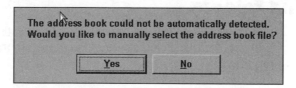

Figure 13-18: If Outlook Express can't find the Address Book, you will have to
search for it.

Continued

STEPS

Importing Information from Other Programs *(continued)*

Step 5. This displays the Open dialog box. Navigate through until you find the folder containing the address book you want to import. (Eudora Pro keeps the contact information in text files.) Select it and click import. The contact information will be added to your Address Book.

The new contacts will be merged in with your existing contacts. Even if you create a new folder and open it, they will go in the main contacts list.

The Outlook Express e-mail import function thinks that Netscape Communicator address books have file extension of.NAB. Communicator 4.6 seems to have changed this to .NA2, and Outlook Express does not know how to import these files, at least in the beta versions.

Organizing contacts

If you have a large number of contacts, you can adopt one of a number of organizational schemes to help find your contact information. Click View ➪ Sort by to select the way in which you want your contacts listed. You can sort by name (either by first name or last name), by e-mail address, and by business or home phone. You also can list your contacts in ascending or descending order.

You also can click the header above a column to sort by that column. The small arrow within the column header indicates the sort order. To reverse the sort order for a column, click the column header again.

Adding folders

If your e-mail contacts fall into a number of separate categories, such as business and personal, or a club or client list, you can organize them into folders.

STEPS:

Adding a Folder to the Address Book

Step 1. In the Address Book, make sure the Folders and Groups panel is displayed. Click View and make sure Folders and Groups is checked.

Step 2.   In the Folders and Groups panel, you should see a Shared Contacts group, plus a folder with your current Outlook Express identity. If you want the contacts in this new folder to be available to your other identities, right-click the Shared Contacts icon, or right-click your identity name icon.

Step 3.   Select New ⇨ New Folder. Give the folder a unique name. (You cannot have folders with the same name under shared contacts and under your identity.)

Step 4.   To move some of your existing contacts into the new folder, click and drag them from the right pane and drop them on the folder. This will be a move: the contact will no longer appear in your regular list of contacts.

Creating mail groups

If you often send a message to the same group of people, you can save time by setting up a mail group. A mail group is nothing more than a collection of other e-mail addresses. Sending a single message to the group sends it to every member of the group. To create a group, follow these steps:

STEPS:
Creating a Mail Group

Step 1.   Open your Address Book, and then click the folder in which you want to create the group — either your own contacts or the shared contacts.

Step 2.   Click File ⇨ New Group, or use the Ctrl+G keyboard shortcut.

Step 3.   This will display the Properties dialog box for the mail group, as shown in Figure 13-19. Give the group a distinctive name in the Group Name text box.

Step 4.   Now you can add members to the group. If the new members are already in your Address Book, click Select Members. This will display your contacts list, from which you can select the members you want to add.

Step 5.   If you have someone you want to add to the group, but they aren't yet in your Address Book, click New Contact. This will let you add them to the Address Book and the group.

Continued

STEPS

Creating a Mail Group (continued)

Step 6. If you want to add someone to your group, but you don't want them cluttering up your main Address Book, type their Name and e-mail address in the two bottom boxes, and then click Add.

Step 7. Click OK to save the group. Later, you can add individuals to or subtract individuals from your group. Right-click the group name in the folder and group list, and then select Properties.

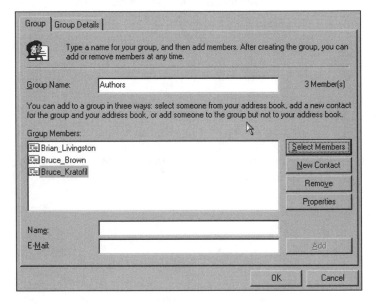

Figure 13-19: Add or subtract members from the Properties box.

Newsgroups

Before there was a World Wide Web, one of the most popular features of the Internet were the Usenet newsgroups. Today, an ISPs news server might carry over 40,000 newsgroups devoted to different subjects and areas of interest.

If you can imagine it, there's probably an Internet newsgroup devoted to it. Music of Barbados? No problem. TV personality Roseanne Barr? Get in line. Obscure C++ programming tricks? All night long.

One of Outlook Express's most useful features is its ability to serve as a newsgroup reader.

News server accounts

When you first set up your Internet connection with Outlook Express, the Wizard optionally asked you if you wanted to set up a news server account. If you didn't do so then, you can set one up now.

Your ISP almost certainly has established a news server for its customers' use. Generally, the news server's name is just the ISPs domain name, but with news at the beginning of the name. For example, GTEs news server is news.gte.net. If using this syntax doesn't work, contact your ISP for the correct news address.

Secret

Most ISPs have software installed that restricts access to their news server. To successfully access the GTE news server mentioned above, for instance, you must dial into the Internet on a GTE dialup account or provide your GTE user name and password.

There are other news servers available that allow public access. For instance, Microsoft's news server carries many individual news groups devoted to its products. To establish an account to access the Microsoft newsgroups, follow these steps:

STEPS:

Establishing a News Account

Step 1. Click Tools ⇨ Accounts to display the Internet Accounts window.

Step 2. Click the News tab to display any accounts you may already have established, as shown in Figure 13-20.

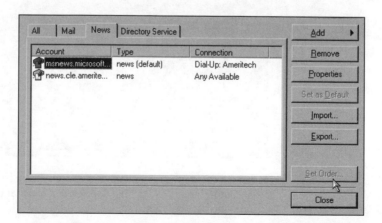

Figure 13-20: The Internet Accounts dialog box will show what accounts you already have established, and it allows you to add more.

Continued

STEPS

Establishing a News Account *(continued)*

Step 3.   Click Add ⇨ News to start the Internet Connection Wizard.

Step 4.   First, the Wizard will ask the name you want to use for this account. Add your name, or the name you want to use, and then click Next.

Step 5.   Next, it will ask for your e-mail address, in case anyone wants to reply directly to you, instead of posting the reply to the entire newsgroup. (See the important Caution that follows.) Click Next.

Step 6.   Fill in the name of the news server on which you wish to establish an account. The name of the Microsoft news server is msnews.microsoft.com. If you want to set up an account with your ISPs server, substitute their information here.

Step 7.   ISPs may want you to log on, providing a user name and password, so that you can establish that you are a customer, as shown in Figure 13-21. If so, select the option My news server requires me to log on. You do not need to do this for the Microsoft news server. Click Next.

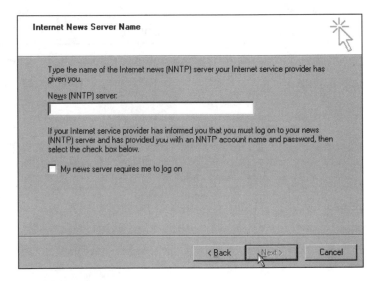

Figure 13-21: Add the name of the news server on which you wish to establish an account. This can be your ISP or a news server that provides public access, such as the Microsoft news server.

Step 8.   Click Finish to end the setup process and establish your account. You will see the news server added to the list in Step 2. When you go back to the main Outlook Express screen, you will see a folder for this server in your Folders list.

Adding newsgroups

Once you have established an account with a news server, you can subscribe to newsgroups. Click Tools ➪ Newsgroups, or use the Ctrl+W shortcut keys to see the Newsgroup selection dialog box.

The left panel has icons representing news servers on which you have created accounts. If you have more than one account, select the server on which you want to view the newsgroups. Click the Reset List button to download all the newsgroups available on the selected server.

Note

News servers for many ISPs might carry 30,000 or more newsgroups. If you have a slow modem, it may take awhile to download the entire newsgroup list.

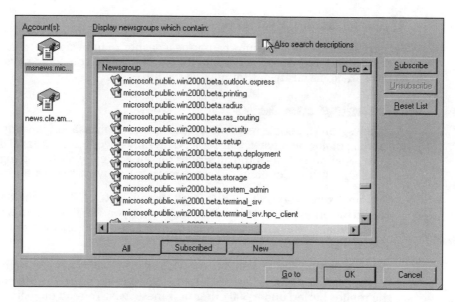

Figure 13-22: Download the list of available newsgroups available on a server.

Once you have downloaded the entire list, you can browse through it to find newsgroups that interest you. If you are searching for newsgroups on a particular topic, type the keyword for that topic in the text box that says Display newsgroups which contain:

Tip

You may have to experiment a little to find the exact keyword for a topic that will yield a successful search. For instance, on the Microsoft news server, typing **Windows 2000** will return no newsgroups. However, typing **win2000** will show that there are over 50 newsgroups devoted to Windows 2000.

When you find a newsgroup you want to view, click Subscribe. Outlook Express will add an icon to the left of the newsgroup that looks like a piece of paper pinned to a file folder, to show that you are subscribed. When you have finished selecting the newsgroups to which you want to subscribe, click OK. When you go back to the main Outlook Express screen, you will see that the Folder list now has a new entry for each of your subscribed newsgroups, branching down from its news server.

You don't have to subscribe to read a newsgroup. To read messages in a newsgroup without subscribing, select the newsgroup window and scroll through the list of newsgroups to find the one that interests you. Click Go To so you view the messages in the newsgroup. If you read through the messages and find that you want to subscribe, you can go back to the newsgroups window, select the newsgroup, and then click Subscribe. From the main Outlook Express window, you can right-click the newsgroup's icon in the folder list (an unsubscribe newsgroup will have a grayed-out folder), and select Subscribe.

Using newsgroups

Participating in newsgroups can bring a gusher of information to your computer. If you tried to deal with it in its raw state, you could never keep up. Here are some strategies for making the job easier.

Reading the news

In newsgroups, people respond to other people's messages, developing a running dialog on a particular topic. Generally accepted Internet slang refers to these as *threads,* as if the messages on one topic are all strung together. To make sure you understand the conversation, you want to read these in order.

Secret

Outlook Express doesn't use the word thread. Instead, it uses the term conversation. Whatever it's called, make sure you use it. Click View ➪ Current View, and make sure that the Group Messages by Conversation option is selected.

Tip

Here's a tip that you'll probably use almost every time you cruise the newsgroups. If you post a question to a newsgroup, it may be difficult to find the replies buried under 300 other new messages. To read only messages that are posted in reply to your messages, set your view for Hide Read Messages. If you want to trace a thread backward, or look for something you saw earlier, switch to Show All Messages.

Most newsgroups are public. Anyone smart enough to configure Outlook Express is allowed to post messages, even if they have nothing worthwhile to say. Since they know they will almost never have to face the other participants face-to-face, behaviors can be quite rude. If you see, over time, that all the posts from Bob Blabbermouth have no redeeming quality, you can set up a message rule (see "Message Rules," earlier in this chapter) to screen out his posts.

Tip If you see a thread that is particularly interesting, select its header and click Message ➪ Watch Conversation. Any new message headers in this conversation will be marked with an icon resembling of a pair of eyeglasses. If you see a conversation that you have no interest in following, click Message ➪ Ignore conversation.

Writing the news

If you are replying to a newsgroup post, it is important to realize the distinction between Reply to Group and Reply to Sender. The former adds another post to the newsgroup. The latter sends off an e-mail message to the sender.

Tip If you post a question to a newsgroup, it may be difficult to find the replies, if they are buried in with 300 new message headers. You can find them by clicking View ➪ Current View ➪ Show Replies to my Messages.

Tip If you subscribe to a number of newsgroups, their headers and messages will eventually begin to take up a lot of space on your hard disk. To see how much, click Tools, Options, and go to the Maintenance tab. Click Clean Up Now. This window will show you the amount of saved information for newsgroups. You can select which Local Newsgroup to check, or you can select all of them, using the Browse button. Click Compact to make more efficient use of the disk storage space. Click Remove Messages to remove the message bodies. Since the Headers remain, you can use them to again download the message bodies from the news server. When you click Delete, both the headers and the messages are removed. Clicking Reset also does this, but will configure Outlook Express to again download these same headers the next time you connect.

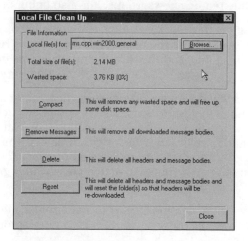

Figure 13-23: To recover disk space from newsgroup activities, right-click a newsgroup folder and select Local Files.

Working Offline

Outlook Express shares its Internet connection tools with the Internet Explorer. Once you establish a connection with one of these programs, you will be able to switch to the other without being prompted for another connection. Like the Internet Explorer, you also can work both online and offline. This is unimportant, if your connection to the Internet is always on, such as when you connect with a cable modem or if you are connecting through a network. With a dial-up connection, however, you often might want to go offline. You might want to do this if you get charged for the time you are connected to the Internet, or so you can free up the phone line you are using.

There are a number of ways in which you can switch between working online and working offline. The way that is always available is to click File ⇨ Work Offline. If your Status bar is enabled, you will see the status of your connection (online or offline); double-clicking will switch you to the opposite mode. You also can add a button to the Toolbar that will let you switch between the two modes.

Note

If you have set your status to Work Offline and you then switch your status, you will not make a connection immediately, although the Status Bar will change. A connection to the Internet will not be started until you give a command that requires a connection, such as sending and receiving e-mail or downloading messages from a newsgroup. If you are online and switch to offline mode, you will be asked if you want to hang up the modem first.

Synchronizing messages

Your synchronization settings determine what gets downloaded—and when—when you read messages. If you have a constant connection to the Internet, synchronization is relatively unimportant. If you aren't charged by the minute for your Internet connection, and you don't have to worry about freeing up a phone line while reading newsgroups, it is also unimportant.

Without synchronization, if you are working online and you click on a newsgroup, Outlook Express will fetch the next batch of headers. (Headers include the sender, the subject line, and the date the message was posted.) When you click a header, the message will then be downloaded for viewing.

Tip

By default, Outlook Express will download 300 message headers at a time when you view a newsgroup. If you want to change this number, click Tools ⇨ Options and select the Read tab. In the Newsgroup section, you can change this setting to retrieve either more or fewer headers at a time. If you have downloaded a group of headers and want to retrieve more, Click Tools ⇨ Get Next 300 Headers. (The number will change to match your header group size.)

A strategy to use to limit your connection time is to synchronize message headers. This will let you download message headers for a newsgroup, or a number of newsgroups. You can then hang up, and then go back and read the downloaded headers offline. Messages that look interesting can be marked to download later.

Just because you subscribe to a newsgroup doesn't mean you need to synchronize its messages. To change the settings for a newsgroup, follow these steps:

STEPS:

Set Synchronization

Step 1. In Outlook Express, select the news server's folder in the Folder pane. This will display all the subscribed newsgroups in the right pane

Step 2. Select the newsgroup that you want to synchronize. Click Settings.

Step 3. The default setting is Don't Synchronize. You can switch this to All Messages (this could be a lengthy process), New Messages, or Headers Only.

Step 4. You can do a Ctrl Select or Shift Select to choose multiple newsgroups and set all their settings at once.

Step 5. To start the synchronization process, click Synchronize Account. If you want to synchronize when you aren't at this window, click Tools ⇨ Synchronize Account.

Outlook Express Keyboard Shortcuts

You can speed your way through Outlook Express with the keyboard shortcuts listed in Table 13-3. Most will work in both the mail portion and the news portion of Outlook Express.

Table 13-3   Outlook Express Keyboard Shortcuts

Work in Main, View Message, and Send Message Windows	
F1	Opens the Help dialog box.
Ctrl+A	Selects all messages.
F5	Refreshes news messages and headers.

Continued

Table 13-3   *(continued)*

Main and View Message Window

Del	Deletes an e-mail message (also Ctrl+D).
Alt+Enter	Displays properties of the selected message. This lets you see the message header, which is otherwise hidden.
Ctrl+D	Deletes an e-mail message (also Del).
Ctrl+F	Forwards a message.
Ctrl+G	In news only, replies to all.
Ctrl+I	Goes to your inbox.
Ctrl+M	Sends and receives e-mail.
Ctrl+N	Opens (mail) or posts (news) a new message.
Ctrl+P	Prints the selected message.
Ctrl+R	Replies to the message's author.
Ctrl+U	Goes to the next unread e-mail message.
Ctrl+Y	Goes to a folder (displays a list box from which to choose a folder).
Ctrl+Shift+B	Opens the Address Book.
Ctrl+Shift+R	Replies to the message's author.
Ctrl+Shift+U	Goes to the next unread news conversation (by thread).
Ctrl+>	Goes to the next message in the list.
Ctrl+<	Goes to the previous message in the list.

Main Window Shortcuts

Enter	Opens the selected message (also Ctrl+O).
Tab	Moves between sections of the screen: Folders list (if on), message list, preview pane, Contacts list (if enabled).
Left arrow	Expands a news thread (also the plus sign).
Right arrow	Collapse a news thread (also the minus sign).
Plus sign	Expands a news thread (also Left-arrow).
Minus sign	Collapse a news thread (also Right-arrow).
Ctrl+J	Moves to the next unread newsgroup or folder.

Main and View Message Window

Ctrl+O	Opens the selected message (also Enter).
Ctrl+Q	Marks a message as read (also Ctrl+Enter).
Ctrl+W	Goes to a newsgroup (displays a list of newsgroups available on a news server, not just the subscribed newsgroups).
Ctrl+Enter	Marks a message as read (also Ctrl+Q).
Ctrl+Shift+A	Marks all news messages as read.
Ctrl+Shift+M	Downloads news for offline reading.

Message Window: Viewing or Sending

F3	Finds text.
Esc	Closes a message.
Ctrl+Tab	Switches between the Edit, Source, and Preview tabs.
Ctrl+Shift+F	Finds a message.

Message window (sending only)

F7	Checks spelling.
Alt+K	Checks names (also Ctrl+K).
Alt+S	Sends or posts a message (also Ctrl+Enter).
Ctrl+K	Checks names (also Alt+K).
Ctrl+Enter	Sends or posts a message.
Ctrl+Shift+S	Inserts a signature.

Summary

E-mail is becoming a very important communications tool. Windows 2000 comes bundled with Outlook Express, a full featured e-mail and news reader. You can:

▶ Customize the Outlook Express environment to work productively.

▶ Set up multiple identities, signatures, and connections in Outlook Express.

▶ Manage your e-mail with rules, and store it in folders.

▶ Send HTML formatted e-mail, or plain text e-mail.

▶ Participate in the thousands of Internet newsgroups.

Part IV

Hardware

Chapter 14

Managing Your Computer with the Control Panel

In This Chapter

We learn how to manage and configure your computer with the Control Panel. We will learn:

▶ How to add shortcuts to the Control Panel.

▶ How to add new hardware with the Hardware Wizard.

▶ How to add and remove software applications.

▶ How to add and remove Windows components.

▶ How to change your Regional Settings.

▶ How to change the sounds for your system.

▶ How to make System Properties settings.

▶ How to configure your mouse.

▶ How to handle Power Management.

Taking Control of the Control Panel

There are thousands of individual settings that you can change on an average Windows PC. Almost all of these settings can be accessed from the Control Panel.

You can access the Control Panel from the Start Menu. Click Start ⇨ Settings ⇨ Control Panel to open the Control Panel window and see the icons it contains. The Control Panel looks like an ordinary folder, and the icons it contains look like regular program icons. However, there is a difference. The Control Panel is merely a shell program that uses a special type of program having a .CPL extension, which stands for *control panel* applet. The control panel is also a program you can run by clicking Start ⇨ Run, and then typing control.exe into the Open text box.

When you run control.exe—and when you select it from your Start menu—it searches for all of the .CPL files located in your Windows 2000 folder and then displays their icons for you, as shown in Figure 14-1.

Figure 14-1: The Control Panel is actually a collection of individual applets. Yours may have more or less icons than the example.

Because the Control Panel works in this way, independent software developers can write their own programs that install applets into the Control Panel. In other words, the Control Panel is not an exclusive playground for Microsoft applications.

Instead of having the Control Panel open in a window, you can change it into an expanding menu, just like your Start menu. Click Start ➪ Settings ➪ Task Bar & Start Menu Settings, and then select the Advanced tab. In the list of Start Menu settings, select Expand Control Panel.

This feature is designed to help you reduce screen clutter. Normally, if you wanted to make some adjustments to your mouse settings, for example, you would open your Control Panel, and then click the Mouse icon. The Mouse Properties dialog box would then open, and the Control Panel would still be open in the background. After you closed the Mouse Properties dialog box, you would then have to close the Control Panel. Changing the Control Panel into a cascading menu lets you skip this extra close step.

Control Panel shortcuts

Do you often find yourself accessing the Control Panel to make changes? You can create a shortcut to the Control Panel on your desktop to shorten the time it takes you to access the Control Panel by adding a shortcut to Desktop, as shown in the following steps:

STEPS:

Add a Control Panel shortcut to your Desktop

Step 1. Right-click an empty portion of your Desktop. Then, select New ➪ Shortcut from the context menu.

Step 2. In the location for your shortcut, as shown in Figure 14-2, type the following (if you use a Windows 2000 folder other than winnt, replace it with the name of your Windows 2000 folder):

```
C:\winnt\system32\control.exe
```

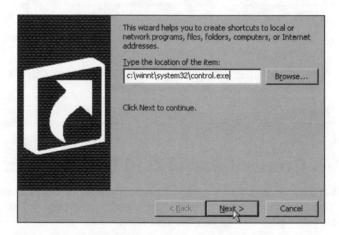

Figure 14-2: Make a desktop shortcut to the Control Panel. If your Windows 2000 folder has a different name, substitute it.

Step 3. Click Next. Name the shortcut Control Panel, instead of the suggested name of control.exe.

Step 4. Click Finish. The icon for this shortcut will be a rather plain rectangle. Right-click the shortcut and select Properties. Click Change Icon.

Step 5. You should be taken to \system32\SHELL32.dll file, which contains a number of common system icons from which you can choose to replace the default icon. If you are not there, navigate to it with the Browse button.

You don't have to make that intermediate stop at the Control Panel if you constantly find yourself accessing the same applet. You can create a shortcut directly to it, instead. Open the Control Panel, and the right-click the applet for which you want to create the shortcut. Then, select Create Shortcut from the context menu. You will then see a message saying that since a shortcut can't be created here, would you like it on the desktop instead.

Since that is what we want, click Yes to finish creating the shortcut. You also can drag and drop shortcuts onto your Start menu, if you would rather preserve a cleaner look on your Desktop. By default, Windows 2000 creates shortcuts that includes some of the basic control panel applets for you, as listed in Table 14-1.

Table 14-1 Shortcuts to System Settings	
For settings . . .	*Do this . . .*
Date/Time	Double-click the clock on the system tray on the far right end of your Taskbar, or right-click the clock and select Properties.
Display Properties	Right-click an empty spot on your Desktop.
System Settings	Right-click the My Computer icon and select Properties.
Network and Dialup Connections	Right-click the My Network Places icon and select Properties.
Printers	Click Start ⇨ Settings ⇨ Printers.

The Control Panel and the Registry

Earlier, we said that thousands of configuration settings are stored in the Registry of a Windows 2000 computer. The System Registry is the central storehouse for most of your system settings.

You can make many system changes by directly editing the Registry. In some cases, that is the only way to make a change. However, that is living dangerously. If you make a mistake and corrupt your Registry, you can totally incapacitate your computer. The various Control Panel applets are designed to help you safely make those changes. (Besides, making a mistake here will probably not disable your whole computer — just part of it!)

Further information on your system configuration is covered elsewhere in this book. Table 14-2 outlines where you can find additional information.

Table 14-2   Control Panel Information in other Chapters

For	See these chapters
Folder Options	7
Display Options	8
Modems	10
Internet Options	12
The Microsoft Management Console and Administrative Tools	15
Editing the Registry	16
Drive management and configuration	17
Printers and fonts	18
Networking hardware and settings	20 and 21

Managing Hardware

One of the major goals of the Windows 2000 operating system was to make the task of managing hardware easier than ever. Windows NT — one of the direct predecessors of Windows 2000 — lacked support for Plug and Play devices and power management support. These two features have been combined into what Microsoft terms the *OnNow design initiative*, which aims to provide a comprehensive approach to control system and device configuration.

Understanding Plug and Play

Plug and Play has been around since Windows 95, although its earliest implementation was a little shaky (it earned the nickname Plug and *Pray*). In Windows 95, Plug and Play device management was implemented either through a Plug and Play (PNP) BIOS or an Advanced Power Management (APM) BIOS. In Windows 2000, Plug and Play support is handled through the Advanced Configuration and Power Interface (ACPI) version 1.0. With ACPI and Plug and Play, all the power management and configuration settings are under the control of the operating system, rather than the BIOS. If you add Plug and Play-compliant hardware to a Windows 2000 computer, the device should be automatically recognized and configured without any user intervention required.

Under the new Plug and Play system, a new type of device driver has been implemented which is called the Microsoft Win32 Driver Model, or *WDM*. The WDM provides a common architecture for both Windows 98 and Windows 2000. Since any WDM driver can do double duty with the two operating systems, hardware manufacturers are expected to adopt this new model driver, which means Windows 2000 will, as a result, have a much greater degree of driver availability than its predecessors.

Through the WDM drivers, Windows 2000 will support USB devices (mice, keyboards, and joysticks), IEEE 1394 (Firewire) buses, scanners, DVD drives, and power management. (Support for all of these devices was missing from Windows NT.)

Note

Windows 2000 will support all legacy Windows NT drivers. However, there will be no Plug and Play support or automatic device recognition for legacy devices. Manual configuration and/or setup programs will be required for devices that use these drivers.

Note

ACPI is an industry standard developed jointly by Intel, Microsoft, and Toshiba. If you are interested in details about ACPI, visit the following web page: http://www.teleport.com/~acpi/.

Secret

The increasing importance of ACPI comes at the expense of the computer's BIOS. More and more, hardware configuration and system management is being done by the operating system and not by the BIOS. Today, one of the major tasks for the BIOS under Windows 2000 is to create tables that ACPI can use to manage the system. Not all BIOS chipsets are equipped to do that correctly (yet), which means that some chipsets will need to be updated for Windows 2000.

Overall, Plug and Play support means the following:

- **Automatic recognition of hardware changes:** This includes both when the system boots, as well as dynamically, such as with USB and IEEE 1394 (FireWire) devices that can be hot-swapped (plugged in and removed while the computer is running).

- **Hardware resource allocation:** Previously, if you installed a device, you would often need to manually assign its resources, hoping that you would avoid conflicts with already installed hardware. Now, when a Plug-and-Play device is recognized by Windows 2000, the Plug and Play Manager looks at all the resource requests from devices, and then dynamically allocates the necessary Input/Output ports, the IRQs, the DMA channels, and the memory locations to each device. All these settings can be changed as other devices are added or removed from the system.

- **Driver loading:** The Plug and Play manager recognizes what drivers are required for a particular device, and then loads the drivers automatically.

To accomplish these feats, the Plug and Play Manager maintains a device tree, from which you can view the assigned settings by using the Device Manager (see the exercise, "Create a hardware profile," later in this chapter.)

All the hardware information is added to the Registry, with device data being stored in the HKEY_LOCAL_MACHINE\SYSTEM\CurrentControlSet\Enum Registry key. The Plug and Play manager looks at this data and decides which device drivers to load. The services list, which you can find in the Registry key HKEY_LOCAL_MACHINE\SYSTEM\CurrentControlSet\Services, obtains much of its information from this key.

Cross-Reference

To learn more about the in's and out's of the Registry, see Chapter 16.

Plug and Play implications

What are the implications of Plug and Play for you? It means that if you have Windows 2000 installed on an ACPI, Plug and Play computer and you add Plug and Play hardware, you spend little or no time dealing with device conflicts and configuration, or in poking around in the Control Panel. You simply install the device, turn the computer on, and then let Plug and Play take over. (At least in theory, that is. In practice, there you might still need to make manual adjustments.)

Tip

To search for components that meet the Microsoft logo requirements for hardware compatibility, go to http://www.microsoft.com/hcl/default.asp. The Hardware Compatibility List you will find there covers all Microsoft operating systems. (Also refer to Chapter 4.) For a list containing only Windows 2000-compatible hardware, go to ftp://ftp.microsoft.com/services/whql/win2000hcl.txt.

Adding hardware

Normally, you need to be logged on as a member of the administrator's group to install hardware. However, if someone from the administrator's group has already loaded the drivers for the device, then you should be able to install the hardware, even if you are not logged on as an administrator.

Installing Plug and Play hardware

To install a Plug and Play device, you must first connect the device to your computer. Normally, you install devices that connect to parallel, serial, or PS/2 ports while the computer is powered off. This is also true for internal components like expansion cards or drives. After following the manufacturer's instructions for installing or connecting the new hardware, turn your computer on.

During the boot up process, Windows 2000 should see that new hardware has been physically installed, and it should then start the Found New Hardware Wizard. After detecting and identifying the new hardware, Windows 2000 will proceed to load the device drivers. If it does not have the drivers, you will be asked to supply a disk or CD-ROM containing the appropriate drivers. The wizard will then complete the detection and installation process automatically.

If you are installing a USB or IEEE 1394 device, you do not need to turn your computer off. You can plug the device in to the appropriate port, and the new hardware should be automatically detected by Windows 2000. If not, you will need to click the Add New Hardware Wizard in the Control Panel. You will need to do the same if you are installing a non-Plug and Play device.

Installing Non-Plug and Play devices

You are not limited to installing only Plug and Play hardware. To install hardware having Windows NT 4.0 drivers, follow these steps:

STEPS:

Installing non-Plug and Play Hardware

Step 1.   If your computer is running, shut down the computer in the normal fashion.

Step 2.   Install the hardware according to the manufacturer's directions.

Step 3.   Turn your computer on again. As your computer boots, Windows 2000 should detect the new hardware and start the Found New Hardware Wizard. If not, click Start ➪ Settings ➪ Control Panel, and then click Add New Hardware to start the Add/Remove Hardware Wizard.

Step 4.   Click Next to move past the splash screen. Select Add/Troubleshoot a Device, and then click Next.

Step 5.   The wizard will first look for new Plug and Play devices. After this search, click Add a New Device and follow the directions on your screen to install the new device. You might need to tell the Wizard what new device type you want to install by choosing a type from the list. Because the Plug and Play manager did not recognize your device, you might also be asked to supply drivers either from a diskette or a CD-ROM, or possibly from the Windows 2000 CD-ROM.

Creating hardware profiles

Windows 2000 supports *hardware profiles,* a system by which you can tell the operating system what devices, drivers, and preferences to load based on the selected profile. When you first start your computer, a selected profile tells Windows 2000 which devices to load, and how they should be to configured. A hardware profile is especially useful with a portable computer. You may choose to load a specifidc profile for your portable computer when you are in your office and have your computer is connected to a network. Other times, you'll choose to load another profile loaded so the computer functions as a standalone computer, such as when you use your computer at home or on the road

STEPS:

Create a hardware profile

Step 1.   Click Start ⇨ Settings ⇨ Control Panel, and then click the System icon.

Step 2.   Select the Hardware tab, and then click Hardware Profiles.

Step 3.   Under Available Profiles, click Original Configuration.

Step 4.   Click Copy, and give your new configuration a name.

Step 5.   Once you have created a new profile, you can customize it in Device Manager. For instance, if the new profile is for a laptop that will not be connected to the network, you will want to disable its network interface card.

Step 6.   You can force Windows 2000 to wait when your computer starts up for you to choose which profile you want to load. Click Wait. Otherwise, you can click Select, and then tell it to use the first profile if you haven't made a selection before a certain number of seconds — which you select in the next step — elapses (see Figure 14-3).

Step 7.   Click OK, and then click OK again to return to the Control Panel.

Figure 14-3: If you have defined a number of common configurations for your computer, you might want to design and use different computer profiles.

Once you have created more than one hardware profile for your computer, each time you start your computer, you will be asked which profile you want to use. To make that choice automatic, make sure you review step 6.

Uninstalling a device

Plug and Play makes uninstalling a device similar to installing a device. If it is a Plug and Play device, you simply unplug — or remove — the device from its expansion slot. (For all except USB and IEEE 1394 hardware, you should first turn your computer off.) When you turn your computer back on, Windows 2000 will recognize that the device has been removed, and it will then adjust your computer's resources accordingly.

If you are removing non-Plug and Play hardware, you will have to use the Add/Remove Hardware Wizard in the Control Panel. You will then need to select Uninstall/Unplug a Device, and then follow the instructions on your screen to complete the uninstall process.

Note

When you uninstall a device, the driver is not deleted from your hard drive. If you are not going to be installing the device again, and you are running out of disk space, you might want to delete any specific drivers that will not be used again.

Tip

If you have accidentally deleted your Fax printer in your Printers folder, you won't need to reinstall it if it is Plug and Play-compatible. The next time Windows 2000 starts, the Plug and Play manager will recognize it as an uninstalled device and reinstall it.

Tip

If you think you might use a Plug and Play device again some day, you don't have to take all the steps to remove it. Instead, you can disable it. While the device will still be connected to your computer, its drivers won't be loaded and no resources will be allocated to it.

STEPS:

To disable a device

Step 1.   Click Start ⇨ Settings ⇨ Control Panel.

Step 2.   Click the System applet, and then select the Hardware tab.

Step 3.   Click Device Manager.

Step 4.   Within the Device Manager, expand the device tree until you see the device you want to disable. Right-click it.

Step 5.   Select disable from the context menu. Click OK twice to return to the Control Panel.

Later, if you want to again enable the device , repeat Steps 1-4. In Step 5, however, select Enable instead of Disable.

If you are connecting a game controller to either a game or a serial port, you will be asked in Step 4 of the Installation Wizard to choose your controller from the list. If yours is not listed, and you have an installation disk, click Add Other. If you don't have a disk, check your manual to see if your controller can emulate another controller that might be on the list and select that controller.

Secret

During the Windows 2000 beta testing period, one of the most popular postings was: "I can't get Windows 2000 to recognize [blank]. Has anybody gotten [blank] to work?" If Windows 2000 couldn't automatically install a driver, success often came from using the older Windows NT 4.0 driver. It wouldn't be Plug and Play, but the device could be added through the Add/Remove Hardware applet in Control Panel.

Cross-Reference

See Chapter 4 for information on specific hardware compatibility issues.

Adding and Removing Programs

The process of adding and removing programs from a Windows 2000 computer is not much different from earlier Windows versions. There are some cosmetic changes in the Wizards, but any experienced Windows user will feel right at home. Behind the scenes, however, a major new feature has been incorporated that will save you from a lot of incompatibility problems.

The Windows Installer Service

This new feature is called the Windows Installer Service (WIS). It is part of the Windows 2000 operating system, and later will be offered in service packs for Windows 95, Windows 98, and Windows NT 4.0. It is also incorporated into the various flavors of Microsoft Office 2000. The purpose of WIS is to take over the job of installing applications. Previously, it was up to each developer to provide his own installation routine for his applications. While some developers relied on existing installation routines, others invented their own.

In the MS-DOS days, most programs installed into a dedicated directory, with all their files located in one place. In Windows 9x and NT, however, an installation program does much more than that. It may create its own directory and copy all its own files there. It also might install files into both the Winnt and Winnt\System32 folders. It also will typically add keys to the Registry, along with uninstall information and shortcuts to the Start menu and the Desktop. Some suite applications will also add a folder — either within the Winnt folder or the Program Files folder — for shared files or applets.

This practice has led to some problems. Some applications installed themselves without much awareness whatsoever of what was already installed on the computer, acting as if they were the center of the computing universe. They may have installed an older version of a given file over a newer version, which led to problems in other applications that required the newer version. Many older installation routines would not maintain shared Dynamic Link Library reference counts, leading to a situation often referred to by Microsoft and others as "DLL Hell." (By the way, Microsoft installation routines are not exempt from these sins.)

WIS implements a number of setup rules, and it requires that a vendor's installation routines present their information in a certain, standardized way, called the Windows Installer format. If the standard format is followed, WIS will then handle all the installation chores. For an application to obtain the "Designed for Microsoft Windows" logo, it will have to call upon the standardized Windows Installer setup.

 Of course, WIS will not help legacy applications written before the WIS format was developed . If you install an older application, you will be using that application routine. Windows 2000 does provide at least a partial safeguard: It has designated certain files as core parts of the operating system, and it will prevent any installation from overwriting those core files with another (older) version.

Installing applications

Most applications distributed today are on CD-ROM media, and most provide an auto-play feature, which also is a Microsoft Windows logo requirement. To install the application, just insert the CD-ROM into the CD-ROM drive and close the door, and the installation routine starts. If it does not, you will need to use the Add/Remove Programs Wizard in the Control Panel.

STEPS:

Manually Installing a Program

Step 1. Click Start ➪ Settings ➪ Control Panel, and then click Add/Remove Programs.

Step 2. The majority of this dialog box will be comprised of programs which have already been installed, and which can be automatically removed. Click the Add New Programs icon on the left side of the dialog box, as shown in Figure 14-4.

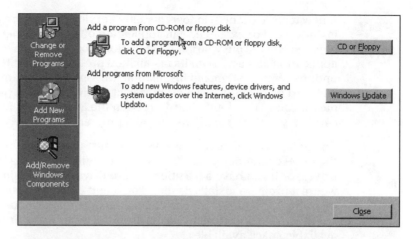

Figure 14-4: To add a program, click the Add New Program icon on the left.

Step 3. The Windows Update service uses your Internet connection to connect you to Microsoft's update site, where you then can download updates or install new features to the Windows 2000 software. If you are installing another application, you would click the CD or Floppy button.

Step 4. The Add/Remove Programs Wizard will then search your floppy drive or your CD-ROM drive for an install.exe or setup.exe program. Since it only searches the root directory of either drive, it will often times be unable to find the installation program. You will be given the opportunity to browse and locate the installation program. If the installation program is not in the root directory of the disk or CD-ROM, it will often be located one or two folders beneath the parent folder, particularly for CD-ROM discs that offer multiple versions of the same program (such as both a Windows 3.x and a Windows 95/98 version).

From this point in the installation process, you simply follow the directions on your screen to complete the installation.

Secret

Often, an application will give you a choice of the type of installation you want to perform. You can choose from a Typical, Standard, or Custom Installation. You should take the time to perform a Custom Installation, because you don't always know how smart the installation program is going to be, and because you can then get a better idea of what is being installed based on the options you select. For example, a Typical installation might insist on installing Internet Explorer 4, even though Internet Explorer 5 is already installed on your computer. In addition, the installation program might list other options that you know you will never use, and you can then clear those selections during the installation process.

A new feature of the Windows Installer Service is a feature called On-Demand installation. For example, if an application offered optional features that you didn't select during your first installation, you would have to close the application and again run its installation program to add those features or options. With On-Demand installation, the option you want to use will be installed on demand—when you select the feature from the application's menu. You will no longer need to re-run the applications installation program. (You may have to supply the original program CD.)

Tip

An application will almost always try to install itself on your system drive—the drive containing your Windows system files. If you have multiple hard drives, or if you have a partitioned hard drive, you can almost always change where a program installs its files. You might consider reserving drive C: for operating system files and its components, and install your applications to another drive or partition, especially if the other drive or partition has more available space available.

Adding and removing Windows components

You can add and remove many of Windows 2000's optional components just as you did in earlier versions of Windows. To do so, follow these steps:

STEPS:

Optional Windows component setup

Step 1. Click Start ➪ Settings ➪ Control Panel.

Step 2. Click Add/Remove Programs, and then click the Add/Remove Windows Components on the left side of the dialog box to start the Windows Component Wizard.

Step 3. Click next to advance to the next screen.

Step 4. Next, you will see a list of the Windows 2000 optional components which you can either install or remove, as shown in Figure 14-5. The choices available to you are described in Table 14-3.

Step 5. Either check the options you want to install, or clear the check box beside those options that you want to remove. The Details option becomes available for those items where additional options can be selected or cleared.

Step 6. After making your selections, click Next and follow the instructions on your screen to install or remove a component. (You might need to insert your Windows 2000 CD-ROM disc during this process.)

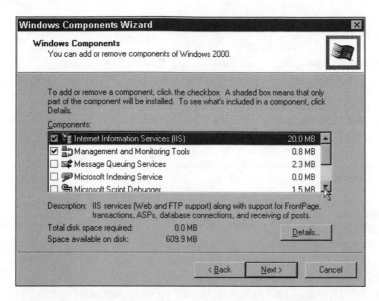

Figure 14-5: Windows Component Installation. These are optional selections available for Windows 2000 which can either add or remove.

Table 14-3 describes the optional components that are available with Windows 2000 Professional.

Table 14-3   Windows 2000 Optional Components

Component Name	Size	Description
Internet Information Services (IIS)	20MB	Provides both Web server software and FTP software. Web server software will allow you to set up your computer to be used as a Web server, and FTP software provides you with simple File Transfer services. IIS also supports both FrontPage and Active Server Pages. The version of IIS included with Windows 2000 Professional is a limited-function version of the full-fledged IIS software included in the Windows 2000 Server edition.
Management and	0.8MB	Provides monitoring tools for network Monitoring Toolsperformance.

Continued

Table 14-3 *(continued)*

Component Name	Size	Description
Message Queuing Services	2.3MB	For loosely coupled and reliable network communication services.
Microsoft Indexing Service	Negligible	For fast full text searching of files.
Microsoft Script Debugger	1.5MB	Client and server side debugging for JScript and VBScript.
Networking Services	0.1MB	Simple TCP/IP services and Routing Information Protocol (RIP) listener.
Other Network File and Print Services	Negligible	Print Services for NetWare.

The ability to pick and choose among the available options is a nice feature. What is surprising, however, is just how sparse the list of options really is. If you viewed the same list in Windows 95 or 98, you would see that you could uninstall many more individual components and options, including Desktop wallpapers, games, Screen Savers, and other things missing from the Windows 2000 list. Maybe this is Microsoft's way of saying they consider Solitaire and Pinball as essential, never-to-be removed parts of Windows 2000. In our opinion, this is bundling taken to the extreme.

Secret

Following is a secret found at Paul Thurott's Windows 2000 Super Site, http://www.wugnet.com/wininfo/win2000/, that allows you to add more parts of Windows 2000 to the list above, so they can be removed.

STEPS:

Uncovering more Windows 2000 Components

Step 1. Click Start ⇨ Programs ⇨ Windows Explorer, and then navigate to the C:\Winnt\Inf folder.

Step 2. Find the SYSOC.INF file, and then right-click and choose Open from the context menu to open the file in Notepad.

Step 3. You should find a section of this file labeled old base components looking similar to the following:

```
; old base components
Games=ocgen.dll,OcEntry,games.inf,HIDE,7
AccessTop=ocgen.dll,OcEntry,accessor.inf,HIDE,7
CommApps=ocgen.dll,OcEntry,communic.inf,HIDE,7
media_clips=ocgen.dll,OcEntry,mmopt.inf,HIDE,7
MultiM=ocgen.dll,OcEntry,multimed.inf,HIDE,7
AccessOpt=ocgen.dll,OcEntry,optional.inf,HIDE,7
Pinball=ocgen.dll,OcEntry,pinball.inf,HIDE,7
MSWordPad=ocgen.dll,OcEntry,wordpad.inf,HIDE,7
```

Step 4. Delete the ,HIDE,7 text at the end of each of these lines, and then save the file.

Step 5. Click Start ⇨ Settings ⇨ Control Panel, and then click Add/Remove Programs. Start the Windows Component Wizard again. You will now have all of these additions available to select and clear in the optional components list. (Refer to Table 14-4, which lists the additional optional Windows components.)

Table 14-4   Additional Optional Windows Components

Component Name	Description
Accessibility Wizard	Programs to help people with visual, audible, and mobility needs.
Accessories	Calculator, Character Map, Clipboard view, Desktop Wallpapers, Mouse Pointers, Paint, Screen Savers, and Wordpad.
Communications	Chat, HyperTerminal, and Phone Dialer.
Games	FreeCell, Pinball, Minesweeper, and Solitaire.
Multimedia	CD Player, Media Player, and sample sounds and schemes.

Caution

If you delete these programs and later want to restore them, you will need your Windows 2000 CD-ROM disc to do so. To be safe, you should back up these files before removing them.

Note in the SYSOC.INF file that if you move up to the section labeled [Components], you will see that the ,HIDE modifier also appears for the Fax, Com, DTC, and ImageVue options, which means you might be able to add them to the list of removable components, as well.

Removing applications

Because applications deposit their files in more than one location, uninstalling them requires that you do more than just delete the program in its home folder. If that's all you do, you will leave behind .DLLs and other shared files in your Windows folder and within the \System32 folder, as well as unneeded Registry entries.

You can leave these leftovers in place, but at the cost of disk and Registry bloat. However, beginning with Windows 95, an application needed to provide a means with which to install itself in order to earn the Microsoft Windows-compatibility logo, even if the uninstall was provided through a standalone program. Some applications would go so far as to leave a shortcut on the

Start menu, with an uninstall shortcut pointing a path to its own destruction. Other times, they were more discreet; the only way to determine how to remove an application was through the Add/Remove Programs dialog box, as shown in Figure 14-6.

As in previous Windows versions, when you open the Add/Remove Programs dialog box, you will see a list of programs that can be automatically uninstalled. However, Windows 2000 gives you even more information about an application, including its size, how often you have used it, and when you used it last.

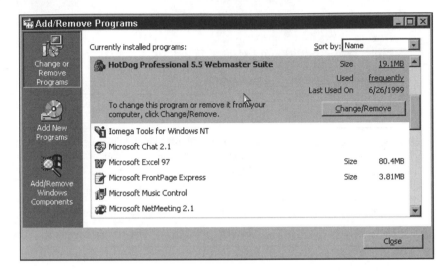

Figure 14-6: The Windows 2000 Add/Remove Programs dialog box gives you more information about your target, including its size and how often you use it.

To judge application usage, Windows 2000 uses three categories to describe how often a program has been used over the past 30 days: rarely, occasionally, and frequently. If you click its score in the dialog box, you will see the rather uninformative definitions that Microsoft uses for usage. For instance, the definition of Rarely Used is: "The program is rarely or never run." (Hopefully, the person who wrote this definition was not the programmer in charge of removing circular references from Excel 2000.)

The list of programs that can be uninstalled by Windows 2000 can be sorted by name, size, frequency of use, or the date last used. That way, if you need to free up some disk space, you can find the appropriate candidates for termination based on one of those values.

Once an uninstall routine starts, you might be asked whether you want to remove certain files that might be need or used by other applications. Since the uninstall routine can't possibly be sure, it asks first. If you don't know the answer to this question (if the program doesn't know, how can you be expected to know?), the safe answer is to always leave the files in place. It might leave your hard drive with a few more files than is absolutely necessary, but your applications should still function properly.

Secret

Even though you uninstall a program, an entry for it might remain on the Change/Remove Programs list. The application isn't consuming any disk space (since the files have been removed), but if your sense of order is being violated by having this extra entry, you can remove it. If you have installed the TweakUI powertoys (see "TweakUI," later in this chapter), select the Add/Remove programs tab to view the same list of programs you see listed on the Change/Remove Programs tab. Select the program you want to remove from the list, and then click Remove. You will no longer see it on the list.

As use of the Windows Installer Service becomes more wide-spread, there should be less uncertainty in uninstall routines.

Adjusting Regional Settings

The Regional Settings icon in Control Panel is where Windows 2000 learns how you want things like date and time, local currency, and other visual interfaces to real life displayed on your computer. What is new in Windows 2000 is its new multiple language capabilities.

Setting your locale

As in previous versions of Windows, you can choose a locale from a list so that Windows 2000 will supply the most obvious settings. A look at the choices in locales gives you an idea of the international scope of Windows 2000. There are over 60 locales from which to choose. In the Western European and US language group alone, the choices range from Afrikaans, Basque, and Catalan through Swahili and Swedish, with 13 different English settings alone — Australia through Zimbabwe.

To widen the scope of locales even further, you can add more language groups. In the Control Panel, select the Regional Settings, and then select the General tab. In the U.S. version of Windows 2000, only the Western European and United States language group is enabled, as shown by the selection in the Language Settings pane in the lower portion of the Regional Settings dialog box shown in Figure 14-7.

Checking the Central European language group adds additional locales, including Polish, Croatian, Slovenian, and Albanian. There are a number of Asian and Middle Eastern languages, as well.

If you choose Polish as your locale from the General tab and then click Apply, you can then select the Currency tab to see that the currency unit is now the zloty, and the date and number settings will be the those which are commonly used in Poland. To switch back to U.S. settings, select the General tab again, select English (United States) as your locale, and then click Apply.

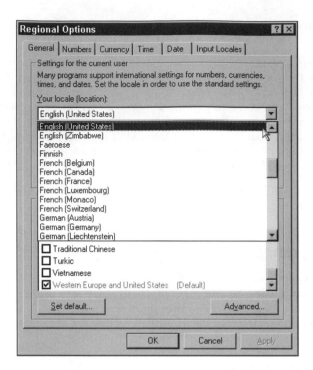

Figure 14-7: Adding Language Groups gives you a wider selection of input locales.

In addition to currency symbols such as the zloty and the dollar, Windows 2000 also can display the symbol for the Euro — the new monetary unit of the European Monetary Union. If you select the Euro as your currency symbol, and then use Microsoft Excel to format cells as currency, you will see the Euro symbol instead of the dollar symbol, as shown in Figure 14-8.

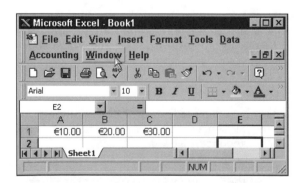

Figure 14-8: If you select the Euro as your currency, applications that check the Regional Settings, such as Microsoft Excel, will use it in place of the dollar symbol.

Multi-language support

If you use the U.S. English version of Windows 2000, you can still work in other languages — such as French or Croatian in your applications. However, application menus, help files, dialog boxes, and tips will still be displayed in English. (There will be 24 localized versions of Windows 2000. The localized versions — French, for example — will display a French user interface, but you will still have the ability to work in English or in other languages. A multilanguage version will allow users to switch the language both for the user interface and for documents.)

The Windows operating system has always had localized editions. Windows 2000 expands that practice by incorporating a new multilanguage support feature with which users can input, view, edit, and print information in over 60 different languages.

Localized versions of Windows 2000 will be available for the following languages: Arabic, Portuguese-Brazilian, Simplified Chinese, Traditional Chinese, Czech, Danish, Dutch, English, Finnish, French, German, Greek, Hebrew, Hungarian, Italian, Japanese, Korean, Norwegian, Polish, Portuguese-Iberian, Russian, Spanish, Swedish, and Turkish.

Unicode support

Windows 2000 Professional uses Unicode 2.1 for its base character encoding. This is an international standard that represents the characters commonly used in the world's major languages. Unicode makes sharing data simpler in a mixed platform environment.

Windows 2000 stores national language support settings in system tables. These tables contain the following data:

- Locale information: date, time, number and currency format, and localized names for days of week and month.
- Character mapping tables: converts local characters in ANSI or OEM format to Unicode format and back again.
- Keyboard layout information.
- Character typing information: for foreign characters.
- Sorting information.

Adding Additional Language Support

To work in another language in the U.S. English version of Windows 2000, follow these steps:

Working in another language

Step 1. Click Start ➪ Settings ➪ Control Panel, and then click Regional Options.

Step 2. Select the Input Locales tab, as shown in Figure 14-9. If you have never installed an additional locale, you will only see your own local language — probably English (United States) — listed in the Installed input locales section of the dialog box.

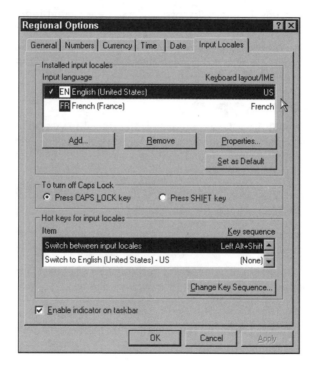

Figure 14-9: Select Regional Options, and then select the Input Locales tab to select another language.

Step 3. To add an additional input locale, such as French, click Add.

Step 4. Select your new locale from the Add Input Locale dialog box, as shown in Figure 14-10. Note that you choices will be limited by the language settings you have selected on the General tab of the Regional Options dialog box. If you want to add Polish, for example, the Central European language must be selected; for Japanese, you need to select the Japanese language.

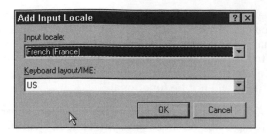

Figure 14-10: Select the Input locale and Keyboard layout/IME type that you want to use.

Step 5.   When you add a locale, you also can select an alternative keyboard type — other than the default QWERTY keyboard — to use.

Step 6.   Make sure that the default language is set to your choice. If not, select the language in the Input language section of the dialog box, and then click Set as Default.

Step 7.   On the lower portion of the dialog box, select the Enable indicator on taskbar check box to add an icon to the System Tray that will indicate the currently selected language. (Clicking this icon will open a window to let you switch between the two languages.)

Step 8.   You also can choose which hot keys you want to use to switch between the two languages. Select one of the items in the drop-down list box, such as Switch to English (United States) - US, and then click Change Key Sequence.

Step 9.   In the Change Key Sequence dialog box shown in Figure 14-11, select the Enable Key Sequence check box to activate the controls, and then choose the key combination you want to use.

Step 10.   Click OK to return to the Regional Options dialog box, and then click OK to close the dialog box.

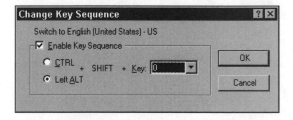

Figure 14-11: You can switch between languages using a combination of keyboard hot keys.

Once you have configured the alternative languages you want to have available, you can either use the Taskbar button or the keyboard hot keys you have enabled to switch between languages. In some cases, it is up to the application to be aware of the language settings. If the application is not configured to use this information, the keyboard hot keys and the alternative language settings will not be functional.

Tip Tired of QWERTY? You can add an English input locale for the Dvorak keyboard. In step 5 above, make sure you choose Dvorak from the drop-down list box. When you click the language indicator in the System Tray, you will see English (United States) and English (United States) United States Dvorak as two of your choices.

Tip You also can access the Input Locale dialog box by clicking Start ⇨ Settings ⇨ Control Panel, clicking Keyboard, and then selecting the Input Locales tab.

W2K meets Y2K

To see how Windows 2000 handles the Y2K problem, click the Date tab on the Regional Settings dialog box, as shown in Figure 14-12. You can configure short, or you can configure it to display long dates, displaying all four digits for the year. To see the available date formats, click the arrows to the right of the date format list boxes. Table 14-5 lists the available date formats from which you can choose the display style you prefer.

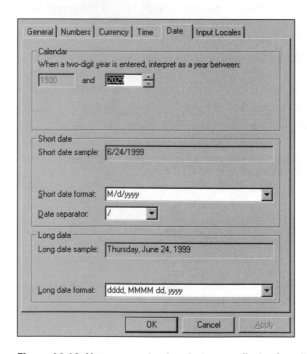

Figure 14-12: You can set the date formats to display four-digit years.

Table 14-5 Date Formats	
Short Date Formats	*Resulting Display*
M/d/yy	6/7/99
M/d/yyyy	6/7/1999
MM/dd/yy	06/07/99
MM/dd/yyyy	06/07/1999
YY/MM/dd	99/06/07
Yyyy-MM-dd	1999-06-07
dd-MMM-yy	07-Jun-99
Long Date Formats	*Resulting Display*
dddd, MMMM dd, yyyy	Monday, June 07, 1999
MMMM dd, yyyy	June 07, 1999
dddd, dd MMMM, yyyy	Monday, 07 June, 1999
dd MMMM, yyyy	07 June, 1999

Secret

If you don't like any of the available date formats, you can create your own format by typing it into the list box. For example, if you modify the last short date format shown earlier in Table 14-5 to recognize Y2K, you would type the format as dd-MMM-yyyy.

Secret

Like Windows 98 — but unlike Windows 95 — you can control how Windows 2000 interprets two-digit dates. There is a movable 100-year window that Windows 2000 uses for any two-digit date it sees. By default, any two-digit year is assumed to fall between 1930 and 2029. When Windows 2000 sees the date 12/7/41, it assumes the "41" to be the year 1941. You can move this window forward or backward, so that if you are still using Windows 2000 in the year 2025, you can move the window forward to compensate for the interpretation.

Assigning Sounds to Windows Events

Earlier versions of Windows allowed you to assign specific sounds to play during events, and that tradition continues in Windows 2000. From the Control Panel, click Sounds and Multimedia. Then, select the Sounds tab to assign sounds to certain events, as shown in Figure 14-13.

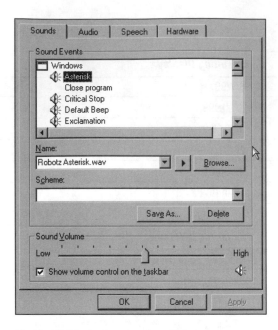

Figure 14-13: Assign sounds to Windows events.

You can assign sounds to Windows 2000 events, such as when Windows starts or stops, when an error has occurred, and so on. When you scroll through the list of sound events in the Sound Events list box, those events that have an assigned sound event display a loudspeaker icon to the left of the event. Highlight one of these events, and the assigned sound file will be displayed in the Name drop-down list box. If you want to preview what the sound sounds like, click the Play button to the right of the Name drop-down list box. To change the assigned sound, click the Name drop-down list box and choose a sound from the list. A number of sound themes have been provided with Windows 2000 for other kinds of sound effects — Robot or Jungle noises, for example.

Other applications often add their events to the Sound Event list, and they often come configured to use their own sounds based on events within the application. You can change the sounds for these events just as you would for Windows 2000 events.

Tip

If you make a lot of custom selections to individual event sounds, you can save your selections as your own theme. Click Save As, and then type a name for your sound theme in the dialog box. If you later make changes to your selections, you can always restore your saved theme by selecting it from the list box.

Note

When you installed Windows 2000, a \Media folder beneath the Windows 2000 folder was created to hold all the sound clips that come with Windows 2000. As you install other applications, they typically also deposit sound files on your hard drive from which you can select different sounds to associate with different events. From the Sounds tab on the Sounds and Multimedia dialog box, click Browse to the right of the Name drop-down list box to search for .WAV files, which are the sound files you use for sound events. You also can click Start ➪ Search, and then search for files with the extension .wav, to locate other files from which you can select to use as sound events.

Tip

Bored with your sounds? You will find a number of web sites on the Internet devoted to sound clips, many of which have .WAV files that you can download and use for your events. An extensive list of sites are available from Yahoo! at http://dir.yahoo.com/Computers_and_Internet/Multimedia/Audio/.

Adjusting Settings with TweakUI

TweakUI is a specialized configuration tool for Windows 95, 98, and NT (see Figure 14-14). It has been described as *the* configuration tool for power users. (While it comes from Microsoft, it is not officially supported.)

Note

In Windows 98, TweakUI was provided with the Windows 98 Resource Kit (in a subfolder called PowerToys). Windows 2000 Beta 3 provided a scaled down version of the Resource Kit on the CD-ROM, but it did not include a copy of the TweakUI program. However, the Corporate Preview Program beta provided an additional CD-ROM disc called the Evaluation and Deployment Kit. This disc contained a larger version of the Windows 2000 Resource Kit, and it also included a copy of the TweakUI program in the Desktop folder.

To install TweakUI, use the Windows Explorer to navigate to the folder containing the TweakUI files. When you find the files, right-click the TWEAKUI.INF file, and then select Install from the context menu. Once the program has been installed on your computer, you will see a TweakUI icon you're the Control Panel from which you can access its many features.

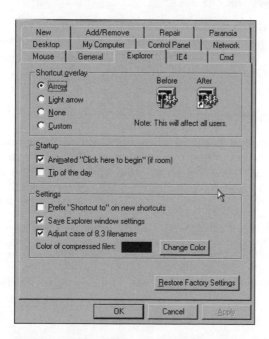

Figure 14-14: TweakUI gives you far more control over the Windows 2000 user interface.

TweakUI helps you fine-tune the Windows 2000 user interface. For example, by clicking the Control Panel tab, you will be presented with the list of Control Panel applets that are available on your system. Clearing the check box next to the name of an applet will prevent it from being displayed in the Control Panel (it doesn't uninstall the applet). Selecting the check box will again enable it to be displayed in the Control Panel.

We will refer to TweakUI in many other parts of this book as we take advantage of its customization abilities.

Adjusting System Properties

The System Properties applet in the Control Panel is a shortcut to a number of different functions and settings in Windows 2000:

- The Network Identification tab contains information about how this machine is known to the network, and will be covered in Part V of this book.

- The Hardware tab is an alternative path to the Hardware Wizard and Device Manager, which was covered in the Hardware section, earlier in this chapter.

- The User Profiles tab provides a portion of the information that is managed more completely with the Users and Passwords applet.

- If you select the Advanced tab, you will find a number of performance settings you can adjust. The Advanced tab contains three buttons that allow you to adjust Performance Options, Environment Variables, and Startup and Recovery Options.

If you are familiar with the System Properties applet in Windows 95 and 98, you will see that some of the options have been moved from the System Properties dialog boxes to the various Administrative Tools in the Microsoft Management Console (see Chapter 15).

Performance options

Click the Performance button. In the Performance Options dialog box, you can make a broad adjustment to how your processor allocates its time. If you select Applications, more time will be allocated to the program that is running in the foreground (the active window). If you select Background services, processor time will be allocated evenly amongst all programs.

According to Microsoft, when you choose Applications, you will be allocating short, variable processor timeslices to all running programs, while Background services will allocate the timeslices in long, fixed amounts. What's best? If you mostly use a single application at a time, without a lot of other programs running in the background, you should choose Applications.

If you are not sure just how your processor time is being allocated, a utility that ships with the Windows 2000 Resource Kit might help (see Chapter 3 for help in installing the Resource Kit). QuickSlice, shown in Figure 14-15, displays in a graphical format the percentage of total CPU time for each process running on your system.

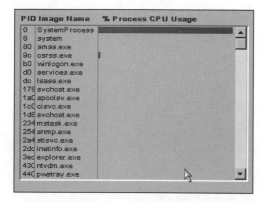

Figure 14-15: QuickSlice shows you what processes are keeping your CPU busy.

Clicking the Change Button in Virtual Memory takes you to the Virtual Memory page, as shown in Figure 14-16. Both Windows 95 and 98 provided a way for you to manage your own virtual memory, or to allow Windows to manage it for you. Windows 2000 provides no similar feature, although it has established default settings for you.

Note

To make changes in your Virtual Memory settings, you must be logged on as the Administrator.

Secret

One step forward and two steps backward: Because the useful, automatic Virtual Memory setting available under Windows 9x is not available in Windows 2000, you should make note of the defaults.

Virtual Memory uses hard drive space to supplement to RAM. When your RAM is filled up, part of your hard drive is pressed into service as temporary RAM. Naturally, this comes at a cost of performance, since information that is read from or written to a drive is much slower than reading from or writing to RAM. Microsoft recommends that you set your Virtual Memory setting to 1.5 times the amount of installed RAM.

Tip

Having a lot of disk space set aside for Virtual Memory might seem like a waste, especially if your hard drive is very full. However, if you often run memory-intensive programs, extra Virtual Memory can help.

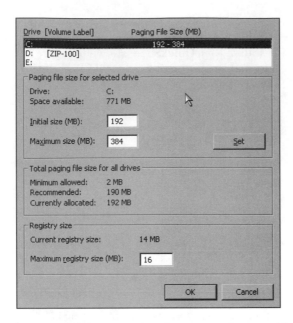

Figure 14-16: You can make adjustments to how your Virtual Memory is managed.

Tip

In the Registry size section of this dialog box, you will find a setting for the maximum Registry size, along with a measurement of how large your Registry actually is. If you are approaching the limit (measured in megabytes), you might want to increase it. Applications often store a large number of settings in the Registry, and you don't want to run out of room.

Environment variables

Environment variables typically contain drive, path, or filename information that controls how various programs work. If you are logged on to your computer using the Administrator account, you can change a number of user and system variables from the Systems, Advanced tab when you click the Environment Variables button. If you are not logged on using the Administrator account, you will only be able to make changes to user variables.

Environment variables are actually stored in the Registry, but they can be modified here. Any environment variables contained in your AUTOEXEC.BAT file are appended to the system environment variable information. When Windows 2000 sets environment variables, it first sets all of the AUTOEXEC.BAT variables, and it then sets all of the system environment variables. Finally, it sets all of the user environment variables. This means that if your AUTOEXEC.BAT file contains a system environment variable that sets the temporary folder to C:\TEMP, and it also contains a user environment variable that sets the user's temporary folder to D:\TEMP, the earlier system environment variable will be overridden by the later user environment variable.

Click Add to create an additional environment variable. You will get a dialog box that asks for the variable's name, and its value. To edit an existing variable, highlight it and click Edit.

Startup and recovery

Click System in the Control Panel, select the Advanced tab, and then click Startup and Recovery to control how Windows 2000 behaves when it starts up, as well as when it crashes. (See Figure 14-17.)

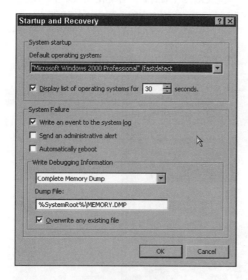

Figure 14-17: Tell Windows 2000 what to do when it crashes. Gathering diagnostic evidence can be important.

If you have multiple operating systems installed on your computer, you will see a textual menu displayed on your screen from which you can choose which operating system you want to boot to. You also can select which one will be your default operating system from this dialog box.

You also can specify how Windows 2000 should continue should you experience an unexpected stop (a crash). At a minimum, you should at least be sure that the event is written to the system log, which will later provide you with clues as to what happened. Looking for clues is another reason why you should instruct Windows to write debugging information to a file, although this takes longer than writing just the details about the event itself. If you are part of a network, you also can send an administrative alert. In addition, Windows 2000 also can be instructed to automatically reboot, or to wait for user intervention.

Adjusting Mouse Settings

There are a number of motion-related changes you can adjust to make mouse movement more comfortable, and there are a number of cosmetic changes you can change to make the mouse more fun to use.

Movement

In Chapter 6 we looked at two basic steps that can make your mouse more useful. If you are left-handed, you can switch the position of the mouse buttons so that the primary button can remain under your index finger. In the Control Panel, click Mouse and select the Buttons tab to choose whether your mouse is a *righty* or a *lefty,* as shown in Figure 14-18.

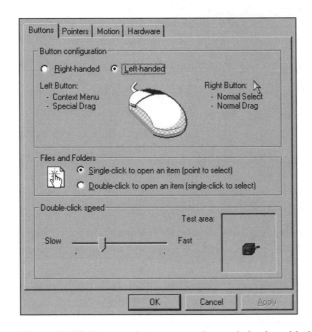

Figure 14-18: You can change mouse button behavior with the button tab.

The other setting we covered in Chapter 6 was the double-click speed. Before adjusting the double click speed, remember that there is a way to drastically reduce the amount of double-clicking you have to do, and that is to click Start ⇨ Settings ⇨ Control Panel, click Folder Options, and then select single-click to select an item. Where you previously needed to double-click, you now only have to single-click. Where you previously had to single-click to select, you now only have to point to an item with the mouse pointer. If you still want to double-click, experiment with the jack-in-the box icon on the Buttons tab to find and select a comfortable double-click speed. The slower the double-click speed, the easier it is to double-click.

Secret

The slowest speed available on the double-click slider is approximately 900 milliseconds, which is 9/10ths of a second. The fastest you can set it to is 100 milliseconds, or 1/10th of a second. (If you can consistently click your mouse button twice within a tenth of a second, maybe you should cut back on your caffeine.)

If you are having trouble with your hand-to-eye coordination (or should it be mouse-to-eye coordination?), there are other specific settings you can change to compensate for this.

Mouse speed

In the Mouse Properties dialog box, select the Motion tab. You can use the speed control to adjust how fast the mouse pointer moves on the screen relative to your mouse's movement. If you set this value slower, the pointer will creep along on the screen, which may give you more precise control when you are trying to click a small screen button. Set it too slow, however, and your mouse will feel like it is dragging a lead weight behind it.

Acceleration

On the Motion tab, the acceleration key gives your screen pointer a speed boost. If you have no acceleration set, the pointer is going to move at the same pace as your mouse. If you increase the acceleration value, the pointer is going to move even faster as you move your mouse. Set the acceleration too high, and you may find yourself overshooting your target.

Sampling

Windows 2000 samples — or checks — your mouse for movement 60 times per second. Any movement you make between those intervals is ignored. By increasing the sampling rate, you may be able to make your mouse a little more responsive. Use the following steps to increase your mouse sampling rate:

STEPS:

Increasing the mouse sampling rate

Step 1. Click Start ⇨ Settings ⇨ Control Panel, and then click Mouse.

Step 2. Select the Hardware tab, and then click Properties.

Step 3. In the Mouse Properties dialog box , select the Advanced Settings tab.

Step 4. If you increase the sampling rate, the time interval between samples will go down. This means that more attention will be paid to the mouse. The maximum sampling rate is 100 times per second.

On the Advanced tab, you will find the mouse input buffer location setting. This shows how much information regarding your mouse position is being stored. If your mouse begins to act strangely, try increasing the buffer size.

Sensitivity

If you often find yourself moving things on your screen when you didn't intend to, your mouse might be too sensitive. For example, you click an icon and the icon's position moves on the screen instead of activating the application.

Windows 2000 thinks you are trying to move something when you move the pointer two pixels on the screen. The problem is that as bigger and better monitors allow people to work at higher screen resolutions, the pixel just isn't what it used to be. In fact, it is much smaller, which means that accidental movement becomes easier to do. To adjust this, you need to use the TweakUI configuration tool.

Secret

Microsoft has hidden some of the mouse control, such as movement controls, in TweakUI, an unsupported Microsoft applet.

Here's how: Click Start ⇨ Settings ⇨ Control Panel, and then click TweakUI. Select the Mouse tab, as shown in Figure 14-19. Here, you will find two mouse sensitivity adjustment settings. The first, Double-click, specifies how close (in milliseconds) any two clicks must be in order to be considered a double-click action. The second, Drag, specifies the distance your mouse pointer must be moved in order to be considered a drag action. If you have trouble keeping your mouse in a fixed position as you click, you can increase these two values. You can click in the Test Icon area to test the effects of any changes you make.

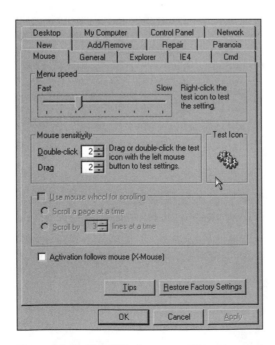

Figure 14-19: TweakUI gives you additional control over your mouse settings.

Mouse menu speed

The mouse menu speed setting adjusts how fast cascading menus — such as the Start ⇨ Programs menu — appear when your mouse hovers over them. You can set this to a hair-trigger response by moving the slider all the way over to the Fast setting, but you then run the risk of accidentally cascading menus as you bypass them. If you set the slider all the way over to the Slow setting, a secondary menu won't appear until you click a submenu choice.

Mouse wheels

Windows 2000 directly supports mouse devices having an internal roller ball, called a wheel, for devices like the Microsoft IntelliMouse or the LogitechMouse + Wheel. In fact, you should not add the included software, such as the Microsoft Intellipoint or Logitech MouseWare software, that accompanies these mice. According to Microsoft, this software may interfere with the power management functions in Windows 2000.

If your wheel isn't working properly, the following exercise might help to wake it up:

STEPS
Enabling your Mouse Wheel

Step 1. Click Start ⇨ Settings ⇨ Control Panel, and then click Mouse.

Step 2. Select the Hardware tab. If there are multiple mice listed, select yours, and then click Properties.

Step 3. Select the Advanced Settings tab. Make sure — under Wheel Detection — that Assume Wheel is Present is selected. Click OK.

Step 4. Click OK again to close the Mouse Properties dialog box. You might have to restart your computer for this change to take effect.

Mouse cosmetics

No, this doesn't mean we advocate putting make-up on your mouse. But there are ways to make the screen pointer look nicer.

Mouse shadows

Compared to the change between Windows 3.x and Windows 95, there was no huge makeover to the appearance of Windows 2000 — the changes were more subtle this time. An unscientific reading of the Windows 2000 newsgroups indicates that the makeover that elicited the most comments similar to "cool" was the topic of mouse shadows.

To enable mouse shadows, click Start ➪ Settings ➪ Control Panel, and then click Mouse. Select the Pointers tab. At the bottom of the dialog box, you will find a check box you can select to enable mouse shadows. Click to enable this feature, and it will almost immediately appear that your mouse pointer is casting a shadow below the pointer. It adds no functionality at all to Windows, but it enhances the 3D effect of the pointer, making it look as though it is hovering over the page.

Mouse pointers

To add even more visual interest to your pointer, you can choose from different pointers to use onscreen. Windows 2000 comes with a number of different pointer schemes, including 3D White, 3D Bronze, Conductor (musical-themed pointers), Dinosaur (at least there are no purple ones), Old Fashioned, and others (see Figure 14-20). Many of the these are animated pointers. Now, you don't have to stare at an hourglass as you wait for something to be completed; instead, you can stare at an hourglass whose sand runs from the top to the bottom, and then flips over to start again.

Tip

More important than dinosaurs, if you are working on a laptop with a dim screen, you might want to try the large or extra large pointer schemes, especially if you are having problems seeing the pointer on the screen.

Note

If you are working on a laptop and have trouble finding your pointer, enable the mouse pointer trails option.

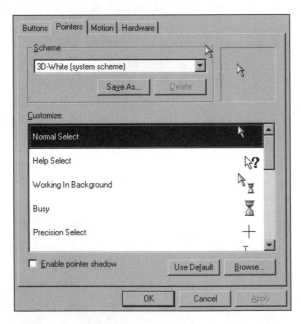

Figure 14-20: You can choose from a collection of mouse pointers, or you can mix and match your own pointer scheme.

All the different pointers are stored in their own folder—C:\Winnt\Cursors—beneath the Windows 2000 folder. Each pointer is actually a file; static pointers use the extension .cur, and animated pointers use the extension .ani. You will see a different pointer in Windows 2000—just as you did in earlier versions of Windows—when you are performing certain tasks. Table 14-6 lists the mouse pointers available in Windows 2000.

Table 14-6   Windows 2000 Mouse Pointers

Pointer Name	Pointer Displayed
Normal Select	The "normal" mouse pointer that you see when moving around the screen.
Help Select	Some dialog boxes have a help button in the upper-right corner that displays a question mark character in the upper right corner. Click the button, and your pointer changes to the Help Select pointer. Then, click something in your application to see a definition or help note about the object you clicked.
Working in background	Windows 2000 is working on something in a background process. You can still do something in the foreground process.
Busy	Windows 2000 is working on something, and you have to wait for it to finish.
Precision select	Usually proves a cross-hair pointer to assist you with precision work.
Text Select	You might know of this as the I-beam. It is used in word processing and other text-oriented programs to select text.
Handwriting	If you have an application that supports handwriting, and you switch to handwriting mode.
Unavailable	You will see this pointer most often in click-and-drag operations. If you are dragging a file or folder to another location, you will see this pointer when you are moving over areas where you cannot drop the selected object.
Resize pointers	This pointer appears in horizontal, vertical, and diagonal flavors. You will most often see these when your mouse pointer is hovering over something (the side of a window or a column header) where you can click and drag to resize.
Move	This pointer appears when you click or select the Move command in a window's system menu. It allows you to move that window using your keyboard the arrow keys.
Alternate Select	According to the previous edition of this book, you will see this pointer in the FreeCell game.
Link select	This is the e pointer you see in your browser or in a help file when you move the pointer over a hyperlink.

Power Management

The Power Management features of Windows 2000 closely depend on the support of your hardware. While a certain number of power support features are offered, not all of them will be available on your computer. In particular, some will be found only on laptop computers that rely on batteries.

While power management depends on the cooperation of your BIOS and Windows 2000, it also can be hindered by a lack of cooperation. The best situation to be in (as far as power management is concerned) is to have a fairly new computer that supports ACPI. That way, you can have Windows 2000 handle power management. Older computers use a power management system called Advanced Power Management (APM) usually version 1.1 or 1.2.

Caution

Why is it better to let Windows 2000 handle power management? The alternative is to let the computer BIOS handle it. To adjust the BIOS settings, you normally do that by first turning off your computer. When you turn it back on, you have to press a special key (it may be the Esc, F2, or Del key) to access your system's CMOS Setup, and you have to press that key prior to the operating system starting to access it. Every computer is a little bit different, so be sure to read your computer's technical reference manual carefully before you go into your system's CMOS Setup. There are many settings that, if configured incorrectly, could disable your computer. Its much easier — and safer — to use the Windows 2000 control panel applets.

Secret

How do you know if your computer is ACPI-compliant? You can determine this in the Device Manager. Do this:

STEPS:

Checking if your computer is ACPI-compliant

Step 1.   Click Start ⇨ Settings ⇨ Control Panel, and then click System.

Step 2.   Select the Hardware tab, and then click Device Manager.

Step 3.   At the top of the device tree, click the plus sign to the left of Computer.

Step 4.   This will expand Computer; beneath, it you will see Advanced Configuration and Power Interface (ACPI) PC. If your computer is not ACPI-compliant, you will not see this entry.

Step 5.   If you right-click ACPI and select Properties from the context menu, you will see the ACPI driver files.

Secret

The Windows 2000 installation will not install the ACPI drivers if the PC's BIOS is not ACPI-compliant. How does it tell? During the Windows 2000 setup, it checks the computer's BIOS and compares it to a good ACPI BIOS list contained in the installation program. According to the Windows 2000 development team, this list has been constantly in flux during the Windows 2000 beta testing period, and it will continue to change right up until Windows 2000 is released to manufacturing.

Secret

ACPI information is also contained in the system Registry. Find the HKEY_LOCAL_MACHINE\SYSTEM\CurrentControlSet\Services\ACPI key and look at the value of the Start key. If this is set to 0, ACPI is enabled.

Power schemes

Power management is built around a number of power schemes. Windows 2000 comes with power schemes for:

- Home/Office Desktop
- Portable/laptop
- Presentation
- Always On
- Minimal Power Management

For each of these schemes, preset times are defined for turning off the monitor and turning off the hard drive. You can choose the scheme that most closely matches your own computer. You can change the settings to match your own preference, and then save the power scheme under a different name, as shown in Figure 14-21.

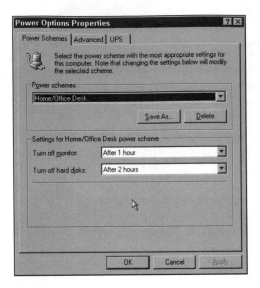

Figure 14-21: You can set these power settings shorter to save power, or longer to save some inconvenience.

Standby

Standby is a power saving mode in which your monitor and hard drive are turned off to conserve power. However, the rest of your computer stays powered on. The contents of RAM will be maintained; when your computer comes up from standby mode, its state will be the same as when standby mode began.

If your computer supports it, you will find a setting in the Power Management dialog box (the computer in Figure 14-21, shown earlier, does not support it) showing how long the computer must be in a period of inactivity before it will automatically enter standby mode. To manually enter standby mode, follow these steps:

STEPS:

Manual Standby

Step 1. Since the contents of RAM are not saved before your computer enters standby mode, you should save any open documents first, in case there is a power failure or the computer somehow crashes coming out of standby mode.

Step 2. Click Start ⇨ Settings ⇨ Control Panel, and then click Power Options. Go to the Advanced tab.

Step 3. Select the option When I press the power button on my computer.

Step 4. Click OK. When the Power Management dialog box closes, you can press the power button on your computer. Instead of turning off, it will go into standby mode.

Step 5. An alternative to pressing the power button is to click Start ⇨ Shutdown, and then select Standby from the shutdown menu.

Hibernation

Hibernation is another optional power mode that is not supported on all computers. The difference between hibernation and standby modes is that before a computer goes into hibernation mode, everything in the computer's memory is saved to the hard drive. When the computer comes out of hibernation mode, the entire system state is then restored.

If hibernation mode is available, you will find a Hibernation tab in the Power Management dialog box. Select that tab, and then enable the check box to enable hibernation mode. Set a time at which the computer will go into hibernation mode after a period of inactivity from this tab.

Note

To manually put your computer into hibernation mode, click Start ⇨ Shut Down, and then select Hibernate from the context menu. While everything should be saved to disk, it's always a good idea to save any open work first.

UPS

If you have an uninterruptible power supply connected to your computer, you will be able to manage it from the UPS tab of Power Management. It will tell you the status of the UPS Service, as well as give an estimate of the UPS runtime and the condition of your battery.

Adjusting Other Hardware Settings

Windows 2000 supports much more hardware than its predecessors, Windows 95/98 and Windows NT 4.0.

Scanners and cameras

Windows 2000 now supports image scanners and digital cameras. If your scanner is on the Windows 2000 Hardware Compatibility List, it is a Plug and Play-compatible scanner and will be automatically recognized when you connect it to your computer. In other words, if your scanner or digital camera is on the HCL, Windows 2000 will have the driver for it.

Once you connect a scanner or a camera to your computer, the Scanners and Cameras applet will appear in the Control Panel. Click it, and then click Properties. In your scanner's Properties dialog box, click Events, as shown in Figure 14-22, to tell Windows 2000 how you want it to manage your scanning activities.

Programs that are installed on your computer—and which are capable of acquiring images from your scanner—will be listed in the application list box. In this list box, you associate certain events (pressing the scan button, for example) with certain applications (such as the Kodak Imaging program, which is bundled with Windows 2000).

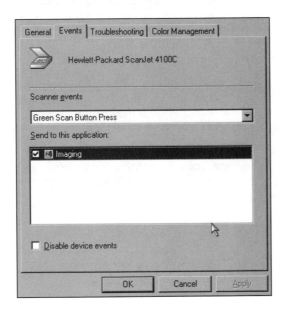

Figure 14-22: You can determine where Windows 2000 will send scans coming from the scanner.

Keyboards

Since most keyboards these days have separate keys for both cursor movement and numeric entry, you normally want to enable the Num Lock key so that you can quickly type numbers from the numeric keypad. The status of the Num Lock key at startup is set for each individual user, and is disabled by default in Windows 2000. If you want the Num Lock key to be enabled, as well as to be enabled before a user logs on, follow these steps:

STEPS:

Enabling the Num Lock key before Logon

Step 1. Open the Registry Editor. If you don't have a shortcut to RedEdit on your Start menu or your Desktop, click Start ⇨ Run, type regedit in the Open text box, and then press Enter or click OK.

Step 2. Locate the following registry key:

```
HKEY_USERS\.DEFAULT\Control Panel\Keyboard
```

Step 3. In the right pane, right-click InitialKeyboardIndicators, and then select Modify from the context menu.

Step 4. Change the value 0 to the value 2.

Step 5. Close the Registry Editor.

Changing keyboard speed

Only a few settings allow you to customize the way your keyboard behaves. Go to the Control Panel, select the Keyboard icon, and go to the Speed tab. If you often hold down a key to get it to repeat (when you hold down an arrow key to move the cursor in a document, for instance) you may want to change the delay before the repeat starts. Make this too short, and you run the risk of accidentally setting it off. You can also increase the speed at which you get the repeating characters. You can test your settings in the text box, until you find a comfortable combination of settings.

The other adjustment you can make is for the cursor blink rate. This is the cursor that will show up in word processing documents, spreadsheets, and other application that have an insertion point.

Remapping keyboard keys

In the Regional Settings section, we saw how to substitute a whole new keyboard layout for another. Instead of swapping keyboards, you can make smaller changes with RemapKey, a utility that comes with the Windows 2000 Resource Kit. (See Chapter 3 for information about installing the Resource Kit.) RemapKey changes keyboard layouts by remapping the scancode of keys. The utility places two keyboards onscreen, one representing your current keyboard, and another that shows what you want. You can change

Chapter 15

Managing Your System with the Microsoft Management Console

In This Chapter

We look at the Microsoft Management Console (MMC), which is a framework for accessing other computer management tools. We will learn:

▶ What the Microsoft Management Console is.

▶ How to create custom MMC consoles.

▶ How to manage computer security using MMC snap-ins.

▶ How to view system information using MMC snap-ins.

The Microsoft Management Console

The Microsoft Management Console is a shell program that provides a common framework for administrative tools. Just as the Windows Explorer provides a common way to view and manage files and folders, the MMC is a common way in which to view and manage networks, computers, services, and system components.

The MMC itself provide no administrative functions. Instead, it is a container for the tools which you will use to perform administrative functions. These tools are called *snap-ins*, and they are available from both Microsoft and other software vendors. In addition to snap-ins, MMC consoles can hold ActiveX controls, links to Web pages, folders, and so forth. In addition to managing a Windows 2000 computer, MMC consoles can be used to control many typical Windows 2000 Server management functions. (Both the Windows 98 and Windows 2000 Resource Kits are also MMC consoles.)

Windows 2000 includes a number of MMC consoles that have already been configured with some of the more important system administration tools. One of the most important of these tools is the Computer Management Console. To open it, follow these steps:

STEPS:

Open the Computer Management Console

Step 1. Click Start ⇨ Settings ⇨ Control Panel.

Step 2. Click Administrative Tools. This folder is a special system folder, much like the Printers and Network and Dial-up Connections folders. It holds shortcuts to a number of preconfigured MMC consoles.

Step 3. Click Computer Management to open it, as shown in Figure 15-1.

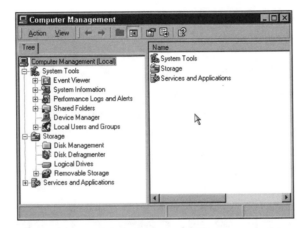

Figure 15-1: The Microsoft Management Console can be configured to hold different tools. This console, called Computer Management, holds a number of useful snap-ins for managing your computer.

Step 4. While a console opens like a regular window in Windows 2000, it does not contain the typical File option on its menu. To close the console, either click the Close icon in the upper-right corner, or click its System Menu and select Close.

Tip   Another way to open the Computer Management Console is to right-click My Computer, and then select Manage from the context menu.

Tip   You also can use the keyboard shortcut Alt+F4 to close the console if it is the active window.

Many of the individual tools within the Computer Management Console will be covered later in this chapter. However, some common characteristics exist with which you use the tools within the MMC. By default, any of the MMC consoles — such as the Computer Management Console — have two panes, resembling the Windows Explorer.

The left pane is the console tree, and it displays the tools and other items available in the console. Just like the Windows Explorer, you will see a hierarchical arrangement of tools, further arranged in nodes. To expand a node, click the plus sign to the left of a node, just like you would expand a folder in the Windows Explorer. Each console tree might contain a number of levels, and each one can be expanded in turn.

The right pane is the details pane. When you select an item (a snap-in) in the console tree, its contents will display in the right pane. What you will see in the details pane also depends on the selected snap-in.

Most MMC consoles contain only two menu commands: Action and View. These are context-sensitive menus, and each will display different menu commands depending on the selected snap-in. Alongside these two commands are a number of toolbar icons. The exact icon selection will also differ depending on the tool that is selected.

Note

Often, an item in the console tree will have a plus sign next to it. When you click the plus sign to expand the tree, the plus sign will disappear and you will see that there are no subfolders beneath it.

Secret

There are so many useful tools in the Computer Management Console that you really should create a shortcut to it on your Desktop so that you can quickly access it when you need it. It may well be that the Computer Management Console is *the* most important new tool in Windows 2000.

STEPS:

Create a shortcut to the Computer Management Console

Step 1. Click Start ➪ Settings ➪ Control Panel.

Step 2. Click Administrative Tools.

Step 3. Right-click Computer Management, and then select Create Shortcut from the context menu.

Step 4. A shortcut labeled Computer Management (2) will appear in the Administrative Tools folder. Click and drag it to your Desktop.

Step 5. If you want, you can right-click the icon on your Desktop and then select Rename so you can delete the (2) appended to the shortcut's name.

Step 6. If you want the shortcut to appear on your Start menu, drag and drop the Computer Management shortcut onto your Start button.

Running MMC and consoles from the command prompt

Consoles that are used in the MMC have the extension .MSC (management saved console). You can run the Computer Management Console by clicking Start ⇨ Run and then typing the following in the Open text box:

```
C:\winnt\system32\compmgmt.msc
```

As an alternative to typing the exact path, you also can type the command as:

```
%systemroot%\system32\compmgmt.msc
```

In both cases, the Computer Management Console will open, just as if you had followed the previously described steps in "Opening the Computer Management Console". (If you created a shortcut to the Computer Management Console using the preceding steps, right-click the shortcut and select Properties. You will see that the target resembles the latter example.)

Instead of opening one of these consoles from the command prompt, you can first open MMC itself, either to create a new console or to modify an existing console. The syntax for this command is as follows:

```
mmc {path\filename.msc} {/a} {/s}
```

The MMC parameters are outlined in Table 15-1.

Table 15-1   MMC Command-Line Parameters

Parameter	What It Means
{path\filename.msc}	Starts MMC and opens the specified .MSC file. If this parameter is left blank, MMC will start with a new, empty console.
/a	Opens the console file in author mode so that you can make changes to it.
/s	Turns off the splash screen that you would normally see when starting MMC. In Windows 2000, the splash screen is automatically suppressed when you open an existing console file.

Secret

The console (msc) files that ship with Windows 2000 can be found in c:\winnt\system32, but there might be others on your system. If you have installed the Windows 2000 Resource Kit (see Chapter 3), its console files will be located in the Resource Kit directory which, by default, is c:\Program Files\Resource Kit. Since software vendors can use the MMC framework to handle their own snap-ins, you might find console files in other directories, as well. You can search for console files by following these steps:

STEPS:

Searching for console files

Step 1. Click Start ➪ Search ➪ For Files and Folders.

Step 2. In the text box labeled Search for files or folders named, type ***.msc.**

Step 3. Click Search Now.

Step 4. If you want to open one of the consoles listed in Search Results dialog box, click the filename.

Tip

If you only run the **mmc** command with no arguments, the Computer Management Console will open with an empty MMC window. From there, you can use the Console ➪ Open command to open any existing console files.

Creating a new console

You can easily create your own console file. You might want to do this so that you can gather your own collection of snap-ins in a customized format, rather than relying on one of the preconfigured consoles that accompanies Windows 2000. (Also, as the snap-in model for computer controls spreads, you may find more third-party snap-ins that you can add to the configuration tools that accompany Windows 2000.)

STEPS:

Creating your own console file

Step 1. Click Start ➪ Run and type **mmc /s** in the Open text box.

Step 2. This opens an empty console inside the MMC window. (Until you add some snap-in tools to the console, the MMC window will be empty.) To add tools to your console, click Console ➪ Add/Remove Snap-in.

Step 3. Click Add. This will display a list of available snap-in tools from which you can select tools to add to your new console, as shown in Figure 15-2.

Step 4. Scroll down the list until you find System Information. Select it and click Add.

Continued

Figure 15-2: All the available snap-ins on your computer
will be listed in the Add Standalone Snap-in dialog box.

Step 5.   If your computer is on a network, you will be asked which
computer you want this tool to manage. This can be either your
local computer or another computer on your network. Choose

Local Computer. If you will be managing another computer on the
network, you will need to have appropriate permissions.

Step 6.   The list of available snap-ins will remain open. Select Device
Manager, as well as Local Computer.

Step 7.   Close the Available Snap-in list to return to the Add/Remove Snap-
in dialog box (see Figure 15-3). Selecting one of the snap-ins listed
in the dialog box will display a description of the snap-in tools'
function in the Description pane.

Step 8.   Click OK to return to the Console Root dialog box. You will then
see the two tools you selected to add listed in the dialog box.

Step 9.   Click Console ⇨ Save As, and save the new console as
Console1.msc

Figure 15-3: The tools you have selected will be displayed in the Add/Remove Snap-in dialog box.

Computer Management

For most users, the Computer Management Console will be the most important console, holding a number of very important tools they will use on a daily basis. When open and viewed at the console tree, three nodes will be displayed: System Tools, Storage (covered in Chapter 17), and Server Applications and Services.

System Tools

In its default configuration, System Tools has six nodes, as shown in Figure 15-4.

Each System Tool is briefly described here:

- **Event Viewer:** Tracks many different events that occur on your computer. Events are recorded in a log that can be viewed for troubleshooting purposes.

Figure 15-4: Some of the most important management and troubleshooting tools can be found in the Computer Management Console's System Tools node.

- **System Information:** Displays hardware configuration information, as well as running software. This tool can play an important role in troubleshooting problems.

- **Performance Logs and Alerts:** Allows you to track hardware usage and system services.

- **Shared Folders:** Displays resources on your computer that are available to other users on the network, as well as what resources are in use.

- **Device Manager:** Provides a graphical view of the hardware attached to your computer, as well as the tools for managing it. (Device Manager was covered in Chapter 14.) The Windows 2000 Professional Device Manager is similar to the Device Manager in Windows 98.

- **Local Users and Groups:** Allows you to manage individual users and groups for a Windows 2000 Professional computer.

The tools available in the Computer Management Console play an important role in three main areas: security, information gathering, and managing your computer.

Security

Windows 2000 Professional provides many important security features, even if the computer is not connected to a Windows 2000 network. Snap-in tools available in the Computer Management Console, Local Users and Groups, and Shared Folders all allow you to configure a Windows 2000 computer in any number of ways for sharing or limiting access to data.

In small offices, where a number of users might share access to a computer or a group of computers on a peer-to-peer network, Local Users and Groups can be used to safeguard important settings or data. It also can be used in a home/office, where you might allow your staff or temporary help to update some contact and accounting information, without providing any access to sensitive financial information and data files. For your home computer, you can restrict your children's access to the computer for games and word processing only, for example, while also restricting their access to your work data files and your configuration information.

The User accounts tool is used to configure security when several individuals share the same computer. It also can be used to configure security for a computer that is installed on a simple peer-to-peer network. (When a Windows 2000 Professional computer is connected to a Client/Server network controlled by a Windows 2000 Server, the Server's Active Directory tools provide much — if not all — of the security configuration.)

Secret

One other reason you should spend more time managing system security is directly related to the growing availability of Internet connections that are "always on," such as those provided by cable modems and DSL connections. Not only do both of these technologies provide an open path *from* your computer to the Internet, they also provide an open path *to* your computer from the outside world, potentially allowing access to your computer and your sensitive data to outsiders.

Groups

When you perform a clean install of Windows 2000 Professional to an NTFS-formatted drive, or when you upgrade from Windows 9x to Windows 2000, security will be set to the default file system and Registry permissions settings. If you upgrade from Windows NT 4.0 to Windows 2000 Professional, security is not set to the default settings; rather, your Windows NT settings are maintained. You can, however, change to the default settings. See "User and Group Management" later in this chapter for more information.)

Of the six user categories available in Windows 2000, the three most important categories are Administrators, Power Users, and Users. Specific rights and permissions for all six user categories are listed in Table 15-2.

Table 15-2   Default Groups in Windows 2000

Groups	Description
Administrators	Administrators are close to omnipotent beings in Windows 2000. The default security settings do not restrict their powers. They can perform any function supported by the operating system. If they come across a right or permission which has not been granted to them, they can give themselves that permission. (Apparently, not even Kryptonite can stop them.)
Power Users	Power Users are in an intermediate step between the all-powerful Administrators and the ordinary Users. The default security settings for Power Users are backward-compatible with the Users category in Windows NT 4.0. They can customize system-wide resources like printers and date and time settings using most of the Control Panel applets. They can create other User accounts (but not Administrator accounts), but they cannot add themselves to the Administrator group. They also can remove any Users they might create. They cannot, however, take ownership of files, load drivers, or manage security. They can install applications for other users, but some pre-Windows 2000 applications might not recognize this.
Users	Users have full control over their own data files and settings. If you perform a clean install of Windows 2000 to a system using an NTFS drive, Users should not be able to compromise the integrity of the operating system or of installed applications. They should be able to run any applications, which have been installed either by Administrators, Power Users, or themselves. They will not, however, be able to run applications installed by other users, nor will they be able to install these applications from a central-ized source. This means that a user should not be able to introduce a virus program to a Windows 2000 system.
Guests	The Guest user level allows temporary access to guest users. A password is not needed to log on as a guest. If you are using the computer as a Web server, you might want to use the Guest account for Web access. Guests can shut down a computer.
Backup Operators	Backup Operator security allows backup and restore capability for files on the computer, no matter who the file owner is. This user level also can shut down the computer, but security settings cannot be changed.
Replicator	This is used to support file replication in a domain.

Secret

The default security settings for a Windows 2000 Professional installation can be found in the winnt\inf\defltwk.inf file.

A Windows 2000 user assigned to the User level should be able to run any program written to conform to the Windows 2000 Application Specification. However, he or she cannot run legacy applications. You must be assigned to the Power User level to run legacy applications.

Default user rights

Table 15-3 lists the default user rights after performing a clean install of Windows 2000 Professional onto an NTFS drive, or when you install Windows 2000 as an upgrade from Windows 9x.

Table 15-3   Default User Rights in Windows 2000

Rights/Permissions	Administrators Group	Power User Group	Users Group	Backup Operator Group
Access another user's private data	X			
Access computer from network	X	X	X	X
Assign user rights	X			
Back up files and directories	X			X
Change system time/date	X	X		
Configure password policy	X			
Create a paging file	X			
Create administrative accounts	X			
Create and delete nonadministrative file shares	X	X		
Create local users and groups	X	X		
Create, manage, delete, and share local printers	X	X		
Debug programs	X			
Force shutdown from a remote system	X			
Format a hard drive	X			
Increase quotas	X			
Increase scheduling priority	X			

Continued

Table 15-3   *(continued)*

Rights/Permissions	Administrators Group	Power User Group	Users Group	Backup Operator Group
Install applications that modify Windows system files	X			
Install operating system	X			
Install service packs, hot fixes, and Windows updates	X			
Install system services	X			
Install, configure, load, and unload device drivers	X			
Log on interactively	X	X	X	X
Manage audit and security logs	X			
Modify firmware environment variables	X			
Modify groups or accounts created by other users	X			
Modify users and groups they create	X	X		
Profile a single process	X		X	
Profile system performance	X			
Remove computer from docking station	X	X	X	
Repair operating system	X			
Restore files and directories	X			X
Shut down the system	X	X	X	X

Users are given write access to only a portion of the Registry on a Windows 2000 computer. They have control of the following items:

- **HKEY_CURRENT_USER:** Full control of their section of the Registry.

- **%UserProfile%:** Full control of their user profile directory.

- **All Users\Documents:** Can modify any shared documents stored here that are shared documents.

- **All Users\Application Data:** Can modify any shared application data.

- **%Windows%\Temp:** Work-around for service-based applications to work more efficiently.

Except for these keys, a user assigned to the Users group will have no more than read-only access to the rest of the computer, and this level can be restricted even more. Individuals assigned to the Power Users group have similar rights to their own sections of the Registry and their User Profile.

Caution

By default, there are no permissions assigned to the root directory. Whatever permissions might have existed before installing Windows 2000 will be maintained, which means that everyone has full control. You might need to change these settings to effect a more secure system. (Changes in permissions are discussed in "Shared folders," later in this chapter.) However, do not change these settings without first exploring the consequences. Changing the default permissions can cause multiple problems throughout your system, as discussed in Chapter 17.

Secret

The reason the root directory is not secured, according to Microsoft, is because the Windows 2000 Access Control List Inheritance Model would recursively configure all subdirectories from the root. If there are non-Windows 2000 directories located on the install partition, their security settings might change in ways you won't anticipate.

Restoring default settings

If you installed Windows 2000 by upgrading from Windows NT 4.0, your computer will not start with the default security settings. Instead, the NT 4.0 security settings will be used. If you want to use the default security settings, you must use the Security Template snap-in. Follow these steps:

STEPS:

Restore the default Windows 2000 security settings

Step 1.   Click Start ⇨ Programs ⇨ Command Prompt.

Step 2.   At the command prompt, type the following commands and then press Enter after each line (*windows* is your Windows 2000 folder)

```
cd windows
cd security
cd templates
```

Step 3.   Still at the command prompt, type the following and press Enter:

```
Secedit /configure /cfg basicwk.inf /db basicwk.sdb /log
basicwk.log /verbose
```

This command-line program can either configure or analyze the system security settings using the Security Template tool. It makes use of templates that are stored as plain text INF files, that can be swapped, edited, or merged together to copy security settings from one computer to another.

The syntax for using this tool to configure System Security is as follows:

```
Secedit /configure /DB filename {/CFG filename} {options}
```

The optional parameters for Secedit are listed in Table 15-4.

Table 15-4   Security Editor Configuration Parameters

Parameter	Description
/DB *filename*	Required argument; displays the path to the database for the security template that should be applied. The database files have an .sdb extension.
/CFG *filename*	Path to the security template that you want imported into the security editor database and then applied to the system. If this argument is missing, the template that is already in the database will be used.
{*options*}	Options can be any of the following:
/overwrite	Valid only when used with the /CFG *filename* switch. If this switch is used, the template specified in the /CFG argument will overwrite any template that is already in the database. If this switch is not used, the /CFG filename will be appended.
/area	Separate security areas exist in the system. If this argument is not used, the default is all areas. You also can specify the following areas, with each area separated by a space:
SECURITYPOLICY:	Local and domain policies for the system.
GROUP_MGMT:	Restricted group setting for any groups specified in the security template.
USER-RIGHTS:	Specifies the user logon rights and grants privileges.
REGKEYS:	Sets security on local registry keys.
FILESTORE:	Sets security on local file storage.
SERVICES:	Sets security for all defined services.
/log *logpath*	Displays the path to the log file. If the logpath value is not specified, the default path is used. Default logs are kept in the c:*windows*\security\logs folder.
/verbose	Displays more detailed progress information.
/quiet	Disables all screen and log output.

The Security Editor also can be used to analyze system security settings. It compares the security settings on your computer against a stored security configuration. To perform an analysis, follow these steps:

STEPS:
Perform a security analysis

Step 1.   Click Start ⇨ Programs ⇨ Command Prompt.

Step 2.   At the command prompt, type the following commands and press Enter after each line (*windows* is your Windows 2000 folder):

```
Cd windows
cd security
cd templates
```

Step 3.   Then, type the following command and press Enter:

```
secedit /analyze /DB filename {/CFG filename} {options}
```

The parameters for the analyze command are listed in Table 15-5.

Table 15-5   Security Editor Analyze Command Parameters

Parameter	Meaning
/DB *filename*	Required argument that displays the path to the database holding the security configuration that you want to compare against. The database files have a .sdb extension.
/CFG *filename*	The security template that should be imported into the database. If this filename is not specified, the analysis will be conducted against the template already contained in the database.
{*options*}	Options can be any of the following:
/log *logpath*	Displays the path to the log file. If the path is not specified, the default is used. Default logs are kept in the c:\winnt\security\logs folder.
/verbose	Display more detailed progress information.
/quiet	Disables all screen and log output.

The template files used for the /CFG command are plain text .INF files, which you can edit with a text editor such as Notepad, if you wanted to substitute part of the settings for a different profile. You also can open these files in

Notepad just to examine their settings. The .DB files used in the /DB argument are binary files that cannot be viewed or edited using a text editor.

Tip

The best way to read .INF files is to right-click and use the SendTo shortcut to send the files directly to Notepad (see Chapter 8).

User and group management

Users and groups are managed from the Computer Management Console. Expand System Tools in the console tree, and then expand Local Users and Groups. Two folders listed beneath Local Users and Groups — one holding all the users for the computer, and the other holding the default groups, were discussed earlier in this chapter. For added flexibility in security, however, you can create additional groups.

Note

When you first install Windows 2000, the Administrator account and a Guest account is created for you. The Administrator account is the default account; it cannot be deleted, disabled, or removed. This means that you will never be locked out of your computer, provided you remember the Administrator password.

Caution

When you first log on as the Administrator, you can set up other user accounts. It is a good security practice to log on as something other than the Administrator for your everyday computer use. If you are using your computer as the Administrator, you are more susceptible to security problems. As an Administrator, you have full control over the system settings, which a malicious program might exploit to bring havoc to your computer. If this happens while you are logged on as a standard user, the Windows 2000 security settings will prevent malicious programs from executing.

Run as

If your day-to-day computing tasks involve activities that do not require you to use your Administrator account, but you might often need to perform such tasks as install a programs or tweak a few settings, you normally will need to log off and then log on again as an Administrator to make those changes. Depending on the security settings defined for your standard user account, you might have access to the Computer Management Console from which you can make changes to individual settings. If your security settings do not allow you to make any changes to your security settings, you will see the message shown in Figure 15-5 when you click OK.

Tip

If you want to use the computer as a standard user for security purposes, but you don't want to have to constantly log off and then log on again as an Administrator, use the Run As command. This command can be used from the Windows Explorer, from the command line, or from a desktop shortcut, using the following steps:

Figure 15-5: An individual attempting to change his or her security settings is denied based on his or her having the wrong security settings.

STEPS:

Use the Run As command to start a program

Step 1.   Open the Windows Explorer and navigate to the folder containing the program you want to run.

Step 2.   Hold down the Shift key, and then right-click the program in the right pane.

Step 3.   Choose Run As from the context menu to open the Run as dialog box shown in Figure 15-6.

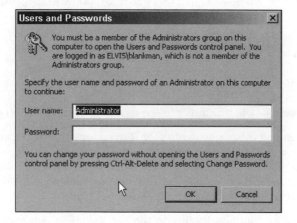

Figure 15-6: After selecting Run as from the context menu, you can select the user you want to log on as by typing in the username and password for that user.

Step 4.   Fill in the name and password. You will not be able to log on and run any programs using the identity of another user if you do not know the correct username or password.

Tip

You might want to use the Computer Management Console to change settings, but you also know that you need to have an Administrator account in order to change most settings. The easiest way to accomplish this while you are logged in as a standard user or a power user is to create a shortcut to the Computer Management Console on your Desktop that you can click in order to open the console as an Administrator, using the following steps.

STEPS:

Create a shortcut using the Run As command

Step 1. Right-click the Desktop.

Step 2. Select New, and then click Shortcut from the context menu.

Step 3. In the Type location of the item text box, type the following (with the quotation marks, but substituting the actual name of this computer for the *computername* value):

```
runas /user:computername\administrator "mmc
%windir%\system32\compmgmt.msc"
```

Step 4. Click Next, type a name for this Desktop shortcut, and then click Finish.

Step 5. When you click this shortcut, you will be prompted for the password of the particular Administrator you added in Step 3.

The window in which you are running the Computer Management Console — or from within the window of any other program you started using the run as command — will not indicate the username under which you have logged on.

Note

You can use this same syntax for Run as for other programs. However, there are a few applications that you cannot start with the Run as command. This includes Windows Explorer, the Printers folder, or a desktop item such as My Computer or the Recycle Bin. According to Microsoft, this is because these items are opened indirectly by Windows 2000.

Tip

The run as command relies on the Secondary Logon Service. If you cannot get the run as command to function properly, it might be that the Service is stopped. To start this Service, follow these steps:

STEPS:

Starting the Secondary Logon Service

Step 1. Start the Computer Management Console. You will need to be logged on as an Administrator to start or stop a service.

Step 2. Locate Services and Applications in the Console tree and expand it. Then select Services.

Step 3. Locate the Secondary Logon Service item in the details pane. Right-click and select Properties from the context menu. The Secondary Logon Service Properties dialog box will appear, as shown in Figure 15-7.

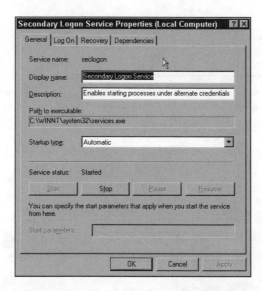

Figure 15-7: The Secondary Logon Service must be running if you want to use the run as command. To make sure it is always available, change its Startup type to automatic.

Step 4. In the Current Status section of the dialog box, click the Start button.

Step 5. To make sure it is always running, ensure that Automatic is selected in the Startup drop-down list box. Click OK.

Adding users

You might want to add additional user accounts to your computer for the following:

- For yourself, so that you won't need to log on to the computer as Administrator to perform everyday tasks.
- For different people who share a computer and who also would like to be able to maintain their own settings.
- For users on a peer-to-peer network so that they can access shared files or printers on this computer.

To create additional users, follow these steps:

STEPS:

Setting up a User Account

Step 1. Click Start ➪ Settings ➪ Control Panel, and click Administrative Tools.

Step 2. Click Computer Management.

Step 3. Expand the Console Tree, and then navigate to System Tools ➪ Local Users and Groups ➪ Users.

Step 4. On the Console menu, click Action ➪ Create User. The Create User dialog box appears, as shown in Figure 15-8.

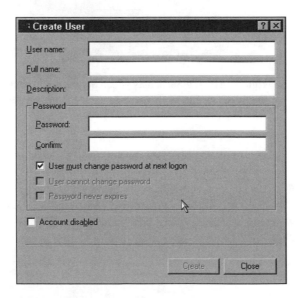

Figure 15-8: Fill in and select options for each user that you create on this computer.

Step 5.   Type the new user's name and password in the appropriate text boxes. If you leave the option User must change Password at next login checked, the option User cannot change password and the option Password never expires then remain disabled. (See "User Names and Passwords, " later in this chapter, for tips on creating user names and passwords.)

Tip

User accounts have a security identifier that stays with the account. This means that you can rename an account without causing the account to lose any properties, such as its password, group memberships, and user profile.

You also can delete user accounts that you have created. Once you delete a user account, all the individual settings and files are deleted, and you cannot restore them using any typical restore operation.

Tip

If you are unsure that deleting a user account will cause something to be lost that might be needed later, you can first disable a user account to lock out the account while still preserving the user account settings. Later, after you are sure that the user account is no longer needed, you can then delete it. In Figure 15-9, the Guest and Internet Guest accounts have been disabled. No one can use these accounts to log on to the computer. To disable a user account, right-click the account in the detail pane, and then select Properties from the context menu. Select Account Disabled, and click OK.

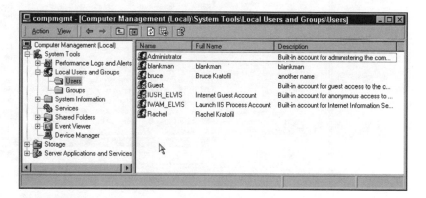

Figure 15-9: Two of the user accounts on this computer — the Guest and Internet Guest accounts — have been disabled, as shown by the x in the lower-right corner of their respective icons in the details pane.

Secret

When you log on, the last name of the user account will be displayed. If you don't want that name displayed, you can disable the setting using the Group Policy snap-in in the MMC.

STEPS

Disabling Last Name display at login

Step 1. Click Start ⇨ Run, and type the following in the Open text box:

```
mmc /s
```

Step 2. Click Console ⇨ Add/Remove Snap-in.

Step 3. Click Add, and then select Group Policy, to start the Select Group Policy object.

Step 4. Select the Local Computer or, if you are on a network, another computer, and then click Finish.

Step 5. Click Close, and then click OK to return to the Computer Management Console.

Step 6. In the console tree, navigate to Computer ⇨ Computer Configuration ⇨ Windows Settings ⇨ Security Settings ⇨ Local Policy ⇨ Security Options, as shown in Figure 15-10.

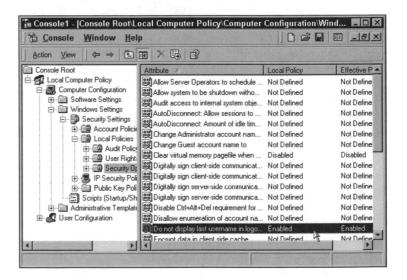

Figure 15-10: In the Group Policy snap-in, navigate to Security Options, and then enable the option Do Not Display Last Name.

Step 7. In the details pane, right-click the option Do not display last name in logon, and make sure this is enabled.

Step 8. Since you might want to use the Group Policy snap-in again, save this console using the Console, Save As command to make accessing it faster the next time you want to use it.

Usernames and Passwords

Each username must be unique, not only from all other usernames, but also to any group names on this computer. A username can be up to 20 characters long, including spaces and periods, but it cannot be *only* spaces and periods, nor can it include any of the following characters: "
/ \ [ ] : ; | = , + * ? < >

Unless this computer will be used by no one else but you, and which will not have any network or Internet access, create a strong and secure password that is difficult for anyone to break. This is especially true for the Administrator password, which allows access to everything on the computer. Passwords can be up to 14 characters long and can include letters and numbers. Passwords also can use the symbols preceding, as well as other symbols.

Never use your name, telephone number, the names of your kids, spouse, or pets, or your social security number for your log-on password. If you have constructed your password the right way, it will be extremely difficult — if not impossible — to hack. Combine letters, numbers, and symbols in a random fashion. For example, the password orxt!@238cMb would be difficult to crack — and difficult to remember, too. By the way, you're not the only person to have ever have watched the Seinfeld television series, so don't use Bosco as your password.

The Group Policy snap-in is designed as a network tool. It can be used on standalone Windows 2000 computers, as well.

Assigning users to groups

By default, when a new account is created, it is assigned to the User group. A new account can be promoted to a higher group.

- If the user account was created by a Power User account, that Power User can log on and add the user to the Power User group.

- An Administrator account is the only account that can promote it to the Administrator group.

To change a group membership when you have the appropriate permissions, follow these steps:

STEPS:

Adding a user to another group

Step 1. Click Start ➪ Settings ➪ Control Panel, and then click Administrative Tools.

Step 2. Click Computer Management.

Continued

STEPS:

Adding a user to another group *(continued)*

Step 3.   In the console tree, navigate to System Tools ⇨ Local Users and Groups ⇨ Users.

Step 4.   In the Details pane, right-click the user, and then select Properties from the context menu.

Step 5.   Select the Member of tab, and then click Add. This will display the Select Groups dialog box, as shown in Figure 15-11.

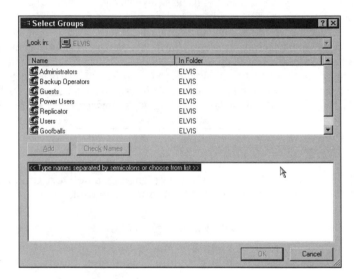

Figure 15-11: By default, new users are added to the User Group. They can be promoted to a more powerful group by another user with the appropriate permissions.

Step 6.   Select the group to which you want the user account added to, click Add, and then click OK to return to the Member of tab.

Once you have created new accounts and assigned the accounts to groups, you can use these settings to manage permissions for various resources on this computer. You can limit access to certain shared folders (see "Shared Folders," later in this chapter) and printers (see Chapter 18) to certain groups or certain users, while limiting access to others.

If you decide that your security scheme needs another group, you can create more groups. To create another group, highlight Groups in the Computer Management Console tree, click Action, and then select Create Group. You will be asked to type a name and description for the group. You can then add users to the new group.

Shared Folders

Shared Folders — in coordination with user groups — allow you to limit access to certain folders on a Windows 2000 computer. They can be used either on a standalone Windows 2000 computer that is shared by a number of users, or when a Windows 2000 computer is connected to a simple peer-to-peer network. (When you are dealing with a full-sized Client/Server network connected to a Windows 2000 Server, there are more powerful security tools available.)

The Shared Folders snap-in allows you to create new shared folders and modify permissions, view users who may be connected to the computer through a network, and see which files have been opened by remote users.

Note

Only Administrators or Power Users can use the Shared Folder tool on a Windows 2000 Professional computer.

To view shared folders, select System Tools ⇨ Shared Folders ⇨ Shares in the console tree. Even if you have not set up shared folders on your computer, you might see that some shares already exist in the details pane. These are special shares that were created by the Windows 2000. Most of these shares will be indicated by the inclusion of a dollar sign ($) appended to their name. Table 15-6 lists the special shares and their purpose.

Table 15-6   Special Shares

Share	Purpose
{*drive letter*}$	A special share that allows an Administrator to access the root directory of a storage device. You might see C$, D$, and so on.
ADMIN$	A resource leading to your system root — the directory into which Windows 2000 was installed. It is used during remote administration of the computer.
IPC$	Allows named pipes — a special segment of system RAM — to be shared. It is also used in remote administration.
PRINT$	Allows remote administration of a printer.
FAX$	Allows fax files from a fax client to be temporarily cached.

Caution

In general, you should not change these shared resource settings. They have been created by Windows 2000, and you might experience problems if you delete or change them.

In addition to these special shares, you might want to share other drives or folders to give other users access to files contained on those drives or in those folders. To create a share, follow these steps:

STEPS:

Creating a shared folder

Step 1. In Computer Management, select System Tools ⇨ Shared Folders ⇨ Shares.

Step 2. On the console menu, click Action ⇨ New File Share.

Step 3. This opens the Create Shared Folder Wizard. You can select an entire drive to share, or you can expand the folder tree and select a particular folder. Click Browse to select the item for which you want to create a shared resource, give it a Share name and description. This name and description will be seen by other users when they attempt a connection to the shared resource. Click Next.

Step 4. Now you need to set the permissions for this new shared resource (see Figure 15-12). You can change these permissions later, so just accept the defaults for now. Click Next.

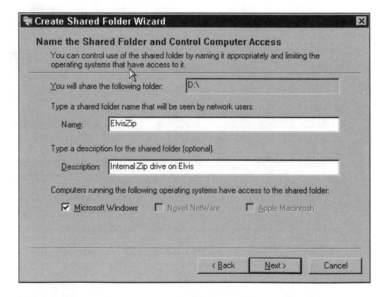

Figure 15-12: Type a name and description for the new shared folder.

Step 5. Click Finish to complete the Wizard. Your new shared resource should now be displayed in the Shares detail pane.

By default, when a shared folder is created, it's permission is set to Everyone. If you did not configure the share correctly when you first created it, as in the example above, you can change it using the following steps:

STEPS:

Change share permissions

Step 1.   In Computer Management, expand Shared Folders, and then select Shares.

Step 2.   Right-click the folder whose permissions you want to change, and then select Properties from the context menu.

Step 3.   Select the Share Permissions tab, as shown in Figure 15-13. If you want to exclude a group from this share, select that group, and then click Remove.

Step 4.   If you want to change permissions for a group, select the group, and then select the Permissions you want to give them (from Full Control to Read, for example). See Table 15-7 for an explanation of access permissions.

Step 5.   Click OK.

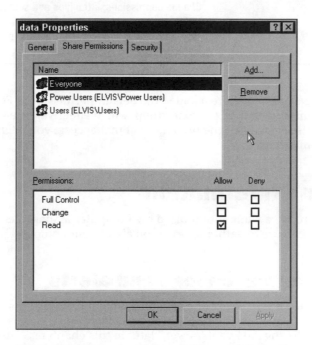

Figure 15-13: You can exclude an entire group of users from a shared folder, or you change their access to read-only.

There are three levels of permissions for a shared folder: Read, Change, and Full Control, in order of escalating importance. Table 15-7 outlines what each level of permission allows.

Table 15-7   **Shared Resource Permission Rights**

Permission Level	Rights
Read	View names of subfolders and files Move to subfolders View the data contained in files Run program files
Change	Everything in Read permissions, plus: Add files and subfolders Change the data in files Delete files and subfolders
Full Control	Everything in Read and Change, plus: Change permissions, if the files and subfolders are in NTFS format Take ownership of files and subfolders, if they are in NTFS format

Tip

When you first share a folder, the default permission is Full Control permission to the Everyone group, which effectively means No Security whatsoever. Given the broadness of that access, you might want to reduce permissions.

Gathering Information

There are a number of tools in the Computer Management console, which you can use to gather information about your computer.

Performance logs and alerts

Windows 2000 automatically keeps a number of logs that let you see what has happened on your computer. You can view these logs using the Event Viewer (see "Using the Event Viewer," later in this chapter). Windows 2000 also can create several optional logs that you can start to monitor some aspect of either the local or remote computer, or to send alerts when a specific event has taken place. The data collected by these logs can be examined using the Performance Monitor snap-in that comes with Windows 2000, or the logs can be configured to save the data in comma-separated value (CSV) files or tab-delimited text files which you can then import into a spreadsheet or database file for further analysis.

To create a new log file, follow these steps:

STEPS:
Create a performance log

Step 1.　Open the Computer Management Console. Expand the Performance Logs and Alerts node, and then select Counter Log.

Step 2.　Right-click the details pane and select Create New Log or alert. You will be asked to type a name for the log. You can use Sample 1 as a name.

Step 3.　Click the Add button to select the counters you want to monitor, as shown in Figure 15-14.

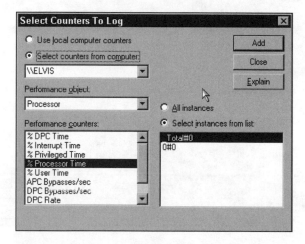

Figure 15-14: From the Select Counter dialog box, you choose the system activities you want to monitor.

Step 4.　Make sure that you have selected the correct computer to monitor by either choosing Use local computer counters, or by choosing the computer by name in the lower-right section of the dialog box.

Step 5.　Select Processor from the Performance object drop-down list box.

Step 6.　In the Performance counters list box, select % Processor Time, and then click Add.

Step 7.　Select System from the Performance object drop-down list box.

Continued

STEPS:

Create a performance log *(continued)*

Step 8. In the Performance counters list box, select File Data Operations/second, and then click Add.

Step 9. Click Close to return to the General screen. You will see the results of your earlier selections, as shown in Figure 15-15.

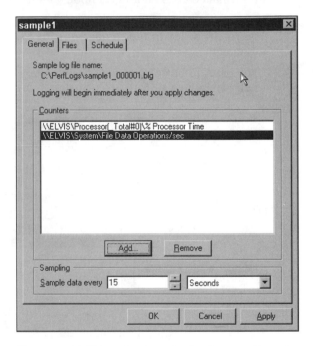

Figure 15-15: This performance log has been configured to track two items: Processor Time and File Data Operations/second.

Step 10. You can adjust how often the counters will be sampled; the default is every 15 seconds. The time increment can be changed from seconds to minutes, hours, or days.

Step 11. Select the Files tab. By default, log files are saved to the C:\PerfLogs folder, although you can change this to any directory you choose. You also can change the default filename.

Step 12. Choose a file type from the drop-down list box. A binary circular file will, when full, begin to overwrite itself. You also can set an upper limit on the size of the log file.

Step 13. Select the Schedule tab. For now, set the log file to start and stop manually, although you also can set it up on an automatic schedule.

Step 14. Click OK to close the dialog box and return to the Computer Management Console.

You can set up more than one counter log. Any logs that are set up— including any default logs created by Windows 2000—will be listed in the details pane if you have selected Counter logs in the console tree. Since we set up the new log for a manual start, its icon should be red, which means it is not running. To start it, right-click and select All tasks ⇨ Start from the context menu.

Tip

You can view logs or watch counters in real time using the Performance Monitor. However, you cannot access the Performance Monitor from the Computer Management Console. It has its own separate MMC console called Performance, which you can set up using the following steps:

STEPS:

To view a counter in the Performance Monitor

Step 1. Click Start ⇨ Settings ⇨ Control Panel, and then click Administrative Tools.

Step 2. Select Performance, and select then Performance Monitor in the console tree.

Step 3. To view current activity on your system, click the Add button. This will open a dialog box similar to the one shown in Step 3 of Creating a Performance Log. Repeat Steps 3 through 9 in the previous exercise to add the same two counters.

Step 4. Right-click the Graph area of Performance Monitor, and then select Properties from the context menu.

Step 5. Select the General tab. In Update Time, select Periodic Update, and then select an interval of one second. Click OK.

The Performance Monitor will now start tracking your two performance indicators. The default view is a line graph, as shown in Figure 15-16. Beneath the graph display, you will see numeric displays of the counters you are tracking. When you have multiple counters like this example displays, select one of the counters from the list on the lower edge of the Performance Monitor dialog box to display its statistics.

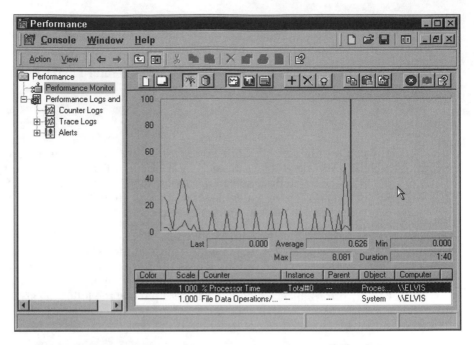

Figure 15-16: The Performance Monitor can be set up to track multiple counters. Current activity is being tracked at the heavy vertical line. When current activity reaches the right side of the graph window, it will wrap around to the left and overwrite the existing display.

Secret

An important principle in Physics says that the act of observing something alters the behavior of what you are observing. Setting up counters to run at periodic intervals will cause system activity which, in turn, will show up on your performance graphs. The very fact that you are monitoring your system increases the system activity beyond what it otherwise would be.

To stop real-time monitoring, click the Stop button. This will halt the display. To restart, click Stop again. To erase the current display, click Clear Display—the second button from the left.

System Information

The System Information snap-in is an information and troubleshooting tool. The first tool available is the System Summary tool, which gives you important information about your computer and about Windows 2000.

Tip

There are two views available in the System Information snap-in: Basic and Advanced. Make sure you are looking at the Advanced view. You want to see as much information as possible about your settings. Click View, and then select Advanced.

Secret

To take a snapshot of your system, navigate to any of the snap-ins under the System Information node, click Action, and then select Save as System Information File. This will save your information in a file with a filename that you provide, in the default .NFO file format (which is a MS.info document). When you click an .NFO file to open it, it will open to the System Information snap-in in a standalone MMC console. These files pack a lot of information, and many can be over 200K in size.

Hardware

The Hardware Resource tool will provide reports on conflicts and resource sharing, direct memory access (DMA), forced hardware, I/O addresses, IRQs, and memory settings. If your peripherals are Plug and Play under Windows 2000, you should not have to worry much about these settings; the Plug and Play Manager will do the worrying for you. However, with nearly infinite hardware combinations—plus legacy hardware—you might still have to do troubleshooting. See Chapter 5 for general troubleshooting procedures.

Components

The Components tool will provide you with information about the various devices on your system and how they are configured (see Figure 15-17). This is much the same information you would see if you use the Device Manager to view the properties of the individual devices.

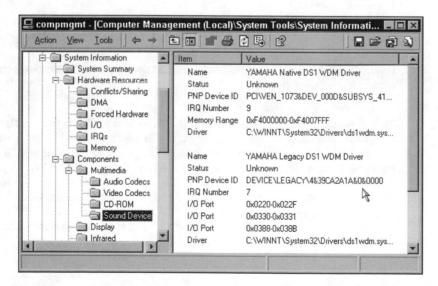

Figure 15-17: The Components tool in the System Information snap-in provides detailed information on device settings. Note that devices, such as this sound card, will display a Plug and Play ID number (PnP Device ID) if they are Plug and Play–compatible devices.

Software

The Software section of the System Information snap-in exceeds the Hardware tool as a source of information. In most cases, you cannot directly manage the software from here, but you can determine what is running, and in some cases, why it is running.

For example, you can select the Loaded Modules report to see what software is currently running on your system. A glance at the details of this report, as shown in Figure 15-18, might show that there are quite a few modules from Intuit running. This might surprise you, particularly if you don't have any Intuit products installed.

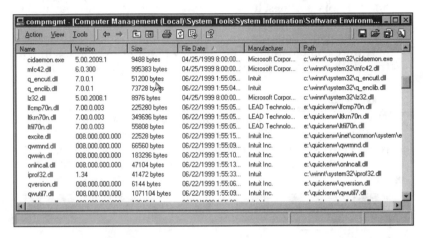

Figure 15-18: A look at the Loaded Modules report displays the software that is currently running on your computer.

To see why these programs are running, look at another report — the Startup Programs report — which is a little bit lower on the console tree. This shows what programs are automatically loaded at system startup, as well as the location from which they are being loaded. As Figure 15-19 shows, programs related to Adobe Acrobat, Microsoft Office, Intuit Quicken, and the Iomega Zip drive are all being loaded. Some are being called from the Startup folder for the current user, some area being called from the Windows 2000 Common Startup folder, and still others are being added by settings contained within the Registry.

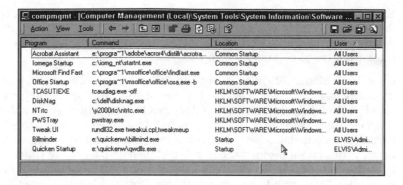

Figure 15-19: Some loaded modules are there because programs are automatically being loaded at system startup.

Each of these programs consumes a certain amount of system resources, however slight, and thus have some impact on your computer's performance. You might want to consider what functionality is lost, if any, by moving these programs out of the Startup group. To test this, while still being able to get back to where you were before, follow these steps:

STEPS:

Moving applications out of the Startup group

Step 1.   Click Start ➪ Settings ➪ Taskbar & Start Menu.

Step 2.   Select the Start menu tab, and then click Advanced. This will open the Windows Explorer to your Start menu settings. In the folder pane, select Start ➪ Programs.

Step 3.   Click File ➪ New ➪ Folder. Name this new folder Notstart.

Step 4.   One by one, drag the shortcuts from the Startup folder into the Notstart folder. Then, restart your computer and try the affected applications to see if they still work.

You could try to move all the shortcuts at once from the Startup to the Notstart folder, but if you do run into problems, it might be difficult to determine which application to blame. (If all else fails, you can try reading the manuals of the applications to see if they say what happens when these programs are not started automatically.)

You don't have to go to the trouble of creating the new folder and dragging the shortcuts there; you could just delete the shortcuts. However, if you decide you want them back in the Startup group, you would need to carefully track what the shortcuts were so that you could recreate them.

Tip

If you have Microsoft Office 95 or 97 installed on your computer, you probably have Microsoft Fast Find as one of your Startup group programs. Fast Find builds an index of Office documents from which you can locate and open documents faster. It does this by building indices in the background (which can consume a hefty amount of resources, and which can often drag down your system performance). It is installed as part of the Office Tools from the Office CD-ROM, which also installs an icon in the Control Panel. If you no longer want it to run, move its icon from the Startup folder to the Notstart folder.

Using the Event Viewer

The Event Viewer is another way in which you can gather information about your computer and its performance. The Event Viewer can be found when you expand the Computer Management System Tools node. Windows 2000 keeps three separate logs that record certain events on your system. These three logs are:

- **Application Log:** Applications or programs can record events in this log. An application written to take advantage of the application log can record error messages here, for example. All users can view this log.

- **System Log:** Windows 2000 system components will record information in this log. For example, if a driver fails to load, or if there is a problem with a service during startup, an event will be recorded here. All users can view this log.

- **Security Log:** Once an administrator specifies events that are to be recorded, the Security Log can keep a record of both successful and unsuccessful logon attempts, or whether resources have been used to create or delete files. By default, the Security Log will not be running, but it can be enabled using the Group Policy snap-in discussed earlier in this chapter. Also, only those users assigned to the Administrators group have access to the security log.

These are the types of events that are recorded in the logs, and they can then be viewed using the Event Viewer. Figure 15-20 shows a sample Application Log, and Table 15-8 outlines the types of events that can be viewed.

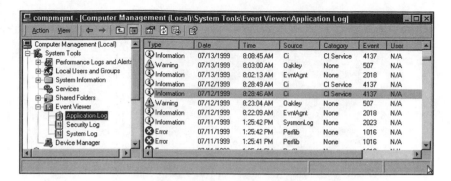

Figure 15-20: Application logs track errors, warnings, and information events.

Table 15-8   Event Log items

Type of Event	Description
Error	What Windows 2000 would deem to be a significant problem that could cause either a loss of data or a loss of functionality. Indicated by a red and white x icon.
Warning	Something that might cause a problem sometime in the future, but not at the present time. Indicated by a yellow triangle with an exclamation point.
Information	Logs the successful operation or logs an application, driver, or service. Indicated by a blue i within a bubble.
Success Audit	When you configure Security Logging to track certain events, this will indicate that one of these events was successful.
Failure Audit	When you configure Security Logging to track certain events, this will indicate that one of these events failed. For instance, if you are tracking logons, and someone enters the wrong password, this will be recorded as a failure.

The Application Log tells you when the event happened, and what triggered it, along with some other cryptic codes, including an Event number. To see the details from a particular event, right-click the event in the details pane. Figure 15-21 displays an error that is detailed in the Error Properties dialog box.

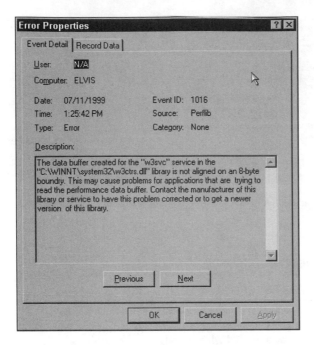

Figure 15-21: Right-click an event to view details and an explanation of what happened.

Secret

While the Warning label makes it sound important and somewhat ominous, many warnings can be safely ignored. For example, you might see this warning in your Application Log: "Failed to obtain Kerberos server credentials for ISAKMP/Oakley service. Kerberos authentication will not function. The most likely reason for this is lack of domain membership." Anytime you start a Windows 2000 computer and it is not connected to a Windows 2000 Server network domain, you will see this warning and you can safely ignore it.

You can sort the events shown in the viewer in the same way you sort in the Windows Explorer. Clicking the column heading will sort by that column; click again to reverse the sort order.

Tip

Since you will probably be most interested in the events that just occurred, make sure the Event Log is sorted by date in descending order. (The arrow in the column header will be pointed downward.)

Event Log properties

Configuring the logs is similar for all three of the logs. To make changes in the configuration — in this example, for the Application Log — follow these steps:

STEPS:

Configuring an event log

Step 1.   Click Start ⇨ Settings ⇨ Control Panel.

Step 2.   Click Administrative Tools, and then select Computer Management.

Step 3.   Expand the System Tools Node, and then expand Event Viewer.

Step 4.   In the console tree pane, right-click the name of the log you want to configure. Since they are similar, right-click Application Log for this exercise.

The Application Log Properties dialog box, shown in Figure 15-22, shows the path and filename for the log. All the logs are kept in the C:\winnt\system32\config folder, and they all have the file extension .EVT . The default maximum log size is 512K, but this value can be increased or decreased. You have a number of choices when you reach this upper limit.

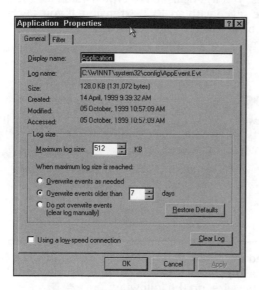

Figure 15-22: The Application Properties dialog box lets you control how large your log files become, and it also lets you control what happens when you reach that upper limit.

You can configure Event Log wrapping so that it can overwrite as much as is needed — so that you are always recording events in your log. You also can set a safety margin by allowing events to be overwritten only if they are older than a specified number of days. In addition, you can set it so that nothing is overwritten, but this means that new events will be overwritten. (You will receive a message when the log becomes full.)

If you set this option, you must remember to periodically empty your log file. To clear it, follow these steps:

STEPS:

Manually clearing a log file

Step 1.   Click Start ⇨ Settings ⇨ Control Panel.

Step 2.   Click Administrative Tools, and then select Computer Management.

Step 3.   Expand the System Tools Node, and then expand Event Viewer.

Step 4.   Select the log you want to clear in the console tree, and then click Action ⇨ Clear All Events.

Step 5.   You will be prompted whether you want to save the old log file. If you say Yes, you will be asked to type a name for the saved log, which will be saved with an .EVT extension. If you say No, your log data will be permanently discarded.

The Security Log

If you use the Event Viewer to view the contents of your log, you will see that the Security Log is empty. By default, it is disabled. If you want to start recording Security Events, follow these steps:

STEPS:

Start the Security Log

Step 1.   If you created the Group Policy MMC in "Disabling Last Name Display at Startup," earlier in this chapter, open it and then jump to Step 7. Otherwise, do the following:

Step 2.   Click Start ⇨ Run and type the following into the Open text box and click OK:

mmc /a

Step 3. Select the Console menu, click Add/Remove Snap-in, and then click Add.

Step 4. Select Snap-in, click Group Policy, and then click Add.

Step 5. For Group Policy Object, click Local Computer, and then click Finish.

Step 6. Click Close, and then click OK. This creates the Group Policy MMC.

Step 7. In the console tree, expand these nodes until you reach Audit Policies: Local Computer Policy ⇨ Computer Configuration ⇨ Windows Settings ⇨ Security Settings ⇨ Local Policies ⇨ Audit Policies.

Step 8. In the details pane, select the event you want to start auditing (logging), and then click Action ⇨ Security.

Step 9. In the Security dialog box, click your selections in Change Local Policy to, and then click OK.

Step 10. Repeat Steps 8 and 9 if you want to audit additional events. Figure 15-23 shows the Audit Policy set up to track logins and policy changes.

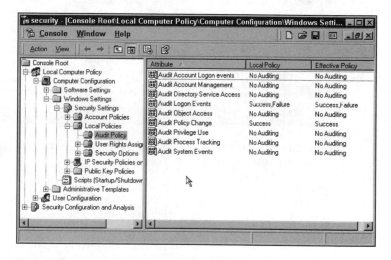

Figure 15-23: To start security logging, open the Group Policy Snap-in, and select Audit Policies. These settings will keep track of all successful and failed logins, as well as any successful changes to policies.

Managing Your Computer

There are a number of other tools available in the Computer Management Console. Some, such as Device Management and Storage Management, are covered in Chapters 14 and 17, respectively. One other important item that an advanced user might want to manage is Services.

Services

There is another snap-in within Computer Management called Services and Applications that reports the status of services and allows you to manage them (see Figure 15-24).

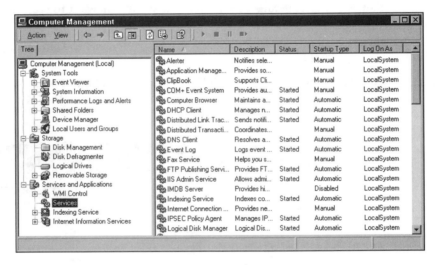

Figure 15-24: The Services snap-in is part of System Tools. It lets you manage services (start, stop, and configure) on your computer.

A service is a background process — or "helper" — program that provides some specific support to other programs. Typically, a user would not directly interact with a service the way they would with a word processing or spreadsheet application. A service runs in the background, and it helps ensure that other programs work as they should.

Note

By default, you have to be logged on as an Administrator to be able to start and stop services.

Tip

Make sure that you can see all the information available with the Services snap-in. Click View ⇨ Choose Columns, and make sure that Name, Description, Status, Start Up, and Account Run under are all selected.

Secret

As in the Windows Explorer, you can sort the information in the Details pane by column. The default view is to sort by name. If you want to sort by status instead—so that you can see which services are running—click the upper portion of the Status column twice. The first click sorts in ascending order and lists the services that aren't running first; their status is blank. The second click sorts the column in descending order.

The Startup column shows if these services are started automatically, or if they are called by some other service or program. For example, we looked at the Indexing Service that compiles indices of files to aid in searches in Chapter 7. When you enable this service from the Search window, you will see the Indexing Service running in the Services window. If you disable this service from the Search window, its status will change to Stop. To see more information about a particular service, right-click the service and select Properties from the context menu. For example, the properties for the Indexing Service are shown in Figure 15-25.

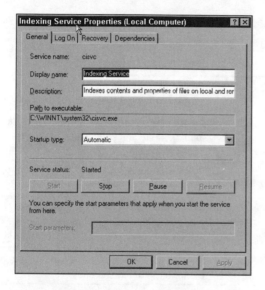

Figure 15-25: The Properties window of the Indexing Service. Its Startup type is Automatic and its Service Status is Started because it has been enabled from the Search Assistant.

You can enable or disable services, or you can pause services from the General tab of the Properties dialog box. You also can use the VCR-like controls in the upper portion of the detail pane. Select a service and these controls become active, and they can be used to start or stop a service.

Caution

Don't stop a service unless you know it is optional. Some services perform vital system functions. You can stop the Indexing Service, because all it does is speed up your searches. However, you do not want to shut down the Plug and Play Service, since it plays a crucial role in managing your hardware.

Some services depend on other services, so shutting down one can cripple another. You can trace service dependencies by right-clicking a service, selecting Properties from the context menu, and then selecting the Dependencies tab. This tab has two panes. The upper pane shows what other services are needed by the service to function. The lower pane shows which other services need the selected service.

Caution

The Dependency tab only traces dependencies among services. Other programs might need services, and those programs will start their required services as needed. If you are going to disable a service, you need to determine if it will affect anything else. For a better idea of the relationships between applications and services, you might want to use the Dependency Walker (see the sidebar, "Dependency Walker," later in this chapter).

Many services are configured by default in Windows 2000. Table 15-9 describes what many of these services do. As a general rule, unless you are sure you can do without a particular service, it is best to leave it alone.

Table 15-9   Default Services in Windows 2000

Service	Provides
Alerter	Will notify specified users or computers of administrative alerts that occur on a system.
CIM Object Manager	Controls the interaction between network management applications and local or remote data or system events.
ClipBook Server	Supports the ClipBook Viewer, which adds functionality to the Clipboard.
Computer Browser	Keeps track of the computers currently on the network, and provides this list to programs that need it.
Content Index	Keeps a full text index of files and folders on a computer to aid in searches.
Directory Replicator	Used when you replicate directories between computers.
Event Log	Provides a list of system, security, and program events on a computer.
Logical Disk Manager	Takes care of all disk management activities, such as disk partitioning and volume creation, logical drive lettering, and formatting.
Media Services Management	Provides services for removable media, such as CD-ROM discs, Zip drives, and Jaz drives.

Service	Provides
Messenger	When the Alerter service sends messages, it uses the Messenger service.
Microsoft Fax Service	Manages incoming and outgoing faxes for both local and network clients.
Microsoft Install Service	Manages application installation. This also includes rollback and repair services.
Net Logon	If a Windows 2000 client participates in a domain, it handles the authentication of logon events.
Network DDE	This provides the transportation and security for network dynamic data exchange.
Network DDE DSDM	DDE Share Database Manager. This supports Network DDE.
NT LM Security Support Provider	If a program uses something other than the named pipe transport, this provides security.
Plug and Play	Handles the installation and configuration of Plug and Play devices. (See Chapter 14.)
Remote Procedure Call Service	Helps distributed programs by providing endpoint mapping and other RPC functions.
Server	Handles file, print, and named pipe sharing. Also provides Remote Procedure Call (RPC) support.
Smart Card Resource Manager	Manages Smart Card devices, which are a new hardware-based security system.
Spooler	Manages the print spooler, which stores documents that are to be printed onto the hard drive, and then sends them to the printer one by one.
Task Scheduler	Supports the Task Scheduler, which you can configure for automated activities.
Telephony	Manages telephony services and devices attached to the computer.
UPS	Manages any uninterruptible power supply that may be attached to the computer.
Workstation	Manages network connections and communications.

Your computer might have more or fewer services available than what is listed in Table 15-9, depending on your configuration.

Dependency Walker

An application running on any of the Windows 32-bit platforms is more than just one big file. An application might actually rely on a number of different files and dynamic link libraries. These might be files that were installed along with the application in the home folder of the application, or they might depend on system DLLs.

One tool to use to view these dependencies is the Dependency Walker, an MMC snap-in that accompanies the Windows 2000 Resource Kit. (If you haven't installed the Resource Kit, see Chapter 3.) To run Dependency Walker, follow these steps:

1. Click Start ⇨ Programs ⇨ Resource Kit ⇨ Tools Management Console.

2. Expand the Tools Categories node in the console tree.

3. Select Diagnostic Tools in the console tree, and then click Dependency Walker in the details pane.

Once you open a particular application in Dependency Walker, it will display all the tasks or DLLs that this application needs. For example, click File ⇨ Open, and then navigate to C:\Program Files\Internet Explorer (or to the folder in which Internet Explorer 5 is installed on your system). Dependency Walker will open this module and then scan it to see what other modules it depends on. Each of these modules are, in turn, scanned to see what modules they depend on. If the Dependency Walker finds a module that it has already scanned, it marks it with an arrow and then stops expanding this particular branch. An example is shown in the following figure.

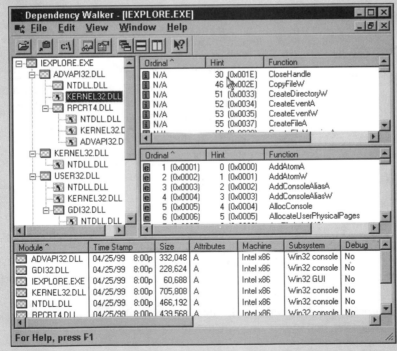

The Dependency Walker displays which modules are needed by a particular program — in this case, Internet Explorer.

While much of the information shown might be of interest only to an application developer, it might also be helpful to an advanced user who needs to know if a particular file is needed.

Device Manager

Another important tool in managing your computer is the Device Manager, which lets you manage your hardware. The Device Manager is very similar to the Windows 98 Device Manager, and is covered in detail in Chapter 14.

Storage Management

Computer Management has a number of tools with which you can manage your storage devices, such as hard drives, floppy drives, and removable drives. Given the importance of these, they are covered in detail in Chapter 17.

Summary

In this chapter we learned how to use tools within the Microsoft Management Console, the new framework for system administration tools. We have learned how to:

▶ Customize tools within the MMC interface.

▶ Manage security using MMC snap-ins.

▶ Gather system information using MMC snap-ins.

▶ Manage the computer with MMC snap-ins.

Chapter 16

The Registry

In This Chapter

We look at the Registry, the storehouse of almost all the settings for your computer, operating system, and much of your software. We discuss:

▶ The Registry structure and see how it stores data.

▶ How to backup and restore the Registry.

▶ Exporting and Importing the Registry keys.

▶ How to use the command-line tools in the Windows 2000 Resource Kit to access the Registry.

A First Look at the Registry

The Windows 2000 Registry is the central repository of configuration information for your installed hardware and software. When you use the Control Panel applets to make changes in your system configuration, when you use TweakUI, and when you make changes using the Computer Management Console (see Chapter 15), those changes are almost always stored in the Registry.

In the days of 16-bit Windows, configuration information was kept in .INI files. Microsoft itself used WIN.INI and SYSTEM.INI to hold specific information. Third-party software often added their settings to these files, and they often created their own .INI files, either in the Windows directory or in the application's home directory. If you wanted to backup your vital configuration information, the settings were always spread all over your computer's hard disk in many different files. The Registry was Microsoft's attempt to bring all this information together into a single place.

While the Registry has been a big part of Windows since Windows 95, it has bulked up considerably in Windows 2000. A computer with a full set of peripherals and a moderate amount of software could have a Registry over 12MB in size.

You can determine the size of your Registry in the Control Panel using the following steps:

STEPS:

Find out the size of your Registry

Step 1.   Click Start ⇨ Settings ⇨ Control Panel, and then click System.

Step 2.   Select the Advanced tab, and then click Performance Options.

Step 3.   Click Change in the Virtual Memory section.

Step 4.   In the lower portion of the Virtual Memory dialog box, shown in Figure 16-1, the current Registry size, in megabytes, is displayed. A value for the Maximum registry size setting also appears.

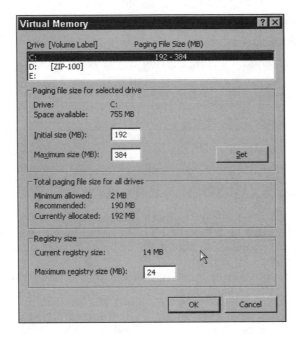

Figure 16-1: You can determine the total size of your Registry, plus its maximum allowable size, from the Control Panel's System icon.

Secret

How much space is enough for your Windows 2000 Registry? One Microsoft Tech Support person in the Windows 2000 beta newsgroups, advocated setting the maximum Registry setting to 64MB to ensure you don't run out of room.

One reason for the expanding size of the Registry is because third-party software developers are now using the Registry to store their own settings and preference information, rather than using .INI files. Every time you use the Windows 2000 Setup program, install additional hardware, or install 32-bit Windows software, data gets stored in the Registry. However, some programs still use .INI files to save their settings. This is supported by Windows 2000 to maintain backward compatibility with older applications.

Editing the Registry gives you an immense amount of power in configuring your system. It also gives you an immense amount of power to screw things up. This is one place where experimentation is not in order.

Caution

While we will be showing you techniques for editing and manipulating the Registry, it is a good practice to only edit the Registry as a last resort. If you can make configuration changes to your system through a Control Panel applet or the Management Console, do so there rather than directly in the Registry. It is far safer to use these configuration tools; if you somehow manage to corrupt the Registry, you might disable your computer altogether. It is also important to know how to restore the Registry.

Secret

If you find that you need to edit your Registry and you have even the slightest hesitation about this potentially dangerous process, you should call technical support at your designated Windows support provider (for many people, this is the computer manufacturer from which they purchased their computer) and insist that they walk you through the procedure.

When disaster strikes

Before we do anything to the Registry, it is important to learn how you can recover from the problem of a corrupted Registry. If your computer cannot boot, and you receive an error message that your Registry has been corrupted, you can restore the Registry. Each time Windows 2000 is able to successfully start, it backs up the last known good version of your Registry files. This way, you have a record of your computer's configuration the last time it started successfully. If you somehow manage to trash your Registry, you can restore the last known good version stored on your system.

STEPS:

Restoring the Registry

Step 1. If your computer won't boot, and you see the error message that the Registry is corrupted, shut down your computer.

Step 2. Wait about ten seconds, and then turn on the power again.

Continued

STEPS:

Restoring the Registry *(continued)*

Step 3. When you see the following message: "Please select the Operating System to Start," press the F8 key. You will only have a brief amount of time to do this — only a second or two.

Step 4. If you press the F8 key in time, you will then see the Safe Mode menu. Use your arrow keys to cursor down and select the following choice: "Last Known Good Configuration." Then press the Enter key.

Step 5. Follow the remaining instructions on your screen.

For more information about the Safe Mode menu, see Chapter 5. Note that if you made any configuration changes or installed any software since the last known good configuration was saved, those changes will be lost.

The Registry Editors

Two different Registry editors ship with Windows 2000: Regedit.exe and Regedt32.exe. Their use is explained in Chapter 9. Since Microsoft provides no menu shortcuts to either of the two Registry editors, you must start them from the Run dialog box or, alternatively create a shortcut to them on your Desktop or one of your menus. Here are steps to add the Registry Editor to your Start Menu:

STEPS:

Creating a Start Menu shortcut to the Registry Editor

Step 1. Click Start ⇨ Settings ⇨ Taskbar & Start Menu.

Step 2. Select the Advanced tab, and then click the Advanced button.

Step 3. This will open a view similar to the Windows Explorer, with your user profile displayed. Expand the Start menu, and then expand the Programs folder.

Step 4. Navigate to the Accessories folder, and then select the System Tools folder.

Step 5. Click File ⇨ New ⇨ Shortcut to launch the Create Shortcut Wizard.

Step 6. In the Type the location of the item text box, type c:\winnt\ regedit.exe and click the Next button. (This is the default name of the Windows 2000 folder — yours may be different.)

Step 7. Name this new shortcut RegEdit, and then click Finish.

The Registry Editor, with its two-pane view, is a convenient way in which to explore the structure of the Windows 2000 Registry.

Registry Structure

The Registry is structured in a topdown fashion, similar to how folders on your hard drive are organized. The Registry consists of five sub-trees, each of which is devoted to holding a certain kind of information (see Figure 16-2). Each sub-tree begins with the word HKEY (see Table 16-1). According to Microsoft, this is a signal to software developers that each is a handle that can be used by a program. The subtrees are the same in name and number to the Windows NT 4.0 Registry, less than the subtrees in Windows 95 and 98 (which have six) but more than in Windows NT Server (which has four).

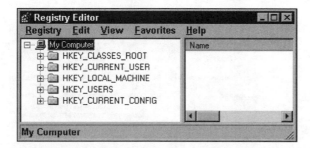

Figure 16-2: The Windows 2000 Registry is divided into five sub-trees, each devoted to holding a certain kind of configuration information.

Each sub-tree within the Registry holds individual keys. A key might contain subkeys, or it might actually hold data. Subkeys can, in turn, hold additional subkeys. You expand and navigate in the left pane of Regedit much like you do in the Windows Explorer. When you select a key or subkey in the left pane, its contents — or value entry — is displayed in the right — or details — pane, as shown in Figure 16-3. A subkey might only have one value entry in the details pane, or it might have many. As an example, expand the HKEY_LOCAL_MACHINE key, and then navigate to Hardware, Description, Central Processor, and then 0. This particular key holds identifying information about the CPU in your computer, including the vendor and model.

Table 16-1   Windows 2000 Registry Sub-trees

Root Key Name	Description
HKEY_CLASSES_ROOT	Contains the associations between applications and file types (i.e., .XLS files belong to Microsoft Excel), OLE Registry information, and file-class associations.
HKEY_CURRENT_USER	Contains the user profile for the individual who is currently logged on. It also contains environment variables, desktop settings, application preferences, network connections, and printer information.
HKEY_LOCAL_MACHINE	Contains information about the local computer system. Settings for hardware and operating system features such as bus type, system, memory, device drivers, and startup control data is located here.
HKEY_USERS	Contains all the actively loaded user profiles. This includes the HKEY_CURRENT_USER and the default Admins profile.
HKEY_CURRENT_CONFIG	Contains the configuration information for the current hardware profile.

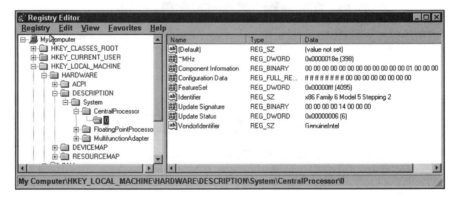

Figure 16-3: There might be many layers of subkeys through which you would need to navigate before you reached any actual data in the Registry.

A Registry key's value entry has three parts: The first part is the name of the subkey; the second is the subkey's data type; and third is the subkey's actual value, as you can see by the three columns displayed in the details pane. There are six data types, as shown in Table 16-2.

Table 16-2	Windows 2000 Registry Data Types
Data Types	**Description**
REG_BINARY	Raw binary data that will typically be displayed in hexadecimal notation, making it difficult for you to read.
REG_DWORD	A four-byte long number that will be displayed in either binary, hexadecimal, or decimal format. This data type is often used for device drivers and services.
REG_EXPAND_SZ	An expandable data string that holds a variable which will be replaced when it is called by an application. It will often look something like: %systemroot%, which will be replaced by the actual folder name containing your Windows 2000 files.
REG_MUTLI_SZ	A multiple string that usually holds a list of values which will be in a human-readable form, rather than being in binary or hexadecimal notation. The values will be separated by a NULL character.
REG_SZ	A text string, which will be in a human-readable form.

Secret

You might also see other data types in the Registry, such as REG_FULL_RESOURCE_DESCRIPTOR, which is shown in Figure 16-3 earlier in this chapter. Other programs can create their own data types to add to the Registry, but the Registry editors will most likely not be able to deal with them.

Cross-Reference

See Chapter 9 for some tips and secrets on navigating in the Registry by quickly expanding and collapsing keys.

Hives

Unlike Windows 95, Windows 98, and Windows NT 3.x, which stored the Registry in two files called System.dat and User.dat, the Windows 2000 Registry is patterned after the Windows NT 4.0 Registry. This means that Microsoft switched metaphors in mid-stream, moving from trees and keys it uses to discuss the parts of the Registry when looked at with RegEdit. When the Registry has been saved to disk, it is actually split into many more parts which were referred to as hives in Windows NT 4.0. Officially, a hive is a "discrete body of keys, subkeys and values rooted at the top of the Registry hierarchy."

Secret

Why hives? Well, to some people at Microsoft, the Registry sub-tree resembles the cellular structure of a beehive.

Actually, not all of the Registry is stored in hives. Hives are those Registry keys that are permanent components of the Registry, not the dynamic parts, such as HKEY_LOCAL_MACHINE\Hardware, which is built only when Windows 2000 boots (see Figure 16-4).

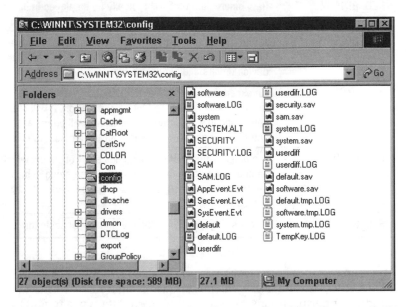

Figure 16-4: The Registry data is split up into a number of files that are called hives.

Most of the hives are stored in the c:\winnt\System32\Config folder. Table 16-3 lists them. For each user profile, there is also a hive in the c:\winnt\Profiles*username* directory with the name Ntuser.dat. Each hive corresponds to a particular segment of the Registry, and is also made up of a number of associated files, each with the same main filename but having a different extension.

In addition to the above, you will also find userdiff and userdiff.log files in System32\Config. These are not associated with a particular part of the Registry. Instead, they are used when you upgrade your operating system, such as from Windows NT 4.0 to Windows 2000 (or from one build of Windows 2000 to another).

As you can see from the Table 16-3, each hive might have either three or four files associated with it. If the file has no extension, it is a copy of the hive. If the file has a .log extension, it is a transaction log showing changes to keys and value entries in the hive. The Software, SAM, Security, System, and .Default hives also have .sav files. These are copies of the hive created at the end of the text mode stage of the Windows 2000 setup. Therefore, they should have file dates corresponding to the date you installed or upgraded Windows 2000.

Table 16-3 Registry Hives in \System32\Config	
Part of the Registry	**Goes with these files**
HKEY_CURRENT_CONFIG	system, system.alt, system.log, system.sav
HKEY_LOCAL_MACHINE\SAM	sam, sam.log, sam.sav
HKEY_LOCAL_MACHINE\Security	security, security.log, security.sav
HKEY_LOCAL_MACHINE\Software	software, software.log, software.sav
HKEY_LOCAL_MACHINE\System	system, system.alt, system.log, system.sav
HKEY_USERS\.Default	default, default.log, default.sav
HKEY_CURRENT_USER	ntuser.dat, ntuser.log (files for each user profile, within the user profile folder)

One hive—HKEY_LOCAL_MACHINE\System—plays such a critical role that an extra backup is created. This backup is created with the filename System.alt. (The other hives do not have .alt files.)

Secret

The Registry contains a list that shows which file goes with which hive. You can find it in the registry at the following key: HKEY_LOCAL_MACHINE\ SYSTEM\CurrentControlSet\Control\hivelist. There is also a list that shows the hive files for each user profile. It is located in the following key: HKEY_LOCAL_MACHINE\SOFTWARE\Microsoft\Windows NT\CurrentVersion\ProfileList.

Registry Roadmap

This section examines the Registry sub-trees, and shows where within Windows 2000 you can change these settings.

HKEY_CLASSES_ROOT

The HKEY_CLASSES_ROOT tree holds the information that relates file types to applications, as well as data types and COM objects, as shown in Figure 16-5. Given the large number of associations that a computer might have, this sub-tree is usually quite large when it is first expanded, and it will grow as you install more software onto your computer. This sub-tree is also where COM object information is stored, which tells Windows 2000 how to find and run software components.

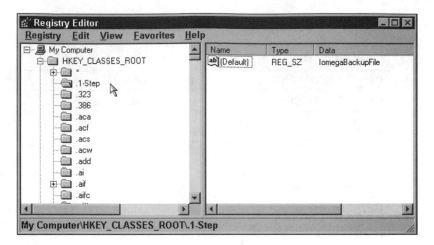

Figure 16-5: HKEY_CLASSES_ROOT is the key in which file association information is stored in the Registry.

File associations are not typically edited in the Registry. Instead, you would edit your file associations by using the Folder Options menu selection from within My Computer or the Windows Explorer by choosing View ⇨ Folder Options from the menu, and then selecting the File Types tab.

Cross-Reference

See Chapter 7 for more information about editing file associations.

HKEY_CURRENT_USER

The HKEY_CURRENT_USER sub-tree holds the information about the user profile for the person who is currently logged on to the computer. Most of the user interface settings that you set through the Control Panel are stored here (see Figure 16-6).

Secret

Some settings here are duplicated by settings contained in HKEY_LOCAL_MACHINE key. If there are different settings for the same environment variable between the two sub-trees, the choice in the HKEY_CURRENT_USER key is given priority.

When a user logs on to a Windows 2000 computer, their user profile is taken from the HKEY_USERS key and copied into the CURRENT_USER key. If no user profile exists for the user who is logging on to the computer (for example, a guest or a new user), Windows 2000 uses the Default User profile.

The subkeys in the HKEY_CURRENT_USER key are typically set from choices you make using the Control Panel applets, or by adjusting other Settings menus. (Information on setting user profiles can primarily be found in Chapters 8 and 14.) Table 16-4 lists the subkeys located in the HKEY_CURRENT_USER key.

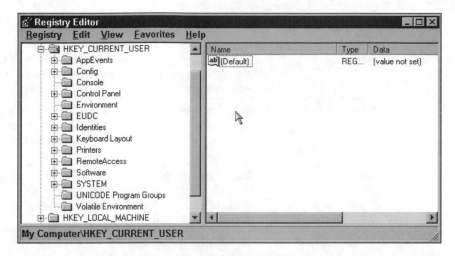

Figure 16-6: The HKEY_CURRENT_USER sub-tree contains the settings for the user who is currently logged on to the computer.

Table 16-4   HKEY_CURRENT_USER Subkeys

Subkey	What information the key contains
AppEvents	Application events that you assign to certain .WAV sound files using the Sounds and Multimedia applet in the Control Panel. They can be Windows 2000 events, or they can be events associated with a particular application.
Console	Sets the window size, along with options for any console tools, such as the Windows 2000 Command Prompt.
Control Panel	Many of the options that you can be using the Mouse, Keyboard, and Display Options applets in the Control Panel are stored in this subkey.
Environment	Environment settings that are set using the System applet in the Control Panel are stored in this subkey. Many of the settings contained here were extracted from the existing AUTOEXEC.BAT file when you installed Windows 2000.
Identities	Multiple identities in Outlook Express 5 are stored in this subkey. The user identies will look something like {0771C1B2-F98C-11D2-AB18-005004707D0A}. Under each subkey, you can find the actual user name belonging to the identity.

Continued

Table 16-4 *(continued)*	
Keyboard Layout	Keyboard language information relating to the Input Locales you choose in the Regional Options applet in the Control Panel are stored in this subkey.
Printers	Printer information is stored in this subkey. Information about each installed physically installed printer can be found here, but there will not be any information contained in this subkey for software-based devices such as fax modems.
Software	Application-specific settings are stored in this subkey. These entries are usually created when you install software. Much of the data here will have a similar structure to the data in the HKEY_LOCAL_MACHINE\Software subkey.
Unicode Program Group	Starting with Windows NT 4.0, this key is no longer used. It is left in place for compatibility reasons.

HKEY_LOCAL_MACHINE

The HKEY_LOCAL_MACHINE key contains the configuration information for your computer. Some of the data in this key is dynamic, meaning that it is created anew each time the computer boots up. The data in this key cannot be edited directly, even using the Registry Editor. There are five subkeys in HKEY_LOCAL_MACHINE, as shown in Figure 16-7.

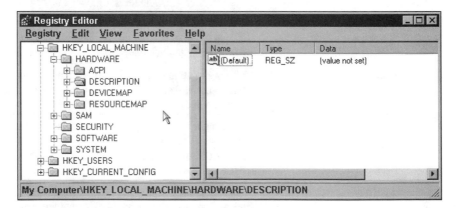

Figure 16-7: The HKEY_LOCAL_MACHINE sub-tree has five subkeys. Each key contains additional subkeys that contain vital system information.

Hardware

The HKEY_LOCAL_MACHINE\Hardware subkey holds the dynamic hardware configuration data for the computer. This subkey is refreshed each time the computer boots up, and the data is then discarded when the system shuts down (it is not stored in a hive file).

Tip

If you want to see your current hardware configuration, it is easier to open the Computer Management Console and view either the System Information or the Device Manager.

Hardware\ACPI is a new subkey in Windows 2000. This subkey holds data on the Advanced Configuration and Power Interface information, a key technology underlying Plug and Play devices.

SAM and Security keys

SAM is the Windows 2000 Security Account Manager. These two keys handle security information, and they play a big role when a Windows 2000 computer is connected to a Windows 2000 network server using the new Active Directory services.

Software

The data contained in the HKEY_LOCAL_MACHINE\Software subkey is configuration information about the software installed on the computer. The subkeys under this key will differ depending on what applications have been installed, but there will always be common subkeys among computers.

The Classes subkey contains another list of file associations like those we found in the HKEY_CLASSES_ROOT key. You will also find a lengthy list of Component Object Model objects. The Microsoft subkey contains information about all the Microsoft applications that accompany Windows 2000.

The HKEY_LOCAL_MACHINE\SOFTWARE\Microsoft\MMC\SnapIns subkey maintains a list of all the snap-ins available on the computer. They are identified by a rather long string of numbers, but if you select a string in the left pane of the Registry Editor, the Details pane on the right will display the plain text name of the snap-in, as shown in Figure 16-8.

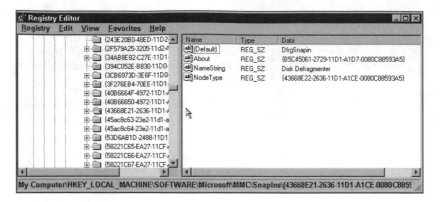

Figure 16-8: A listing of the installed snap-ins that can be used in the Microsoft Management Console.

Note that toward the end of the Microsoft subkey, you will find a subkey called HKEY_LOCAL_MACHINE\SOFTWARE\Microsoft\Windows NT\CurrentVersion. One might think that the Registry designers never got the memo about the name change to Windows 2000. Actually, the name was probably left alone so that there would be a consistent architecture between the Windows NT 4.0 Registry and the Windows 2000 Registry. This subkey holds information about Windows 2000 services, as well as information about the installed version of Windows 2000.

In addition to the common subkeys discussed above, software that you install will create their own subkeys, and the subkeys will often be used to store configuration information specific to the application (in lieu of using .INI files).

System

The HKEY_LOCAL_MACHINE\SYSTEM subkey holds all the data that Windows needs, but that can't be initialized during the startup process. Instead, the information is stored here in the System subkey. Recognizing the importance of this information, this is the one subkey that also has an extra backup file called System.alt. This data is crucial to starting the system; if you make changes with unintended consequences, you can back your changes out, because Windows 2000 automatically keeps a safe backup of this information.

The startup data is kept together in subkeys called *Control Sets*. While there can be up to four control sets — which would be labeled ControlSet001, ControlSet002, and so on — there are usually only two, the current control set plus one backup. This backup is done automatically by the system and normally requires no user intervention. Information on the various control sets is tracked in the HKEY_LOCAL_MACHINE\SYSTEM\Select subkey, as shown in Figure 16-9. There are four value entries in this subkey that track the following:

- **Default:** This is the number of the control set that will be used at the next system startup, unless the LastKnownGood configuration is manually selected (see If Disaster Strikes, earlier in this chapter).

- **Current:** This is the control set that started the system for the current session.

- **LastKnownGood:** This set is an unmodified copy of the last set that was used to successfully start the system.

- **Failed:** This control set was replaced when the LastKnownGood control set was used to start the system.

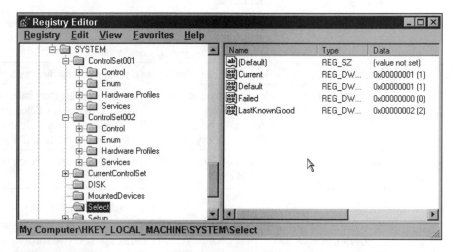

Figure 16-9: The HKEY_LOCAL_MACHINE\SYSTEM\Select subkey keeps track of the control set, or system configuration, that started the computer, as well as the Last Known Good configuration.

If you had a problem starting your computer, the presence of both the bad and the good control set might give you a clue as to what problem occurred. You can views the failed set with the Registry Editor, and then compare it to the functional control set.

Caution

While you can use the Registry Editor to track down the problem, do not use it to change any settings unless you have verified that it is safe to do so. Many of the control set settings are automatically maintained by the system. Presumably, your LastKnownGood control set is working, so you can rely on it to successfully boot your computer.

Secret

What determines a "good" system start? Microsoft's definition of good is if there are no severe or critical errors and at least one user is able to successfully log on. You can actually redefine this standard, either to make it more stringent or to remove a particular criterion. However, that is not as simple a procedure as it sounds. You must create an executable program that will check your system start settings for you in order to determine if your desired conditions have been met. The name of the program with to verify your startup must be specified in the HKEY_LOCAL_MACHINE\SYSTEM\ ControlSet001\Control\BootVerificationProgram key to determine if the startup was a "good" startup.

The control set organizes its data into the subkeys listed in Table 16-5.

Table 16-5   Control Set Subkeys

Subkey	Description
Control	Holds startup parameters for the system. These parameters includes the subsystems to load, as well as the environment variables and the paging file information.
Enum	Holds hardware configuration information for devices and drivers.
Hardware Profiles	Holds information that tracks which configuration information is used with various hardware profiles. You create different hardware profiles by selecting Start ⇨ Settings ⇨ Control Panel ⇨ System, and then selecting the Hardware tab (see Chapter 14).
Services	Holds the information that controls which services are loaded, and in what order.

Tip

If you have created different hardware profiles and you are unsure which numbers correspond to the profile you are running, see the information contained in the HKEY_LOCAL_MACHINE\System\CurrentControlSet\ Control\IDConfigDB key. The value of CurrentConfig will display the currently loaded hardware profile.

HKEY_USERS

The HKEY_USERS sub-tree usually holds two user profiles: the first profile is for the user who is actually logged on to the computer. The key name for the active user will show the Security ID for that user, which will look something like the following:

```
HKEY_USERS\S-1-5-23-527479835-1964818763-2035704189-520
```

The second profile is the default user profile, located in the subkey HKEY_USERS\.DEFAULT, which is in use when no one is logged on to the computer (for example, when the Login prompt is displayed on the Desktop). The structure of the .DEFAULT subkey is similar to the structure of the HKEY_CURRENT_USER section in the Registry. This is not the permanent storage place for the default user profile; that is actually stored in c:\winnt\ Profiles\Default User\NTUSER.DAT, but only when Windows 2000 has been installed in an upgrade.

Note

Each user profile created on a Windows 2000 computer will have its own profile in the c:\winnt\Profiles\ folder if Windows 2000 was installed as an upgrade, or in the c:\Documents and Settings folder if you performed a clean install. Each profile will have its own NTUSER.DAT file which can differ significantly in size, depending on how much a given user does — especially in terms of software installation. For example, on one of the author's computers, the profile that was created for everyday use has an NTUSER.DAT file that is 1500K in size, while a user profile that was created as an illustration for the book (but which was never really used) has an NTUSER.DAT file that is 300K in size.

HKEY_CURRENT_CONFIG

The HKEY_CURRENT_CONFIG key was added to the Windows NT 4.0 Registry — and is also contained in the Windows 2000 Registry — to achieve compatibility with the Windows 95 Registry. It duplicates the information in the HKEY_LOCAL_MACHINE\System\CurrentControlSet\Hardware Profiles\ Current subkey, which is the current hardware profile data. According to Microsoft, programs written for Windows 95 (which may look for information in these keys) will also be able to run under Windows 2000 (and Windows NT 4.0).

Backing Up and Restoring the Registry

The Registry has taken the role of arbitrator of important system settings. It has become even more important as third-party software developers have started using it more and more as a storehouse for their applications' settings, rather than using .INI files. We have now started to keep all our eggs in one basket, which means we have to take really, really good care of that basket (and those eggs).

In addition to the automatic backup of the LastKnownGood Registry copy, you can create additional backups. You might want to do this to place a copy of a backup on an alternate backup media (such as a ZIP disk), so that all of the backup copies are not stored on the same hard drive. You cannot use a regular copy and paste procedure in the Windows Explorer or My Computer, because the Registry files are open while the computer is in use, and you will receive a sharing error, as shown in Figure 16-10.

Figure 16-10: You cannot manually copy the Registry files as a backup without receiving a sharing error.

Windows Backup

One way to back up the Registry is to use the Windows 2000 Backup and Recovery Tools program, a utility that is included with Windows 2000. One of the options of the Backup program is to back up the system state. According to the Backup Help file, when you back up the system state, you will create backup copies of all the data files relevant to your computer. For Windows 2000 Professional, this includes the Registry, the boot files needed to start Windows 2000 Professional (which includes Ntdlr and Ntdetect), and the COM+ class registration database. (Additional files are backed up if you are using Windows 2000 Server.)

Secret

When you back up the system state, in addition to backing up the Registry and the files needed to boot the computer, you also back up all the files that Microsoft has labeled as protected. These are the files — mostly DLLs — that can't be overwritten when you install third-party software. On one of our Windows 2000 computers, backing up only the system state backed up 225MB of data.

To create a system state backup in Windows 2000, follow these steps:

STEPS:

Create a System State backup

Step 1.   Click Start ➪ Programs ➪ Accessories ➪ System Tools ➪ Backup.

Step 2.   Select the Backup tab.

Step 3.   In the left pane, check the System State option to enable it.

Step 4.   In the Backup media or file name text , select the drive to which you want to create your backup (see Figure 16-11). Given the size of the system state data, as shown in the previous Note, the minimum size of your backup media should probably be equivalent to a Zip disk. You would not want to select a floppy drive as the target unless you have a lot of time to feed diskettes into the drive.

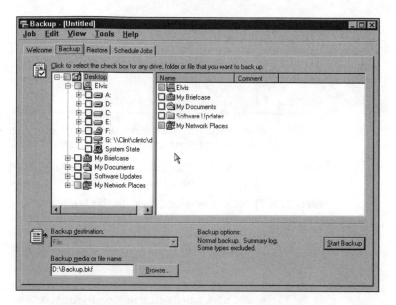

Figure 16-11: You can back up your computer's system state, which includes the Registry, using the Windows 2000 Backup program.

Step 5.   Click Start Backup.

If you need to restore the system state, the procedure is similar to the above steps. However, you will select the Restore in Step 2 instead, and you will then select the backup file from which you want to restore your system state.

RegBack and RegRest

While backing up the system state will back up your Registry, it will also back up many other things. If you just want to create backup copies of the Registry, and to restore these files if necessary, you can use two tools that are distributed with the Windows 2000 Resource Kit. (See Chapter 3 for information on installing the Resource Kit.) These tools are RegBack (for Registry Backup) and RegRest (for restoring the Registry backups). These two programs work on individual Registry sub-trees, and they can back up the registry files while your system is up and the Registry files are open.

To find these tools, follow these steps:

STEPS:

Locating RegBack and RegRest

Step 1.   Make sure you are logged on to the computer either as an Administrator or as a Backup operator.

Step 2.   Click Start ⇨ Programs ⇨ Resource Kit ⇨ Tools Management Console (if you haven't installed the Resource Kit, see Chapter 3).

Step 3.   The Resource Kit comes in the familiar Microsoft Management Console interface. (See Chapter 15 for details on the MMC.) In the console pane, expand Microsoft Resource Kit ⇨ Windows 2000 Resource Kit ⇨ Tools Categories ⇨ Computer Management, as shown in Figure 16-12.

Step 4.   In the details pane, scroll down to find the various Registry tools, which are listed in alphabetical order. (If they are not listed in alphabetical order, click the Tool column heading in the Details pane.)

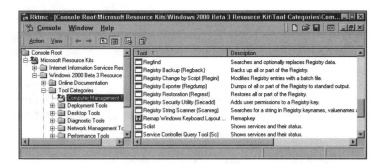

Figure 16-12: The Windows 2000 Resource Kit's Computer Management folder has a number of tools with which to work with the Registry.

When you view the details pane in the console in Figure 16-12 , you see that most of the Registry tools have a plain rectangular icon to the left of their filenames, rather than a customized icon. RegBack and RegRest, as well as most of the other Registry tools in the Resource Kit, are command-line files that are run from the Windows 2000 Command Prompt which, in previous versions of Windows, was called the MS-DOS Prompt. These are indicated by the rectangular icon resembling the Command Prompt/MS-DOS Prompt window. To reach the Command Prompt, click Start ⇨ Programs ⇨ Command Prompt.

You also can run most of these utilities from the Run menu. In many cases, a Command Prompt window will open, the program will run, and the window will immediately close. If you need to see the text, such as those for error or status messages, you might be out of luck using the Run menu.

The syntax for RegBack is as follows:

```
c:\regback [destination] {filename hivetype hivename}
```

The parameters and options are explained in Table 16-6.

Table 16-6	RegBack Parameters
Parameter	*Explanation*
destination	This is the destination of the backup files. The destination can be another drive, another folder on your hard drive, or a network share where you have write permission.
filename	Saves the hive file to this backup filename. If you do not use this option, they are backed up using their existing filenames.
hivetype	This can either be **machine** or **user**. Any other entry here will cause RegBack to fail.
hivename	This is one of the immediate subtrees of HKEY_LOCAL_MACHINE or HKEY_LOCAL_USER. If it is not one of these hive roots, RegBack will fail. If no hivename is given, then all the active hives will be backed up.

If you leave out the optional parameters and type the following command:

```
c:\regback c:\destination
```

all of the active hives will be backed up to the destination folder.

All of the hive files must be able to fit in the designated destination. If they don't, RegBack will fail. Given the size of the hive files, you will not be able to use a floppy drive as the destination. You can either set the target to a larger removable drive, such as a Zip Drive, SuperDisk, or a Jaz Drive, or you can set the destination to some other folder on your hard drive. After RegBack has run, you can then use XCOPY to save the backup files to floppy disks.

Only active hive files are backed up by RegBack. That means that inactive hives, such as the NTUSER files of inactive users, are not backed up. Since these hives are inactive, they are not loaded into memory, and you can back them up without any sharing violations using any regular backup or copying commands. You would want to do this anyway, to avoid any name conflicts, since by default, these hives all have the name NTUSER.

Your target folder cannot hold files with the same name as the files you are going to back up; RegBack will not overwrite files. Instead, it will terminate with an error message (see Figure 16-13). Therefore, if you want to use RegBack in a batch file, you want to ensure that the destination folder is empty first. The batch file will look, in part, something like this:

```
del \destination\*.*
RegBack \destination
```

Figure 16-13: RegBack will display a report of the hives that have been successfully backed up, as well as report those you will need to back up manually.

To restore Registry hives backed up with RegBack, you use the companion RegRest program. RegRest can be found in the same location of the Windows 2000 Resource Kit, and it is also a command line program. You must be logged on as an Administrator or Backup Operator to run RegRest.

Tip

An important difference between RegBack and RegRest is that all the hive files must be on the same volume (drive) as their destination. This is because RegRest doesn't copy the files, it only renames them. So while you can use RegBack to copy the Registry hives from your C: drive to a Zip Drive, for example, you will not be able to restore them from the Zip Drive. You will first have to copy them to another folder on your C: drive and then restore them.

When RegRest restores your backup copy of the Registry, it doesn't throw out the existing copy. Instead, you can save the current version of the Registry to another backup file. The syntax you use to restore a specific part of the Registry using RegRest is as follows:

```
C:\regrest [newfile savefile] {hivetype hivename}
```

The parameters for RegRest are listed in Table 16-7.

Table 16-7	RegRest Parameters
Parameter	*Meaning*
Newfile	This is the backup source filename from which you will be restoring.
Savefile	This is the filename used to save the existing Registry hive that is being replaced.
Hivetype	This must be either **machine** or **user**, or RegRest will fail.
Hivename	This must be a hiveroot, and it must be an immediate sub-tree of the HKEY_LOCAL_MACHINE or HEY_LOCAL_USER keys.

If you want RegRest to restore all the active hive files, type the following command:

```
C:\regrest NewFolder SaveFolder
```

Where *NewFolder* is the name of the source folder to which you backed up the hive files that will replace the files in the System32\Config folder, and where *SaveFolder* the location from which the hives currently in System32\Config will be moved. RegRest is similar to RegBack in that only active hives will be swapped. User profiles will not be restored, but since they are not active, you can use regular file copy techniques to restore them to the appropriate \Profiles folders.

After running RegRest, you must restart your computer to actually see the results of the swapped Registry files.

Other Registry Tools

There are a number of other Registry utilities available in the Windows 2000 Resource Kit that allow you to compare values, search for values, and edit the Registry. Some of the more useful utilities are discussed here.

Compreg.exe

Compreg is a tool with which you can compare two local or remote Registry keys and highlight the differences. It is a 32-bit, command-line utility that should also work with Windows 95, Windows 98, Windows NT, and Windows 2000 Registries. It does not write to the Registry.

To run Compreg, you need to access the Windows 2000 Command Prompt. Click Start ➪ Programs ➪ Accessories ➪ Command Prompt. Then type the following command:

```
compreg key1 key2 {options}
```

The syntax for this program is outlined in Table 16-8.

Table 16-8   Compreg Parameters

Parameter	Meaning
key1	The first of two local or remote Registry keys to compare. The default key is HKEY_CURRENT_USER. There are abbreviations you can use for certain subkeys. You can use CU for the HKEY_CURRENT_USER, CR for HKEY-CLASSES_ROOT, and US for HKEY_USERS.
key2	The second of two local or remote Registry keys that you will be comparing. If you use the name of a computer for *key2,* then whatever key is used in *key1* will be appended to the computer name.
Options:	Additional arguments that can be specified. These are as follows:
-v	A verbose report that prints both matches and differences between keys.
-r	This will recurse subkeys that only exist in one key.
-e	The error code level of the utility will be set to the code in effect when the utility was last used. The default error level is set to the number of differences found.
-d	This will only print the value entry names, not the values.
-q	This sets quiet mode, which will only print the number of differences.
-n	This will suppress color in the output.
-h	This will provide additional help information.

Compreg outputs its results in text form, as shown in Figure 16-14. Here, Compreg was used to compare the Console subkey for the Current_User with the Console subkey for HKEY_USERS\.DEFAULT. In this example, there were two entries found in the first key — CURRENT_USER — that were not found in the second key. The 1 at the beginning of the line indicates that the entry was found only in the first key.

Figure 16-14: Compreg allows you to compare two different keys in a Registry, or two keys on a remote computer.

If the two subkeys have the same entry, but they each have different values, the two entries will be printed as a block, with both the key name and the values, so that you can compare them. If you use the verbose option, you will also get a listing of those keys that are the same, with each line beginning with an X character.

Tip

Compreg can be a useful tool if you are trying to determine why two computers are behaving differently. If the computers are connected to a network, you could compare relevant portions of the Registry to see if there are differences in the settings.

Reg.exe

While RegEdit and RegEdt32 will typically be the Registry editors you want to use, there is another editor provided in the Windows 2000 Resource Kit, Reg.exe, that might sometimes be necessary. Reg is a text-mode Registry editor that works from the Command Prompt, and it might be needed if you are having problems booting your computer and can only boot to the Command Prompt. (See Chapter 5 for more information about troubleshooting and working from the Command prompt.) It lets you add, change, delete, search, backup, and restore Registry entries on both local and remote computers.

The default location for Reg.exe is C:\Program Files\Resource Kit\NTRK. By typing the following command:

```
C:\Program Files\Resource Kit\NTRK\reg /?
```

Windows will display a help file showing you the syntax to use for performing the various Reg functions.

Regmon

Secret

Regmon.exe is a Registry monitoring tool. It does not come in the Windows 2000 Resource Kit. It is a freeware utility available from System Internals, which you can find on the Internet at http://www.sysinternals.com/regmon.htm. The program, written by Mark Russinovich and Bryce Cogswell, tracks Registry activity on your system and displays the results in a window. It also allows you to export the list to a file for later viewing.

Regmon can be used to check out many different entries in the Registry. For example, it can show you just a hint of the incredible amount of activity that a computer goes through while processing your most basic requests. Just clicking the Start button causes over sixty Registry related entries as Windows 2000 checks for various settings and preferences.

Secret

You also can use it to track down where, in the Registry, certain settings are stored. One of the new features of Windows 2000 is personalized menus — called IntelliMenus — in which Windows tracks the programs you most frequently use. To see where this new setting is stored in the Registry, enable Regmon, and then click Start ➪ Settings ➪ Taskbar & Start Menu. Select the

Start menu options tab. Then, in Start Menu settings, change the setting for Personalized menus. Then, immediately open Regmon to see what key was used. Regmon will show you that HKEY_LOCAL_MACHINE\SOFTWARE\ Microsoft\Windows\CurrentVersion\Explorer\StartMenu\IntelliMenus is the location in the Registry in which the IntelliMenu settings are stored, as seen in Figure 16-15.

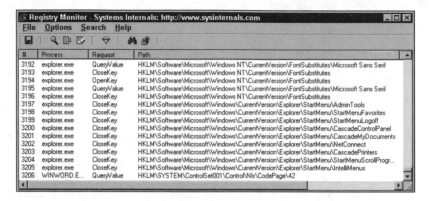

Figure 16-15: Regmon traces Registry activity on your computer.

Tip

You can save Regmon output as an RGD file (it's default output format) so that you can view it later. The RGD file saves the output as tab-delimited text, which can easily be viewed in a spreadsheet, mimicking the column views presented by Regmon.

Registry Tricks and Secrets

Now that we have seen what and where the Registry is, and some of the tools you can use with it, we will look at some of the tricks and secrets that you can use when there is no other way to accomplish a task.

Exporting and importing Registry files

You can export a branch of the Registry, or the entire Registry, to a text file that can be opened in an editor such as Notepad or WordPad. You might want to do this so that you could search for values or perform some involved editing (to take advantage of the advanced editing tools in WordPad, such as Search and Replace), or to import some of the exported data into another Registry file.

Caution

You can export the entire Registry, but remember: it can be 12MB to 14MB in size, which will make it difficult to work with. Unless you have a specific reason to export the entire Registry, it's probably best to export a branch instead.

STEPS:
Exporting the Registry

Step 1. Click Start ⇨ Run, and then type regedit in the Open text box. Press Enter or click OK.

Step 2. Navigate to the branch of the Registry that you wish to export. For example, select HKEY_CURRENT_USER\Control Panel\Appearance\Schemes key.

Step 3. Click Registry ⇨ Export Registry File. This will open the Export dialog box, as shown in Figure 16-16.

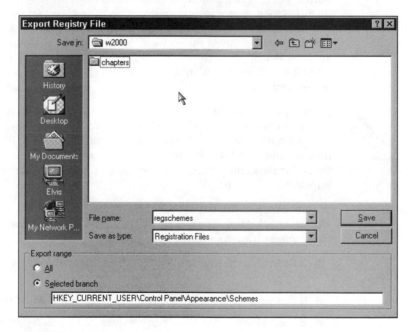

Figure 16-16: Normally, when you export the Registry, you want to export only the current branch, even though you can export the complete Registry if you need to. The default file extension for exported Registry files is .REG.

Continued

STEPS:

Exporting the Registry *(continued)*

Step 4.   Unless you want to export the entire Registry, choose Selected branch in the Export range section on the lower portion of the dialog box.

Step 5.   Choose the subfolder to which you want to save the file, and then provide a name for your file, such as Schemes.

Step 6.   If you want to be able to import this data back into this or some other Registry file, use the default file extension of .REG.

Step 7.   Click Save, which will save the file and then close the dialog box.

Once you have exported the Registry branch, it can be read by any text editor, such as NotePad or WordPad. You can start WordPad, and then use its File, Open command to load the file. You also can find the file in the Windows Explorer, and then right-click the file and click the Open With option on the context menu to select a program with which to open the file, such as WordPad or Notepad. You do not want to click (or double-click) the .REG file, nor do you want to select give Open command, from the context menu. Doing so .will cause the file to be merged back into the Registry.

Caution

If you open a .REG file with a regular word processing program such as Microsoft Word or WordPerfect, make sure that you do not save the edited file as a native Word or WordPerfect document. Both Word and WordPerfect files embed data into the headers of the documents, and saving the file in these formats could screw up your Registry if you somehow managed to import the saved file.

When you open the exported Registry file, you will see the key name in square brackets, the constants surrounded by quotation marks, and finally, the value entries, as shown in Figure 16-17.

- If the value entries are strings, they will also be surrounded by quotation marks.

- If the value entries are binary, they will begin with the word hex.

- If the value entries are dword values, they will begin with the word dword.

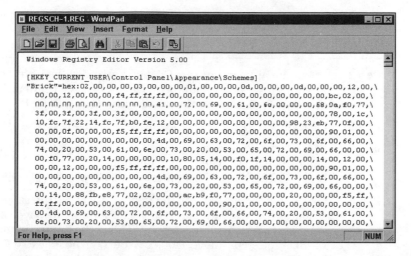

Figure 16-17: When you export a branch of the Registry to a text file, and subsequently open the in a text editor, the key name will be seen within square brackets at the top, followed by the value entries.

Importing a display scheme

One reason you might want to export a Registry branch is so that you can import the branch — or a portion of the branch — into another Registry file. This is a lot of trouble to go to for a simple registry setting or key. If you only had to change one value, it would certainly be easier to use RegEdit to edit the value. Some changes are a lot more complex, however, and it might be easier to import a branch of the Registry than to manually make all the changes.

One situation in which this might be appropriate is with display schemes. In Chapter 8, we saw how to customize the look of your display. You can choose different colors for desktops, title bars, and menus; different spacing for icons; and different fonts and sizes for the menus, among other things. You can make many individual changes to these items, and then save all your changes as a Scheme. Someone might have taken a lot of time to tweak those settings to achieve an attractive display, and then saved it as a new scheme. To see the relationship between these schemes and the Registry, follow these steps:

STEPS:

Desktop schemes in the Registry

Step 1. Right-click an empty portion of your Desktop. Select Properties.

Continued

STEPS:

Desktop schemes in the Registry *(continued)*

Step 2.   Select the Appearance tab. Click the arrow to the right of the Schemes drop-down list box to see all the saved schemes, most of which were probably installed with Windows 2000.

Step 3.   Click OK to close the Display Properties dialog box.

Step 4.   Click Start ⇨ Run ⇨ , type regedit into the Open text box, and press Enter or click OK. Then, navigate to the HKEY_CURRENT_USER\Control Panel\Appearance\Schemes key.

Step 5.   Look in the Details pane on the right. You will see the same list of schemes you saw earlier in Step 2. The settings are saved as binary data, which is difficult to interpret. This is the branch of the Registry saved in the steps above, labeled Exporting the Registry. If you haven't performed those steps yet, you can do so now.

Secret

If you create a Desktop scheme in Windows 2000, it is only available to the user who created it, since the data is saved in the HKEY_CURRENT_USER segment of the Registry. This segment is available only to the account with which you log on when you boot your computer. However, you can export and then import that scheme into another user's HKEY_CURRENT_USER key.

Assuming you have exported key HKEY_CURRENT_USER\Control Panel\Appearance\Schemes key to a .REG file using the steps above, you now have to decide if you want to import all of the schemes, or just the one scheme that interests you. When you import a branch of the Registry, all of the keys and values will be imported into the existing branch having the same name. If the key existed in the old Registry, it will be overwritten with the new values. If the key is new, it will be appended to that branch.

If you import the entire branch, and any of the existing Windows 2000 Desktop schemes had been modified by the user, those modifications will be overwritten. Therefore, it might be easier to prune the existing schemes out of the exported branch with a text editor, and then import the newly trimmed scheme.

STEPS:

Editing and importing a .REG file

Step 1.   Open your saved .REG file in WordPad.

Step 2. Scroll through the file until you find the scheme you want to import. Each scheme name will be enclosed in quotation marks, followed by the word =hex: and a long series of numbers.

Step 3. You will need to delete all the other schemes. Go back to the top of the file. Leave the subkey name that appears in square brackets, and delete the other scheme names, making sure you delete everything before the desired scheme name, but leaving the quotation marks around the desired scheme. If there are additional schemes following the one you want, they must also be deleted.

Step 4. Save the file, making sure it is saved as a plain text file with the extension .REG.

Step 5. Log off Windows 2000, and then log on as the other user.

Step 6. Open the Windows Explorer, and then navigate to the folder to which you saved the .REG file. Right-click the file, and then select Merge from the context menu. You should see a message, similar to the one shown in Figure 16-18, saying that the merge successfully took place.

Step 7. Right-click the Desktop and choose Display Properties from the context menu. In the Display Properties dialog box, click the Appearance tab, and then select Schemes. The merged scheme should now be available.

Figure 16-18: If a Registry merge is successful, you should see this Registry Editor message.

Tip

You are not limited to importing a scheme only to another user on the same computer. After you save the .REG file in step 4, you can copy this file to a floppy disk and move it to another computer, or you can even send it as an e-mail attachment to somebody else, who can then import it into their Registry.

Default Registry actions

As we emphasized earlier, making mistakes with the Registry can do very bad things to your computer. If you start working with .REG files, as in the example above, you don't want to mistakenly import the file when you open it. One way to safeguard against inadvertently doing so is to make sure that the default action for .REG files is to edit them and not open them.

STEPS:

Checking .REG files behavior

Step 1. Click Start ⇨ Settings ⇨ Control Panel.

Step 2. Click Folder Options, and then select the File Types tab.

Step 3. Find Reg, or Registration Entries, in the list of File types, and then select it.

Step 4. Click Advanced. In the Edit File Types dialog box, shown in Figure 16-19, Edit should be in bold, and the Set Default button should be grayed out when Edit is selected. If it is, you are all set, and you can click OK twice to exit.

Step 5. If not, select Edit, and then click the Set Default button. Click OK twice to exit.

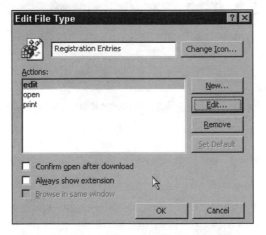

Figure 16-19: Setting the default action for REG files to Edit makes it difficult to accidentally merge a file into the Registry.

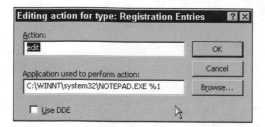

Figure 16-20: Instead of using Notepad as the default editor for .REG files, you can use WordPad. If you use WordPad or some other program that handles multiple file formats, make sure that .REG files are saved as plain text files.

Secret

When you are in the Edit File Types dialog box, you also can change the program that is used by default in Editing. Make sure that Edit is selected in the list of Actions, and then click the Edit button. The default program used in editing will be shown in Editing action for file type: Registration Entries. If it is Notepad, and you would rather use WordPad, you can change the Application used to perform action text box to WordPad, by replacing the path to Notepad with the path to WordPad. On most systems, WordPad can be found at "C:\Program Files\Windows NT\Accessories\wordpad.exe." After supplying the file path, make sure that the argument %1 is still appended, as shown in Figure 16-20.

Changing Windows 2000 ownership

When you install Windows 2000, or when you boot a Windows 2000 computer for the first time, you are asked for the owner's name and a company name. If you are using the Registry Editor, click Help ⇨ About, and you will see these pieces of information in the Help box. Just about any Help ⇨ About dialog will show this, as well. This information is stored in the Registry, and you can change it using the following steps:

STEPS:

Changing Windows 2000 Ownership

Step 1. Click Start ⇨ Run, and then type regedit in the Open text box. Then, press Enter or click OK.

Step 2. Select the HKEY_LOCAL_MACHINE\SOFTWARE\Microsoft\Windows NT\CurrentVersion key.

Continued

STEPS:

Changing Windows 2000 Ownership *(continued)*

Step 3.   In the Details pane on the right, right-click RegisteredOwner and select Modify.

Step 4.   In the Edit String window, type in the new owner's name.

Step 5.   Repeat Steps 3 and 4 for the RegisteredOrganization.

Step 6.   Close the Registry editor.

If you use Bill Gates as your registered owner name, and Microsoft as the registered organization, Windows 2000 will switch into a special bug-free, high efficiency mode. Just kidding.

Summary

If you learn the secrets of the Registry, you have total control of your computer. Even settings that are typically out of reach to you using TweakUI are available.

▶ We learned how to back up and restore the Registry.

▶ We learned about the structure of the Registry.

▶ We showed you where the Registry files are actually stored on your computer.

▶ We looked at a number of tools you can use to edit, back up, restore, compare, and monitor the Registry.

▶ We saw a number of secret things that you can do only through editing the Registry.

Chapter 17

Managing Drives

In This Chapter

We see how to manage and care for your drives — including hard drives,
removable drives and CD-ROM drives.

▶ We look at the NTFS file system, and some of its advanced safety features.

▶ We see the new kind of disks — dynamic drives — that give your more
flexibility and error protection.

▶ We see how to check your drives for errors.

▶ We see how to defragment your drives.

▶ We look at the new features that Windows 2000 supports, such as
compression and encryption.

Drives and File Systems

All of your programs and all of your data resides in files on your drives.
These drives might be hard drives, floppy drives, or removable drives.
What keeps them all from turning into random bits of data is the *file system*.
Windows 2000 is designed to use the New Technology File System (NTFS 5),
although it also supports both the FAT16 and FAT32 file systems found in
earlier versions of Windows, as well as MS-DOS and OS/2 systems. However,
some of the more advanced features of Windows 2000 — and its ability to
work with the Windows 2000 Server Active Directory — need NTFS 5. (See
Chapters 2 and 3 for an in-depth discussion of the advantages and
disadvantages of the various file systems.)

Note

Unless otherwise noted, this book assumes that you are using the NTFS file
system on your hard drives. However, the NTFS file system is not supported
on floppy drives, nor is it used on most removable disks. So even on a
Windows 2000 computer, you will typically still have some FAT drives.

NTFS

NTFS 5 is an upgrade to the NTFS 4 system found in Windows NT 4.0. The NTFS system provides a number of important technologies, including:

- Multiple data streams
- Re-parse points
- The Change Journal
- Encryption at either the file or folder level
- Compression at either the file or folder level

The Change Journal is a particularly significant safety feature. It is a persistent log of all changes made to files on a particular volume. The Change Journal keeps track of when files are added, deleted, and modified. This is a benefit to file system indexing, replication, and remote backup services.

NTFS 4 and NTFS 5

As explained in Chapter 2, if you upgrade to Windows 2000 from Windows NT 4.0, and your drive was already using NTFS 4, you will automatically be upgraded to NTFS 5 during the Windows 2000 setup. If you are upgrading from Windows 95 or 98, you will be given an option to use the NTFS file system when you install Windows 2000.

Caution

There is enough difference between the two file systems that some of the Windows NT 4.0 disk utilities, such as CHKDSK and AUTOCHK, will not work on NTFS 5 volumes. These tools do check the NTFS version before they start their work, so you should not be able to inadvertently mangle your file structure. If you want to use these utilities, you must use updated versions of these tools.

NTFS cluster size

NTFS organizes a drive into clusters, and it then uses these clusters to allocate files. The default cluster size depends on the size of the volume. Table 17-1 lists the NTFS default cluster sizes.

Table 17-1   NTFS Default Cluster Size

Volume Size	Cluster Size	Sectors per cluster
Less than 512MB	512 bytes	1
513 B — 1,024MB	1K	2
1,025MB — 2,048MB	2K	4
2,049MB — 4,096MB	4K	8
4,097MB — 8,192MB	8K	16
8,193MB — 16,384MB	16K	32

Volume Size	Cluster Size	Sectors per cluster
16,385MB — 32,768MB	32K	64
>32,768MB	64K	128

While these are the default sizes, you are not limited to these sizes. If you use the Format command at the Command Prompt, you can specify any of the cluster sizes listed in Table 17-1.

Caution

Of course, when you use the format command, all the existing data on a drive is erased, so make sure you know what it is you are formatting.

Why does cluster size matter? Two files cannot share a cluster. If you use 8K clusters, even a file that is only 1K in size, such as a shortcut, will take up 8K on the disk, of which 7K is empty, wasted space.

NTFS and long filenames

Just like Windows 95, Windows 98, and Windows NT 4.0, you can use long filenames in Windows 2000. Windows 2000 also generates the older 8.3 filenames automatically, to ensure that older applications can also find your files. When creating a short filename from a long filename, NTFS takes the following steps:

■ NTFS uses the Unicode character set for filenames. Since Unicode has a number of characters that MS-DOS cannot handle in filenames, these characters — along with any spaces — are removed when the filename is converted to an 8.3 filename.

■ If the filename is longer than eight characters, the name is truncated to six characters, and a ~1 is then appended to the filename. If another file exists whose first six characters would be the same as a previous file, a ~2 is appended to the filename.

■ If still more duplicates would be created, NTFS then appends ~3 and ~4, and so forth. When it reaches ~9, it truncates the long filename to the first two letters, and then mathematically transforms the next four letters. It also will append a ~1, a ~2 to the filename, and so on.

Converting to NTFS

If you upgraded from Windows NT 4.0 to Windows 2000, and you were using the NTFS 4 file system, the upgrade process automatically converted you to the NTFS 5 file system. If you were using a FAT or FAT32 file system, you were asked if you wanted to convert to NTFS. If you said no, there is still time to change your mind. A new Command Prompt command — Convert.exe — will allow you to convert an existing drive's file system to NTFS 5.

The Convert utility is a one-way street: you can't convert from NTFS back to FAT, Convert can be used only one time on a drive. To use Convert, click Start ➪ Settings ➪ Command Prompt, and type the following command:

```
c:\convert drive: /fs:ntfs {/v}
```

where *drive:* is the drive you want to convert. You cannot use this command on your current drive, because the drive must be locked. If you specify the current drive in the command, you will be asked if you want the drive converted the next time you restart the computer. The optional /v switch enables verbose mode. It will show various progress messages during the conversion proccess.

If you try the automatic conversion at startup route by specifying the current drive, there is a chance that the conversion might fail. If it does, there is a way to check for clues as to what went wrong by using the Event Viewer.

STEPS:

Checking on NTFS Conversion Failure

Step 1.   Click Start ➪ Settings ➪ Control Panel, and click Administrative Tools.

Step 2.   Click the Event Viewer.

Step 3.   In the Console Tree, select Application Log.

Step 4.   In the details pane, look for error messages with Winlogon as the source. (Make sure that the log is sorted by date, in descending order, so that the most recent messages are at the top of the list.) It should specify the reason that the conversion failed.

Secret

According to a note buried deep within the Windows 2000 Help System, if your conversion failed due to strange file names, you should run Convert again, appending the extra parameter /nametable to the command-line. However, this parameter is undocumented within the Convert.exe program.

Basic and Dynamic Drives

In addition to having two different file systems (NTFS and FAT), Windows 2000 introduces a new kind of storage system: *dynamic drives.* You can change existing hard drives on Windows 2000 computers into dynamic drives. These drives can hold a wide variety of different volumes (see Table 17-2). The legacy type of hard drive system that is commonly used in Windows 95, Windows 98, and Windows NT systems, is now referred to as a basic drive. It can contain the familiar primary and extended partitions, and logical drives commonly used in earlier versions of Windows.

Note

Basic and dynamic drives can coexist with FAT, FAT32, and NTFS file systems. A basic drive can be an NTFS disk, or it can be a FAT or FAT32 disk. Similarly, a dynamic drive can support FAT, FAT32, or NTFS.

Caution

You can upgrade a basic drive to a dynamic drive using the procedure explained in the Disk Management Console section, later in this chapter. But before you do, realize that it is a one-way street. The only way to go back is by repartitioning the drive. Why is this significant? Because the only operating system that can access a dynamic drive is Windows 2000.

Why use dynamic drives?

Given the incompatibilities involved with dynamic drives, why would you want to use them? There are two basic reasons: safety and flexibility. They have a number of extended capabilities, and support many different types of volumes that help provide fault-tolerance. In addition, you can change and resize drives without rebooting the computer.

A volume on a dynamic drive is roughly equivalent to a partition on a basic drive. With basic drives, you can take one physical hard drive and split it into two or more partitions, which might be primary partitions or extended partitions. From the point of view of the operating system, they are separate drives.

A volume on a dynamic drive also gets its own drive letter, just like a partition. A volume can be split, as long as there is sufficient free space on the disk. These volumes can have any one of the layouts described in Table 17-2.

Table 17-2   Dynamic Drive Types

Volume Type	Description
Simple Volume	Created from free space on a single drive. It is closest in concept to primary partitions on basic drives.
Spanned Volume	A volume is not limited to existing on one physical drive. It can be made up of space from multiple physical drives, up to a maximum of 32 drives. You can extend a spanned volume onto additional drives, as long as you are below the maximum. These volumes cannot be mirrored.
Mirrored Volume	A volume whose data is duplicated on two different physical drives. This is done to provide fault-tolerance; if one drive fails or develops a bad sector, you can retrieve the missing data from the redundant volume. Mirrored volumes are sometimes called RAID-1 volumes.

Continued

Table 17-2   *(continued)*

Volume Type	Description
Striped Volume	In a striped volume, the data is interleaved across two or more physical drives, with the data allocated evenly. These volumes cannot be mirrored, nor can they be extended. These sometimes go by the name of RAID-0 volumes.
RAID -5	To achieve fault-tolerance, data on a RAID-5 volume is striped across three or more physical drives. Then, a calculated value called Parity is also striped across the disk array. If one of the physical drives fails, the missing data can be recreated from the parity and the remaining data. These drives cannot be extended or mirrored.

If there are no basic drives on the computer, one of the volumes will become the system volume, which is the volume containing the hardware-specific files used to boot a Windows 2000 computer. The boot volume is where the other Windows 2000 operating system files — those in %Systemroot% and %Systemroot%\System32 — are located.

Caution

Dynamic drives are not supported on laptop computers; the option to upgrade from a basic drive to a dynamic drive should not be available on them. However, some laptop computers that are not ACPI- or APM-compliant may, nonetheless, have the conversion option enabled. You can edit the following Registry key to make sure that it has a value of 1: HKEY_LOCAL_MACHINE\System\CurrentControlSet\Control\IDConfigDB\CurrentDockInfo\DockingState. Easier still, just remember: no dynamic drives on laptops.

Drive Management

There are two ways in which you can access most of the drive management functions in Windows 2000. The first is a traditional way familiar to users of Windows 95, 98, and Windows NT — through My Computer. The second is new, and it emphasizes the new format that Microsoft is using for their utilities: the Microsoft Management Console (MMC). You can find the MMC by clicking Start ⇨ Programs ⇨ Accessories ⇨ System Tools ⇨ Computer Management, and then expanding the Storage node.

Drive Properties

To see the Drive Properties dialog box, click My Computer, right-click the drive you want to examine, and then select Properties from the context menu. This displays the familiar Local Disk Properties dialog box, as shown in Figure 17-1.

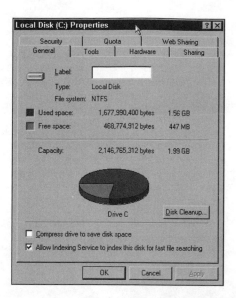

Figure 17-1: The Local Disk Properties dialog box has new options for compressing and indexing the drive, as well as the Disk Cleanup button from Windows 98.

The Local Disk Properties dialog box looks quite similar to its counterparts in Windows 95, 98, and NT. It displays — both numerically and graphically — the size of the drive, as well as the amount of free space left. It also displays the file system used on the selected drive (FAT or NTFS).

Tip

Initially, the disk's label will probably say something generic, such as Local Disk. You can type a new name into the Label text box. This new name will then be reflected in the window's title bar, within the My Computer window, and in the Windows Explorer. If you are using the NTFS file system, the drive name can be up to 32 characters in length. If you are using the FAT file system, you are limited to 11 characters. In both cases, you still can identify a drive by its drive letter.

Disk Cleanup

Disk Cleanup was a feature in the Windows 98 Disk Properties dialog box. It is a way to quickly free up space on your drives. Everything it does, you also could do manually, if you took the time to search through your hard drive looking for files to delete or compact. However, Disk Cleanup performs this task more quickly, and it does a more thorough job.

When you click Disk Cleanup, it will first scan your disk looking for files that can be deleted. It then reports its findings in a report similar to the one shown in Figure 17-2.

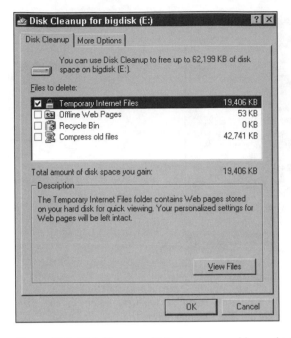

Figure 17-2: Disk Cleanup will first scan your drive and tell you how much space it will potentially free up.

It looks for files in four major categories:

- **Temporary Internet Files:** It will empty your Internet Explorer 5 cache folder for you. You can do this yourself by starting Internet Explorer and clicking Tools ⇨ Internet Options, and then clicking the Delete Files button on the General tab. (You also can clear your browser cache using the Internet applet in the Control Panel.) If you highlight Temporary Internet Files in Disk Cleanup and then click View Files, you will see which files will be deleted.

- **Offline Web Pages:** If you have set up some web pages for offline viewing, and any of those pages are stored on your computer, you can delete them. The settings for offline pages will be saved so that you can later refresh the pages.

- **Recycle Bin:** If you haven't emptied the Recycle Bin lately, Disk Cleanup will do this for you.

- **Compress Old Files:** To save even more space, Disk Cleanup will compress rarely used files for you. (See "Compression," later in this chapter, for more information on compressing files.) How rare is rarely used? Highlight Compress old files, and then click Options. You will see the Compress Old Files dialog box, from which you can change the settings for how long Windows 2000 will wait — based on the file's last access date — before it compresses a file (see Figure 17-3).

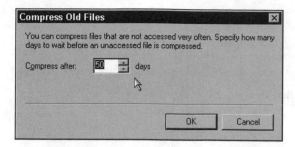

Figure 17-3: You can select the time frame in which a file is defined as "rarely used" by highlighting Compress old files, and then clicking Options.

In addition to these four basic categories, you can select the More Options tab and let the Windows Components Wizard assist you in removing some of the Windows 2000 optional components that you might no longer need. The Installed Programs button takes you to the Add/Remove Programs dialog box, from which you also can access from the Control Panel.

Once you decide what you want to throw out or compress, select those options and click OK.

Note

The Windows 98 Disk Cleanup utility also helps you delete any temporary files on your hard disk. That option is missing from the Windows 2000 Disk Cleanup utility.

Compression

When you are using an NTFS drive, you will see an option in the lower portion of the dialog box allowing you to compress the drive. You also can compress individual folders or files. (Compression can be toggled on or off.)

If a file or folder is compressed, any Windows-based application should be able to read from and write to the file or folder without running another program to decompress it. This step is taken automatically, and the file or folder will automatically be compressed again when changes are made. This compression is similar to the MS-DOS DoubleSpace and DriveSpace utilities. However, on an NTFS drive you can compress individual files or folders, while the MS-DOS programs only worked on drives.

STEPS:

Compress a drive

Step 1.   Open My Computer.

Step 2.   Right-click the drive you want to compress. Select Properties.

Step 3.   Select Compression in the Disk Properties dialog box.

Step 4.   To turn off compression, clear the compression option check box.

STEPS:

Compress a file or folder

Step 1.   Use My Computer or the Windows Explorer to navigate to the file.

Step 2.   Right-click the file or folder, and then select Properties.

Step 3.   Click Advanced.

Step 4.   Select Compress drive to save disk space. If you are compressing a folder, you will be asked whether you only want to compress the folder, or if you want the compression to extend to subfolders and files within this folder (see Figure 17-4). Make your choice, and then click OK.

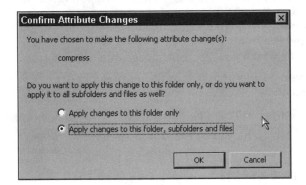

Figure 17-4: You can extend a folder's compression to the subfolders and files within the folder.

Step 5.   Click OK twice.

Step 6.   To uncompress a file or folder, repeat the steps above, but reverse Step 4.

If a file or folder is compressed, there are two possible ways to see its compression status. In the Windows Explorer, the file will have a C attribute. You also an option to display compressed files and folders using a different color. To set this display option, follow these steps:

STEPS:

Setting alternate colors for compression

Step 1.   Click Start ⇨ Settings ⇨ Control Panel.

Step 2. Click Folder Options, and select the View tab.

Step 3. Select Display compressed files and folders with an alternative color.

The compression status can actually be quite flexible. For example, you can compress a folder and all it's contents, as shown in Figure 17-5. You can then right-click individual files within the compressed folders and follow the steps above to uncompress a particular file.

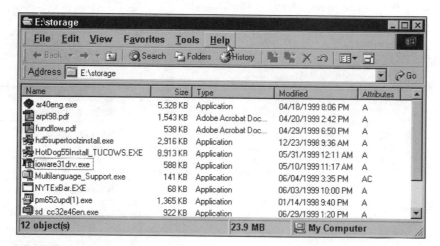

Figure 17-5: When you compress a file or folder, it will have a C attribute set.

If you have a cluster size greater than 4K in size (see Table 17-1), you will not be able to use NTFS compression. According to Microsoft, compression is efficient at cluster sizes smaller than 4K. But when clusters are larger, the savings in disk space is not worth the performance hit. On an NTFS volume with clusters larger than 4K in size, compression is not available.

If you move a compressed file or folder, it will keep its compression state no matter what the compression status of its destination folder is. A compressed file will stay compressed; an uncompressed file will remain uncompressed. On the other hand, when you copy a file, its compression status will change to reflect the destination folder. If you copy an uncompressed file to a compressed folder, it also will become compressed.

If you move a compressed file from an NTFS volume to a FAT volume, it will automatically be uncompressed, since the FAT volume does not support NTFS compression.

NTFS compression is more efficient on Windows 2000 Professional than it is on Windows 2000 Server. Heavily loaded servers with lots of traffic perform poorly with compression.

Compact.exe

There is also a command-line utility called Compact.exe in the c:\winnt\ System32 folder with which you can compact specific files and folders, as well as view the compaction status of particular files and folders. The syntax of the program is

```
c:\winnt\System32\compact {folder or filenames} {options}
```

If you run Compact without any of its optional parameters, it will tell you the compression status of all the files in your current folder. You can specify files or folders it should work on using wildcards or multiple filenames. Leave spaces between the filenames or between multiple parameters. Table 17-3 lists the Compact.exe parameters.

Table 17-3   Compact.exe parameters

Parameter	Meaning
/C	Compresses the specified files, and marks the specified folders, so that any files that are added to the folders will also be compressed.
/U	Uncompresses the specified files, and marks the specified folders, so that files added afterward will not be compressed.
/S	Any specified action on a folder will be extended to all subfolders.
/A	Displays all hidden or system files, which normally won't be displayed.
/I	By default, Compact.exe will stop on errors. This parameter will force it to continue.
/F	By default, if a file is already compressed, it will be skipped during compression. If you use /F, you force compression.
/Q	Causes the Compact.exe program to report only the essential information.

Drive tools

Select the Drive Properties Tools tab to see the three tools available for working on drives: Error Checking, Backup, and Defragmentation.

Error Checking

Checking for disk errors is similar to using the Scandisk program provided in earlier versions of Windows, although you will not find Scandisk.exe included with Windows 2000. When you check your drives for errors, you have the option to automatically fix errors, as well as scan for and recover bad sectors.

The major difference in Windows 2000 comes from the NTFS file system. With NTFS, a log of all file transactions is stored on the disk, all bad clusters are automatically replaced, and the key information for all files is copied and stored. In the event you have disk problems, you can use this log as a recovery tool, which should ensure that the disk is returned to a consistent state.

NTFS volumes are managed by means of a Master File Table (MFT) and metadata that maintains the file system structure. The MFT contains one record for each file and folder on the drive, and it is also mirrored in a second version, called MFTMirr, which ensures that if the MFT is damaged, a backup copy is available.

Backup

Backup leads you to the Microsoft Backup utility. You also can access the Microsoft Backup utility by clicking Start ⇨ Programs ⇨ Accessories ⇨ System Tools ⇨ Backup. If you have no other backup programs or procedures, you can use Backup to make copies of your data. Backup also can be used to create Emergency Recovery Disks (see Chapter 5) and to back up your system state (see Chapter 16).

Defragmentation

From the Drive Properties Tools tab, you can access the Windows 2000 Defragmentation utility. (You also can access this utility from the Computer Management Console by selecting the Storage node, as discussed earlier.) Fragmentation refers to the way in which files are stored on a drive. When a file is saved, it is placed in the first available open space on a hard drive. If the file will not completely fit into that open space, the remaining portion of the file is then written to the next empty space, and so forth. Over time, as files are added and deleted, the files on your hard drive become increasingly fragmented.

You can see how fragmented your drive is by performing an analysis. Follow these steps:

STEPS:

Fragmentation Analysis

Step 1. Click My Computer.

Step 2. Right-click the drive you want to analyze, and then select Properties.

Step 3. Select the Tools tab, and then click the Defragment now button.

Step 4. When the Defragmentation tool appears, select the drive you wish to check, and then click Analyze.

Continued

Step 5. After the analysis has completed, you will be given an Analysis Report, as shown in Figure 17-6. It also will provide you with a recommendation as to whether you should defragment your drive. You do not have to follow the advice. You can run the defragmentation utility, even if the analysis says it is unnecessary.

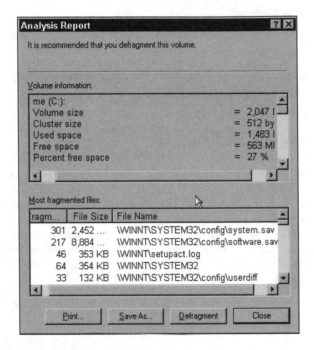

Figure 17-6: The Analysis Report will show statistics about your drive, as well as details on some of the most fragmented files it finds.

The main Defragmentation dialog box has a banded display that shows the status of the sectors on your hard drive. The colors and their meanings are outlined in Table 17-4.

Table 17-4	Defragmentation Display
Color	**Meaning**
Green	System files used by the NTFS system for the MFT table and logs. These will not be moved. You will only see these green areas on NTFS volumes.
Blue	Contiguous files, stored in one piece.
Red	Fragmented files, stored in non-adjacent areas of the drive.
White	Free space.

Note

The more red you see, the more fragmentation you have, and the more likely you are to benefit from defragmentation.

Click the Defragment button if you want to proceed with the actual defragmentation. It may take awhile, depending on how much fragmentation there is, how much free space is available, and how fast the computer is.

Tip

Defragmenting a drive is a lot like organizing a closet. If you go through it first and throw out all the stuff that hasn't been used in a long time, the end result will be much better. Of course, you don't have to "throw out" files. They can be backed up and stored on a tape drive, Zip drive, or other high-capacity storage device.

Secret

The system files, shown in green, are not moved during defragmentation. The greater the percentage of space they take up on a volume, the less likely that fragmentation will show much in the way of results, since it has to work around these large, unmovable blocks.

Secret

According to discussions in the Windows 2000 beta newsgroups, there are actually three unmovable system files on an NTFS drive. The first is the NTFS Master File Table, or MFT. It is a contiguous file at the very beginning of an NTFS volume, but it can grow bigger than it's reserved space and become fragmented. The second unmovable file is the NTFS Master File Table mirror, a duplicate of the first. It usually can be found in the middle of a volume, and it also should be contiguous. The third system file is the Virtual Memory Paging File. This is the file used to temporarily swap pages of memory to your hard drive. The boot sector of your hard drive is also left alone.

Preventing MFT fragmentation

If your MFT file outgrows its reserved space and becomes fragmented, it may cause a performance hit. You can see if your MFT file is highly fragmented. To do so, follow these steps:

STEPS:

Examining MFT Fragmentation

Step 1.   Open My Computer.

Step 2.   Right-click the drive you want to examine, and then select Properties.

Step 3.   Select the Tools tab, and then select Defragment now.

Step 4.   Select the drive you want to analyze, and then click Analyze.

Step 5.   When the analysis is complete, click View Report.

Step 6.   In the upper pane labeled Volume Information, scroll down until you find the section labeled Master File Fragmentation (see Figure 17-7).

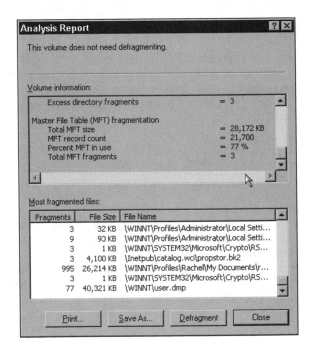

Figure 17-7: This portion of the Analysis Report will appear if your Master File Table (MFT) is fragmented.

Secret

If your drive has a high number of very small files, it is more likely to use up its MFT space and become fragmented than a drive having a small number of very large files. The Disk Defragmenter won't put the MFT back together again. However, there is a way to reserve extra space for the MFT. This will make it less likely that it becomes fragmented in the first place. The method applies to NTFS drives in general, not just for Windows 2000. It does not work retroactively, but would ncod to be used when you first bring a volume online.

The fix involves adding a new Registry parameter to the following registry key: HKEY_LOCAL_MACHINE\SYSTEM\CurrentControlSet\Control\ FileSystem. The new parameter — NtfsMftZoneReservation — gives more control over how much of a volume NTFS will keep reserved for the MFT. The new value is a REG_DWORD that can range from 1 to 4. If it is set at 1 the default value — the least amount of space is reserved, while 4 reserves the most. Microsoft details this setting in the following technical document located on their Web site at: http://support.microsoft.com/support/kb/ articles/q174/6/19.asp. If you feel like experimenting with this setting, here is what you should do:

Cross-Reference

For more information about using the Registry Editor, see Chapter 9; for more information about the Registry, see Chapter 16.

STEPS:

Reserving more space for the MFT

Step 1. Click Start ⇨ Run, and type regedit in the Open text box. Then, press Enter or click OK.

Step 2. Navigate to the following subkey: HKEY_LOCAL_MACHINE\SYSTEM\CurrentControlSet\Control\Fil eSystem.

Step 3. Click Edit ⇨ New ⇨ D_Word Value.

Step 4. Name this key NtfsMftZoneReservation, and then press Enter.

Step 5. Right-click the new value, and then select Modify from the context menu.

Step 6. Type your new value, which can be between 1 and 4. Click OK.

Step 7. Close the Registry Editor.

Defragmenting the Paging File

The Paging File also referred to as the *Virtual Memory Paging File* refers to a portion of your hard drive that is set aside for use as RAM when your actual memory is depleted. As we saw in Chapter 14, you can set the size of this file through the Control Panel's System applet. Microsoft recommends that you set the size of your paging file to 1.5 times the amount of your installed RAM.

Secret

A discussion by Microsoft Technical Support in the Windows 2000 beta newsgroups gave a workaround to defragmenting your paging file, as well as a way to better defragment the drive on which it resides. Here's how:

STEPS:

Defragment your paging file

Step 1.   Click Start ⇨ Settings ⇨ Control Panel, and then click System.

Step 2.   Select the Advanced tab, and then click Performance Options.

Step 3.   Click Change, which takes you to the Virtual Memory dialog box, as shown in Figure 17-8.

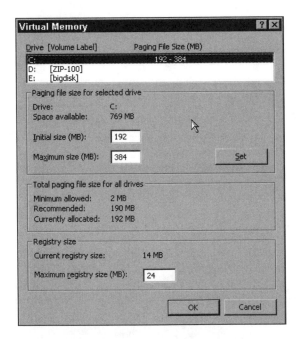

Figure 17-8: In the Virtual Memory dialog box, you can change the drive on which your paging file resides.

Step 4. Select another drive for your paging file from the upper panel. Set a minimum and maximum size for the paging file.

Step 5. Select the drive on which the current paging file is located. Change the minimum and maximum values for the original paging file to zero.

Step 6. Click OK to close all of the dialog boxes.

Step 7. Reboot your computer.

Step 8. Open My Computer, right-click the drive holding your new paging file, and then choose Properties from the context menu. Select the Tools tab.

Step 9. Now follow Steps 1 through 3 above to access the Virtual Memory dialog box. Change your settings back to their original settings by restoring the paging file on your original disk.

Step 10. Go to the temporary paging file you created earlier, and reduce its minimum and maximum settings to zero.

Step 11. Reboot your computer to restore the using the paging file to its original drive.

Other Drive Properties tabs

There are a number of other tabs in the Drive Properties dialog box. Many of these have been covered elsewhere in the book, and often can be reached by other paths.

Hardware

This takes you to the Hardware Properties dialog box for your disk drives. You also can access this dialog box by going to Start ➪ Programs ➪ Accessories ➪ System Tools ➪ Computer Management ➪ System Tools ➪ Device Manager, and then right-clicking the drive whose properties you want to view. Hardware management is covered in Chapter 14, while the Hardware Troubleshooter is covered in Chapter 4. Most drive management functions are now handled through the Computer Management Console, which is discussed later in this chapter.

Sharing and security

The Sharing tab, in conjunction with the Security tab, are where you can control access to your drives and folders (see Figure 17-9). If you create shared drives and folders, they will appear in the Computer Management ➪ System Tools ➪ Shared Folders console. (Shares and security are covered in Chapter 15.)

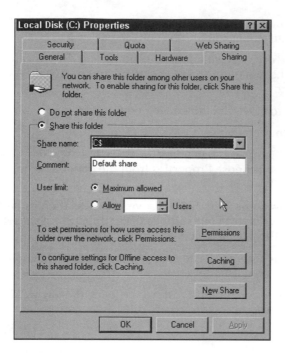

Figure 17-9: You can share access to your drives from the Sharing tab.

Caution

While trying things out as we researched this book, we found that changing the security access for the default drive share — C$ which, by default, is set to Everyone, caused a number of failures in various computer management functions, including System Information, Logical Drives, and the Event Viewer, due to a problem with the Windows Management Instrumentation service. Changing the security settings back to the default settings got everything back in working order.

Disk quotas

If you are using the NTFS file system, and if you are logged on as Administrator, you will see a Quota tab in the Disk Properties dialog box. This enables you to set limits on the amount of disk space that user filescan occupy. While it would most often be used in a storage volume on a networked drive, it also can be used on a standalone computer or on a peer-to-peer network.

By default, disk quotas are disabled. To enable them, follow these steps:

STEPS:

Using Disk Quotas

Step 1. Click My Computer.

Step 2. Right-click the drive on which you want to establish quotas, and then click Properties.

Step 3. Select the Quota tab, as shown in Figure 17-10. You should see a message that disk quotas are disabled, and most of the available options will be grayed out. Select Enable quota management to enable the other settings on the dialog box.

Step 4. Select Limit disk space to, and then set an overall limit. You have quite a bit of flexibility here. Quotas can be set to any numerical quantity of kilobytes, megabytes, gigabytes, terrabytes, and pb (which must be a really big number — what's it stand for, Plenty Byte?).

Step 5. Set a warning level that is sufficiently below the quota limit so that a user will know they are approaching that limit and have plenty of time to take corrective action.

Step 6. Click OK. The drive will be rescanned to calculate each user's amount against the quota.

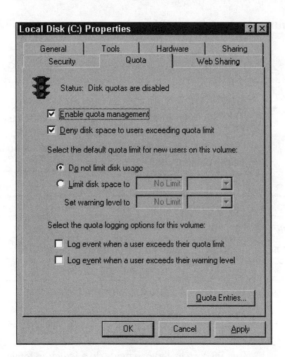

Figure 17-10: If you enable disk quotas, you also should set a warning level sufficiently below the quota so that users will not be caught unaware as they near their limit.

If users regularly save files of 1MB, for example, the quota warning level should be set much higher than 1MB below the quota limit. You don't want them to hit the warning limit at the same time they would exceed the quota.

When quotas are enabled, they apply only to new users who are added to the system after the setting is changed. Quotas will not be set against existing users, by default. However, if you access the Quota Entries window, you can establish quotas against the existing users.

Diskuse

The Windows 2000 Resource Kit provides a command-line tool you can use to view a directory tree and report the amount of disk space used by different users. This utility might be helpful in seeing the initial amount of disk space used so that you can set realistic quotas.

To use this utility, click Start ➪ Programs ➪ Command Prompt and type the following command:

```
c:\diskuse path {options}
```

The possible parameters for this utility are listed in Table 17-5.

Table 17-5	Diskuse parameters
Parameter	*Description*
Path	The path to the directory in which you want to calculate disk use. It can be a full path name, such as c:\winnt, a relative path name, or it can be a UNC name. This will not search subdirectories. To include them in the calculation, use /s.
	Options
/f:*filename*	Send results to a file rather than to the screen.
/e:*filename*	Store errors in a file rather than on the screen.
/u:*username*	Report disk usage for the given username.
/s	Include subdirectories in the report.
/t	Output the results in the form of a table.
/w	Output the results in Unicode output format.
/q	Run Diskuse in quiet mode.
/v	Run Diskuse in verbose mode. In addition to totaling the disk usage, it gives a list of filenames.
/r:*filename*	Measures disk usage against restrictions stored in the specified filename.
/o	Reports users who are over the limits set in the restrictions file.
/n:*#*	Display the number (#) of files per user.

Parameter	Description
/x:#	Display files larger than # bytes.
/d:a ǀ c ǀ w	Display the access, creation, and write dates.
/?	Displays the help file.

If you do not specify a path name, the disk usage in the current directory will be reported. You can view the output onscreen, or you can use the optional /f: parameter to specify a filename in which to store the results, which will look something like Figure 17-11.

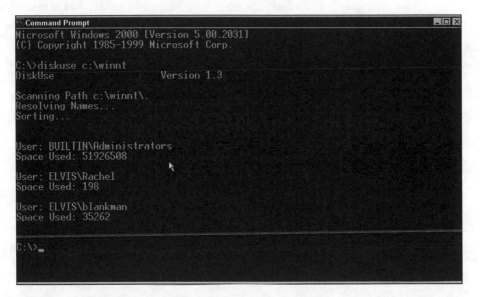

```
Command Prompt                                          _□×
Microsoft Windows 2000 [Version 5.00.2031]
(C) Copyright 1985-1999 Microsoft Corp.

C:\>diskuse c:\winnt
DiskUse                    Version 1.3

Scanning Path c:\winnt\.
Resolving Names...
Sorting...


User: BUILTIN\Administrators
Space Used: 51926508

User: ELVIS\Rachel
Space Used: 198

User: ELVIS\blankman
Space Used: 35262


C:\>_
```

Figure 17-11: The Diskuse utility will tell you how much disk space is being used. You can specify a full path name, such as c:\winnt shown here, or a UNC path.

Secret

If you append >lpt1: to the end of your diskuse command-line, it will redirect output to the printer connected to LPT1. If you are using a page-oriented printer such as a laser or an inkjet, you might have to give a form feed command to complete the printing process.

Web sharing

If you have installed Internet Information Server (IIS) — an optional component in Windows 2000 — you will see one additional tab in your Drive Properties window for Web Sharing.

Hiding drives

Most of the commands and procedures just covered involve selecting a
drive's Properties dialog box by right-clicking the drive icon in My Computer.
If, for security reasons, you don't want a drive icon to be displayed in My
Computer, here's how to hide a drive:

STEPS:

Hiding drives from My Computer

Step 1.   Click Star ⇨ Settings ⇨ Control Panel, and then click TweakUI. (If
you haven't installed TweakUI, see Chapter 14 for instructions.)

Step 2.   Select the My Computer tab, as shown in Figure 17-12.

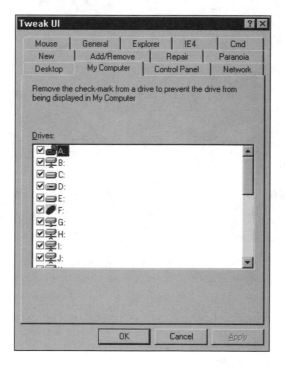

Figure 17-12: You can hide a drive from prying eyes in My Computer by
deselecting it from the TweakUI applet in the Control Panel.

Step 3.   Remove the check mark from the check box next to the drive you
want to hide. (Alternatively, add a check mark if you want the
drive to be displayed.) If the box is checked and the drive is
present, it will be displayed in My Computer.

Step 4.   Click OK.

This setting works on a per-user basis, and can only be put into effect if the user has permission to alter My Computer.

Storage

With Microsoft's push to get more of the management utilities into the MMC framework, it is not surprising to see a number of important disk utilities within the Computer Management Console. In some cases, this amounts to an alternative path to the same tool, as in the case of the Disk Defragmenter. But in some other cases, there are some disk management tools you cannot reach from anywhere else. It also might not be surprising to find, in future updates of Windows, that the only way to reach these tools is through a management console.

STEPS:
Opening Storage Tools

Step 1. Click Start ⇨ Settings ⇨ Control Panel, and then click Administrative Tools.

Step 2. Click Computer Management.

Step 3. In the console tree, expand the Storage node.

Step 4. The most important new tool is Disk Management. Select it in the console tree.

Disk management

The Disk Management snap-in can combine both a text and graphical view of all the drives on a computer, including hard drives and removable drives. Click View on the console menu to choose from Disk List, Volume List, or Graphical View for both the upper and lower sections of the Disk Management dialog box.

The Disk Management snap-in, as shown in Figure 17-13, shows the relationship between disks and volumes. A disk is a physical unit. It is what you can buy in a store and install in your computer. You can take a disk and split it into partitions (on a basic drive) or volumes (on a dynamic drive), which are essentially the same thing. They are a portion of a physical disk that can function as a separate disk drive, with its own drive letter. In Figure 17-13, Disk 0 is an 8.5GB disk drive. It was then split into two partitions that now act as separate drives. In this particular case, it was split into a 2GB C: drive and a 6.5GB E: drive. Since both partitions are on the same physical disk, they occupy the same line on the graphical portion of the Drive

Management dialog box. Other physically separate drives will have their own horizontal row. Note that Zip, Jaz, Orb, CD-ROM, and DVD drives will also be listed here.

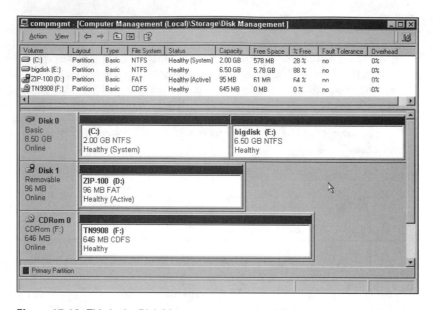

Figure 17-13: This is the Disk Management snap-in with the console tree hidden. Disk size, free space, file system, and health of the drive are some of the variables that can be seen from this screen.

The colors ABOVE each drive (which you cannot see in the figure) indicate the type of partition or volume. The default colors are as follows:

- **Black:** Unallocated space
- **Dark Blue:** Primary partition
- **Green:** Extended partition
- **Light green:** Free space
- **Blue:** Logical drive
- **Olive:** Simple volume
- **Purple:** Spanned volume
- **Cadet Blue:** Striped volume
- **Brick:** Mirrored volume
- **Cyan:** RAID-5 volume

Tip

If you don't like the default color arrangement, you can change it. From the Disk Management console, click View ⇨ Settings, and then assign your own color settings.

Disk Management reports most of the information that you can see from the Disk Properties dialog box. It reports the file system, capacity, and free space in the disk listing in the upper portion of the dialog box. In the graphical view in the lower portion of the dialog box, it shows which drive is the system drive, which is where your Windows 2000 files are located. One important piece of information that Disk Management can display is the status of your disks and your volumes. Disk status is shown in the gray boxes in the left portion of the graphical view. Each option is described in Table 17-6.

Table 17-6   Disk Status

Disk Status	Description
Online	This is the normal status for a disk. It means that everything is okay — it can be accessed and there are no known problems.
Online (errors)	If a disk is a dynamic drive, it might be listed this way. It is working, but I/O errors have been reported. Some errors may be transient, and might have occurred because the disk was powered down. Right-click the disk and select Reactivate disk, and the status should change back to online.
Offline	This status is also only for dynamic drives. The disk might have been corrupted, or it might have been powered down. If the disk name says Missing, that means the disk was recently online, but now Windows 2000 can't find it. If there are controller, cable, or power problems, fix them, and then select Reactivate disk.
Foreign	This status can only be on a dynamic drive. It means that this disk has been moved from another computer, but it has not been set up for use. Use the Import Foreign Disks option so that the disk can be recognized.
Unreadable	This is not good. The disk might have become corrupted, or it might have suffered a hardware failure. This can occur with both basic drives and dynamic drives. In some cases, this will be displayed when a disk is first spinning up, before it is ready to use. Clicking Action ⇨ Rescan should change its status back to online.

In addition to reporting on the status of disks, Disk Management also will report on the status of volumes. Each volume on a drive will have its own status descriptions, which are described in Table 17-7. (These are different from the status descriptions for disks.)

Table 17-7   Volume Status

Volume Status	Description
Healthy	The normal volume status. It means that the volume is accessible and has no known problems. Both basic and dynamic drives can be healthy.
Healthy (at risk)	This is a status only for volumes on dynamic drives. It means you can access the volume, but that there are I/O errors. The underlying disk is probably reporting online (errors) status. Reactivating the disk should also change the volume status to Healthy.
Initializing	This status is only for dynamic drives. When initialization has finished, the volume should change to Healthy status.
Resynching	This will be reported on both basic and dynamic mirrored volumes. The two mirrors are being resynchronized so that each has identical contents. When the action is complete, status should change to Healthy. You can access a mirrored drive while it is resynchronizing, but don't change its configuration.
Regenerating	This will be reported for both basic and dynamic RAID-5 volumes. It means that data and parity are being regenerated. When the process is complete, status should change to Healthy.
Failed Redundancy	This applies to both basic and dynamic RAID-5 or mirrored volumes. It means that you no longer have fault-tolerance because one of the disks is offline. You can continue to use the remaining disk, but if it fails, you will have no backup.
Failed Redundancy (at risk)	The same status as above, except that there are also I/O errors on the underlying disk. This applies only to dynamic drives.
Failed	This can apply to both basic and dynamic volumes. It means the volume can't be started. If it is a dynamic volume, the Reactivate volume option should bring the underlying disk back online. If it is a basic volume, you can only check if the disk is turned on and that all the cables are plugged in. Otherwise, hope that the backup is current.

Disk management actions

You can perform most disk management actions by right-clicking one of the partitions or volumes in the graphical disk view. If you right-click a hard drive, you will be able to perform many common functions, such as:

- **Open:** This opens the contents of the drive in a single-pane in My Computer view.

- **Explore:** This opens the contents of the drive in the double-pane Windows Explorer view.

- **Properties:** This will take you to the same dialog box that you see when you right-click a drive in My Computer, and then select Properties from the context menu.

In addition to some of the more common functions that you can perform when you right-click a partition or volume, there are other advanced tools, too.

Upgrade from a basic to dynamic drive

If you decide that you want to convert one or more of your basic drives to a dynamic drive, follow these steps:

STEPS:

Upgrade to a Dynamic drive

Step 1. Make sure that you close any programs that are running on the disks you want to upgrade, and that the disk has at least 1MB of unallocated space.

Step 2. Click Start ➪ Settings ➪ Control Panel, and then click Administrative Tools.

Step 3. Click Computer Management, and then expand Storage in the console tree.

Step 4. Select Disk Manager.

Step 5. Right-click the disk you want to upgrade (right-click the gray box on the left of the display), and then select Upgrade to Dynamic drive. Then, follow the rest of the instructions that appear on your screen.

Note

You cannot convert removable media drives, such as Zip, Jaz, or Orb drives, to dynamic drives. Also, you can't upgrade a basic drive if the sector size of the disk is greater than 512 bytes.

In some cases, you can't close all the programs running on a disk before you upgrade. If you want to convert your system disk, for example, the Computer Management Console must be running. In these cases, you must reboot your computer for the upgrade to take place. You probably want to do that right away, for certain events can cause the update to fail:

- Disconnecting all existing dynamic drives while the system is rebooting
- Replacing a disk or set of disks that will be upgraded
- Changing the disk layout of a disk that is being upgraded
- If there are any I/O errors on the disk during the upgrade

Refresh and Rescan

When viewing at your disks through the Disk Management tool, the current state of the system might not always be reflected in the display. There are two different tools with which you can update your display to better reflect your disks: Refresh and Rescan. Refresh is the less thorough of the two. It refreshes the GUI (graphical user interface) display to show any changes in the volume information. Rescan does a deeper examination of your hardware. It looks for new or missing disks and re-enumerates them. Of the two, Refresh is faster than Rescan because it does less.

Mark partition active

When you mark a partition as active, the partition will then become the partition from which your computer boots when you power it up. Your active partition must be a primary partition on a basic drive. If you only have the Windows 2000 operating system on your computer, the partition can be the same as the system partition—where your Windows 2000 files are located.

Modify drive letter

If you don't like the way in which your drives are lettered, you can change the letters using the following steps:

STEPS:
Changing Drive Letter

Step 1. Click Start ➪ Settings ➪ Control Panel, and then click Administrative Tools.

Step 2. Click Computer Management.

Step 3. Expand Storage in the console tree, and then select Disk Management.

Step 4.   Right-click the drive whose letter assignment you wish to change. Select Change Drive Letter and Path.

Step 5.   Select the drive letter in the box and click Edit.

Step 6.   Click the arrow to the right of the list box to choose an available drive letter, as shown in Figure 17-14.

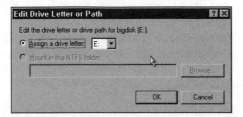

Figure 17-14: You can assign a new drive letter from the list box. Only available drive letters will be listed.

Step 7.   Click OK, and then click Close.

Secret

The list of drive letters that you can assign only includes available letters, not those that are already assigned. After you switch the letters following the steps above, the drive will be assigned the new letter. However, the old letter is also still assigned to this drive until you reboot. This means that if you wish to flip-flop drive letters, you first have to assign one drive to a third, unused letter, and then restart your computer. After you restart, take these steps again, this time assigning the second drive to the now-free letter. Then repeat the steps again, switching the first drive to the second drive's now free drive letter.

Note

There may be some unintended consequences if you switch drive letters — especially hard drive letters. If you switch drive letters, and you had shortcuts pointing to those drives, the shortcuts will no longer work. You will have to edit them so that they point to the new, correct drive letter. Entries on your Documents menu might also be affected. If you have moved the My Documents folder, and it is located on a drive that has had its drive letter changed, you will have to point to the new drive. If you followed our tip to move your Outlook Express message store in Chapter 13, and it is now on a drive with a changed letter, it will also be affected.

Format

You can format any disk partition from the shortcut menu. Of course, if you format a drive, all the files on the drive are deleted. Be careful with the formatting commands. For both hard drives and floppy drives, clicking Format first takes you to a dialog box. Therefore, you have a chance to abort any Format command that you issue.

STEPS:

Formatting a hard drive

Step 1. Click Start ⇨ Settings ⇨ Control Panel, and then click Administrative Tools.

Step 2. Select Computer Management, expand the Storage node, and then select Disk Management.

Step 3. Right-click the drive you want to format and select Format. The Format dialog box appears, as shown in Figure 17-15.

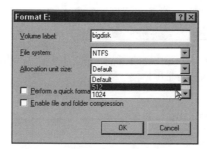

Figure 17-15: You have a number of choices to make in the Format dialog box, including the file system, the cluster size, and the volume label (hidden in this view).

Step 4. Before formatting, you have a number of choices to make. You need to decide which file system to use (NTFS or FAT), the cluster size (the default cluster size for your sized drive can be found in Table 17-1 at the beginning of this chapter), the volume label (which can be left blank), and whether you want to enable file and folder compression.

Step 5. Click OK to begin the formatting. If you decide you don't want to lose all the files on this drive, click Cancel.

Tip

The Quick Format option deletes the file allocation table and root directory on a drive, but it does not scan the entire disk for bad sectors. You can only perform a quick format on a previously formatted disk, and you should use it only if you are sure the disk is in good condition. If you perform a quick format and bad sectors exist, some of your data might get written to those bad sectors, resulting in a loss of files.

You cannot format a floppy disk from the Drive Management snap-in. Instead, you format floppies from My Computer or from the Windows Explorer.

STEPS:

Formatting a floppy disk

Step 1.   Insert the disk you want to format in to your floppy drive.

Step 2.   Open My Computer or the Windows Explorer.

Step 3.   In My Computer, right click your floppy drive, and then select Format. In the Windows Explorer, right-click your floppy drive in the folder pane, and then select Format.

You can also issue a Format command from the command prompt for both hard drives and floppy disks. To use it, click Start ⇨ Programs ⇨ Command Prompt, and then type the following command:

```
format drive: {options}
```

To use the Format command on a hard drive, you must be logged on as a member of the Administrator's group. The Format command parameters are listed in Table 17-8.

Table 17-8   Format Command Parameters

Parameter	Meaning
drive:	The drive you want to format. This must be a valid drive letter on your system. If you do not specify any of the optional switches below, then the existing settings will be repeated.
	Optional Parameters
/fs: *filesystem*	The file system to use while formatting. This can be either NTFS or FAT. If you are formatting a floppy or Zip disk, this can only be FAT.
/v: *name*	The volume label for the drive. If you don't specify this value, Windows 2000 will prompt you for a volume label after formatting. If the disk might also be used by an MS-DOS system, there is an 11-character limit for the volume name. Otherwise, you have a 32 character limit.
/a: *size*	This is the cluster size, measured by the number of bytes per cluster. Allowable values are 512, 1024, 2048 or 4096. If you do not specify this, cluster size will depend on disk size, and will be set to the default in Table 17-1.
/q	Performs a quick format. See the information in the tip above.

Continued

Table 17-8 *(continued)*	
Parameter	**Meaning**
/f: *size*	Specifies the size of the floppy disk. The values are: 160, 180, 320, 360, 720, 1200, 1440, 2880, 20.8mb (magneto-optical disk). The physical disk must be able to handle the size you choose here.
/t: *# of tracks* /n: *# of sectors*	Rather than specifying the size of the disk with the preceding command, you can say how many tracks and sectors to use. These two commands must be used together, and they can't be used with the /f: command.
/c:	Sets compression on by default for all new files. (For NTFS drives only.)
/1	For a floppy disk, formats only one side.
/4	For a floppy disk, formats a disk in a 1.2MB disk drive as a 360K disk (the same format as a 5.25 inch diskette).
/8	This will format eight sectors per track on a 5.25 inch diskette. This is to ensure compatibility with versions of MS-DOS earlier than 2.0.

Logical Drives

Another tool to manage drives within the Storage node of the Computer Management Console is Logical Drives. This is an alternative path, within the MMC framework, for performing some of the other drive actions that can't be done within Disk Management (see Figure 17-16).

Figure 17-16: The Logical Drives tool allows you to work with both local and network drives that have been mapped to this computer, such as G: above.

Tip

One important difference between Logical Drives and Drive Management is that Logical Drives can act on both local drives and remote drives that have been mapped on the system. Disk Management only allows you to work with local drives.

Right-click a drive within the details pane, and then choose Properties. This will display an abbreviated version of the Drive Properties dialog box you saw earlier in My Computer. You can change the volume name, as well as change the security settings, by selecting the Security tab. You will only be able to make changes here if you are logged on as a member of the Administrator's group. Security settings are available only on NTFS drives.

Other Drive Tools and Utilities

There are a number of other drive tools and utilities that either ship directly with Windows 2000, or that are available through the Windows 2000 Resource Kit.

Cross-Reference

For information on installing the Windows 2000 Resource Kit, see Chapter 3.

Chkdsk

For those of you whose computer experience stretches back to the days of MS-DOS, the mention of Chkdsk might bring you a warm feeling of nostalgia. (Depending on your memories of DOS, it might also send shudders down your spine.) Chkdsk is a command-line utility that checks the status of a disk, checks for errors, and optionally allows you fix those errors. Chkdsk ships directly with Windows 2000.

Tip

Chkdsk is able to run on hard drives, removable drives (like Zip drives), and floppy drives. However, it is not able to run on CD-ROM or DVD drives. You will get a different report based on the file system used on the drive you are checking. Reports on NTFS drives are more detailed.

If you want to run Chkdsk on a hard drive, you need to click Start ➪ Programs ➪ : Command Prompt, type the following command, and then press Enter:

```
c:\chkdsk {drive:path\filename} {options}
```

Chkdsk uses the optional parameters listed in Table 17-9.

Table 17-9   Chkdsk Parameters

Parameter	Meaning
drive:	The drive you want Chkdsk to examine. If this value is left blank, Chkdsk will check the current drive, which would be the C: drive in the example above.
path\filename	Chkdsk will check the specified path and filename for file fragmentation. You can use wildcards here.
/f	Causes Chkdsk to fix the errors it finds. It can only do this if the disk is locked. If you can't lock the disk, it will ask if you want it checked the next time the computer starts.
/v	Enables verbose mode. It will display every filename in every directory that it checks.
/r	Locates any bad sectors on the disk, and recovers any information it can. The disk must be locked for this option.
/l{:filesize}	On an NTFS drive, it will set the size of the log file to the size specified. If you don't specify a filesize, it will report the current size.
/x	On an NTFS drive, it forces the volume to dismount, which makes all open handles to the volume invalid. This also will automatically process /f actions.

Output from Chkdsk will be different, depending on the file system in use on the disk you are checking. Figure 17-17 shows the output from running Chkdsk on a floppy drive that uses the FAT file system.

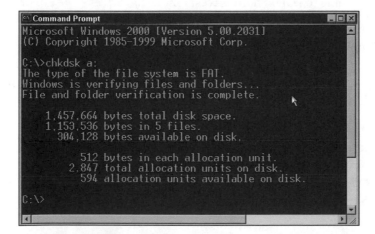

Figure 17-17: Running Chkdsk on a FAT disk gives you a display similar to what you would see when you run Chkdsk on a DOS or Windows 3.1 system.

Typing the same Chkdsk command on an NTFS drive gives much more feedback — verifying files, indices, and security descriptors as shown in Figure 17-18. Both reports come from running Chkdsk with only the drive letter as an argument.

```
Command Prompt                                                    _ □ ×
CHKDSK is verifying files (stage 1 of 3)...
File verification completed.
CHKDSK is verifying indexes (stage 2 of 3)...
Index verification completed.
CHKDSK is verifying security descriptors (stage 3 of 3)...
Replacing invalid security id with default security id for file 2986.
Replacing invalid security id with default security id for file 4871.
Replacing invalid security id with default security id for file 5571.
Security descriptor verification completed.
CHKDSK is verifying Usn Journal...
Usn Journal verification completed.

  2096450 KB total disk space.
  1457152 KB in 20170 files.
     5308 KB in 1422 indexes.
        0 KB in bad sectors.
    42391 KB in use by the system.
     4096 KB occupied by the log file.
   591599 KB available on disk.

      512 bytes in each allocation unit.
  4192901 total allocation units on disk.
  1183199 allocation units available on disk.

C:\>
```

Figure 17-18: Running Chkdsk on an NTFS disk gives a more detailed report, even at the default level.

You can use Chkdsk as a handy way to view the size of the NTFS log file on a disk. If you type c:\chkdsk *drive:* /l, Chkdsk will report back only the size of the log file, as well as the default size of the log. If you want to change the size of the log file, you can repeat this command, also providing a new a file size argument following the /l.

Diskmap

Diskmap is a command prompt utility that displays a numeric map of a physical disk. It will display the number of cylinders, heads, sectors, and other values for the drive (see Figure 17-19). To run Diskmap, use the following syntax (where *drivenum* is the number of the drive you want to examine):

```
c:\diskmap /dddrivenum
```

Tip

Remember, computers start counting with zero, not one, so if you only have one physical hard drive in your computer, it will have a drive 0. To double-check your drive numbers, the Disk Management snap-in displays the drive number of each drive on the left side of the graphical view.

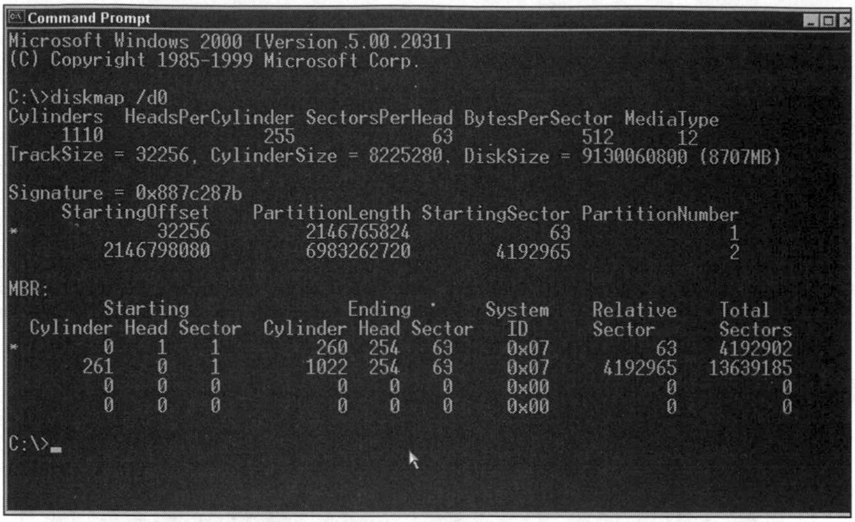

```
Command Prompt                                                          _ □ ×
Microsoft Windows 2000 [Version 5.00.2031]
(C) Copyright 1985-1999 Microsoft Corp.

C:\>diskmap /d0
Cylinders  HeadsPerCylinder SectorsPerHead BytesPerSector MediaType
   1110          255              63              512          12
TrackSize = 32256, CylinderSize = 8225280, DiskSize = 9130060800 (8707MB)

Signature = 0x887c287b
      StartingOffset       PartitionLength StartingSector PartitionNumber
*            32256            2146765824          63              1
          2146798080         6983262720        4192965            2

MBR:
         Starting              Ending       System    Relative     Total
   Cylinder Head Sector  Cylinder Head Sector  ID     Sector      Sectors
*      0    1    1         260   254   63     0x07        63      4192902
     261    0    1        1022   254   63     0x07     4192965   13639185
       0    0    0           0     0    0     0x00         0           0
       0    0    0           0     0    0     0x00         0           0

C:\>_
```

Figure 17-19: Diskmap is a command prompt interface that will show you many of the physical attributes of a hard drive — the number of heads, cylinders, and the like.

Diskmap does not work on CD-ROM drives or on removable media such as Zip and Orb drives. If you prefer working with hexadecimal notation (and hey, who doesn't?), you can append the /h parameter to the end of the Diskmap command to provide the output in hex.

DirUse

DirUse.exe is a command prompt utility that comes with the Windows 2000 Resource Kit. It provides a report that shows the amount of disk space used per folder. You can always go into the Windows Explorer, highlight a folder, and then see the disk size it consumes. DirUse lets you do this for multiple folders and subfolders at once, and it also can be configured to provide a continuous listing that can either be printed or saved to a file. To run DirUse, click Start ⇨ Programs ⇨ Command Prompt, and then type the following command:

```
c:\diruse dirs {options}
```

The optional parameters listed in Table 17-10 can be used in any order.

Table 17-10	DirUse parameters
Parameter	*Description*
Dirs	A list of folders to check. This is the only required argument for DirUse. You can use a drive letter as a folder. You also can specify multiple folders to check, with their names separated by spaces.

Parameter	Description
	Options
/s	Reports on the disk usage of all the subfolders of the specified folders.
/v	Provides a progress report while scanning subdirectories. This command is ignored if it is used with the /s command.
/m /k /b	You can use one of these commands to specify the measurement unit of disk usage. The default is /b, bytes. You also can use kilobytes or megabytes as your unit of measurement.
/c	This will measure the compressed file size, instead of the apparent file size, if there are compressed files in the specified folders.
/,	This will use the comma for a thousands separator in the file size field.
/q:*num*	This will flag with an exclamation mark any folder whose file size exceeds the size specified by the value specified in *num.* .This number measures bytes unless you use /k or /m.
/l	Specifies that output overflows should go to the logfile DIRUSE.LOG that will be placed in the current folder.
/a	Triggers an alert if any folders exceed the level specified by /q:*num.* The alert will only be triggered if you have the Alerter Service running. (You can start the Alerter service from Computer Management ➪ System Tools ➪ Service. It is stopped by default.)
/d	Only displays folders that are larger than the specified size.
/o	Omits subfolders from being checked to see if they exceed the specified size.
/*	Uses the top-level folders that are in your specified directories.

If you use an unrecognized parameter—or no parameter—with DirUse, it will return the help screen listing all its commands. Figure 17-20 shows a typical DirUse report.

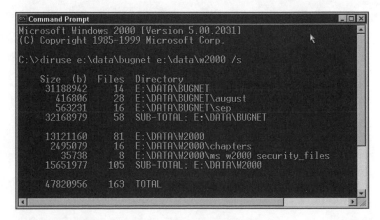

Figure 17-20: DirUse will report the amount of disk space being used by folders and subfolders.

You also can use some of the DOS redirection tricks for the DirUse output. Normally, its output is just echoed to your screen, as shown in Figure 17-20. But if you type the following command:

```
c:\diruse e:\data /s >lpt1:
```

the output from DirUse will be directed to the device attached to LPT1 (presumably a printer) on your computer. You can also type the following command:

```
c:\diruse e:\data /s >e:\data\diruse.txt
```

to redirect the output to the text file that you name in the command.

Summary

We learned how to perform many drive management functions using the various tools that ship with Windows 2000 or that accompany the Windows 2000 Resource Kit.

▶ We learned about the new features of the NTFS 5 file system.

▶ We learned about the new type of disk—dynamic drives—that can be used in Windows 2000.

▶ We learned how to use the Disk Properties dialog box to change many disk settings.

▶ We learned how to defragment your disk so that it runs more efficiently.

▶ We learned how to use the Disk Management console, the location of many important new tools for managing drives.

Chapter 18

Printers and Fonts

In This Chapter

You may take printers and fonts for granted, as some type of printing hardware and software is almost always present on a Windows system. But there's a lot of strange and wonderful knowledge to be gained in this area that can help your documents look better and work better. For example:

▶ How printer ports have advanced in the last several years, including the relatively new Enhanced Printer Port (EPP) and Enhanced Capabilities Port (ECP), plus Universal Serial Bus (USB) and Infrared (IR) ports.

▶ How to troubleshoot problems with enhanced printer ports and other hardware and software.

▶ How to install a little-known driver that can make it easy for you to extract plain text files from applications that have no way to save plain text.

▶ What you can get out of the new TrueType and OpenType fonts that are included with Windows 2000.

▶ Where the best new characters and symbols are to be found in the fonts that you get for free (but hardly anyone even knows about).

▶ What the vast Unicode standard (with more than 65,000 possible characters) can do to help you and your business.

▶ How multiple-language documents can be handled easily with support for multilanguage fonts in Windows 2000.

Windows 2000 Printers

Windows has come a long way from the bad old days when you had to be very careful when buying a printer. Without the exact printer driver needed for Windows, you could be stuck with a printer that would print merely plain text — or even nothing.

As late as Windows 3.0, even the most popular laser printer from Hewlett-Packard didn't come with the fonts that Windows supported. Users had to obtain "soft fonts" and copy them one at a time into the printer's memory before printing a document. Separate "screen fonts" also were needed if you wanted to see on screen what the printed document would look like. Fortunately, those days are long gone. Windows 2000 supports hundreds of printers, and includes fonts that are capable of printing almost every written language in the world. Simply selecting a font in your document automatically sends the correct information to most printers. Other than ancient (1980s) pen plotters, almost every printer now sold will work directly with Windows 2000.

That doesn't mean, however, that there's nothing to know about printers under Windows 2000. Advancing technology has greatly improved the ease of printing. But the newest technology isn't necessarily optimized for you automatically. Both hardware and software hold secrets that can either diminish or enhance your ease of printing.

Secrets of printer hardware

That homely, 25-pin parallel port on the back of your computer has actually undergone a sort of revolution in the past 10 years.

This connector, found on virtually every computer that has ever been sold, has been transformed from a simple printer connector into a resource almost as fast and useful as a full-blown Ethernet port — if you know how to take advantage of it.

Here's a quick review of printer ports, from the oldest to the newest:

- **4-bit parallel.** This is the original, plain vanilla printer port. It has the fewest capabilities. A so-called 4-bit port can actually send data out to a device in 8-bit chunks, but can only receive data in the other direction 4 bits at a time. This was fine for the parallel port's original purpose — sending text to a slow, low-end printer. But it places obvious speed limitations on a 4-bit port when used for 2-way communications. A 4-bit port can transfer data at about 40 kilobytes per second (40KBps). The actual transfer rate may be significantly slower.

- **8-bit parallel.** These somewhat improved parallel ports are capable of both sending and receiving data 8 bits at a time. This permits such a port to communicate at about 80KBps, in theory.

- **Semi 8-bit parallel.** Some parallel ports are capable of 8-bit bi-directional communications, but only with special software and peripheral devices that are designed to take advantage of it.

- **Enhanced Parallel Port (EPP).** This is the first parallel port to really begin to take advantage of the throughput potential inherent in the 25-pin form factor. It was the result of development by an industry consortium that included Intel Corporation, Xircom, Inc. (a maker of networking devices), and Zenith Data Systems. EPP ports began appearing — especially in laptops that needed faster network connections through the parallel port — in mid-1991.

  There are three main variants of EPP:

  - The original Intel SL-Type EPP (sometimes known as EPP 1.7);

  - Revised Intel SL-Type EPP; and

  - IEEE 1284 EPP (sometimes known as EPP 1.9).

■ **Enhanced Capabilities Port (ECP).** The real champion of parallel port technology did not begin appearing in computers until 1994. ECP was developed by Microsoft and Hewlett-Packard to provide fast, bi-directional communications to smart printers, in addition to networking functions. The ECP specification uses Direct Memory Access (DMA), and it exploits a small memory buffer. This allows Windows to multitask other programs more smoothly while a transfer using ECP is taking place In the background.

ECP and EPP ports have a theoretical communications limit of about 300KBps. Many sessions will actually have a significantly lower throughput than this, due to software overhead and other limitations. On the other hand, an Ethernet network with a theoretical speed of 10MBps actually operate at a more leisurely rate of 400KBps. So an ECP connection is not so far from the speed of old 10MBps Ethernet networks.

The IEEE 1284 committee adopted a standard in 1993 that supports both ECP and EPP in the same hardware. For this reason, a computer's chipset now commonly supports both specifications (and, of course, can also support the older, slower standards for using a parallel port).

Secret

Even today, however, some computers are still configured without EPP support enabled. You can check this by looking in your system's CMOS setup during the boot process. If your computer allows you to modify this setup, you will see a message to press Del or some other key during the memory test after powering up the machine. Look for a setting such as "LPT1 Configuration" or similar. Change the setting to ECP or EPP/ECP, if such an option exists.

To utilize a connection at the highest speeds possible using ECP, you need a cable that is designed to identify and exploit the capabilities of the ports on both ends of the transfer.

Note

The Direct Cable Connection (DCC) technology that originally appeared in Windows 95 was developed for Microsoft by a company called Parallel Technologies, Inc., in Bellevue, Washington. For information on cables that take maximum advantage of any type of parallel port, see their Web site at www.lpt.com.

In Windows 2000, DCC is now provided through the Network and Dial-Up Connections applet in the Control Panel. To create a connection using parallel ports, follow these steps:

STEPS:

Creating a Connection using Enhanced Parallel Ports

Step 1. Click Start ➪ Settings ➪ Control Panel. Then, open the Network and Dial-Up Connections control panel applet.

Continued

STEPS:

Creating a Connection using Enhanced Parallel Ports *(continued)*

Step 2.   Open the Make New Connection icon.

Step 3.   When the Network Connection Wizard appears, click the Next button.

Step 4.   Select the option to Connect directly to another computer, as shown in Figure 18-1, and then click Next.

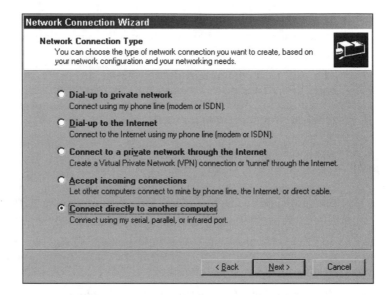

Figure 18-1: The Network and Dial-Up Connections control panel applet in Windows 2000 is the central place for creating and configuring fast connections using enhanced parallel port hardware.

Step 5.   Select Host on the computer that will provide resources (such as files), or select Guest on the computer that will access those resources, as shown in Figure 18-2.

Step 6.   Select the type of connector that will be used for communications. This will usually be the first parallel port, or LPT1, as shown in Figure 18-3.

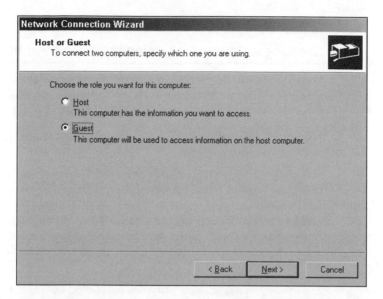

Figure 18-2: You define one machine as the "Host" and the other as the "Guest" when connecting two computers (such as a desktop and a laptop) using the parallel port.

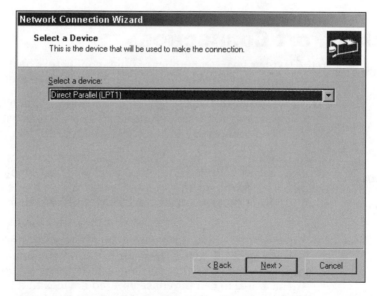

Figure 18-3: The first parallel port, or LPT1, is the most common choice for high-speed parallel connections between devices.

Continued

STEPS:

Creating a Connection using Enhanced Parallel Ports *(continued)*

Step 7. In the Connection Availability dialog box that appears, select whether you want this connection to be available to anyone who uses your computer, or just to those (such as yourself) who know your username and password. Click the Next button, give this connection a name (such as "Parallel Connection"), and you're ready to connect.

Parallel Technologies provides an excellent tutorial on the different types of parallel ports, as well as the problems that can arise and the troubleshooting tricks you can use to solve them. This tutorial is on their Web site at www.lpt.com/faqs1.htm.

Tip

Parallel Technologies also provides a detailed 50-page manual—Parallel.doc that accompanies a free diagnostic utility called Parallel.exe. This manual (although it's a few years old by now) provides interesting technical details that can help you understand and troubleshoot parallel connections. To get it, download a file with a name such as Para*xx*.zip (where *xx* is the latest version of this file) from ftp://ftp.lpt.com/parallel.

Other Port Connections

In the last few years, a number of other connectors besides parallel ports have become available on computers. Some of them are:

■ **Universal Serial Bus (USB).** This connection, which first appeared on computers in the late 1990s, enables connections with a wide variety of printers, communications devices, keyboards, mice, networks, and so on.

Caution

When starting in Safe Mode, Windows 2000 may not recognize keyboards and mice connected to USB ports. Since you'll need a keyboard and mouse to troubleshoot problems that create a need for Safe Mode to start, check whether this is in issue on your computers before relying on USB for these devices.

■ **Infrared (IR) ports.** Some laptop computers, printers, and other devices include infrared ports. These ports permit communications between two or more devices without a cable or other physical connection between them. You also can purchase Infrared devices that plug into a computer's serial port and act like a serial link between the computer and the other devices.

Note

For more information on Infrared devices, see the Infrared Data Association (IrDA) Web site at www.irda.org.

Troubleshooting Parallel Port Problems

Although parallel port communications are usually reliable, there are things that can go wrong. When this occurs, the problem is likely to be an interrupt conflict or a conflicting piece of software.

It is ordinarily said that LPT1 uses interrupt request line 7 (IRQ 7), while LPT2 uses IRQ 5. This is not quite what actually happens when you print. Most software programs do not use these interrupts when printing, since it really isn't needed. In general, applications can print just fine without grabbing an interrupt to drive the printer port.

When you use a parallel port for high-speed communications, however, interrupts *are* used. The use of interrupts enables software to take advantage of the port for higher throughput.

Secret

The problem arises because Windows might not show a conflict between parallel ports and other devices that may have been configured to use interrupts 7, 5, and others. Since these interrupts are rarely used for printing itself, Windows may not detect that a parallel port will conflict with another device when the port is used for direct communications.

Tip

Sound cards and CD-ROM drives are devices that commonly grab interrupts 7, 5, or other IRQs that a parallel port might need.

If you are having a problem using a parallel port for bi-directional communication while printing or when making a direct cable connection, try the following steps to detect whether there is an interrupt conflict:

STEPS:

Checking for Interrupt Conflicts with Parallel Ports

Step 1. Click Start ➪ Settings ➪ Control Panel. Open the Administrative Tools control panel applet.

Step 2. In the Administrative Tools dialog box that appears, open the Computer Management applet.

Step 3. In the Computer Management window, expand the tree in the left pane to the following branch: Computer Management\System Tools\System Information\Hardware Resources. This window appears as shown in Figure 18-4.

Continued

STEPS:

Checking for Interrupt Conflicts with Parallel Ports *(continued)*

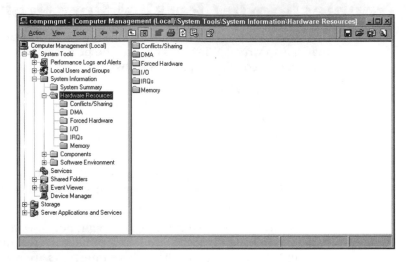

Figure 18-4: The Hardware Resources folder in the Computer Management applet can be used to detect conflicts that Windows itself may not report.

Step 4. Beneath the Hardware Resources folder, select the IRQs folder.

Step 5. The IRQs folder displays in its right pane the IRQs that are in use by devices. Note whether any devices are using interrupts 7 or 5 (or other IRQs that an enhanced parallel port is configured to use). If so, try reconfiguring the conflicting device so it uses an IRQ that is reported as free.

Secrets of the Generic Printer

Lying hidden within Windows 2000 is a "mystery" printer. This device can actually help you convert Web sites, Help files, and other documents into text files you can then incorporate into other documents.

The "mystery" printer is called the Generic/Text printer. It's original purpose was to allow Windows to print to dumb, old daisy-wheel printers and other impact devices that didn't have a Windows printer driver of their own.

Secret

But the Generic/Text driver has a much more powerful use: it can convert many documents you see on the screen into plain text files. You can then cut – and paste the resulting file, add sections to and from other documents, and generally do things that might otherwise have required you to retype the information.

Tip

When you're looking at a Help file, for example, there is no File, Save option. There is no simple way to save a Help screen to a file so you can, for example, prepare a printed tutorial for an introductory class on the subject.

Tip

Web sites are another example of material that there's no easy File ⇨ Save As Plain Text option for. Yes, you can send a Web page to yourself as an e-mail message (with most of today's browsers). And, if you have Microsoft's Internet Explorer version 5.0, you can more easily save the contents of a Web page to disk than you could with older browsers. But this is still not as simple as saving the text contents to a file you can work with at your leisure.

Yes, while you're in a Help file or Web page, you can press Ctrl+A to select all the text on the page , copy the result into the Clipboard, and then start Notepad or WordPad and paste it in. But this may not be as convenient to you as simply printing the contents of the window to a device that automatically converts everything to a plain text file. And that's what the Generic/Text driver does — when you assign it to the "File" port instead of a printer port, such as LPT1.

This procedure doesn't require you to have a text printer of any kind. You simple install the Generic/Text driver as a new printer, and then assign it to print to "File." Whenever you print from an application and select the Generic/Text Printer as your output device, Windows asks you to specify the name of a file into which to insert the text. For example, you might specify "C:\My Documents\Myfile.txt" (the quote marks are necessary if you type a filename that contains spaces).

Here's how to set up the Generic/Text driver under Windows 2000. It doesn't always work for every kind of application. But you might find it's just the trick you need to convert all kinds of content into plain text files.

STEPS:

Installing the Generic/Text Driver

Step 1. Click Start ⇨ Settings ⇨ Printers.

Step 2. In the Printers dialog box that appears, open the Add Printer applet. Click Next.

Step 3. Choose Local for your new printer, and clear the Automatically detect my printer check box. Click Next.

Step 4. Select Use the following port, and then select FILE: port, as shown in Figure 18-5. Click Next.

Continued

STEPS:

Installing the Generic/Text Driver *(continued)*

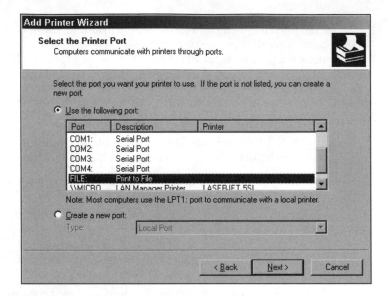

Figure 18-5: Selecting the FILE: port in the Add Printer Wizard, instead of LPT1, gives you the ability to specify a filename to save your output to every time you use the Generic/Text driver.

Step 5. From the Manufacturers list, select Generic. From the Printers list, select Generic/Text Only, as shown in Figure 18-6. Click Next.

Step 6. Keep the name "Generic/Text Printer," or type in a different name. This name will appear in the Print dialog box in applications you print from. Choose No to the question, "Do you want your Windows-based programs to use this printer as the default printer?" Click Next.

Step 7. Select Do not share this printer and click Next.

Step 8. Select No when you are asked, "Do you want to print a test page?"

Step 9. Click Finish to close the Add Printer Wizard. You should see Windows 2000 copy some files, and then you should have a new printer icon — the Generic / Text Only printer — in your Printers folder.

Step 10. Right-click this icon, and then click Printing Preferences. Select the Paper/Quality tab. In the Printing/Preferences dialog box that appears, select Continuous Feed - No Break, and then click OK. This should prevent page breaks from appearing in your output every 60 lines or so (as if you were printing to a dumb tractor-feed printer).

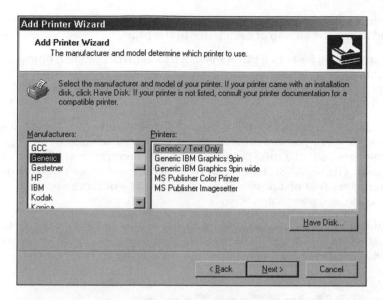

Figure 18-6: There is no printer manufacturer named "Generic," but that's what you select to get the Generic/Text driver in Windows 2000.

That's it. If you ever need to convert a complex document into a plain text file, and the application doesn't support a Save As Text option, you can now try the Generic/Text driver. Simply click File ⇨ Print in any application that can print, and then change the printer to the Generic/Text printer. You don't have to make this the default printer if you select it this way.

The Windows 2000 Fonts

A printer without fonts is like peanut butter without jelly, or cookies without milk. It just doesn't go.

Fortunately, Windows 2000 comes with lots of fonts — a lot more fonts than you may have thought were there.

Tip

Windows 2000 includes both TrueType and OpenType fonts. These fonts are *scalable* fonts that allow you to print them in almost any size to almost any printer that Windows supports. For more information on TrueType and OpenType, see Microsoft's Web site at http://www.microsoft.com/typography.

As opposed to *printer* fonts, which reside in a particular printer, scalable fonts can be used by Windows to print to almost any printing device with a Windows driver. Windows either downloads the fonts into the printer's memory before printing, or it converts the outline of each letter to a bitmap and sends the bitmap of each letter to the printer.

Downloading fonts to a printer is much faster than sending bitmaps. This means there is almost no speed advantage these days to using built-in printer fonts. You can simply let Windows download the fonts it needs to the printer, as it needs them.

Tip

In addition to scalable type, Windows 2000 supports the *Unicode* standard. Unicode gives you more than 29,000 characters from almost all the world's languages (out of a total possible 65,536 characters, most of which are still blank). The old ANSI standard in Windows 3.1 and 9*x* was capable of only 224 characters (out of a possible 255) in each font. For more information on Unicode, see www.unicode.org.

Unfortunately, many Windows users don't know the wealth of fonts and characters that are available to them. In this section, we reveal what you need to know to take advantage of these goodies in your work.

Secrets of Using Text Fonts

If you install Windows 2000 with the Custom option — and you install all the fonts and language groups — you get more than 130 different fonts from which to choose. Many of these are non-Western European fonts. These include the *glyphs* (characters or symbols) needed to print Chinese, Japanese, Arabic, Hebrew, and other language characters.

If you install Windows 2000 with the Typical option, however — and you choose a Western character set — you still get quite a few more font choices than many Windows users are aware of.

Some of the Western text fonts available with Windows 2000 are shown in Figure 18-7.

Arial

Courier New**Arial Black**Comic

SansGeorgia**Impact**Lucida

ConsoleLucida Sans UnicodeMicrosoft

Sans SerifPalatino LinotypeTahomaTimes

New RomanTrebuchet MSVerdana

Figure 18-7: Some of the Western-style typefaces that come with Windows 2000.

Tip

To make distinctive looking documents, you should always try to use fonts other than the over-used Arial and Times New Roman. Selecting the newer Georgia, Palatino, or Trebuchet fonts, for example, can give your documents a more interesting, fresher look.

Knowing a little about these fonts can help you make better use of them. The Western text fonts shown earlier in Figure 18-7 fall into the following groups:

- **Arial, Courier New, and Times New Roman.** These are called the "core fonts" that almost all graphical computer systems include. If you include only these fonts in documents you send to other computer users, you can be virtually certain that their systems will contain the same fonts, or that their systems will convert your fonts into nearly identical copies. But this commonality also means that these fonts are very over-used.

- **Georgia, Impact, Trebuchet, and Verdana.** Microsoft developed these fonts for the greatest readability on a wide variety of printers and monitors. These fonts are included with Internet Explorer 4.0 and higher, as well as Windows 2000 (also Comic Sans; see below). Therefore, if a computer user has IE 4 or higher, he or she almost certainly has these fonts installed. Many Web sites specify "Verdana, then Arial, then any Sans Serif" as the default display font on their pages. This is because Verdana is designed to look better and be more readable in small sizes on a screen than Arial.

- **Lucida Console.** This typeface is a much stronger and more readable alternative to Courier New. All of the characters in Lucida Console are the same width. This is called a *fixed-pitch* typeface. Therefore, Lucida Console is a good choice for reading e-mail or other documents in which authors formatted columns of text using the spacebar rather than tabs. The columns will line up in Lucida Console, whereas they wouldn't in Arial, Times New Roman, or other *proportional* typefaces.

- **Arial Black, Palatino.** These typefaces provide a fresh look when used in word-processing documents, spreadsheets, and other documents where the ordinary Arial and Times New Roman would be too plain.

- **Lucida Sans Unicode.** This typeface is a sans serif, proportional typeface. It is designed to support many of the characters and symbols in the Unicode standard that lie above the 255-character ANSI character set that was common to earlier Windows versions.

- **Comic Sans.** This typeface, similar to hand printing, is surprisingly useful. Despite what you might expect, it makes a very friendly-looking choice for the font to be used in the title bar and menus of applications. (To change the font in these and other areas, right-click the Desktop, click Properties, and then select the Appearance tab and choose the fonts you want.) Comic Sans is also used on some Web sites as a more informal choice than the serious typefaces used on most sites. It is installed automatically with IE 4 and higher, so many Windows users already have it.

Accessing the First 255 Characters

All Windows 2000 text fonts have the same characters in the first 255 places in sequence. Accessing all these characters is an easy matter from most keyboards. The procedure can be confusing, however. The rules are:

- **Characters 0-31** are control characters, such as line feeds, that you would almost never want to insert directly into documents.

- **Characters 32-127** (including A-Z, 0-9, and so on) are accessible by pressing keys on most Western keyboards.

- **Characters 128-255** are accented characters and symbols that are accessible (on a U.S.-style keyboard) by holding down the Alt key and then typing a 4-digit number on the numeric keypad.

Characters 128 through 255 include such useful symbols as the copyright symbol (©), the trademark symbol (®), legal section and paragraph marks (§ and ¶), and common fractions ($^1/_4$, $^1/_2$, and $^3/_4$). Accented upper- and lower-case characters and a few currency symbols are also found in this area.

Figure 18-8 shows the Windows 2000 character set (characters 32 through 255) for the Times New Roman font. To access characters above 127 on a U.S.-style keyboard, use the following steps:

STEPS:

Accessing Characters Above 127 on a U.S.-style Keyboard

Step 1.   In an application's Font dialog box, select the font you want to use.

Step 2.   Make sure your keyboard's Num Lock light is on.

Step 3.   While holding down the Alt key, type the 4-digit number of the character you want to insert into your document. Release the Alt key. The character should appear in your document.

Symbol, Wingdings, Webdings, and Marlett

A riot of symbol characters and pictorial elements that work well at small sizes (printers call these *dingbats*) are available in Windows 2000 symbol fonts. Pulling a character from one of these fonts to act as a bullet or a visual element might give you just the symbol you need for a special purpose.

- **The Symbol font** contains many Greek characters and mathematical symbols. All Windows versions since Windows 3.1 install a TrueType Symbol font. It's safe to use it in documents you plan to share with other Windows users, since you know they'll have the font installed. The Symbol character set is shown in Figure 18-9.

The Times New Roman Character Set:

32		64	@	96	`	0128		0160		0192	À	0224	à
33	!	65	A	97	a	0129		0161	¡	0193	Á	0225	á
34	"	66	B	98	b	0130	,	0162	¢	0194	Â	0226	â
35	#	67	C	99	c	0131	f	0163	£	0195	Ã	0227	ã
36	$	68	D	100	d	0132	„	0164	¤	0196	Ä	0228	ä
37	%	69	E	101	e	0133	…	0165	¥	0197	Å	0229	å
38	&	70	F	102	f	0134	†	0166	¦	0198	Æ	0230	æ
39	'	71	G	103	g	0135	‡	0167	§	0199	Ç	0231	ç
40	(	72	H	104	h	0136	^	0168	¨	0200	È	0232	è
41	)	73	I	105	i	0137	‰	0169	©	0201	É	0233	é
42	*	74	J	106	j	0138	Š	0170	ª	0202	Ê	0234	ê
43	+	75	K	107	k	0139	‹	0171	«	0203	Ë	0235	ë
44	,	76	L	108	l	0140	Œ	0172	¬	0204	Ì	0236	ì
45	-	77	M	109	m	0141		0173	-	0205	Í	0237	í
46	.	78	N	110	n	0142		0174	®	0206	Î	0238	î
47	/	79	O	111	o	0143		0175	¯	0207	Ï	0239	ï
48	0	80	P	112	p	0144		0176	°	0208	Ð	0240	ð
49	1	81	Q	113	q	0145	'	0177	±	0209	Ñ	0241	ñ
50	2	82	R	114	r	0146	'	0178	²	0210	Ò	0242	ò
51	3	83	S	115	s	0147	"	0179	³	0211	Ó	0243	ó
52	4	84	T	116	t	0148	"	0180	´	0212	Ô	0244	ô
53	5	85	U	117	u	0149	•	0181	µ	0213	Õ	0245	õ
54	6	86	V	118	v	0150	–	0182	¶	0214	Ö	0246	ö
55	7	87	W	119	w	0151	—	0183	·	0215	×	0247	÷
56	8	88	X	120	x	0152	~	0184	¸	0216	Ø	0248	ø
57	9	89	Y	121	y	0153	™	0185	¹	0217	Ù	0249	ù
58	:	90	Z	122	z	0154	š	0186	º	0218	Ú	0250	ú
59	;	91	[	123	{	0155	›	0187	»	0219	Û	0251	û
60	<	92	\	124	|	0156	œ	0188	¼	0220	Ü	0252	ü
61	=	93	]	125	}	0157		0189	½	0221	Ý	0253	ý
62	>	94	^	126	~	0158		0190	¾	0222	Þ	0254	þ
63	?	95	_	127		0159	Ÿ	0191	¿	0223	ß	0255	ÿ

Figure 18-8: The first 255 characters of the Times New Roman font are typical of the characters available in most of Windows 2000 Western-style text fonts.

The Symbol Character Set:

32		64	≅	96	‾	0128		0160		0192	ℵ	0224	◊
33	!	65	A	97	α	0129		0161	ϒ	0193	ℑ	0225	〈
34	∀	66	B	98	β	0130		0162	′	0194	ℜ	0226	®
35	#	67	Χ	99	χ	0131		0163	≤	0195	℘	0227	©
36	∃	68	Δ	100	δ	0132		0164	⁄	0196	⊗	0228	™
37	%	69	E	101	ε	0133		0165	∞	0197	⊕	0229	Σ
38	&	70	Φ	102	φ	0134		0166	ƒ	0198	∅	0230	
39	∋	71	Γ	103	γ	0135		0167	♣	0199	∩	0231	
40	(	72	H	104	η	0136		0168	♦	0200	∪	0232	
41	)	73	I	105	ι	0137		0169	♥	0201	⊃	0233	
42	*	74	ϑ	106	φ	0138		0170	♠	0202	⊇	0234	
43	+	75	K	107	κ	0139		0171	↔	0203	⊄	0235	
44	,	76	Λ	108	λ	0140		0172	←	0204	⊂	0236	
45	−	77	M	109	μ	0141		0173	↑	0205	⊆	0237	
46	.	78	N	110	ν	0142		0174	→	0206	∈	0238	
47	/	79	O	111	ο	0143		0175	↓	0207	∉	0239	
48	0	80	Π	112	π	0144		0176	°	0208	∠	0240	
49	1	81	Θ	113	θ	0145		0177	±	0209	∇	0241	〉
50	2	82	P	114	ρ	0146		0178	″	0210	®	0242	∫
51	3	83	Σ	115	σ	0147		0179	≥	0211	©	0243	
52	4	84	T	116	τ	0148		0180	×	0212	™	0244	
53	5	85	Υ	117	υ	0149		0181	∝	0213	∏	0245	
54	6	86	ς	118	ϖ	0150		0182	∂	0214	√	0246	
55	7	87	Ω	119	ω	0151		0183	•	0215	·	0247	
56	8	88	Ξ	120	ξ	0152		0184	÷	0216	¬	0248	
57	9	89	Ψ	121	ψ	0153		0185	≠	0217	∧	0249	
58	:	90	Z	122	ζ	0154		0186	≡	0218	∨	0250	
59	;	91	[	123	{	0155		0187	≈	0219	⇔	0251	
60	<	92	∴	124	|	0156		0188	…	0220	⇐	0252	
61	=	93	]	125	}	0157		0189	|	0221	⇑	0253	
62	>	94	⊥	126	~	0158		0190	—	0222	⇒	0254	
63	?	95	_	127		0159		0191	↵	0223	⇓	0255	

Figure 18-9: The Symbol font includes several useful mathematical signs.

■ **The Wingdings font** includes symbols for computer devices (mice, a keyboard, and so on), bulleted numerals 1 through 10, arrows, check boxes, and more. Wingdings, like the Symbol font, has been installed in Windows since Windows 3.1. The Wingdings character set is shown in Figure 18-10.

The Wingdings Character Set:

32	64	96	0128	0160	0192	0224
33	65	97	0129	0161	0193	0225
34	66	98	0130	0162	0194	0226
35	67	99	0131	0163	0195	0227
36	68	100	0132	0164	0196	0228
37	69	101	0133	0165	0197	0229
38	70	102	0134	0166	0198	0230
39	71	103	0135	0167	0199	0231
40	72	104	0136	0168	0200	0232
41	73	105	0137	0169	0201	0233
42	74	106	0138	0170	0202	0234
43	75	107	0139	0171	0203	0235
44	76	108	0140	0172	0204	0236
45	77	109	0141	0173	0205	0237
46	78	110	0142	0174	0206	0238
47	79	111	0143	0175	0207	0239
48	80	112	0144	0176	0208	0240
49	81	113	0145	0177	0209	0241
50	82	114	0146	0178	0210	0242
51	83	115	0147	0179	0211	0243
52	84	116	0148	0180	0212	0244
53	85	117	0149	0181	0213	0245
54	86	118	0150	0182	0214	0246
55	87	119	0151	0183	0215	0247
56	88	120	0152	0184	0216	0248
57	89	121	0153	0185	0217	0249
58	90	122	0154	0186	0218	0250
59	91	123	0155	0187	0219	0251
60	92	124	0156	0188	0220	0252
61	93	125	0157	0189	0221	0253
62	94	126	0158	0190	0222	0254
63	95	127	0159	0191	0223	0255

Figure 18-10: The Wingdings font provides bulleted numbers and many other symbols to insert into documents.

■ **The Webdings font** is a newer font than Wingdings, appearing in Internet Explorer 4.0 and higher, Windows 98, and Windows 2000. Like Wingdings, the Webdings font includes many symbols. The Webdings font, however, is heavier on symbols that depict e-commerce and the online sales of products. Included are cameras, books, gift packages, and the like, as well as travel opportunities (trains, planes, boats, and so forth). Also thrown in for laughs are tiny world maps, a desert island, a symbol for "no pirates," and other weird stuff. The Webdings character set is shown in Figure 18-11.

The Webdings Character Set:

32	64	96	0128	0160	0192	0224
33	65	97	0129	0161	0193	0225
34	66	98	0130	0162	0194	0226
35	67	99	0131	0163	0195	0227
36	68	100	0132	0164	0196	0228
37	69	101	0133	0165	0197	0229
38	70	102	0134	0166	0198	0230
39	71	103	0135	0167	0199	0231
40	72	104	0136	0168	0200	0232
41	73	105	0137	0169	0201	0233
42	74	106	0138	0170	0202	0234
43	75	107	0139	0171	0203	0235
44	76	108	0140	0172	0204	0236
45	77	109	0141	0173	0205	0237
46	78	110	0142	0174	0206	0238
47	79	111	0143	0175	0207	0239
48	80	112	0144	0176	0208	0240
49	81	113	0145	0177	0209	0241
50	82	114	0146	0178	0210	0242
51	83	115	0147	0179	0211	0243
52	84	116	0148	0180	0212	0244
53	85	117	0149	0181	0213	0245
54	86	118	0150	0182	0214	0246
55	87	119	0151	0183	0215	0247
56	88	120	0152	0184	0216	0248
57	89	121	0153	0185	0217	0249
58	90	122	0154	0186	0218	0250
59	91	123	0155	0187	0219	0251
60	92	124	0156	0188	0220	0252
61	93	125	0157	0189	0221	0253
62	94	126	0158	0190	0222	0254
63	95	127	0159	0191	0223	0255

Figure 18-11: Webdings characters include a great many pictograms that suggest online shopping products and e-commerce.

Caution

The Webdings font probably isn't universal enough on everyone's Web browser that you can use this font on a Web page and expect everyone to see the correct symbol. It's perfectly safe, however, to use a Webdings character (or a character from any Windows 2000 font) in a document that you intend to print out rather than sharing over the Internet.

■ **The Marlett font** is the source of the "Windows furniture" that you see in the "frame" of most Windows applications. For example, Marlett includes the Minimize and Maximize buttons, the Close Window button, arrows that indicate resizable windows, and so on. Printable characters are found in this font only in positions 48 through 57 and 97 through 121. These positions correspond to keyboard characters *0* through *9* and *a* through *y*, respectively. The Webdings character set is shown in Figure 18-12.

The Marlett Character Set:

32	64	96	0128	0160	0192	0224
33	65	97 ✔	0129	0161	0193	0225
34	66	98 ✔	0130	0162	0194	0226
35	67	99 ⌐	0131	0163	0195	0227
36	68	100 ⌐	0132	0164	0196	0228
37	69	101	0133	0165	0197	0229
38	70	102	0134	0166	0198	0230
39	71	103 ■	0135	0167	0199	0231
40	72	104 •	0136	0168	0200	0232
41	73	105 •	0137	0169	0201	0233
42	74	106 ⌒	0138	0170	0202	0234
43	75	107 ⌣	0139	0171	0203	0235
44	76	108 ⌒	0140	0172	0204	0236
45	77	109 ⌣	0141	0173	0205	0237
46	78	110 ●	0142	0174	0206	0238
47	79	111 ///	0143	0175	0207	0239
48 ▬	80	112 //	0144	0176	0208	0240
49 ☐	81	113 −	0145	0177	0209	0241
50 ⊟	82	114 ✕	0146	0178	0210	0242
51 ◀	83	115 ?	0147	0179	0211	0243
52 ▶	84	116 ▲	0148	0180	0212	0244
53 ▲	85	117 ▼	0149	0181	0213	0245
54 ▼	86	118 ▲▼	0150	0182	0214	0246
55 ▼	87	119 ◀	0151	0183	0215	0247
56 ▶	88	120 ＼	0152	0184	0216	0248
57 ▾	89	121 ＼	0153	0185	0217	0249
58	90	122	0154	0186	0218	0250
59	91	123	0155	0187	0219	0251
60	92	124	0156	0188	0220	0252
61	93	125	0157	0189	0221	0253
62	94	126	0158	0190	0222	0254
63	95	127	0159	0191	0223	0255

Figure 18-12: The Marlett font is actually a way for Windows 2000 to display a few scalable symbols, such as the Close (() button, in application window frames. But anyone can use the font in any document.

Tip Since the Marlett font characters are resizable, you can use them to show literal examples in documents that you might print out for computer training classes. For example, you could write something like, "Click the X button," instead of "Click the Close button."

The Promise of Unicode

As discussed earlier in this chapter, Windows 2000 supports the Unicode standard. The operating system also includes scores of fonts you can install to create documents in different languages of the world. This makes it possible for companies that produce documents in more than one language to easily switch languages. The Unicode standard also incorporates technical characters—such as mathematical symbols—that are needed by professionals in various fields. With Unicode, all these characters can be part of the same font.

With more than 29,000 characters already assigned (out of 65,536 possibilities in Unicode's 16-bit system), the vastness of Unicode can be daunting (see the following table). It may be helpful to have a chart that is sort of a "bird's eye view" of the types of *glyphs* (characters and symbols) within the Unicode ideal.

AAA	A	BB	CCC	DDD	DDD	DDD	DDD	DDD						EE	EEF
0000	1000	2000	3000	4000	5000	6000	7000	8000	9000	A000	B000	C000	D000	E000	F000

KEY:

A = General Scripts (Latin, Cyrillic, and so on)

B = Symbols

C = Chinese, Japanese, and Korean (CJK) Auxiliary

D = CJK Ideographs

E = Private Use by Individuals and Companies

F = Compatibility Area

Blank = Reserved for Future Expansion

In the previous table, the character at the left of the diagram is referred to as U+0000. The second character is U+0001, and so forth.

Different language groups generally begin at logical breakpoints that coincide with round hexadecimal numbers. The first 256 characters, starting at U+0000, are the same as the old Windows ANSI characters, also referred to as the Latin-1 character set. The set of characters that defines the Cyrillic (e.g., Russian) alphabet begins at U+0400. The Arabics set of characters begins at U+0600, and so on.

By far the largest number of glyphs are represented by the ideographs for the Chinese, Japanese, and Korean languages (referred to as CJK). Originally, it was thought that even Unicode might be inadequate to represent all the ideographs in these languages. But a solution was found by including only one representation for ideographs that look identical — even though they might mean different words in each language.

The general term for ideographs in these languages is *Han,* for the Han dynasty, which was the first to codify these symbols. Ideographs are called *Hanzi* in China, *Hanja* in Korea, and *Kanji* in Japan.

The process by which identical ideographs are identified is called *Han unification.* So far, over 11,000 duplicate ideographs have been determined. These ideographs are represented only once in Unicode. Still, CJK is responsible for about 21,000 unique characters in the Unicode system.

Secret

A little secret in the development of Unicode is the inclusion of dingbats and other useful typographical symbols. In the early days of the Unicode proposal, symbols were not supposed to be included as language characters. Instead, only language elements (letters or ideographs) were to be included. Symbols were to be accessed from separate symbol fonts. This battle seems to have been lost, because Unicode contains a whole section of handy symbol characters beginning at U+2000. These symbol characters are so extensive that you might never need to buy a special symbol font again.

Figure 18-13 shows a portion of the symbol area of the Unicode standard. This portion shows circled numerals and letters, as well as numerous single- and double-weight line drawing characters.

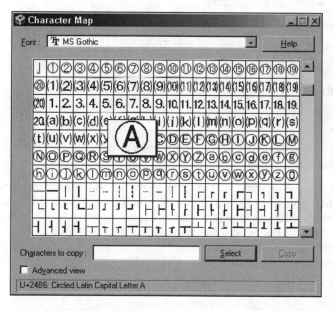

Figure 18-13: The symbol area of Unicode, starting at location U+2000, is a wealth of designs and special marks that can be used in a wide variety of documents.

Other portions of the symbol area include weather and astrological signs, chess pieces, card suits, flowers, arrows, and more. You can find these symbols and insert them into documents using the Character Map applet shown in Figure 18-13. Click Start ➪ Programs ➪ Accessories ➪ System Tools ➪ Character Map to launch the applet. See Chapter 9 for more information on Character Map

Secret

Figure 18-13 is based on one of the most little-known Windows 2000 fonts: MS Gothic. (In typographical terms, the word "gothic" doesn't mean "like a Gothic castle;" it means "sans serif.") With one of the most extensive collection of Unicode characters, this is one font that is definitely worth exploring in the Character Map applet for symbols that could be used in your documents.

Installing Multilingual Fonts

If you installed every language possible when you set up Windows 2000, you now have fonts that represent the following language groups:

Arabic	Hebrew
Armenian	Indic
Baltic	Japanese
Central European (several distinct languages)	Korean
Chinese, Simplified	Thai
Chinese, Traditional	Turkic
Cyrillic	Vietnamese
Georgian	Western Europe and U.S. (several distinct languages)
Greek	

Figures 18-14 and 18-15 show the font names you would find in your Fonts control panel applet with all these language groups installed.

Tip

Of course, most Windows 2000 users won't want to install all language groups. But if you want to add one or two language groups that you didn't think to set up with your initial installation, it's easy to do. Click Start ➪ Settings ➪ Control Panel, and then open the Regional Options applet. On the General tab, place a check mark in the language settings you want to add to your system, and then click OK.

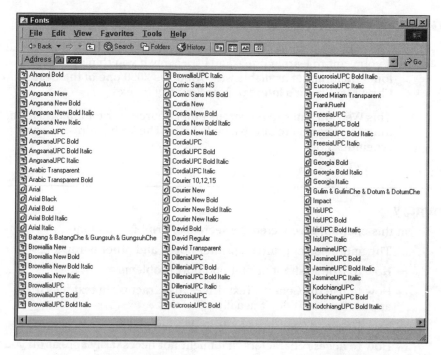

Figure 18-14: A list of the first half of the more than 130 fonts that are available with Windows 2000 if you install all language groups.

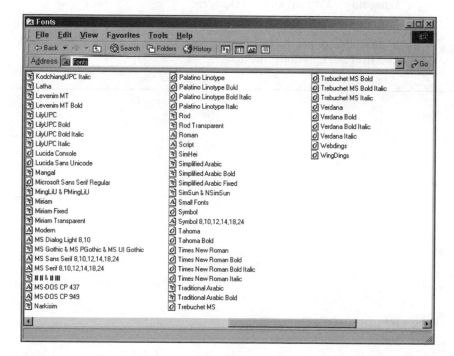

Figure 18-15: The second half of the list of all fonts that are available with Windows 2000.

How to Get More Fonts

The subject of Windows fonts could easily fill up a book this size all by itself. If you want to learn more—and especially if you think you might want more fonts than the set available with Windows 2000 one of the best sources is Chris MacGregor's Internet Type Foundry Index.

This Web site links to numerous other sources for font information, free fonts, and commercially available fonts. The Web address is www. typeindex.com.

Summary

In this chapter, we covered the secrets of printing and fonts.

▶ The underside of printers, printer ports, and other hardware.

▶ How to troubleshoot printer and port problems.

▶ How to use the Generic/Text driver to extract plain text files from applications that don't usually allow this.

▶ TrueType and OpenType fonts in Windows 2000.

▶ How to access characters that might not necessarily appear on your keyboard.

▶ Useful fonts that go beyond Arial and Times New Roman, including Symbol, Wingdings, Marlett, and MS Gothic.

▶ Finding the most useful characters within the vast Unicode system.

▶ Installing support for language groups that you might not have selected when you first set up Windows 2000.

Part V

Networking with Windows 2000 Professional

Chapter 19

Networking Basics

Defining a Network

A network consists of two or more computers — whether they are desktop computers, notebooks or laptops, hand-held computers, Macintoshes, or others — connected together so they can share information and peripherals. Networked computers are attached to each other using cables or wires, and it is across those cables that the shared information, commands, and queries pass. You also can attach computers by wireless methods, as described later in this chapter.

In addition to the cables, or the method of connection, there are other pieces of networking hardware you need, such as network interface cards, hubs, and perhaps routers or switches. Additionally, you might attach printers, digital cameras, and other peripherals as part of your network. This equipment can be shared between all of the users on the network.

Computers on a network communicate with each other by sending data and information over the network cables; but as you can imagine, network communication is more complicated than just that.

About packets

The data that transmits over a network might consist of text, images, user authentication, and so on. Before the data can travel from one computer to another, it must be divided into smaller pieces for easier distribution.

Data is sent over a network in *packets*. Each packet contains not only pieces of the data, it also contains the name of the sender and the receiver, along with some error-control information, to help make sure the packet reaches its destination in one piece.

Note

A packet is also called a *frame* or a *block*. All three terms refer to a unit of transmitted information that includes addresses, data, and error-checking codes.

Packets may be of fixed or variable length. Each packet contains only a portion of the data being sent. Your networking software disassembles the data, places it into packets, and then sends it across the network. (It is the number of packets traveling over the network that makes up the network traffic.) When the packets get to the designated computer, the packets are then reassembled to form the data you sent. Naturally, this is all completed in split seconds.

Multiple packets travel simultaneously. If a packet is lost or becomes corrupted on its journey, the receiving computer notifies the sending computer and the packets must be re-sent to complete the data.

About transmission

Different topologies and technologies send different types of packets — and provide various error correction and control methods — to make sure the packets are complete when they reach their destination. The topology of the network refers to how you arrange the cables, the networking hardware, and the computers. Technology refers to the type of wiring and hardware you use and the general speed of the network.

Networks can be made up of single or multiple segments. One segment might consist of ten or fifty workstations and one or two servers connected together to share data and peripherals. A second segment of the network might consist of another server or two, plus ten, twenty, or fifty more workstations. The two segments can use the same network operating system or different systems; they might share peripherals and files between them, or they might not.

The topology and technology of the network determines how the network packets are distributed, not only to the computers in one segment, but also in how the packets are distributed to computers in multiple segments.

The ISO/OSI model

For a network to work properly between segments, operating systems, computers, and networking hardware and software, certain stand-ards must be followed. International Standards Organization/Open Systems Interconnect (ISO/OSI) is a set of standards that define network func-tionality. ISO/OSI sets standards for cabling, network interface cards (NIC), protocols, and so on.

A seven-layer model defines computer-to-computer communications, from the application data to the most basic of the networking hardware. The layers work independently, yet they are connected because each layer builds on the functions of the layers below.

Following is a brief explanation of each layer:

- **Layer 1**. The Physical layer defines the cabling, hubs, and other equipment that amplifies and carries the electrical signal.

- **Layer 2**. The Data-link layer controls the flow of data through the network cards, bridges and switches, and other devices that connect the physical layer and the actual data stream. This layer also checks to ensure that all data is received and that it's usable.

- **Layer 3**. The Network layer defines the protocols for data routing, to ensure that the data gets to the correct destination. Such protocols include IP and IPX.

- **Layer 4**. The Transport layer defines protocols for error-checking and message formation. If data is too large, the Transport layer divides and numbers the data so that it can transmit the data in smaller pieces. The numbered data helps the layer reassemble the pieces after it gets to the other computer, segment, or other receiving end.

- **Layer 5**. The Session layer maintains the connection — or session — for as long as it takes to transmit the packets. It also performs security and administration functions.

- **Layer 6**. The Presentation layer identifies the way in which the data is formatted. This layer encrypts and decrypts information, for example, and translates data to ensure that one system can understand the data from another system.

- **Layer 7**. The Application layer defines how the applications interact with the network. This layer receives and delivers requests from applications on one computer to those on another computer.

The model's layers work together to send requests from a client to a server, for example. The layers might send a file from the server to the client in answer to a request. When a computer sends a request over the network, it begins on Layer 7, the Application layer, and works its way to Layer 1, the Physical layer. The request then travels across the networking cable to its destination using the network protocol to carry the packets. Figure 19-1 illustrates how the ISO/OSI layers work.

When the packets reach the remote computer, they enter on Layer 1 and move up to Level 7, the Application layer, where the request is passed on to the process or service responsible for answering the request. Then the cycle starts over again.

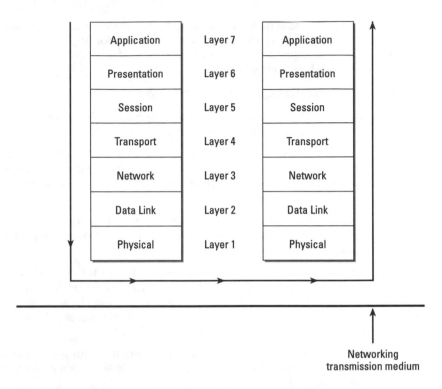

	Layer 7	
Application		Application
Presentation	Layer 6	Presentation
Session	Layer 5	Session
Transport	Layer 4	Transport
Network	Layer 3	Network
Data Link	Layer 2	Data Link
Physical	Layer 1	Physical

Networking
transmission medium

Figure 19-1: The ISO/OSI layers define networking functionality standards.

Understanding the Advantages and Disadvantages of a Network

For the most part, you'll find that networking your computers will benefit everyone in your business by enabling them to share files, folders, schedules, expensive printers, and so on. Sharing resources makes your business more efficient and effective, and gives the network users more equipment with which to work.

Networking also presents some disadvantages. The cost may be too high, or security issues might be a problem. Fortunately, there are enough options and solutions available with networking as to make the good outweigh the bad.

Considering the advantages

You can connect from two to ten computers in a small office in a simple peer-to-peer network that is easy to install, administer, and operate. If you have more than ten computers to connect, you can use a client/server network. Networking hardware and software is flexible, scalable, and easy to fit to your needs.

You also can expand the network as your needs grow. Adding computers, servers, hubs, and segments when you want to add new users or services is called scalability. Most networking equipment is built for expansion, as are most network operating systems and software.

Windows 2000 includes the networking software you need to set up any type of network. It includes the protocols, clients, services, and drivers for most network interface cards (also called network adapters or NICs). Following are a few more advantages to networking your computers.

Tip

Windows 2000 Professional not only includes everything you need to set up your network, it also will automatically configures itself to work on a TCP/IP network. All you have to do is install a network card and power up a Windows 2000 Professional computer; the program locates other computers on the network and configures itself to join the workgroup or domain automatically.

Cross-Reference

For more information about installing a network card, see Chapter 20. For more information about Windows 2000 Professional's automatic network configuration, see Chapter 21.

Sharing files

You can share files with everyone on the network. You might share letters, spreadsheets, reports, digital photographs, accounting files, and other business documents with your co-workers.

In addition, file transfers are quicker across a network than when they are saved to disk. Extremely large files are easier to transfer, as well, especially since it is often impossible to copy some large files to diskettes. You might transfer or copy application files, large image files, Web documents, and so on from another user's drive or from a server. When using the network for these tasks, you can complete the procedure almost instantaneously.

Sharing disk space

Disk space is always at a premium. Graphic and image files, large application files, and data files are getting larger and larger. You can use a network drive or server drive for storing both your large and small files.

In addition to sharing hard drives, you can share file storage drives — tape drives, Zip and Jaz drives, and even floppy drives. If your computer doesn't have a Zip or Jaz drive, for example, but someone else on the network does, you can save files to that drive if sharing is enabled.

Tip

Use a Zip disk to back up your important files so you can access them whenever you need them, even if your files are backed up to a network tape drive. Retrieving files from a Zip disk is much easier than retrieving them from a tape.

You also can share CD-ROM drives across the network. If your computer has a 24X CD-ROM drive and another computer on the network has a 44X CD-ROM drive, use the 44X drive to install software to your computer. The faster CD-ROM drive means the installation process will be faster.

Creating backups

Backing up your data files is important. You should always keep an extra copy of important files in case your hard disk goes bad, a file becomes corrupted, or someone accidentally deletes your work. You can back up all of your data quickly and easily over the network—either to a storage disk or to another hard disk. Restoring that data is also quick and easy over the network.

Peripherals

Expensive peripherals—such as a color inkjet printer or a laser printer— are more affordable if everyone in the office can use them. If a printer isn't networked, only one person has continual use of that piece of equipment. Naturally, others can move to the computer to which the printer is attached; but that may not always be convenient or appropriate. If the printer is attached to the network, however, everyone can make use of it. You'll save money and time, and you'll do more with less.

Secret

Keep your old printers—dot-matrix or inkjet, for example—and connect those to individual computers that might be able to make use of them. You wouldn't necessarily want to use a dot-matrix printer over the network because it's slow, noisy, and cumbersome. But if one person can use it to print draft reports or other documents, that takes some of the load off the network printer and eases network traffic.

Considering the disadvantages

Planning and installing a network is a scary proposition. You'll need to invest time and money. You'll have to learn about various networking hardware and software. Sharing equipment and files can pose problems, as well. Following are some of the disadvantages to setting up and using a network.

Investing time and money

One obvious problem with installing a network is that you must invest time. When you learn something new, it takes time to understand all the intricacies. Installing hardware and software also takes time. Teaching networking procedures to the office staff might take your time, as well.

Tip

Find the people in your office who understand how computers work and teach them about the network. Then let them teach the others to use the network and to be a help desk, of sorts, when users have questions. This will save you time and effort, and it will promote teamwork.

Administering the network will likely take the most time. No matter what type of network you install, you must first configure the networking hardware and software, and you must then maintain the network so that people can use it daily with no problems. You must consider security, backups, printing and file sharing, permissions, and so on. Naturally, the smaller the network, the easier the administration.

Money is another consideration. You might not want to invest a lot of money in your computer system, or you might have the means to install a model network, with all of the bells and whistles. It all comes down to priorities. If a network helps you speed your work and make the office more efficient, you will spend more money, time, and effort in setting up the network.

Fortunately, there are multiple levels of networking from which you can choose. You can purchase a kit, for example, for less than $100 that allows you to set up a small and simple network between two computers and a printer. Even though it might not be the fastest or the most efficient network, it will at least provide simple file- and printer-sharing with a small investment of time and money.

If you want to install a higher-level network for working with multimedia files, sharing expensive equipment, and providing services for your users, you can install a faster, more efficient network.

Maintaining and troubleshooting the network

Network maintenance includes keeping reliable connections between the computers and peripherals, troubleshooting connection problems between computers, and providing the available services (like e-mail or printer services) to all computers on the network. The more equipment you connect to the network, and the more services you offer, the more difficult maintaining the network will be.

Network maintenance can often be a huge disadvantage, especially if you must take time to constantly troubleshoot problems. You can avoid some problems with equipment and software by understanding how the network is put together, as explained in this chapter and the next two.

Solving security problems

Another disadvantage to running a network is system security. You don't want just anyone opening payroll files, for example. Customer records, accounting files, reports, inventory, and so on, are just some of the types of files you should protect on the network.

Fortunately, Windows 2000 Professional offers the option of setting access limits for files, folders, printers, and other resources. You can choose not to share any of your resources with others on the network. You also can set certain limits to those resources to protect them from only certain network users or groups.

Cross-Reference

See Chapter 21 for information about setting shares and permissions.

Sharing equipment and files

When you're sharing your equipment over a network, such as a printer or a Zip drive, you take the chance that the equipment won't be readily available when you need it. A co-worker, for example, just sent a 24-page color document to a networked inkjet printer. You have to wait your turn to print, and that could take a while, depending on the network setup, printer speed, and so on.

There are some solutions to these problems. You can speed up your network so that printing and other processes don't take as long. As another example, you might be able to change the order of the documents being printed to rush your job to the front of the line.

Secret

You can use a print server to manage the printing for all users on a network. A print server can be a program or a hardware device that attaches to the network. The print server provides shared access to the printers attached to the network. When a user sends a print job to a network printer, the print server places the job in a queue with other jobs. When a printer is available, the print server sends the next job to the printer.

Considering network traffic

One final disadvantage you might notice when working on a network is a general slowing of all applications and processes. Depending on the type of network equipment, the types of applications, and your uses for the network, networking computers can sometimes slow your work considerably. Some methods of networking are built for speed, while others are built for simple sharing at a rather slow pace.

Secret

There are many things you can do to keep your network running smoothly and quickly. For example, consider the quality of your networking hardware; if you use cheap network cards and second-rate cabling, your network performance will suffer. If the cabling is out in the middle of the floor where people trample it, you're putting your network connections at risk. Check the cabling periodically for damage. Check all connectors, routers, hubs, and other devices periodically to make sure connections are secure. Keep backups of your data and, from time to time, test the backups to make sure they're reliable.

Exploring Network Types

The three basic network types are Client/Server, Peer-to-Peer, and Dial-Up Networking. The type you choose depends on your networking goals, the equipment you want to install, your experience level, and the time you plan to invest. Each type of network provides distinct advantages and disadvantages.

If this is your first network, or you only want a small and simple network, you can choose to set up a peer-to-peer network. A peer-to-peer network is simpler to operate and less expensive than a client/server network. After you gain experience, however, you may want to switch over to a client/server network, using your peer-to-peer network as a foundation.

The client/server network provides multiple services for many users. Whereas a peer-to-peer network is limited to ten or fewer users, a client/server network can include ten, a hundred, or thousands of users. It is also more difficult to install, administer, maintain, and troubleshoot than a peer-to-peer network.

You might set up a dial-up network to accommodate the needs of only a few users. Telecommuters or home-based workers can easily dial up a computer at the office and transfer files, print, and collaborate with co-workers.

Using a peer-to-peer network

In a peer-to-peer network, all computers share their resources — including files, folders, drives, and printers — with all other computers on the network. Each computer also runs its own local applications and programs; it just has access to additional resources.

A peer-to-peer network usually contains two to ten connected computers. You could include more computers than ten (up to 25), with the right hardware and software; however, when you have more than ten computers on a peer-to-peer network, you slow the performance of every computer on the network, as well as limit network speed, security, and efficiency.

Figure 19-2 illustrates a peer-to-peer network. Three computers share their files, printers, CD-ROM drives, and other resources.

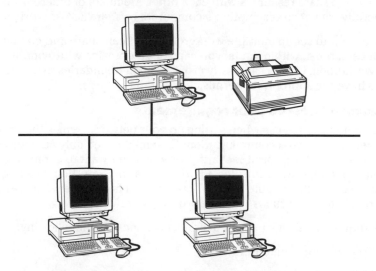

Figure 19-2: Peer-to-peer networking makes all resources available to everyone on the network.

Peer-to-peer networks present some disadvantages. Obviously, using a peer-to-peer computer means the users must trust each other — to be careful of files and programs, to responsibly use printers and other equipment, and to dependably make their computer available to everyone else.

File security can be a problem on a peer-to-peer network. You do, however, have the option of not sharing all your files and folders, and you can set permissions for the use of your resources.

Looking at peer-to-peer networking

A peer-to-peer network is easy to maintain and set up. It's also cost effective, especially for small business use. There are a wide range of cabling and networking solutions for a peer-to-peer network. Some solutions provide fast and powerful networking, while others offer slower connections but with reliable service.

Understanding the workgroup

The computers connected in a peer-to-peer network are called a workgroup. Members of a workgroup usually trust each other to share resources and to responsibly take care of those resources.

It is also possible to have multiple network segments with peer-to-peer networking, and thus set up multiple workgroups. The members of one workgroup share resources with each other. Members of different workgroups generally cannot see each other's computers or share across workgroups.

Note

If you want to set up multiple workgroups that can share and communicate with each other, within limits, you can set up domains with Windows 2000 Server Edition. Clients can easily cross domain boundaries using trusts, if they have the appropriate permissions and passwords.

Examining peer-to-peer requirements

The equipment you use when setting up your network defines the speed and efficiency of network communications. You might need only an intermittent connection for file or printer sharing, or you might want to connect to another computer for more routine file and printer sharing. You should decide how you want to use each computer on the network, and how those resources will be shared, before you choose your networking hardware.

The requirements of a peer-to-peer network include the following:

- Two or more computers
- A network interface card for each computer
- Cabling or alternative equipment to enable the computers to communicate, plus networking hardware when applicable
- A compatible (peer-to-peer) operating system—Windows 2000 Professional
- Optionally, a printer and other peripherals for sharing

The type of networking equipment you use dictates the performance of your network. You can start out with a fast and efficient network or you can upgrade as necessary. The type of cabling, network cards, and other networking hardware you use will dictate the speed of the network.

Assigning computer duties and resources

As you plan your peer-to-peer network, you should think about which computers will perform which tasks on the network. Some tasks include file storage, backing up data files, and resource usage. Use the best computer for each job so the entire network will run efficiently and economically.

Items to consider include computer memory, disk space, and specialty hardware for use with attached resources. In addition to using computers that operate efficiently, you might need to add hardware to computers that will perform special network tasks.

To decide how to assign computer duties and resources, follow these steps:

STEPS:

Assigning Computer Duties and Resources

Step 1. Determine the duties you expect from your computers. A computer can store files — word processing, database, graphics, application, data, and other files — for any or all of the users on the network. A computer can store backup files for any or all of the computers on the network. The difference between normal file storage and backup file storage not only determines the amount of hard disk space used, but it also influences network traffic.

Step 2. Consider each computer's hard disk space before deciding which computer to use for file storage and backups. A computer with only one or two gigabytes of disk space could comfortably store word processing and spreadsheet documents, but it would not be appropriate for storing multimedia or other large files. Most new computers come with large hard drives now. It's not unusual to see drives that offer ten or more gigabytes of space.

Step 3. Consider, too, the power and memory of each computer on the network. A very slow machine — a Pentium 120, for example — is not the appropriate choice for storing files that need to be accessed often. A computer that processes slowly will slow the rest of the network when accessed frequently. Similarly, computers with less memory react more slowly than those with more memory.

Step 4. For each resource you add to the network, determine which computer best suits that resource's requirements. Consider the requirements for printers, CD-ROM drives, tape drives, and so on. Remember, too, that when you share a resource, the computer attached to that resource will take a performance hit whenever the resource is being used.

Secret

You must be sure to arrange for backups in an office setting. You should include two sets of backups using different computers or even mass storage devices, like a tape drive. You have to weigh the inconvenience and expense of backing up against the inconvenience and expense of re-creating your accounting, payroll, and customer information when a hard drive crashes or some other disaster occurs.

Understanding peer-to-peer limits

Peer-to-peer networks offer many advantages to the office; but you also can experience some real problems with a peer-to-peer network, including the following:

- Peer-to-peer networking can place a strain on individual computers and resources, especially if the requests for services are many.

- If network traffic is high, the entire network slows and performance is impaired.

- Peer-to-peer networking offers little security to files and data.

- It limits the number of computers you can attach to the network.

Considering security issues

If you have a small office and everyone gets along well, you won't have to worry much about security issues with your peer-to-peer network. There are, however, a couple of issues to consider:

- First, accidents happen. Someone could accidentally access your hard drive and delete a few files, a folder or two, or even your entire hard drive's contents. This is a security issue.

- Second, someone who fancies himself to be a hacker could get into your office computers and cause problems with your network or access files.

- Third, if you have an Internet connection, there is always the possibility someone could hack into your system and compromise your data from the Internet.

Windows provides some safety measures that can protect your files from access by others on the network. You can choose which files you share and which remain private, and you also can set permissions to both your computer and resources. Also, many third-party applications enable you to control the contents of your computers on the network.

As you plan your network, remember the possible problems and solutions and build them into your plan.

Boosting network performance

A peer-to-peer network can be efficient for many networking duties. When only two or three people are using the network, the network traffic should not hamper any one computer's performance. Network traffic encompasses any data sent from computer to computer, as well as to printers and other resources.

However, when more people access resources on the network and traffic increases, or the network tasks become increasingly more complex, individual machine performance may suffer. Computers with minimal power, memory, and disk space not only exhibit slow performance for the user, but also can slow the entire network if multiple people use its resources.

The best way to avoid problems with network traffic is to start your network with computers that are capable of operating efficiently as standalone computers. A Windows 2000 Professional computer has both minimal and recommended requirements. If you can afford a computer that fits the optimum requirements or better, you'll see much better network performance, as well as general computer performance.

Using a client/server network

A server generally stores all data files, and sometimes applications, and it normally controls the distribution and use of peripherals and resources. Some networks contain one server, while others might contain multiple servers. The number of servers depends on the number of clients and the number of services offered. Figure 19-3 illustrates a client/server network.

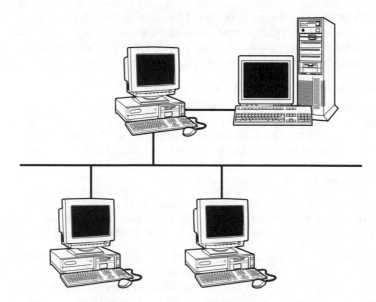

Figure 19-3: The server(s) supply services to the clients.

Some larger networks have multiple servers to provide a wide variety of services to the clients. In addition to multiple servers, some client/server networks use multiple segments to separate users and resources in manageable groups.

Servers generally use faster processors and have more memory and disk space to perform the management tasks of the network. Servers perform multiple duties, including the following:

- Authenticating users
- Allowing access to resources (files, folders, printers, and so on)

- Providing Web access
- Tracking resource usage
- Logging security breaches
- Distributing e-mail
- Providing application access and data

Understanding client/server

Both the server and the client on the network use an operating system that enables them to communicate. An example of a client operating system is Windows 2000 Professional. An example of a server operating system (also called a network operating system) is Windows 2000 Server. The client and server operating systems enable the client to request services and the server to grant the requests.

The client/server network is designed for large networks (more than ten clients) and for tasks that require a host computer, such as Internet access or database management. Each network operating system has its own method of organizing users and resources. Windows 2000 Server organizes users into domains.

Understanding the domain

A domain consists of one or more computers assembled together in a group for naming purposes. The domain of your network affects you when you log on to the network and when you want to access a resource in another network segment. When you log on to the network, Windows asks you for your username, password, and your domain or workgroup (when using peer-to-peer networking).

At least one server in your domain authenticates you as a member of that domain. When the server identifies you as a member of the domain, you can then access the resources in the domain for which you have permissions.

Each domain must have one server that can authenticate users and manage resources. Often, a domain also has a backup server that keeps copies of all records for the domain, in case the first server crashes or has other problems. Domains might also have servers that manage printers, files, Internet access, applications, and so on.

Examining the multi-segment network

As a network grows in clients, servers, and services, you can add multiple segments to help manage and organize the resources. Each segment added to a network is usually formed into a separate domain for administration purposes, although you can use one domain to contain multiple segments.

Each new domain, or segment, must have a server that authenticates the users within that domain. Users from one domain cannot necessarily access the servers in another domain. Two or more domains can, however, create a trust relationship in which the users can access resources when permitted.

Looking at client requirements

The requirements for the clients on a client/server network are similar to those on a peer-to-peer network. For each client computer on the network, you need a network adapter card. Compatible cabling is also necessary, as well as any other networking hardware—a hub, for example.

You can add printers and other resources to the network, as well. When you add resources, you choose whether to attach them to a local computer or to the server computer. For example, you might have a laser printer you attach to the server and let everyone access. You might have a color inkjet or an old dot-matrix printer, on the other hand, that you attach to just one machine for use by that one computer. A network operating system doesn't share resources attached to the clients, only those resources attached to the network or to the server are shared.

In addition to the client and networking hardware, you'll need to obtain and set up a server computer.

Tip

You should always use an Uninterruptible Power Source (UPS) on the server, so you can properly shut the server down before a power outage affects it.

Considering server requirements

A server computer must have sufficient processor speed, RAM, and disk space to provide various services to the clients. The server's hardware configuration depends on the type of services it will offer and the number of clients on the network.

In addition to hardware, the server needs a compatible operating system. You can use a network operating system such as Windows 2000 Server. You also can choose other network operating systems, such as Novell NetWare or Banyan VINES. A network operating system supplies more management, security, and other features and tools that make operating the network efficient.

Tip

You can purchase server computers, complete with operating system, that are built specifically for the job. These computers have all of the hardware compatible for the chosen operating system. You might want a supercomputer, which is a computer that has massive amounts of RAM, caching, and disk space. You might only need a computer with extra memory and disk space for storing files and accessing the Internet.

The hardware you choose for your server must first and foremost be compatible with the network operating system (NOS). You should first choose the operating system you will use, and then purchase the server computer. Each NOS requires specific amounts of memory and disk space, and perhaps certain types of drives—such as Small Computer System Interface (SCSI) or Integrated Drive Electronics (IDE)—and other such requirements.

IDE versus SCSI

IDE, a popular hard disk interface standard that provides only medium to fast data transfer rates, isn't always a good interface for server applications because it's slow and has other limitations in functionality that hamper a server's operations. However, you can use an IDE interface in some server circumstances, depending on the NOS.

On the other hand, SCSI is a high-speed parallel interface. In addition to being fast and extremely practical for server use, SCSI devices are used to connect a personal computer to up to seven peripheral devices at a time using a single port. SCSI devices include hard disks, tape drives, CD-ROM drives, other mass media storage devices, scanners, and printers.

Secret

If you decide you need a server in your business, you should also consider a backup server. It doesn't take long for a server to become indispensable to a company, and the data stored there is often irreplaceable. A backup server running a network operating system keeps an up-to-date replication of all data on the other server. If the original server crashes or becomes inoperable for some reason, the backup server can take over without a loss in time, money, or data.

Examining network operating systems

A network operating system (NOS) is one designed specifically for a server. An NOS offers many features and tools that help you manage the network, clients, applications, security, and other facets of the network.

You might want to use an NOS for any of a variety of reasons. Perhaps you have specific networking needs — security problems, home business, Web business, and so on.

Another reason to choose a particular network operating system is that you're using an application that requires it. For example, Internet Information Server (IIS, a Web server) works best with the NT Server or Windows 2000 Server network operating system. Some vertical-market applications, such as programs for selling and listing real estate or managing an insurance business, might require a specific NOS.

Following are some features found in network operating systems:

- All network operating systems include a tool for naming the users of the network and limiting their access to certain resources. Through user accounts, you can choose which files and folders a user may access, which resources he or she may use, and limit access to other computers or servers, as well.

- A good network operating system should include some sort of printer management tool. This tool helps you direct print jobs to the appropriate printer, cancel and delete jobs, and otherwise control printing on the network.

- Most network operating systems include diagnostic tools for examining the network components, such as protocols and connections. When something goes wrong with a connection, these tools make it easier to find the problem.

- Tools and utilities for gathering network data and analyzing it might be important to you. Some NOSs log application errors and security breaches, for example. Others use optimization utilities to help you determine where the network connections are slow.

- Some NOSs include Web utilities and support for browsers. You might want to create your own Web server, for example, for displaying company home pages over the Internet.

Following is a list of the most popular computer network operating systems:

- Windows 2000 Server
- Microsoft Windows NT Server
- Microsoft LAN Manager
- Novell NetWare/IntranetWare
- IBM LAN Server
- IBM OS/2 Warp Server

Looking at dial-up networking from the client's point of view

Remote access defines attaching to a network from another location and accessing resources from the remote computer. For example, you might attach to your work computer from home or from the road in order to access a file or your e-mail. Using remote access, you can access files, programs, printers, and any other resource on your work computer and other computers on the network for which you have permission. Using remote access to keep in touch with the office is called telecommuting.

Tip

Companies save office space, insurance, and spend less time and money on remote workers than office workers. In addition, the remote worker saves wasted commuting time, sets his or her own schedule, and has better morale than if her or she were stuck in an office all day.

Cross-Reference

For information about installing and using Windows 2000 Dial-Up Networking, see Chapter 11.

Filling the client's needs

You will need certain equipment in your home or remote office to enable you to work efficiently. Your company might supply the equipment you need, or you might have to purchase it yourself. Generally, you'll need the following:

- Computer and modem
- Communications software
- A fast connection to the office
- Printer
- Phone line
- Backup media such as Zip disks or a tape drive
- Virus protection

Secret

If you are on the road and travel a lot with your work, keep a kit with you at all times that contains such things as an extra computer battery, a spare phone cord, a list of support numbers, spare floppy disks, your Windows 2000 installation CD, and so on.

Establishing the client's duties

Make sure you understand how your company defines telecommuting and any guidelines they set for use of the equipment. Also, ask about insurance for the equipment, inquire about how upgrades and repairs are to be handled, and so on.

If you are working away from the office, your first responsibility is to stay in touch with your co-workers to make sure everyone is on the same page. You might need to telephone or e-mail daily, for example, to discuss projects, procedures, or other factors affecting you and others who remain in the office.

Understanding Network Topologies and Technologies

Topology describes how the cables, networking hardware, and computers are arranged and located. Technology refers to the type of wiring and hardware you use. Topology and technology are closely related. The topology you choose must use a specific technology.

Defining topologies

Basically, there are three topologies you might choose to use in your business: bus, spanning tree (or star), and ring. When you choose a topology, you also must choose the technology that best suits the topology, plus the connectors, protocols, and hardware that uses that technology.

Examining bus

The bus topology connects computers along one length of cable. Bus topology limits the network in that only 30 or so users can be connected to a segment. Another problem with the bus topology is that the network is slow because only one network packet can be sent at a time. Figure 19-4 illustrates the bus topology; computers attach along a single length of cable.

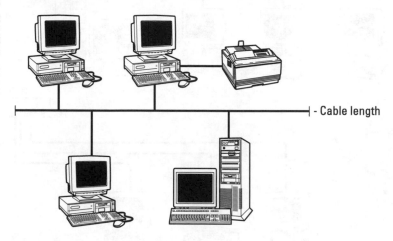

— Cable length

Figure 19-4: The bus topology isn't flexible or scalable.

When there is a problem within the network — say a cable connecting two computers goes bad — the problem cable can be difficult to locate. The entire network must be shut down until the cable is found and fixed. One final problem with the bus topology is that it's not scalable. If you want to expand it the future, it is difficult to add equipment because of the way the network is set up.

Exploring Star or Spanning Tree

A spanning tree (also called star) topology connects all computers through a central hub. All packets of data must pass through the hub before they can reach their destination. The hub is a box that contains ports in which to plug networking cables; each computer plugs into the hub with a separate cable. When the hub receives a signal from a computer on the network, it modifies and then distributes the signal to all the other computers on the network.

Figure 19-5 shows a spanning tree network. Hubs make it possible to extend the network so that more workstations can access the resources.

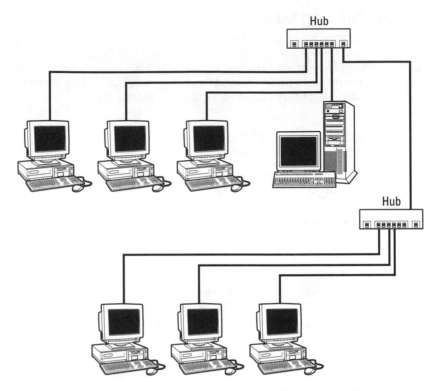

Figure 19-5: A spanning tree network branches out with the use of hubs.

Tip

Spanning tree is the perfect topology for small business offices. You can start with three to seven computers, for example, and keep adding hubs to expand the network as needed. Additionally, spanning tree is the perfect solution for a client/server network; you can add clients and servers on various segments of the network whenever you hire new employees or add to your networking hardware.

Considering Ring

Ring networks are usually large because the technology can cover great distances. In addition, ring networks often use fiber optic cable. Figure 19-6 illustrates a simple ring network.

The ring topology passes packets from one computer to the next, in one direction only: around a circle (ring). When one computer wants to send data to another, it must first capture a token which passes around the ring, waiting for someone to transmit information. The token picks up the destination address and the message and then travels around the ring until the destination computer picks it up.

One problem with a ring network is that if a cable or card fails, no data can pass around the network until the problem is corrected.

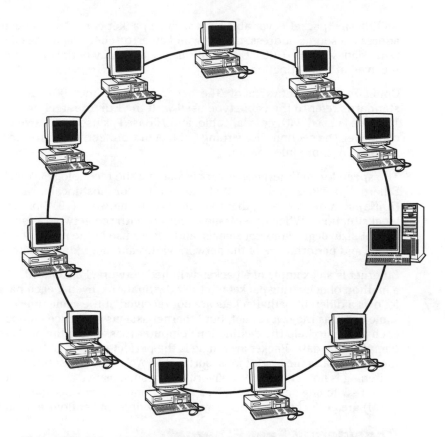

Figure 19-6: A ring network enables token passing from one computer to the next.

Defining network technologies

Network technologies refer to the architecture and protocols used on certain networks; Ethernet and Token Ring are two common technologies. The technology you choose governs the speed of the network, the type of cabling you use, and the network cards you install to your computers. Additionally, you must use networking hardware to match the technology you choose.

Identifying Ethernet

Ethernet is a protocol and cabling scheme that can use the bus or the spanning tree topology connected with various cabling types, as described later in this chapter. Ethernet transfers data at the rate of 10 megabits per second (Mbps), which means it can transfer 10 million bits of information from one networked computer to another per second.

An Ethernet packet is variable-length, and a packet consists of a destination address, a source address, the data, and an error-checking mode called cyclic redundancy check (CRC). CRC confirms the accuracy of the data after it's received at its destination.

Common implementations of Ethernet are 10Base2 and 10BaseT. These standards refer to the cable type used with the Ethernet technology. 10Base2 is used with coaxial cable, and 10BaseT is used with twisted-pair cable. See the section, "Regarding Cable and Connections," later in this chapter for more information.

The speed for an Ethernet network is fast and the technology is flexible. Ethernet provides effective data transfer rates for most local area networks (LANs). Realize, however, that the speed of the network (10Mbps) works in ideal situations. When other issues interfere with the network—such as packet size, degradation of signals, and excess use of the network—the speed and performance of the network varies and degrades somewhat.

Secret

Ethernet is an example of a packet-switched network. Packet switching is a method of delivering packets to their destinations, even if each packet follows a different path. Packets are not received at the same time or in the same order as they were sent, but Ethernet assigns sequence numbers to each packet to help the destination computer reassemble the packets to complete the data. Packet switching is the perfect method of transmission for such data as files, print jobs, surfing the Web, and so on; however, packet switching is not efficient for delivering data such as live audio and video. Circuit switching networks such as Asynchronous Transmission Mode (ATM) are perfect for delivering audio and video applications and files.

Considering Fast Ethernet

Ethernet technology also includes Fast Ethernet. Fast Ethernet's rates are 100Mbps. Fast Ethernet uses cabling, network cards, hubs, and other networking equipment to match the 100 Mbps speed and works well with the spanning tree topology.

The common standard implementation for Fast Ethernet is 100BaseTX, although 100BaseT4 is growing in the market. 100BaseTX requires Category 5 twisted-pair cabling, and 100BaseT4 can work with either Category 5 or Category 3 twisted-pair. For more information, see the section, "Regarding Cable and Connections," later in this chapter.

Fast Ethernet may be a viable choice for your office network. You should consider Fast Ethernet if someone on the network plans to use large graphics, audio, or video files consistently, or if you plan to upgrade your network to add more clients, a server or two, and more services. Fast Ethernet provides more bandwidth to your network to accommodate these larger, processor-intensive file types. You also can use Fast Ethernet as a backbone for multiple workstations and servers. Bandwidth is a measurement of the amount of information or data that can pass through any given point on the network: cabling, hub, network cards, and so on. The wider the bandwidth, the more data that can pass through.

Secret

You can start your network with Ethernet and easily upgrade to Fast Ethernet, if necessary. You can purchase network cards and hubs that work with either a 10Mbps or a 100Mbps network, called 10/100 cards. First, buy 10/100 cards for your network. You can use these cards with the cabling and 10Mbps hubs for a 10Mbps network. When you can afford the more expensive 100Mbps hub, simply buy and install it. The 10/100 network cards and the cabling can then be used to create a 100Mbps network.

Examining Token Ring

The Token Ring protocol uses the token passing methodology and a ring topology, and it can transmit data at 16Mbps and 100Mbps. Token Ring is usually used for larger networks. The networking hardware and wiring is expensive and complicated to install and is therefore often used for large client/server networks.

Secret

Token Ring networks have several advantages over Ethernet networks: they support larger packets and therefore more data within a given period of time, for example. Token Ring networks are also very efficient because of the order and method of data transmission. Use Token Ring when you consistently move very large files over the network.

Computers on a Token Ring network take turns sending data. A token (a special network packet) is passed from computer to computer. When a computer has the token, it is that computer's turn to transmit data. The data, plus the token, move to the next computer, and so on.

Problems in a Token Ring network occur when one node — or computer on the network is down or has connection problems. Unless the ring is maintained, tokens cannot pass through and communications stop until the cable or computer is repaired.

Multistation Access Units (MAUs) are often used to keep the ring working when a workstation fails. MAUs are a series of stacked hubs connected together to bypass the workstation and continue passing the token.

Exploring FDDI

Fiber Distributed Data Interface (FDDI) networks also use the token-passing method of data transmission on the star or ring topology. FDDI most often uses two interconnected rings to create a communications network. The dual rings provide a guarantee that communications continue if one ring fails.

Tip

FDDI can use only one ring; two rings create a fault tolerance safeguard.

FDDI uses fiber optic cabling, although it also can use Category 5 twisted pair to the desktop. See the section, "Regarding Cable and Connections," later in this chapter for more information. FDDI is often used for servers and backbones, as opposed to local area networks.

Looking at backbones

A backbone manages the majority of network traffic. Not all networks need a backbone — only large networks with excessive traffic. Backbones often connect multiple network segments across offices and buildings. Backbones support a high-speed protocol and use different cabling than a LAN, so that masses of data can quickly pass through.

A backbone might provide connections between server rooms and tele-communications closets. Server rooms are a convenient area set off from the rest of the office where multiple servers reside for easier troubleshooting, upgrading, as well as for better security over the equipment. A telecommu-nications closet is the room or area in which all hubs, routers, and other networking equipment is located for easy troubleshooting and maintenance.

Gigabit Ethernet

Gigabit Ethernet (also called 1Gbps Ethernet) operates at 1000Mbps and makes a perfect backbone for a corporate network. The standard implementation for Gigabit Ethernet is 1000BaseSX, which is perfect for a single office or building; 1000BaseSX could, however, be a problem with longer distances.

Tip

Gigabit Ethernet was created to compete with ATM. ATM has been around longer than Gigabit Ethernet, but ATM vendors continue to disagree on standards for the technology; thus ATM hasn't really come into its own.

Gigabit Ethernet runs over fiber optic cabling, although it can use twisted-pair from servers or telecommunications closets, for example. When used with twisted-pair, Gigabit Ethernet is limited in distance to 70 feet or less. With fiber cabling, the distances range as far as 1600 feet.

ATM

ATM can manage live video and audio files, video conferencing, large graphics, and other such data that requires high speed and high performance. With ATM, only one transmission takes place at a time, so large file transfers don't collide with other network traffic.

ATM also uses a fixed cell (packet) size for all data transmission, which makes the network traffic more foreseeable and more easily managed than the variable packet networks, such as Ethernet. In addition, ATM's packet size is nearly three times as large as any Ethernet packet size, resulting in a more efficient transfer of data and fewer bottlenecks.

Tip

A bottleneck is any component on the network that slows the transmission of data. A bottleneck might be the speed difference between the client computer and the server; or it could be a server's slow hard disk transferring only one-half of the packets it receives per second. Applications, image files, RAM, and even the difference between network cards can all cause bottlenecks.

Regarding Cable and Connections

Cabling provides the physical connection between computers. Cabling is used for transmitting and receiving information over the network. You can connect your network with any of various types of cabling, including traditional cabling such as coaxial or twisted-pair, fiber optic, and even radio signals or infrared.

Tip

When preparing to cable your office network, check with your city for any applicable building codes. Some building and commercial codes prohibit laying cable without specific permits and permissions.

The cable you choose must be suited for the distance between your computers. Some cables work better with short distances, while others reach farther between machines. You also choose the type of cabling to match the network cards and other networking hardware.

Network cabling and other equipment have standards that are set by the Institute of Electrical and Electronics Engineers (IEEE) to ensure interoperability of products and services from vendor to vendor. The IEEE 802 series of standards sets computing and electrical engineering standards. Check standards before you buy. Following is a list of the common IEEE (pronounced eye-triple-E) 802 standards defining local area network criteria:

802.1	Network management and bridging
802.2	LAN data-link protocols
802.3	Ethernet standards
802.4	Bus topology using token passing
802.9	Integrated data and voice networks
802.10	LAN security
802.11	Wireless connections

Using coaxial and twisted-pair cabling

The decision you make on the type of cable depends on the speed you want for your network. Consider how difficult or easy the cable is to install, how expensive the cabling solution is, the distance between computers, and your security issues.

Defining coaxial

Coaxial — or coax — cable is inexpensive to use on a network; however, it is used less frequently today because it is not upgradeable. Don't use coax for your business network unless you only plan to connect a few computers and you never expect to upgrade, add computers, or add users.

Secret

Thin coax works well with Ethernet; however, it can't work with Fast Ethernet. If you choose to upgrade your Ethernet to Fast Ethernet later, you'll have to throw out all of your 10Base2 cabling and hardware and start from the beginning to build a faster network.

The cable consists of a plastic jacket surrounding a braided copper shield, plastic insulation, and a solid inner conductor. Coaxial cabling is also called thin net, or thin Ethernet cabling, and it's used with 10Base2 standard implementation. The data-transfer rate for 10Base2 is 10Mbps over 185 meters. The 185 meter limit (around 610 feet) describes the maximum cable segment length.

Thin Ethernet doesn't require a hub because you can use special connectors for joining two or more computers. You can use T-connectors to attach the thin coaxial cable to a BNC connector on the Ethernet network interface card.

Defining twisted-pair

Twisted-pair cabling is similar to common phone wire, but it is a higher grade of cabling that allows high-speed data to travel over it. The majority of networks today use twisted-pair because it's relatively inexpensive and it offers high rates of data transfer.

Twisted-pair cable consists of two or more pairs of insulated wires twisted together. In each twisted pair, one wire carries the signal and the other wire is grounded. The cable can either be unshielded twisted-pair (UTP) or shielded twisted-pair (STP).

Shielded twisted-pair cable has a foil shield and copper braid surrounding the pairs of wires. STP provides high-speed transmission for long distances. Unshielded twisted-pair cable also contains two or more pairs of twisted copper wires; however, UTP is easier to install, costs less, limits signaling speeds, and has a shorter maximum cable segment length than STP.

Twisted-pair uses 10BaseT standard implementation over UTP wiring and uses RJ-45 connectors. 10BaseT provides data transfer speeds up to Mbps. You use the star topology with twisted-pair so that each computer on the network connects to a central hub. The maximum cable segment length for twisted-pair is around 100 meters, or 330 feet.

Tip

If you use the 10BaseT cabling scheme, you have to buy network cards that accept 10BaseT, or twisted-pair cabling. You'll also need to buy a 10BaseT hub — one with jacks for twisted pair plugs.

There are categories — or levels — of twisted-pair cabling. Each level describes the performance characteristics of the wiring standard. Of the levels of twisted-pair cabling, Category 3 (Cat 3) and Category 5 (Cat 5) are the most common. Cat 3 is less expensive than Cat 5, but its transfer rate isn't as fast.

Secret

Cat 5 works equally well with 10BaseT or with 100BaseTX. You might want to start your network with Cat 5 cabling and 10BaseT hardware — 10Mbps network cards and hub. Then, when you're ready, upgrade to 100BaseTX hardware.

Tip

You also can purchase network cards—called 10/100 cards—that operate at both 10Mbps and 100Mbps. Use these cards and Cat 5 cabling for a network speed of 10Mbps. Then, when you're ready, you can upgrade with the purchase of a Mbps hub.

Choosing the right cabling type

Consider the following if you have any doubts as to the type of cabling you want to use in your network:

Choose coaxial cabling if you:

- Have fewer than ten computers
- Don't have any portable computers (laptops, notebooks) on the network
- Plan to never expand the network

Choose 10BaseT cabling with a hub if you:

- Have fewer than ten computers
- The computers are within 330feet or so of each other
- Have portable computers to connect to the network
- Might, at some point, need to add computers to the network

Choose 100BaseTX (Fast Ethernet) cabling with a hub if you:

- Plan to use large graphic files, streaming audio, and/or video

Using wireless connections

A wireless connection creates a network using technologies other than conventional cabling. Microwave, radio signals, infrared beams, and laser links use electromagnetic signals to create these links. Speeds vary from 1Mbps to 10Mbps in wireless networks, although manufacturers are working to increase the speed of their products.

Wireless connections have become a standard for many networks, not only with desktop computers, but especially with the use of portable computers. Wireless connections provide connection without physical limitations.

Manufacturers have established and adhere to universal standards for connecting computing devices through wireless technologies. Set standards guarantee that hardware from different vendors will be compatible.

On the other hand, interference from the atmosphere, obstacles, and other technologies make wireless connections less predictable than cable connections. Additionally, data transfer rates are slower with wireless than with cable, although new technologies are in the works for the future.

Secret

Even though standards have been set for wireless network connections, not all wireless manufacturers meet those standards. The IEEE standard for wireless network connections is 802.11. Check before you buy.

There are four common methods of communication to wireless networking — infrared, radio signals, microwave, and laser links. The most popular wireless connections for business networks are radio signals and infrared connections. Microwave and lasers might have a use in large corporate, educational, or government networks.

Secret

It's common to use wireless connections in conjunction with other cabling methods. You might want to use Cat 5 twisted-pair cabling for the majority of your network, and add a few wireless connections where appropriate, such as for mobile workers or separate buildings.

Understanding infrared

Infrared works similarly to a television's remote control. The connection must be line-of-sight; infrared cannot penetrate obstacles. The cone of the infrared beam is highly directional and ensures that the infrared connection doesn't spill to other nearby devices. The transmission distance for infrared is relatively short.

Secret

When two infrared devices are within range of one another, Windows 2000 automatically detects the second device and establishes an automatic connection.

One of the major benefits of infrared transmission is increased bandwidth for each user. Instead of shared bandwidth, as with cables, each user receives dedicated bandwidth. Infrared also provides a safe, invisible light wave for transferring data.

Breaking the cone of infrared light might disconnect the infrared connection, depending on the length and severity of the break. If the data transmission is interrupted however, the protocol resubmits the data repeatedly until the data is successively transmitted or the limit is exceeded.

Examining Radio Frequency

Radio Frequency (RF) describes the number of times per second that a radio wave vibrates. Radio signals are accessible to most users throughout the world. However, Federal Communications Commission (FCC) licensing and equipment approval aren't always easy to acquire, and the bandwidth of radio signals is low to moderate.

Radio signals penetrate light obstacles, such as thin walls. Spread-spectrum signals , a type of radio signal, can pass through heavy walls, even though the transfer rate is slow.

Spread-spectrum signals are fairly secure against tampering from outside sources. Additionally, spread-spectrum products provide 1 to 2Mbps data rates at a range from 50 to 1000 feet, depending on the building construction, interference sources, and other factors. Radio frequency systems are generally slower than 10Mbps Ethernet, and they are often quite expensive.

Using fiber optic cable

Fiber optic cable is often used as the backbone cable for large networks; however, it might become useful in smaller networks in the near future as data speed requirements increase and the price of fiber drops. Fiber optic cabling is reliable, fast, and expensive. Fiber optic cables are difficult and expensive to install and to repair.

Fiber optic cabling works by transmitting pulses of light through a glass or plastic core. A plastic shield of PVC or Plenum protects the fibers. Fiber optic cable can transmit at speeds of 655Mbps and even 1Gbps for up to 6562 feet.

All fiber transmissions take place in one direction only; fiber can either send or receive, but it cannot receive while it is sending—or vice versa. However, because the transmission speeds are so great, the direction problem is only a minor one.

Discovering Other Networking Hardware

Networking hardware includes network interface cards, hubs, routers, and switches. This is the equipment you use to build your network. You insert network interface cards into each computer. Additionally, you must use a hub if you connect three or more computers. You might not use routers and switches in your network; it depends on the size and purpose of your network.

Tip

When choosing networking hardware, make sure it is compatible with the IEEE standards, as listed previously.

Examining Network Interface Cards

A network interface card (also called a NIC—pronounced "nick", network card, or network adapter card) is a printed circuit board that plugs into a slot inside the computer and connects the computer to the network. The network card also connects to the network media (cable), which in turn connects all of the network interface cards to the network so the computers can communicate.

Tip

The connections between the network card and the cable depend on the cable type. Coaxial cable uses a BNC connector, while twisted-pair cabling uses an RJ-45 connector.

A network card usually comes with a disk that includes any network driver software used to configure the network card. The card translates commands so that it can manage the placement of the flow of data to and from the computer.

Secret

After you purchase a network interface card, go to the card manufacturer's Web site on the Internet and download the most updated software driver for that particular card. Manufacturers are always updating the drivers to make the card work more efficiently. The latest driver will be on the Web, not on the disk that comes with the new card.

Network cards can cause problems upon installation. Depending on the other devices in and software on a computer, it might be difficult to get a card to work. Sometimes it's the brand of the card, and sometimes it's from other problems.

See Chapter 20 for more information about troubleshooting network cards.

Determining when to use hubs, bridges, repeaters, switches, and routers

Most networks require a hub, and many networks can make use of switches, bridges, repeaters, and routers. These devices extend services, interpret data, boost performance, and provide other benefits to the network.

Table 19-1 provides a brief summary of the uses of each hardware device.

Table 19-1   Hardware Devices and Uses

Device	Use
Hub	Extends the network by adding computers
Bridge	Connects networks that use different protocols
Repeater	Extends the length a network cable can reach
Switch	Connects similar networks to add speed to the network
Router	Connects similar or dissimilar networks to add speed through intelligent addressing

Hubs

A hub is a device that modifies network transmission signals, thereby allowing you to extend the network for additional workstations. There are two kinds of hubs: an active and a passive hub. An active hub amplifies the transmission signals to help extend cable length. A passive hub splits the transmission signal so another client computer can be added.

Tip

Use hubs with twisted-pair cabling in a star or spanning tree topology. You must also match the hub type with the network technology. For example, if you use 10BaseT twisted-pair cabling and cards, you must also use a 10BaseT hub.

Figure 19-7 illustrates how a hub acts as a central device to which all computers are attached. Signals travel from computer to hub and then to the destination computer.

Hubs come with a certain number of ports, including 4, 5, 8, 16, and 24. You plug one computer into each hub. The hub protects other computers on the network because the other computers aren't hindered by one bad connection.

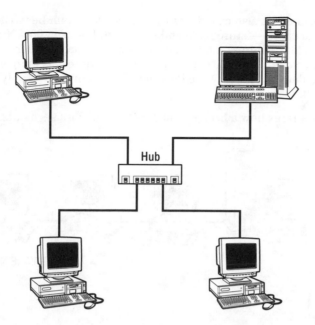

Figure 19-7: You must use a hub when you connect more than two computers.

Tip

Choose a hub with more ports than you think you'll need for your business network. Consider doubling the number of ports; for example, if you think you'll only need 12 ports, consider buying a 24-port hub. You'll be surprised how quickly a network can grow.

Stackable hubs are reasonable for most businesses to use. With stackable hubs, you can add a hub as you need it—say as your network grows. One hub stacks on top of the next. You can save money by buying the hub size you need; an 8-port hub, for example. Then, as your network grows, you can add another 8- or 12-port hub and link the hubs together.

Secret

When buying stackable hubs, consider buying managed—or intelligent— hubs. Managed hubs include software that allows you to communicate with the device and check the status of the ports, send out alerts, and so on. This monitoring software makes troubleshooting hub problems easier and helps you get back online more quickly.

Bridges

Use a bridge to connect to network segments or LANs that use different protocols or different wiring, in most cases. The bridge examines a packet to see if its destination is on the same network. If the destination is not on the same network, the bridge forwards the packet to another segment. As a bridge monitors messages and reads packets, it learns where each network system is located. It constructs a table of the media access control (MAC) addresses that are accessible by its ports and uses those addresses to regulate the flow of traffic on the network.

An Ethernet address is also called a MAC address. It's a number written as 12 hexadecimal digits — 0 through 9 and A through F — as in 0080001021ef. Alternatively, a MAC address might have six hexadecimal numbers separated by periods or colons, as in 0:80:0:2:21:ef. The MAC address is unique to each computer and does not identify the location of the computer — only the computer itself.

Figure 19-8 illustrates how a bridge connects two network segments.

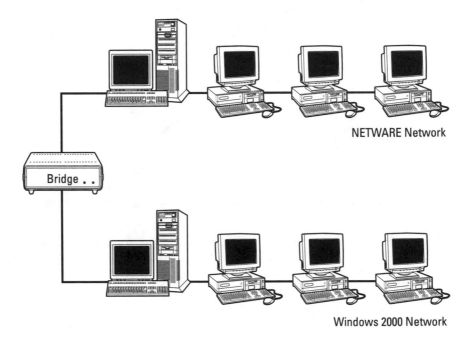

Figure 19-8: A bridge connects network segments using different protocols.

Translating bridges (Brouters) connect networks with different architectures, such as Macintosh and UNIX.

Bridges can cause traffic problems on large networks because they do forward all packets for which they don't know the destination address. However, bridges are less expensive than routers, and they are also easier to install and configure.

Don't use bridges and routers on the same network. Traffic gets jammed because bridges are less discriminating than routers, and packets often must bounce back and forth to reach the appropriate destination.

Repeaters

Use the inexpensive repeater to extend cable lengths. You can double the length of a network cable by positioning a repeater half-way between the cable lengths. You can even use multiple repeaters to extend the distance to the maximum that the specifications allow.

Figure 19-9 shows how a repeater can extend twisted-pair cabling in an Ethernet network.

You use the star topology with twisted-pair so that each computer on the network connects to a central hub. The maximum cable segment length for twisted-pair is around 100 meters, or 330 feet.

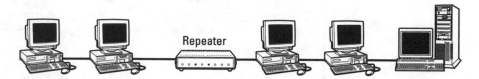
Repeater

Figure 19-9: Repeaters amplify the signal so it can travel longer distances over the transmission medium.

A repeater is a signal amplifier. Whatever signal the repeater receives, it then boosts it and sends it on its way. Repeaters don't examine or verify packets; they don't determine data quality. They simply amplify the signals and transmit it to another computer.

Switches

Switches are a cross between a hub and a bridge. Switches connect similar network segments or LANs. Switches filter data and speed the flow between networks by keeping track of the MACs attached to each port, and then routing traffic destined for a certain address.

Tip

To increase bandwidth, use switched hubs instead of shared hubs. Hubs operate on the machine level and cannot discern addresses or errors in packets. Adding a switch to the hub device makes the hub more efficient and speeds traffic on the network.

Routers

A router is an intelligent connecting device that sends packets to the correct LAN or network segment. The router knows the addresses of all computers on the network. When it reads a destination address in a packet, the router can choose the best available path for the packet to travel to get to its destination.

Figure 19-10 shows a router connecting multiple network segments.

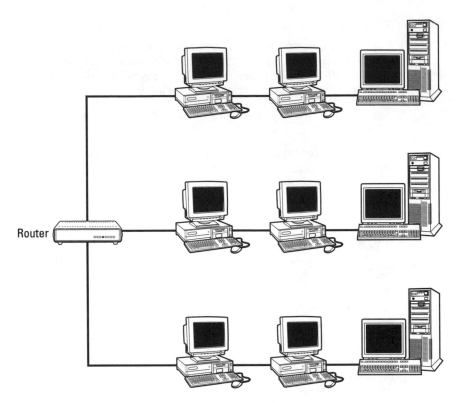

Figure 19-10: Use routers to quickly send the packets to their destinations.

Router configuration is complex because it involves setting functions, protocols, hardware interfaces, and parameters. LAN connections are usually easier to configure; Wide Area Network (WAN) connections are a bit harder. With a WAN connection, the line ending is one you don't normally control because the ending is located at the phone company, for example.

Routers keep track of a packet's movement. That tracking information is stored in the routing table. Each protocol on the network uses its own separate routing table. Also, routers perform error-checking services to make sure bad packets aren't sent through the entire network.

Secret

Routers are different from bridges in several ways. Routers build tables based on network (IP and other) addresses, whereas bridges build tables based on MAC addresses. You cannot change a MAC address; to alter the address patterns, you have to move computers when you use a bridge. Routers block traffic to unknown addresses but bridges forward it, thus adding to the network traffic. Also, routers block broadcast traffic, while bridges cannot block broadcast traffic. The more broadcast traffic, the more bandwidth used, and the slower the network.

Understanding the Network Software

Even with the networking hardware—cables, cards, and so on—attached to your computers, they cannot communicate with each other without networking software. The networking software installed on the computer enables the hardware to do its work.

Windows 2000 automatically adds a client, protocol, and services when it detects a network card in the computer. You can add additional network components and reconfigure components to each network connection, if you want.

Tip

Windows 2000 automatically sets up the default network connection for you; however, there are times when you might need to change configurations or components in the Networking and Dial-up Connections dialog box. See Chapter 21 for more information.

Defining adapters

In networking, an adapter refers to the software driver that makes the network interface card work. Windows locates your adapter and configures it for you; however, you can install a new adapter or change the configuration for an existing adapter in Windows 2000.

Tip

You should always install the latest version of the NIC driver to ensure that the card works efficiently with Windows. It's important to note that the drivers on the manufacturer's disk accompanying the NIC is not necessarily the most recent driver version. For the best solution, check the manufacturer's Web site on the Internet.

Note

When you first turn your computer on after installing a Plug and Play network card, Windows detects the card and prompts to install the network driver. You can let Windows install the driver and complete the task. Later, you can add an updated driver, change the driver, or leave the adapter configured as is.

Any time you add a new or change an old device—such as a network card—you can cause your computer to stop working. Each device has it's own settings. If you add another device that tries to take those settings, you have a hardware conflict.

The three settings you must consider are the Interrupt Request (IRQ), Direct Memory Access (DMA), and Input/Output (I/O) addresses. Hardware lines carry a device's signal to the processor. When a device wants to communicate with the processor, it causes an IRQ to gain the processor's attention. The I/O is the means by which data is transferred between the computer and its peripheral devices. DMA is a method of transferring information directly from a hard disk, for example, into memory by bypassing the processor.

Tip

In Windows 2000, the IRQ is called the Interrupt Request; the DMA is called the Memory Range; and the I/O is called the Input/Output Range.

IRQs

Most computers have fifteen IRQs. Some IRQs are assigned to specific devices, and others are free for cards and devices you install. Following is a list of IRQs and some devices that commonly assigned to specific IRQs:

Tip

To locate the IRQ for your devices, including the network card, check the Device Manager in Windows 2000.

Interrupt Request	Device
1	Keyboard Controller. IRQ1 is never available to other add-in cards. If there's a conflict with IRQ1, it probably means the system board is bad.
2	Tied to IRQs 9-15. Don't use this IRQ if you can help it. IRQ9 uses it to communicate with the CPU.
3	COM 2. Shares IRQ3 with COM4; serial ports use mice, modems, and other such devices.
4	COM1; Shares IRQ4 with COM3, so you cannot assign a device on COM1 and COM3 at the same time.
5	LPT2 or sound card; A secondary printer port; if no secondary printer, then used for sound card.
6	Floppy disk controller. Not available for other uses if you have a floppy drive.
7	LPT1. First parallel port is used for attached printer.
8	Clock. Reserved for the internal real-time clock. Never available. If conflict arises, could mean you have a bad motherboard.
9	Cascades from IRQ 2. A high priority IRQ since it talks directly to the CPU. Often used for network cards.
10-11	Unused. Open for network cards, sound cards, and other devices.
12	PS/2 mouse. If you use a PS/2 port mouse, this is its IRQ. If not, you can use it for something else.
13	Coprocessor or Numerical Processing Unit (NPU). Never available for anything else.
14	Primary IDE hard disk controller. Not available for other devices.
15	Unused or secondary IDE hard disk controller. Generally not available for other devices.

I/O addresses

I/O addresses refer to locations in a computer's memory map. Addresses are in hexadecimal format, which is a base-16 numbering system that uses the digits 0 to 9, followed by the letters A to F. Hexadecimal numbers represent the binary numbers that computers use internally (they all fit into the 8-bit byte).

The following common devices are assigned to certain I/O addresses:

I/O Address	Device
130h	SCSI host adapters
140h	SCSI host adapters
170h	Secondary IDE interface
1F0h	Primary IDE interface
220h	Sound Blaster cards
240h	Sound card alternate
278h	LPT 2 or LPT3 (and generally IRQ 5)
280h	Network interface cards
2A0h	Alternate for NIC
2E8h	COM 4 (with IRQ 3)
2F8h	COM 2 (with IRQ 3)
300h	Network interface cards
320h	Network card, SCSI adapter, or MIDI device
330h	SCSI adapter
340h	SCSI adapter
360h	Network card, unless first parallel printer port is using this address
378h	LPT1 with color systems (with IRQ 7)
3BCh	LPT1 with monochrome systems
3E8h	COM3 (with IRQ 4)
3F8h	COM1 (with IRQ 4)

DMA channels

DMA (Direct Memory Access) channels might be an area for hardware conflicts. Plug and Play systems use DMAs. The most commonly assigned devices for DMA channels are as follows:

0   Assigned internally for system board. Not available.

1   No specific assignment; may be used for sound cards and SCSI adapters.

2   Diskette drives.

3   No specific assignment; may be used for sound cards, network interface cards, and SCSI adapters.

4   No specific assignment.

5   No specific assignment; may be used for Sound Blaster cards.

6   No specific assignment.

7   No specific assignment.

Defining the network client

The network client is the software that enables your computer to become a member of a network. Each network type — Windows peer-to-peer, NT Server, Novell NetWare, and so on — has its own specific client. You install the client software for the network type to a computer to allow the computer to communicate over the network. Microsoft supplies clients for Microsoft networks, plus clients for NetWare. You also can add a network client.

Novell NetWare also supplies clients for its NOS. If you set up a client/server network with NetWare, you may want to use Novell's client because it offers more features on that particular network than the Windows NetWare client. However, the Novell client also has more compatibility problems with Windows.

Cross-Reference

See Chapter 21 for more information about installing clients for client/server and peer-to-peer networks.

Defining protocols

Protocols are languages that define procedures for transmitting and receiving data over the network. Protocols define the format, timing, sequence, and error-checking used on the network. There are many protocols that work on many levels in networking. For example, Ethernet is both a networking technology and a protocol, as is Token Ring. These are communications protocols that guarantee the synchronization and flow of data from computer to computer.

Transport protocols send messages and data from one computer to another over the network. The common transport protocols include Transmission Control Protocol/Internet Protocol (TCP/IP), Internet Packet Exchange/Sequenced Packet Exchange (IPX/SPX), and Network Basic Input/Output /System Extended User Interface (NetBEUI, also called NetBIOS).

Note

Windows 2000 enables you to install TCP/IP and NetBEUI; plus the following: AppleTalk, DLC, and OSI-LAN. In addition, Windows 2000 uses a compatible IPX/SPX protocol called NWLink IPX/SPX/NetBIOS Compatible Transport Protocol.

Choose the transport protocol that works best with your network. For example, if you're using a client for a small Windows network, NetBEUI is a good protocol because it's efficient and easy to configure. If you're using a Novell NetWare client, you should use IPX/SPX. NT Server or Windows 2000 Server clients generally use TCP/IP, as well as peer-to-peer networks and sometimes NetWare clients.

Secret

Don't install and configure multiple protocols unless you have a specific reason to do so, such as if you're a member of an integrated NetWare and NT network, or you must occasionally communicate with a Macintosh computer. When you install more than one protocol to your workstation, each protocol is checked for every network connection, thus slowing the response time to network transmissions.

NetBEUI

NetBEUI is a Microsoft protocol you can use with any Windows operating system — Windows for Workgroups, Windows 95, Windows 98, Windows NT, and Windows 2000 Professional. NetBEUI stands for NetBIOS Extended User Interface. NetBIOS stands for Network Basic Input/Output /System. NetBEUI defines how the software should send and receive messages when NetBIOS is the transport method.

Secret

NetBIOS also works with other protocols and various network types. NetBIOS is an interface for the network protocol; it provides the Transport and Session layer services for the protocol with which it's working. NetBIOS isn't routable, meaning it cannot reach computers located in segments other than its own.

NetBEUI is perfect for small networks. It's easy to set up, provides good performance, and is a fast protocol. NetBEUI uses very little memory and also provides good error detection over the network. If you're setting up your first network and you want an easy job of it, use NetBEUI as your networking protocol.

NetBEUI is not a routable protocol, so it can only work on one segment of the network. That's why it's best used with small networks of 150 computers or fewer.

IPX/SPX

IPX/SPX is the protocol used with Novell NetWare networks, although you also can use it with Microsoft networks. IPX/SPX is a protocol stack, or group of protocols that work together.

IPX is used to transfer data between a server and workstations on the network. IPX packets carry the packets used in Ethernet and in Token Ring networks. IPX doesn't guarantee the delivery of data, nor the sequence in which the data is delivered.

SPX is a set of Novell NetWare protocols that adds to the capabilities of IPX. SPX guarantees packet delivery, for example, by requesting verification from the destination computer.

Tip

IPX/SPX supports many of the Windows' features, including NetBIOS, Windows sockets, and others.

IPX/SPX is a routable protocol; however, there are some problems with routing. For example, routing tables are not always accurate because of the way they're built. In addition, routing tables are vulnerable to errors because of the time it takes to circulate packets to other segments.

NWLink IPX/SPX/NetBIOS Compatible Transport Protocol is Windows 2000 IPX/SPX-compatible protocol. NWLink supports routing and Novell NetWare client/server applications.

AppleTalk

AppleTalk is the Apple Computer networking protocol used to connect Macintosh clients to an Ethernet network. Windows 2000 Server networks with Macintosh computers attached use the Services for Macintosh feature to enable Macintosh computers to communicate with IBM-compatible computers on the network using the AppleTalk protocol. In addition, the AppleTalk protocol enables file and information shares across an AppleTalk internet, or a collection of AppleTalk networks.

AppleTalk uses the MAC address to locate computers for packet delivery. The AppleTalk Address Resolution Protocol (AARP) is the protocol that finds MAC addresses by sending out a network broadcast containing the address for which it is searching. When the system replies, AARP adds the MAC address to its mapping table.

DLC

DLC (Data Link Control) uses MAC addresses to provide communications between applications and computer hardware. DLC is not a routable protocol; it works only within one segment.

Tip

You might use DLC if you're connected to an IBM mainframe or if your network uses a print server, for example. When you install DLC, it automatically adds additional printer port drivers.

TCP/IP

Transmission Control Protocol/Internet Protocol (TCP/IP) is actually a set (stack or suite) of network protocols designed by the government's Advanced Research Projects Agency (hence the name ARPAnet) in the 1970s. Each of the protocols that make up TCP/IP make it an efficient and fast communications language for the Internet and for local and wide area networks.

TCP/IP works with a variety of hardware and software products. You can use it on UNIX, Macintosh, and IBM-compatible computers using Windows, NetWare, OS/2, and more. Many manufacturers and vendors support TCP/IP because it is so widely used.

TCP/IP protocols

Some of the other protocols in the TCP/IP suite include the following:

- **IP (Internet Protocol)** enables network packets to move data between network segments and travel across routers. IP is a routing protocol. IP chooses the path the packets take across routers and networks. IP regulates packet forwarding by tracking Internet addresses, recognizing incoming messages, and routing outgoing messages. However, data in these packets (called datagrams) may arrive at the destination in any order or they may not arrive at all.

- **TCP (Transmission Control Protocol)** is a higher-level protocol than IP. It provides continuing connections between programs. TCP also makes IP datagrams smaller and faster. TCP divides datagrams into smaller segments to fit the physical requirements of the servers on the network. Then it uses IP to transmit the segments of data. TCP inserts a header into each segment that is used to track every segment from one port to the other. TCP guarantees that every byte sent arrives and without duplication or loss. After the segments arrive at the target host, TCP checks for errors. If it finds any corrupted data, it discards it and requests the data be transmitted again.

- **UDP (User Datagram Protocol)** is similar to TCP in that it divides some datagrams into segments and sends them over the network using IP. UDP is a primitive version of TCP.

- **PPP (Point-to-Point Protocol)** enables connections between hosts and networks and the nodes (routers, bridges, and so on) in between.

- **SMTP (Simple Mail Transfer Protocol)** is for exchanging e-mail.

- **FTP (File Transfer Protocol)** is for transferring files. FTP lets one computer transfer a file to another using TCP.

- **SMB (Server Message Block)** lets a computer use network resources as if they were local.

- **NFS (Network File System)** enables a computer to use files as if they were local.

- **TELENET** is a terminal emulation protocol that lets you connect to a remote service while in Windows.

- **ARP (Address Resolution Protocol)** translates 32-bit IP addresses into physical network addresses, such as 48-bit Ethernet addresses.

- **RARP (Reverse Address Resolution Protocol)** translates physical network addresses into IP addresses.

- **ICMP (Internet Control Message Protocol)** helps IP communicate error information about the IP transmissions for routers.

- **IGMP (Internet Group Management Protocol)** allows IP datagrams to be broadcast to computers that belong to groups.

Tip

Some of the TCP/IP protocols are also applications. FTP, TELNET, and SNMP, for example, are programs that you can use over the network because they're included with the TCP/IP suite.

Examining an IP address

An IP address identifies the computer or other node (router, printer, server, or other) on the network. Each IP address on a network must be unique.

An IP address is a binary number that is written in a series of four decimal digits, known as dotted decimal. Four period-delimited octets, consisting of up to 12 numerals, forms an IP address. For example, Microsoft's home page IP address is the dotted decimal number: 207.46.131.137. The numbers represent decimal notations for each of the four bytes of the address; the address identifies the computer.

The IP address is really made up of two parts: the network number and the host number. The network number identifies the general location of the computer on the network, and the host number pins it down to the exact computer. In Microsoft's IP address, 207.46 is the network address. 131.137 represents the host number. Each class of address uses a different manner of dividing the octets. Microsoft is a Class B network.

The highest value in any octet is 255 because of the way the binary format translates to dotted decimal.

IP addressing is divided into five categories, or classes. Three of the classes — Class A, Class B, and Class C — are in use today. The following list describes each of these classes:

- **Class A** is used for large networks. To identify a Class A network address, the first octet uses the numbers from 1 to 126. Class A networks have an 8-bit network prefix; therefore they are currently referred to as /8s (pronounced slash eights) or just "eights."

- **Class B** is mainly used for medium-sized networks and the first octet values range from 128 to 191. Class B network addresses have a 16-bit network prefix; thus they are referred to as /16s.

- **Class C** is reserved for smaller networks. To identify a Class C network, the values range from 192 to 223. Class C networks have a 24-bit network prefix and are referred to as /24s.

Universities and corporations have already taken the Class A addresses. Class B addresses are assigned to companies and institutions with a minimum of 4000 hosts. If you apply for an Internet address, you will likely receive a Class C address. Each class defines its own 32-bit address boundaries. In Class C, the first three octets are for the network address; the last octet represents the host address.

Looking at the subnet mask and gateway

A subnet mask is part of the IP addressing system. A subnet mask creates subnetworks that allow a computer in one network segment to communicate with a computer in another segment of the network. The main reason for subnetting (or creating subnets on a network) is to divide a single Class A, B, or C network into smaller pieces.

The subnet mask is a 32-bit address that hides, or masks, part of the IP address so as to add to the number of computers added to the network. All networks must use a subnet mask, even if it doesn't connect to another network. If a network isn't divided into subnets, the default subnet mask is used. The default depends on the IP address class.

Class A networks use a default subnet mask of 255.0.0.0.

Class B uses 255.255.0.0.

Class C uses 255.255.255.0

The gateway is a bridge between two segments of a network. Messages travel between network segments through the gateway. A gateway is a combination of hardware and software; it creates a shared connection between say, a LAN and a larger network.

Setting up a TCP/IP network

There are several IP addresses that are reserved for private use. Following are the three blocks reserved for IP addresses:

10.0.0.0 to 10.255.255.255

172.16.0.0 to 172.31.255.255

192.168.0.0 to 192.168.255.255

You should change numbers only in the last octet of the IP address for a business network. If your corporate network is very large, you can make other changes to the IP addresses, as long as they are consistent.

In addition to IP addresses, you also need a subnet mask. Use the same subnet mask for all computers on the network.

Defining services

In networking, server machines offer services — such as printing, Internet access, backup and restore, authentication, and so on. In client computers, however, services are limited. Windows 2000 Professional offers services for file and print sharing, file replication services, and routing and remote access services, for example. You also can add services from disk.

Summary

In this chapter, we describe the networking hardware and software you need to set up a network.

▶ You can choose the type of network that works best for your business.

▶ You learn the networking topologies and technologies so you can choose the right networking layout for your company.

▶ You can decide which networking speeds and transmission media best suit your networking needs.

▶ You learn about the various networking protocols you can use to set up your network.

Chapter 20

Installing Networking Hardware

Purchasing and Installing a Network Interface Card

When you choose a network interface card for a computer, make sure you match the card to the network cable and the technology you're using. If, for example, you plan to use an Ethernet cabling scheme, you must also use an Ethernet network card. If you set up wireless connections, you must choose the appropriate network card for that type of network.

Installing the network card is fairly easy, as is installing a hub. Installing the cabling is a bit more difficult. Installing and configuring a router is the toughest job of all.

The difference between Legacy and Plug and Play

Legacy is a wonderful term that has come to the fore — oddly enough — in the computer age. It was originally used to describe outdated computer applications, devices, adapter cards, and so on, but it has come to have wider use.

For instance, the traditional print version of the *New York Times* is an example of legacy media. Newt Gingrich is an example of a legacy politician, and *60 Minutes* is an example of a legacy TV show.

In the Windows 2000 universe, *legacy hardware* refers devices that must be manually configured. The alternative is *Plug and Play*, an alluring, but still somewhat vaporous Microsoft effort designed to make computer setup easier.

With Plug and Play, you theoretically plug a card—video, sound, network, or whatever—into a computer slot. Then, when you start your computer, Windows detects the new device and automatically installs and configures the driver. Plug and Play also can refer to printers, modems, and other devices that identify themselves and declare their resource needs to the computer's operating system and BIOS.

Note

You can physically install some Plug and Play devices in or to a Windows 2000 computer—such as a printer, joystick, or USB port—and without rebooting, Windows will recognize and install the necessary drivers for you. You should always turn off the computer before opening the case so that you don't get an electrical shock while removing screws.

Often, Windows cannot find Plug and Play devices, or it installs a driver that isn't the best choice for the device. It's a good idea to check with the manufacturer of the card to make sure you have the latest driver that works with Windows 2000 Professional.

Windows 2000 Professional's Plug and Play manager is more reliable than in previous Windows versions. The Plug and Play manager identifies a new device and then assigns it the needed system resources. Whenever there is a change to the system, the Plug and Play manager automatically reconfigures resource assignments.

Tip

If the card requires a bus master slot and you don't have one available, the card won't work as efficiently. Bus mastering enables advanced bus architectures to assign control of the data transfers between the CPU and peripherals. Using bus mastering with network interface cards supplies the card with higher data transfer speeds. However, you might need your bus mastering slot for another device, such as a drive or controller.

Legacy

Legacy cards are often older ISA cards that Windows 2000 can't identify or automatically configure. A legacy card might have fixed resources, in which case you cannot manually change the settings; or a card might supply switches or jumpers for the manual setting and configuration of the resources. In cases like these, make sure you assign the slot as an ISA slot in your computer's CMOS.

Although Windows is built for use with Plug and Play devices, the Registry contains information about legacy devices that it can use in order to accurately detect some legacy hardware. The Registry also attempts to prevent resource conflicts for legacy devices by keeping track of the resources used for the those devices and then blocking Plug and Play devices from using those resources.

Plug and Play

To use Plug and Play, you need both hardware and software support. First, the device must be able to identify itself to the BIOS and the operating system, and it must be manually configurable. Second, the BIOS must support Plug and Play. And last, the operating system must be able to assign system resources, such as IRQs, to the devices or cards.

Tip

Most any device made for the newer buses — PCI, EISA, or PCMCIA — is a Plug and Play device. In addition, some newer ISA cards also support Plug and Play.

A Plug and Play BIOS starts the automatic configuration of Plug and Play devices. During POST (Power-on Self Test), the BIOS determines the resource needs for Plug and Play devices, checks the resources assigned to legacy devices, and then determines which resources are free for assignment to the Plug and Play devices.

Secret

With Windows 2000 Plug and Play support, the BIOS must be compliant with Advanced Configuration and Power Interface Specification (ACPI). In general, the runtime services portion of the BIOS is replaced by ACPI.

When Windows detects a Plug and Play device, it consults the Registry, recognizes the device, and then configures it. Windows 2000 provides a set of bus drivers for nearly every type of common I/O bus that can be found in a computer.

In the real world, some devices are more compatible with Plug and Play than others. Both PCI and EISA meet more Plug and Play requirements than ISA devices because they provide the standard information needed by the system for identification and configuration.

Tip

Usually, a PCI bus is secondary to a primary bus. If that is the case, both the primary bus and the PCI bus must support Plug and Play to enable Plug and Play.

Looking at NIC types

PCI and ISA are the two most common bus types. If you have a choice between PCI and ISA, you should definitely choose PCI. PCI network cards are particularly well suited to Windows 2000 because of Plug and Play, and because they maximize the functionality of multitasking operating systems.

If you're using a portable computer, you'll need a PC Card NIC to fit the available card slot. Read your documentation to determine the type of card you can use with your portable computer.

Secret

You can find network cards that are combination card, such as a modem and network card, and the deal may seem like a good one, especially if you don't have enough slots to accommodate two separate cards. However, if you have enough PC slots, purchase two separate cards. With combination cards, if one card becomes damaged or quits working, you have to replace both cards.

Depending on your computer, you can use network cards that connect to an external port (such as the parallel port), that fit into a PC Card slot on a laptop or portable , or that are installed internally and connect to a bus.

Secret

Parallel port network cards do not perform well on a network; don't use one of these unless it is the only way with which you can connect tot he network. USB external network adapters — which are new products on the market — might be worth a try since they're easy to use and might yield better performance than parallel cards.

Following are the common card types (some of the following cards are still available in older computers but may not be found on newer ones):

- **PCI (Peripheral Component Interconnect).** PCI is the most popular, common, and fastest bus architecture today. PCI is an Intel specification defining a local bus that allows up to ten PCI-compliant expansion cards to be plugged into the computer. PCI is Plug and Play on most systems, as well as being the least expensive card listed here.

- **ISA (Industry Standard Architecture).** ISA is a 16-bit bus design and the slowest bus architecture of the list. ISA can perform at speeds of 10Mbps for file and printer sharing. Some 100Mbps ISA cards are also available, but the bus is too slow to benefit from the additional bandwidth.

- **EISA (Extended Industry Standard Architecture).** EISA is a 32-bit extension to the ISA standard bus. EISA can easily run at speeds of 10Mbps but also has some trouble with 100Mbps speeds.

- **MCA (Microchannel Architecture).** MCA is a 32-bit expansion bus designed for multiprocessing. Expansion boards identify themselves, thus eliminating any conflicts created by manual configuration. These cards are supported only by IBM, so there are fewer card options available. (MCA cards are no longer used on newer computers.)

- **VESA (Video Electronics Standards Association).** VESA is an enhanced EISA 32-bit design that runs ten times faster than ISA. Unfortunately, VESA is no longer in use on newer computers because it just didn't catch on.

- **PCMCIA (Personal Computer Memory Card International Association).** PCMCIA is a standard for portable computers. The card is usually the size of a credit card. There are several versions — or types — of PCMCIA cards; the types define the thickness and uses of the card.

- **PC (Personal Computer).** A PC card conforms to the PCMCIA standard and offers high performance on the network. PC cards use a 68-pin connector with longer power and ground pins.

Buy PCI

PCI cards support bus mastering, especially for the use with Pentium Pro-class processors. Bus mastering is a technique in which the advanced bus architectures controls the flow of data between the CPU and peripheral devices. This means that the NIC receives greater system bus access and higher data transfer speeds.

Here are some other reasons to PCI, if you can:

■ PCI drivers are tuned for 32-bit performance, which matches the PCI bus architecture and the Windows operating system.

■ PCI takes advantage of the performance and power capabilities of the Pentium-series processors. ISA and EISA buses are older standards, adequate for older 386 and 486 CPUs but not as sophisticated as PCI.

■ PCI was designed for 32-bit and 64-bit data paths, meaning faster throughput on the network.

Purchasing the Network Interface Card

Your first priority when choosing the NIC you want is to match your computer's slots with the type of network you plan to use. Other things to consider when purchasing a network card are price, brand name, warranty, and the type of connectors on the card.

Tip

Buy the same brand of NIC for all the computers on your network. Using the same brand of NIC with the same type of network software makes installing, configuring, and troubleshooting network connections easier.

Tip

When buying a NIC, buy a known brand instead of a bargain-bin special. The more expensive cards made by superior manufacturers are of better quality, they last longer, and they generally always have better warranties. Support is better, too, and believe me — you will need support.

Cable and technology types

When you choose a network interface card, consider the speed of the cabling and card, as well as the technology types. If you're using Ethernet cabling, you must use Ethernet cards. If you've chosen Ethernet, you also must also match the network card and the hub with the speed — either 10Mbps or 100Mbps, for example. Either speed can work with Cat 5 twisted-pair cabling. Most network cards today are rated as 10/100, meaning that you can use them at either speed — 10Mbps or 100Mbps. For more information, see Chapter 19.

If you're building an Ethernet network, definitely buy the 10/100 cards. You can use the 10Mbps now and upgrade later to 100Mbps, if you choose. Most newer 10/100 cards have an autosensor that detects the network speed so you don't have to reconfigure the workstations.

You also must consider connectors on the network card. If your cable is coax, the card needs to have BNC connectors. If the cable is twisted-pair, make sure the card has RJ-45 connectors. Note that a portable computer often uses a different type of connector and card than a desktop computer. Check your documentation before buying a NIC for a portable computer.

Brand and quality

Consider the network card's brand, price, warranty, and the technical support offered. Most network adapter cards cost about the same, between $30 to $40 each.. Avoid any network interface cards that are considerably cheaper and avoid network card sales; these cards may be obsolete or damaged.

Warranties range from a few months to a lifetime. Always buy a card with a lifetime warranty. If the card you have in mind doesn't offer a lifetime warranty, don't buy it. There are many cards available from which you can choose. Also check for other features and advantages included with the card. For example, the manufacturer should supply a cross-shipping service when you return a bad card for replacement while it is under warranty.

Buy products from manufacturers who have a good reputation for their products and support. Adaptec, 3Com, Digital Equipment, and Linksys are just a few manufacturers of Ethernet adapter cards. IBM, DEC, Proxim, and Xircom are a few of the companies that manufacture wireless cards.

Installing a Network Interface Card

When you install a NIC, you go through two steps. First, you physically install the card into the computer. Second, you install the network card's driver or, rather, you let Windows do that for you.

Cross-Reference

See Chapter 21 for information about installing and configuring the network card's driver.

Tip

Portable computers have a door or slot for network cards that you can reach from the outside. Check your computer's documentation for more information.

Inserting a card into a desktop computer

Be careful when touching the network card. Natural oils from your skin can damage the card. Touch only the edges of the card, and not the gold-edged connector on the bottom of the card..

STEPS:

How to install a network interface card

Step 1. Before you install the network card, consult your computer's documentation to see if there are any special instructions you need to for installing cards.

Step 2. Make sure your computer is powered off and the power cord has been removed from the back of the computer.. You should also unplug all of the plugs from the back of your computer, including the cable that connects to the display, modem, printer, and so on.

Step 3. Remove the computer's case. If you have trouble removing the case, consult the computer manual for instructions. Most cases are connected with screws, or they have a snap-on lock or button to press with which you can release the case.

Step 4. Look inside the computer for a row of slots along the back edge. Some slots will already have cards installed in slots.

Step 5. Remove the screw that secures the slot cover to the frame above the slot into which you will be inserting the network card. A slot cover is a metal strip that keeps dust out when there's no card installed in the slot. Keep the screw.

Step 6. Holding the card only from the top and side edges, carefully position it over the slot and gently push it straight down. Check to see that the card fits into the slot before seating the card.

Step 7. To seat the card, firmly push the card down into the slot. Push the card just a little bit harder than you think you should so that you can hear it snap into place.

Step 8. Insert the screw to hold the card in place. Be careful not to over-tighten the screw. The screw head should be flush with the top metal tab of the card, and the card's tab should be flush with the top of the case.

Step 9. Next, check that you didn't accidentally disconnect any wires or cables from other devices — such as hard drives — inside the case. Remember to remove all the tools you've used up to this point.

Step 10. *Do not touch the computer during the next step.* Plug the computer in and apply power to it. Be alert for smoke or the smell of plastic burning. Make sure the computer boots properly. If you detect any problems, immediately power off the computer and reseat the card. Then, try again.

If you powered the computer on and everything seems okay, you can continue with Step 11.

Continued

STEPS:

How to install a network interface card *(continued)*

Step 11.   Power off the computer again and disconnect the AC power cord from the computer. Replace the case and secure it with screws, if applicable. Reattach all external cables you might have disconnected.

If the card isn't seated properly, the computer won't boot — you won't even see anything on your display.

You can power up the computer and configure the card now, if you want (see Chapter 21 for more information). Next, attach the network cables to the card, as explained in the following section.

You should read the documentation that comes with your NIC, plus any readme files that might be on the floppy disk or CD-ROM that comes with the card. If you didn't receive a disk containing the driver software for the NIC, check the manufacturer's Internet site for the latest available drivers.

Connecting the cabling to the card

The next step is to connect the cabling to your network card. Again, the computer should be turned off for this process. To be safe, you want to unplug the AC power line, too.

The cable you purchased should have the correct connector on the end — RJ-45, BNC, or other connector. All you have to do is plug the connector into the network card you just installed. Make sure the connection is secure.

You should use a patch cable to connect the card to a hub or wall jack if you're using Ethernet cabling. Patch cables are short cables (one or two feet long) that you use to ease the strain on the longer length of cable connecting the hub to the computer. (See the following section about cabling a hub for more information about patch cables.)

Finally, you can power up your computer. Windows 2000 will automatically configure the computer to communicate with the network. (For more information, see Chapter 21.)

Purchasing and Installing a Hub

You need a hub if your network is Ethernet and it connects three or more computers together. If you've connected two computers together using Ethernet technology, cabling, and network cards, you can do that without a hub; however, it would be a faster and more efficient connection if you use a hub. For more information, see "Connecting Two Computers," later in this chapter.

Tip

Hubs run independently of the types of computers attached to the network, so you could have a PC and a Macintosh plugged into the same hub to run on an Ethernet network.

There are two types of hubs: stackable and chassis. *Stackable* hubs are flat on the top and bottom. In larger networks, you can stack one hub on top of another to expand the network. *Chassis* hubs are larger, one or two feet tall and up to two feet wide. Chassis hubs are often used in huge networks — 200 users, for example — and they present some disadvantages over stackable hubs.

Stackable hubs (see Figure 20-1) are the best choice for a small to medium network. You can install one or two stackable hubs and then add others to it as the network grows. A stackable hub has between 3 and 24 ports to which you connect network cables. Stackables are inexpensive and flexible. You can move them around. You can locate them throughout the network or stack them together. You also can mix and match the brands of hubs you use and the number of ports that each hub contains.

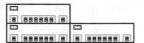

Figure 20-1: Stackable hubs make the network expandable.

A major advantage to using stackable hubs is that if one hub fails, the rest of the hubs are not affected. Most network users can continue to work on the network until you can add a replacement hub.

A chassis hub is different than a stackable hub. Chassis hubs are made for sizable networks with scores of connections (200 or more). A chassis hub is made to mount into a network rack so that it displays slots along the front. The slots are for installing cards quickly and easily. The cards have multiple RJ-45 connectors for attaching cabling to the hub. The main problem with using a chassis hub is that if the hub goes down, all of the users connected to it lose the network connection.

Purchasing a hub

The first step in purchasing a hub is to determine the speed of the technology you plan to use. For example, if your network cards are 10Mbps Ethernet, your hub must be 10Mbps Ethernet. If your network cards are 100Mbps Ethernet, your hub must also be 100Mbps. You can use 10Mbps cards, however, with a 100Mbps hub.

The next step is to determine the number of devices you need to connect to the network. List all computers, printers, servers, and such. You also might want to connect your printer to a computer for print management, or directly to the hub.

Tip

You can connect printers directly to the network hub with the help of a network interface, such as Hewlett Packard's JetDirect NIC.

Buy a hub that supplies a port for every device you plan to connect to it. In addition, plan for the near future by buying a hub with more ports than you currently need. It's less expensive to buy a hub that allows your network to grow than to buy a new hub later.

Secret

When looking for a hub, search for one with a cross-over port to connect another hub. That way, you can build your spanning tree (also called cascading) topology as your network grows.

Hub prices vary, but generally, they are inexpensive. While you are comparison shopping, price a hub per port instead of per complete hub. Ethernet hubs should sell for less than $20 per port.

Hub warranties range from a couple of months to a lifetime. As with the network card, make sure you get a hub with a lifetime warranty. Look for other benefits like cross-shipping of replacement parts and products, technical support, and so on.

Here are some more features you should look for in a hub:

- LED lights indicate when the hub is turned on, when it's working, and the hub's collision status. Collisions are quite common with some networking technologies. A collision occurs when two or more computers try to transmit data simultaneously. Both computers stop transmitting and retransmit after a random period of time. If the LED that indicates collisions is constantly lit, you know you have a problem.

Note

Chassis hubs do not have LED lights.

- IEEE 802.x specifications mean the hub will comply with a full set of processes as required by the IEEE. The processes might involve collision-handling, retransmitting packets, link tests, and other functions.

- Repeater functions refer to the retransmission of network packets when a collision or timing problem takes place. Timing losses can occur when there is distortion due to cabling interference, signal loss, jitter, or other problems. Data transmission is more reliable when a hub has repeater functions.

Installing a hub

Place the hub in a central, convenient location. After plugging the network cable into the network card, you can run the cable to the hub and plug it into any open port. If you have a cross-over port on the hub, use it only for connecting to another hub, not for connecting to a computer or printer. You can use patch cables to make the computer connections more reliable and strong.

Tip

You should label each cable on the hub with a number or name so you know where it leads to, in case you have trouble with that computer's connection.

If you plan to use the hub to connect only computers, that's easy. If you plan to use the hub to connect another hub so you can extend your network, check the hub's documentation to discover how to set the hub for this function. Here's some technical hints, in any event.

For two hubs to communicate with each other, the transmitter of one device must be connected to the receiver of the other device. Most hubs provide a cable switch that accomplishes this task. If you do not find the switch on your hub, you can use a crossover cable to do the same thing.

You can purchase a crossover cable for use with hubs. Crossover cables are wired differently than straight-through cables but are still made of unshielded twisted-pair cabling. Straight-through cables are your normal UTP cables for use from computer to hub.

Cabling to the hub

In an office, you often move computers, hubs, and users around. Any stress at all on the cabling between the hub and the computer can cause network transfer interruptions. You should not run the cable from the computer directly to the hub; you need to use patch cables, instead, to cable to the hub. Patch cables are short (three to five feet long), flexible, twisted-pair cables that connect the NIC to the hub. Patch cables cut down on the twisting and kinking of the solid cabling you use to connect computers.

Note

Most wiring specifications require the use of patch cables and jacks, especially in offices and businesses.

The twisted-pair cabling you use for networking can be either a solid or a stranded cable. Solid cabling is used for the majority of the cabling because it distributes the data quickly and efficiently. It's not a good idea, however, to attach the solid cabling directly to your network card or hub. If the solid cabling is moved around very much, the cable can become twisted or kinked. Kinking the cable can make your network connection irregular, or stop the connection altogether.

Normally, you use the solid cabling for room-to-room connections, and switch to the stranded cable (patch cable) to connect to the computer or hub. The stranded cable is much more flexible than the solid cable, so you don't have to be as careful when moving the cable, computer, or hub.

As an example of using solid and stranded cabling, you might bring the solid cabling through the wall, attach a jack to the cabling, and cover it with a faceplate. From the wall outlet, you attach a patch cable that then plugs into the network card on one end. On the other end, attach a jack and faceplate, and then use a patch cable to attach the jack to the hub.

If you make the patch cables yourself, you need a special punch to terminate the cabling and attach the jacks. You might want to outsource this part of the cabling. Call the telephone or a telecom service in your area to obtain quotes and help installing the twisted-pair cabling.

Tip

Networking kits come with the connectors and jacks attached to cables, ready for you to plug in to your network. You also can buy pre-terminated cables, patch cables, and other equipment for your cabling job.

If you have many connections to a hub, you might want to use a device called a patch panel in your office network. Patch panels contain 8, 12, or 24 jacks within a strip for easy connection to solid cables. You can attach the patch panel to the wall, insert the solid cables, and then insert the patch cables on the other side leading to your hub for safe and effective wiring of your network.

Managing Routers

Often, a bridge or a switch can automatically configure themselves, but configuring a router is more complex. Routers are intelligent devices that direct network traffic by following a strict set of rules in order. These rules define how the router will deal with each packet of information; for example, the router might accept certain destination addresses and drops others.

You set the router's rules using a cryptic command-line interface. If you mistype a rule, you could mislead the router. If a hacker breaks into your system, he or she could send fake Internet Control Message Protocol (ICMP) packets that tell your router to change its default rules. Bad rules or mistaken filters can slow the router's performance and thus, decrease network throughput. Therefore, routers are extremely difficult to set up and configure.

Here's a list of things you should think about when you configure a router:

- Configure the physical interface by enabling support for traffic protocols for LAN or WAN connections. WAN connections are obviously more difficult to configure because they encompass more nodes.

- Configure the link for the framing protocols, such as PPP, frame relay, HDLC, or other Layer 2 protocol.

- Define routing tables or configure the support for automatic routing tables. You have one routing table per network protocol that you use on the network. You must define static routes if you configure the tables manually, which makes the process more difficult, but saves network traffic over dynamic (automatic) routing. Alternatively, you can configure the router for dynamic routing tables or use a combination of static and dynamic routing.

■ Define filters or rules for each interface/protocol combination. In general, everything that is not explicitly permitted is prohibited, or everything that is not explicitly prohibited is permitted. Different routers present different methods of setting security filters; check the router documentation.

Tip

If you need to add a router to your network, I suggest you hire someone to install and configure the device for you. Even professionals have trouble defining router tables and designing rules and filters.

Installing Cable

Installing cable can be as easy or as difficult as you want to make it. You can run the cable through walls or under the carpet to hide it. You might want to purchase raceway, a plastic casing that covers the cable and attaches it to the wall.

Tip

If you don't want to install the cable yourself, you can hire someone to do it. Check the yellow pages for telecom or telephone services, network consultants, or network technicians for prices.

Secret

Before installing cabling, make sure you check building codes and AC power line placement and standards for that building. If you're renting the office space, make sure you check with the owner of the building.

Making a network map

The first step is to plan where the computers will be located. Next choose a central location for the hub. Finally, decide how and where you will place the cables within the room or building. Examine the walls and ceilings to see if you can run the cable through the ceilings and make drops (a wire run) at each computer station or group of computers. Perhaps you can run the cabling through the walls without much trouble.

Draw a map of the network as you plan it. Sketch locations of the computers, printers, wiring, hubs, patch panels, and any other equipment you add to the network. A network map can come in handy later for locating problem areas and troubleshooting connections.

You can sketch a network map, use a drawing program, or just list text labels for each computer, peripheral, and cabling. Figure 20-2 illustrates a network map. The sketch helps identify hub and cable placement, and the text identifies computers and other peripherals.

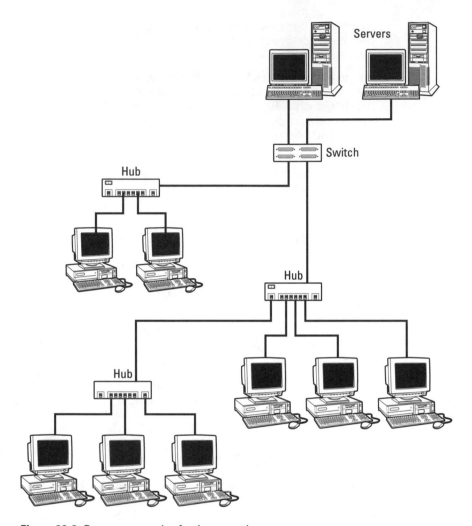

Figure 20-2: Draw out your plan for the network.

Tip

If you outsource your cabling, make sure to tell the installers you want a complete map of the cabling when they are done. Question the installers to make sure you're getting the type of cabling, connectors, placement, and other things that you want from the cabling job.

Laying the cable

Make sure you have the appropriate ends on the cable you choose. If you bought a kit or pre-made cables, the cables and connectors should be fine. If you made your own cables and attached the connectors yourself, you should test the cabling before you begin installing it.

Running cable through walls and under floors requires some special equipment — snakes and fancy drill bits, for example — as well as taking two people to pull the wire. You might need to go through cinder block walls or heavily insulated walls. Watch that you don't drill through the studs in a framed wall.

Caution

If you plan to go behind walls or under the floors, hire an electrician to help you pull the wire. For one thing, you want to avoid drilling any power lines. If you're not sure where the power lines are, do not drill or pull cabling until you find out.

When you're ready to actually lay the cable, label both ends of each cable with a number or name. For example, number the first cable 1 on each end. That way, it will be easier to test the cable at the hub or jack and to know which computer the cable is attached to.

Following are some more tips for installing your cable:

- Don't kink the cable. Kinks in the cable can cause connection problems, as well as ruin the cable.

- Don't use a staple gun or staples of any type to install cabling. You can nick the cable, which ruins it.

- If you use plastic or metal ties to hold several cables together, don't pull the ties too tightly. You might kink a cable and interfere with the connection. Also, use plastic instead of metal ties, because the metal ties could cut the cable over time.

- Don't install cabling so it runs beside AC power lines of any sort. The power can interfere with the data traveling over the network cable.

- Don't install cabling close to florescent lighting (within two feet). Florescent lights can interfere with the network signal.

- If you must cross a power line, cross it at a right angle only to guarantee you get the least interference.

- Don't coil excess cabling when the cabling is in use. If, for example, you install the cable and have several feet left over, don't coil it up. Instead, lay the cable out as straight as possible. Coiling the cable can cause interference in the data transmission.

- If you use raceway along the walls to help hide the cabling and make it look neater, consider using screws to attach the raceway to the walls. If you use glue, you might not be able to get the raceway off easily when you need to.

Checking the cabling

Modern cables are very seldom the problem when it comes to a network connection; however, there are a couple of instances where the cable might be the root of your problem. Sometimes the connectors or terminators aren't attached properly, especially if you added the hardware yourself. Check connections before you run the cable.

Another problem area is if the cable is coiled or kinked, or if there's a nick or cut in the cable. Make sure the cabling is in good shape before you lay it. You also should make sure not to lay the cabling in an area where it can easily become damaged with nicks or cuts.

After the network is set up, checking a cable connection is fairly easy. If the lights on the network card and/or hub are all lit, the cable connection is good.

Another way to test the cable is with an inexpensive ($8) cable tester called a continuity tester. You connect one end of the continuity tester to a pin on one end of the cable; then connect the other end of the tester to the corresponding pin on the other end of the cable. After verifying (the green tester lights light up) the continuity between the same pins, check to see if any other pin has continuity with the first. Pin one, for example, should only display continuity with pin one, pin two only with pin two, and so on.

A Time Domain Reflectometer (TDR) is another cable tester, but this equipment's cost ranges from $1,000 to $10,000, depending on the quality. For more information about cable testers, see "Troubleshooting Hardware," later in this chapter.

Connecting Two Computers

You might have need for file sharing, but you have no interest in putting a lot of time, money, and effort in setting up a network. You can share resources between two computers — two desktop computers, for example, or a desktop and notebook computer — for less than $35.

Note

You must designate files, folders, and printers as shared before you can use them over any network. (See Chapter 21 for more information.)

Cross-Over Cable

You can connect two computers that have Ethernet network cards with a cross-over cable for sharing files and printers. This method of networking computers is accomplished without the use of a hub; however, it applies only to connecting two computers. If you want to connect more, you need to set up a hub and the cabling that goes along with it.

Newer Ethernet network interface cards have one of the following types of cable connections: a BNC port for use with coax cable or an RJ-45 connector that you use with twisted-pair cabling. To use the card with a cross-over cable, you must buy a card with the RJ-45 connector.

A cross-over cable is a Cat 5 cable with the transmit and receive connections reversed. You can purchase pre-made cross-over cables. Alternatively, you can make your own cross-over cable (from Cat 5 solid wire cable) if you have a meter and a crimping tool to attach the RJ-45 plugs to the cable.

Table 20-1 shows the pin numbers on the RJ-45 connectors and the colors of the wires for both connectors of the cross-over cable. Notice that only four wires are used. On connector #1, wires 4 (blue), 5 (white/green), 7 (white/brown), and 8 (brown) are not used. On connector #2, wires 4 (brown), 5 (white/brown), 7 (white/green), and 8 (green) are not used.

Table 20-1   Cross-Over Cable Ends for Connectors #1 and #2

Pin (Color)	Pin (Color)
1 (white/orange)	3 (white/orange)
2 (orange)	6 (orange)
3 (white/green)	1 (white/green)
6 (green)	2 (green)

STEPS:

Set up a network between two computers using a cross-over cable

Step 1.   Power off the computers and unplug them. Install the network cards to the computers. If the network card has more than one transceiver (connection for the network cable), enable the RJ-45 transceiver and disable others on the card. Consult the card's documentation for more information about the transceiver.

Step 2.   To each network card's transceiver, attach the custom cable connector.

Step 3.   Plug the computers back in and power them up. Windows will automatically configure the cards and the network.

Bus and coax link

You can create a bus topology to network two computers without a hub. You need to install a network interface card with BNC transceivers to each computer. You also need a BNC T-connector for each computer, two BNC terminators, and the coax cable.

You can actually create a peer-to-peer network using this method—called daisy chaining the computers together. However, don't attach more than ten computers together in this manner; network performance suffers greatly when you add more computers to a bus topology.

STEPS:

Set up a bus topology network between two computers

Step 1. Power off the computers and unplug them. Install the network cards to the computers. If the network card has more than one transceiver (connection for the network cable), enable the BNC transceiver and disable others on the card. Consult the card's documentation for more information about the transceiver.

Step 2. To each network card's transceiver, attach a BNC T-connector. On one end of each T-connector, attach the cable; on the other end, attach a terminator.

Step 3. Plug the computers back in and power them up. Windows will automatically configure the cards and the network.

Alternatively, you can use RJ-45 connectors and twisted-pair cabling in the bus network.

USB Link

If you have two computers that both have USB ports, you can buy a kit to network those two computers. The two computers must be in the same room, no more than 16 feet apart. Because you're using USB ports, you don't have to shut down Windows to plug in the device; Windows automatically recognizes the device.

For $90 to $130, Anchor Chips, ADS, Belkin, and Entrega make USB kits. Kits usually include a linking device that plugs into one computer, plus ten to sixteen feet of cable that plugs into the other computer. You also should get an installation guide and a CD-ROM with the installation software.

The performance of the USB kits doesn't equal an Ethernet system; however, it is faster than phone line kits. The maximum data transfer rate of the USB data exchanges is 3Mbps to 7 or 8Mbps. You can share both files and printers with a USB kit.

Computers are often shipped with USB support disabled. Before you try to install the USB networking kit software, make sure that USB support is enabled. Enable USB support in your computer's CMOS.

Follow the directions in the USB kit for installing the equipment and connecting the cable.

Phone line kits

Using your phone lines to network two computers is a technology you might want to explore. You can use the telephone cabling and RJ-11 modular phone jacks already in place., without rewiring.

You also can connect multiple computers to a phone line network, but in an office, I wouldn't recommend it. Data transfer rates are too slow for use in business.

A phone line network enables you to share all resources on the network, including files, printers, applications, games, CD-ROM drives, and other peripherals. Most phone line networks run at 1Mbps, which is a lot slower than Ethernet's 10Mbps. If you want to work with multimedia, large graphic files, or complex calculations over the network, you should consider a faster network technology.

A phone line network uses standard telephone wire to connect your computers. The ends for the phone wire use RJ-11 jacks, just like the lines to your telephones. All you have to do is plug the RJ-11 jacks into an extra phone jack in the wall.

The special network adapter card you insert into your computer essentially divides the data traveling over the lines into separate frequencies — one for voice, one for network data and, if applicable, one for high-bandwidth Internet access such as DSL. Digital Subscriber Line (DSL) is a technology that transmits data in both directions simultaneously over copper lines.

You might want to use the phone line network to complement any other networking media you use, such as Ethernet Cat 5 or wireless, in certain circumstances.

Telephone lines are copper lines; most phone lines are now Cat 3. The phone line networking frequencies can coexist on the same telephone line without impacting the phone service.

You can buy phone line networking kits from manufacturers such as LinkSys, Tut, and Artisoft.

Direct Cable Connection

A direct cable connection (DCC) is the connection you make between the I/O ports of two computers with a single cable. You use a cable that directly connects the two computers without the use of network cards, hubs, or other hardware equipment. The DCC connection is slow, but it's also inexpensive and very handy.

Tip

You could use DCC networking at the office to connect your laptop to your desktop. If your desktop is already connected to an Ethernet network, for example, you can transfer files from the laptop, to the desktop, to a server or other computer on the network, and then back again. Extending the network to your laptop in this way can save time, money, and networking headaches in many situations.

Naturally, there are limitations to DCC. In addition to a slow connection, you cannot share a printer; however, you can transfer a file from one computer to another and then print from the computer attached to the printer. One other hindrance with DCC is that the two computers must be close together — at least in the same room, and perhaps on the same desk or table. This limit is imposed by the cable; direct cables are generally no longer than fifty feet.

Physically connecting the computers

You can connect two computers using a cable or a wireless connection. Both methods are relatively inexpensive to use. Each method has its advantages and disadvantages.

To connect the two computers using cable, you can use a parallel file-transfer cable, also called a high-speed direct parallel cable. The cable costs around $30, and it connects to the parallel port (LPT) on each computer. Alternatively, you can use a serial cable, which costs only about $10, but which transfers data at a slower rate than a parallel cable.

Additionally, use any of these cables for a direct connection:

- **A standard RS-232 cable.** The RS-232 cable transmits data at about a 20Kbps. A serial cable generally used for connecting a computer to a peripheral device, the RS-232 has a maximum cable limit of 15 meters, or about 50 feet. A null modem cable is an RS-232-C cable. It connects two computers so they can communicate without the use of a modem. A null modem cable connects the serial ports.

Note

A serial port transmits data slower than a parallel port, one bit at a time. Serial cables transmit data sequentially over only one pair of wires. Since parallel cables transmit data simultaneously over multiple lines, parallel is the faster of the two connection methods.

- **A standard 4-bit cable, such as LapLink or InterLink cables.** Four-bit cables are bi-directional, parallel cables.

- **An extended capabilities port (ECP) cable.** Using this cable with an ECP-enabled parallel port and allows data to transfer more quickly than standard cables. The ECP port must be enabled in the BIOS (Basic Input/Output System).

Secret

ECP and EPP (Enhanced Parallel Port) are enhancements to the original parallel port on the computer. Both provide faster data transfer rates than the original parallel port, bi-directional operation with 8 instead of 4 input bits, and other support for faster data transfer speeds. Although ECP offers the highest speed block transfers, it works better with printers and scanners than the EPP port. The EPP port is specially suited for interactive communications, such as the data transfers that take place with network card adapters. To find out if you're using the ECP or EPP enhancement, check your computer's CMOS. Many computers offer the option to change the parallel port configuration from ECP to EPP and back.

- **A universal cable module (UCM) cable.** A parallel cable, the UCM supports connecting different types of parallel ports.

STEPS:

Physically connecting the two computers by cable

Step 1. Power off the both computers and unplug them.

Step 2. Connect one end of the cable to one computer and the other end of the cable to the other computer.

Step 3. Plug in the power cables to both computers power them up. Configure the Direct Cable Connection software by following the instructions in the next section.

Alternatively, you can set up a direct cable connection using Infrared, as opposed to using a physical cable. Infrared uses high-frequency light waves instead of cabling to transmit data. With Infrared, there must be a clear line of site between the two computers since the light waves cannot penetrate obstacles.

Infrared does supply high bandwidths, and it's an inexpensive technology. However, if you don't use a fairly short transmission distance, interference can be a problem. Infrared connections are usually limited to one meter (about 3 feet), but some manufacturers offer connections up to 3 meters (about 10 feet).

Tip

You configure an Infrared connection the same as you would a Direct Cable Connection, except that when you are asked about the port, you choose the Infrared communications port.

If you install Infrared ports on your computers, Windows 2000 is supposed to automatically detect another Infrared device and establish the connection. If the connection should be broken or interrupted, Windows signals the problem with an audible signal and automatically tries to reestablish the signal for a period of time.

Configuring Direct Cable Connection

Windows 2000 Professional includes a wizard in the Network and Dial-Up Connections dialog box to help you set up the Direct Cable Connection.

STEPS:

Configure the Direct Cable Connection in Windows 2000

Step 1.   Choose Start ⇨ Settings ⇨ Network and Dial-up Connections. In the Network and Dial-up Connections dialog box, click (or double-click) Make New Connection to show the Network Connection Wizard. Click Next.

Step 2.   In the Wizard dialog box for Network Connection Type, choose Connect directly to another computer. Click Next.

Step 3.   When connecting two computers, one computer is the Host and the other becomes the Guest. The Host/Guest assignments relate to a client/server network — one computer (the Host) acts as a server to the other (the Guest). On the first computer, choose the Host option. On the second computer, choose the Guest option. Set up the Host first. Click Next.

Step 4.   Choose the connection device, such as the COM1 or LPT1 (see Figure 20-3). Click the Properties button to set properties on the port, if necessary. Click Next.

Step 5.   Because you're adding only one computer to your network, you should add the user of that computer to the list of users who are allowed to connect. Add the user by clicking the Add button. Enter the user's name and the password you want to assign to that user. When you enter the properties for the user, that user's name appears in the list (see Figure 20-4). When you set up the Guest computer, enter your name and a password to use to connect. Click Next.

Step 6.   Name the connection so you can identify it in the Network and Dial-up Connections dialog box. Click Finish and close the dialog box.

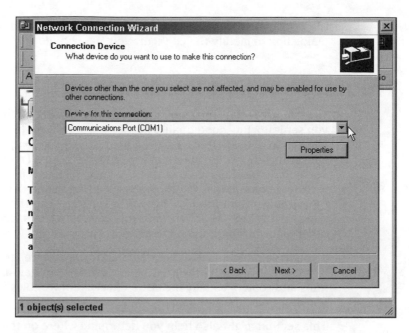

Figure 20-3: Set the port for DCC.

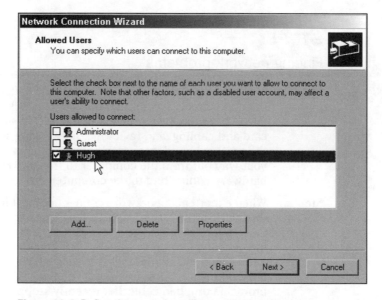

Figure 20-4: Define the user who will connect to your computer.

Tip   Click or double-click the connection in the Network and Dial-up Connections
dialog box to modify the configuration at any time.

Troubleshooting Hardware

You can prevent many problems in your network if you plan a little before
you set it up. Buy good quality networking hardware instead of the cheapest
you can find; the better quality equipment will last longer and work more
efficiently. Always document everything and keep all equipment information,
documentation, instructions, and receipts. Fill a notebook for each computer
with such information as processor speed, hard disk size, RAM amount and
type. Define cabling, network cards, and hubs. Keep the documentation that
comes with CD-ROM drives, hard drives, sound cards, printers, and every
other piece of equipment in your network.

If you have problems with your networking hardware, use the documentation
that came with the hardware to determine if there's a problem. For example,
hubs and routers usually include a checklist of troubleshooting steps to help
you determine the problem.

This section might also help you determine where on the network the
problem is occurring and how to alleviate the problem.

STEPS:

Finding network problems

Step 1.   Network connection problems sometimes affect one computer,
but often affect all computers on the network. Check the computer that's having a problem first; check it's network interface
card and cabling, and review it's networking software to make sure
the protocol or adapter aren't causing the problem. Then work
your way out from the computer to the hub, repeater, or other
hardware connecting to the computer that is having problems.

Step 2.   When experiencing network connection problems, ask yourself
the following questions to help diagnose the problem. Did the
connection work before, or did it just recently stop working? If it
just recently stopped working, what equipment or software have
you added? Did something happen or change since it last worked?
If the connection never worked, you probably have configuration
problems or a bad cable. If it recently stopped working and you
added something new to the network, remove that added equipment and see if the situation improves. If nothing's changed and it
quit working all of the sudden, check network cards, cabling, and
hubs, in that order.

Step 3.   When you have hardware trouble with the network connections, physically check all cabling, plugs, and network LEDs on cards, hubs, and other devices. You don't want to waste hours of time checking software details, only to find that a connector was loose or unplugged.

Step 4.   If you're using a hub, bridge, switch, or router, power all computers down, turn off the hub or other device, and then power back up again. Often, resetting the connection devices is all that's needed to get the connections up and running again.

Step 5.   If you still have problems, try to narrow it down. Check to see, for example, if some connections are working and others are not. Check to see if only one computer has problems, or if a group of computers cannot connect.

Step 6.   To determine if a particular piece of equipment is causing the problem, swap parts with another computer. For example, you can swap network cards, patch cables, network jacks, and so on.

Tip

You can use a Windows 2000 feature to help you diagnose problems. Use Safe Mode to start the system without certain device drivers and services to discover if it's the network software causing the problem. For example, you can start a computer in Safe Mode with or without networking to determine if it is networking hardware that's causing the problem. Figure 20-5 shows a Windows 2000 computer in Safe Mode.

Secret

Here's a low tech trick that really solves a surprising number of network problems, especially if you've got more than one hub chained together: simply turn off everything (all computers on the network and all hubs), and then turn everything on again.

Troubleshooting tools

You can troubleshoot your networking problems without the use of tools and equipment, but if you have a few tools, the job is easier. Here are some tools you can buy and use for testing the network.

Basic cable checkers apply a small voltage to each wire in the cable, and they then verify whether the voltage is detected on the other end of the cable. You use a basic cable checker before you lay or disconnect the cable from the network to test it.

Cable scanners — or cable testers — check all of the cabling in your network and tell you how far it is to the problem. You can trace the problem — such as interference in the line or cable length — to its location. Cable scanners are a sophisticated cable checker; they also check wire length, signal loss along the cable, interference from other conductors, and impedance of thinnet terminators.

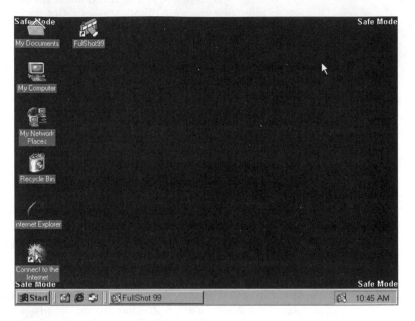

Figure 20-5: Use Safe Mode to diagnose problems.

Voltmeters and multimeters test voltage, signal strength, and power supplies. Use a voltage checker to help determine if a NIC is defective and unable to maintain the proper voltage.

Time Domain Reflectometer (TDR) is expensive and only worth the money if you have a large, multi-segmented network. TDRs report broad information about cabling problems, such as shorts, opens, splices, splits, ground faults, crimps, cuts, shortened conductors, and many other problems.

Protocol analyzers detect shorts and electrical interference, collisions and bottlenecks, and routing information contained in data packets.

Network cards

You can check to see if the network card and hub are working by checking the LEDs on both. Most network cards have a green light that displays on the back of your computer when the card is working. If the card isn't working, it may display an amber or red light. The corresponding jack in the hub should also be lit up with a green light if the connection is working, or with an amber or red light if it isn't.

If the network card isn't working, you should turn the computer off, remove the case, and reseat the card. This is the most common reason a network card doesn't work initially. Next, check the software that comes with the NIC. Often, manufacturers include diagnostic software to help you discover NIC problems.

Device Manager

Check a network card to make sure it's working by checking the lights on the card or by checking in the Windows' Device Manager.

STEPS:

Check the network interface card status in the
Device Manager

Step 1. Choose Start ⇨ Settings ⇨ Control Panel. Click or double-click the System.

Step 2. In the System Properties dialog box, choose the Hardware tab and then click the Device Manager button.

Step 3. Click the plus sign to the left of Network Adapters to display your network interface card's adapter. If there is a splat on the card, you know you have a problem. If the adapter has a red circle and an exclamation point through it, double-click the device and read the Device Status area of the Properties dialog box. The device status area tells you if there is a problem and what it is. If the adapter has a red X through it, it's been disabled. You can enable the adapter by double-clicking the adapter in the list. The Device Properties dialog box will appear. On the General tab, make sure the current configuration is correct, as shown in Figure 20-6. Click OK.

Step 4. If there are no splats beside the network card, right-click the card and choose Properties to view information about the card. On the General tab, check the Device status to determine if there's a problem with the card. You can then click the Troubleshooter button to use Windows' help to solve the NIC problem.

Continued

Check the network interface card status in the Device Manager *(continued)*

Step 5.   If the card is working properly but you're still having trouble, you might check the card's driver by clicking the Driver file. You can update the driver, uninstall the current driver, or view the current driver's details before checking on the Web for a newer version.

Step 6.   If you think there's a problem with the IRQ, I/O range, or DMA settings, click the Resources tab and view the settings. Figure 20-7 shows the Resources tab for a network card. Check in the Conflicting device list if you think you have an IRQ conflict.

Step 7.   If the card still doesn't work, try switching the card with another one and see if the second card works. If the second card works, the first card might be bad. If the second card doesn't work, try another slot. Again, make sure you're seating the card properly.

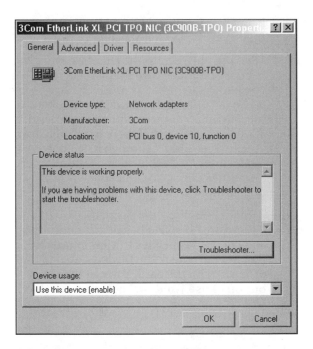

Figure 20-6: Check a device's configuration.

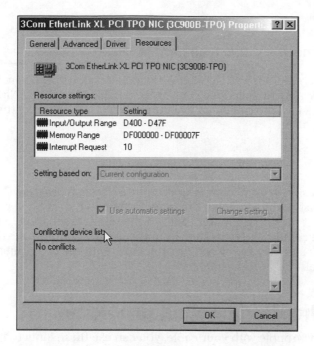

Figure 20-7: Check your NIC for conflicts and problems.

General check list

If you can narrow your problem to the network card and the connection to the network, you're doing well.

STEPS:

Check the network interface card

Step 1. Check all of the NIC hardware and software settings, including I/O address, IRQ, DMA, slot settings, primary or secondary settings, speed settings, and incompatibilities with the cable type, connector, and other networking devices.

Step 2. Run NIC diagnostics from the NIC manufacturer or from a third-party vendor.

Continued

STEPS:

Check the network interface card *(continued)*

Step 3. Swap the NIC with another NIC and try connecting again. If the original problem doesn't go away, replace the original NIC and look into the cabling or the port as a possible cause of the problem.

Secret

Test the port using another computer running a terminal program (the computers must both be running the same settings — parity, baud rate, and so on). Connect the two computers and set the terminal program to receive on the second computer. Try to send from the first computer. If the data is sent, the cable and port are okay. The problem is with the NIC configuration or the protocol.

Troubleshooting cabling problems

If you're having trouble with your cable, you can use these hints to help you determine what the problem is and how to take care of it. The first step to fixing any problem is to try and avoid it.

First, make sure you use the best wiring you can afford. Don't skimp on cabling, connectors, wiring blocks, and so on. Poor quality cable connectors can cause as many problems as poor quality cabling.

Second, terminate voice and data wires to separate them; don't run voice and data on the same cable. Also, when terminating your own cable, tightly twist up to the termination point at the punch blocks, wire plates, and connectors. Don't use too many terminations along a length of cable; follow recommended standards for your cabling type.

Symptoms of cabling problems

Cabling problems are not usually the first thing you look for when trouble-shooting a network connection. However, some symptoms point directly to faulty cables. Here are some of the things you want to keep an eye out for:

- The entire network doesn't come up.
- A connection doesn't come up, or it doesn't stay up.
- Data isn't being sent or received from any computer.
- Traffic seems heavier than usual and remains constant thereafter.

Here are some things to check when experiencing connection problems you think are related to cabling:

- Cables located near motors, fluorescent lights, or power lines are often affected by noise and poor transmission rates. If you have intermittent connection problems or disconnections, they could be caused by crosstalk.

- Cables connected directly from the wall plate to the computer often become twisted or kinked and cause transmission problems. Use patch cables to connect the computer to a wall plate or hub. Keep patch cables short (two to three feet long) for more Near End Cross Talk.

- Using too long a length of cable causes dropped and corrupt transmissions. Follow the IEEE standards for the cable type and don't run the cable to the maximum lengths; add some leeway by keeping the lengths under the limits. Similarly, too short cables also can cause problems.

- If the connectors you use are cheap or old, that could be a source of problems in transmission. Replace connectors when they're looking shabby.

Secret

If you upgraded your 10BaseT network to 100BaseTX, make sure you upgrade the cabling, as well. Often, 10BaseT networks use Category 3 wiring, which is fine for 10BaseT. However, Cat 3 doesn't meet the required specifications for 100BaseT networks; you need to use Cat 5 cabling and connectors. Using the wrong cabling can cause a huge drop in performance.

Coaxial problems

Check all of the cables in the system for nicks or breaks first. Also check all of the terminators to make sure they are securely fastened to the cable and to the computers. If all looks okay, you might still have a break in the connection; it's difficult to tell with coaxial cabling.

You can try replacing the terminators and T-connectors, if you're comfortable with that. You also can try swapping out one cable with another, unless your cabling goes into walls or under flooring.

You also can use a cable tester, if you have one. Cable testers are devices that test for loose connections, faulty cables, and other cabling problems.

Twisted-pair cabling problems

Twisted-pair cabling usually displays a link light on the back of the computer, in the area of the network card port. As long as the link light is lit, you don't have a problem with the cable.

Again, check for physical problems with the cable: cuts, crimps, coiled cable, and so on. Check the connectors. If you have a cable tester, use it. If all else fails, you can call a cable professional to test the cabling for you and replace it as necessary.

Ethernet problems

Ethernet technology can cause traffic and bandwidth problems. Here are some things to keep in mind when working with Ethernet:

- Make sure the cable lengths are no longer than 385 feet per run. Longer cable lengths can slow traffic and even drop connections.

- Don't overload the number of users on a segment. Overloaded segments mean longer response times and, perhaps, corruption of large files. Try to keep the number of users per segment to no more than 12.

- Collisions increase as more traffic appears on the Ethernet network. When packets collide, the network retransmits them, thus causing more collisions and more retransmissions. Again, keep the number of users per segment to no more than 12; if the traffic is still to heavy, add another segment to divide users and open some bandwidth.

- Redundant paths cause more traffic because Ethernet doesn't support multiple data paths; it sends data over all paths instead of choosing one. If you have jumper cables, for example, that connect two hubs, you're creating a redundant path that can slow your network response time.

- If you find you have many CRC (Cyclic Redundancy Check) errors or link errors, you likely have a bad connection between the hub and the NIC causing collisions and corrupted data. Check the adapter first, then the hub, then the cabling between the two.

- A network with constant collisions might caused by a terminating resistor that is damaged or missing. Late collision errors might be occurring because the cable is too long.

- Excessive noise on the network indicates the cables might be damaged.

Hardware devices

Hardware devices, such as hubs, bridges, repeaters, and so on, usually have problems specific to the brand and model of the device. You should first check the manufacturer's documentation for any methods for checking configuration and diagnostic testing.

Tip

If you have a problem in one segment of a network, but not in a segment connected to the first with a bridge, hub, repeater, or other device, check the device dividing the two segments first.

Many hardware devices can collect statistics and record network errors. You can use this information to diagnose specific hardware problems and to locate problems in other areas of the network.

Hub

If you have only one hub on your network and it fails, the entire network goes down. If you have multiple hubs on a network and one fails, only the segment serviced by that hub fails.

It's also possible that one port on a hub will fail and that affects only one computer. That is a difficult situation to troubleshoot because you usually start diagnosing the computer, network card, and cabling before you get to the hub. If you start at the hub instead, you might be able to better diagnose the problem. Try using another port for the workstation to see if the problem is in the hub's port or closer to the computer itself. If one port works and another does not, the problem is the port.

You also can remove one workstation from the hub at a time to see if the other computers work on that one port, or on multiple ports. If removing one workstation eliminates the problem, there's something wrong with that workstation's cable.

Switches

Many switches include monitoring software that helps you determine problem areas. Some switches, for example, report the peak throughput levels daily so you can monitor traffic patterns. Other reports might include the number of frames processed per Ethernet port, the number of transmission errors, overall bandwidth utilization, error reporting on a per port basis, and utilization per port.

Repeaters

As with most hardware devices, you can tell if you're having trouble with a repeater by the LEDs on the front of the device. First check the lights to makes sure they're blinking. Next, check to make sure a device on one side of the repeater can see a device on the other side. If these tests work, the repeater is most likely okay.

If you have trouble with traffic going through a repeater, check the segment cable leading into the repeater first, and then the connections between the last computer that feeds into the repeater. Finally, check the NIC on the computer leading into the repeater.

Bridges

You can retrieve information from a bridge to help you diagnose network problems. Before buying a bridge, make sure it can report on such information as the number of frames received and forwarded per port, the number of errors per port, and the number of collisions per port.

If a bridge seems slow or to not be working, check to see if the bridge is overloaded. A bad bridge generates bad packets that create a slow down on the network. You can use a protocol analyzer to diagnose an overloaded bridge.

Router

Routers also can monitor the network; they collect information about network traffic. Routers should collect, at the least, the following information: the number of frames received and forwarded per port, the number and type of errors per port, the number of collisions per port, and the number of frames with an excessively high hop count. Hop count defines the number of segments a packet travels before it gets to its destination.

Secret

Be careful when using a router with an intelligent hub. That can cause bad packets, a slow network, and a high rate of collisions.

Tip

If you're using Ethernet technology within a segment connected to a router, you can run into some router-specific problems. For example, if you receive CRC errors constantly and you have checked other possible causes, the problem could be that the cable to the router is not shielded or the line isn't clean enough for transmission requirements. Similarly, framing errors also could indicate unshielded cabling, an improperly designed cable, or a cable that is too long.

Routers often experience problems with equalizing the amount of traffic sent and received between segments. You adjust the router's configuration so it can better manage packet sizes, network traffic, and input and output capacities. If, for example, you discover input drop problems (dropped packets) in a network connecting faster interfaces and serial interfaces, the router might be dropping packets because the traffic is too congested. You can check the router's documentation to determine how to increase the input hold queue size.

Other router problems include clocking conflicts, framing errors, rejected packets, restarts, disconnects, and intermittent connectivity. Table 20-2 describes some general problems caused by router configuration, and the settings you should check when the network experiences these problems.

Table 20-2   Router Configuration Problems

Problem	Check Setting
Excessive, continuous traffic	Clocking
Chronic loss of service	Clocking
Generally degraded performance	Clocking
Reduced all-over performance and intermittent failures	Buffers
Dropped packets	Queuing
Intermittent connectivity	Timing, buffers
Lost connections at peak periods	Queuing, buffers
Lost connections after normal operation	Routing tables, buffers
Users cannot connect	Access lists, network address space assignments

Bottlenecks

Bottlenecks are usually caused by a mismatch of networking components. If all your networking hardware works well together, you won't have bottlenecks. If you do, you need to locate the problem and alleviate it.

Memory is always a prime suspect for a slow computer or network. A server, for example — or a workstation that carries most of the load — could be a bottleneck on the network. When everyone accesses one computer, its processes slow. Adding memory can improve the situation.

Applications often create a bottleneck if they're faulty or a little buggy. Make sure you use the latest upgrades to any program installed on your computers. If you think a program is running slowly, check with the manufacturer to see if there is an available upgrade or a patch that solves the problem. Also check the manufacturer's Web page for information and patches.

When anyone on the network transfers several large files — images, sound clips, or motion files — from one computer to another, that can cause a log jam. You might wave those files to a zip disk or CD-RW drive to help ease a network traffic problem.

Here are some ways to alleviate bottlenecks on a Windows 2000 Professional workstation:

- Use SDRAM, when you can, to match the higher bus frequencies. If possible, you can use the newer memory SLDRAM (SyncLink DRAM) or RDRAM (Rambus DRAM), to speed processes.

- Make sure the L2 caches are adequate on the workstations to keep the traffic off the main I/O bus.

- Use the Accelerated Graphics Port (AGP) instead of the PCI bus to quadruple graphics throughput.

Summary

In this chapter, you learned about installing networking hardware and troubleshooting hardware problems. Specifically, you learned the following:

▶ How to buy and install a network interface card.

▶ How to buy and install a hub to the network.

▶ How to install cable to the network.

▶ How to connect two computers in a simple network.

▶ How to troubleshoot some common hardware problems.

Chapter 21

Windows 2000 Workstations on Third-Party Networks

Microsoft is really banging the gong for the idea of Windows 2000 networks, where Windows 2000 Professional workstations dance cheek-to-cheek with Windows 2000 servers. To take advantage of all the whiz-bang new features in Windows 2000 Server, such as Active Directory, you essentially must be running Windows 2000 everywhere.

The trouble is, Windows 2000 hardware requirements are so high that most users of older versions of Windows (even Windows NT 4.0 and Windows 98) will simply have to scrap all their existing PCs and replace them lock, stock, and barrel.

For this reason, many organizations may initially deploy Windows 2000 as a workstation on heterogeneous, existing networks running under other operating systems — Novell NetWare, UNIX, Linux, and earlier versions of Windows NT — either directly or by means of dial-up Virtual Private Networks. Fortunately, Windows 2000 readily connects to other networks.

Setting Up Windows 2000 Professional on a Peer-to-Peer Network

Setting up Windows 2000 for peer-to-peer networking with a workgroup of Windows 95, Windows 98, and Windows NT machines is almost as easy as Microsoft advertises.

When Windows 2000 Professional boots, one of the first things it does, by default, is look for a DHCP server from which to obtain an IP address. If it can't obtain an IP address, it will assign itself a private IP address that is unique to the network, and continue in NetBIOS naming broadcast mode to enable communication with the hub and other PCs on the network.

Microsoft promises that "users can have their network up and running in a few minutes," and this is true in many cases — but not all. Sadly, some people are still going to need to manually configure their Windows 2000 Professional workstations, which means manually assigning a unique IP address, and other similar delights.

Establishing a network share

Welcome to the black hole of the PC universe. The amount of time and money that has been squandered configuring networks over the last decade is beyond human comprehension. The reason? Networks — even simple peer-to-peer star networks with a single hub — are difficult to set up and can require a lot of trial-and-error modification of settings. So don't despair if everything doesn't come together on the first try. You are definitely not alone.

Good news: if you have experience setting up a peer-to-peer network with Windows 95, Windows 98, or Windows NT 4, the basics of Windows 2000 Professional setup will be immediately familiar to you.

STEPS:

Manually Assigning a Unique IP Address

Step 1. Boot Windows 2000 Professional and log in as Administrator.

Step 2. Right-click My Network Places and select Properties, as illustrated in Figure 21-1.

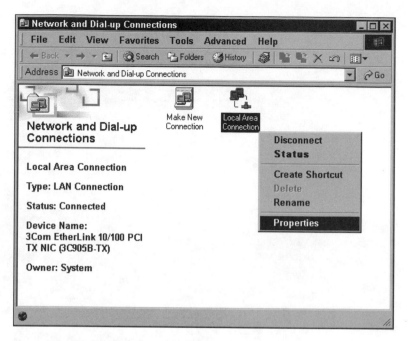

Figure 21-1: Network and Dial-up Connections.

Step 3. Right-click Local Area Connection and select Properties.

Step 4. Select Internet Protocol (TCP/IP) and click the Properties button. If your network has a DHCP server, it may be recognized automatically. If not, enter the IP address of your DNS server. If your network doesn't have a DHCP server, you must enter an IP Address, a subnet mask, a default gateway, and the IP address of your DNS server, if your network has one. The IP address will be a sequence of four groups of as many as three numbers separated by periods (for example, 207.179.9.196, as shown in Figure 21-2).

Continued

STEPS:

Manually Assigning a Unique IP Address *(continued)*

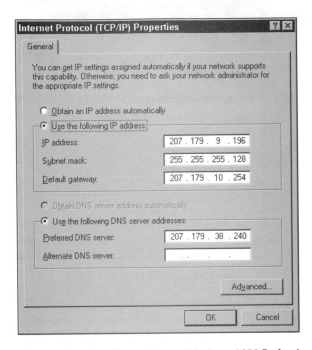

Figure 21-2: Manually assigning a Windows 2000 Professional workstation's IP address, subnet mask, Default gateway, and DNS server.

Undocumented

The sequential number of a given workstation on the network or workgroup is often shown in the last three digits of the assigned IP address. In the example shown in Figure 21-2, this workstation with IP 207.179.9.196 is number 196 on the network. The one before has been assigned 207.179.9.195, and so forth. Depending on your network's size and configuration, you might only need to type in the unique assigned IP address on this screen.

STEPS:

Mapping a Network Drive

Step 1. Right-click My Network Places.

Step 2. Click Map Network Drive, as shown in Figure 21-3.

Step 3. Fill in the letter of the drive you want to make available on the network. You also can map a specific folder on the drive, rather than the entire drive. If you want to have the computer automatically reconnect to the network at boot, be sure to check the Reconnect at logon check box.

You can now map a folder or a subfolder on a drive to the network, rather than simply mapping to the entire drive (share) itself.

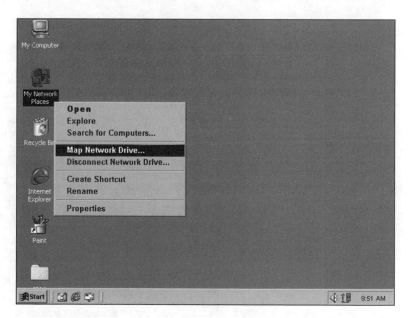

Figure 21-3: Map Network Drives is available by right-clicking My Network Places.

Connecting to a network printer

Once you have installed a printer, you need to share the printer with the rest of the network if you want other machines on the network to be able to use it. By default, when you add a printer to your network, it is not shared.

STEPS:

Sharing a Printer

Step 1.   Click Start ➪ Settings ➪ Printer.

Step 2.   Highlight the printer you want to share on the network.

Step 3.   Right-click the printer and choose Properties from the context menu.

Step 4.   Select the Sharing tab, as shown in Figure 21-4.

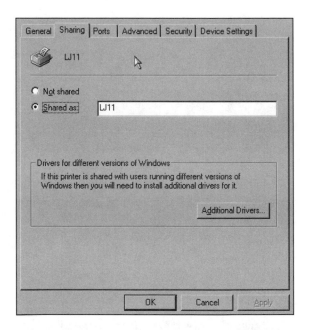

Figure 21-4: The Sharing tab in the Print Properties dialog box.

Once you designate the printer as shared, it will be available to all users on a network. To refine this availability, you access the Properties ⇨ Security tab.

Managing access to this printer relies on the user accounts set up with your general network security (see Chapters 15 and 19). You can set a permission level for a printer to either an individual user or to a group. There are four levels of permissions: No Access (set through the Sharing Tab), Print, Manage Documents, and Manage Printers. The rights belonging to each level are shown in Table 21-1, and are cumulative, so that any rights belonging to a lower level are allowed to all higher levels

Table 21-1   Printing Permissions

Level	Rights
No Access	None.
Print	Print documents on this printer.
Manage Documents	Control settings for documents; Pause, resume, restart, and delete documents.
Manage Printers	Change the printing order of documents; Pause, resume, and purge the printer; Change printer properties; Delete a printer; Change printer permissions.

How to print to a network printer

Once network printing has been set up and configured, network users have many options for their printing jobs. To find the printer you want, you can:

- Browse the network for printers using Network Neighborhood.

- Browse for printers using the Add Printer icon in the Printers folder.

- Select a printer through the Print Setup dialog box in any Windows 2000 or Windows 95/98 application. All available printers will be shown in the drop-down menu.

- Make a networked printer your default printer. Click Start ⇨ Settings ⇨ Printers, right-click the networked printer, and then select Set as Default from the context menu.

Tip

You can set the times of the day that a printer is available to the network on the Advanced print tab, as shown in Figure 21-5.

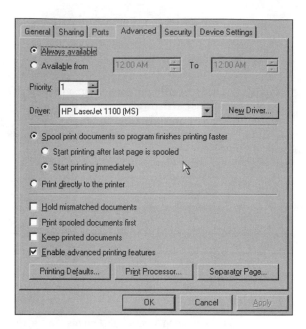

Figure 21-5: The Advanced print tab in the Print Properties dialog box, where you can control the times of the day a printer is available to the network.

Changing your network configuration

So what happens if you need to change something in your network configuration? Many settings — such as the ability to change the name of a workstation — are accessed through My Computer. They also can be accessed through the System applet in the Control Panel.

Please be aware, however, that changing a system name can cause problems on a network — for instance, it can muck up server configurations.

Changing the Name of a Workstation

Step 1. Make sure you're in the local admin group, and then right-click My Computer and select Properties.

Step 2. Select the Network Identification tab.

Step 3. Click the Advanced button to change the name of the computer.

Step 4. Type the computer's name and the name of the workgroup that the computer will be participating in.

Step 5. Click OK to accept the changes.

Step 6. Click OK when Windows 2000 tells you that the computer must be rebooted for the changes to take effect.

Step 7. Click OK to close the Properties dialog box.

Step 8. Click Yes when it asks you to restart your computer.

Step 9. When the computer has restarted, it will be part of the workgroup.

Setting Up Windows 2000 Professional on a UNIX Network

Windows 2000 Professional workstations are no different than any other Windows workstation in a UNIX environment. In order to communicate with other workstations on the network, Windows 2000 Professional workstations need to be running the same protocols.

Typically, the UNIX network could be running the TCP/IP transport protocol. On top of this, the network could be running the NFS application protocol, and SAMBA, which is based on the Server Message Block application (SMB) protocol. Installing SAMBA makes the UNIX server look like a Windows 2000 server to Windows 2000 Professional workstations.

Most Windows 2000 features translate across into the SAMBA-enabled UNIX environment, including the Windows Explorer, Windows shortcuts, drive letter mapping, and My Network Places.

Here's a nifty feature that will surely simplify your life at some point. Recently accessed file shares are automatically stored in My Network Places so you can easily return to the file share you established before without having to map the drive letter.

Connecting Windows 2000 Professional to a UNIX network

The first thing you need to do when connecting to a UNIX share is make sure that your network is configured correctly. If you are using a DHCP server on your network, Windows 2000 should set up everything you need by default. If not, you will need to set up your TCP/IP information. If you right-click My Network Places on your Desktop, and select Properties, you will be shown a screen with different protocols and services. Select Internet Protocol (TCP/IP) and click the Properties button. Then, follow the procedure for manually assigning a unique IP address, as described earlier in this chapter in the peer-to-peer networking section.

Mapping a drive to a UNIX server

In order to make drives and the data they contain available to others on the network, you have to map it to the server. There are several ways to do so, as shown in the following exercises.

STEPS:
Mapping a Drive to UNIX Server #1

Step 1. Right-click My Network Places and select Map Network Drive.

Step 2. In the Map Network Drive dialog box, select the drive letter that you want to map to (this is you own personal preference). You also can specify the folder you are mapping from. The format for this follows UNC (Universal Naming Convention) standards. The format is like this:
\\SOLARIS_SERVER_NAME\SHARENAME
where SOLARIS_SERVER_NAME is the exported name of the Solaris server, and SHARENAME is the name of the share to which you want to connect.

Tip

If you need to connect as a different user, you can click "different user name" and type in a new name. By default, Windows will try to connect to the share using the same username and password with which you last logged on.

STEPS:
Mapping a Drive to UNIX Server #2

Step 1. Click (or double-click) My Network Places.

Step 2. Click (or double-click) Entire Network.

Step 3. On the Entire Network screen with the contempo network graphic, as shown in Figure 21-6, select "Search for a computer," type in the SOLARIS_SERVER_NAME described above, and then click Search. You will be shown a list of computer names that match the name you typed. If you click the name of your Solaris server, you will be taken to a window with the list of the shares on that server.

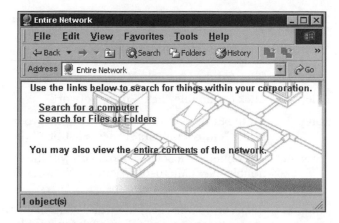

Figure 21-6: The Entire Network Window, where you can search for a computer on the network.

Step 4.   Click the share to which you want to connect and select Map Network Drive, as shown in Figure 21-7. All the information should be filled out by default. All you might have to do is change your username and click Finish.

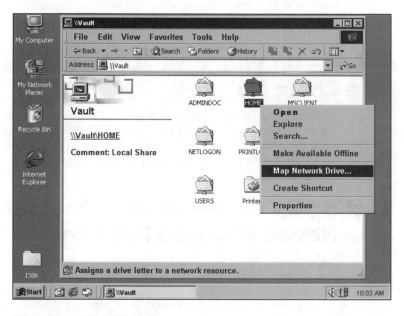

Figure 21-7: Map Network Drive

STEPS:

Mapping a Drive to UNIX Server #3

Step 1.   Click (or double-click) My Network Places.

Step 2.   Click (or double-click) Entire Network.

Step 3.   On the Entire Network screen with the groovy network graphic, select "entire contents" to see a list of all the available networks.

Step 4.   To connect to a Solaris share, you will then want to click (or double-click) Microsoft Windows Network. This will take you to a list of all known workgroups.

Step 5.   Click (or double-click) the workgroup name that your Samba server belongs to, and then click (or double-click) your Samba server name when it comes up. Whether you search for the server or browse the entire contents for it, you will be taken to the next screen where you will find a list of available shares.

Step 6.   Click the share to which you want to connect and select Map Network Drive. All the information should be filled out by default. All you might have to do is change your name and click Finish.

Setting Up Windows 2000 Professional on a Linux Network

Networking Windows 2000 Professional workstations on a Linux network is virtually identical to UNIX (see above). The main difference is that support for the SMB protocol is native to Linux (as it is to Windows NT and OS/2), so you shouldn't have to install anything additional.

Setting Up Windows 2000 Professional on a Novell NetWare Network

Windows 2000 Professional workstations connect to Novell NetWare networks pretty much like any other Windows client. In order to communicate with other workstations on the network, Windows 2000 Professional workstations need to be running the same protocols. Typically, the NetWare network could be running IPX as the base protocol, with the NCP application protocol for file and print services running on top of that.

Microsoft has included a crippled Novell NetWare client in Windows 2000, but it won't be very useful to organizations where NetWare functionality actually matters. Although it does boast a single logon feature for both NetWare and Windows 2000, Microsoft Client Services for NetWare won't work with Novell Z.E.N. Works, Novell Distributed Print Services, or Novell Storage Management Services — which makes Microsoft three-for-three in torpedoing major functionality in a competing network.

Fortunately, Novell supplies a NetWare Client for Windows 2000, which is significantly more functional than Microsoft's client — although not without foibles of its own. Check Novell's Web site at www.novell.com for the latest version.

 Windows 2000 Professional makes it easier to connect to numerous different — even wildly different — networks by means of the Per-Connection Settings feature, which allows every dial-up, VPN, or direct network connection to have completely separate configurations, including networking protocols, scripts, and security.

Connecting Windows 2000 Professional to a NetWare network

The first thing you need to do when connecting to a NetWare network is make sure that your network is correctly configured. Then, you need to install the Novell NetWare client for Windows 2000.

STEPS:
Installing Novell's NetWare Client for Windows 2000

Step 1. Right-click My Network Places and select Properties.

Step 2. Right-click Local Area Connection and select Properties. This will take you to a list of protocols and services that are installed on the computer, as shown in Figure 21-8.

Continued

STEPS

Installing Novell's NetWare Client for Windows 2000 *(continued)*

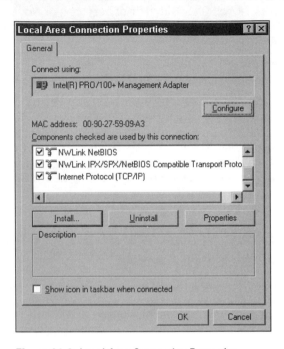

Figure 21-8: Local Area Connection Properties.

Step 3. Click the Install button, select Client in the Select Network Component Type dialog box, and then choose Add, as shown in Figure 21-9.

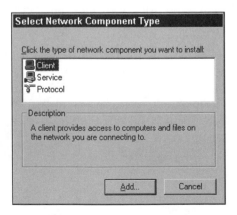

Figure 21-9: Select Network Component Type (in this case, Client) dialog box.

Step 4. Select the Have Disk button. Now, type the path or browse to the location where you downloaded the Novell NetWare Client for Windows 2000 (for example, c:\temp).

Step 5. Select the Novell client and click OK.

Step 6. After various files have been extracted and installed, and you have rebooted the computer, you should see the NetWare login box that prompts you to press Ctrl+Alt+Delete to log in.

Secret

Windows 2000 Professional workstations are supposed to automatically shut down and reboot during the installation of Novell's NetWare Client for Windows 2000, but this doesn't always happen. According to KeyLabs, who tested this for us: "We have never seen the machine shut down by itself after installing this client. It is safest to wait 15 minutes and then power down the machine yourself. If you shut it down too quickly, everything doesn't get set up correctly, and you will not be able to log in when you restart your computer."

Mapping a drive to a NetWare volume

Mapping a network drive to a NetWare volume is very similar to mapping a drive to a Windows share.

STEPS:

Mapping a Drive in NetWare

Step 1. First, right-click My Network Places and select Novell Map Network Drive, as shown in Figure 21-10.

Step 2. If you know the path to the volume, you can just type it in and select Map. If you're not sure, you can click Browse to use the NetWare Resource Browser.

Step 3. Locate the volume you want in the NetWare Resource Browser, and then click OK. This will take you back to the Map Drive dialog box with all the path information filled in.

Step 4. Now you just need to select Map, and you will be able to use the files on the NetWare volume just as if they were on a local drive (provided you have the proper rights).

Continued

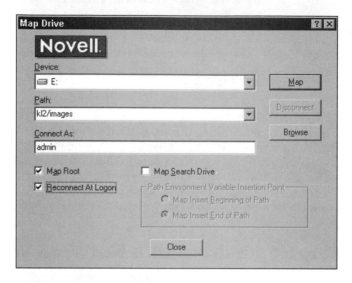

Figure 21-10: Novell Map Drive dialog box.

Windows 2000 provides legacy print support for Novell NetWare 2.x, 3.x and 4.x. Network printer connections can be established by mapping the LPT port or the UNC port where the printer resides.

Sharing a printer on a NetWare network

If you have successfully connected your Windows 2000 Professional workstation to a Novell NetWare network using Novell's Client for Windows 2000, you should have a rich range of enhanced printing services available, courtesy of Novell's Distributed Print Services. These include bi-directional printer communication, single seat printer administration, and automatic printer driver installation.

STEPS:

Installing a Network Printer in NetWare

Step 1. Once the NetWare Distributed Print Services printer has been installed and configured on the NetWare server, the Windows 2000 workstation finds the printer by browsing My Network Places in the Windows Explorer.

Step 2. Right-click the network printer you want to install and click Connect.

Step 3. The server should now install and configure the printer for the Windows 2000 Professional workstation so that it is available to it.

Setting Up Windows 2000 Professional and Virtual Private Networks

Realizing the tremendous attraction of virtual private networks to businesses of all sizes, Microsoft has beefed up Windows 2000's VPN capabilities, while streamlining and simplifying setup.

Windows 2000 supports the point-to-point tunneling protocol (PPTP), as well as the more advanced Layer 2 tunneling protocol (L2TP). In the default setting, Windows 2000 will first attempt to establish a VPN connection through L2TP, and then roll back to PPTP if it doesn't initially succeed.

Windows 2000 claims enhanced support for Virtual Private Networks (VPNs) in a Novell NetWare environment, thanks to support for Layer 2 Tunneling Protocol and Novell's BorderManager software, and third-party solutions like Raptor Firewall and Cisco PIX 520.

The thing that makes VPNs so attractive, of course, is that they allow very cheap extension of the network—especially to travelling personnel—by means of a simple dial-up connection to the Internet.

Setting up the VPN host

To create a VPN, you need two things: a host (or a computer that's set up to receive the incoming calls), and a client (or a computer that's set up to place the calls). Here's how to set up the host in Windows 2000:

STEPS:

Enabling Incoming VPN Connections in Windows 2000

Step 1.   Click My Network Places, and then click Properties.

Step 2.   On the Network and Dialup Connection screen, select Make New Connection.

Step 3.   Click Next until you get to the Network Connections Wizard introduction, as shown in Figure 21-11.

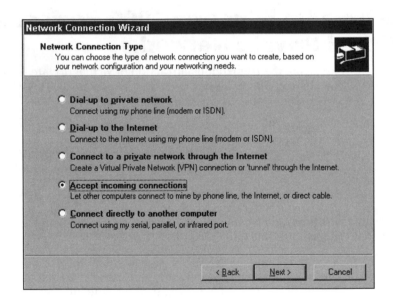

Figure 21-11: Network Connection Wizard

Step 4.   Make sure the Accept incoming connections radio button is enabled, and then click Next.

Step 5. The Network Connection Wizard will show you the Devices for Incoming Calls screen, from which you can select what devices you want to use for VPN connections. Please note, though, you don't *have* to select any check box here. If you leave the check boxes cleared, Windows 2000 will handle everything automatically. Either check the checkbox next to a device or leave them all blank and click Next.

Step 6. Next, the Windows 2000 Network Connection Wizard will allow you to enable virtual private connections. Select the Allow virtual private connections radio button and click Next, as shown in Figure 21-12.

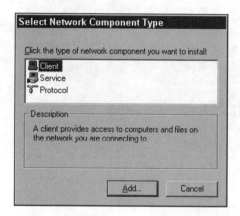

Figure 21-12: Enabling a VPN in the Network Connection Wizard.

Step 7. The next step is to set permissions for the virtual private network— in other words, identify who can get in. You can do this several ways. One is through the Network Connection Wizard, which will let you select users by placing a check in a check box next to their name, during the initial setup process. Another way is through the Microsoft Management Console (MMC), where you can select users.

Using the Microsoft Management Console to allow VPN access

If you need to give VPN access after you've left the Network Connection Wizard, you can do so through the Microsoft Management Console, as shown in Figure 21-13.

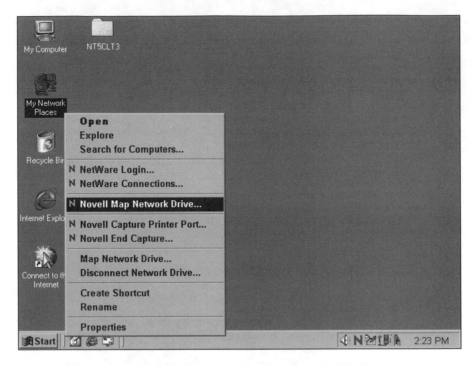

Figure 21-13: Opening the Microsoft Management Console to Set VPN Permissions.

STEPS:

Using the MMC to allow VPN access

Step 1.   Click Start ⇨ Programs ⇨ Administrative Tools ⇨ Computer Management.

Step 2.   Once Computer Management has launched, find the local users list. It will probably be under System Tools ⇨ Local users and Groups, Users in the left-hand pane.

Step 3.   Select the users you want to allow access to the VPN from the names in the right pane, as shown in Figure 21-14. Right-click the user you want to set up, and then select Properties.

Step 4.   Be sure to change the remote access permission by selecting the Allow access radio button on the Dial-in Tab in the Administrative Properties dialog box.

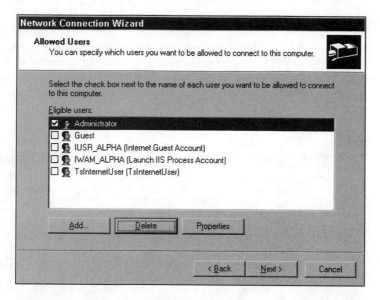

Figure 21-14: Using the Microsoft Management Console to select users to allow VPN access.

Setting up the VPN client

It's really easy to set up your Windows 2000 laptop—or any other Windows 2000 computer—to be a VPN client to initiate outgoing VPN connections.

STEPS:

Enabling Outgoing VPN Connections in Windows 2000

Step 1. Click My Network Places, and then click Properties.

Step 2. On the Network and Dialup Connection screen, select Make New Connection.

Continued

STEPS:

Enabling Outgoing VPN Connections in Windows 2000 *(continued)*

Step 3. Click Next until you get to the Network Connections Wizard introductory screen, as shown in Figure 21-15. Make sure you've selected the radio button for Connect to a private network through the Internet.

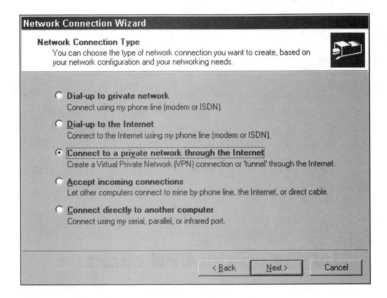

Figure 21-15: Back to Connection Type in Network Connection Wizard.

Step 4. In the Destination Address dialog, type in the URL or IP address of the server with which you will to connect.

Step 5. Choose the type of connection you want to use (if you're on the road or at home, you'll probably want to choose Dial-up Connection). Once the Wizard has finished, all you have to do in order to start a VPN connection is click (or double-click) the VPN shortcut icon, which is added to your Desktop by default. Finally, after you have dialed into the Internet, you will be asked for your VPN username and password.

Windows 2000 synchronization

A new feature in Windows 2000 is the Synchronization Manager, which replaces the late and not too lamented Briefcase feature in Windows 9x and Windows NT 4. Synchronization is designed to make it easier for mobile computer users to synchronize the files on their laptop with the files on their network. It also works with Web pages, over the Internet, and so on.

Further, you can use Synchronization to take files offline when you are no longer connected to the network or the Internet. Files and folders designated for offline use appear as if they were still connected to the network, except that they are visually highlighted.

You can designate specific files, folders, and even entire network drives for synchronization at scheduled intervals, manually, at logon or logoff, or when the machine is idle. Even better, you can control synchronization by connection type. For instance, you can set up Synchronization so that a huge database file is only synchronized when you are connected to the LAN using a high speed connection, while Web pages are synchronized when connected using a dial up connection.

Setting up Windows 2000 to use offline files

Synchronization Manager isn't *quite* as straightforward and intuitive as you might hope, though. For instance, your first impulse might be to select a file or folder for synchronization. Wrong. The first thing you need to do is set up your Windows 2000 computer to use offline files. By default, the Enable Offline Files check box is selected in Windows 2000 Professional, while it is cleared in Windows 2000 Server.

STEPS:

Setting Up Windows 2000 to Use Offline Files

Step 1. Click My Computer, select the Tools menu, and then select Folder Options.

Step 2. On the Offline Files tab, ensure that the Enable Offline Files check box is selected.

Step 3. Choose Synchronize all offline files before logging off to get a full synchronization of all files selected for offline use. If you leave Synchronize all files cleared, you'll get a quick synchronization.

Tip

Windows 2000 Quick Synchronization doesn't really synchronize. According to Microsoft, "a quick synchronization ensures that you have complete versions of all your offline files, though they may not necessarily be the most current versions."

Selecting files and folders for offline use

Now that you've set up Windows 2000 to use offline files, you can actually start designating the files you want synchronized, as well as the schedules for synchronization.

STEPS:
Selecting a File for Offline Use #1

Step 1.   In the Windows Explorer, right-click the file you want to make available offline.

Step 2.   Select Make available offline, and choose the settings you want.

Tip

You can only use Windows 2000 Synchronization Manager on a Novell NetWare network if the NetWare server has SMB capabilities installed.

STEPS:
Selecting a File for Offline Use #2

Step 1.   In the Windows Explorer, choose Tools ➪ Synchronize. Click the box next to the files you want to make available for later use offline, as shown in Figure 21-16.

Step 2.   Click Setup to specify when you want synchronization to take place, as shown in Figure 21-17.

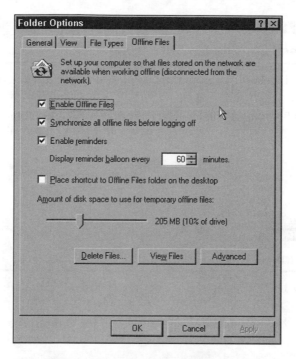

Figure 21-16: Folder Options in Synchronization.

Figure 21-17: Items to Synchronize in the Synchronization Manager.

STEPS:

Selecting a File for Offline Use #3

Step 1. In My Computer or My Network Places, click the shared network file or folder that you want to make available for later use offline.

Step 2. On the File menu, click Make Available Offline. Note: the Make Available Offline option will appear on the File menu only if your computer was set up to use Offline Files.

STEPS:

Listing All Files Selected of Offline Use

Step 1. To see a list of all of the network files that are available offline, open the Synchronization Manager.

Step 2. Select Folder Options, select the Offline Files tab, and then click View Files.

STEPS:

Deselecting A File for Offline Use

Step 1. Decide you don't actually want to have a file synchronized for offline use? To undo making a file or folder available offline, right-click the item in the Windows Explorer, and then click Make Available Offline again to clear the check mark.

Summary

Windows 2000 Pro workstations work well on non-Windows 2000 networks. In this chapter, we learned:

▶ How to setup Windows 2000 Professional as a workstation on a peer-to-peer Windows 95/Windows 98/Windows NT network.

▶ How to setup Windows 2000 Professional as a workstation on a Solaris UNIX / Samba network.

▶ How to setup Windows 2000 Professional for Virtual Private Network (VPN) access to a network.

▶ How to setup Windows 2000 Professional as a workstation on a Novell NetWare network.

▶ How to use Windows 2000 Synchronization Manager.

Appendix

What's on the CD-ROM

The CD-ROM that comes with *Windows 2000 Secrets* contains this entire book in a machine-readable format. You can search the text to find topics of interest, and you can print out sections you may need to refer to separately.

You can install the book onto your hard drive, or you can run the e-book from the CD-ROM without installing anything. It's up to you.

Note

The e-book is licensed for use on a single machine and may not be copied or distributed without written permission from IDG Books Worldwide.

Installing the E-Book from the CD-ROM

You may choose to install the book to your hard drive, read it online, or exit at any time. To begin, follow these steps:

1. Insert the CD into your CD-ROM drive. The Setup program should run automatically. If it does not begin automatically, see Step 2.

2. If the Setup program doesn't begin automatically, browse to your CD-ROM drive in Explorer, then open the Setup.exe file you find in the root folder of the CD.

Index

IDG Books Worldwide, Inc.
End-User License Agreement

5. **Limited Warranty**.

   (a) IDGB warrants that the Software and Software Media are free from defects in materials and workmanship under normal use for a period of sixty (60) days from the date of purchase of this Book. If IDGB receives notification within the warranty period of defects in materials or workmanship, IDGB will replace the defective Software Media.

   (b) **IDGB AND THE AUTHORS OF THE BOOK DISCLAIM ALL OTHER WARRANTIES, EXPRESS OR IMPLIED, INCLUDING WITHOUT LIMITATION IMPLIED WARRANTIES OF MERCHANTABILITY AND FITNESS FOR A PARTICULAR PURPOSE, WITH RESPECT TO THE SOFTWARE, THE PROGRAMS, THE SOURCE CODE CONTAINED THEREIN, AND/OR THE TECHNIQUES DESCRIBED IN THIS BOOK. IDGB DOES NOT WARRANT THAT THE FUNCTIONS CONTAINED IN THE SOFTWARE WILL MEET YOUR REQUIREMENTS OR THAT THE OPERATION OF THE SOFTWARE WILL BE ERROR FREE.**

   (c) This limited warranty gives you specific legal rights, and you may have other rights that vary from jurisdiction to jurisdiction.

6. **Remedies**.

   (a) IDGB's entire liability and your exclusive remedy for defects in materials and workmanship shall be limited to replacement of the Software Media, which may be returned to IDGB with a copy of your receipt at the following address: Software Media Fulfillment Department, Attn.: *Windows 2000 Secrets*, IDG Books Worldwide, Inc., 7260 Shadeland Station, Ste. 100, Indianapolis, IN 46256, or call 1-800-762-2974. Please allow three to four weeks for delivery. This Limited Warranty is void if failure of the Software Media has resulted from accident, abuse, or misapplication. Any replacement Software Media will be warranted for the remainder of the original warranty period or thirty (30) days, whichever is longer.

   (b) In no event shall IDGB or the authors be liable for any damages whatsoever (including without limitation damages for loss of business profits, business interruption, loss of business information, or any other pecuniary loss) arising from the use of or inability to use the Book or the Software, even if IDGB has been advised of the possibility of such damages.

   (c) Because some jurisdictions do not allow the exclusion or limitation of liability for consequential or incidental damages, the above limitation or exclusion may not apply to you.

7. **U.S. Government Restricted Rights**. Use, duplication, or disclosure of the Software by the U.S. Government is subject to restrictions stated in paragraph (c)(1)(ii) of the Rights in Technical Data and Computer Software clause of DFARS 252.227-7013, and in subparagraphs (a) through (d) of the Commercial Computer — Restricted Rights clause at FAR 52.227-19, and in similar clauses in the NASA FAR supplement, when applicable.

8. **General**. This Agreement constitutes the entire understanding of the parties and revokes and supersedes all prior agreements, oral or written, between them and may not be modified or amended except in a writing signed by both parties hereto that specifically refers to this Agreement. This Agreement shall take precedence over any other documents that may be in conflict herewith. If any one or more provisions contained in this Agreement are held by any court or tribunal to be invalid, illegal, or otherwise unenforceable, each and every other provision shall remain in full force and effect.

Installing the CD-ROM

The CD-ROM that accompanies Windows 2000 Secrets contains the entire book in a machine-readable format. You can search the text to find topics of interest. You can also print out sections if you need to refer to them separately.

To read the e-book from the CD-ROM or install the e-book on a hard drive, run Setup.exe from the CD-ROM. On most PCs, Setup.exe will start automatically when you insert the CD into the CD-ROM drive. It's also easy to uninstall the e-book if you wish to do so (see the instructions below).

To run the setup, follow these steps:

1. Insert the CD into your CD-ROM drive, such as D.

2. The Windows 2000 Secrets e-book setup should start automatically. You will be given the choice of installing the e-book on your hard drive, or only installing small DLL files that allow the e-book to be read from the CD-ROM.

3. If your system is configured so the setup procedure does not start automatically, click Start ⇨ Programs ⇨ Accessories ⇨ Windows Explorer. In Windows Explorer, double-click the file Setup.exe on your CD-ROM drive.

4. If you chose to install the e-book, you can run it at any time by clicking Start ⇨ Programs ⇨ Windows 2000 Secrets ⇨ Windows 2000 Secrets.

Once the e-book is open:

- You can read the book by opening any chapter in the left pane and selecting any topic.

- You can jump to any topic by clicking the Index tab.

- You can search for any word or phrase by clicking the Search tab.

To uninstall the e-book, follow these steps:

1. Click Start ⇨ Settings ⇨ Control Panel ⇨ Add/Remove Programs.

2. Select Windows 2000 Secrets and click the Remove button.

3. You will receive the choice of two options: Automatic or Custom uninstall. The Automatic uninstall option removes all signs of the e-book. The Custom uninstall option allows you to remove individual features of the e-book.